ELLIOTT ERWITT

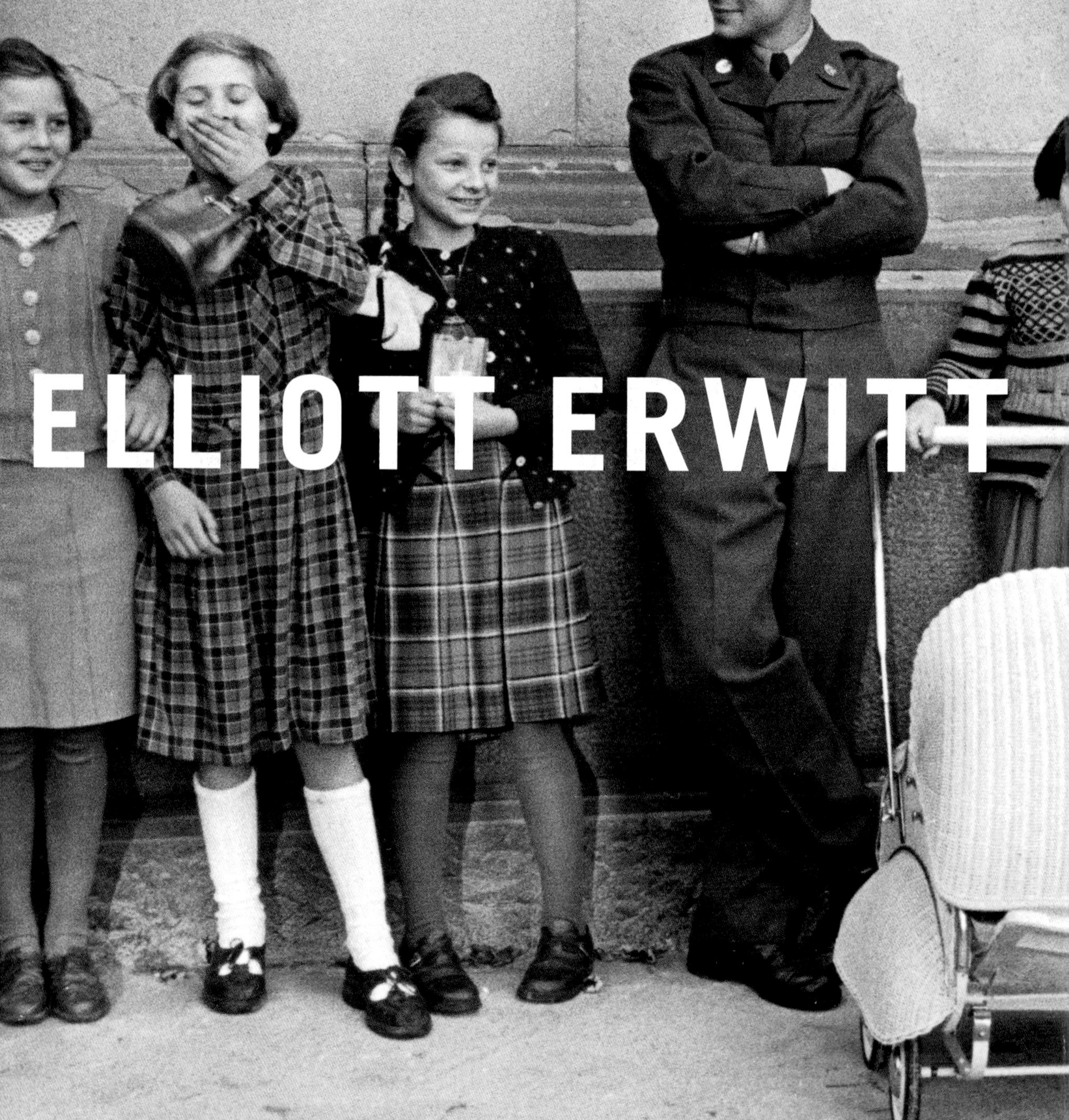

Frauen
ELLIOTT ERWITT

PERSONAL BEST

teNeues

Elliott Erwitt's photographs (as well as his life) are more complicated than they seem. Likewise, a book of his pictures called *Personal Best* would appear to be a simple, straightforward expression. Not so.

In Erwitt's photographic lexicon, "personal" means pictures he has been determinedly making for himself while earning a living as a working photographer. Whether, as a teenager, in the lab of a Hollywood publicity mill ("One week I washed and dried 25,000 Ingrid Bergmans!") or, later in New York, as a member of the distinguished photo co-op Magnum shooting annual reports of Fortune 500 companies, six-figure advertising campaigns for Madison Avenue or breaking news for Paris *Match*, Erwitt has been working professionally for others yet still finding time to be an amateur photographer for himself. For him, "amateur" is hardly pejorative; he points to the Latin root of the word *amo* (to love). This is photography for the love of it. Or, as he might say, photography made difficult.

For a profile on Erwitt many years ago I asked one of his mentors, Henri Cartier-Bresson, to comment on this duality and he said, "Elliott has to my mind achieved a miracle working on a chain-gang of commercial campaigns and still offering a bouquet of stolen photos with a flavor, a smile from his deeper self." This, from an icon who, like Stieglitz before him, could not reconcile a photographer working for anybody but himself.

Few of the commercial works are included here. Most of the pictures in this volume Erwitt shot for himself (usually with a classic Leica rangefinder and in black and white) in between commercial assignments. And now, at 78, after some 60 years of doing so, he has compiled his best.

I first encountered Erwitt in a 1970 exhibit at the Smithsonian in Washington which I reviewed for *Life*. I was struck by a quick mind—and even quicker reflexes—that could capture juxtapositions that ranged from the sardonic (page 44) to the whimsical (page 165) all found in the commonplace across the globe. That was Erwitt the ironist.

Later photographs would inspire other critics to point out that, with the possible exception of the late Robert Doisneau, no 20th Century photographer had a sense for humor; i.e., Erwitt saw things in the human condition that evoked everything from wry smiles to outright guffaws. Erwitt, the wit.

Then there are the canines. Knowing an audience's affection for an underdog, he has made scores of photographs—enough to sustain five monographs over the years—of man's best friend. Writing about them P.G. Wodehouse said, "There's not a sitter in his gallery who does not melt the heart...and no beastly class distinctions, either. Thoroughbreds and mutts, they are all there." Erwitt, the shooter of dogs.

Most often overlooked is the candid, world class magazine photojournalism that includes the infamous "kitchen debate" between Nikita Khrushchev and Richard Nixon that Nixon later used (without Erwitt's permission) in the 1960 presidential election campaign to support his platform of being strong on Communism. (The level of the so-called debate was "ridiculous" according to Erwitt, with each man bragging, with increasing vehemence, about their country's wealth and power. As the son of Russian émigrés, Erwitt understood what both men were saying despite the best efforts of their translators to be diplomatic. "At one point Nixon was getting so irritating I thought I heard Khrushchev say in Russian, 'Go fuck my grandmother'.")

Then, in 1966 during a testy period when Charles DeGaulle was making his NATO allies nervous, Erwitt covered the French president's trip to the Soviet Union and was able to slip unnoticed into a back room in Moscow where DeGaulle was seen informally with the Soviet leadership.

Erwitt, the invisible insider.

In the past decade, however, there have emerged from Erwitt's archive many more pictures that might be defined as social realist documentary photography of the kind most famously attributed to Robert Frank but also of the so-called New York School of photography that included, among others, William Klein, Louis Faurer and Helen Levitt. (Diane Arbus, Lee Friedlander and Garry Winogrand would emerge as the next generation in this line.)

In the 1990s Erwitt was increasingly showing images—many that hadn't been shown publicly since they were created in the late 1940s and early 50s—that put him squarely in the firmament of this revered period of fine art photography. They demonstrate a conscious breaking of the rules for the then-contemporary photographic standards—perfect exposure, full tonal range, sharp focus, traditional composition—coupled with an existential "tough love" treatment of America, cloaked in the aura of the *film noir* motion pictures of the period that hung over this generation of photographers. And, like his peers of that time, there is the unselfconscious striking out to create a deliberate style or signature of his own. *Personal Best* gathers together many of those and many more that have never been published.

So what is it that has allowed Erwitt to achieve such prominence in so many ways that few of us have seen, until now, as a whole? Clouding the picture is his commercial success as not only a photographer but, for some twenty years, a documentary filmmaker whose efforts could be found on the cable television network HBO. The stigma of Stieglitz (and Cartier-Bresson) regarding commercial success still haunts parts of the art establishment which ignores the fact that both men were independently wealthy so they could afford to make such pronouncements. (They also didn't have six children!)

Erwitt, however, the only child of displaced Russians, was not so fortunate. He found himself in New York at the age of 11 after being born in Paris, raised in Milan and fleeing Europe on the last boat out of free France. Then, at 16, he was on his own in Los Angeles where his parents had decamped, then split up and took off. There must be a TV sitcom in the story of a teenager steeped in the cultures of Russia, Italy, France and New York City attending Hollywood High and living in a rented bungalow with friends.

Erwitt survived all that and has used the experience to become an uncanny observer of others, highly sensitive to the vicissitudes of life and, when necessary, utterly charming and disarming. (Witness him as the handsome young GI in 1951 working the line of young *mädchen* outside a ladies room (see frontispiece). So is it any wonder that he developed into one of the most acute, perceptive and individualistic eyes in 20th century photography?

Sean Callahan

Die Fotografien von Elliott Erwitt sind genau wie sein Leben komplizierter, als sie auf den ersten Blick erscheinen. Ebenso scheint der Titel eines Buches mit seinen Bildern mit dem Namen *Personal Best* eine einfache, direkte Aussage zu sein. Stimmt nicht.

Nach Erwitts fotografischem Lexikon sind „persönliche" Bilder jene, die er in erster Linie für sich selbst gemacht hat, während er sich seinen Lebensunterhalt als Fotograf verdiente. Ob er als Teenager im Labor einer Werbemühle in Hollywood gearbeitet hat („In einer Woche habe ich 25.000 Ingrid Bergmans gewaschen und getrocknet!") oder später in New York als Mitglied der angesehenen Foto-Kooperative Magnum jährliche Berichte über die Fortune-500-Firmen geschossen hat, sechsstellige Werbekampagnen für Madison Avenue realisierte oder Eilmeldungen für Paris *Match* lieferte, immer arbeitete Erwitt professionell für einen Auftraggeber und fand daneben noch Zeit, als „Amateurfotograf" eigene Projekte umzusetzen. Für ihn hat der Begriff „Amateur" nichts Abwertendes; er verweist auf die lateinische Wurzel des Wortes *amo* (lieben). Dies ist Fotografie um der Fotografie willen. Oder, wie er es ausdrücken würde, Fotografie verkompliziert.

Als ich vor vielen Jahren für ein Profil über Erwitt einen seiner Mentoren, Henri Cartier-Bresson, darum bat, diese Dualität zu kommentieren, antwortete er: „Elliott hat meiner Meinung nach ein Wunder vollbracht, indem er in den Zwängen kommerzieller Kampagnen arbeitete und trotzdem mit einem Strauß erhaschter Bilder aufwarten kann, mit einem Duft, einem Lächeln aus seinem tiefsten Selbst." Diese Aussage stammt von einem Meister, der eigentlich, wie Stieglitz vor ihm, nicht mit einem Fotografen übereinstimmen konnte, der nicht ausschließlich für ihn arbeitete.

Nur wenige kommerzielle Arbeiten sind hier aufgenommen worden. Die meisten Bilder in diesem Band hat Erwitt für sich selbst gemacht (gewöhnlich mit einer klassischen Leica Sucherkamera und in Schwarzweiß), zwischen seinen kommerziellen Aufträgen. Nun, mit 78 Jahren, nachdem er etwa 60 Jahre auf diese Weise gearbeitet hat, stellt er die Besten davon zusammen.

Ich traf Erwitt zum ersten Mal 1970 auf einer Ausstellung im Smithsonian in Washington, die ich für *Life* besprechen sollte. Ich war von seinem schnellen Verstand – und seinen noch schnelleren Reflexen – fasziniert, der Nebeneinanderstellungen einfangen konnte, die vom Sardonischen (Seite 44) zum Verschmitzten (Seite 165) reichen konnten und überall auf dem Globus im Alltäglichen gefunden wurden. Das war Erwitt, der Ironische.

Spätere Fotografien würden andere Kritiker zu dem Hinweis inspirieren, dass – vielleicht mit Ausnahme des verstorbenen Robert Doisneau – kein Fotograf des 20. Jahrhunderts Sinn für Humor hatte; Erwitt aber sehe Dinge im menschlichen Wesen, die von einem schiefen Grinsen bis hin zu Lachsalven alles hervorrufen könnten. Erwitt, der Witzige.

Dann gibt es die Hunde. Da er die Zuneigung des Publikums zu den Unterlegenen kannte, machte er unzählige Fotos vom besten Freund des Menschen – genug, um über die Jahre fünf Monographien zu füllen. P.G. Wodehouse sagte: „Es gibt nicht ein Modell in seiner Galerie, bei dem einem nicht das Herz schmilzt ... und es gibt auch keine tierischen Klassenunterschiede. Rassehunde und Köter, sie sind alle da." Erwitt, der Hundefotograf.

Wenig beachtet werden meist seine Momentaufnahmen, die Meisterleistungen des Fotojournalismus darstellen, darunter auch die berüchtigte „Küchendebatte" zwischen Nikita Chruschtschow und Richard Nixon. Diese benutzte Nixon 1960 für seinen Präsidentschaftswahlkampf (ohne das Einverständnis von Erwitt), um seinen harten Kurs gegen den Kommunismus zu untermauern. (Das Niveau der so genannten Debatte war nach Erwitts Aussage „lächerlich", da jeder der beiden Männer mit steigender Vehemenz prahlte, wie reich und stark sein Land sei. Als Sohn russischer

Einwanderer verstand Erwitt, was beide Männer sagten, trotz der Bemühungen ihrer Übersetzer um Diplomatie. „An einem Punkt wurde Nixon so provokativ, da dachte ich, ich hätte Chruschtschow auf Russisch sagen hören: ‚Geh und fick meine Großmutter'.")

1966, während einer kritischen Periode, in der Charles de Gaulle die NATO-Alliierten nervös machte, berichtete Erwitt über die Reise des französischen Präsidenten in die Sowjetunion und konnte in Moskau unbemerkt mit in ein Hinterzimmer schlüpfen, wo de Gaulle informell mit der sowjetischen Führung zu sehen war.

Erwitt, der unsichtbare Insider.

Im vergangenen Jahrzehnt sind aus Erwitts Archiv jedoch auch Bilder aufgetaucht, die man als sozialrealistische Dokumentarfotografie bezeichnen kann, wie man sie eher von dem berühmten Robert Frank kennt, aber auch von der so genannten New York School of Photography, zu der unter anderen William Klein, Louis Faurer und Helen Levitt zählten. (Diane Arbus, Lee Friedlander und Garry Winogrand würden zur nächsten Generation dieser Reihe gehören.)

In den 1990er Jahren zeigte Erwitt verstärkt Bilder – von denen viele seit ihrer Entstehung in den späten 40ern und frühen 50ern noch nicht öffentlich gezeigt worden waren –, die ihn geradewegs an den Himmel der in dieser Zeit so verehrten Kunstfotografen katapultierten. Sie zeigen den absichtlichen Bruch der Regeln für die (nach damaligen zeitgenössischen fotografischen Standards) perfekte Aufnahme (volles Tonwertspektrum, scharfer Fokus, traditioneller Bildaufbau) – verbunden mit einem existenziellen, liebevoll-strengen Blick auf Amerika, und eingehüllt in die Aura des *Film noir* jener Zeit, die generell über den Bildern dieser Generation von Fotografen hing. Wie bei seinen zeitgenössischen Zunftkollegen, finden wir auch bei ihm das unbefangene Bestreben, einen eigenen Stil oder eine eigene Handschrift zu entwickeln. *Personal Best* versammelt viele dieser und anderer Bilder, die noch nie veröffentlicht wurden.

Was also befähigt Erwitt, auf so vielen Gebieten berühmt zu werden, wie es nur wenige von uns bislang als Ganzes erlebt haben? Das Bild wird getrübt durch seinen wirtschaftlichen Erfolg nicht nur als Fotograf, sondern auch während seiner nahezu zwanzig Jahre als Dokumentarfilmer, dessen Ergebnisse im Kabel-TV-Netzwerk HBO zu finden sind. Die Stigmatisierung von kommerziellem Erfolg durch Stieglitz (und Cartier-Bresson) spukt immer noch durch Teile des Kunstbetriebs, der die Tatsache ignoriert, dass diese beiden Männer unabhängig und reich waren und sich solche Äußerungen deshalb leisten konnten. (Sie hatten auch keine sechs Kinder!)

Erwitt war als einziges Kind russischer Einwanderer nicht so vom Glück gesegnet. Er wurde in Paris geboren, wuchs in Mailand auf und floh auf dem letzten Schiff aus dem freien Frankreich und aus Europa, bis er mit 11 Jahren in New York ankam. Mit 16 lebte er allein in Los Angeles, wo seine Eltern die Zelte abbrachen, sich trennten und die Stadt verließen. Die Geschichte hat Potenzial für eine TV-Komödie: Ein Teenager, der von den Kulturen Russlands, Italiens, Frankreichs und New York Citys geprägt wurde, in Hollywood zur Schule geht und mit Freunden in einem gemieteten Bungalow lebt.

Erwitt überlebte dies alles und nutzte diese Erfahrungen, um ein unbestechlicher Beobachter der Anderen zu werden. Er reagierte hochsensibel auf die Wechselfälle des Lebens und konnte, wenn nötig, überwältigend charmant und entwaffnend sein. (Schauen Sie sich nur das Foto an, auf dem der hübsche junge GI 1951 mit einer Reihe von jungen Mädchen vor einer Damentoilette schäkert (siehe Titelbild)). Ist es also ein Wunder, dass er sich zu einem der intensivsten, scharfsinnigsten und individualistischsten Fotografen des 20. Jahrhunderts entwickelte?

Sean Callahan

Les photos (tout comme la vie) d'Elliott Erwitt sont bien plus compliquées qu'elles ne le paraissent. De même un album de ses photos intitulé *Personal Best (Le Meilleur de moi-même)* pourrait paraître une expression simple et facile. Ce n'est guère le cas.

Dans le lexique photographique d'Erwitt, « personnel » cela signifie des photos prises pour lui-même alors qu'il gagne sa vie comme photographe. Pendant son adolescence, dans le laboratoire d'une agence publicitaire d'Hollywood (« En une semaine j'ai lavé et séché 25 000 Ingrid Bergman ! ») ou, plus tard à New York, en tant que membre de la célèbre co-op Magnum pour laquelle il a réalisé les reportages photographiques annuels du magazine « Fortune 500 Companies », six campagnes publicitaires pour Madison Avenue ou les scoops pour Paris *Match*. Erwitt a travaillé en professionnel pour beaucoup de monde, tout en trouvant le temps de faire des photos d'amateur pour son propre compte. Selon lui, le terme « amateur » n'est pas péjoratif ; il souligne l'origine latine du mot *amo* (aimer). C'est faire de la photo pour le plaisir. Ou, comme il aimerait à le dire, compliquer la photographie.

Afin de faire un portrait d'Erwitt, il y a plusieurs années de ça, j'ai demandé à l'un de ses mentors, Henri Cartier-Bresson, de commenter cette dualité et il m'a répondu : « Elliott a accompli, à mon avis, un miracle en travaillant simultanément sur des campagnes commerciales et des bouquets de photos volées où l'on perçoit le parfum et le sourire de son moi profond. » Ceci d'un maître de la photo qui, tout comme Stieglitz avant lui, ne supportait pas qu'un photographe puisse travailler pour quelqu'un d'autre.

Quelques-unes de ses œuvres commerciales figurent ici. La plupart des photos de ce volume, ont été prises par Erwitt pour son propre plaisir (d'ordinaire en noir et blanc avec son fameux Leica télémètrique) et ce entre divers contrats commerciaux. À 78 ans, après 60 années et quelque de photographie, il produit aujourd'hui une compilation de ses meilleures créations.

J'ai rencontré Erwitt, pour la première fois en 1970, à l'occasion d'une exposition de la Smithsonian à Washington dont je devais rendre compte pour le magazine *Life*. J'ai été impressionné par la vivacité de son esprit (et ses réflexes encore plus rapides) qui pouvait capter des juxtapositions allant du sarcastique (page 44) au fantaisiste (page 165), présents dans des scènes de la vie commune du monde entier. Autant pour le côté ironique d'Erwitt.

Des photographes plus récents inspireront d'autres critiques qui signaleront qu'à l'exception, peut-être, du regretté Robert Doisneau, aucun photographe du XXe siècle n'a su porter un regard humoristique sur le monde ; Erwitt voit dans la condition humaine de quoi susciter des réactions qui vont des sourires ironiques aux francs éclats de rire. Erwitt, l'homme d'esprit.

Et puis il y a les chiens. Connaissant l'affection du public pour la gent canine, il a fait de nombreux clichés du meilleur ami de l'homme (de quoi remplir cinq monographies au long des années). À leur propos, P.G. Wodehouse a écrit : « Il n'y a pas de sujet de cette galerie qui ne mette le cœur en émoi... et sans le moindre préjugé de classe encore. Chiens de race et humbles toutous, ils sont tous là. » Erwitt, photographe des chiens.

Ce qu'on omet le plus souvent c'est le photojournalisme de classe mondiale qui comprend en particulier le notoire « débat dans la cuisine » entre Nikita Khrouchtchev et Richard Nixon. Ce dernier l'utilisera plus tard (sans la permission d'Erwitt) dans sa campagne électorale pour les présidentielles de 1960 pour soutenir son programme de lutte anti-communiste. (Le niveau du soi-disant débat fut franchement « ridicule » selon Erwitt, chacun des participants se vantant, avec une véhémence croissante, de la richesse et de la puissance de son propre pays. En tant que fils d'immigrés russes, Erwitt comprenait ce que les deux hommes disaient malgré les gros efforts de leurs interprètes pour préserver un ton diplomatique. « Confronté à la truculence de Nixon, Khrouchtchev lui a lancé, à ce qu'il m'a semblé, l'équivalent russe de : 'Va te faire foutre.' »)

Puis en 1966, lors d'une période tourmentée où Charles de Gaulle mettait les nerfs de ses alliés à rude épreuve, Erwitt couvrit le voyage du président français en Union soviétique et put se glisser discrètement dans les salons privés où de Gaulle s'entretenait de façon informelle avec les dirigeants soviétique.

Erwitt, l'invisible initié.

Au cours des dix dernières années, ont émané des archives d'Erwitt de nombreuses photos qui pourraient être définies comme des photos documentaires de réalisme social, dans le genre de celles attribuées au fameux Robert Frank mais aussi à la célèbre Ecole de photographie de New York qui comptait notamment au nombre de ses élèves, William Klein, Louis Faurer et Helen Levitt. (Diane Arbus, Lee Friedlander et Garry Winogrand feront partie de la génération suivante de ce courant photographique.)

Dans les années 90 Erwitt exposait de plus en plus d'images – dont beaucoup n'avaient pas été montrées publiquement depuis leur création à la fin des années 40 et début des années 50 – qui le haussaient carrément au firmament de cette période vénérée de la photographie artistique. Elles démontrent une violation délibérée des règles des normes photographiques de l'époque – pose parfaite, gamme de tonalités complète, image nette, composition traditionnelle – à laquelle s'ajoute une thérapie existentielle de l'Amérique, dans le genre « amour sans concessions », empreint de l'atmosphère du *film noir* du cinéma de l'époque qui s'attachait à cette génération de photographes. Et, tout comme chez ses pairs de cette période, il se débat sans complexe pour créer un style audacieux et personnel. *Personal Best* réunit beaucoup de ces images et beaucoup d'autres publiées pour la première fois.

Qu'est-ce qui a donc permis à Erwitt d'atteindre une importance telle dans tant de domaines que quelques-uns d'entre nous considéraient, jusqu'à présent, comme un tout ? Brouillant l'image, il y a son succès commercial, non seulement en tant que photographe mais encore en tant que documentariste dont les films passent sur HBO, la chaîne de télévision par câble. Le mépris de Stieglitz (et de Cartier-Bresson) à l'égard du succès commercial continue de hanter le monde artistique qui ignore le fait que les deux hommes étaient financièrement indépendants et qu'ils pouvaient donc se permettre de faire de telles déclarations. (Ils n'avaient pas non plus six enfants à nourrir !)

Erwitt, cependant, fils unique d'immigrés russes, n'avait pas cette chance. Il se retrouva à New York à l'âge de 11 ans après être né à Paris, avoir grandi à Milan et fui l'Europe à bord du dernier bateau au départ de la France libre. À 16 ans, il se retrouva seul à Los Angeles après la séparation de ses parents, qui partirent chacun de leur côté. Il y a sûrement une sitcom à faire qui raconterait l'histoire d'un adolescent imprégné des cultures de la Russie, de l'Italie, de la France et de New York, qui rêve d'atteindre le succès à Hollywood dans un bungalow loué avec des amis.

Erwitt a survécu à tout cela et s'est servi de cette expérience pour se transformer en perspicace observateur de l'autre, très sensible aux vicissitudes de la vie et, au besoin, tout à fait charmant et désarmant. (Voyez l'élégant et jeune GI en 1951, observant les jeunes filles à l'extérieur des toilettes des dames (voir frontispice). Alors, rien d'étonnant qu'il soit devenu l'un des photographes les plus perspicaces, perceptifs et originaux du XXe siècle?

Sean Callahan

Las fotografías de Elliott Erwitt, como su vida, son más complicadas de lo que parecen. De igual modo, *Personal Best*, un libro con sus imágenes, podría parecer una expresión sencilla y directa, pero no lo es.

En el léxico fotográfico de Erwitt, «personal» significa las imágenes que ha venido tomando decididamente para sí mismo mientras se ganaba la vida como fotógrafo profesional. Ha trabajado para otros como fotógrafo contratado, pero siempre encontró tiempo para ser un fotógrafo aficionado para sí mismo, tanto en su adolescencia cuando trabajaba en el laboratorio de una fábrica de publicidad rápida de Hollywood («En una semana, lavé y sequé 25.000 fotos de Ingrid Bergman.») como más tarde en Nueva York, cuando era miembro de la afamada agencia Mágnum, tomando fotos para los informes anuales de las empresas incluidas en la lista de Fortune 500, las campañas publicitarias de seis cifras de Madison Avenue o las noticias de actualidad de la revista Paris *Match*. Para Erwitt, «amateur» no es una palabra en absoluto peyorativa, sino que nos recuerda el significado de la raíz latina del vocablo: *amo* (amar). Es la fotografía por amor a ella o, como puede que diga él, la fotografía en difícil.

Hace muchos años, durante mi preparación de una biografía sobre Erwitt, pedí a uno de sus mentores, a Henri Cartier-Bresson, que comentara esta dualidad. Me respondió: «En mi opinión, Elliott ha logrado un milagro: trabaja en una cadena de producción de campañas comerciales pero continúa ofreciendo un ramillete de fotos robadas a la realidad que regalan un aroma, una sonrisa desde su yo más profundo». Y eso lo ha dicho un icono que, como Stieglitz antes que él, no admite que un fotógrafo trabaje para nadie, excepto para sí mismo.

Este libro incluye pocas de sus obras comerciales: la mayoría de las imágenes que aparecen en él fueron tomadas por devoción entre trabajos contratados, generalmente con una Leica clásica con telémetro, en blanco y negro. Ahora, a los 78 años de edad, cuando lleva unos 60 años tomándolas, ha reunido las mejores.

Conocí a Erwitt en 1970, en una exposición en el Smithsonian en Washington que estaba cubriendo para la revista *Life*. Me impresionaron la gran rapidez de su mente y la superioridad de sus reflejos, capaces de capturar yuxtaposiciones que iban desde lo sardónico (página 44) a lo caprichoso (página 165), todas ellas en los lugares más comunes del mundo. Era Erwitt, el irónico.

Las fotografías posteriores inspiraron a otros críticos a señalar que, con la posible excepción del difunto Robert Doisneau, ningún otro fotógrafo del siglo XX poseía ese sentido para captar el humor, es decir, Erwitt veía características en la condición humana que provocaban desde sonrisas secas hasta grandes carcajadas. Erwitt, el ingenioso.

Después, la raza canina. Conocedor del afecto del público por los perros desvalidos, ha tomado cientos de fotografías del mejor amigo del hombre, las suficientes para la publicación de cinco monografías con ese tema en distintos años. Sobre ellas, P.G. Wodehouse escribió: «No hay un modelo en esta galería que no te derrita el corazón… y sin distinción de clases entre estos animales. Están todos aquí, de pura raza y mestizos.» Erwitt, el fotógrafo de perros.

Sus trabajos de fotoperiodismo en publicaciones de talla mundial, los cuales se pasan por alto con frecuencia, incluyen el tristemente célebre debate entre Nikita Kruschev y Richard Nixon en 1959 conocido como «debate en la cocina», imágenes que después éste último utilizó (sin permiso de Erwitt) en la campaña presidencial de 1960 para explicar la firme posición de su plataforma frente al comunismo. (Según Erwitt, el nivel del llamado debate fue «ridículo», pues los dos hombres se limitaron a lanzar frases jactanciosas cada vez más vehementes, sobre la riqueza y el poder de los países de cada uno. Como hijo de emigrantes rusos, Erwitt comprendía perfectamente lo que decían ambos, a pesar de los nobles esfuerzos diplomáticos de sus intérpretes. «Hubo un

momento en el que Nixon se volvió tan irritante que creo haber oído como Kruschev decía, en ruso, ‹Vete a joder a mi abuela›.»).

Después, en 1966, Erwitt fue el encargado de cubrir el viaje del presidente francés Charles de Gaulle a la Unión Soviética, en un periodo difícil durante el cual puso nerviosos a sus aliados de la OTAN. El fotógrafo logró entrar sin llamar la atención a una pequeña sala en Moscú donde la dirigencia soviética recibió, de manera informal, a de Gaulle.

Erwitt, el infiltrado invisible.

Sin embargo, durante la pasada década, el archivo de Erwitt ha producido muchas imágenes más que pueden definirse como fotografía documental social-realista, del tipo atribuido especialmente a Robert Frank y de la llamada New York School of Photography, que incluía, entre otros, a William Klein, Louis Faurer y Helen Levitt, y cuya siguiente generación vendrá formada por Diane Arbus, Lee Friedlander y Garry Winogrand.

En los años 90, Erwitt mostró cada vez más imágenes, muchas de las cuales no se habían presentado al público desde su toma a finales de los 40 y principios de los 50, que lo colocaban decididamente en el firmamento de este respetado periodo de la fotografía como parte de las bellas artes. Estas tomas demuestran una ruptura consciente de las normas de la fotografía contemporánea de la época —exposición perfecta, gama tonal completa, enfoque nítido, composición tradicional— junto con un tratamiento existencial de «amor duro» por los Estados Unidos, revestido del aura de las películas de cine negro del periodo que cubría a los fotógrafos de esta generación. Y, como en sus compañeros del momento, se produce el golpe inconsciente para crear un estilo deliberado o una firma propia. *Personal Best* reúne muchas de estas fotografías, junto con muchas otras que nunca se habían publicado.

Entonces, ¿qué ha hecho que Erwitt alcance tal fama en tantos modos diferentes que pocos de nosotros hemos visto, hasta el momento, como un todo integral? Esta imagen se ve nublada por su éxito comercial, no sólo como fotógrafo, sino también, durante unos veinte años, como director de documentales cuyas obras se exhibían en el canal de televisión por cable HBO. El estigma de Stieglitz (y de Cartier-Bresson) relacionado con el éxito comercial continúa obsesionando a ciertos sectores del grupo dominante en el mundo del arte que pasan por alto el hecho de que ambos fotógrafos eran económicamente independientes, lo cual les permitía expresarse de ese modo. (¡Y tampoco tenían seis hijos!).

Erwitt, sin embargo, hijo único de una familia rusa desplazada, no tuvo esa suerte. Se encontró en Nueva York con 11 años, después de haber nacido en París, crecido en Milán y escapado de Europa en el último barco que zarpó de la Francia no ocupada. Después, a los 16 años, quedó solo en Los Ángeles, donde sus padres habían levantado el campamento, se habían separado y se habían marchado. Debe existir alguna serie de televisión con la historia de un adolescente inmerso en las culturas de Rusia, Italia, Francia y la ciudad de Nueva York, que asista al instituto Hollywood High y viva en una casita alquilada con un grupo de amigos.

Erwitt sobrevivió a todo esto y utilizó la experiencia para convertirse en un asombroso observador de los demás, extremadamente sensible a las vicisitudes de la vida y, en caso necesario, totalmente atractivo y encantador. (Contemplen a ese joven y guapo soldado raso en 1951 trabajando la línea de señoritas a la puerta de los baños para señoras [véase el frontis]). Entonces, ¿es de extrañar que su mirada se haya convertido en una de las más agudas, sensibles y distintivas de la fotografía del siglo XX?

Sean Callahan

Le fotografie di Elliott Erwitt (così come la sua vita) sono molto più complesse di quanto sembri. Così pure la raccolta di sue immagini chiamata *Personal Best* potrebbe sembrare un modo di esprimersi semplice e diretto. In realtà non è così.

Nel lessico fotografico interpretato da Erwitt, il termine "personal" è riferito alle foto scattate espressamente per sé stesso quando si guadagnava da vivere come fotografo professionista. Sia da adolescente, nel laboratorio di una squallida agenzia pubblicitaria di Hollywood ("Una volta ho lavato e asciugato 25.000 foto di Ingrid Bergman in una settimana!") o in un secondo tempo, a New York, in qualità di membro della celebre agenzia fotografica Magnum dove, tra i vari progetti, si è occupato di raffigurare i rapporti annuali delle società incluse nell'elenco Fortune 500, le campagne pubblicitarie milionarie per Madison Avenue o le notizie di primo piano per Paris *Match*, Erwitt ha sempre lavorato con grande professionalità per i propri clienti riuscendo comunque a trovare il tempo per rimanere un fotografo amatoriale per sé stesso. Per lui, il termine "amatoriale" non è affatto peggiorativo; egli si sofferma infatti sulla radice latina della parola *amo* (dal verbo "amare"). La fotografia per il gusto di amarla. O, come lui stesso direbbe, la fotografia complicata.

Allo scopo di farmi un'idea più chiara su Erwitt, parecchi anni fa chiesi a uno dei suoi maestri, Henri Cartier-Bresson, di esprimere un parere a proposito di questo suo dualismo e mi disse: "Secondo me, Elliott ha ottenuto il massimo seguendo un percorso lavorativo obbligato attraverso le campagne commerciali e continuando comunque a proporre una gamma di immagini rubate e sprigionanti un aroma, un sorriso dal suo intimo più profondo." E ciò, da un'icona che, come Stieglitz prima ancora di lui, non poteva accettare l'idea di un fotografo che lavorasse solo per sé stesso.

Sono poche le opere commerciali incluse in questo volume. La maggior parte delle fotografie qui raccolte sono state scattate da Erwitt per sé stesso (abitualmente con una classica telemetrica della Leica e rigorosamente in bianco e nero) tra un incarico commerciale e l'altro. Ora, a 78 anni e dopo quasi 60 di professione, ha voluto riunire il meglio dei suoi lavori.

Incontrai Erwitt per la prima volta nel 1970, durante una mostra che recensivo per la rivista *Life* allo Smithsonian Institute di Washington. Ciò che mi colpì maggiormente fu la prontezza della sua mente – ed ancor più dei suoi riflessi – in grado di cogliere le giustapposizioni che vanno dal beffardo (pagina 44) allo stravagante (pagina 165) e tutte ritrovate nei più comuni luoghi della Terra. Erwitt l'ironista.

Le fotografie più recenti avrebbero ispirato altri critici a sottolineare che, fatta forse eccezione per Robert Doisneau, nessun altro fotografo del ventesimo secolo ha avuto la sensibilità per l'umorismo; in altre parole, Erwitt captava situazioni della condizione umana che sapevano evocare tutto, dai sorrisi sardonici alle sghignazzate sincere. Erwitt, lo spiritoso.

A questo punto arrivano i cani. Percependo l'affetto del pubblico nei confronti di un perdente, Erwitt scatta innumerevoli fotografie – abbastanza per creare cinque monografie nel corso degli anni – aventi come oggetto il migliore amico dell'uomo. A tal merito P.G. Wodehouse disse: "Non c'è modello in questa sua galleria fotografica che non riesca a commuovere... e non esistono distinzioni di classe "bestiale". Cani di razza e bastardini, ci sono proprio tutti." Erwitt, il fotografo dei cani.

Più spesso trascurato è invece lo schietto fotogiornalismo da rivista a livello internazionale che comprende l'infame "dibattito in cucina" tra Nikita Khrushchev e Richard Nixon, che quest'ultimo utilizzò in un secondo tempo (senza l'autorizzazione di Erwitt) nel corso della campagna per le elezioni presidenziali del 1960 per sostenere la sua piattaforma di solidi ideali anti-comunisti. (A detta di Erwitt, il livello del cosiddetto dibattito era "ridicolo" – due uomini che si vantavano, con crescente irruenza, sul benessere ed il potere del proprio paese. Figlio di emigranti russi, Erwitt capiva cosa si stessero dicendo i due uomini nonostante gli enormi sforzi dei rispettivi interpreti per cercare di mantenere un minimo di diplomazia. "Ad un certo punto, quando Nixon stava davvero diventando insopportabile, mi pareva di aver sentito Khrushchev dire in russo, 'Vai al diavolo!'").

In seguito, nel 1966, durante un periodo molto critico in cui il comportamento di Charles De Gaulle innervosiva gli alleati della NATO, Erwitt produsse il reportage fotografico del viaggio in Russia del presidente francese e, giunto a Mosca, riuscì a passare inosservato e ad intrufolarsi in un retro stanza dove De Gaulle fu visto assieme al leader sovietico in veste non ufficiale.

Erwitt, l'agente segreto invisibile.

Tuttavia, nel corso dell'ultimo decennio, dall'archivio di Erwitt sono emerse ancora moltissime fotografie che potrebbero essere definite come un documentario fotografico socio-realista simile a quelli più noti attribuiti a Robert Frank ma anche alla cosiddetta New York School of Photography alla quale appartengono diversi artisti, tra i quali citiamo William Klein, Louis Faurer e Helen Levitt. (Diane Arbus, Lee Friedlander e Garry Winogrand sarebbero poi emersi nella generazione successiva).

Negli anni novanta Erwitt esibiva sempre più spesso immagini – molte delle quali mai pubblicate dalla loro creazione, avvenuta verso la fine degli anni quaranta e l'inizio dei cinquanta – che gli vinsero l'accesso al firmamento di quel venerato periodo della fotografia d'arte. Tali fotografie rappresentano una cosciente violazione delle regole dei canoni fotografici dell'epoca – esposizione perfetta, gamma tonale completa, messa a fuoco precisa, composizione tradizionale – associati ad un trattamento esistenziale di "amore coriaceo" nei confronti dell'America, dissimulato sotto l'alone dei film noir appartenenti al periodo che incombeva su questa generazione di fotografi. Inoltre, come per i suoi coetanei, si percepisce questo slancio deciso verso la creazione di un determinato stile ed impronta del tutto personale. *Personal Best* riunisce molte di queste immagini ed un numero anche maggiore di fotografie fino ad oggi inedite.

In breve, cosa ha portato Erwitt a conseguire tale importanza in così tanti modi che, fino a oggi, pochi di noi hanno visto nell'insieme? Ad offuscare ulteriormente il quadro della situazione è il suo successo commerciale non solo come fotografo ma, per quasi vent'anni, anche come regista di documentari, trasmessi dalla rete televisiva HBO. Lo stigma di Stieglitz (e di Cartier-Bresson) relativo al successo commerciale tormenta ancora alcuni settori dell'ambiente artistico che ignora il fatto che i due uomini erano indipendentemente agiati e che quindi potevano permettersi di divulgare certe dichiarazioni (per giunta, non avevano sei figli!).

Tuttavia, Erwitt, figlio unico di emigrati russi, non fu così fortunato. A 11 anni si ritrovò a New York dopo essere nato a Parigi, cresciuto a Milano ed essere fuggito dall'Europa a bordo dell'ultima nave partita dalla Francia ancora libera. In seguito, a 16 anni, visse da solo a Los Angeles dove i suoi genitori si erano inizialmente rifugiati, separandosi, per poi partire. Si può individuare una commedia televisiva nella storia di un adolescente immerso nella cultura russa, italiana, francese e newyorkese, che frequenta il liceo a Hollywood High e vive in un bungalow affittato con degli amici.

Erwitt è sopravvissuto a tutto questo ed ha fatto uso della sua esperienza per diventare uno straordinario osservatore degli altri, estremamente sensibile alle vicende della vita e, ove necessario, totalmente affascinante e disarmante. (Eccolo nel 1951 nei panni del giovane e bel soldato a corteggiare le giovani *mädchen* in fila fuori dalle toilettes (vedi frontespizio). C'è quindi da sorprendersi se Erwitt è divenuto uno degli sguardi più acuti, percettivi e individualisti della fotografia del ventesimo secolo?

Sean Callahan

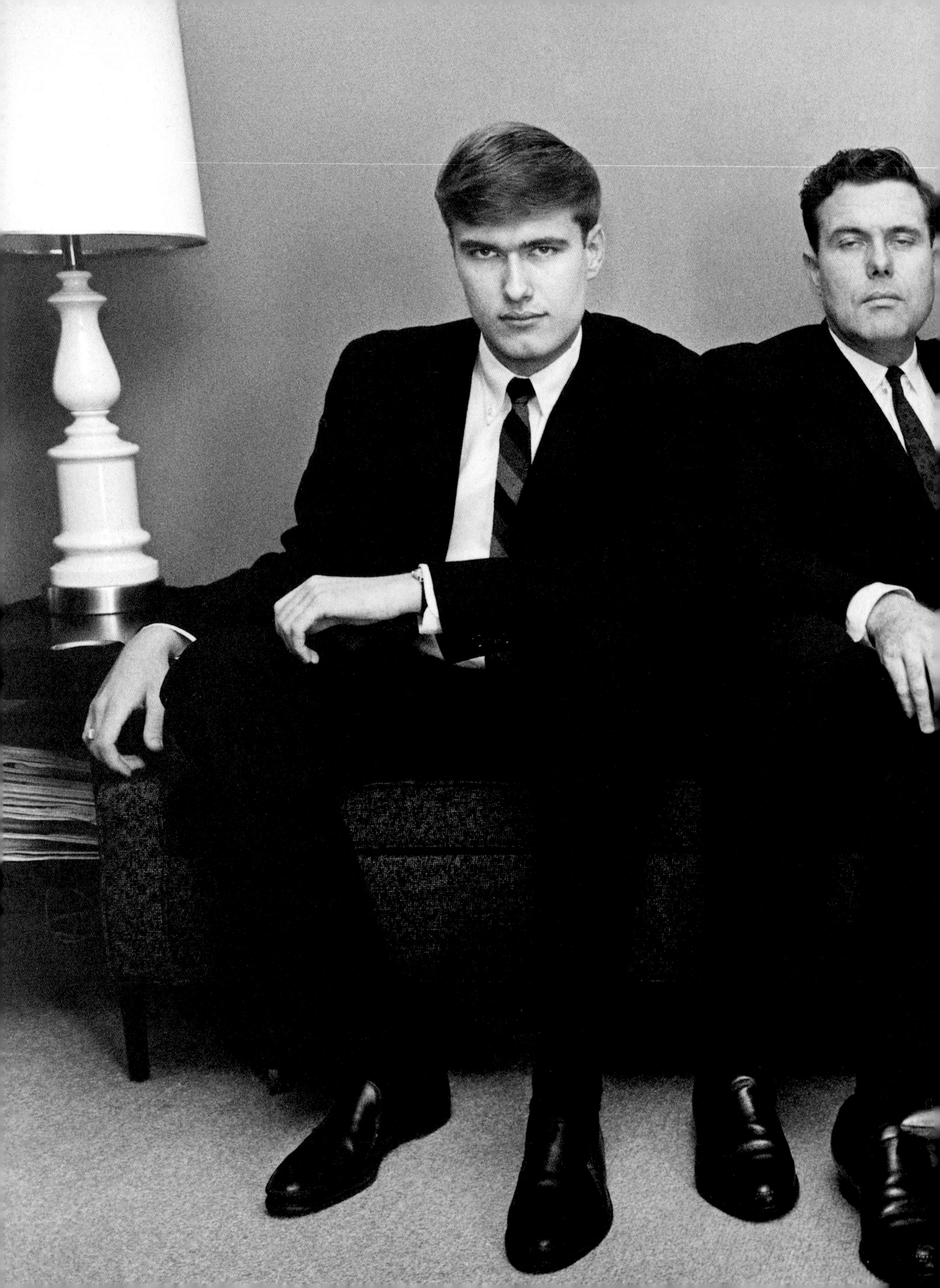

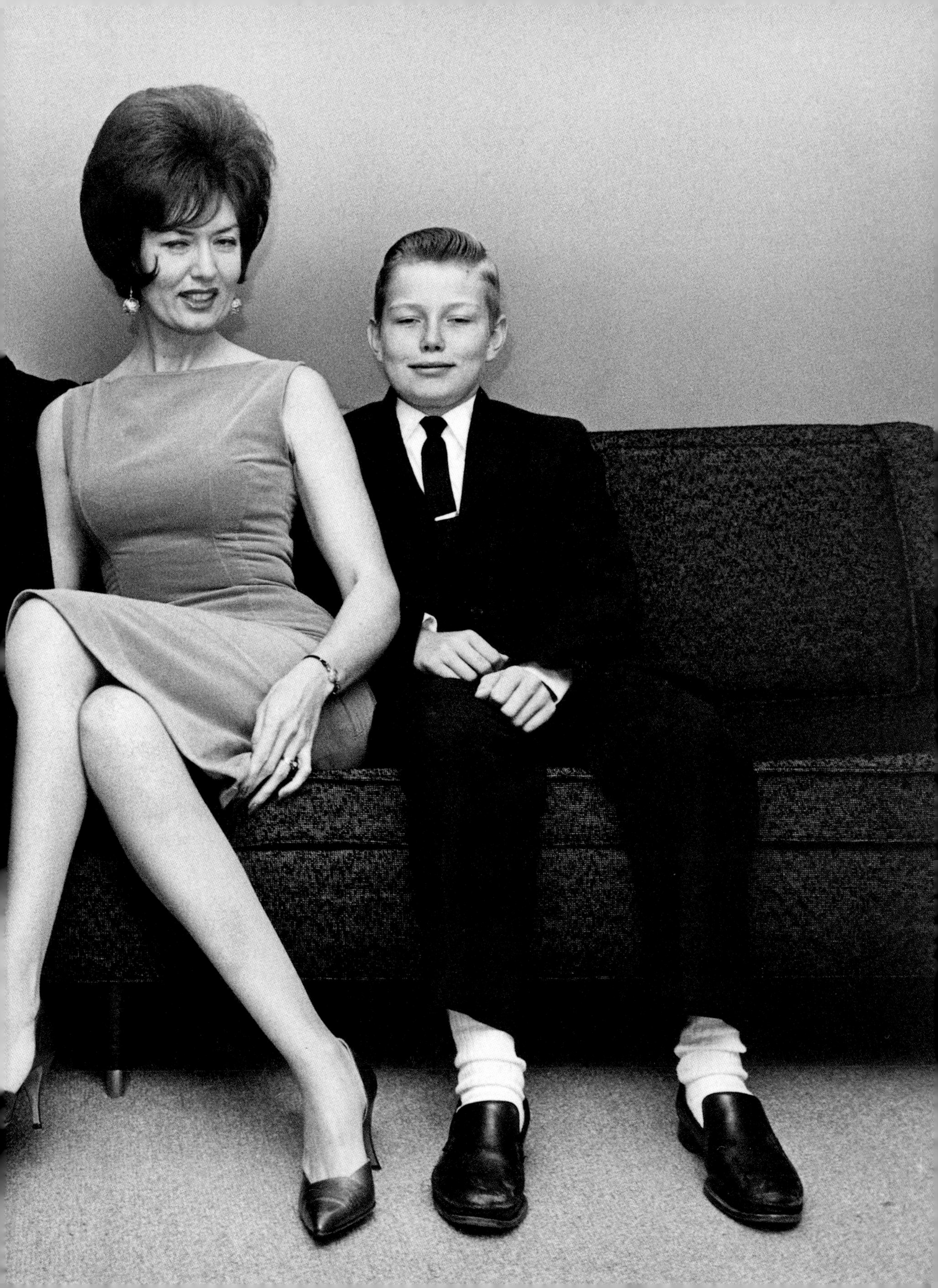

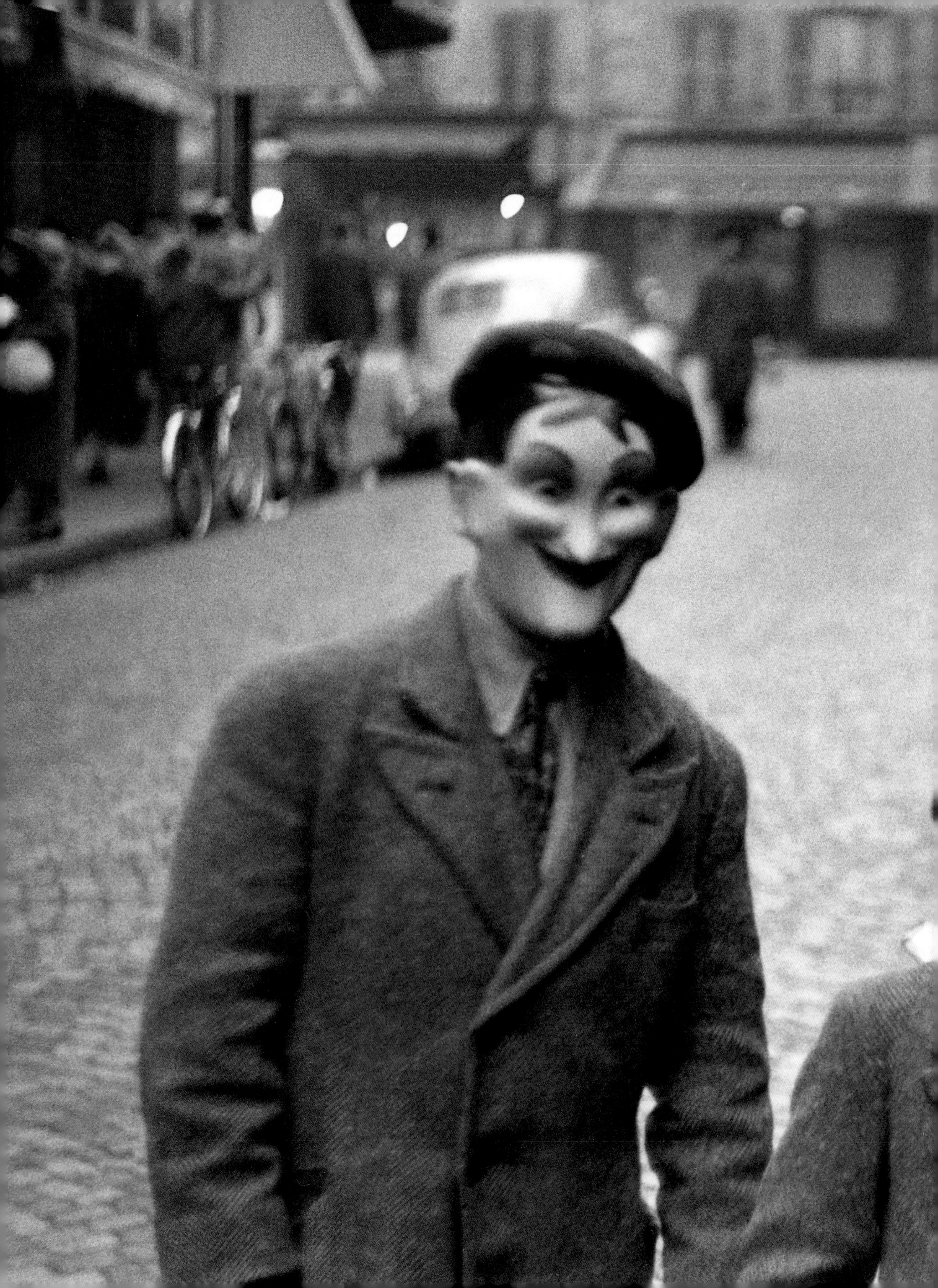

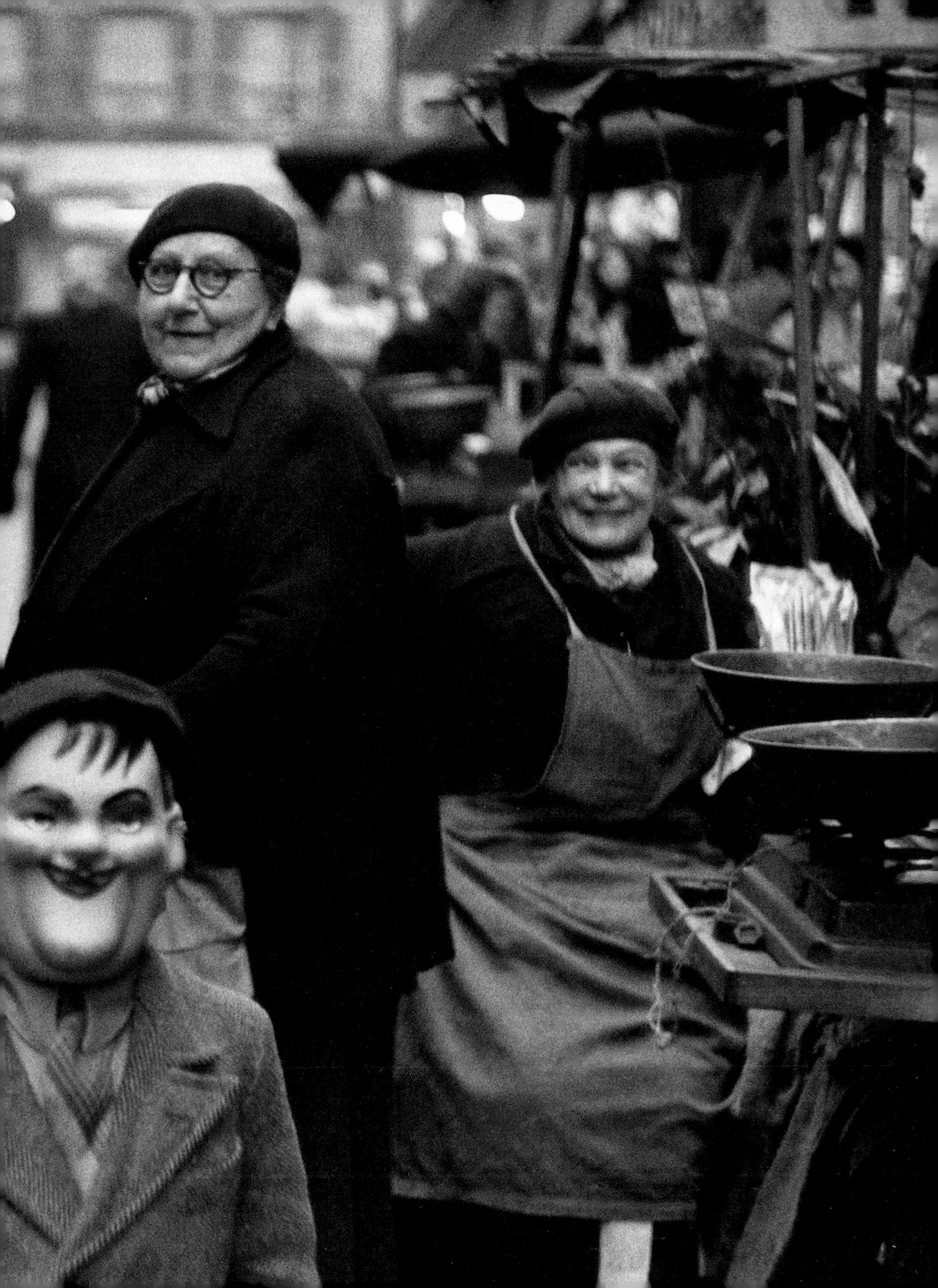

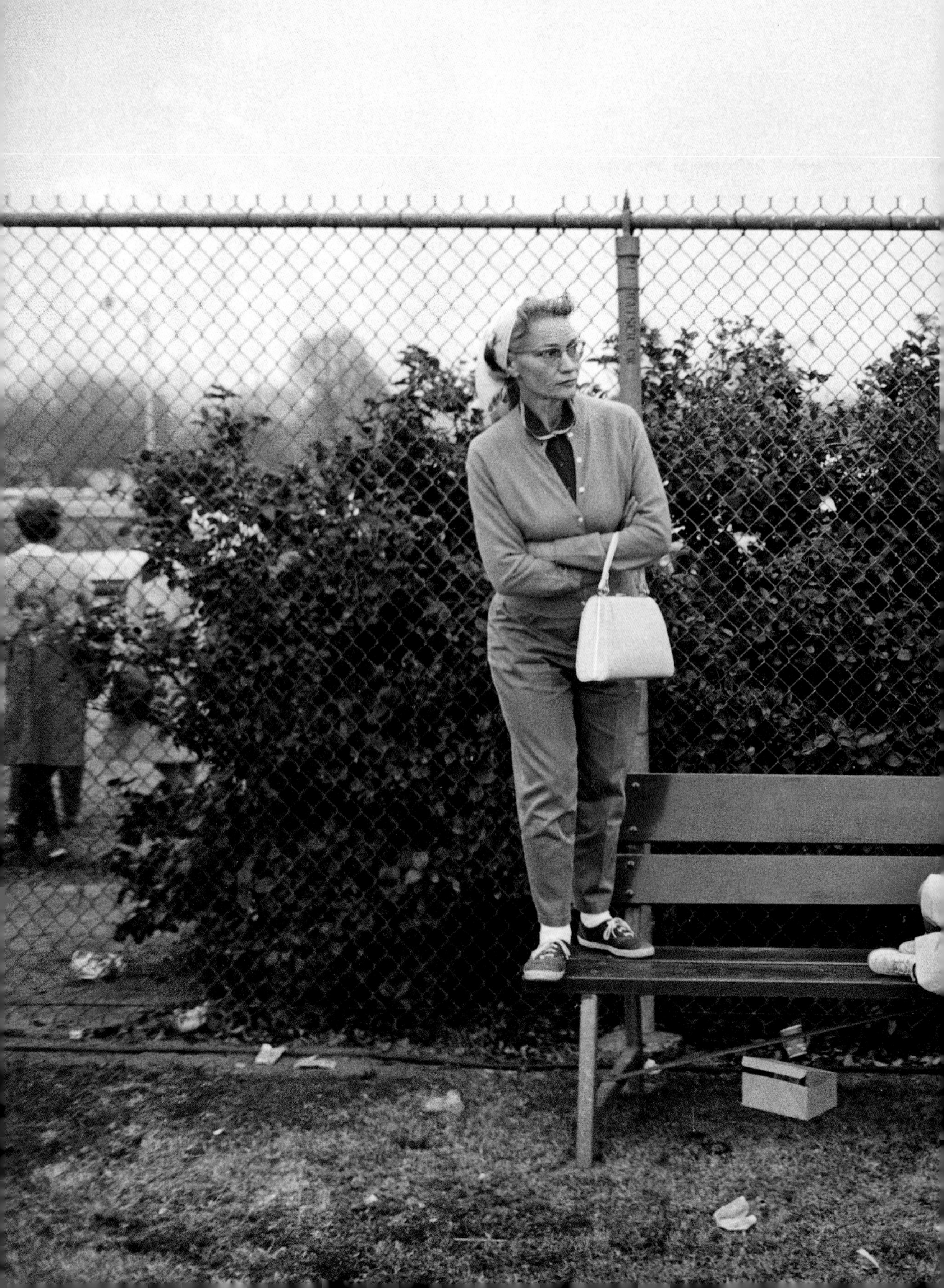

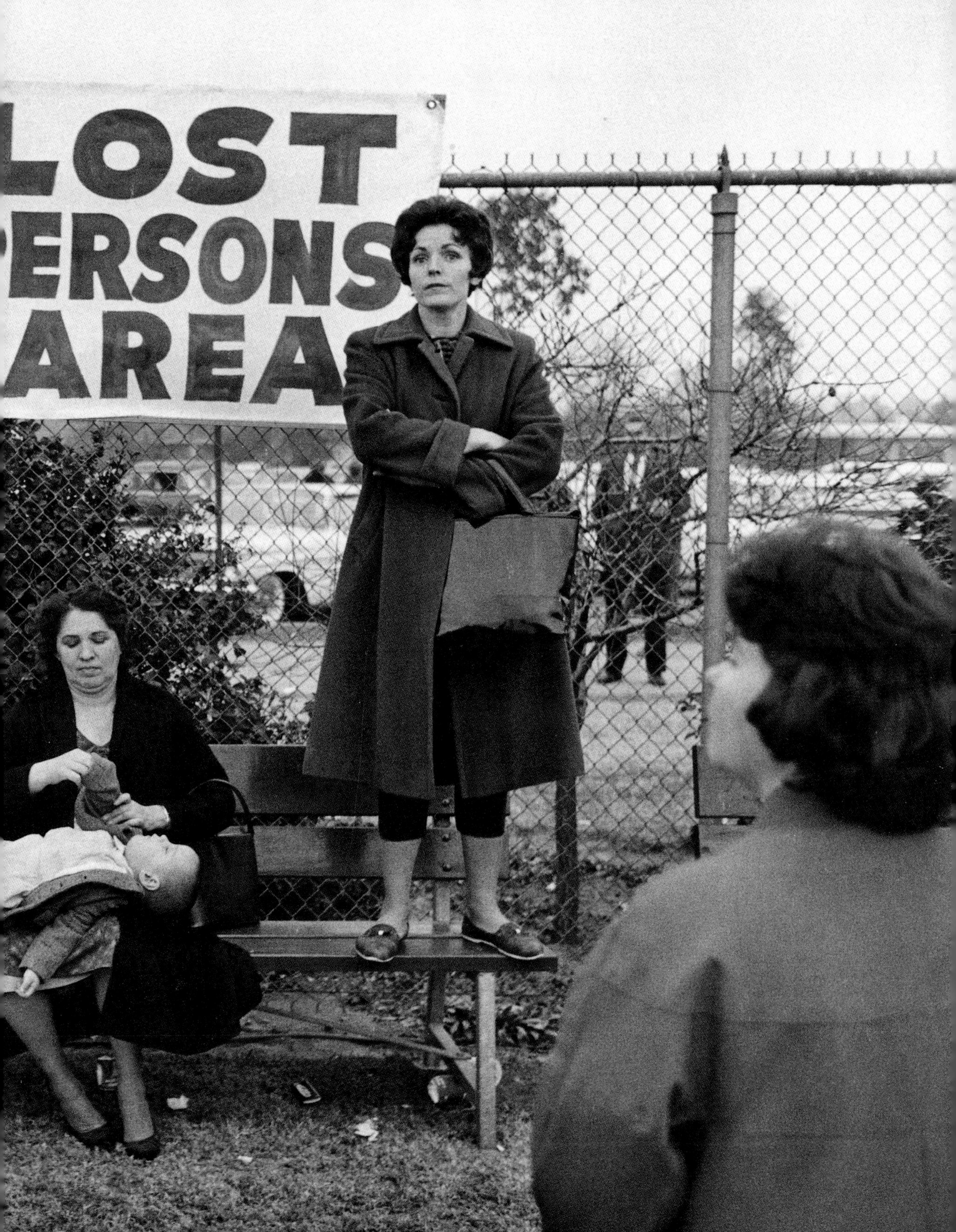

LOST
PERSONS
AREA

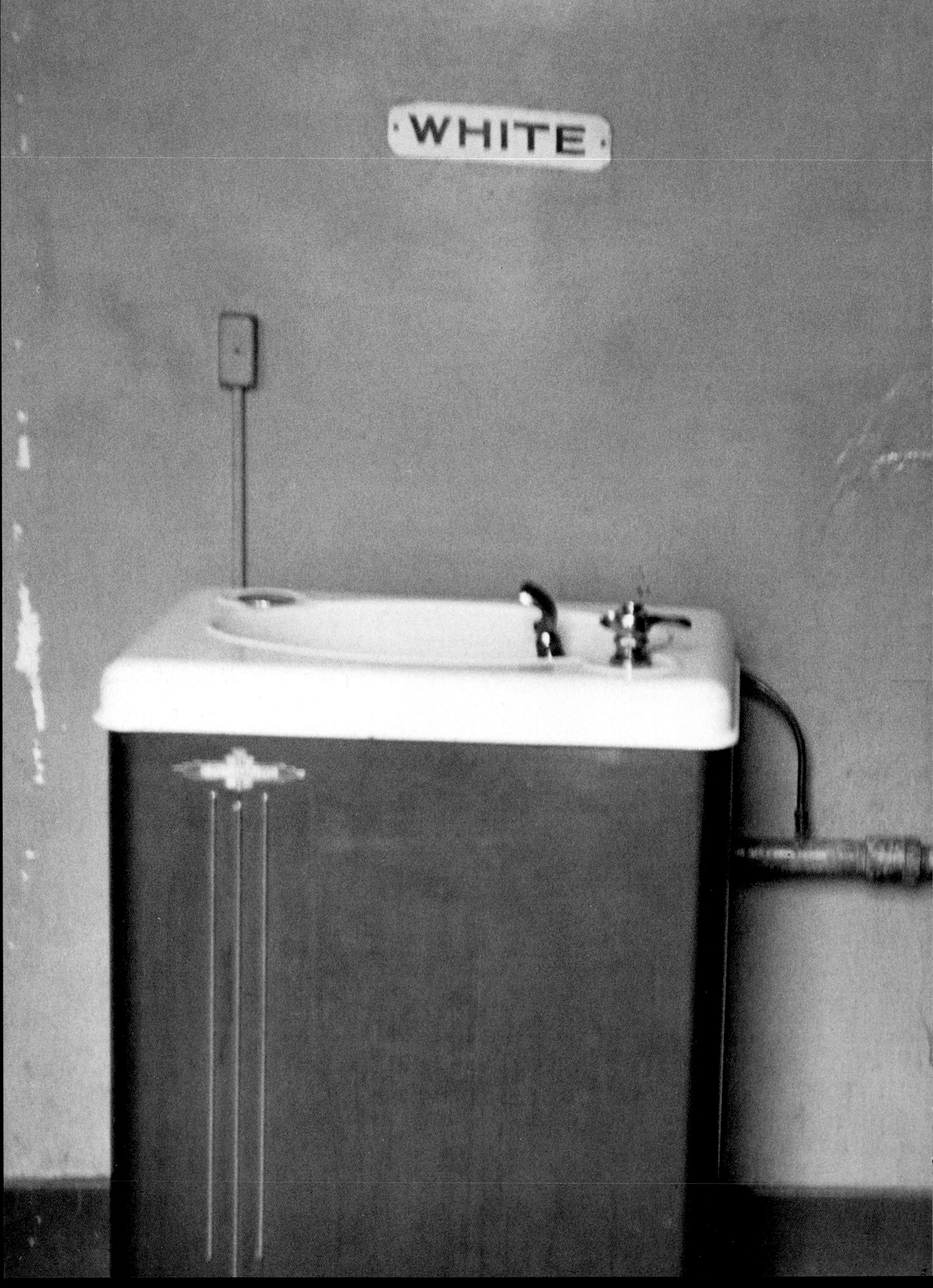
·WHITE·

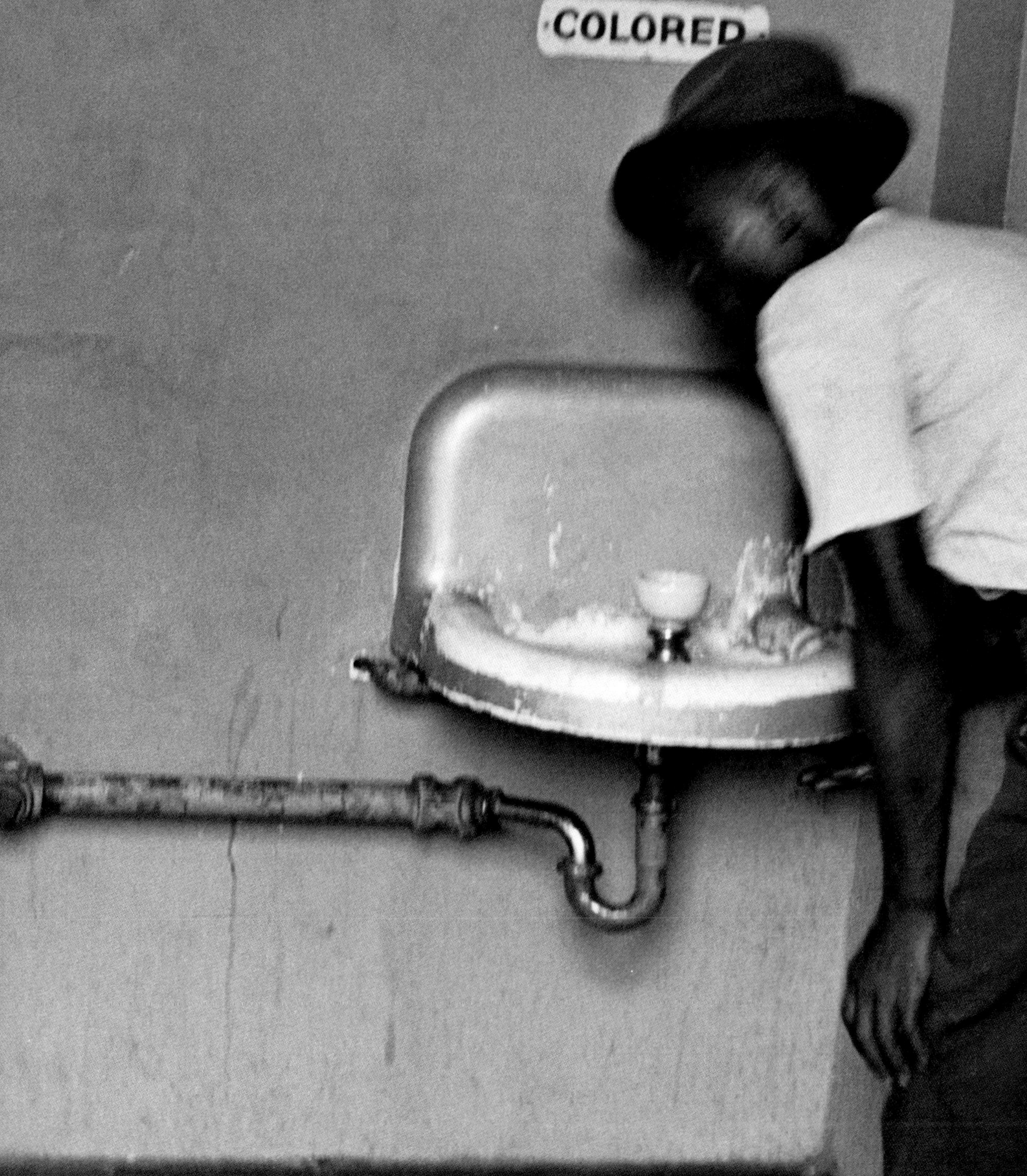
COLORED

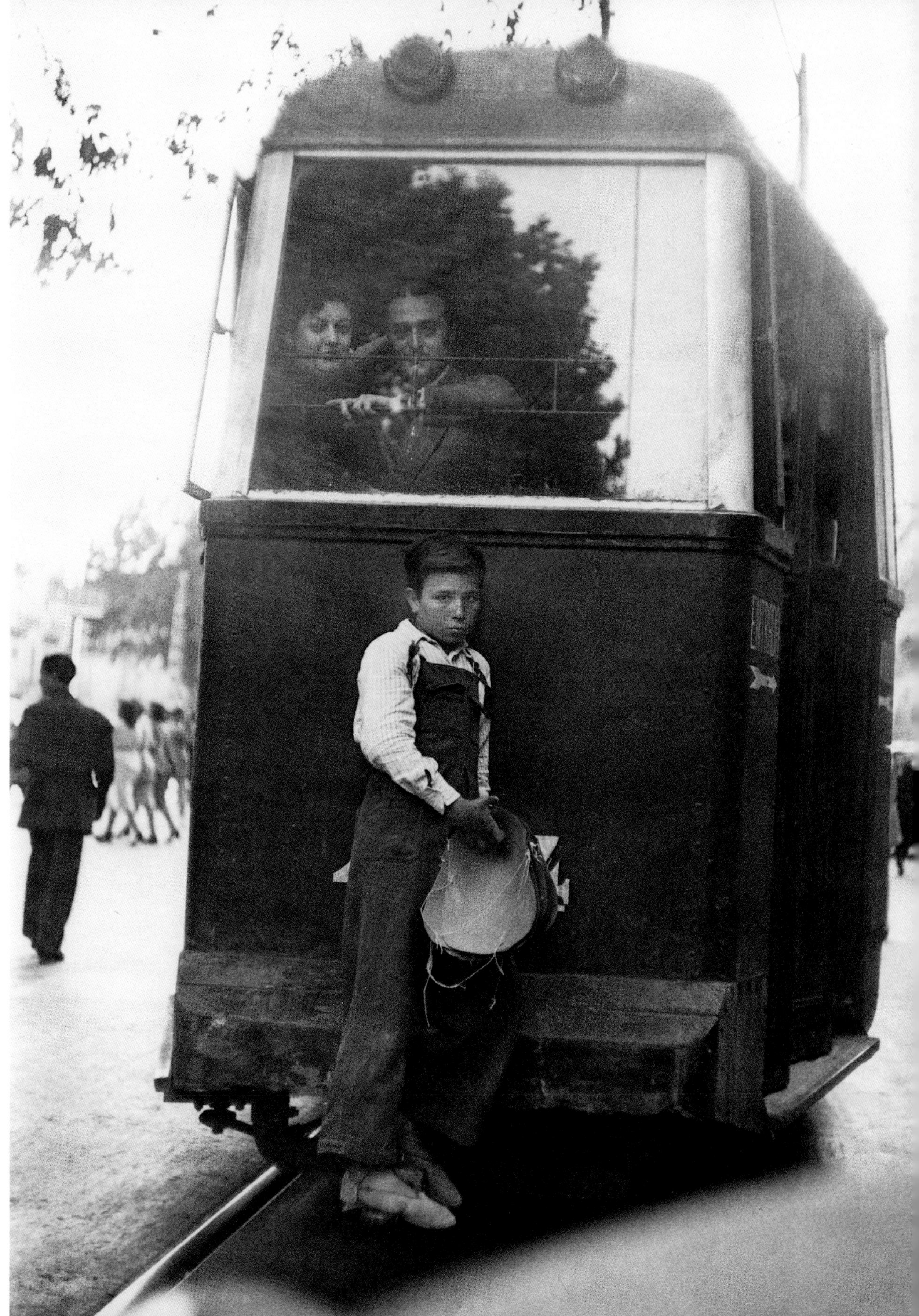

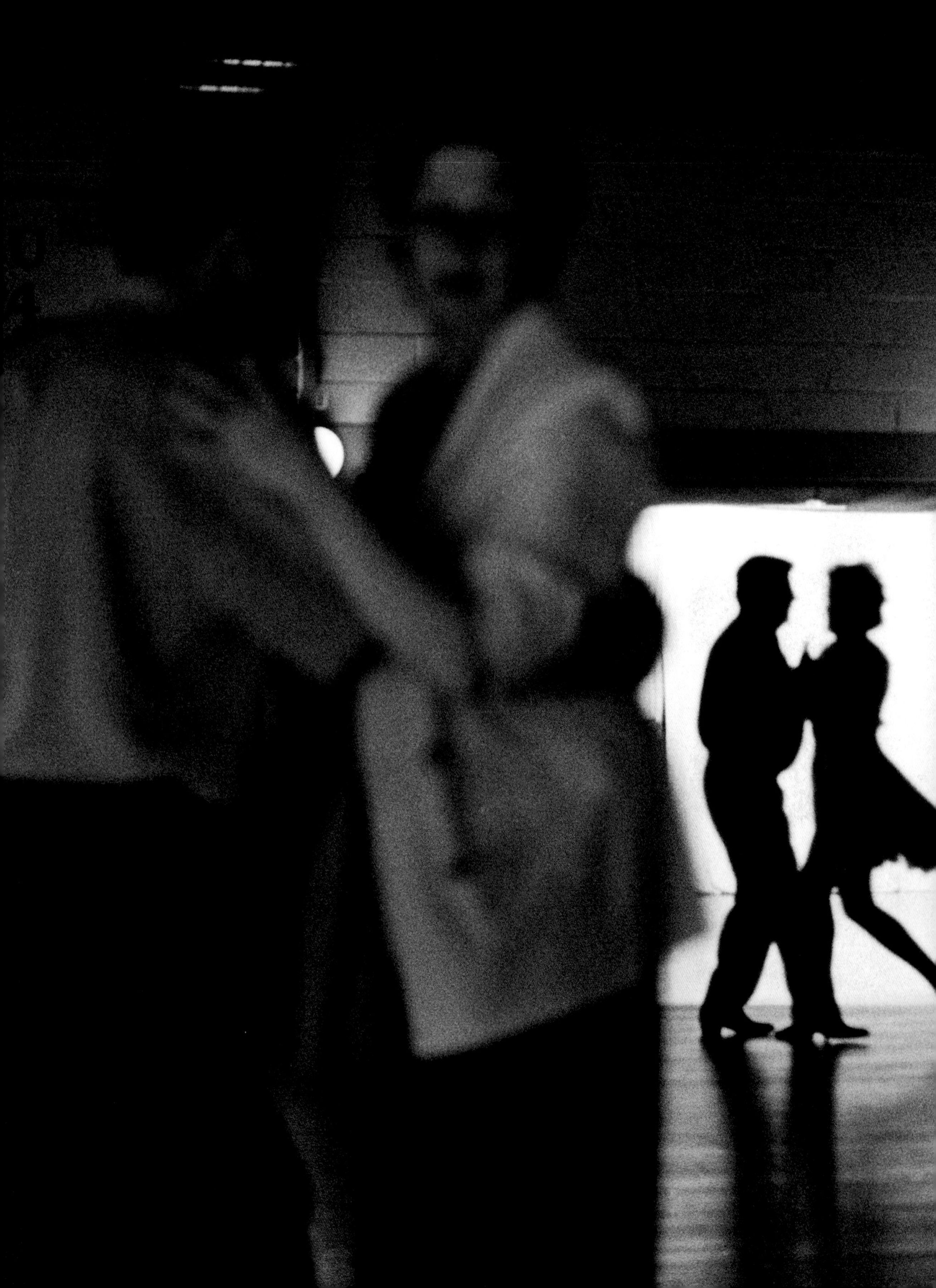

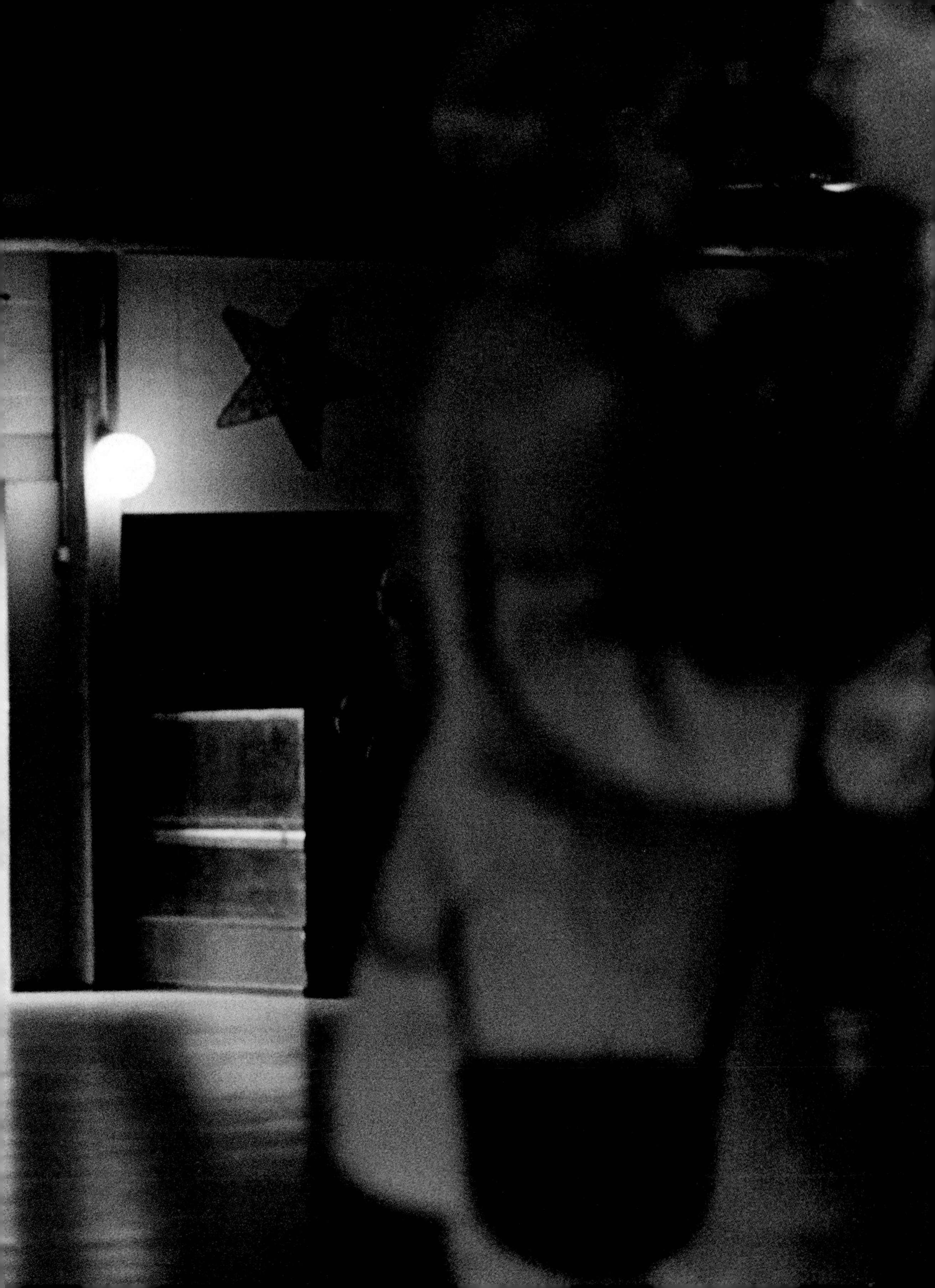

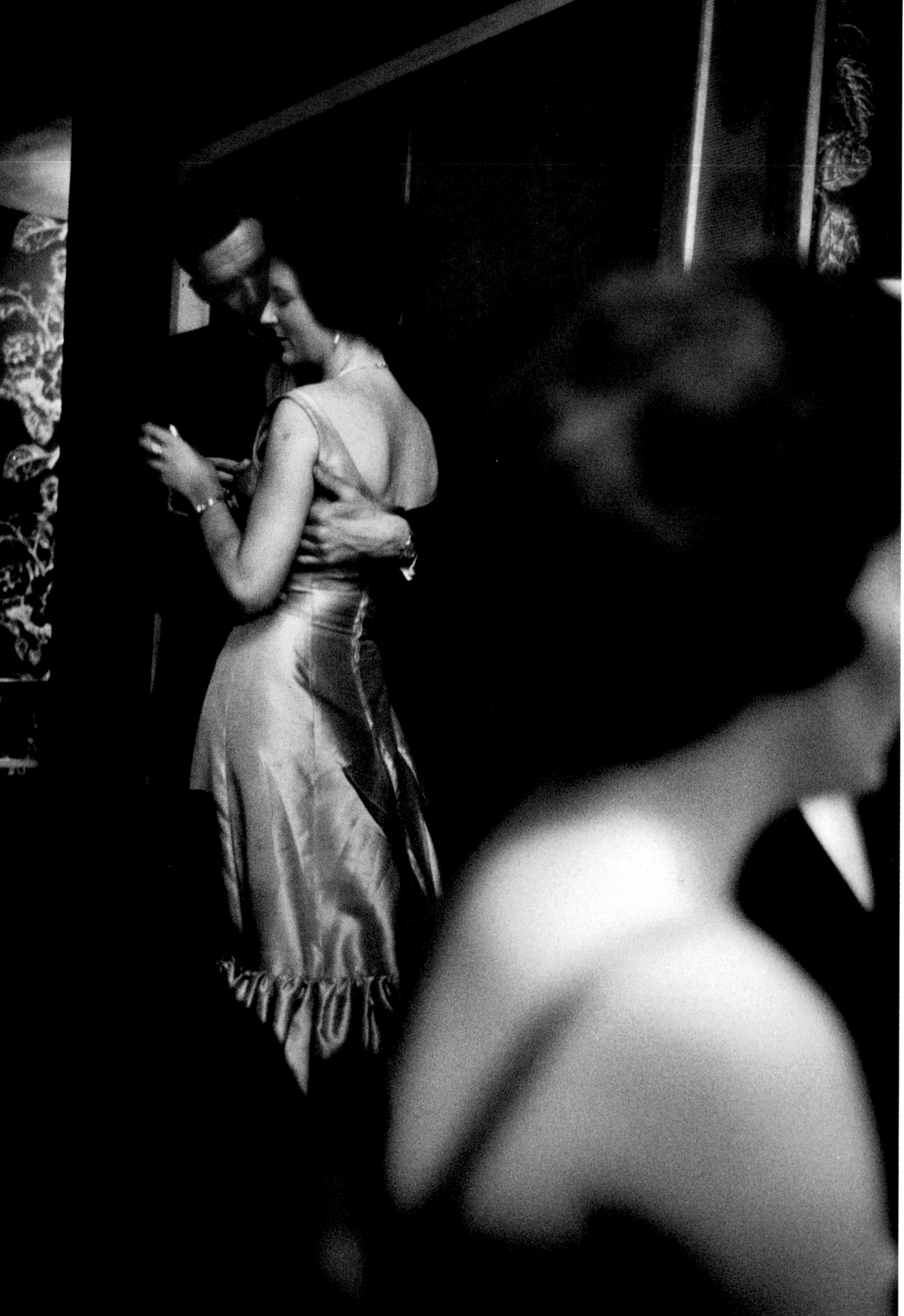

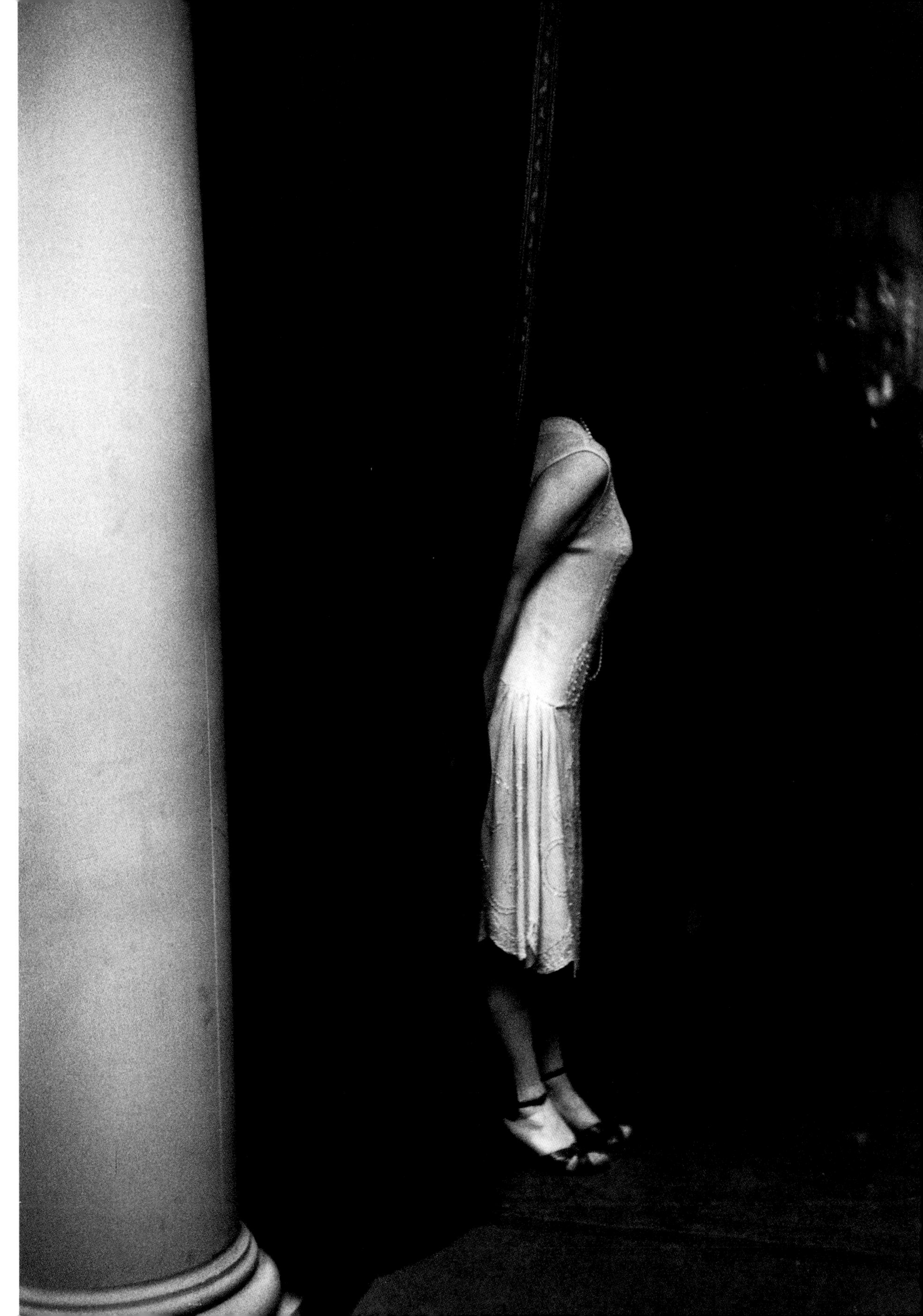

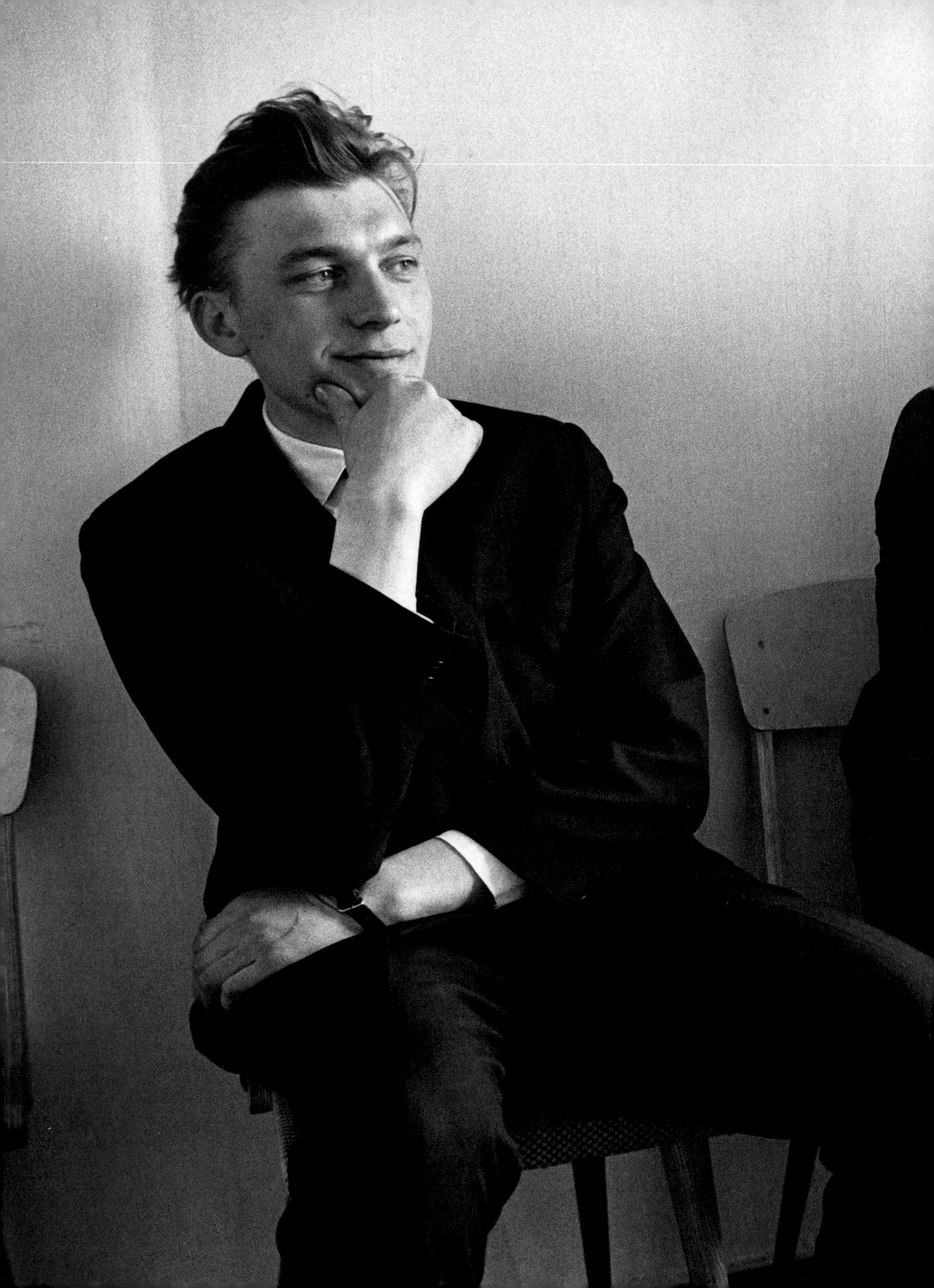

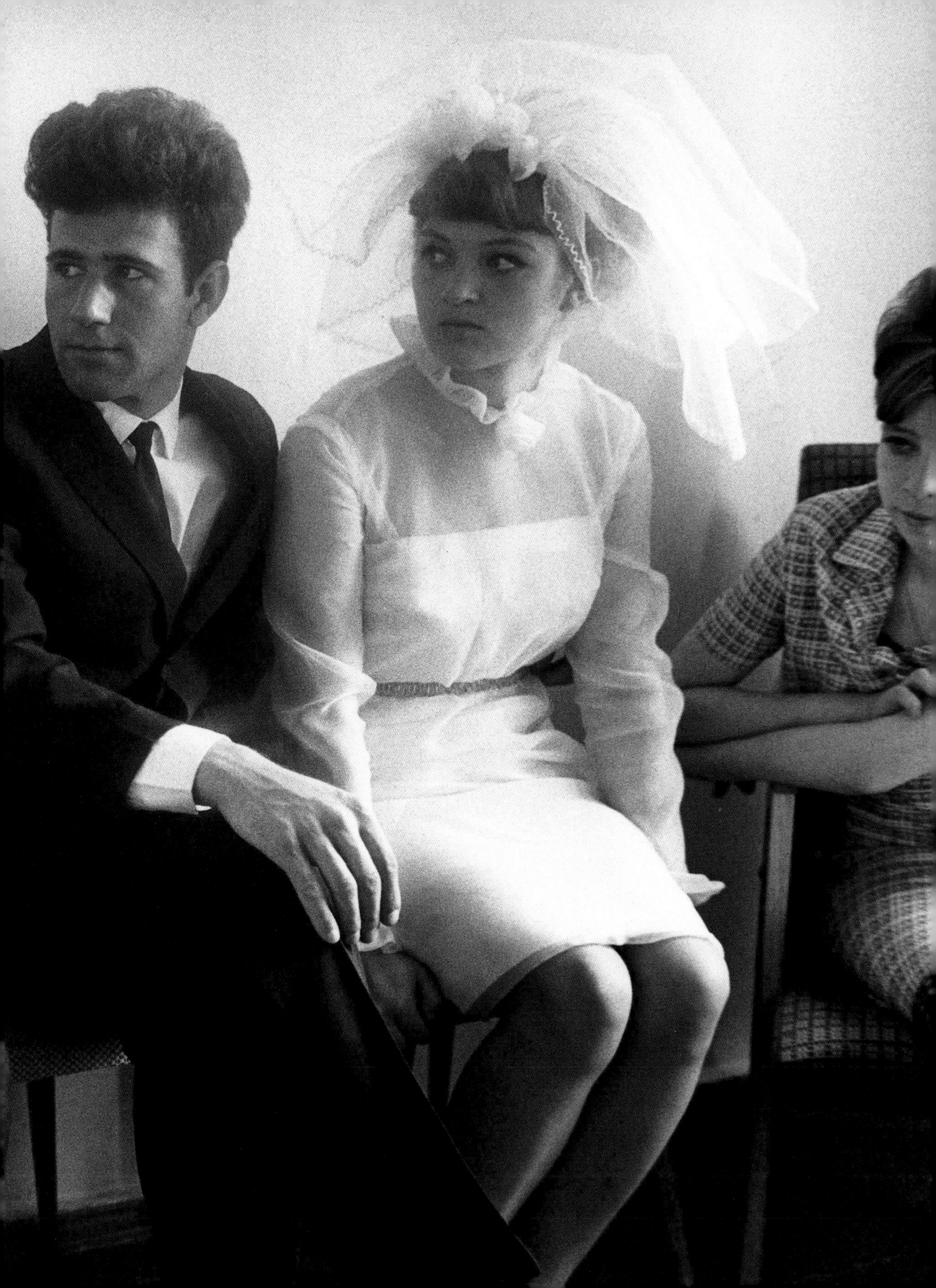

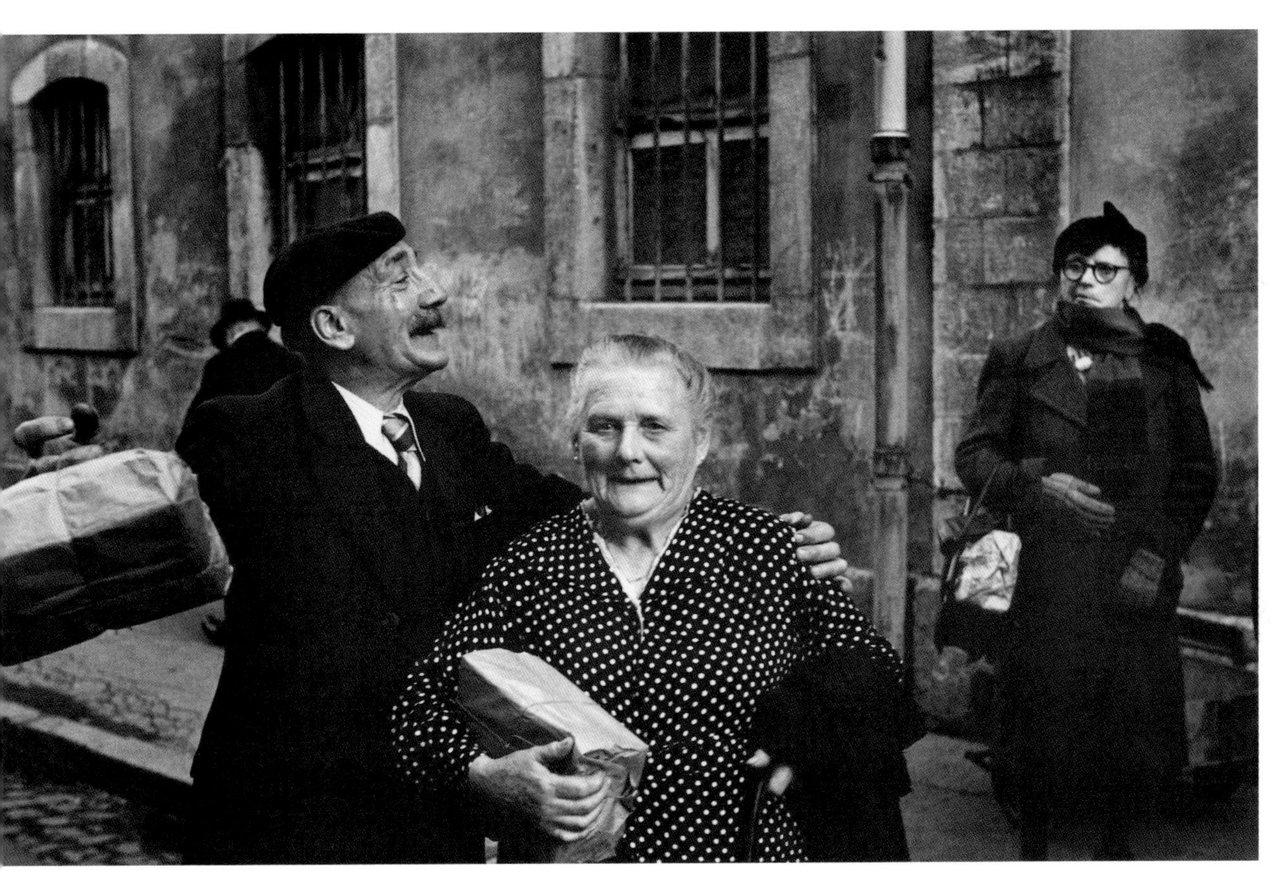

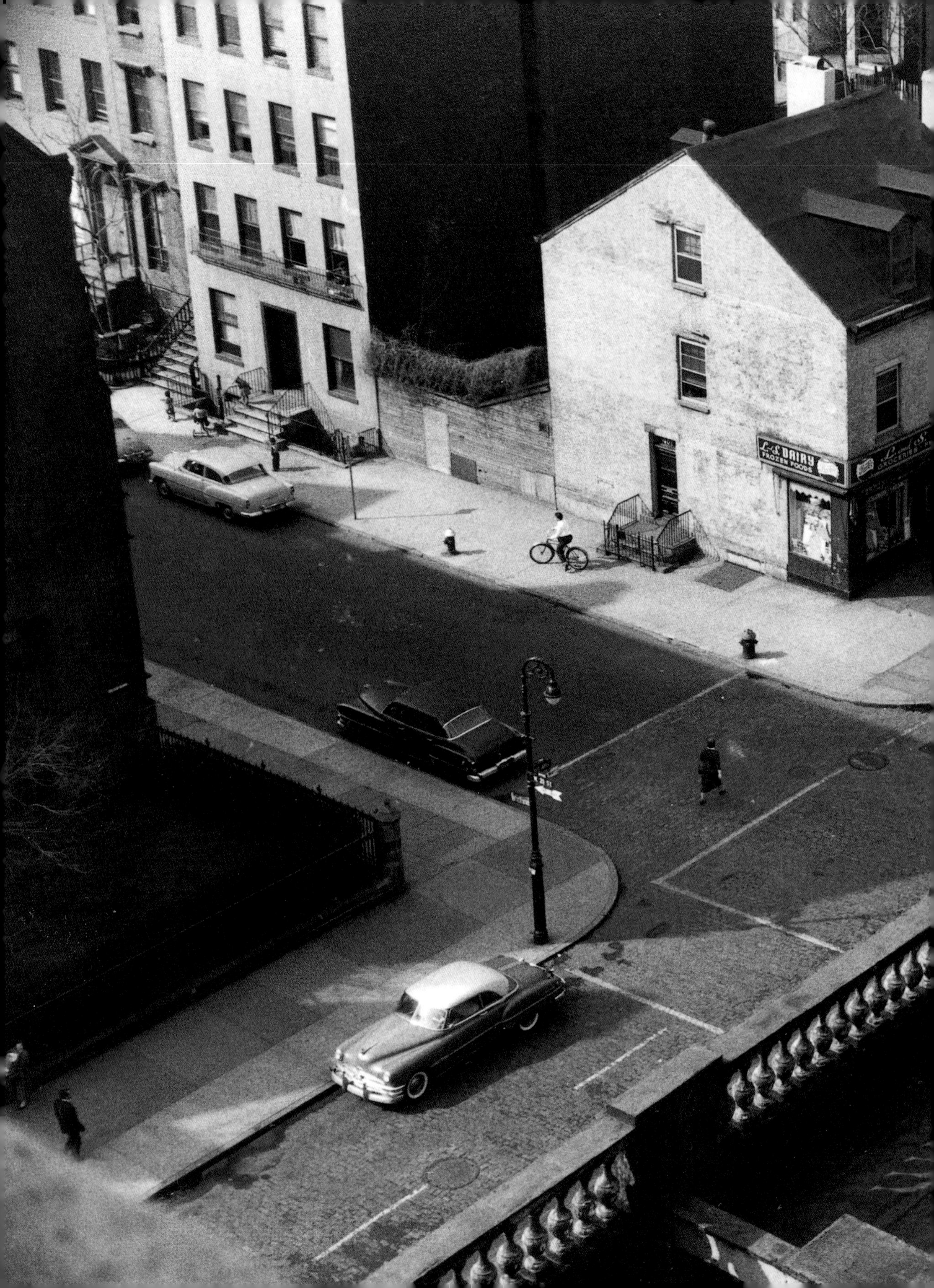

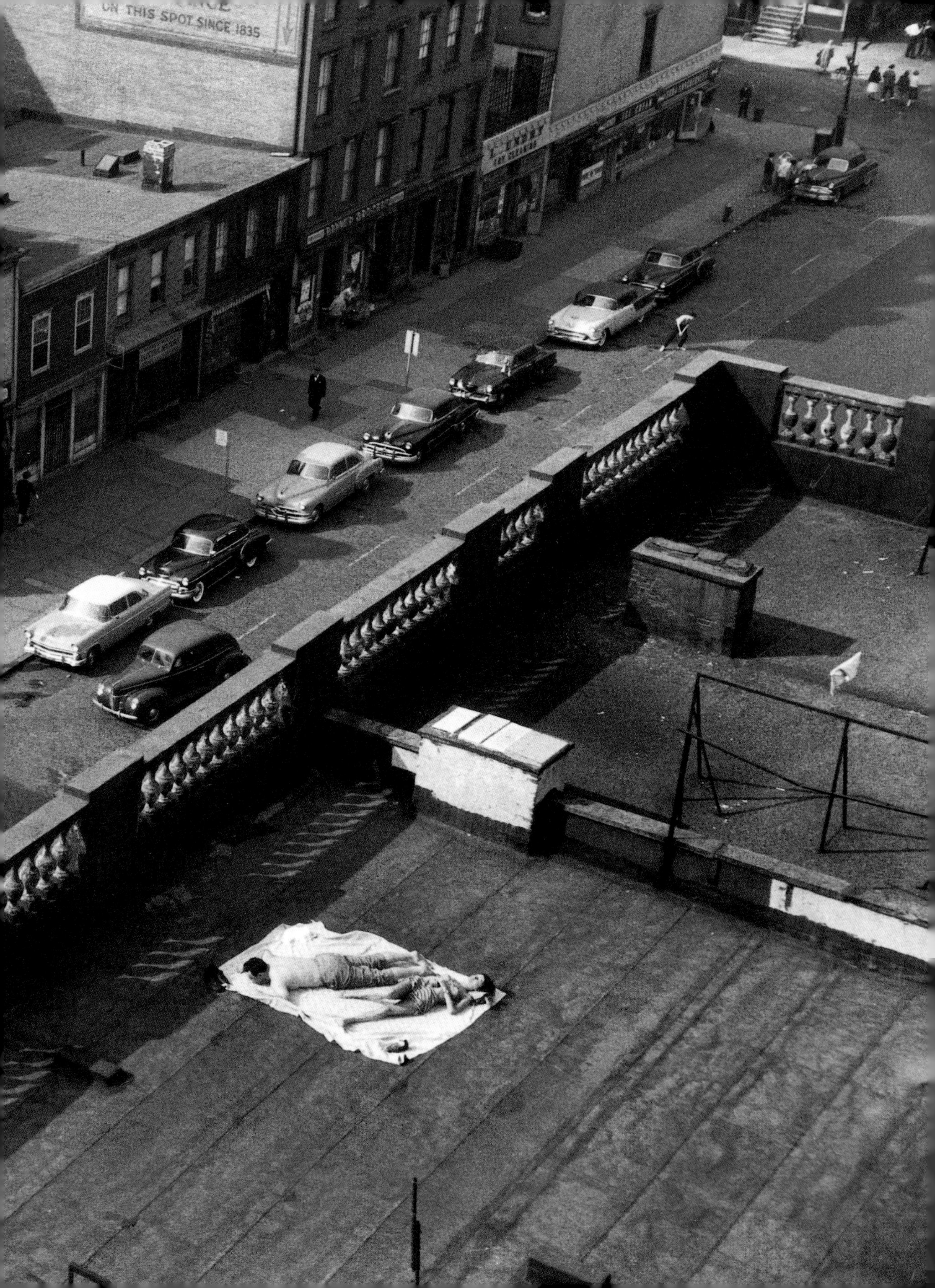
ON THIS SPOT SINCE 1835

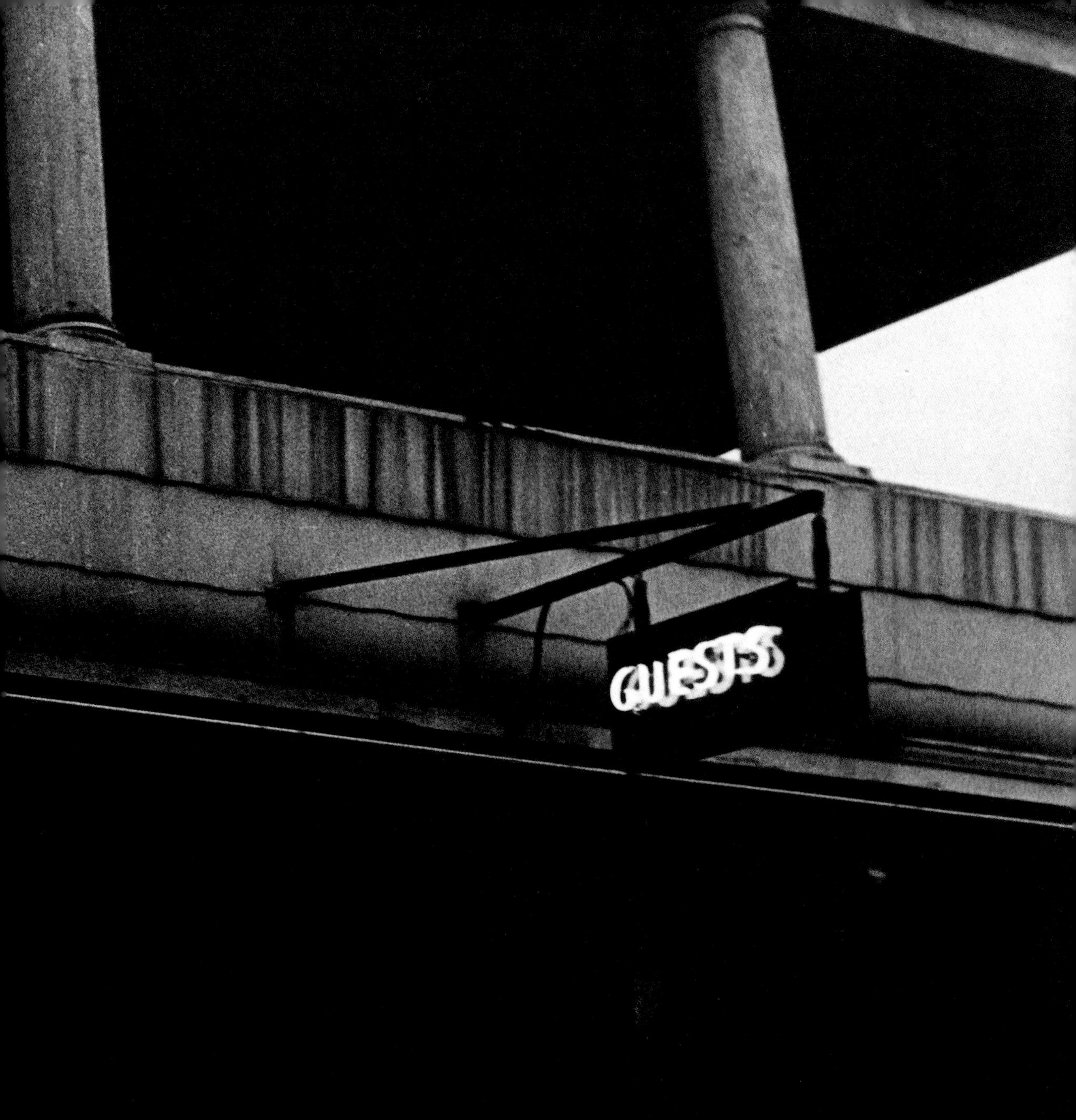
GUESTS

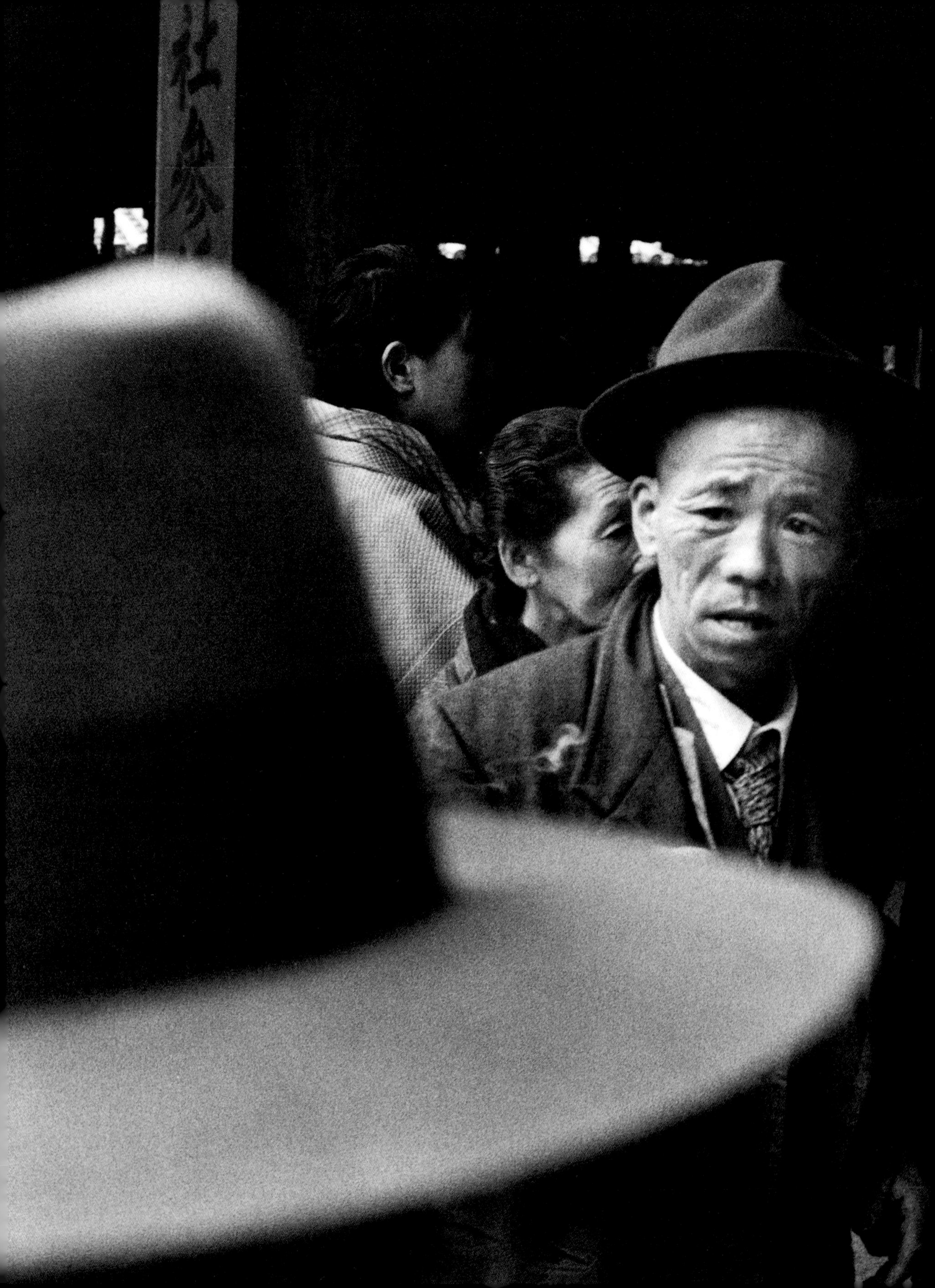

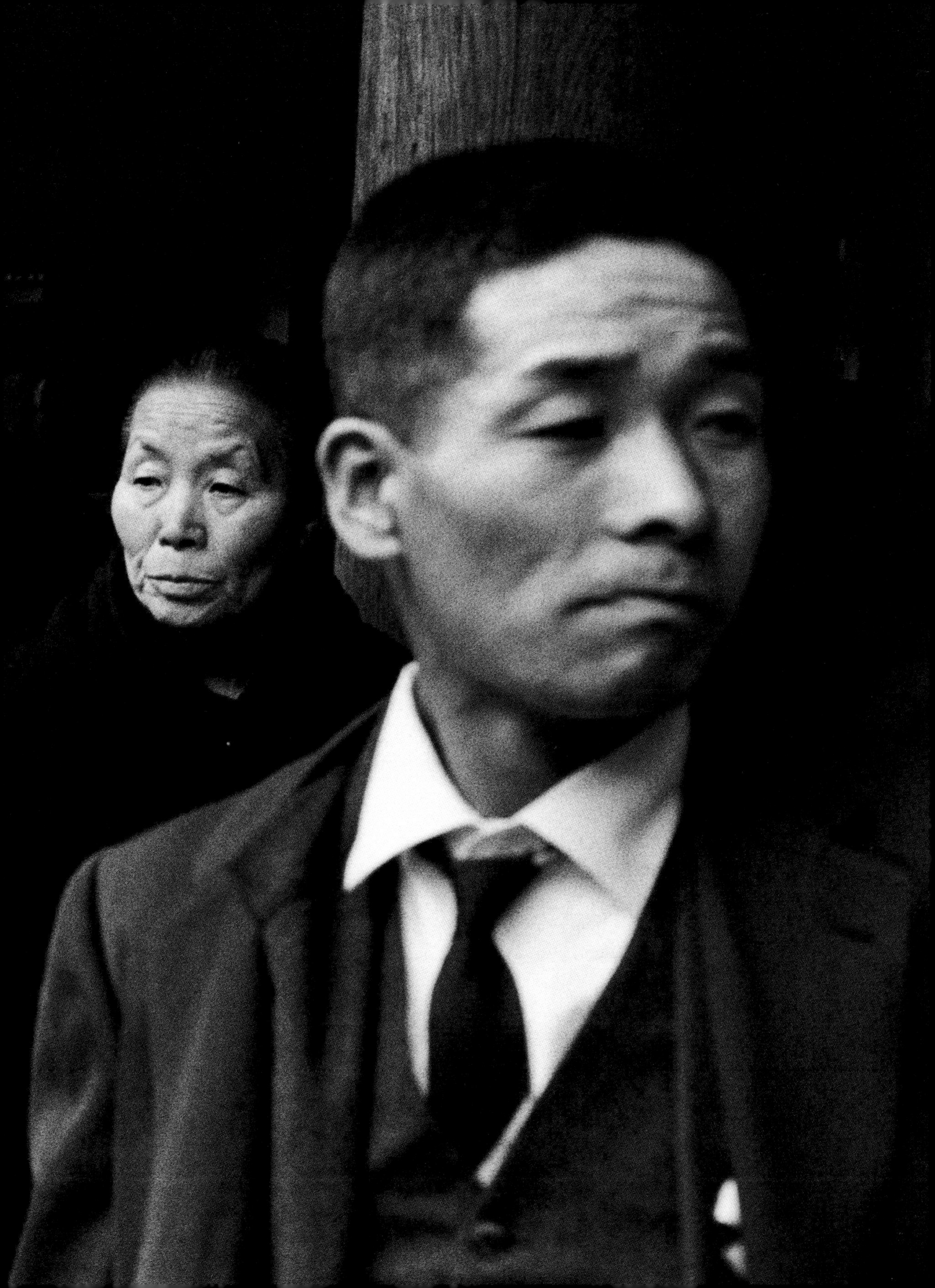

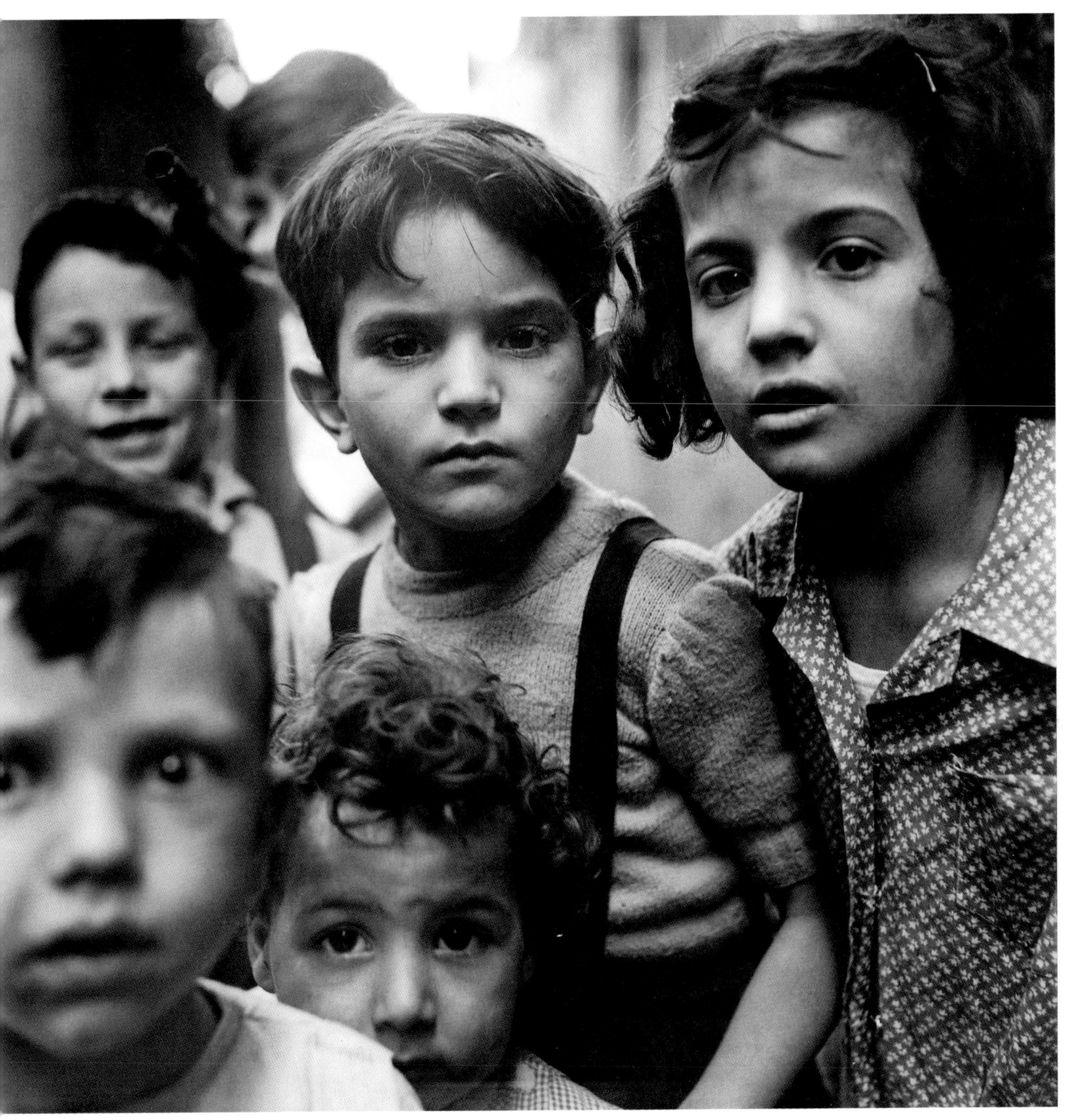

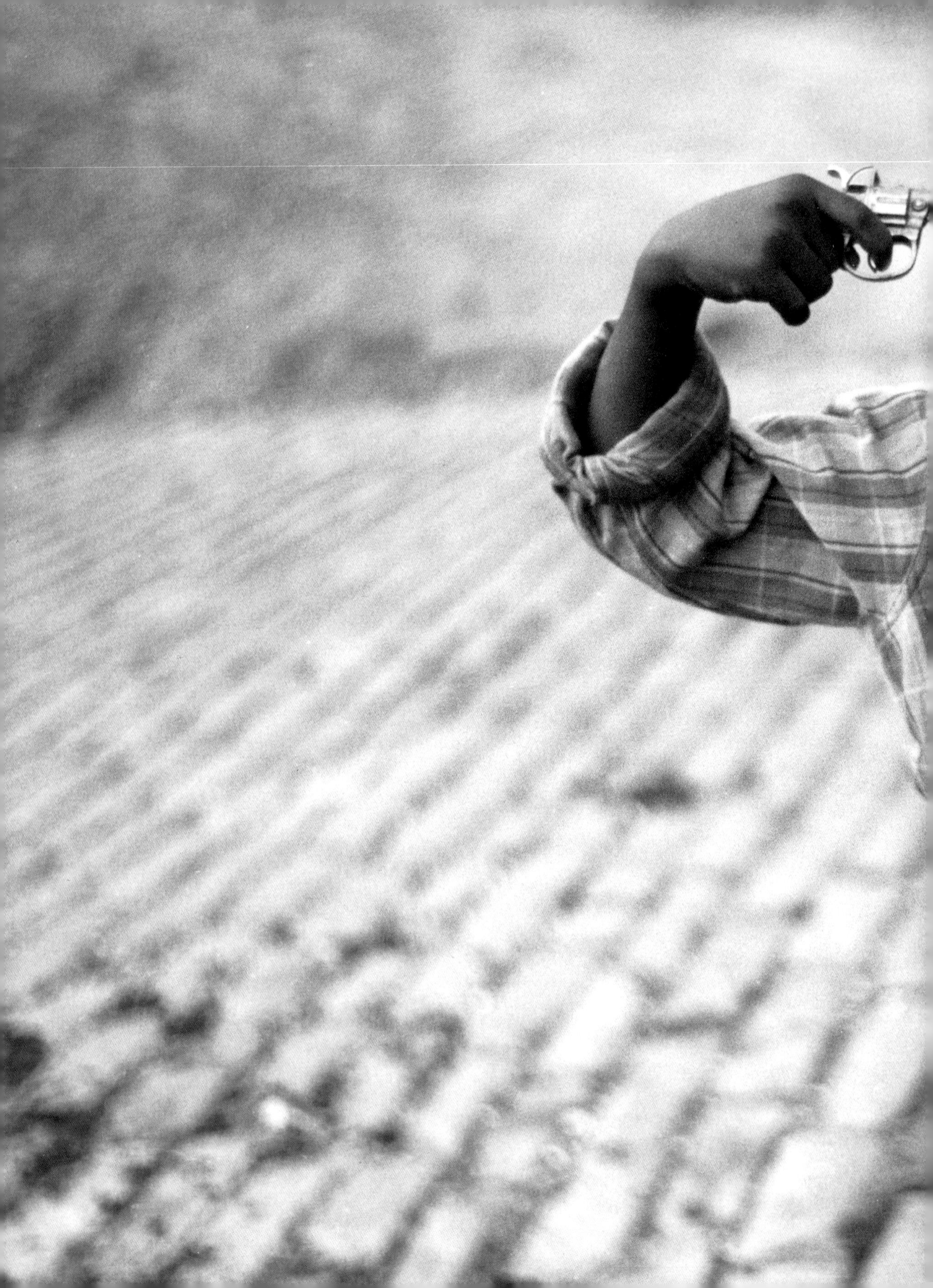

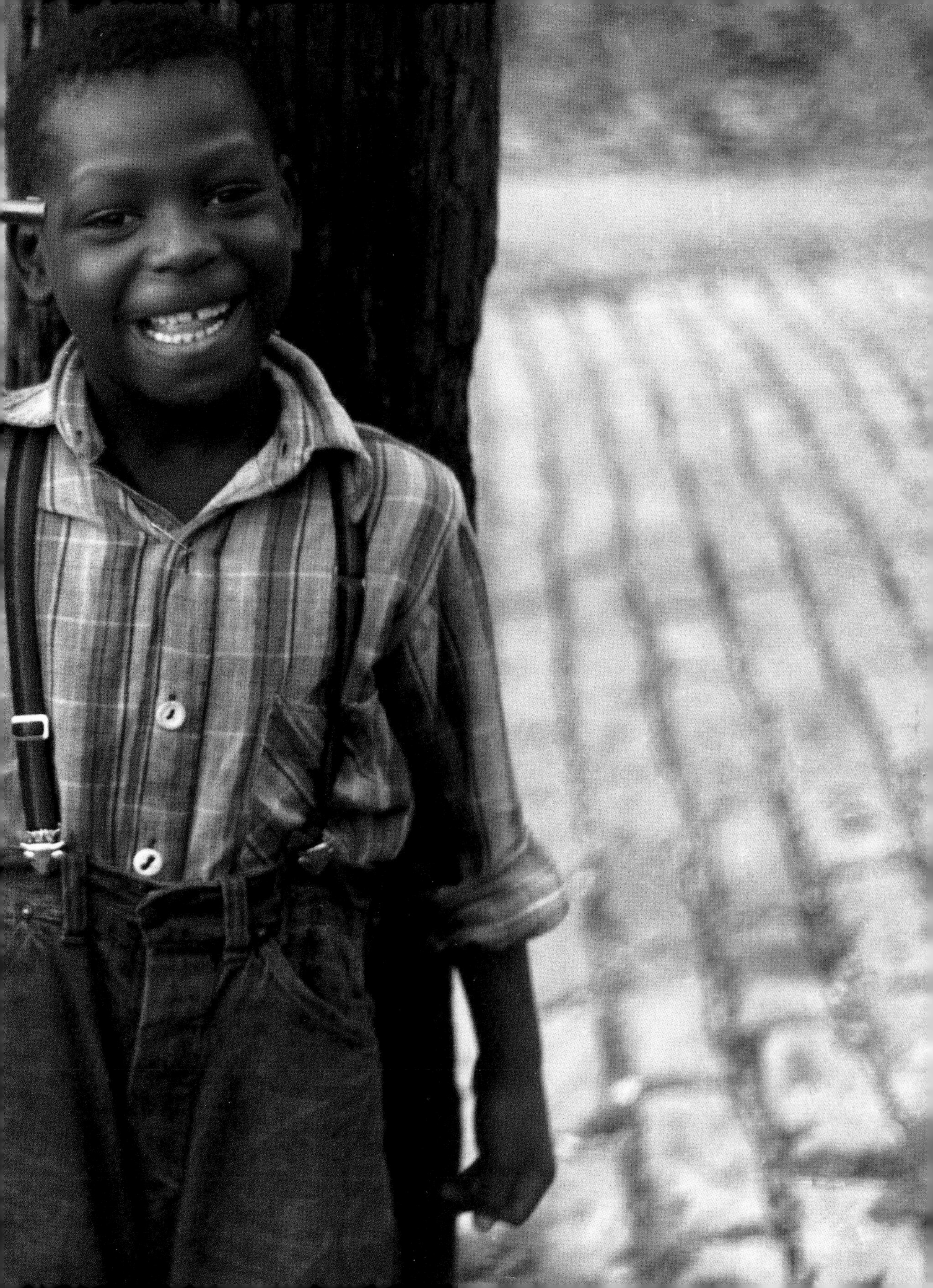

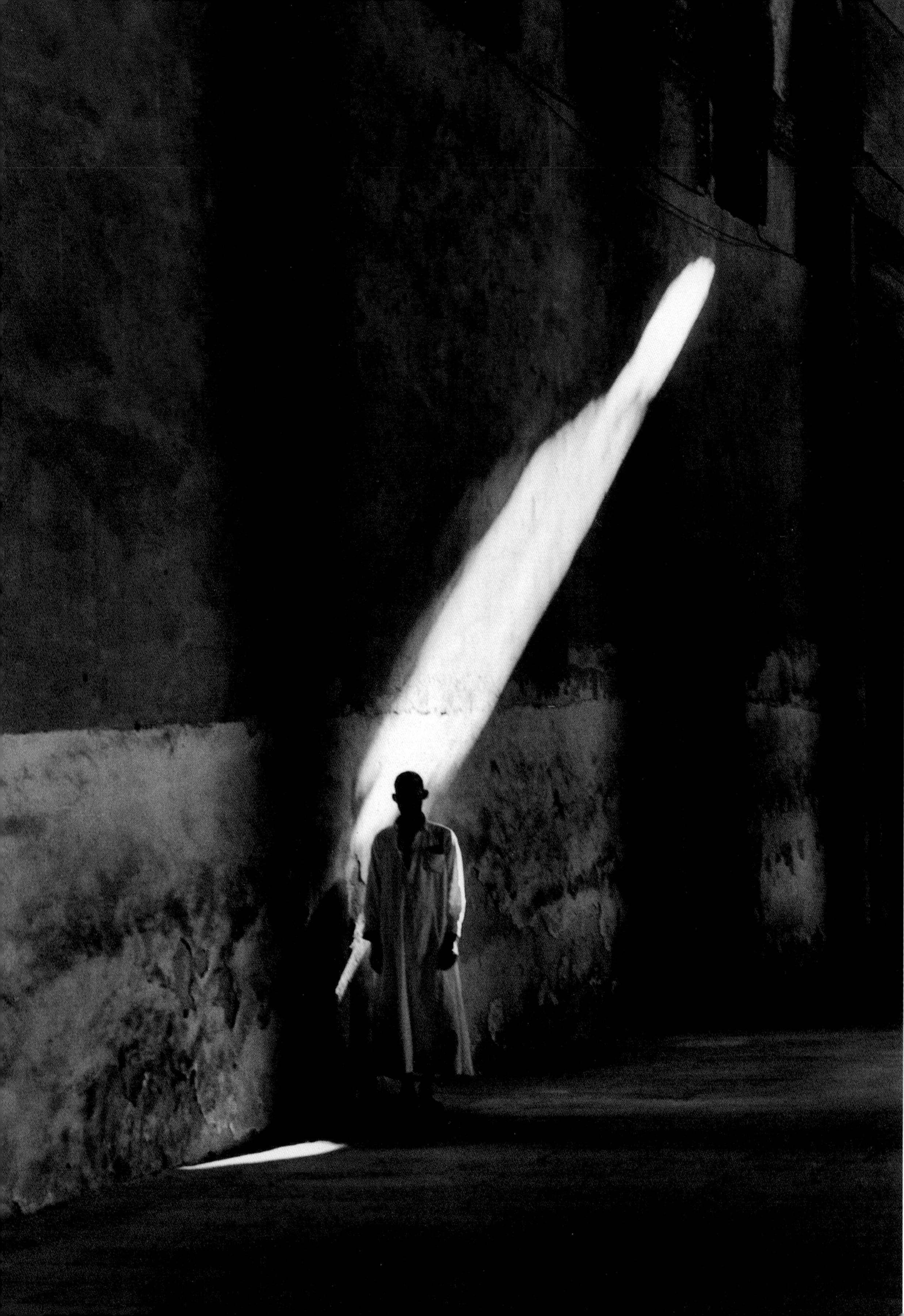

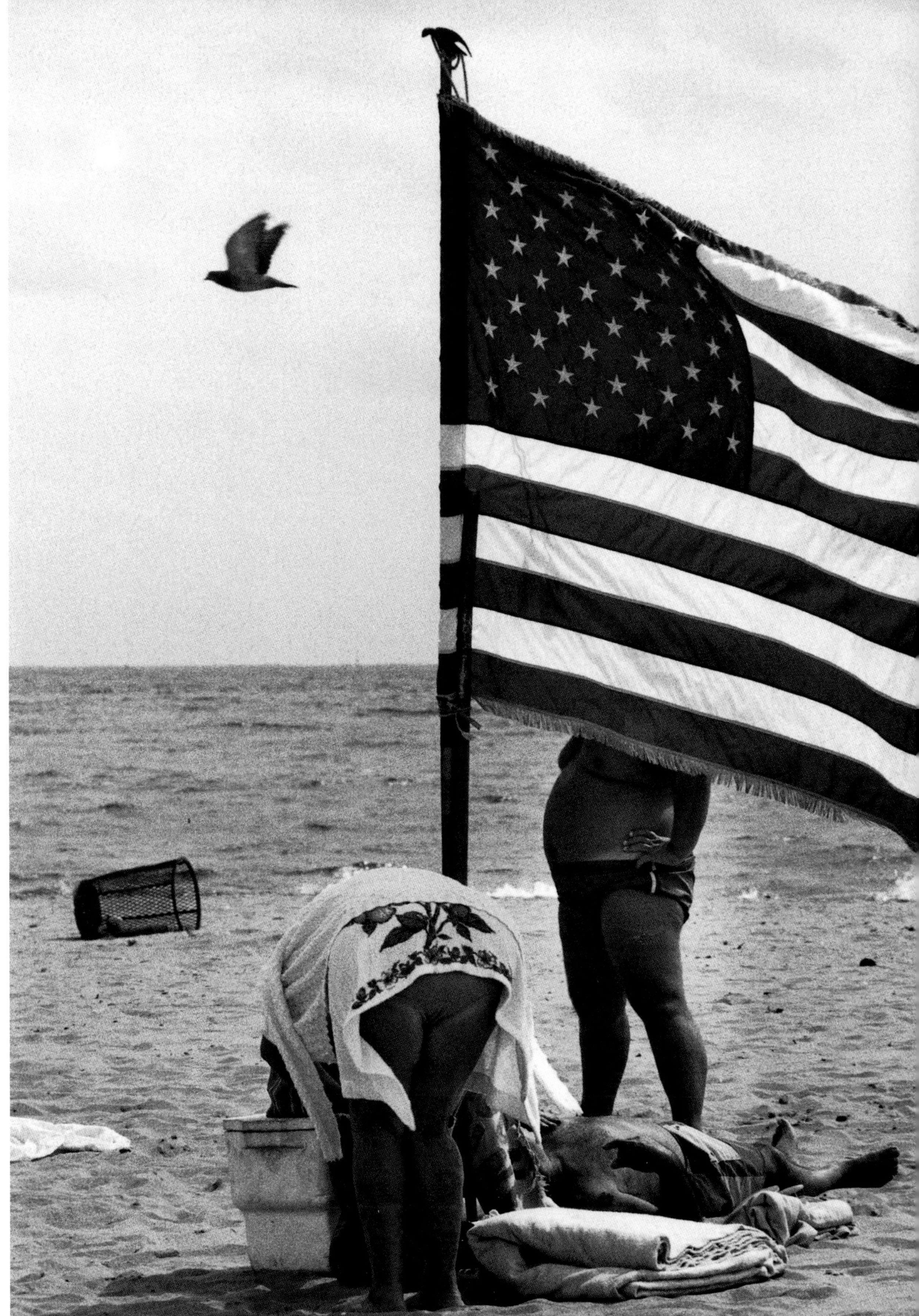

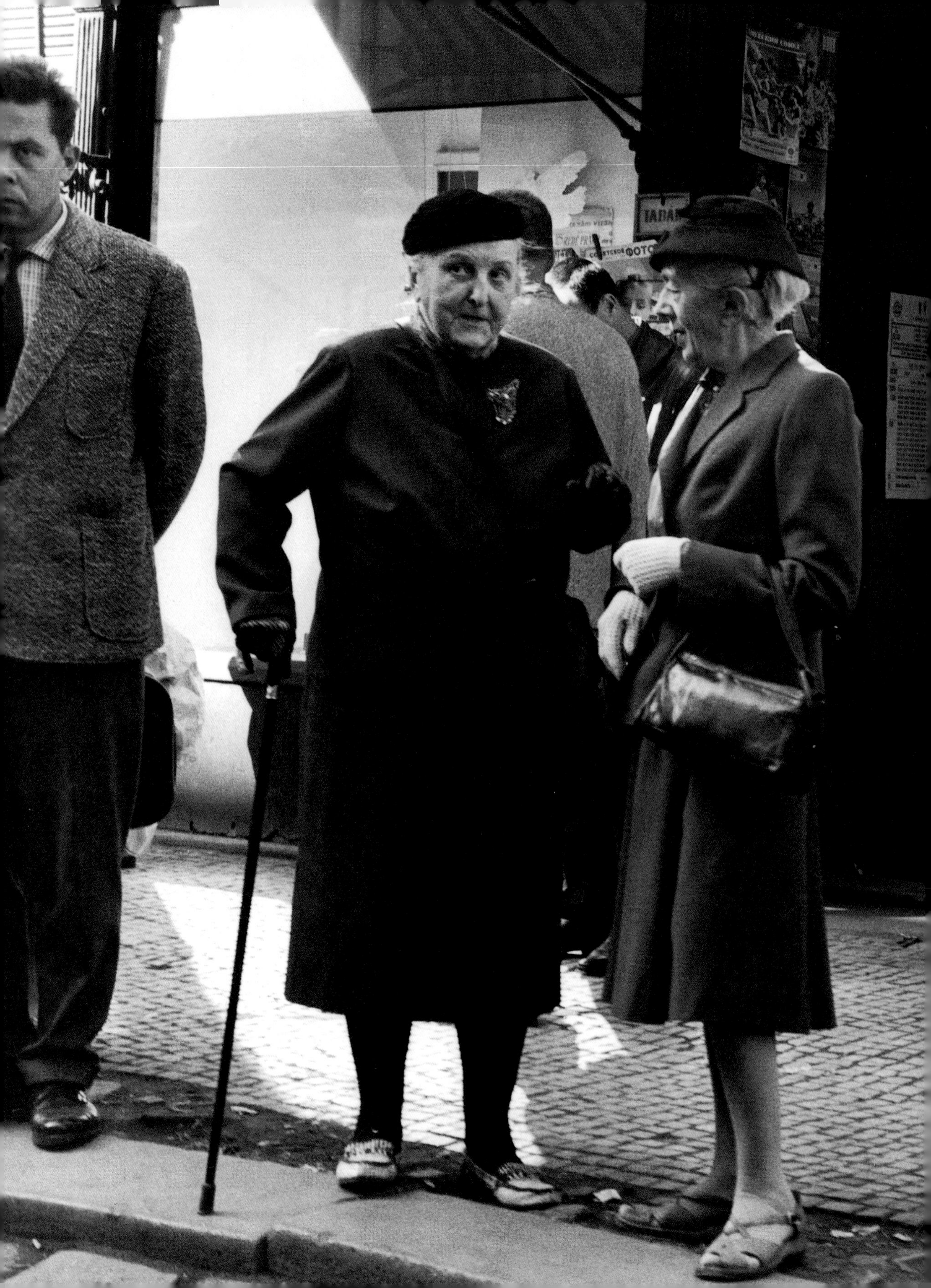

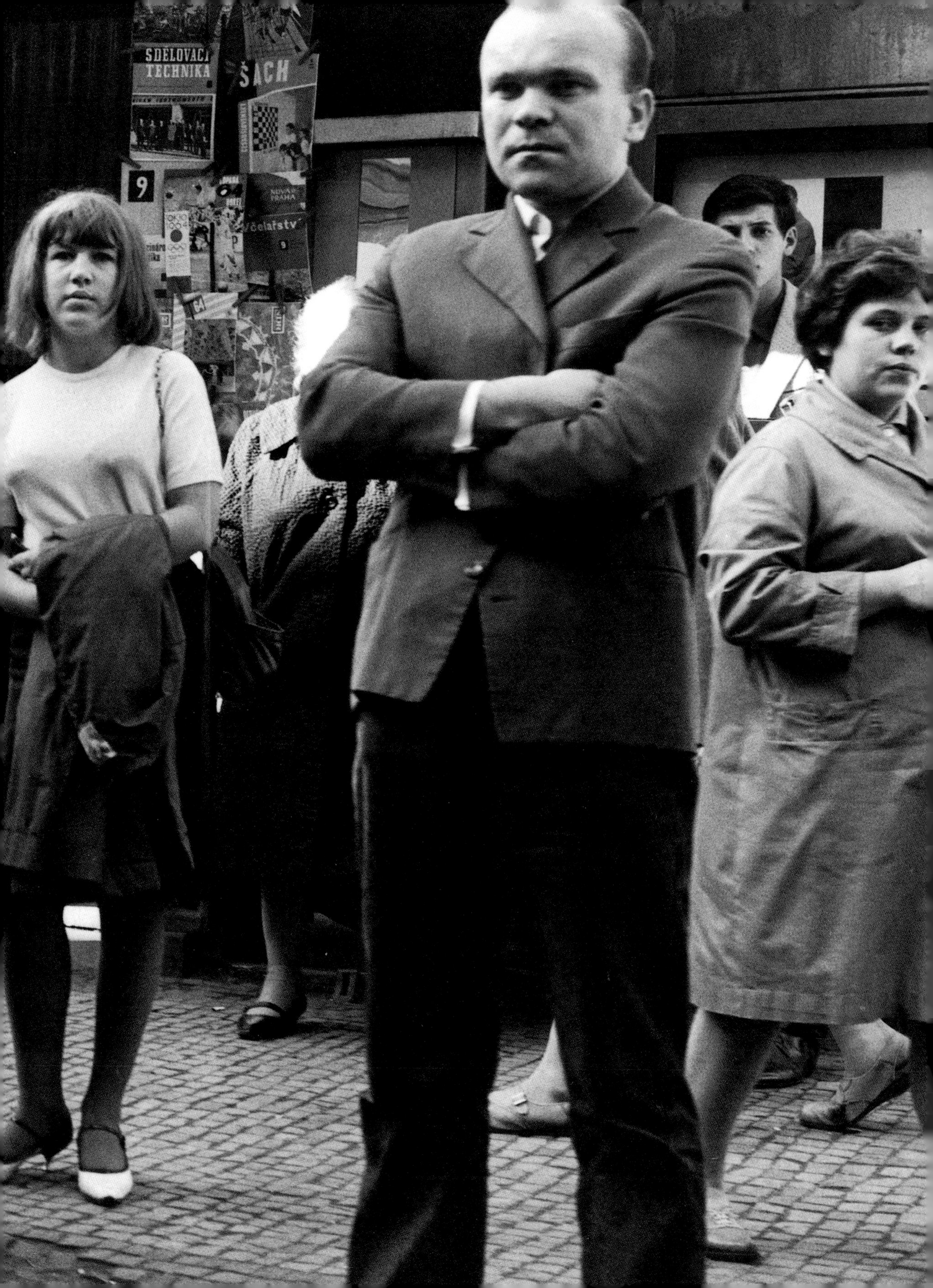

SDĚLOVACÍ TECHNIKA
ŠACH
9
NOVÁ PRAHA
včelařství
9
64

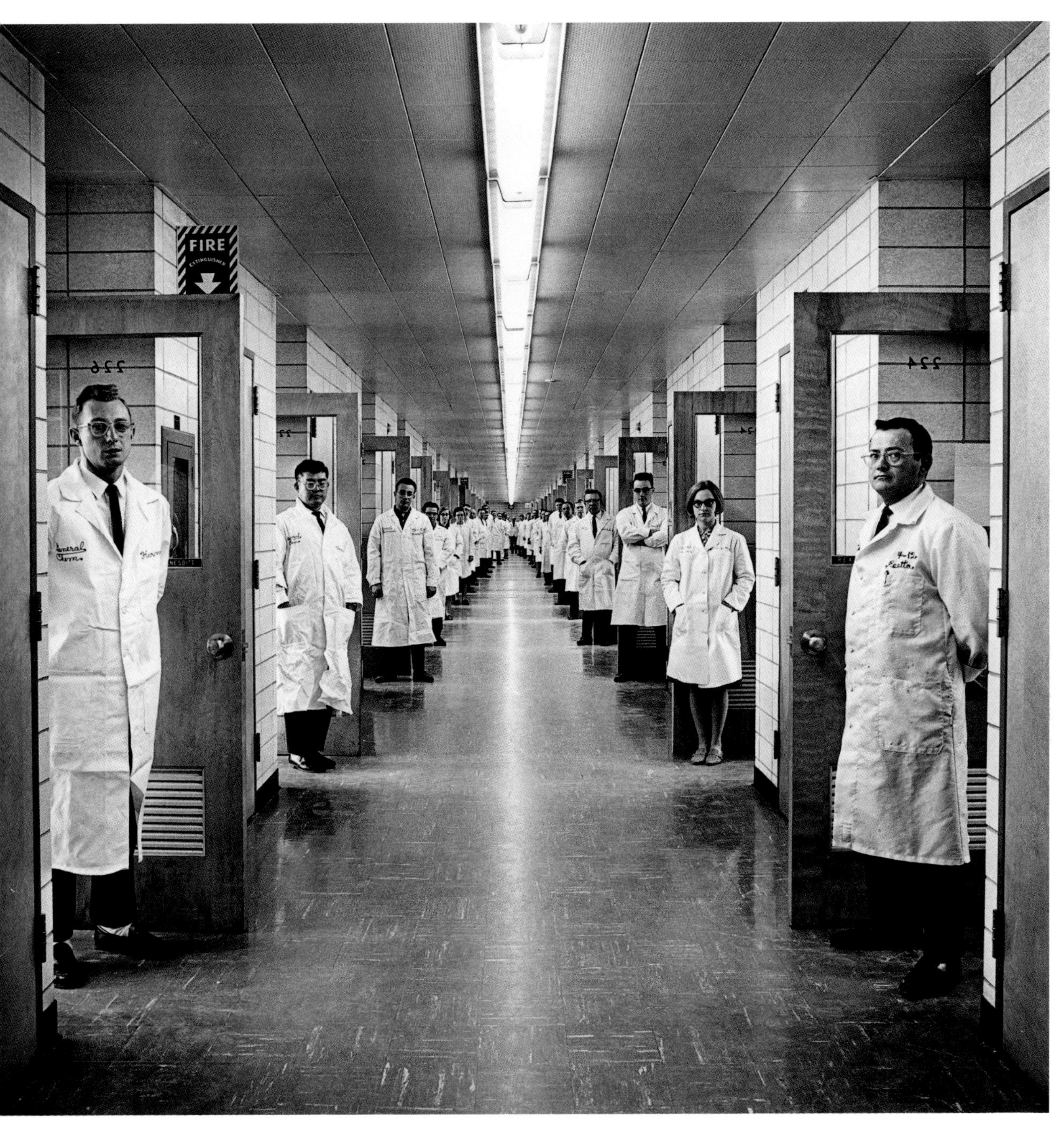

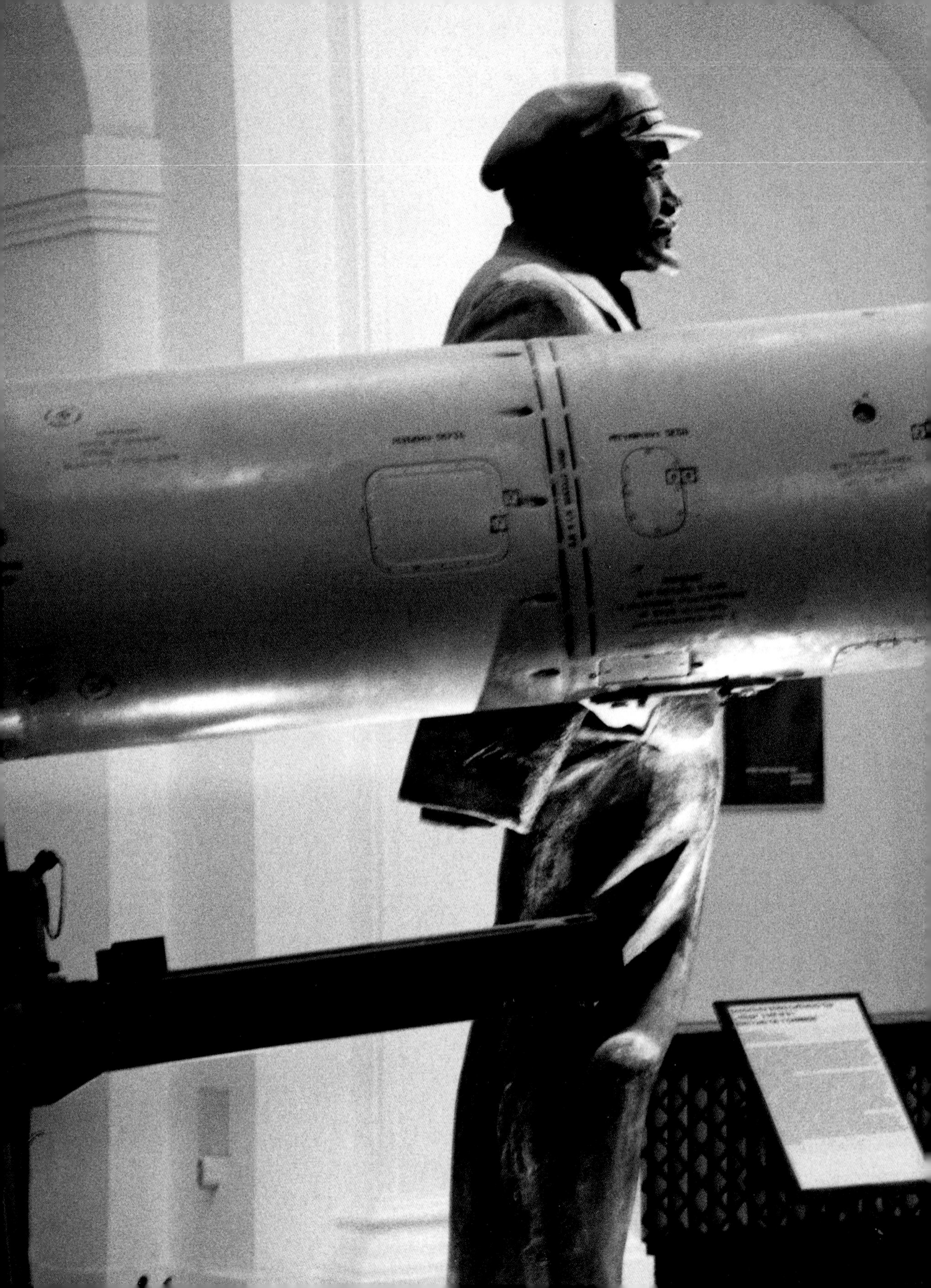

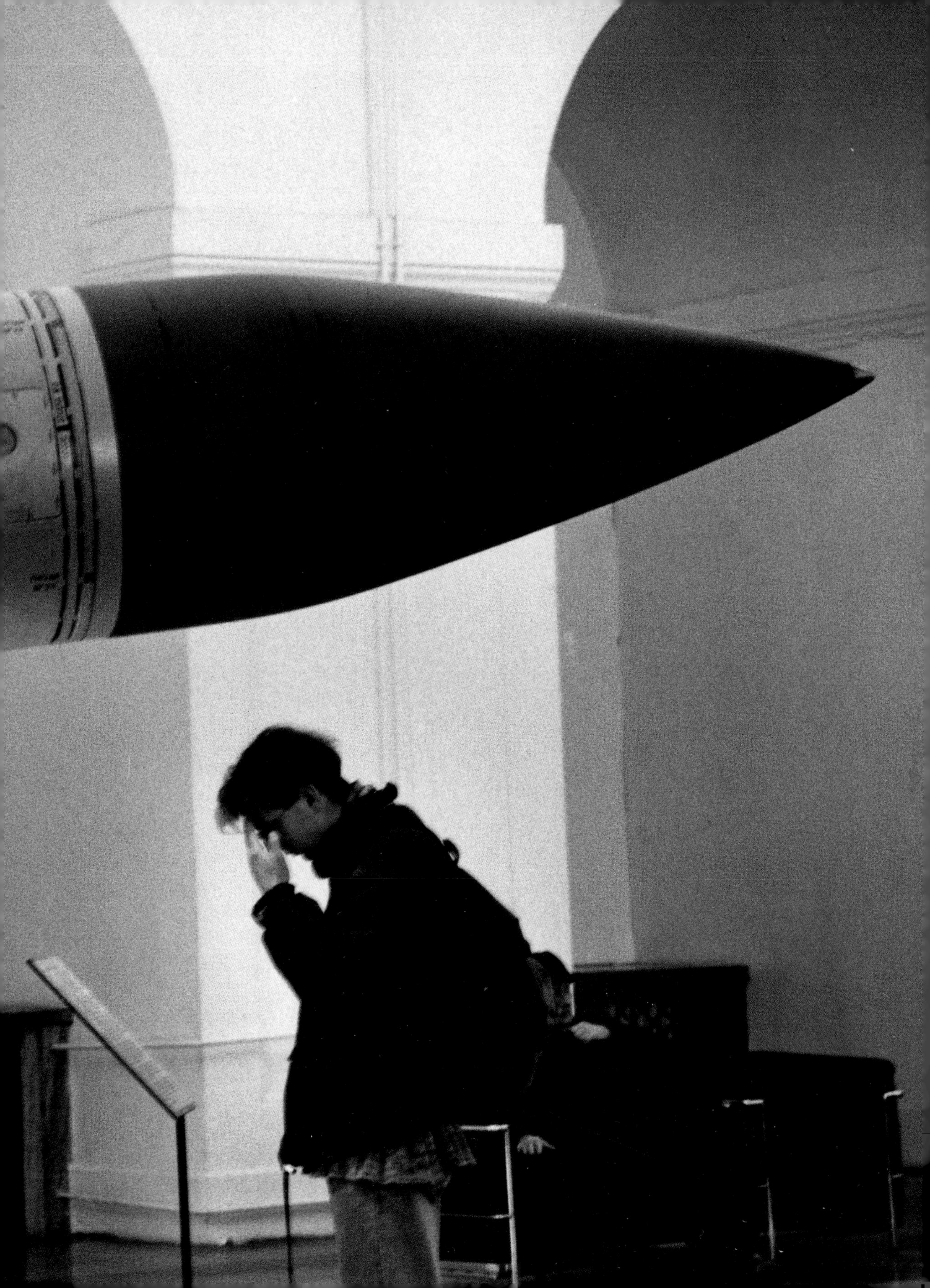

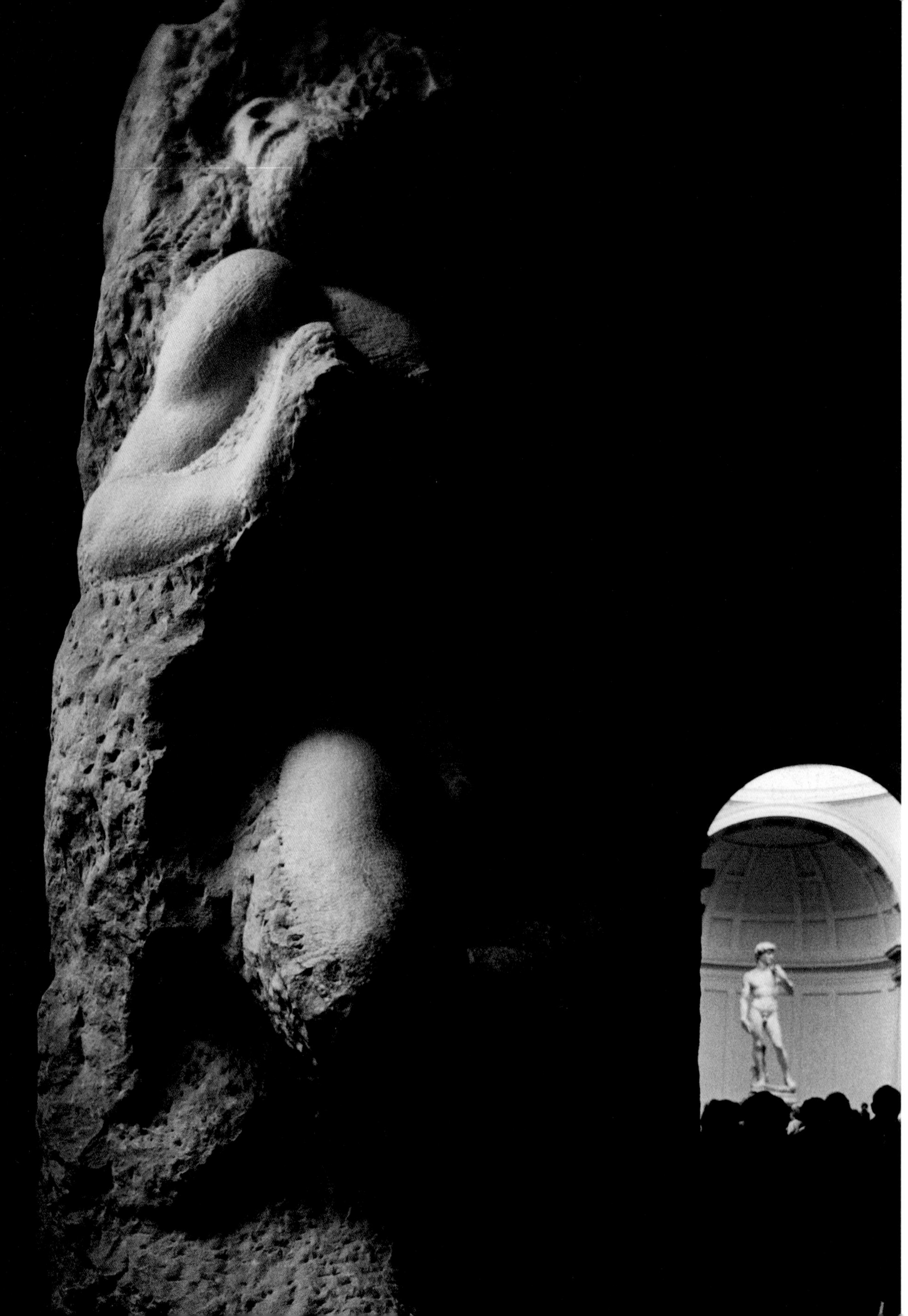

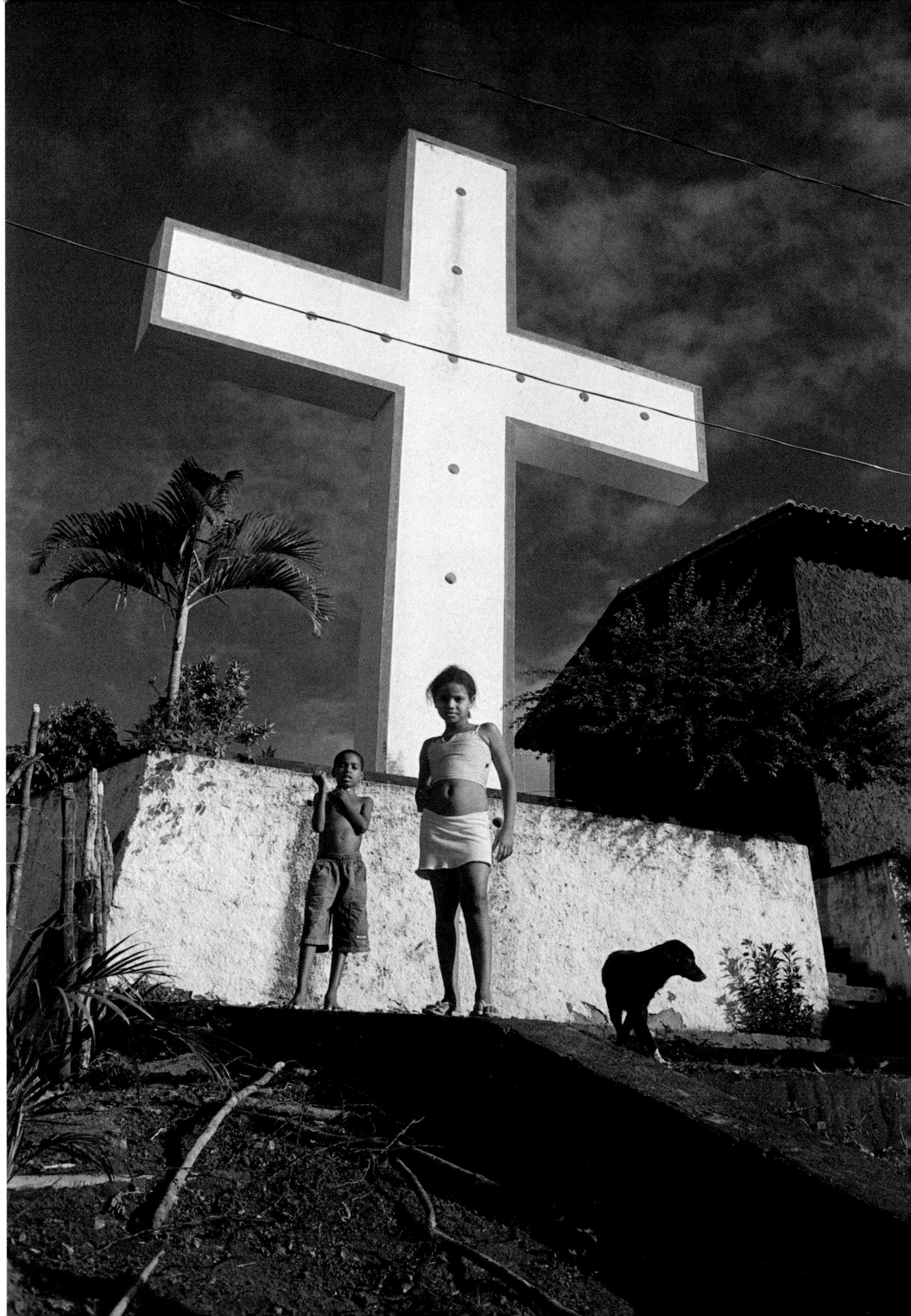

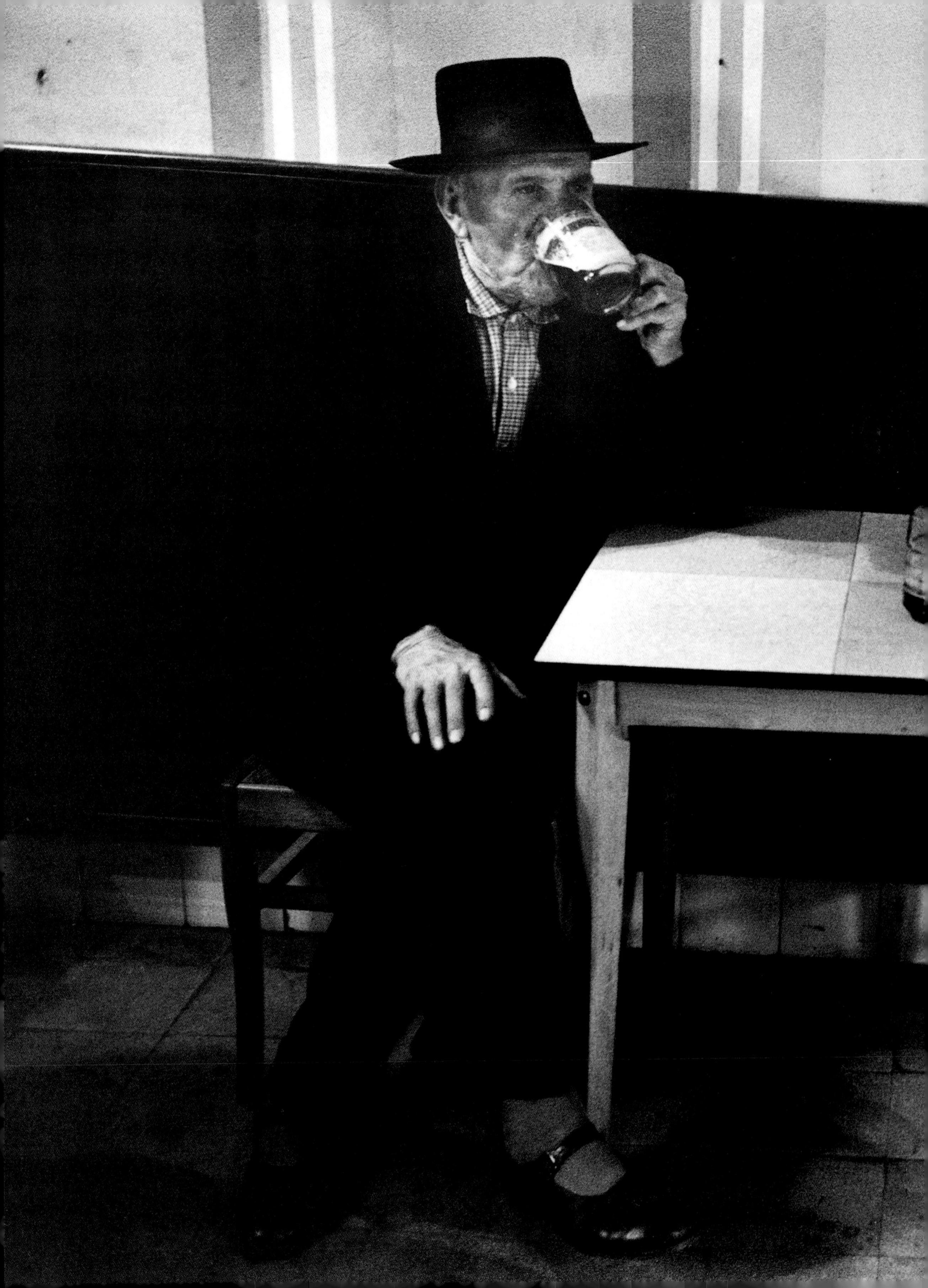

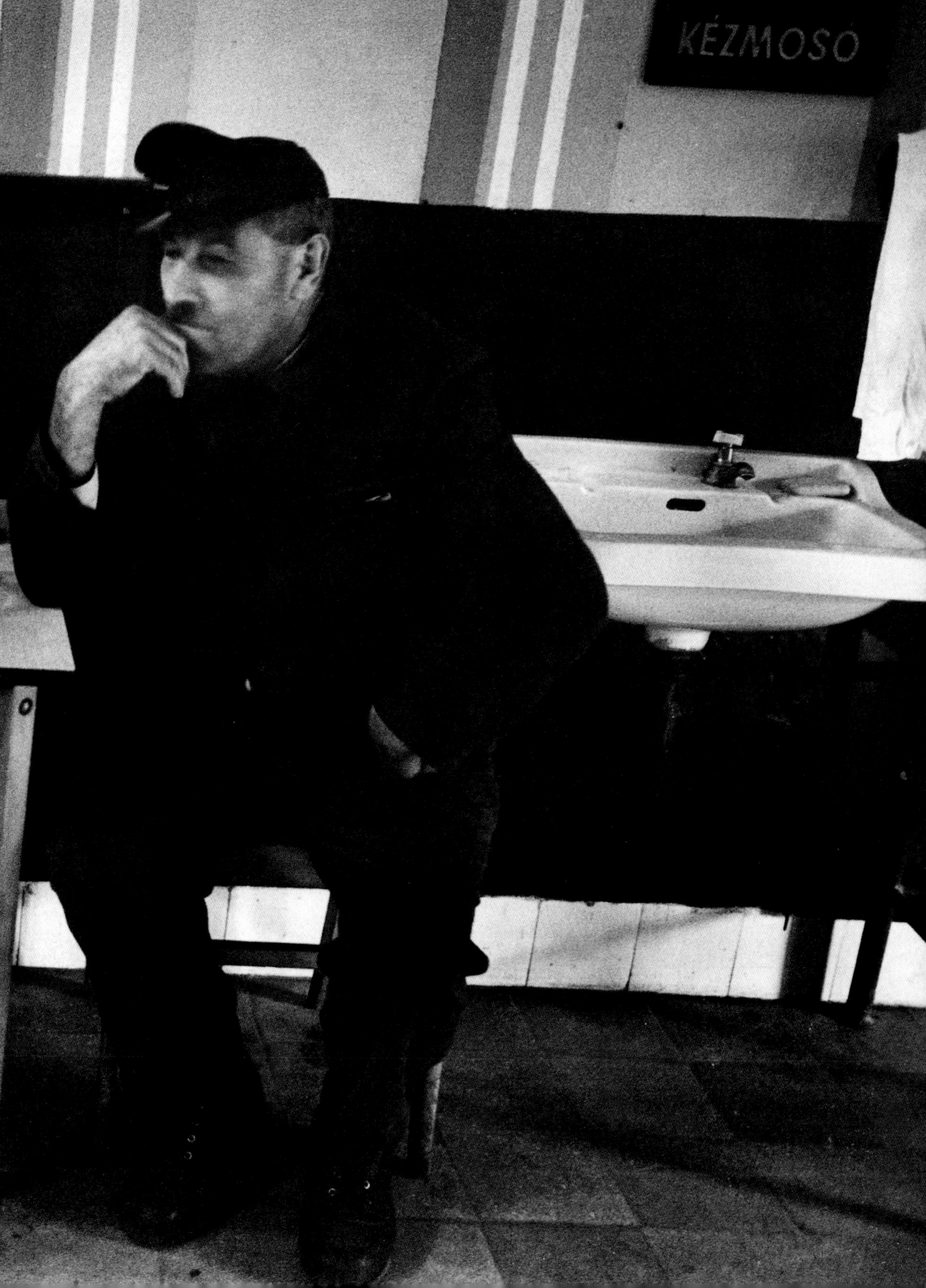

KÉZMOSÓ

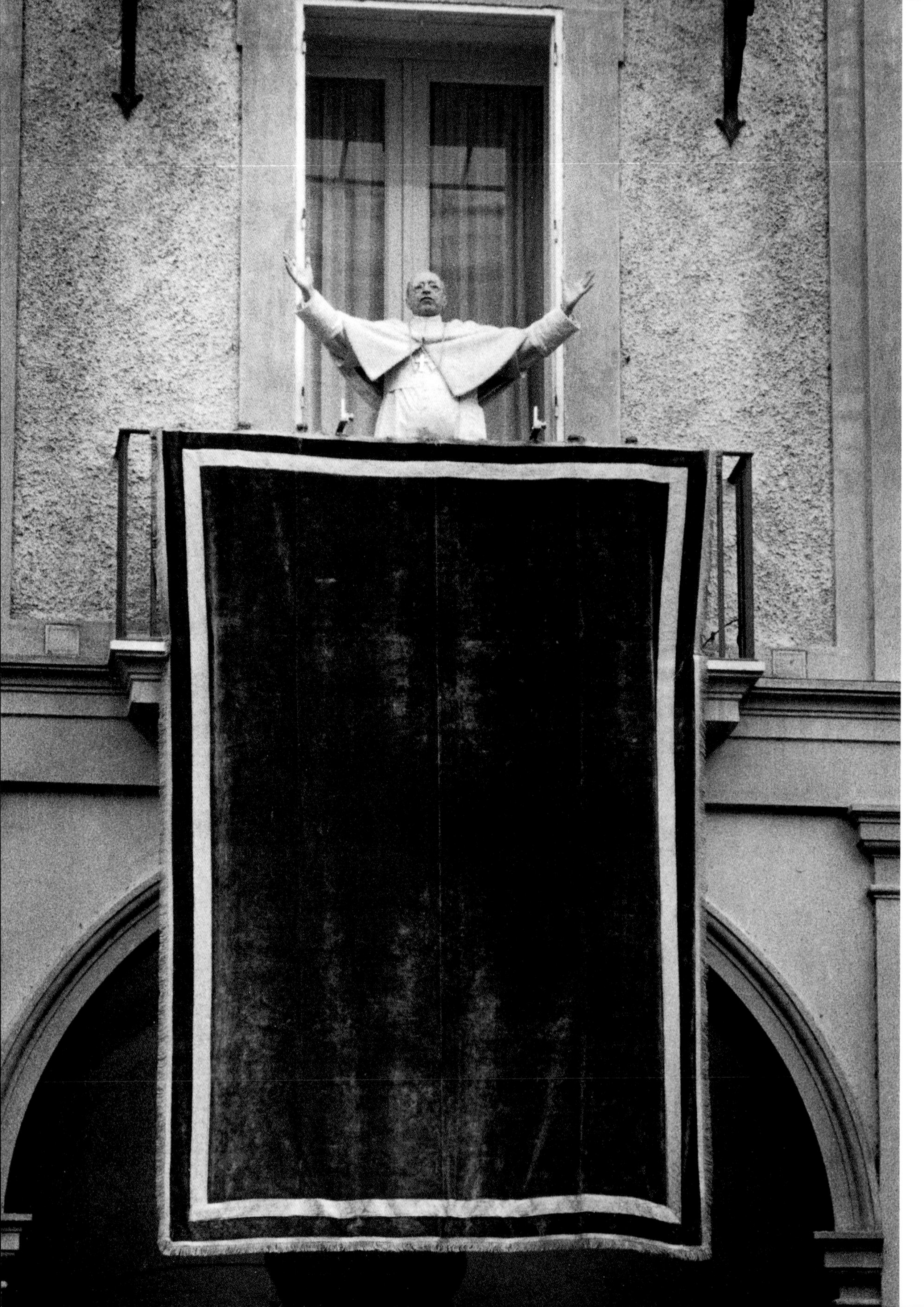

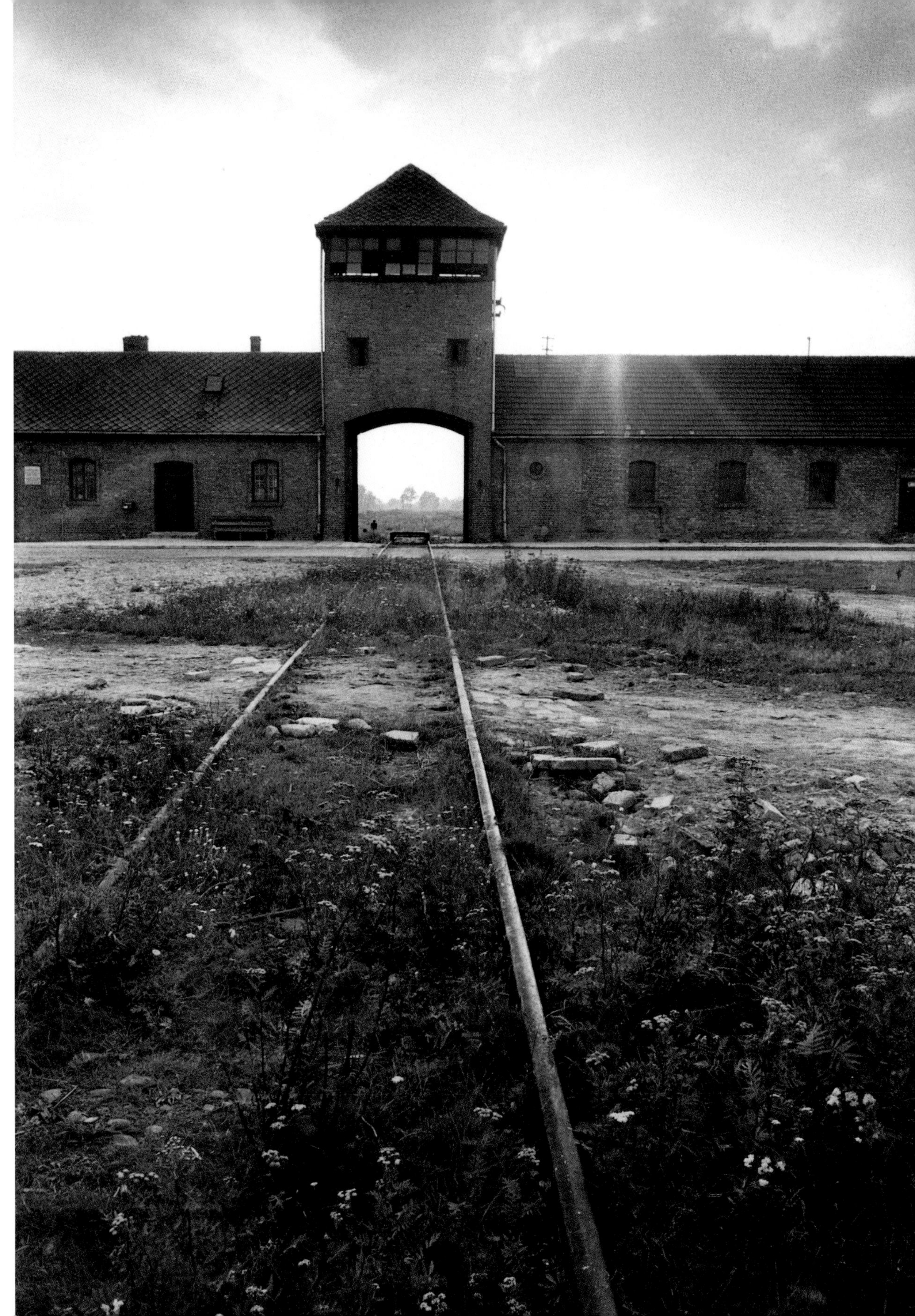

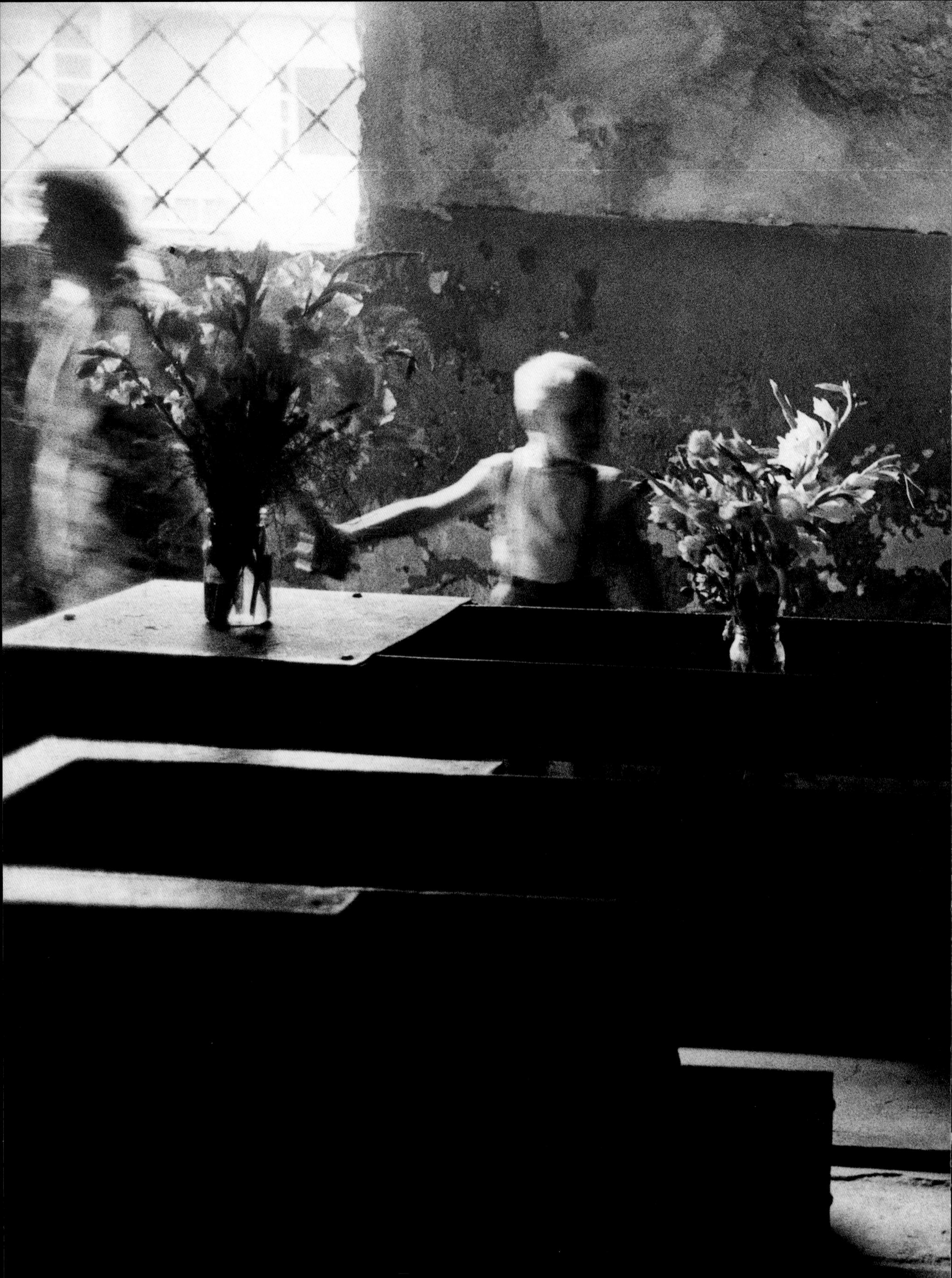

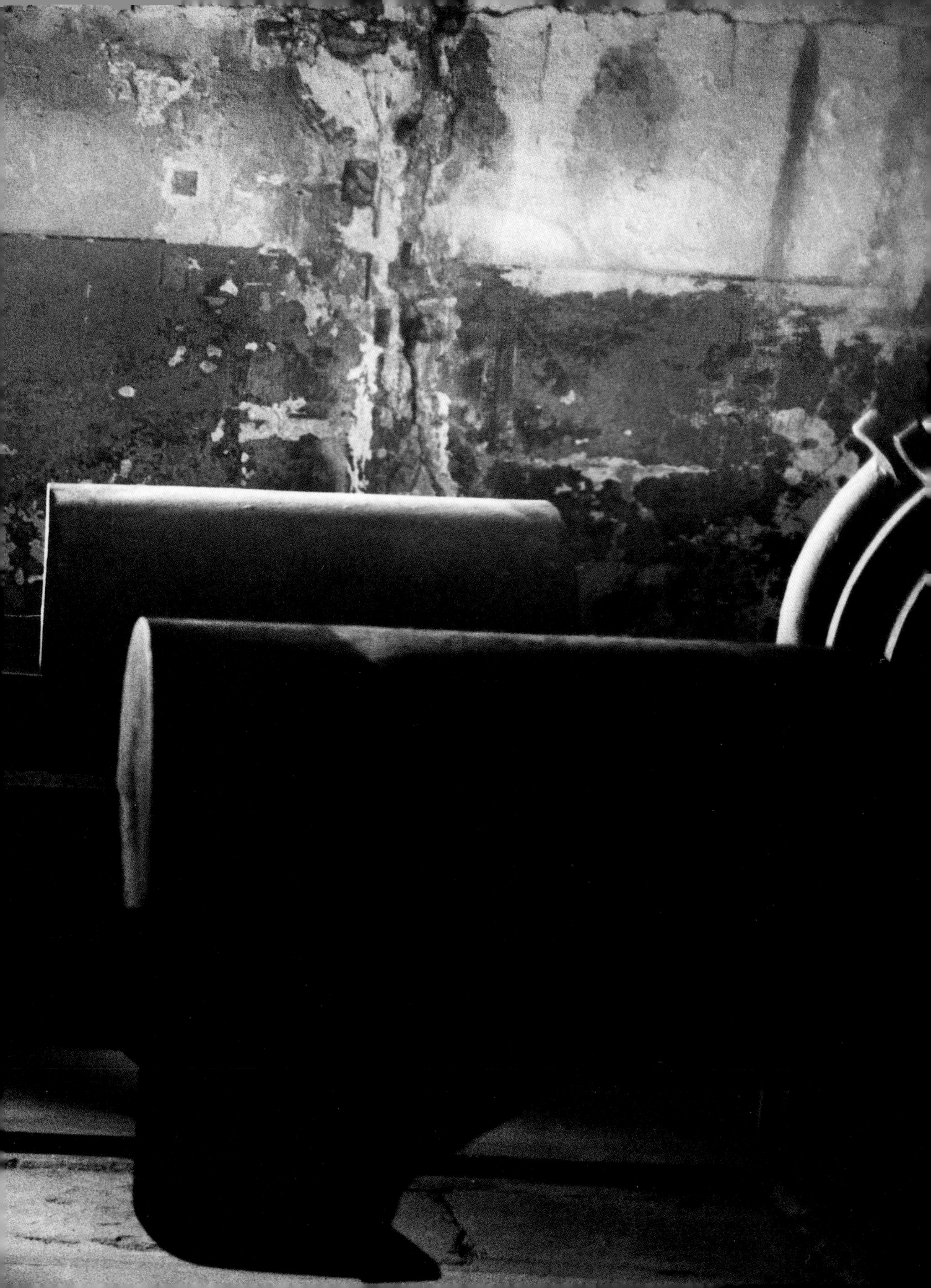

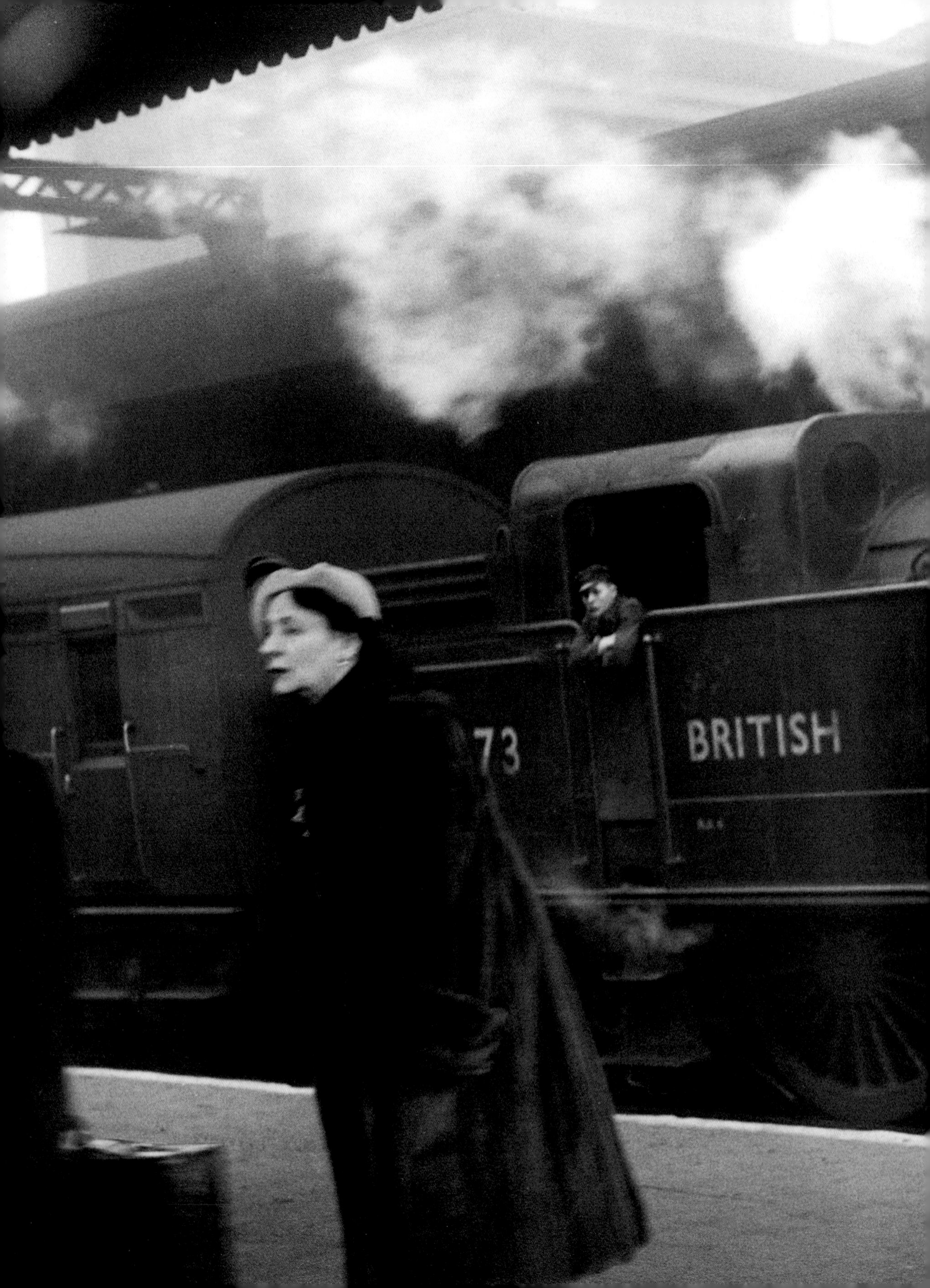
73
BRITISH

WAYS

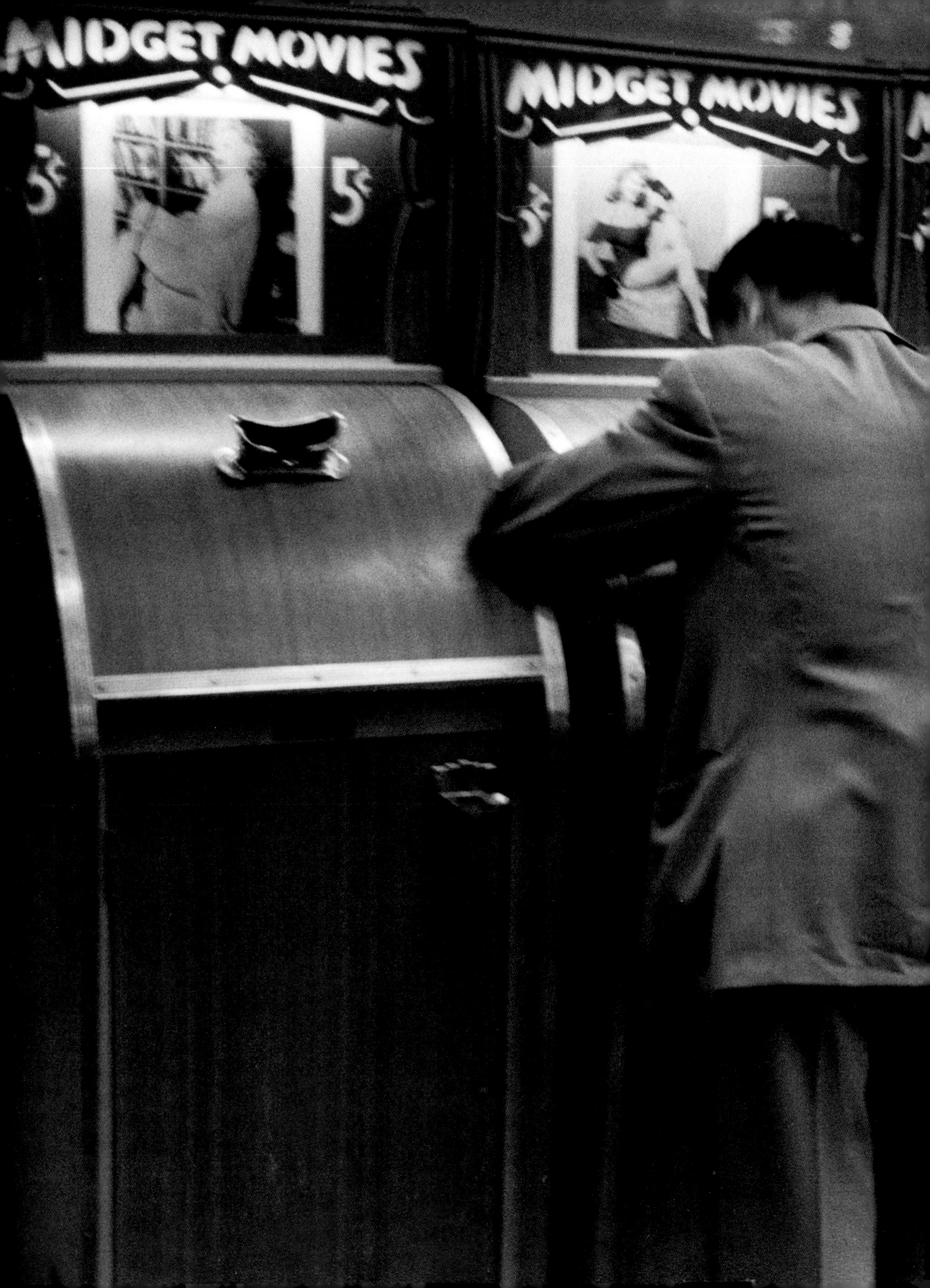

MIDGET MOVIES
5¢
5¢
MIDGET MOVIES
5¢

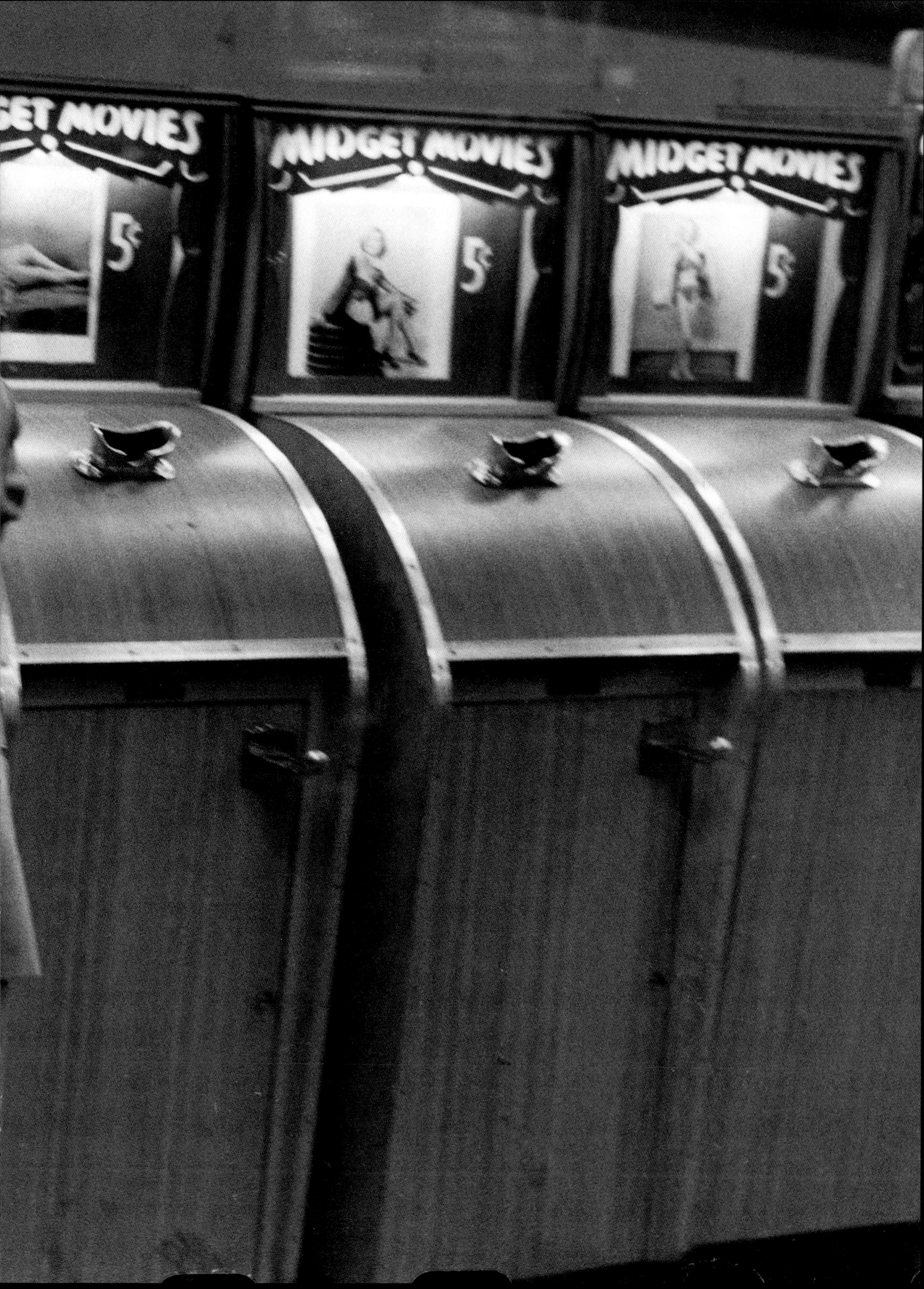
GET MOVIES
MIDGET MOVIES
MIDGET MOVIES
5¢
5¢
5¢

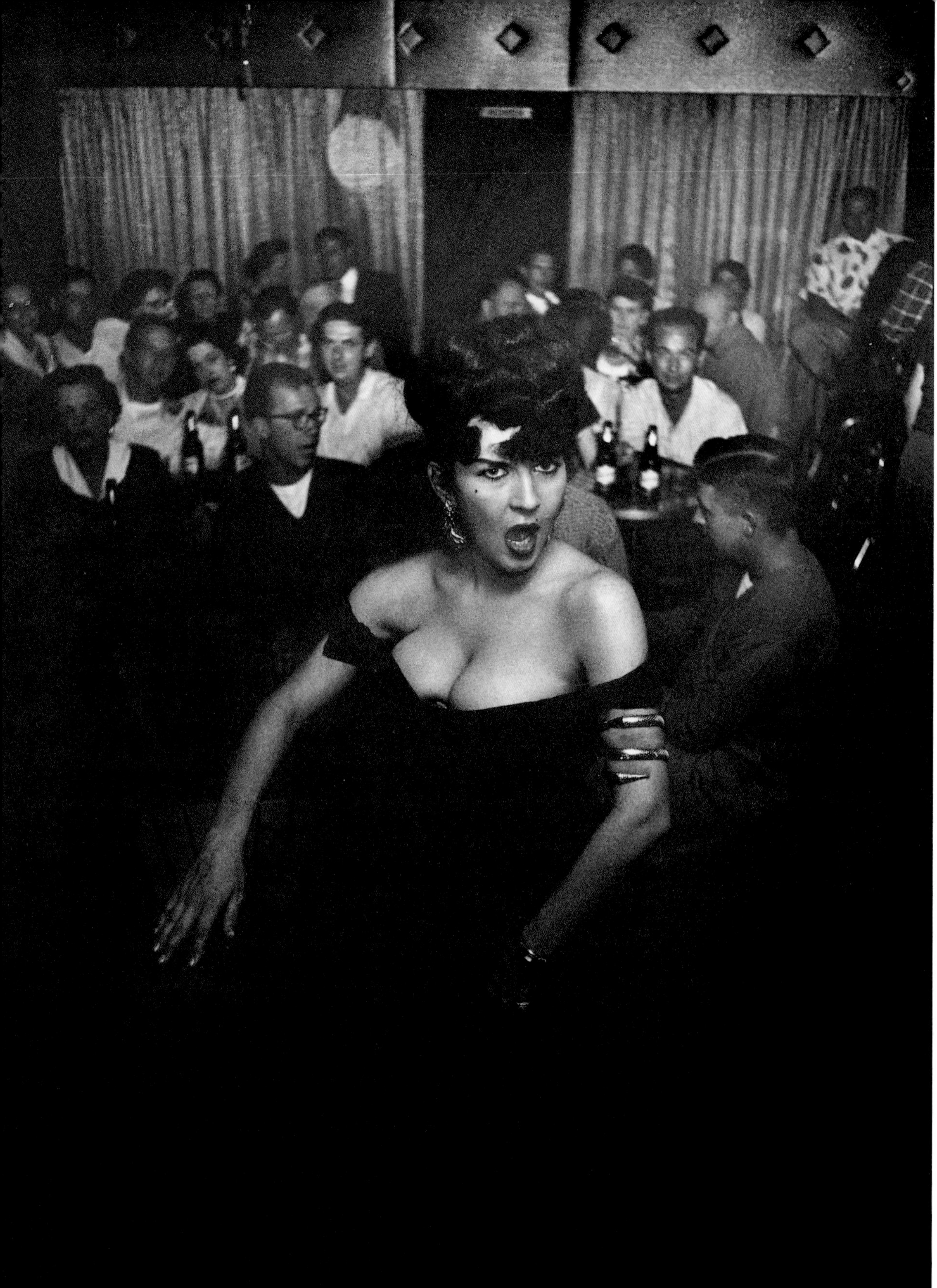

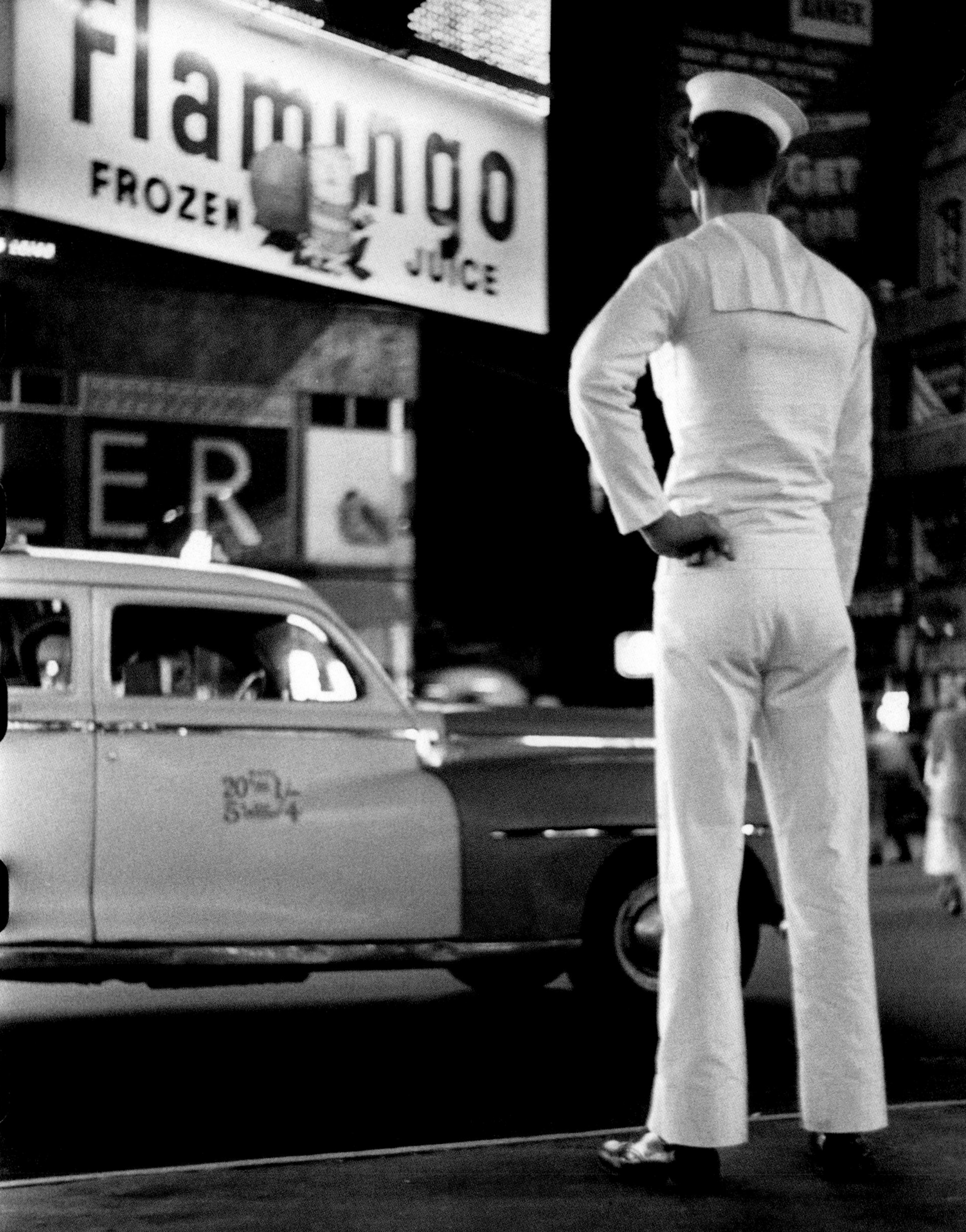

Flamingo
FROZEN
JUICE
ER

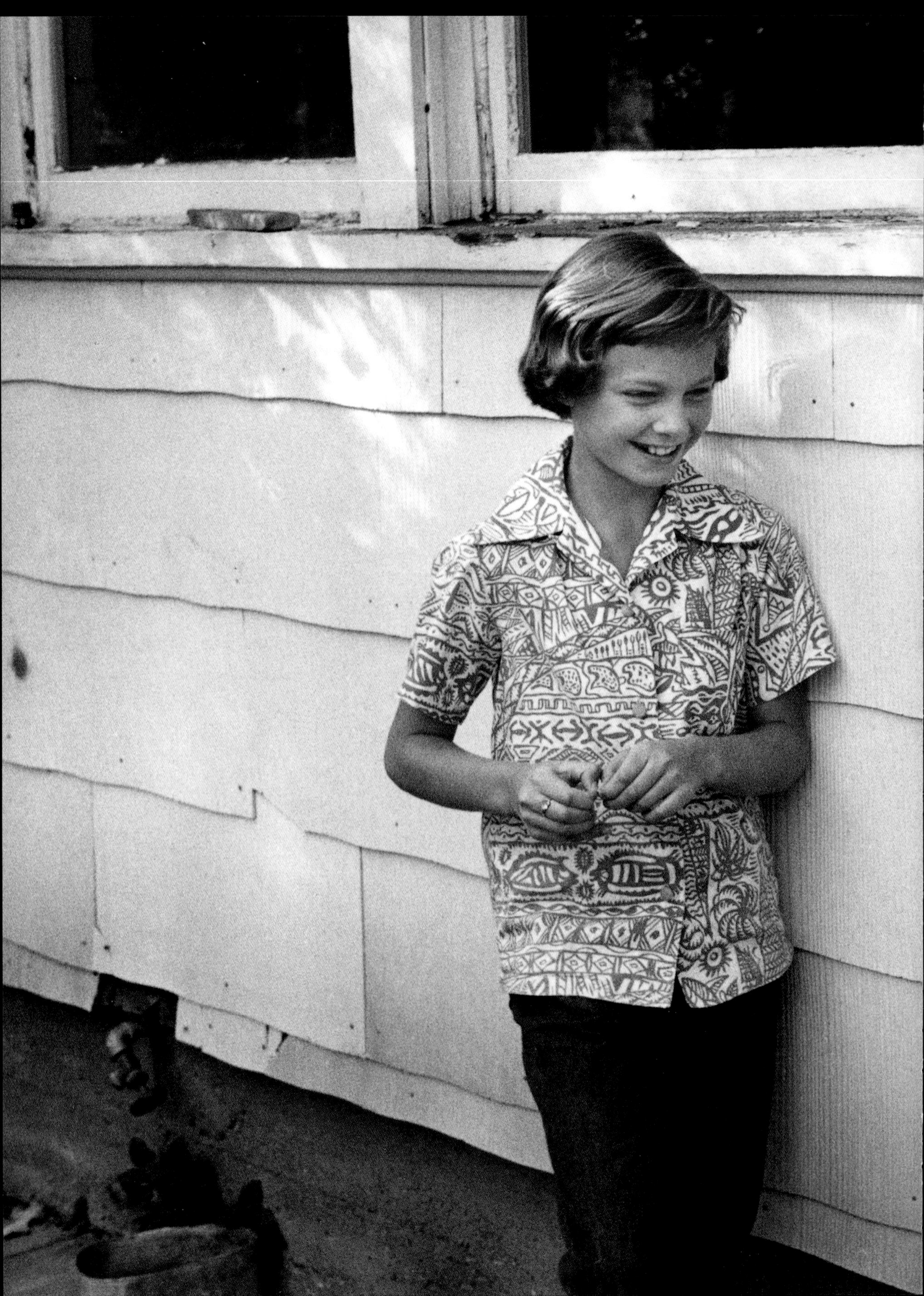

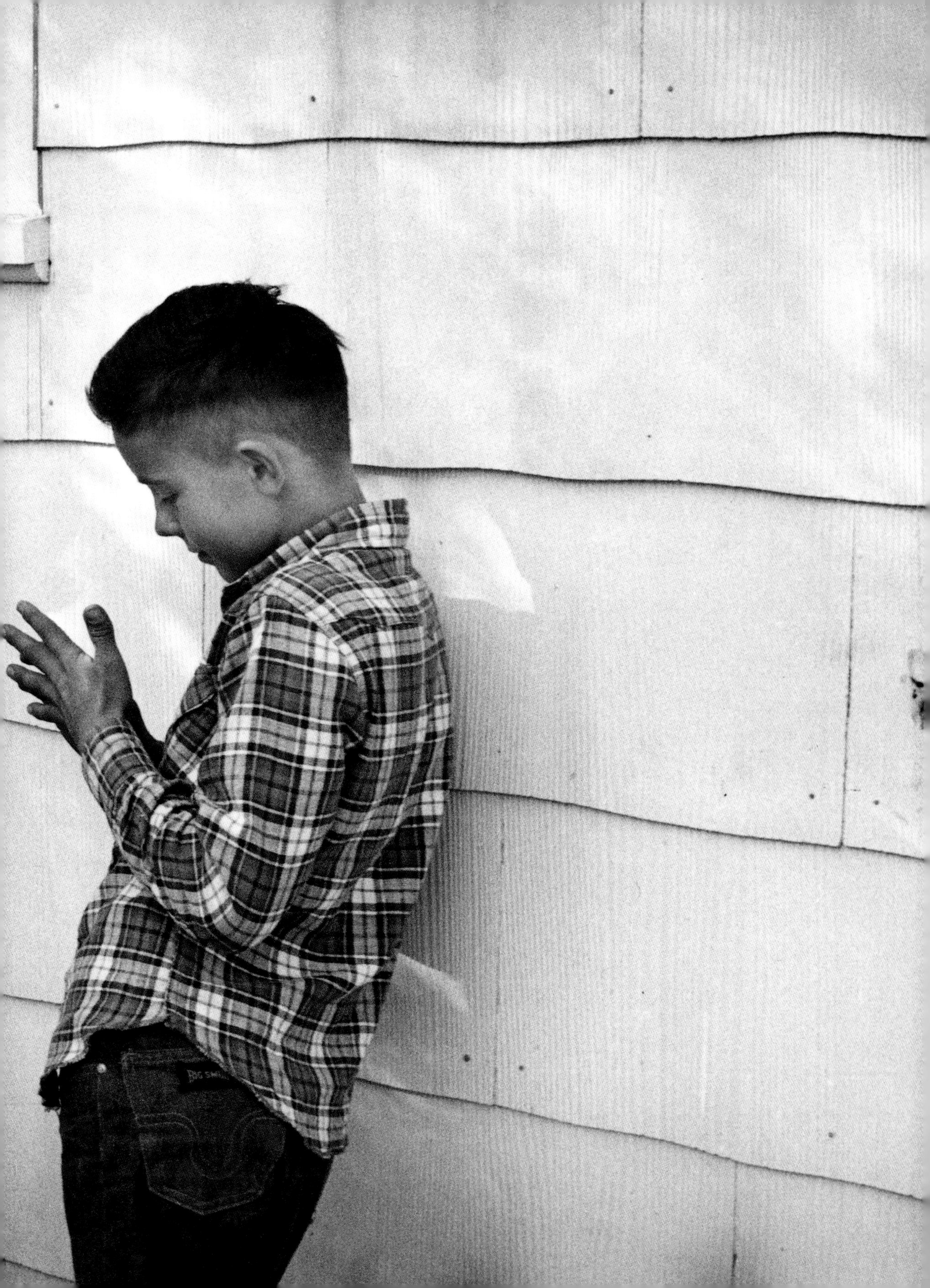

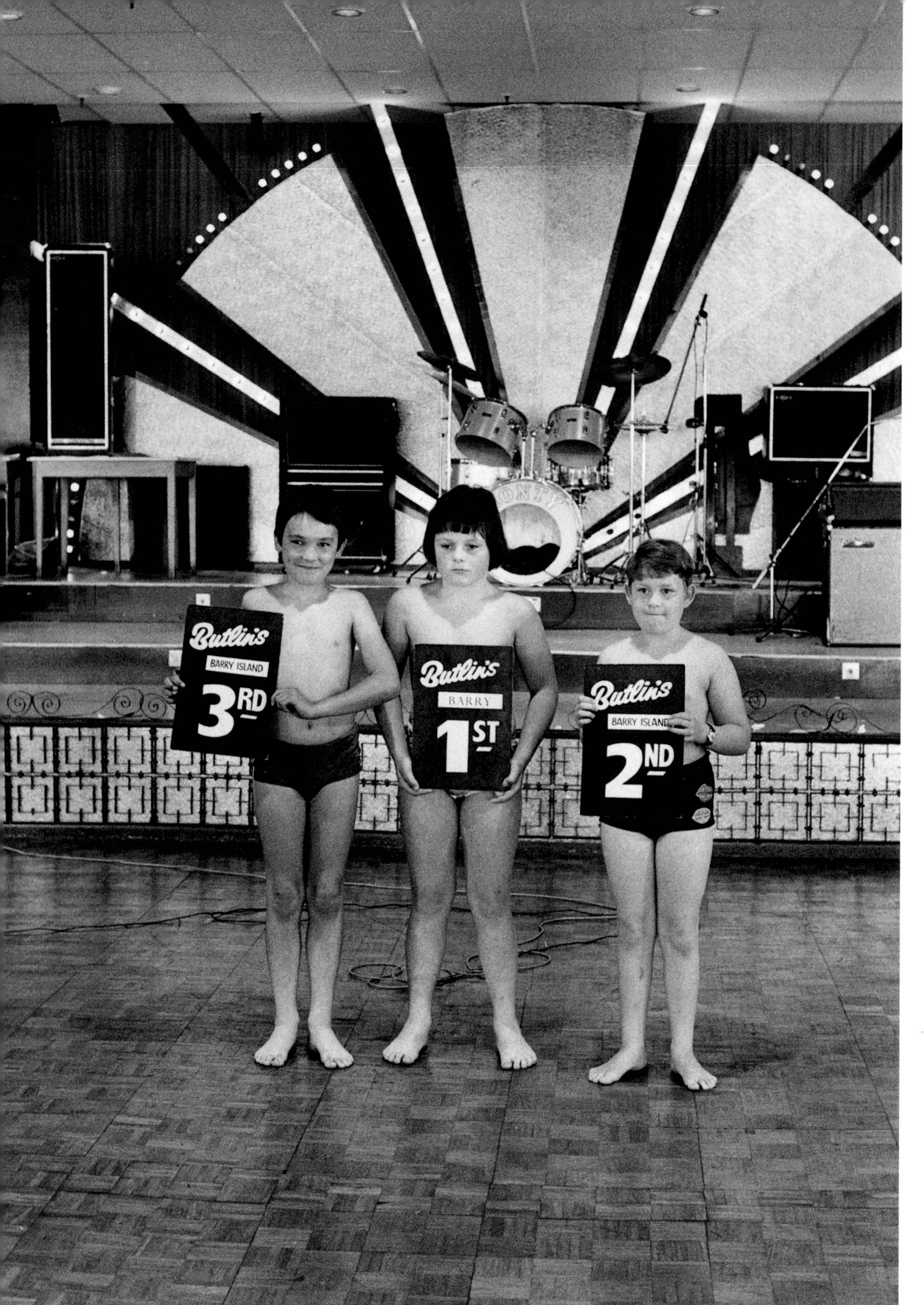
Butlin's
BARRY ISLAND
3RD
Butlin's
BARRY
1ST
Butlin's
BARRY ISLAND
2ND

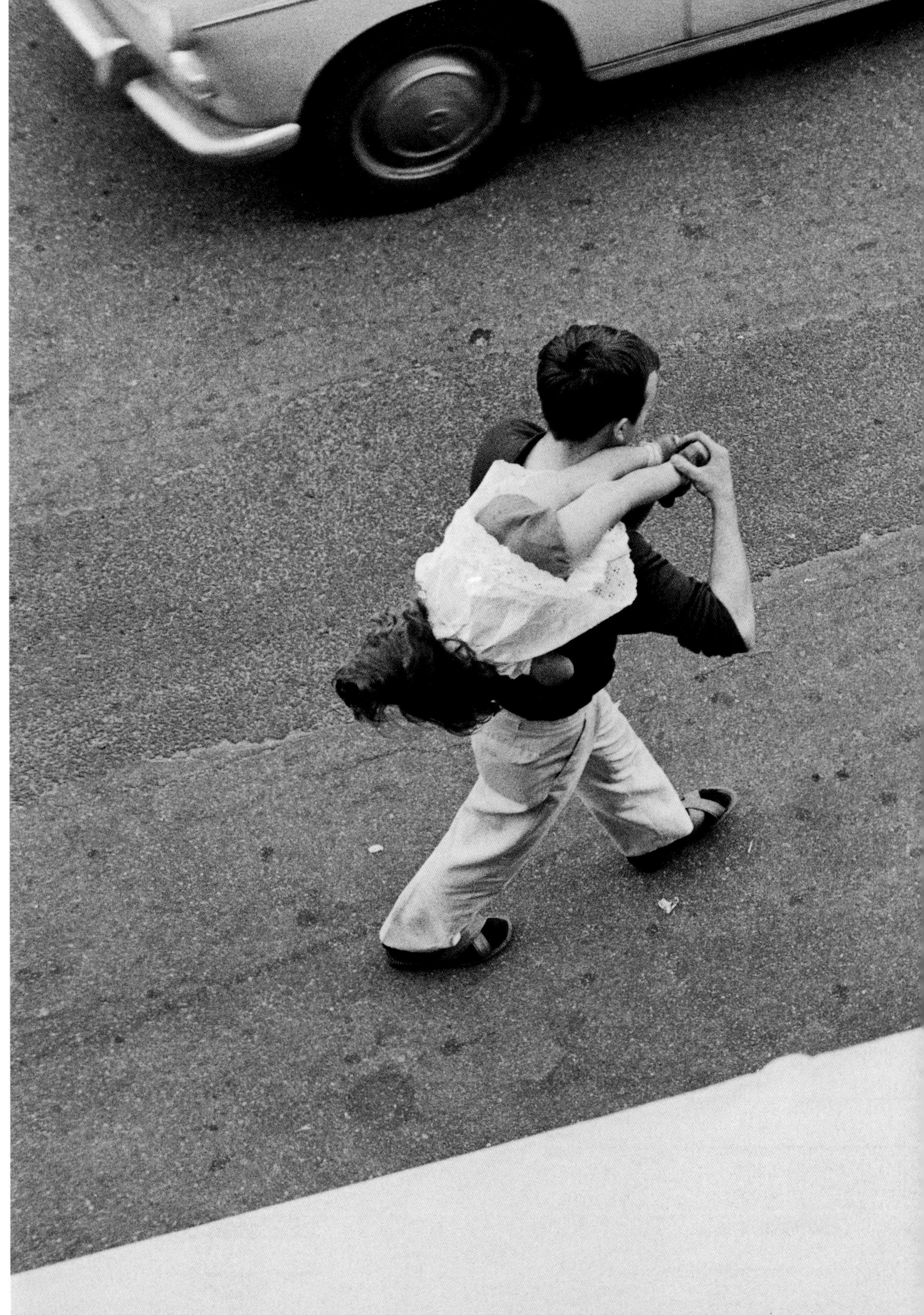

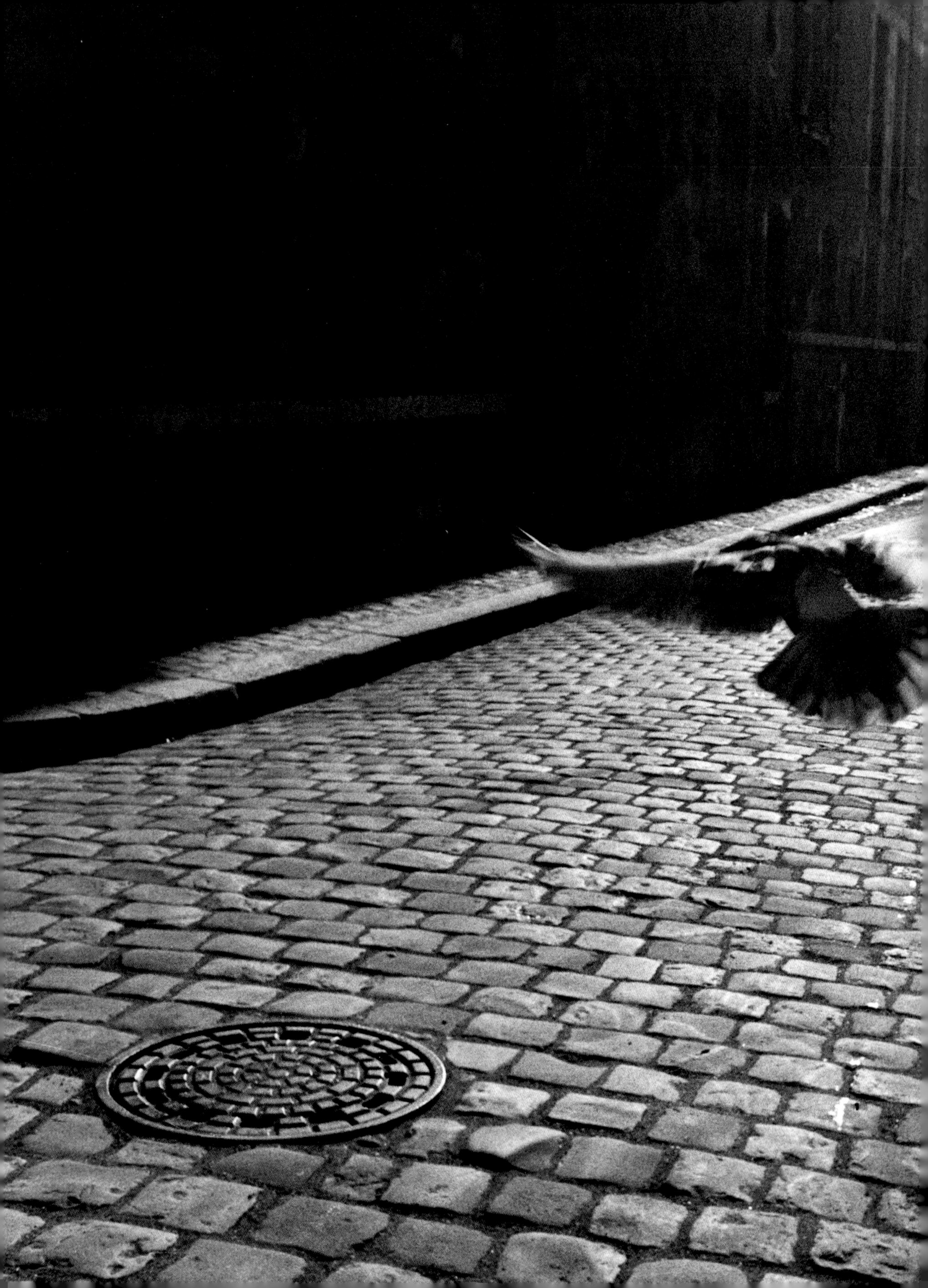

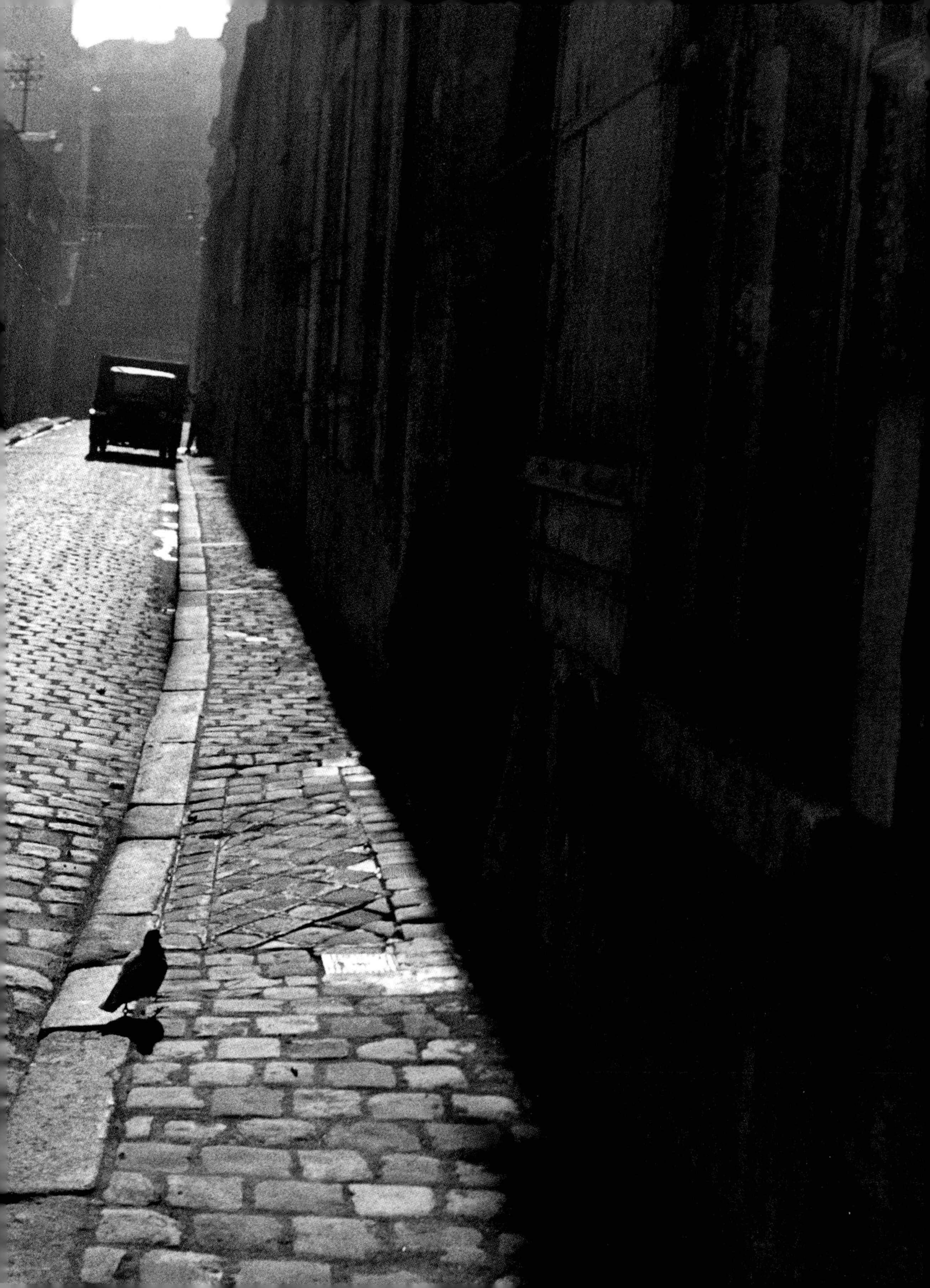

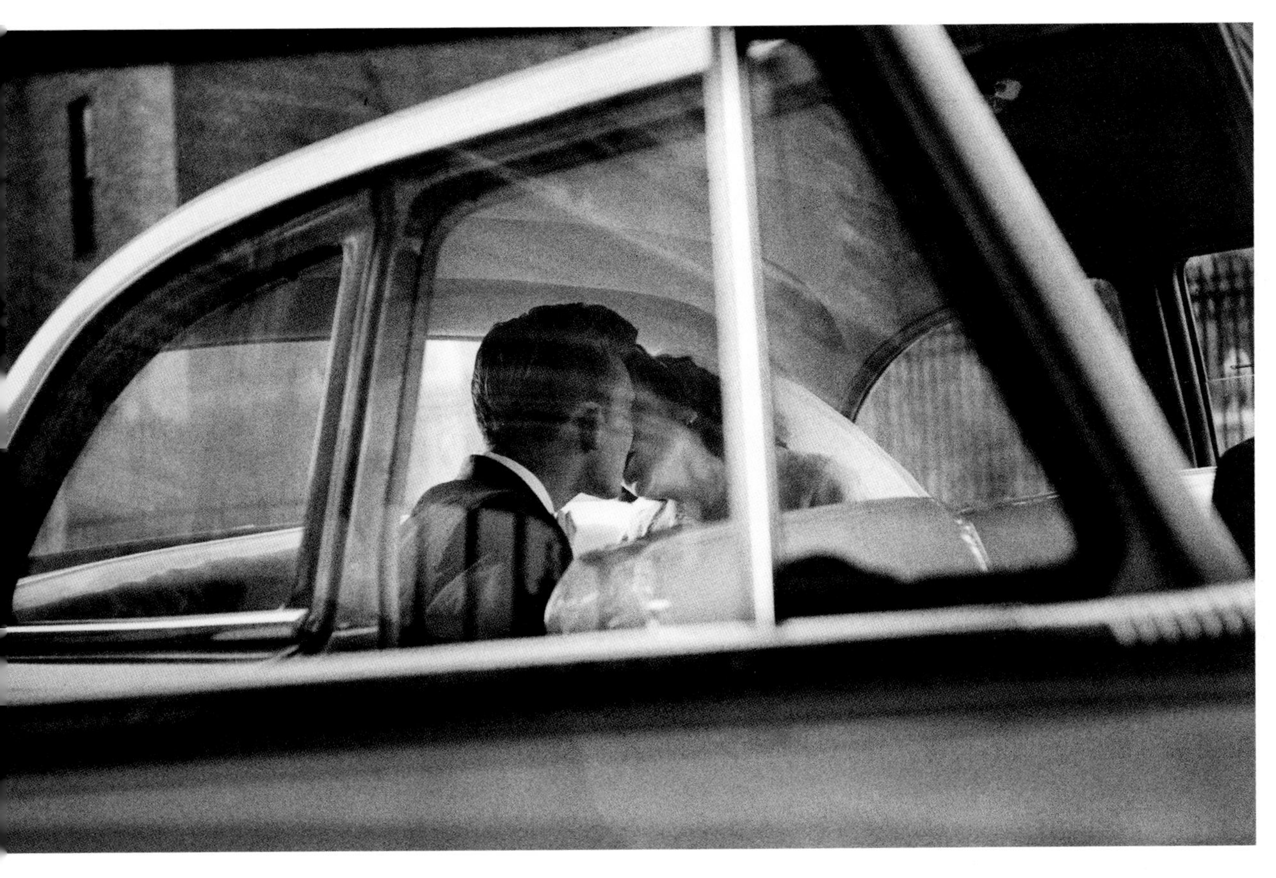

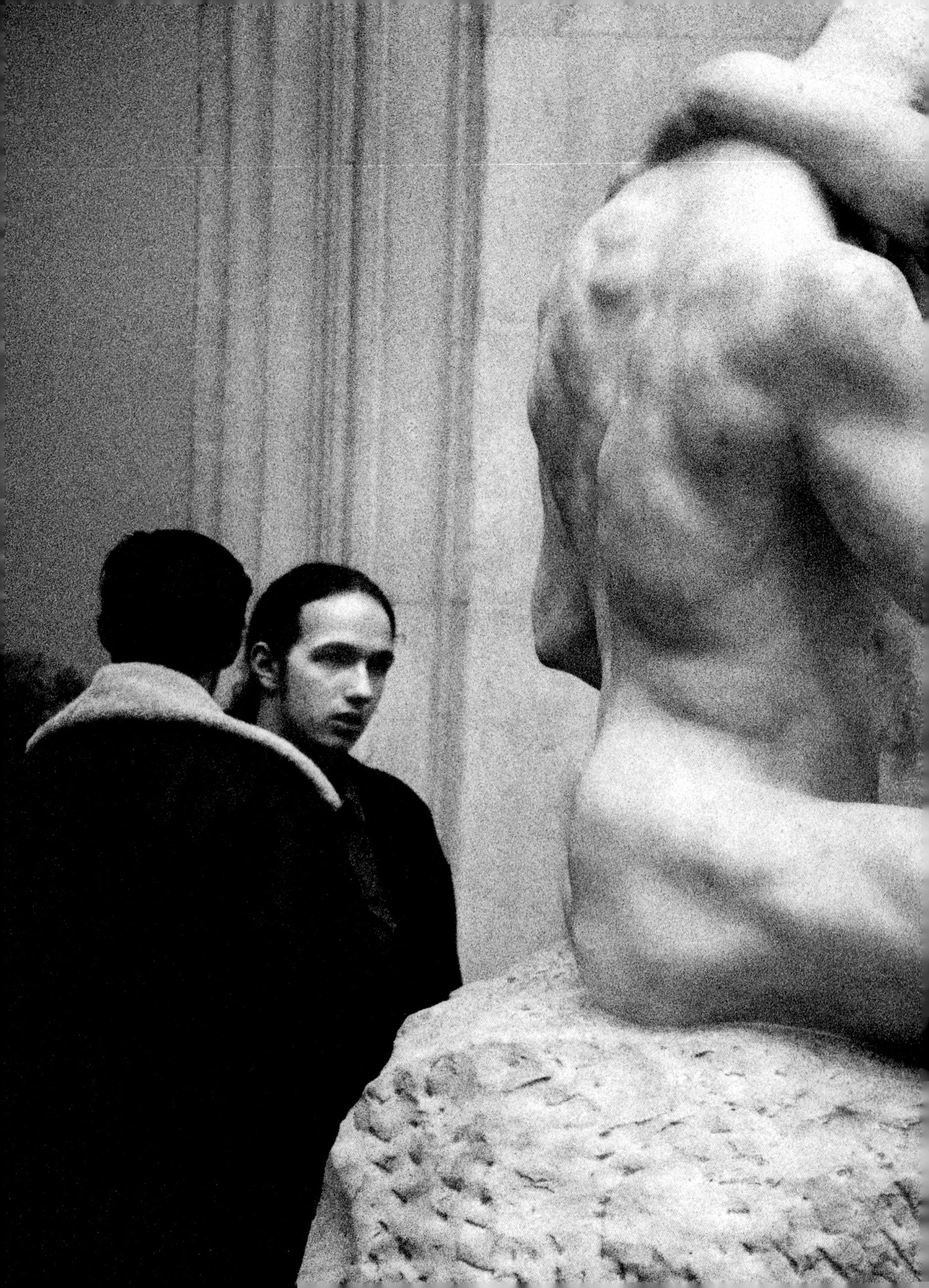

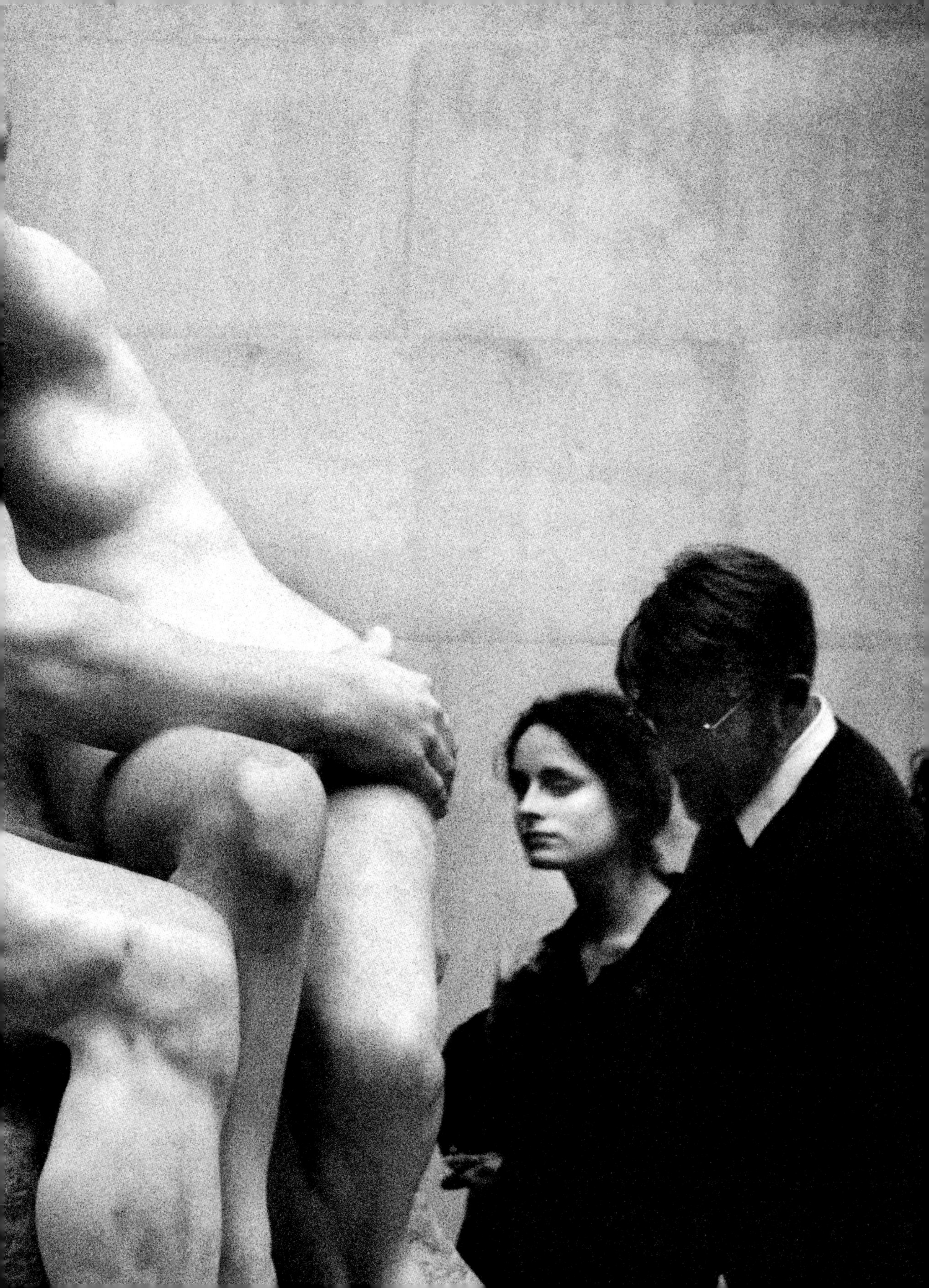

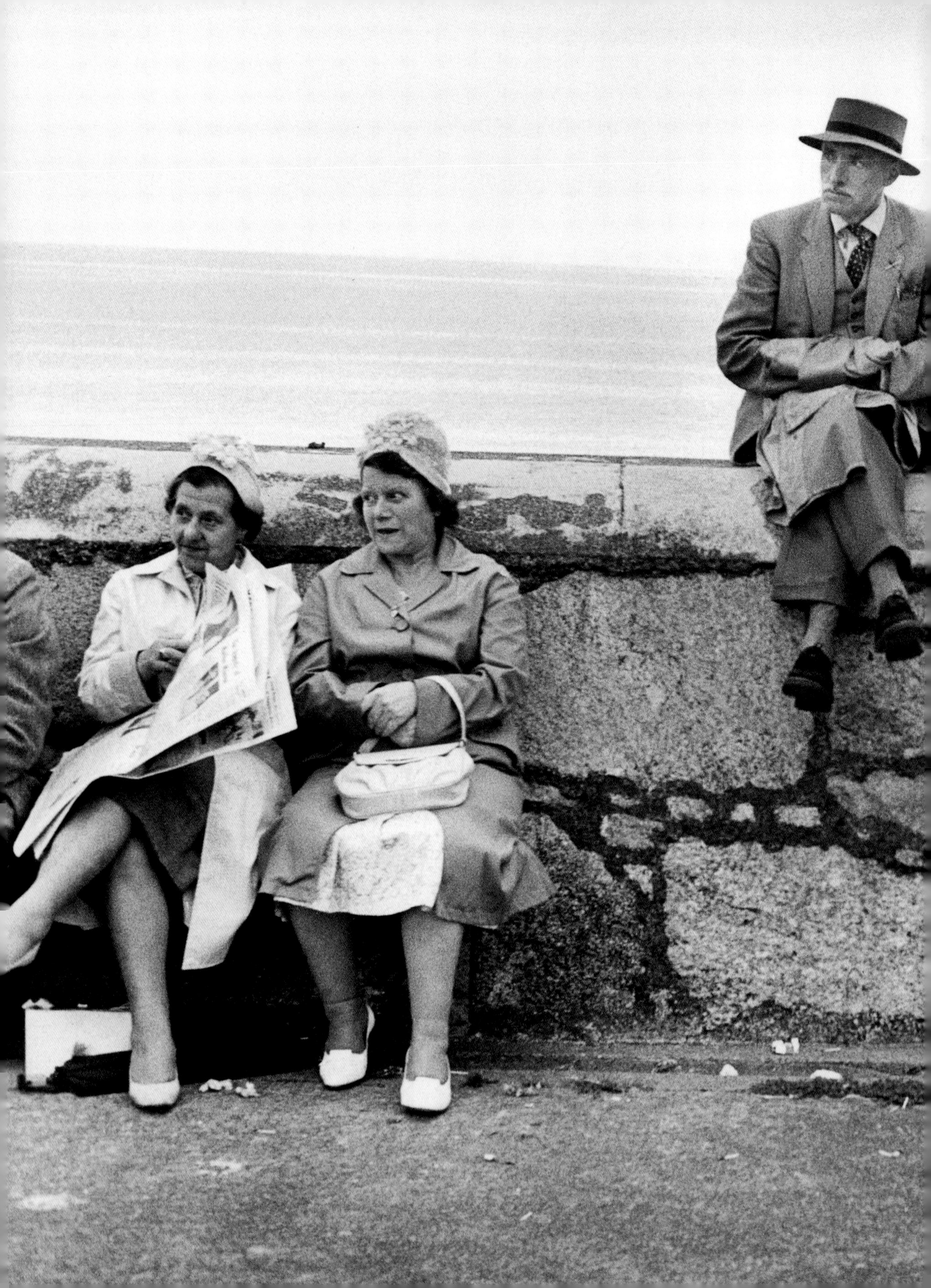

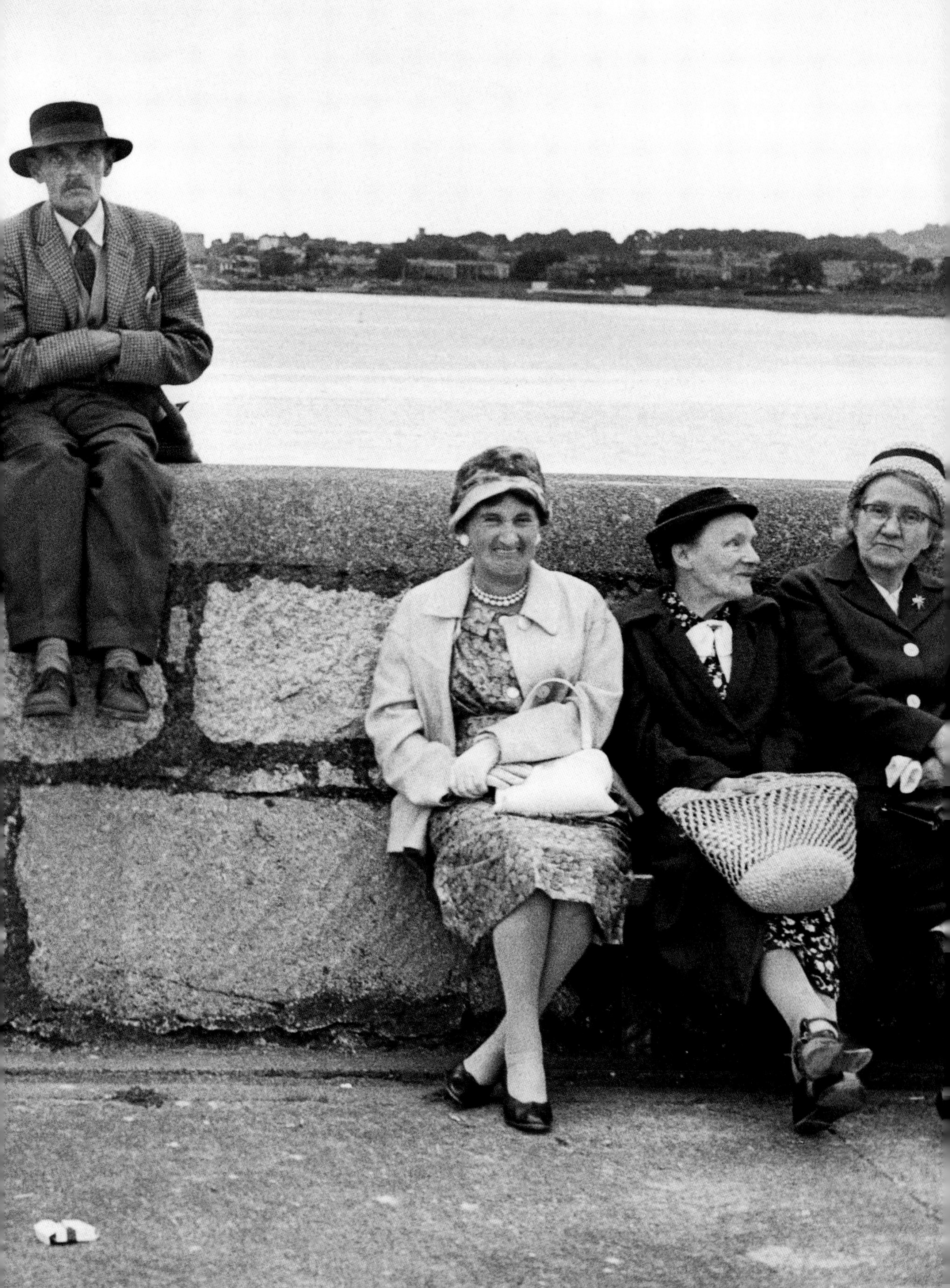

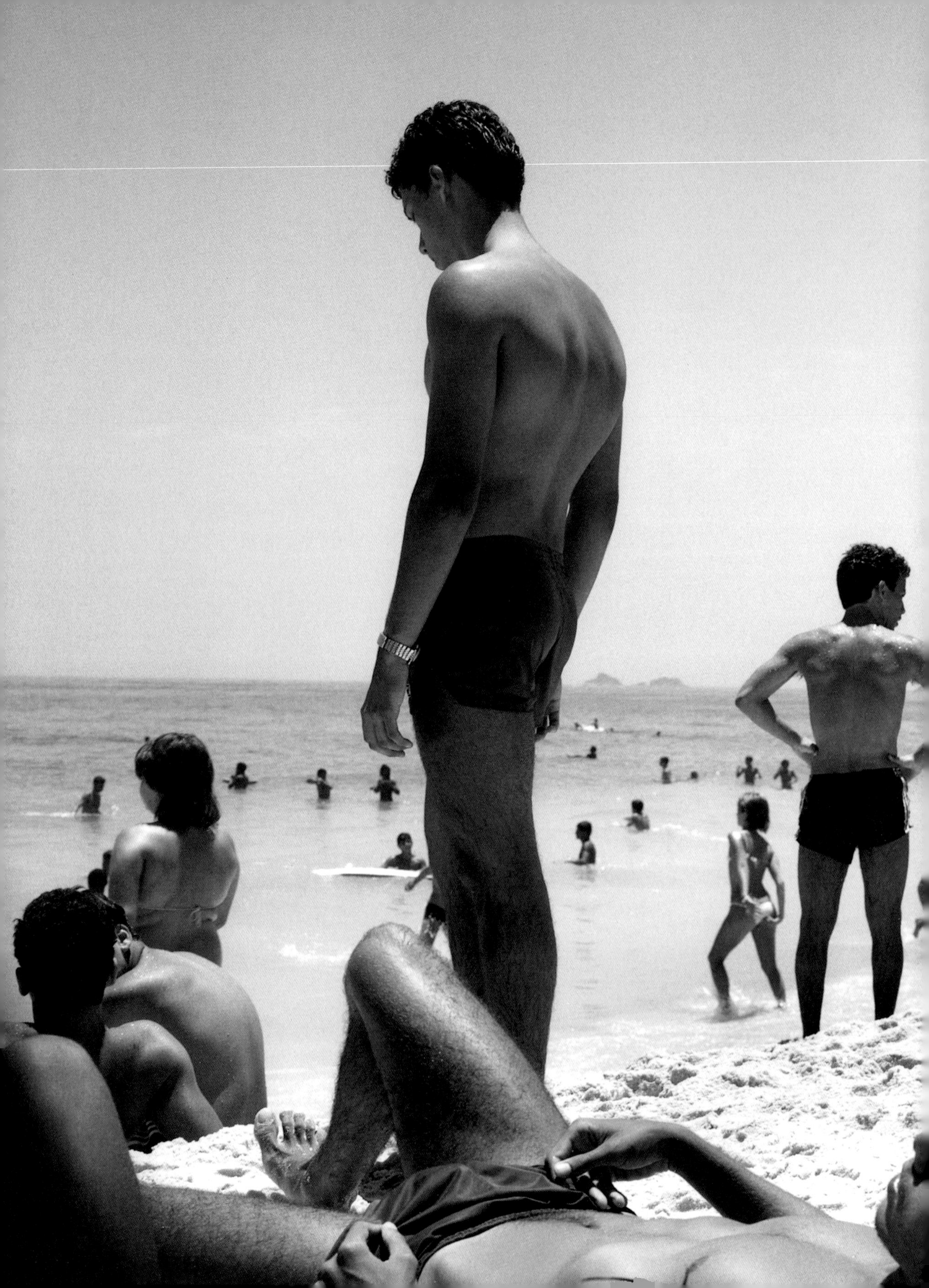

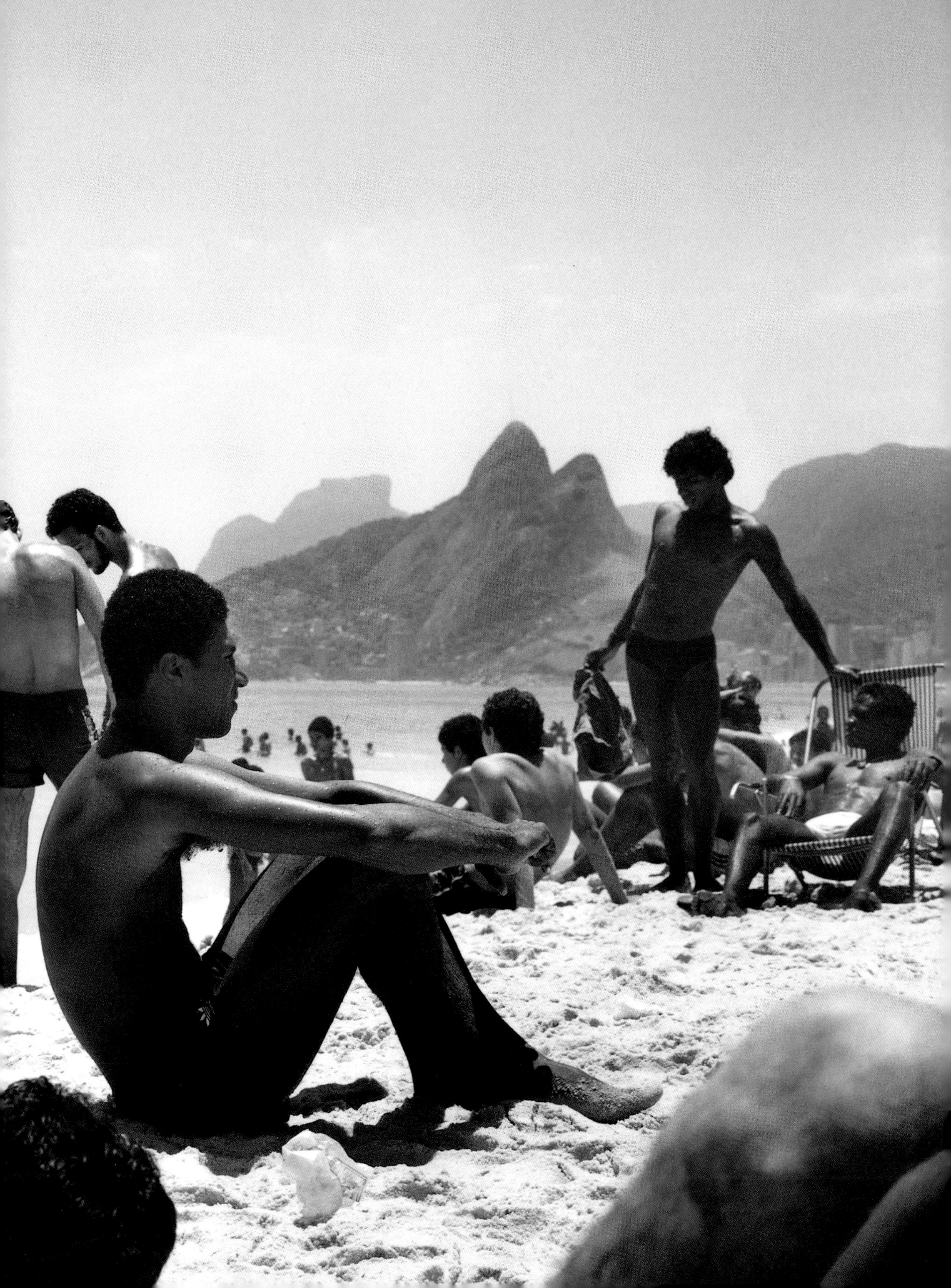

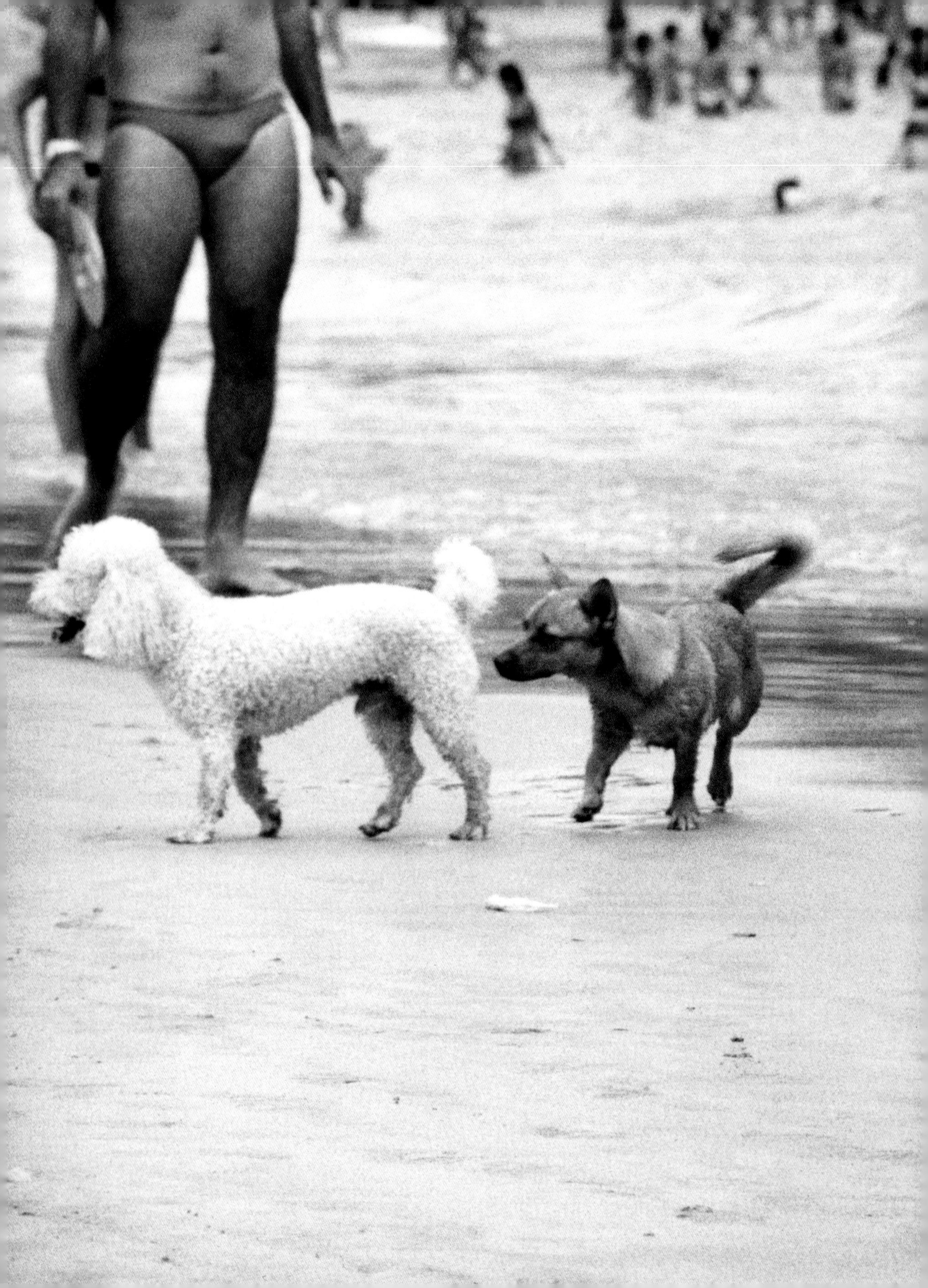

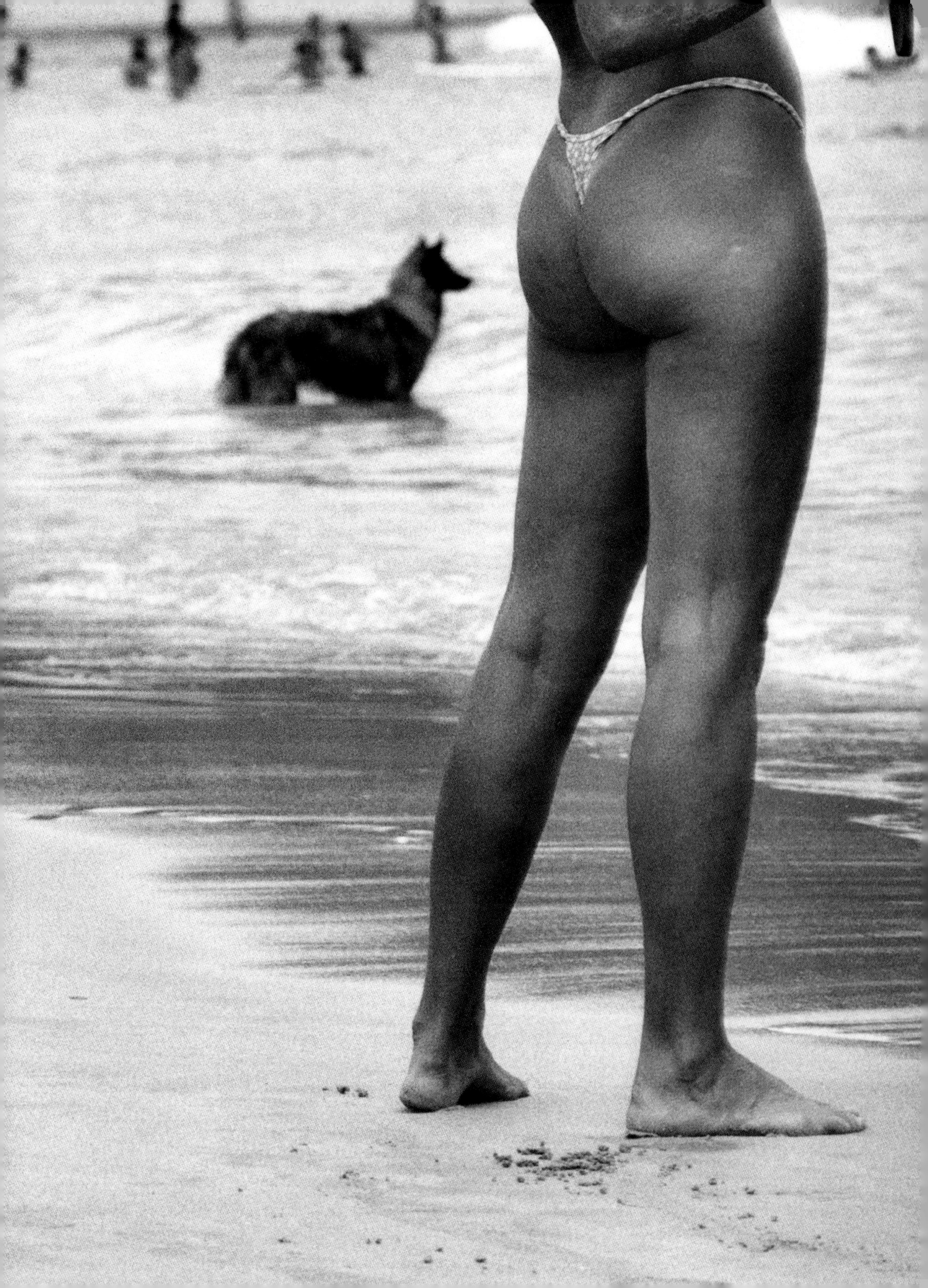

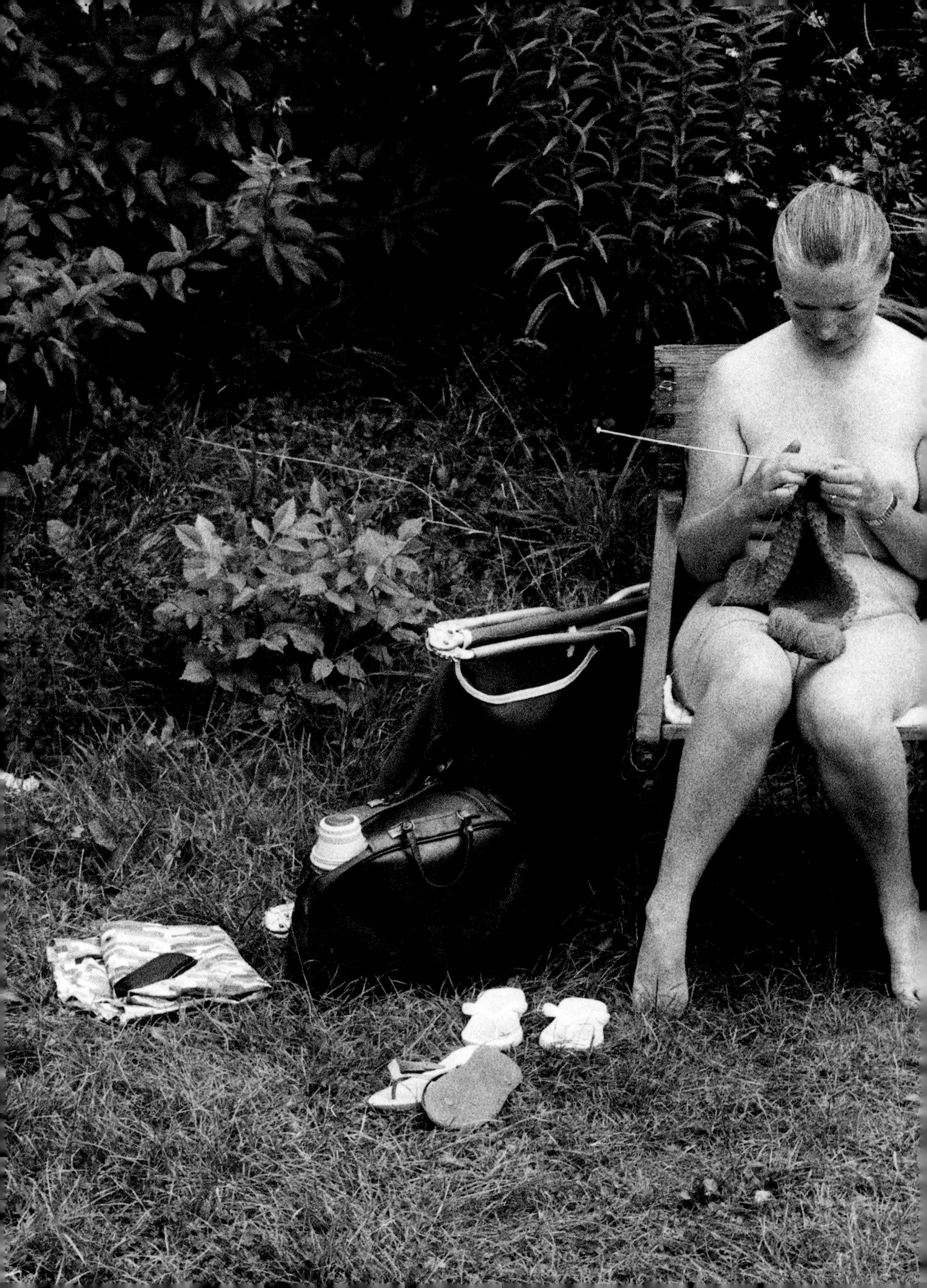

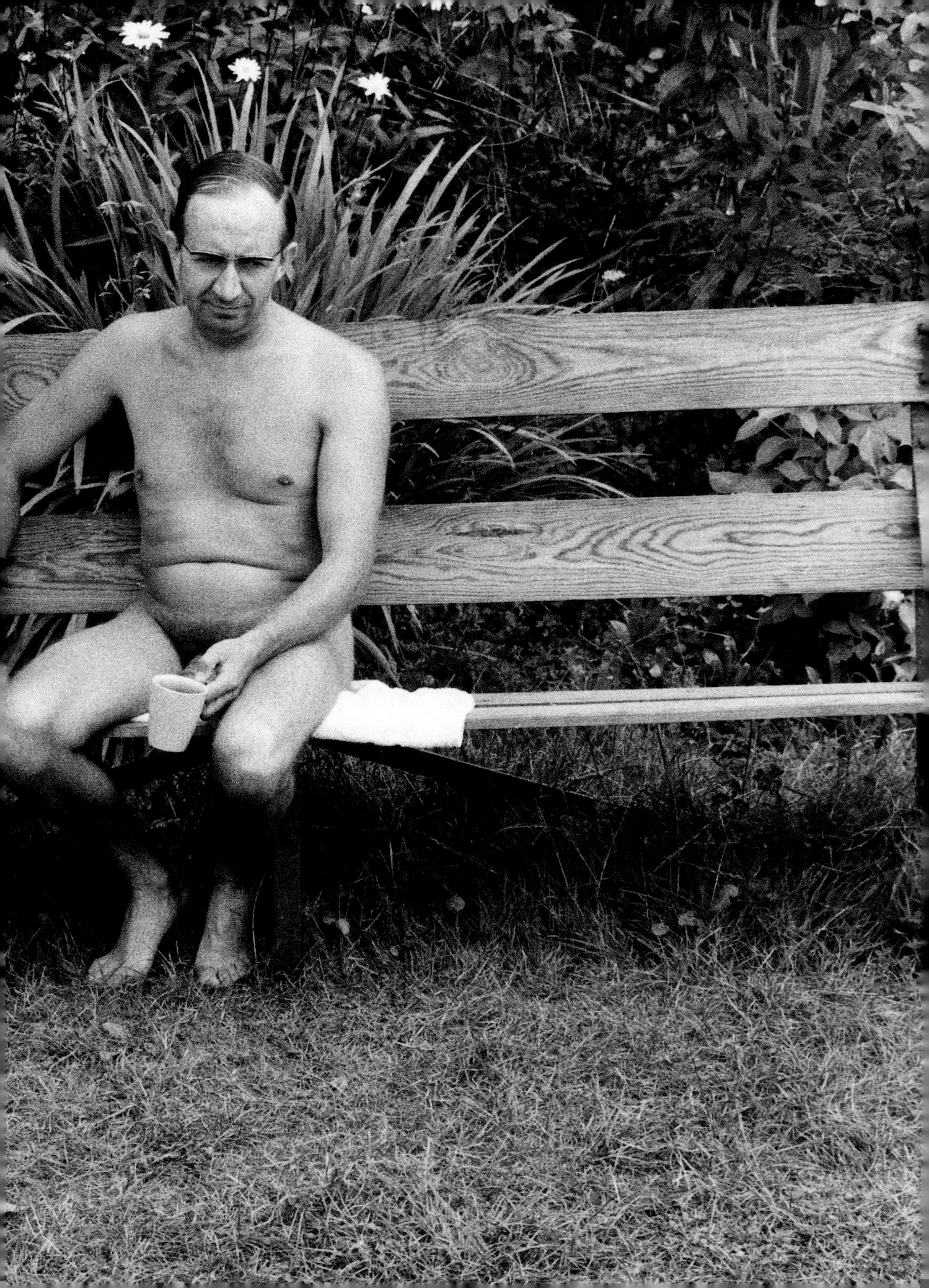

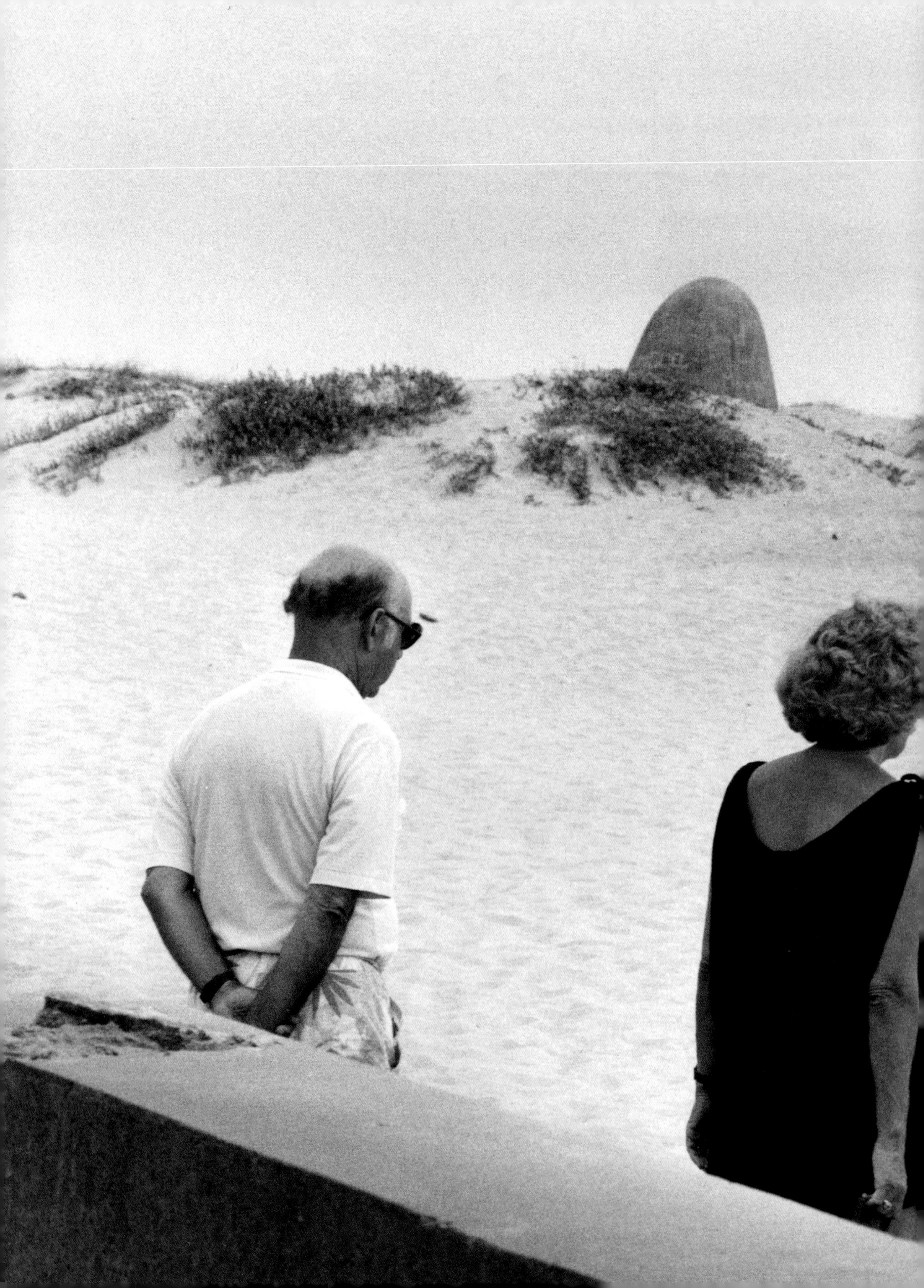

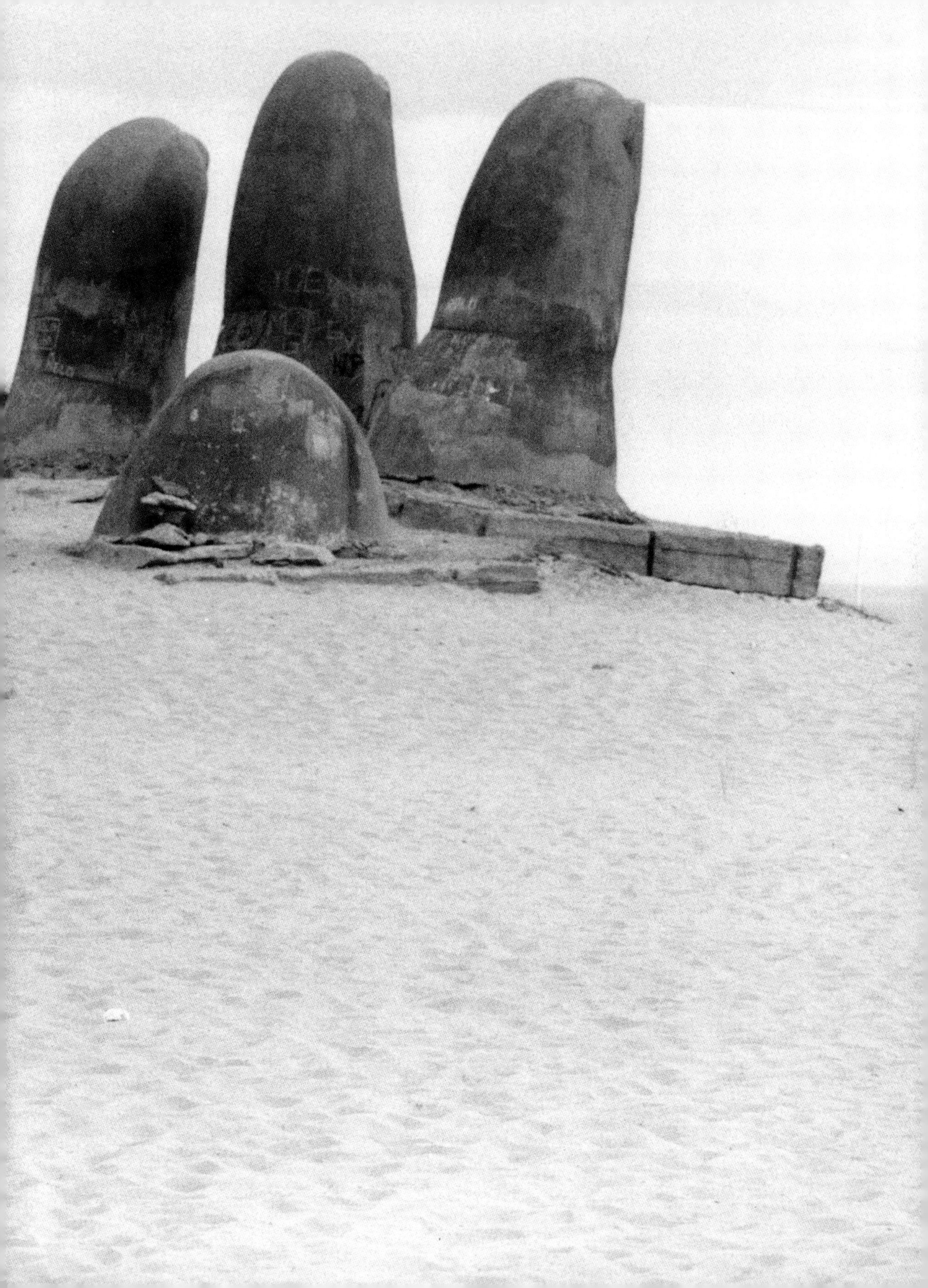

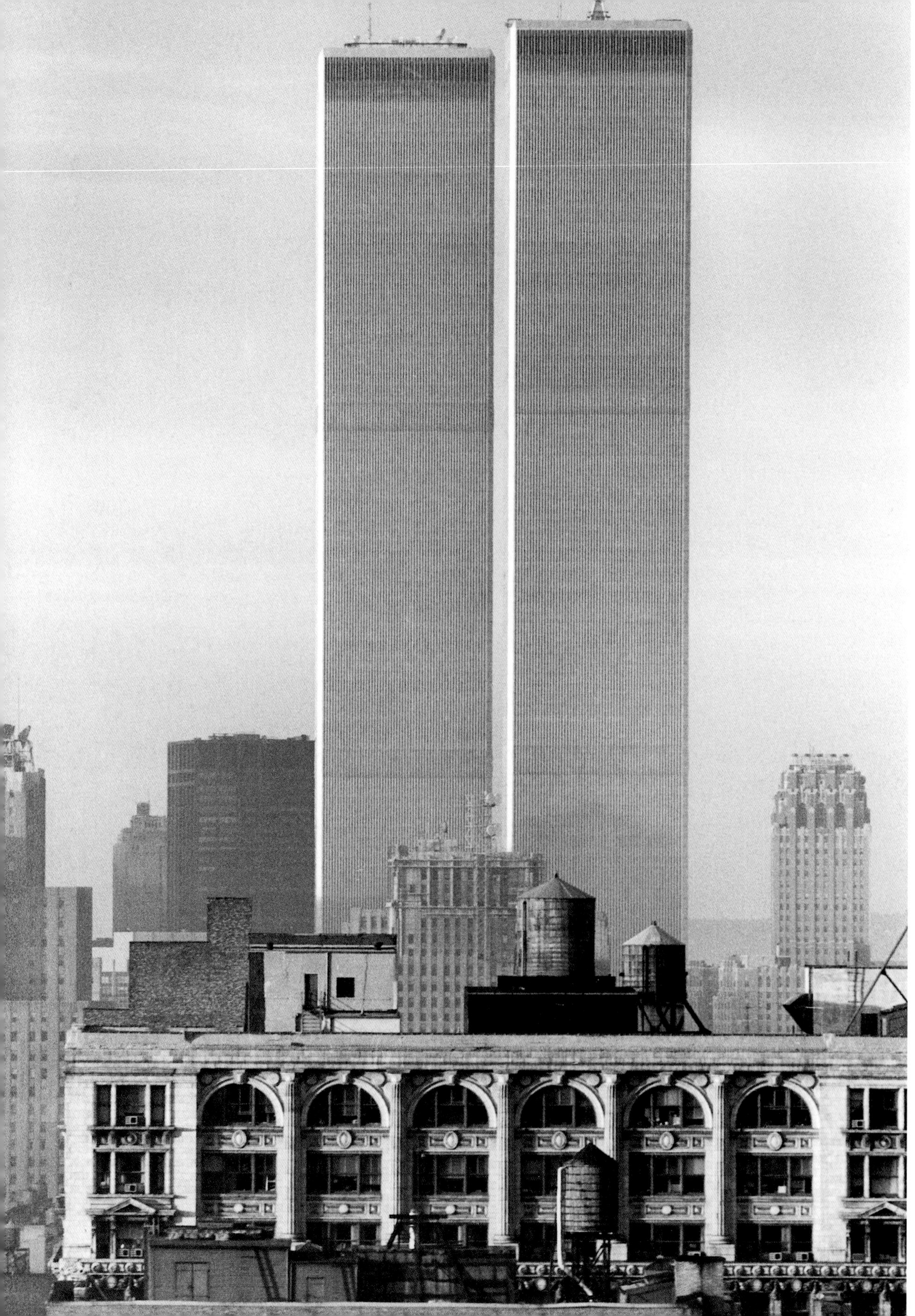

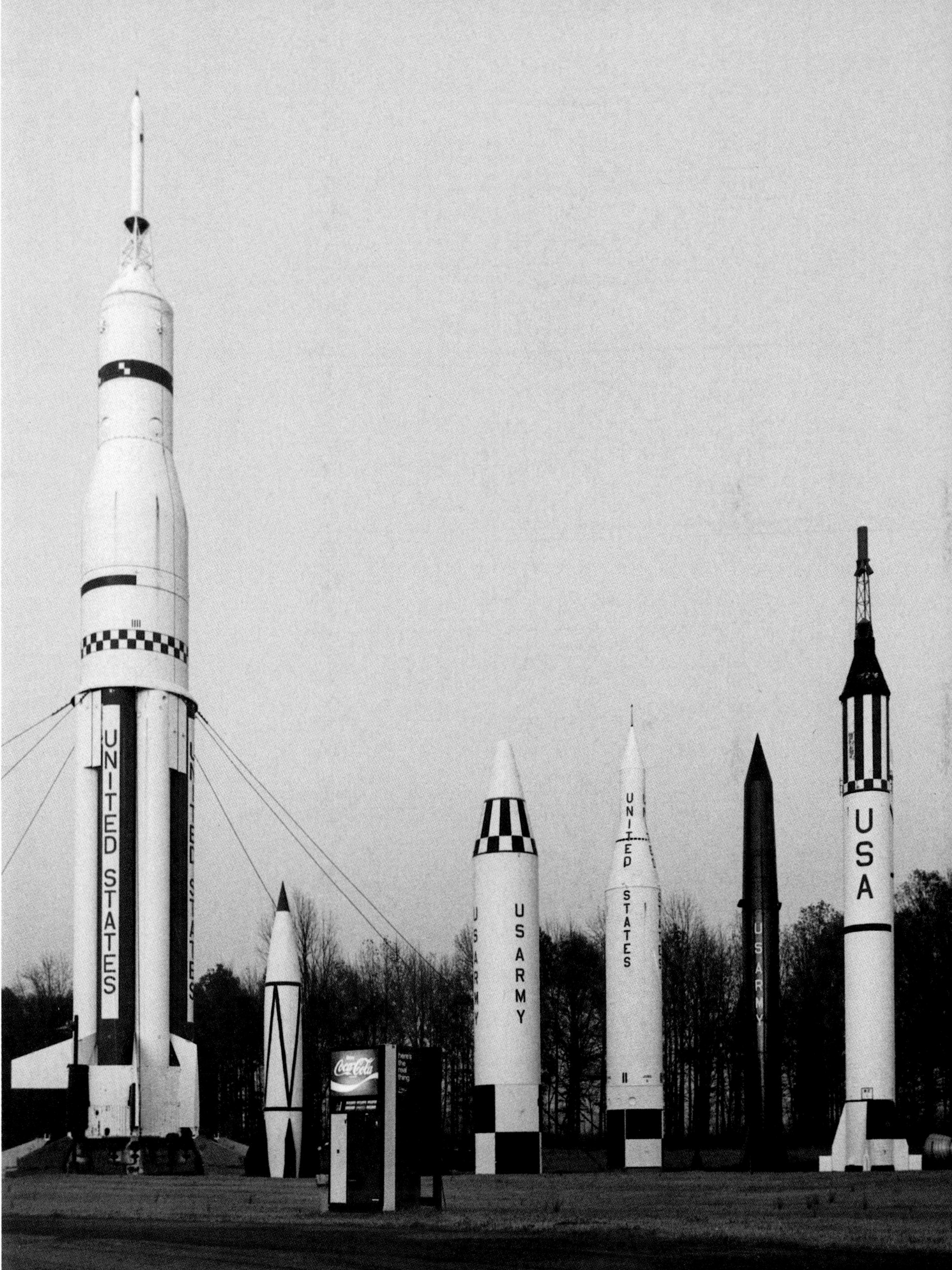
UNITED STATES
UNITED STATES
US ARMY
US ARMY
UNITED STATES
US ARMY
USA
Coca-Cola
here's
the
real
thing

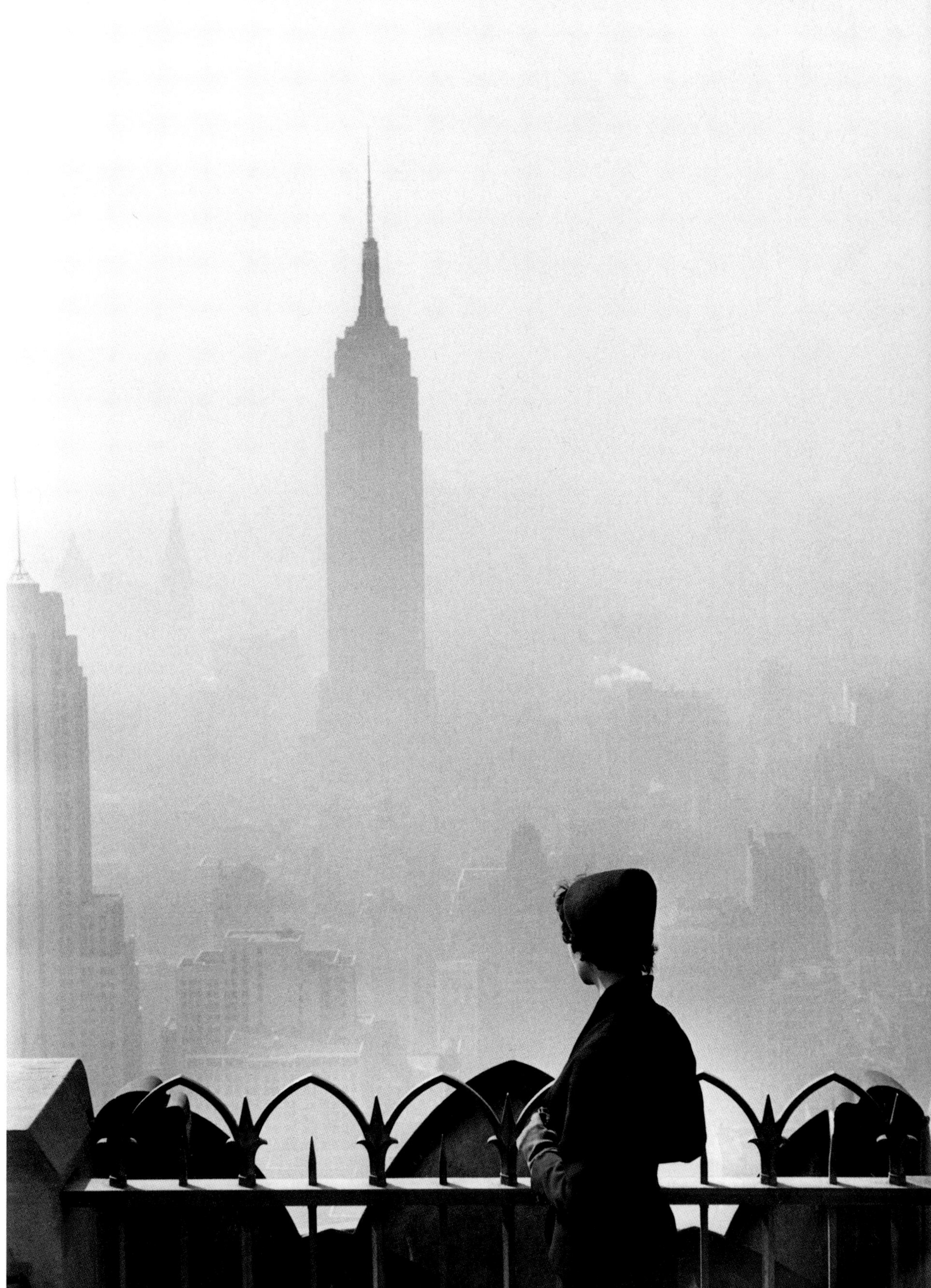

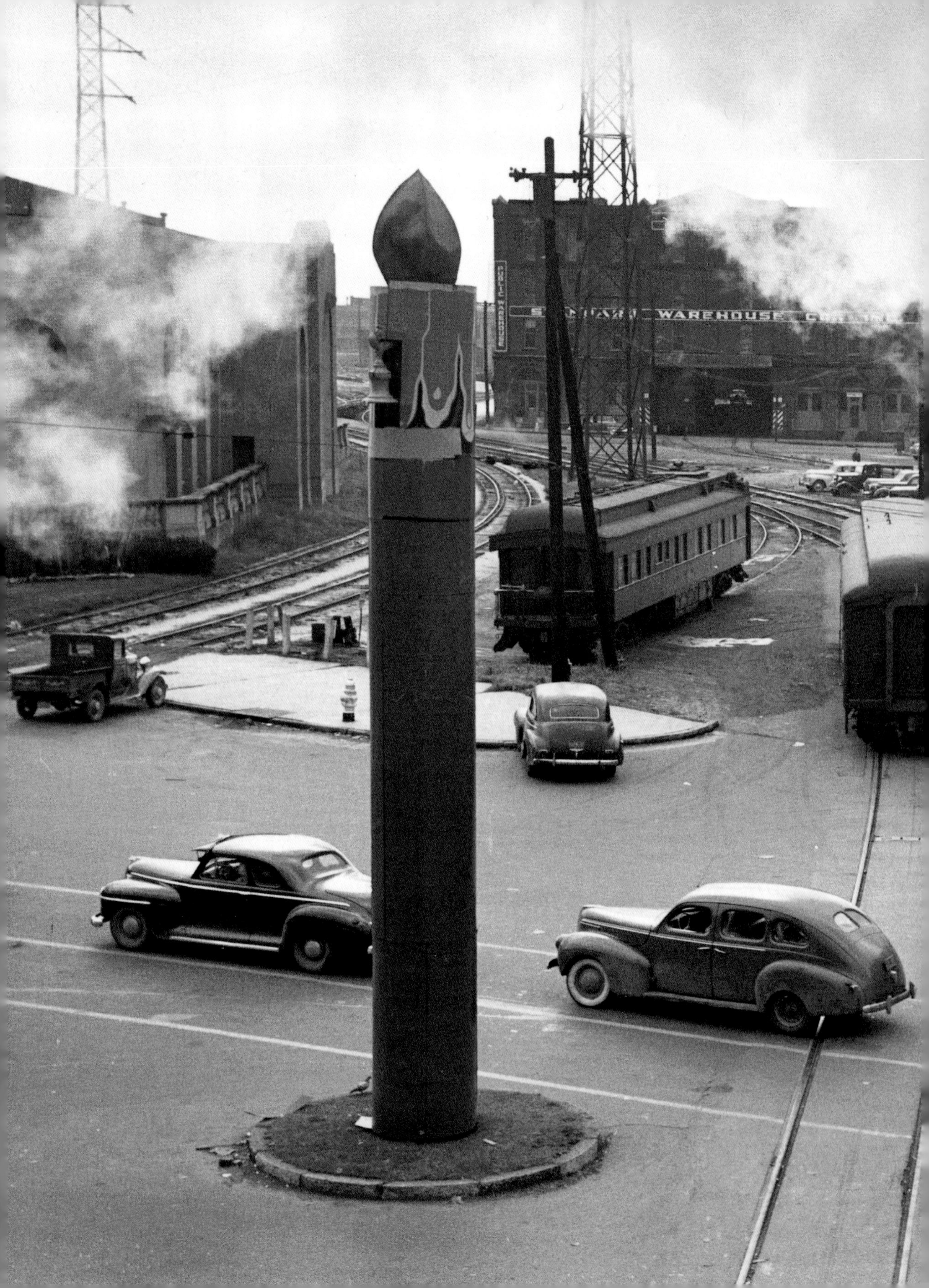
STANDARD WAREHOUSE COMPANY
PUBLIC WAREHOUSE

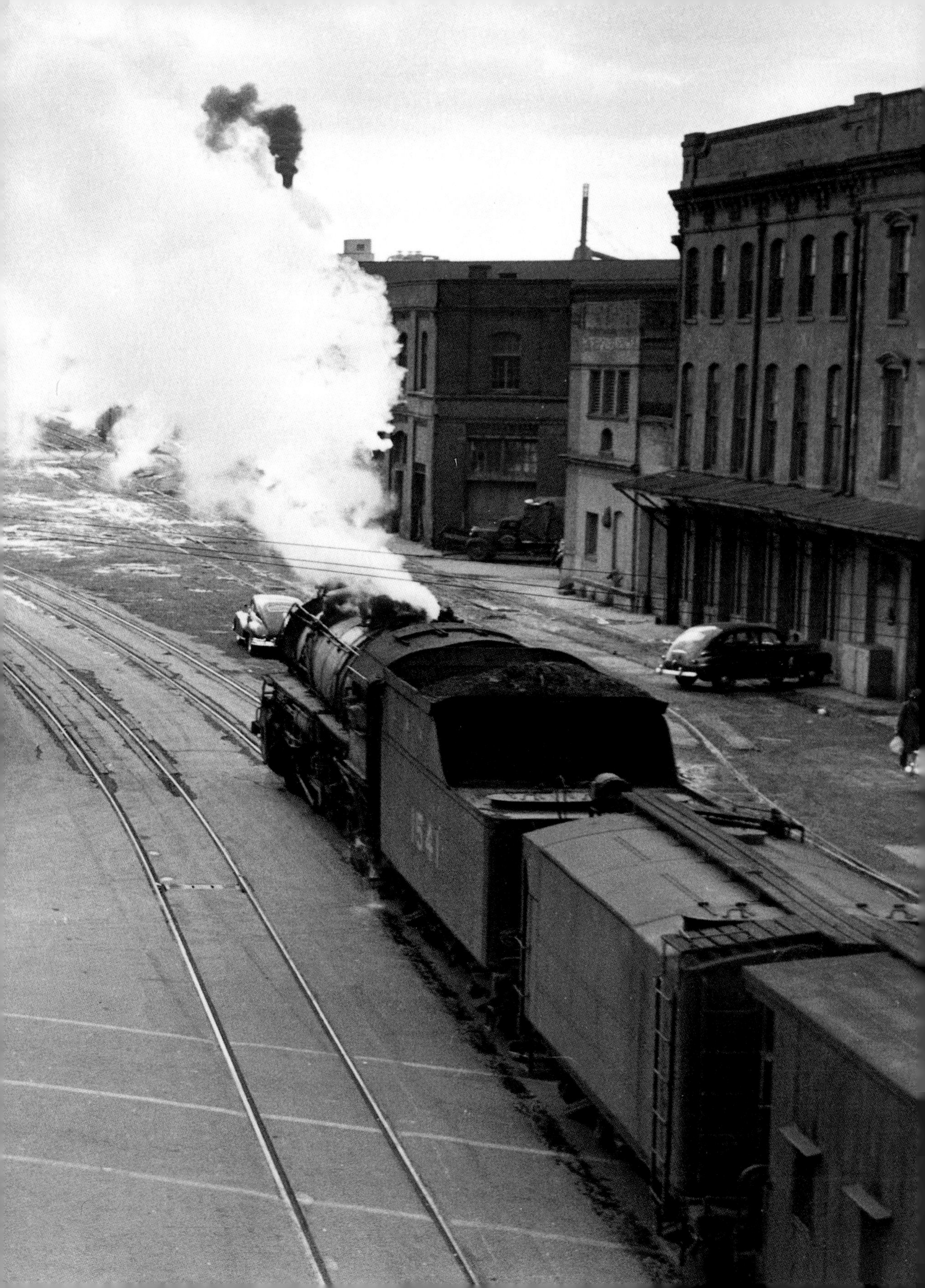

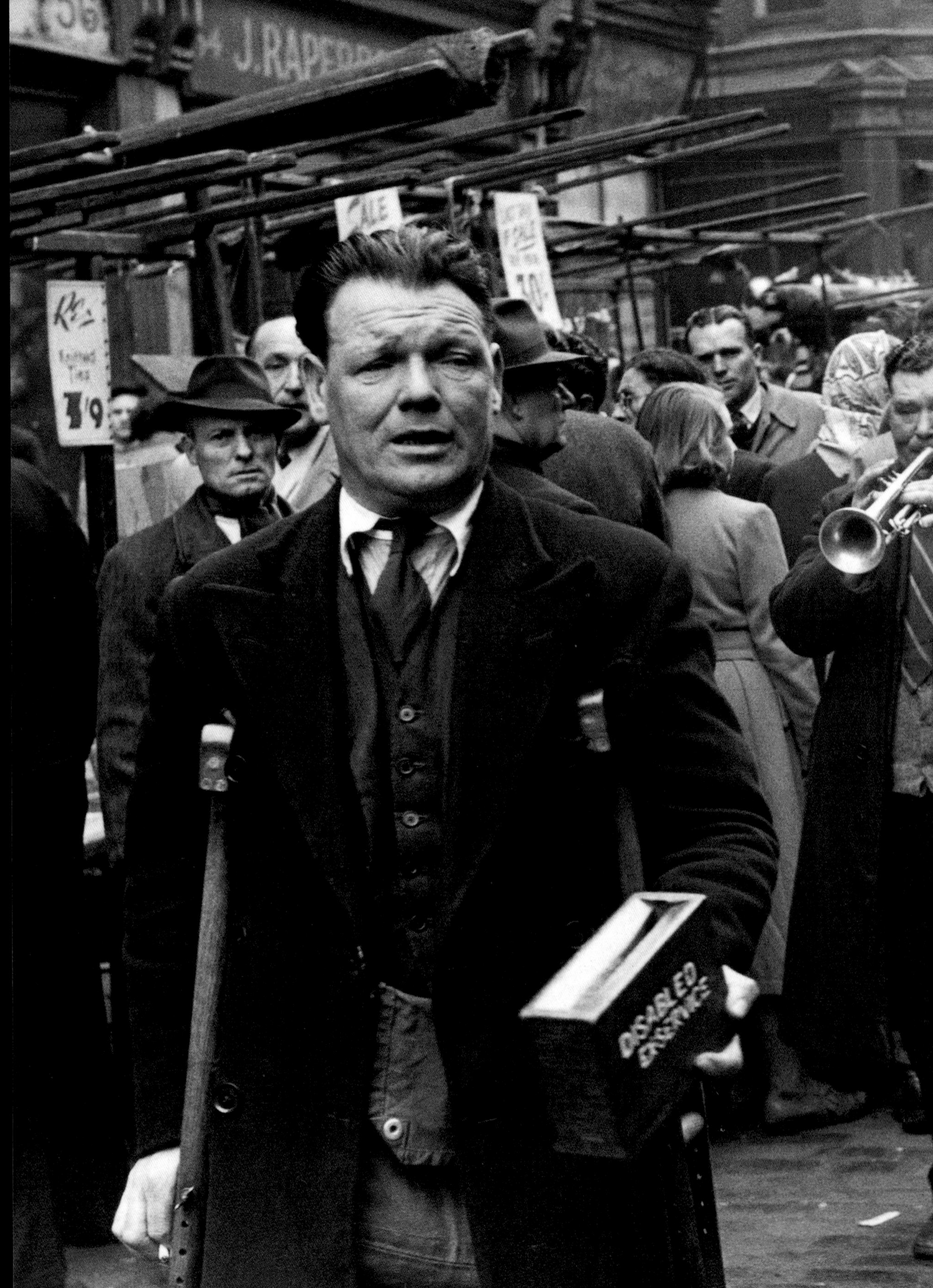

J. RAPE
ALE
DISABLED EX-SERVICES

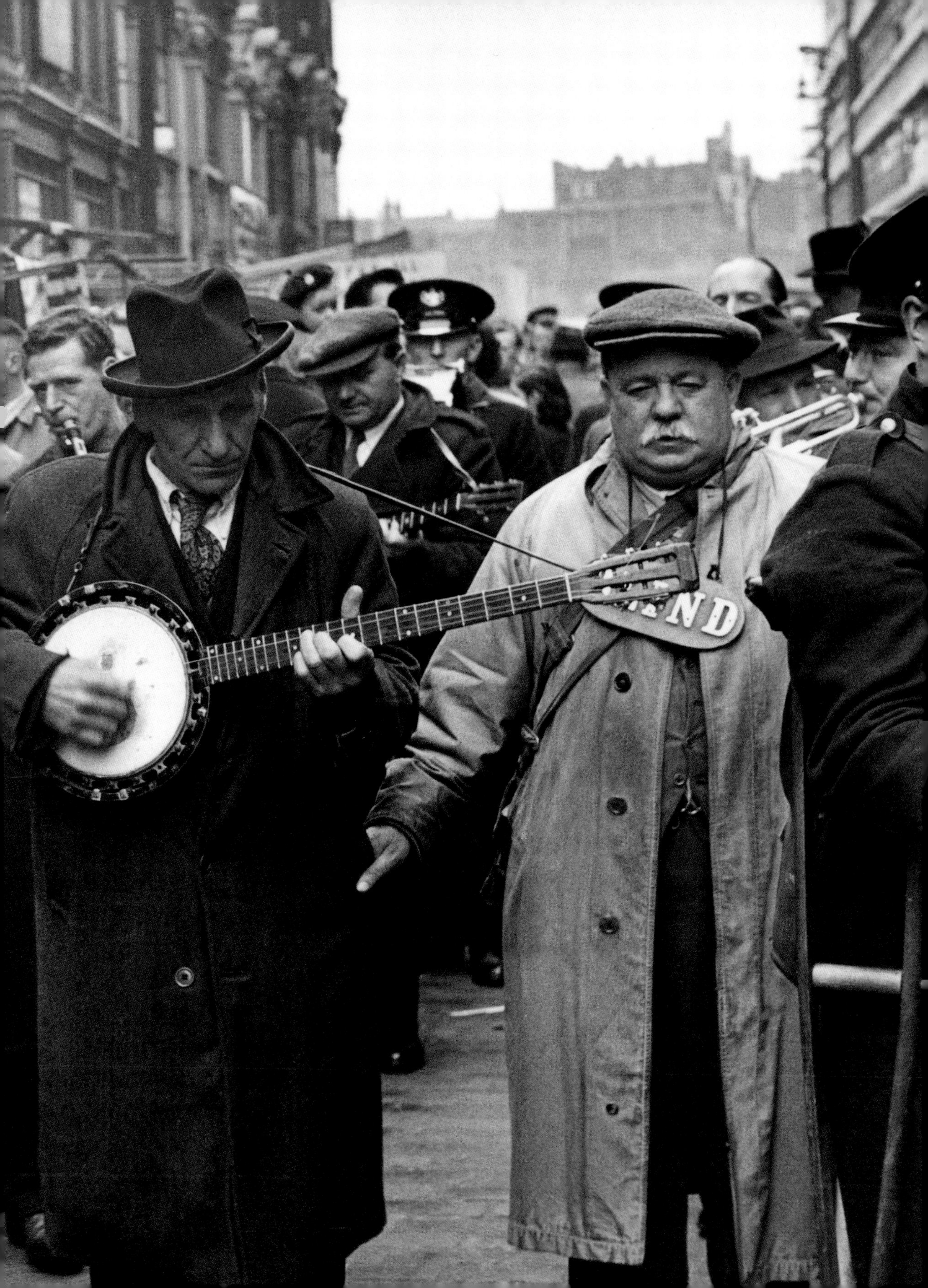

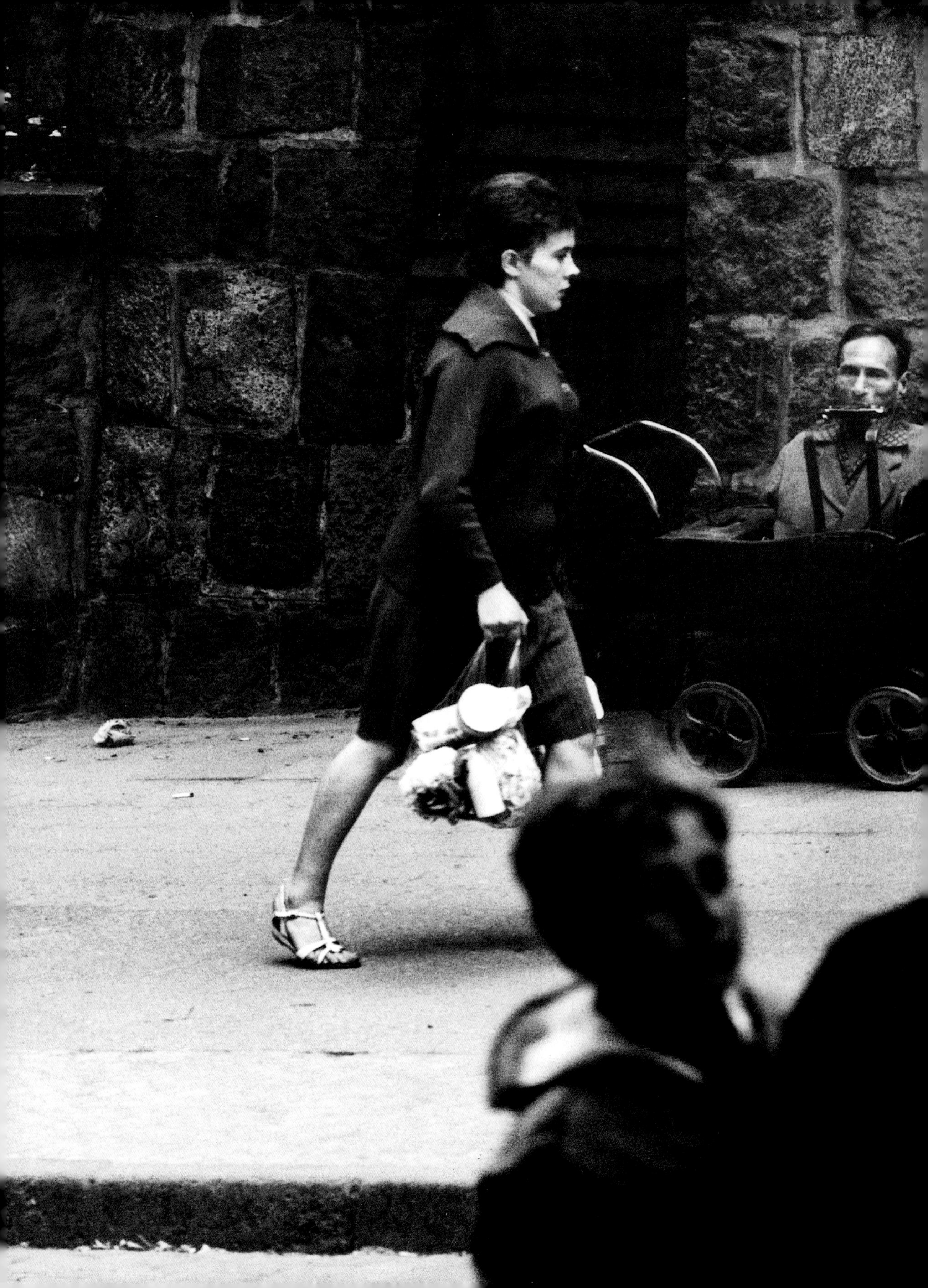

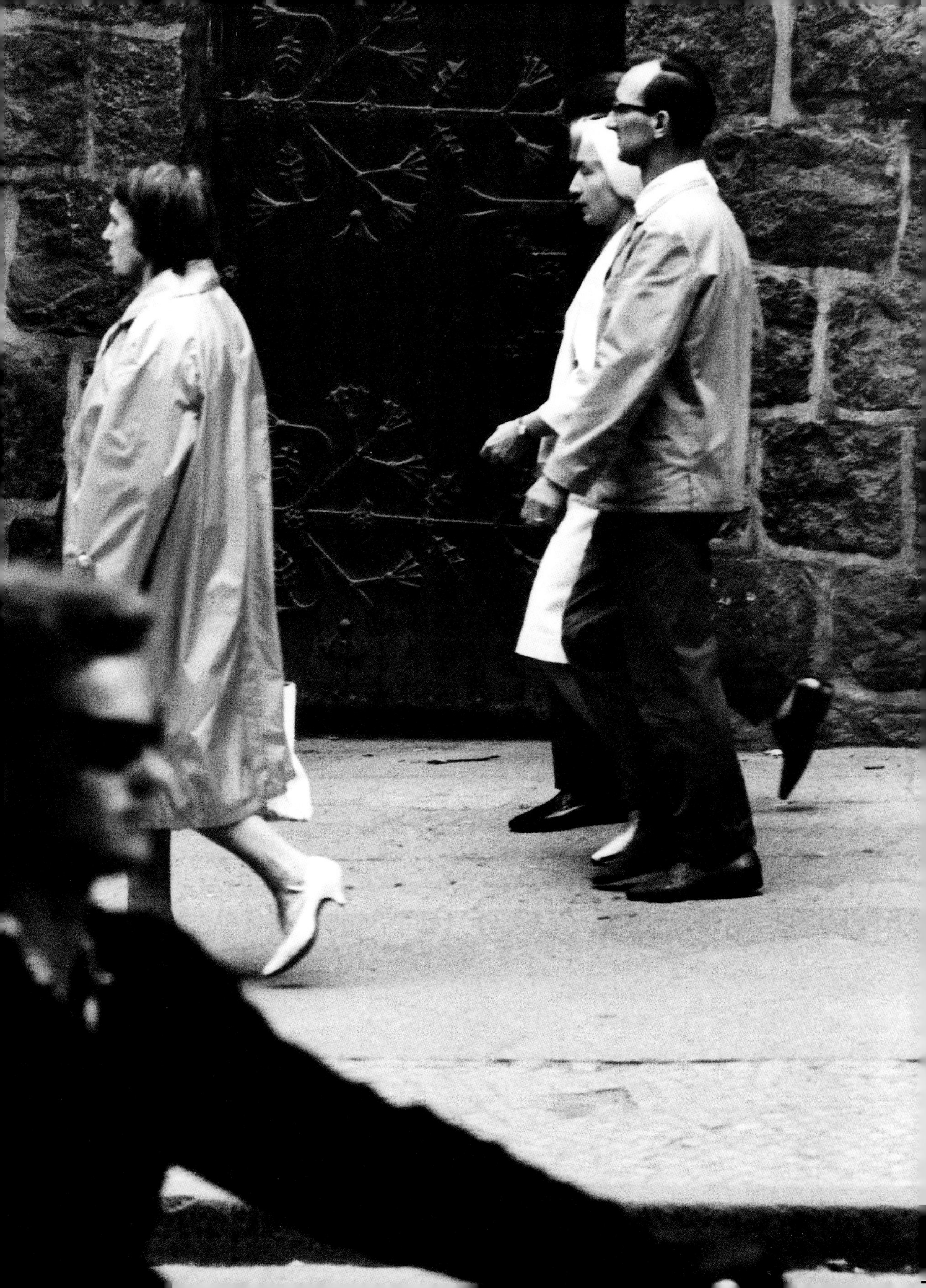

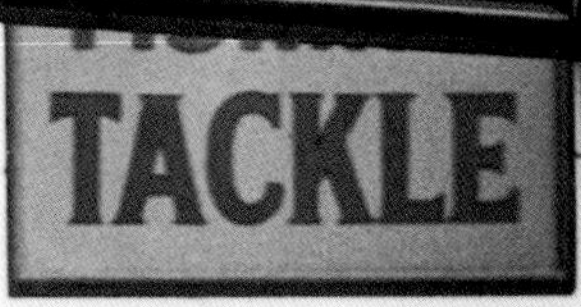

Carola PHOTO STUDIO
TACKLE
LIBE
983   983
FOR SALE
MENS SUITS
&
OVERCOATS
LADIES
FUR COATS
LIBERAL
BAR
PASSPORTS
ATLANTIC CARTING CO

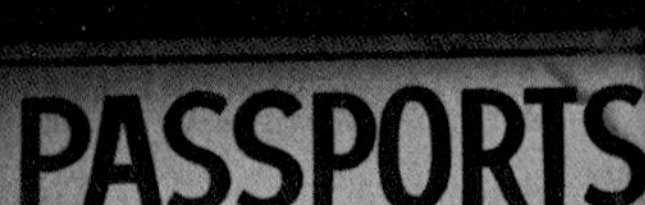
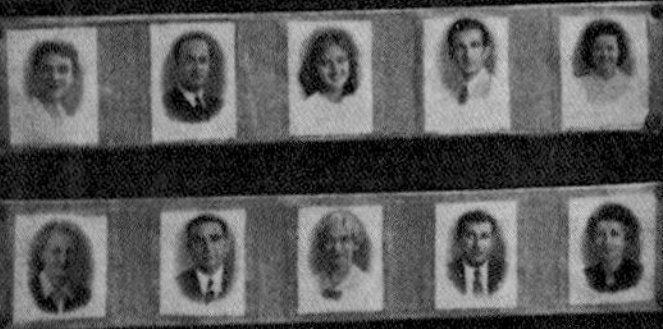
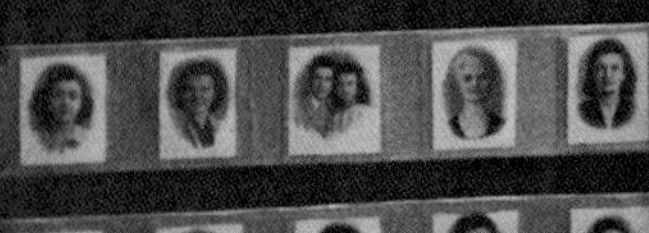
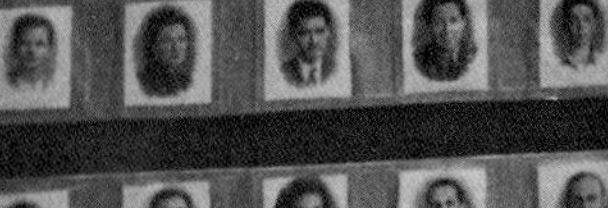
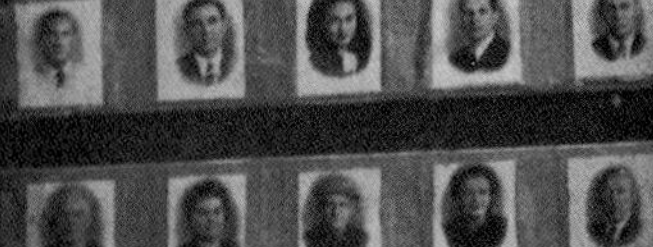

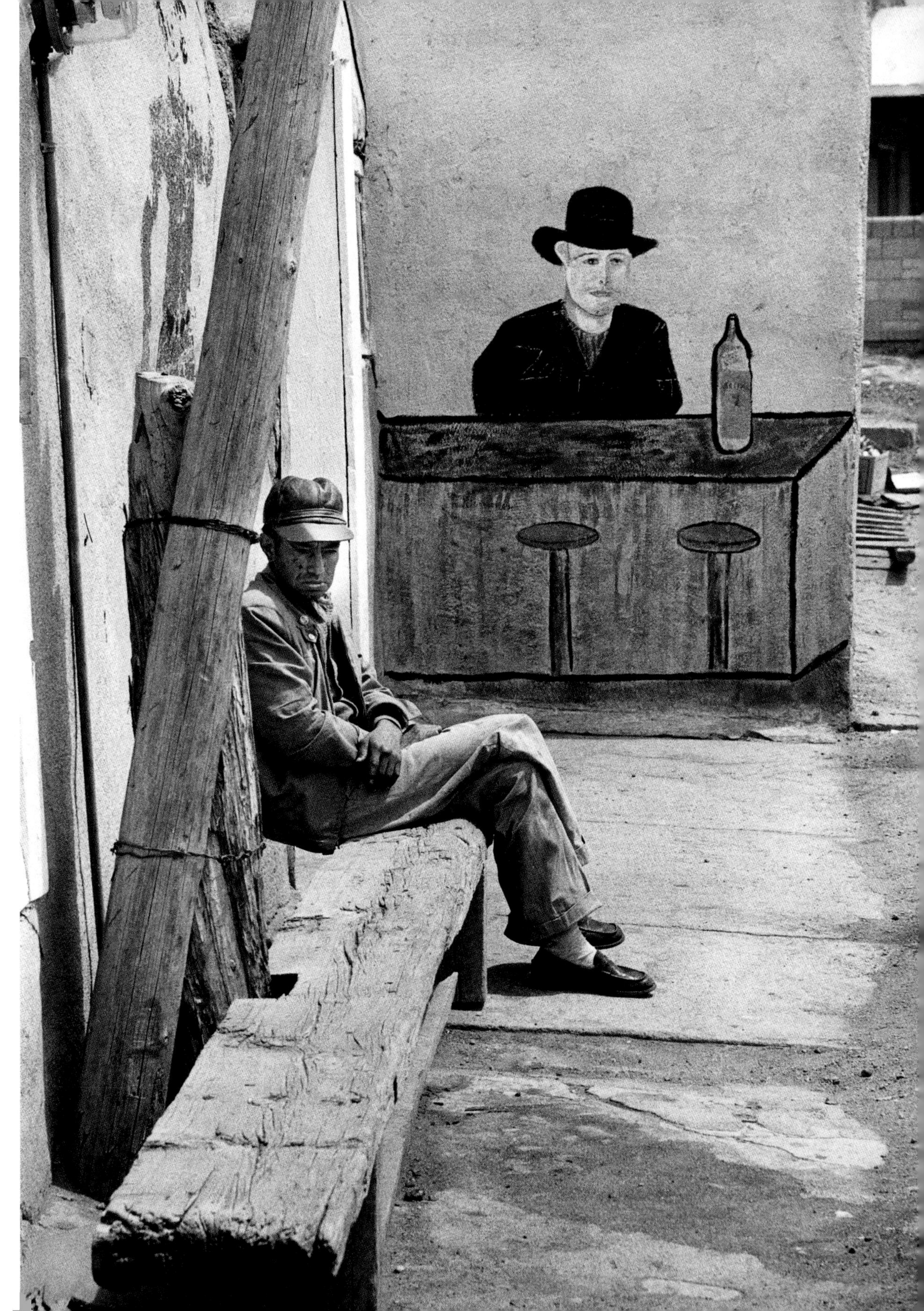

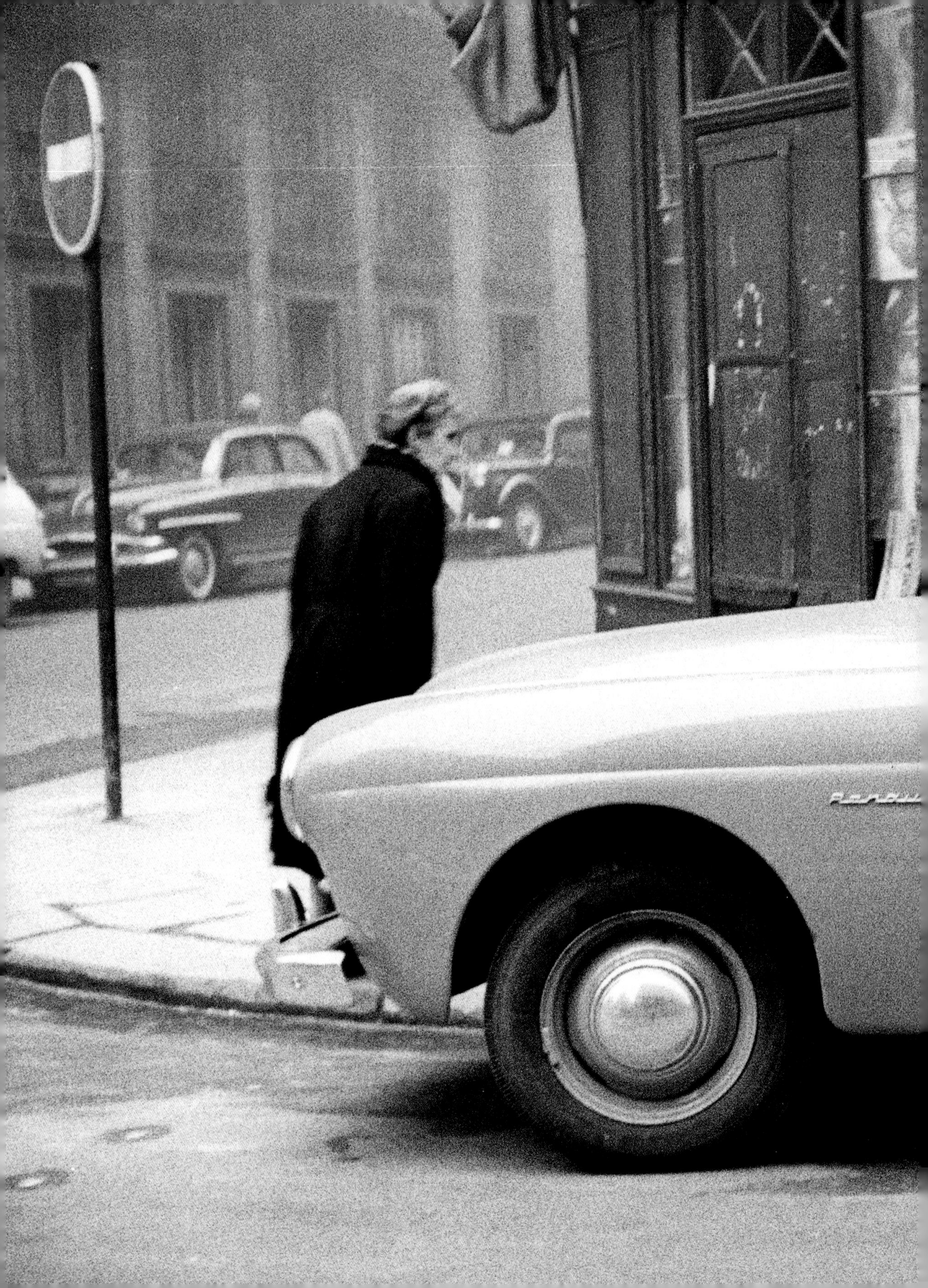

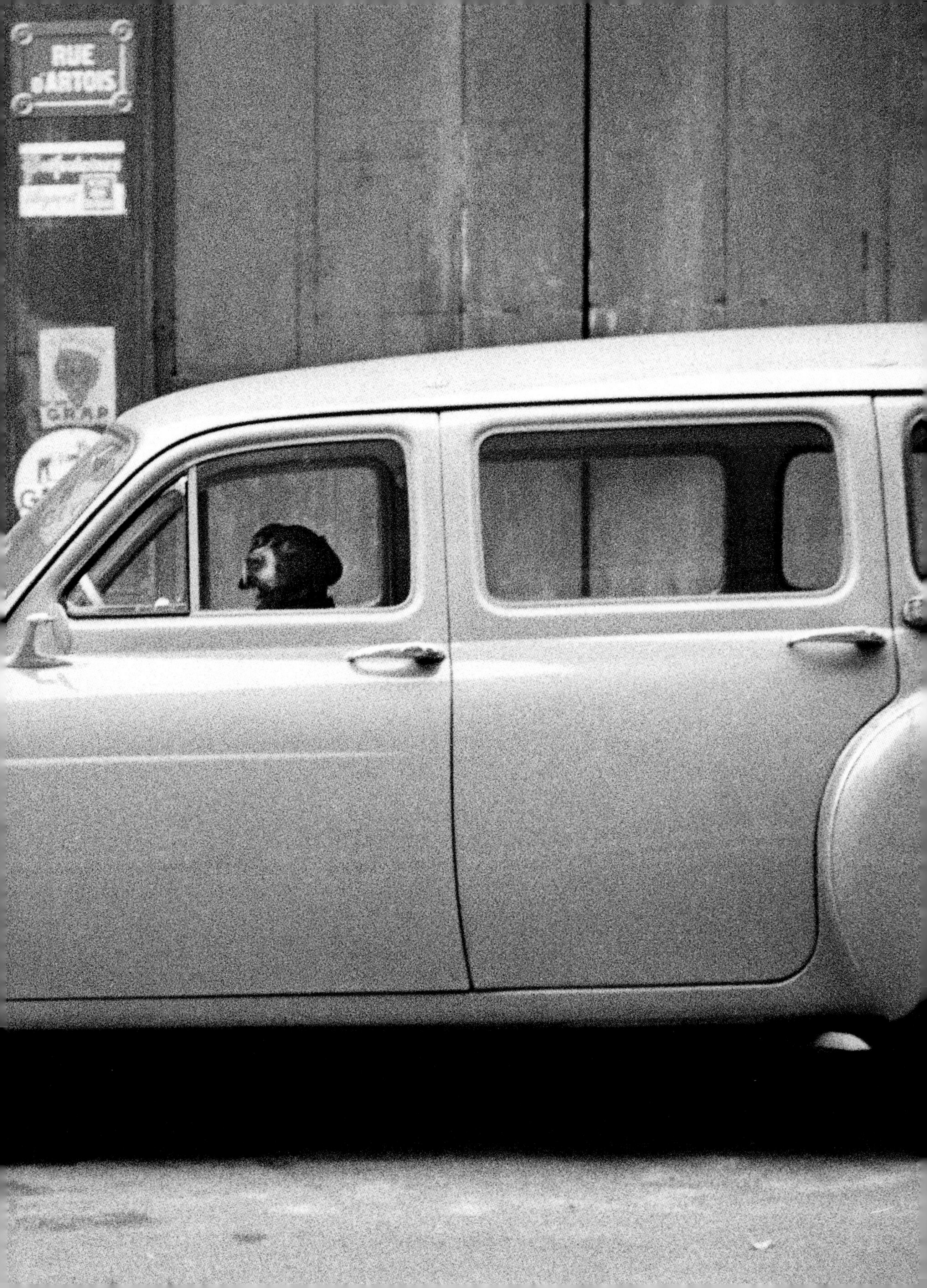

RUE D'ARTOIS

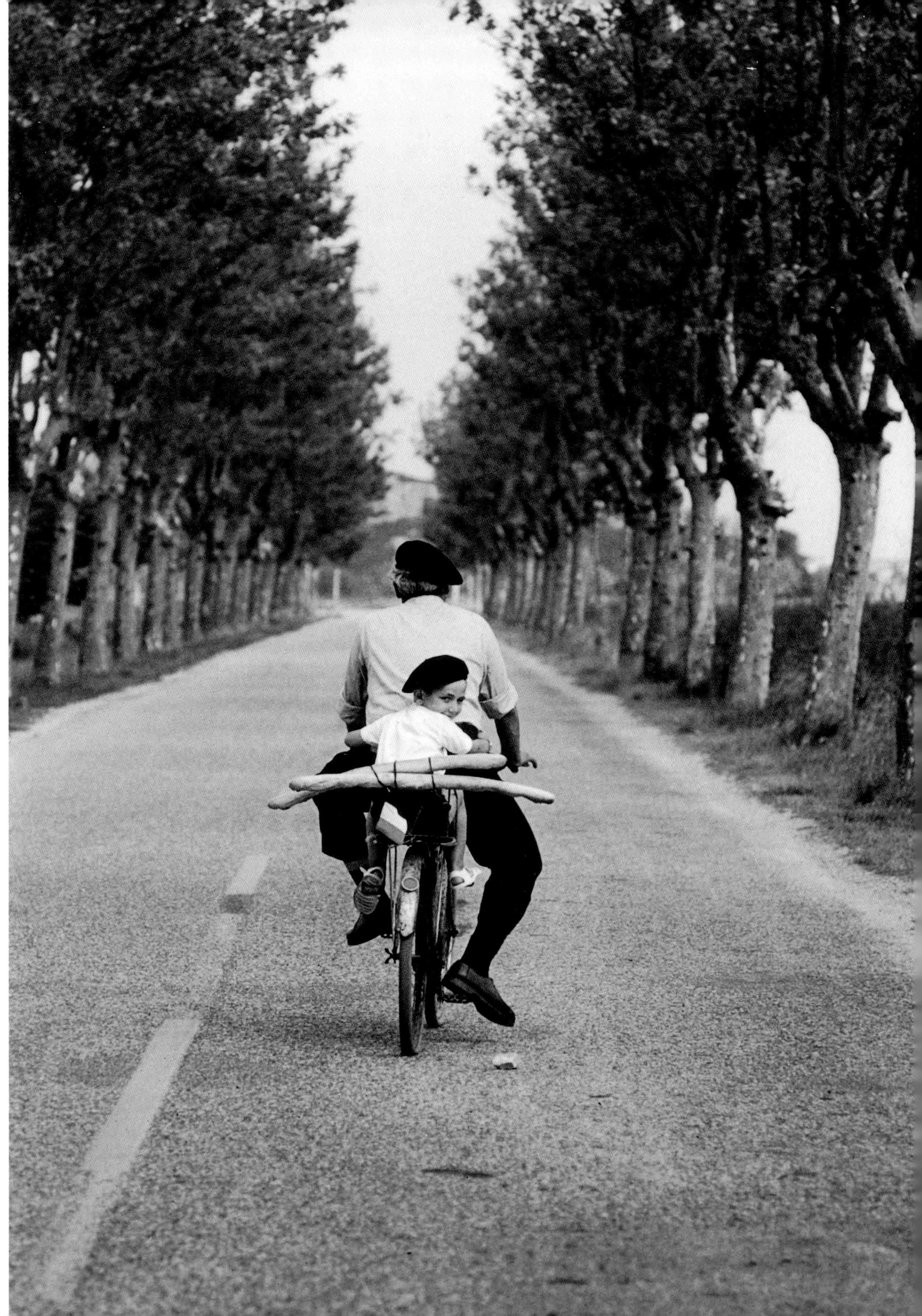

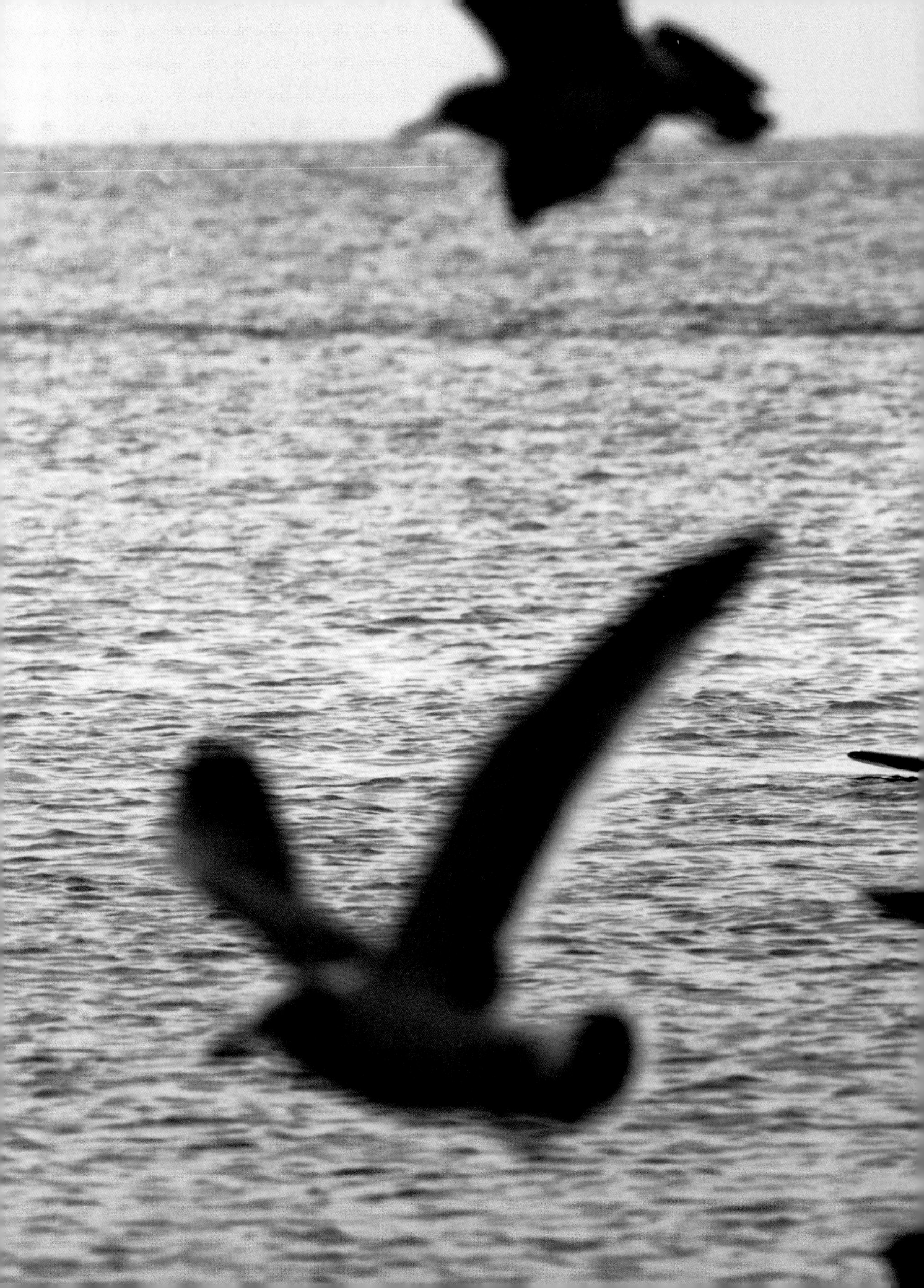

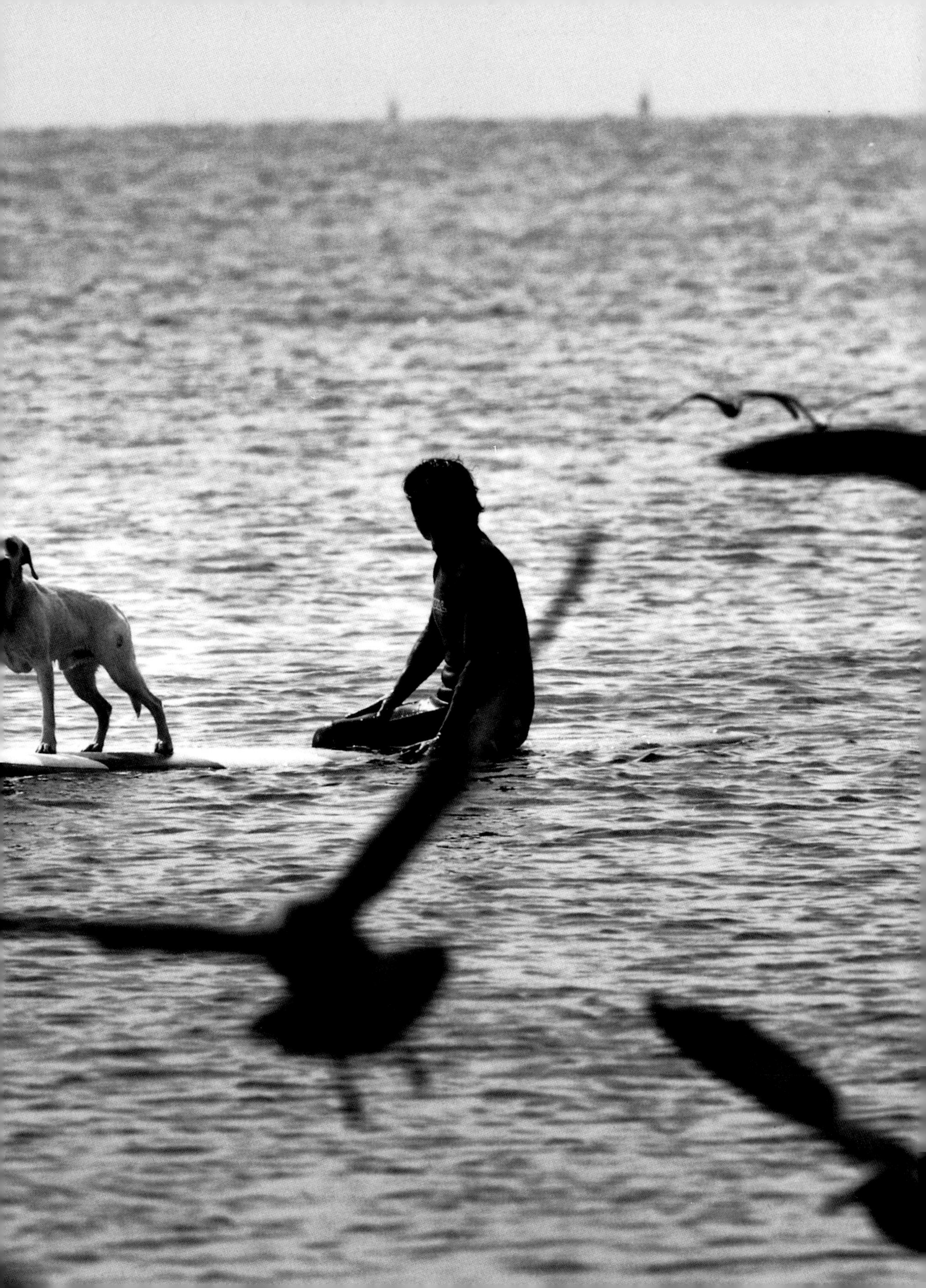

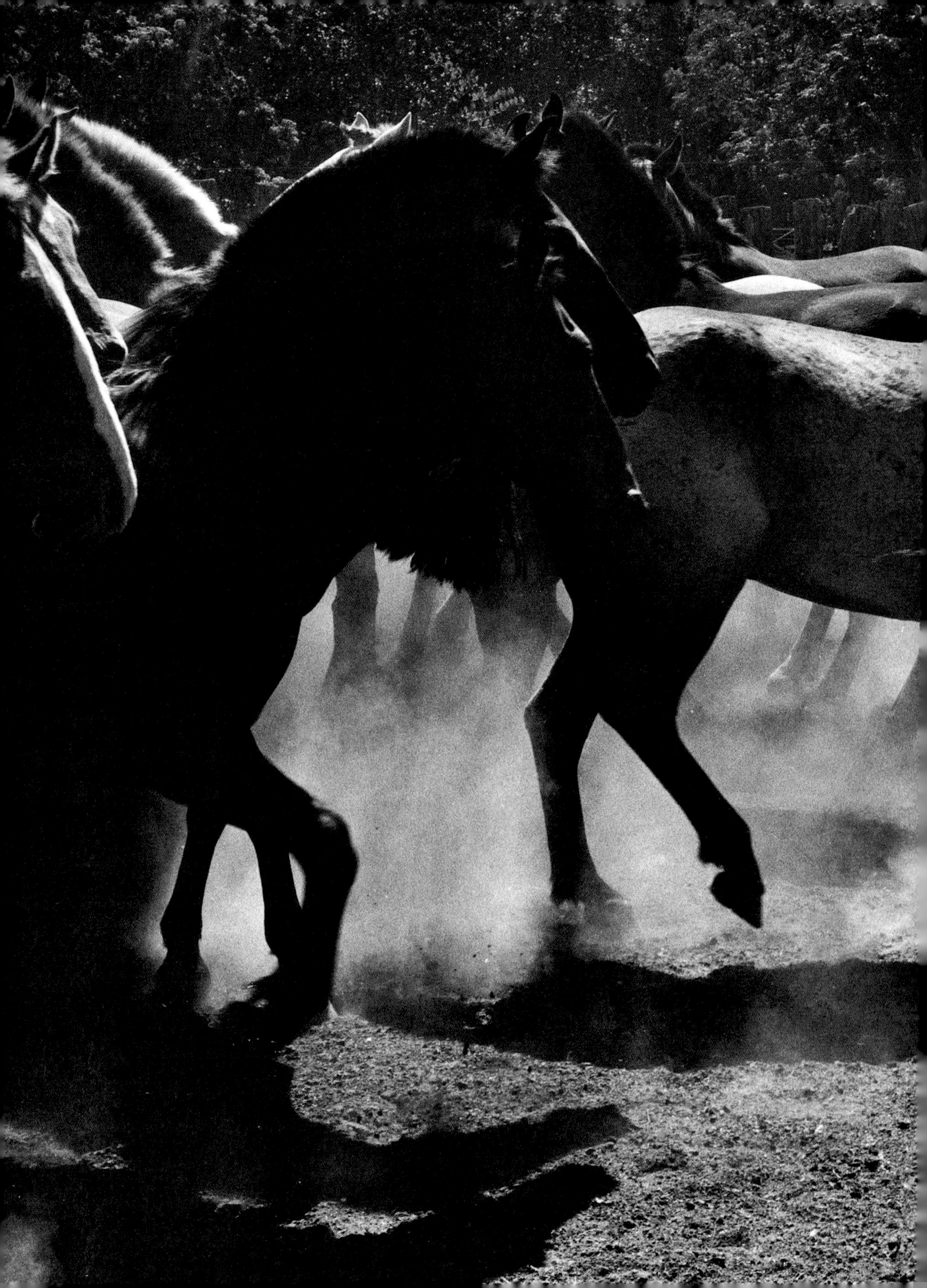

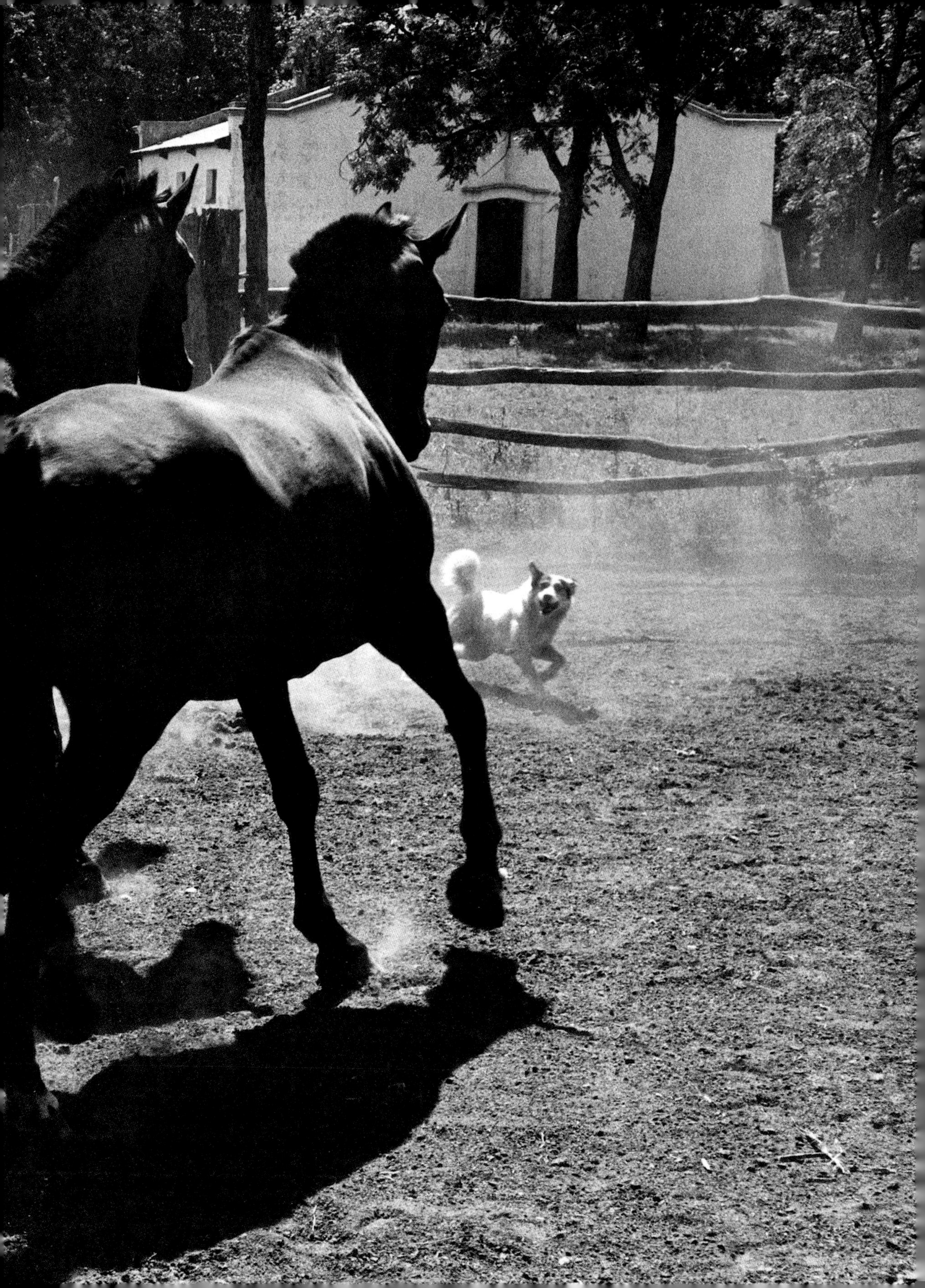

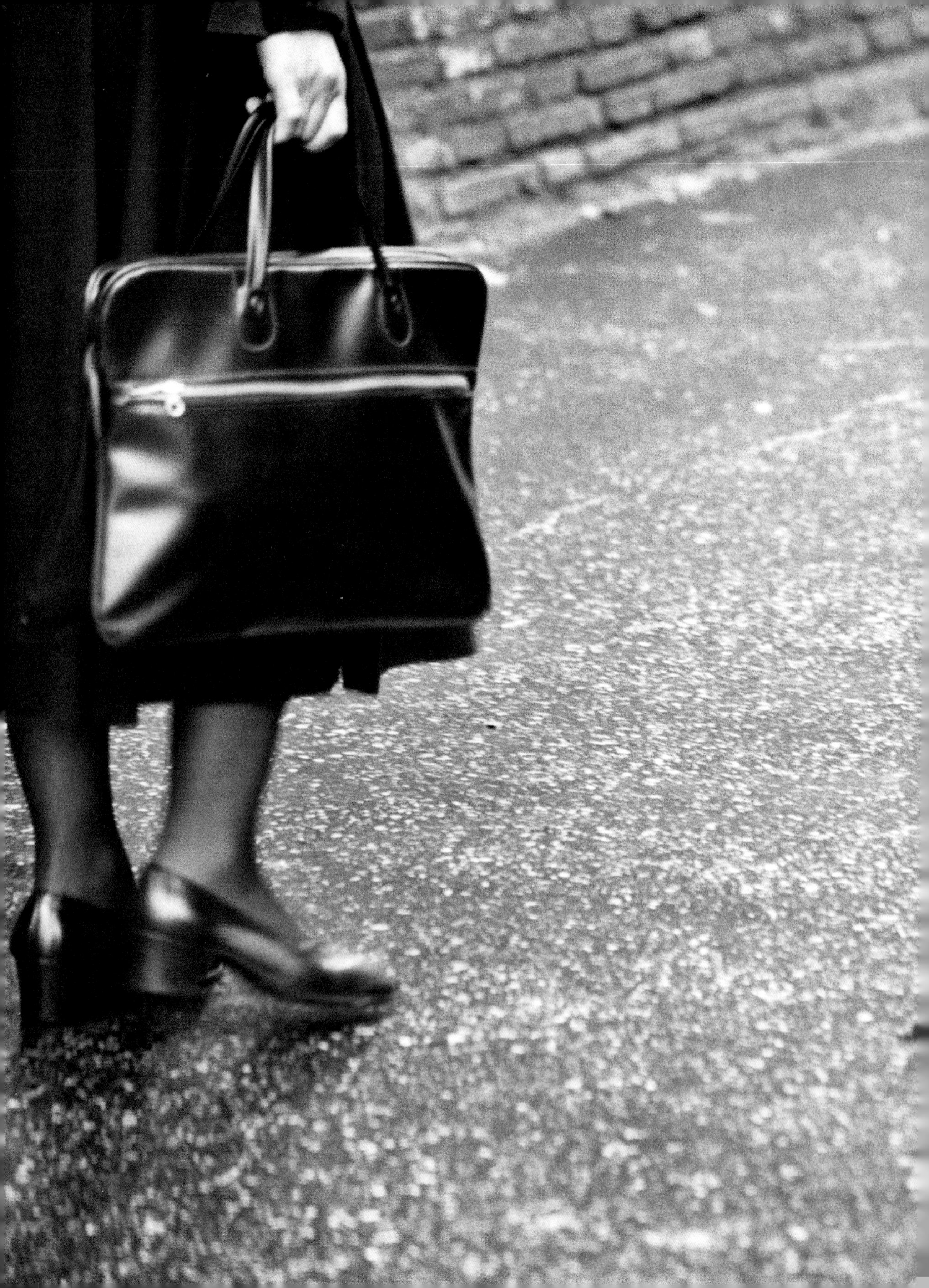

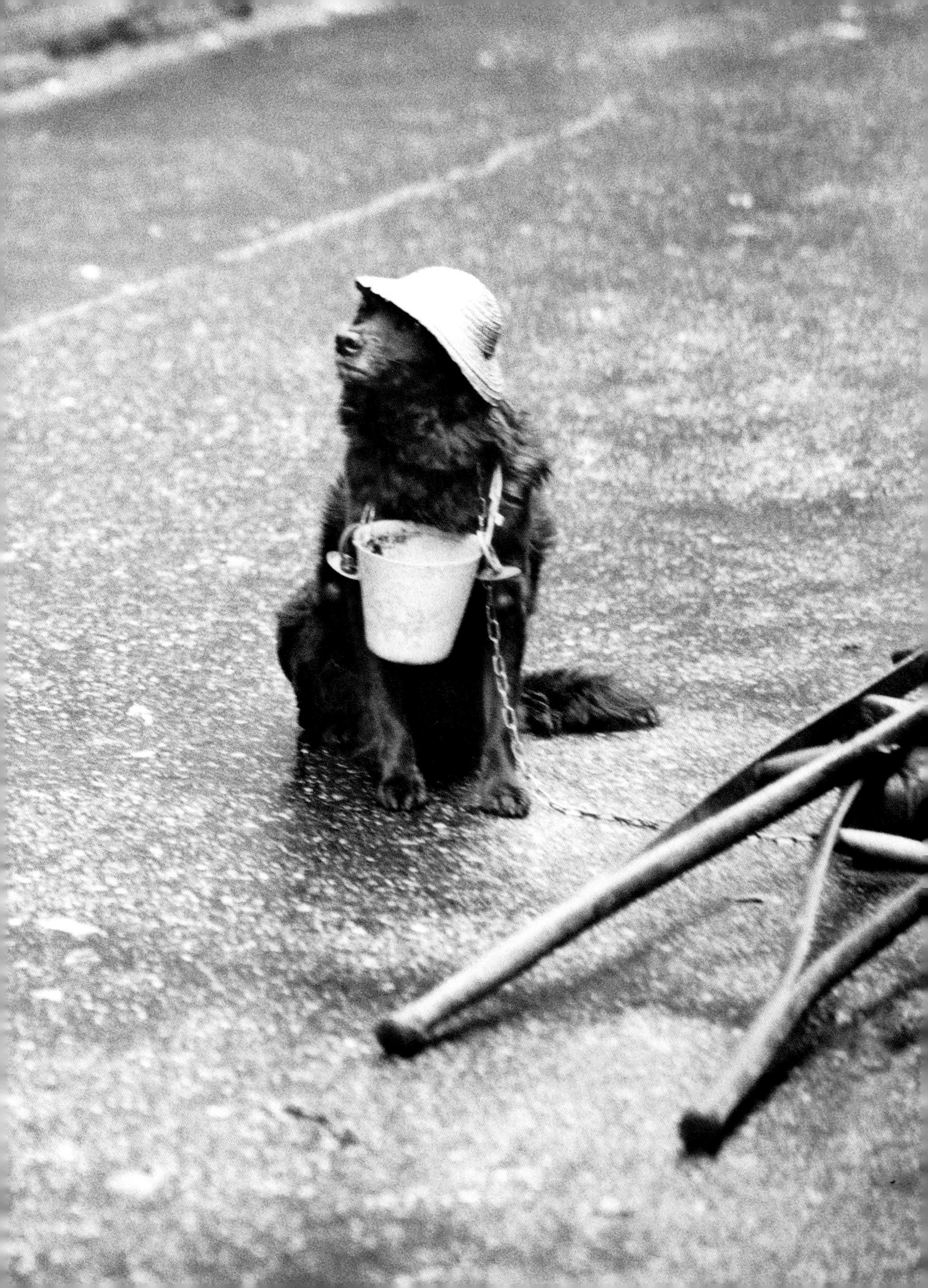

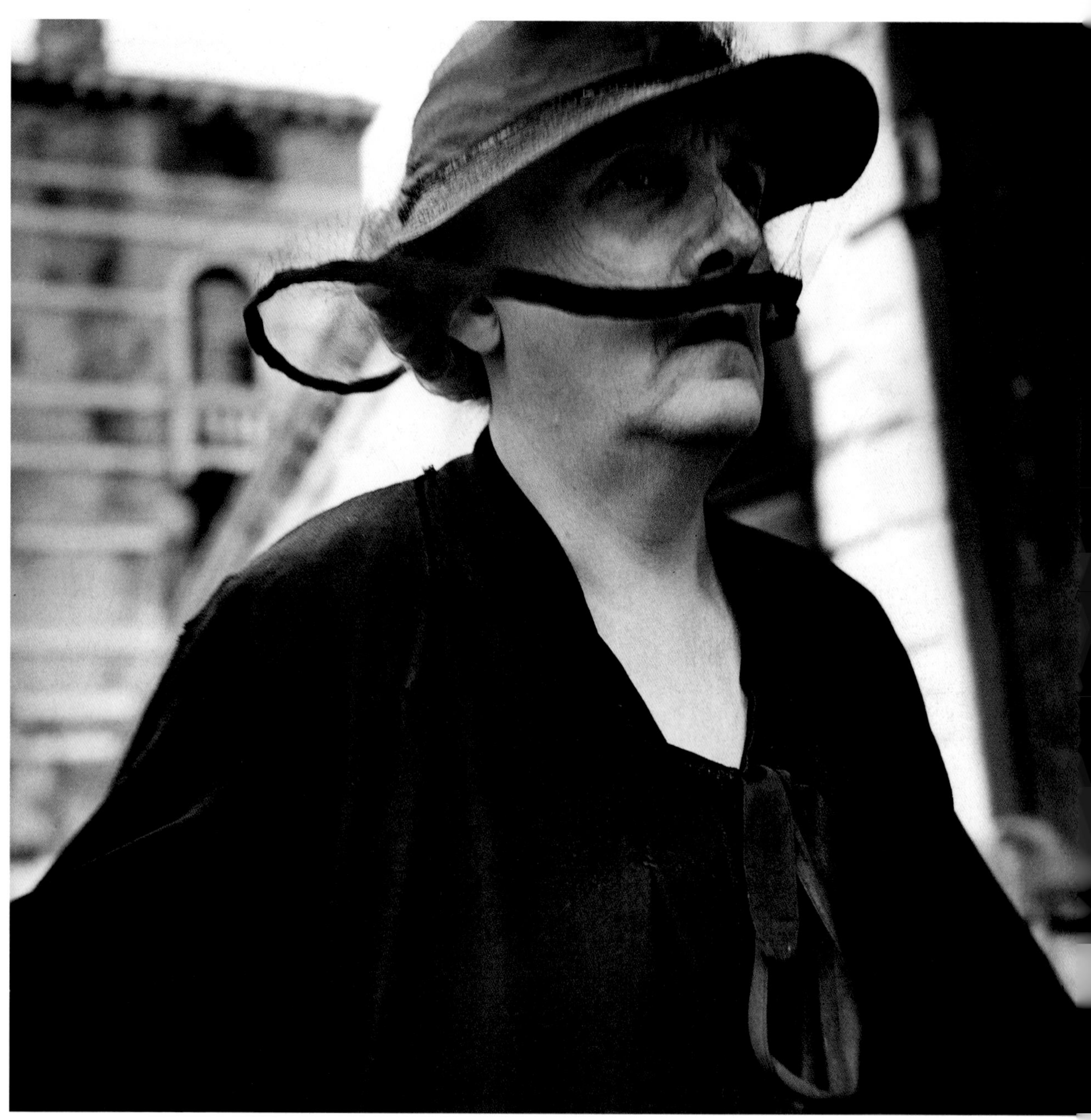

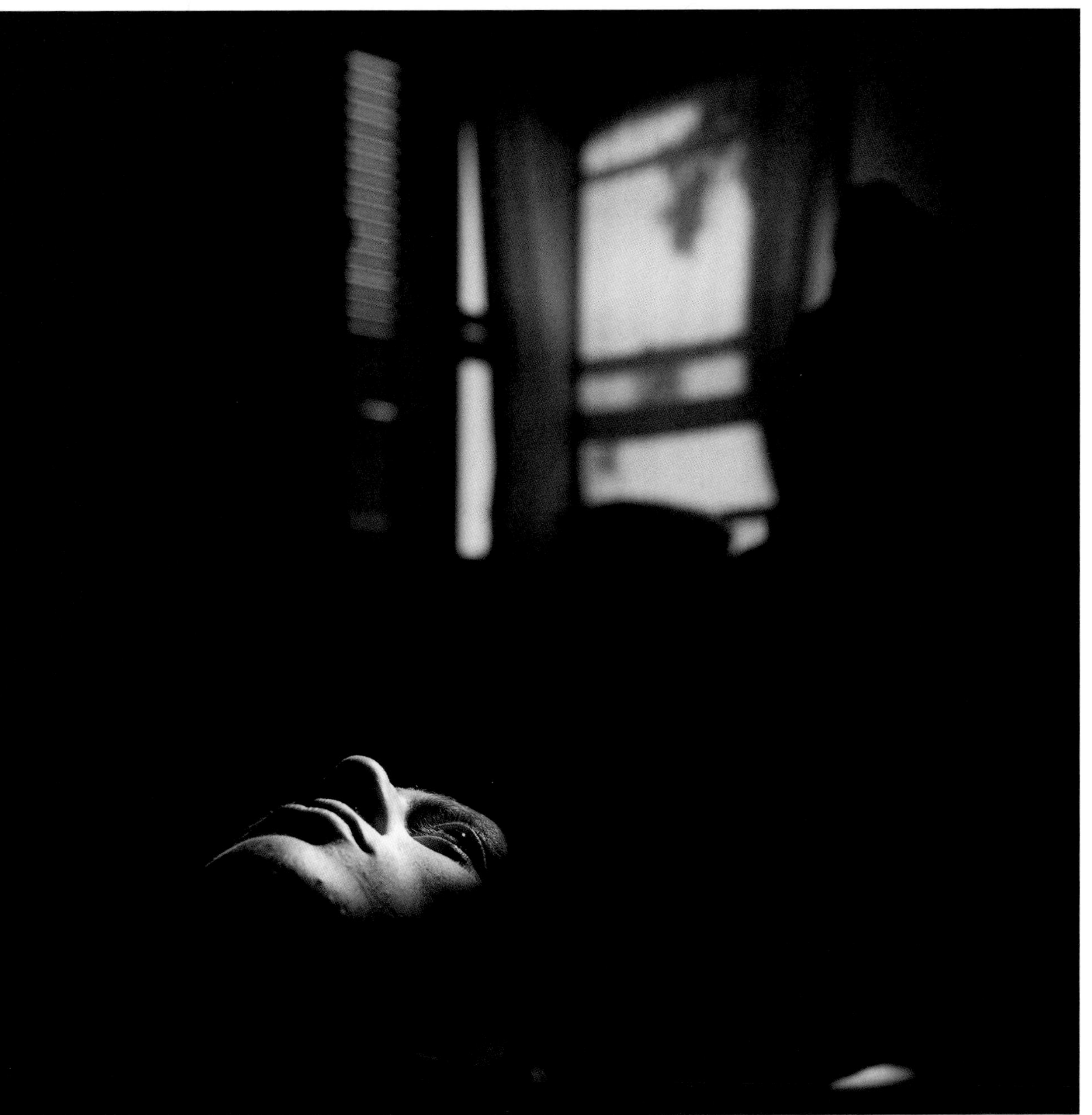

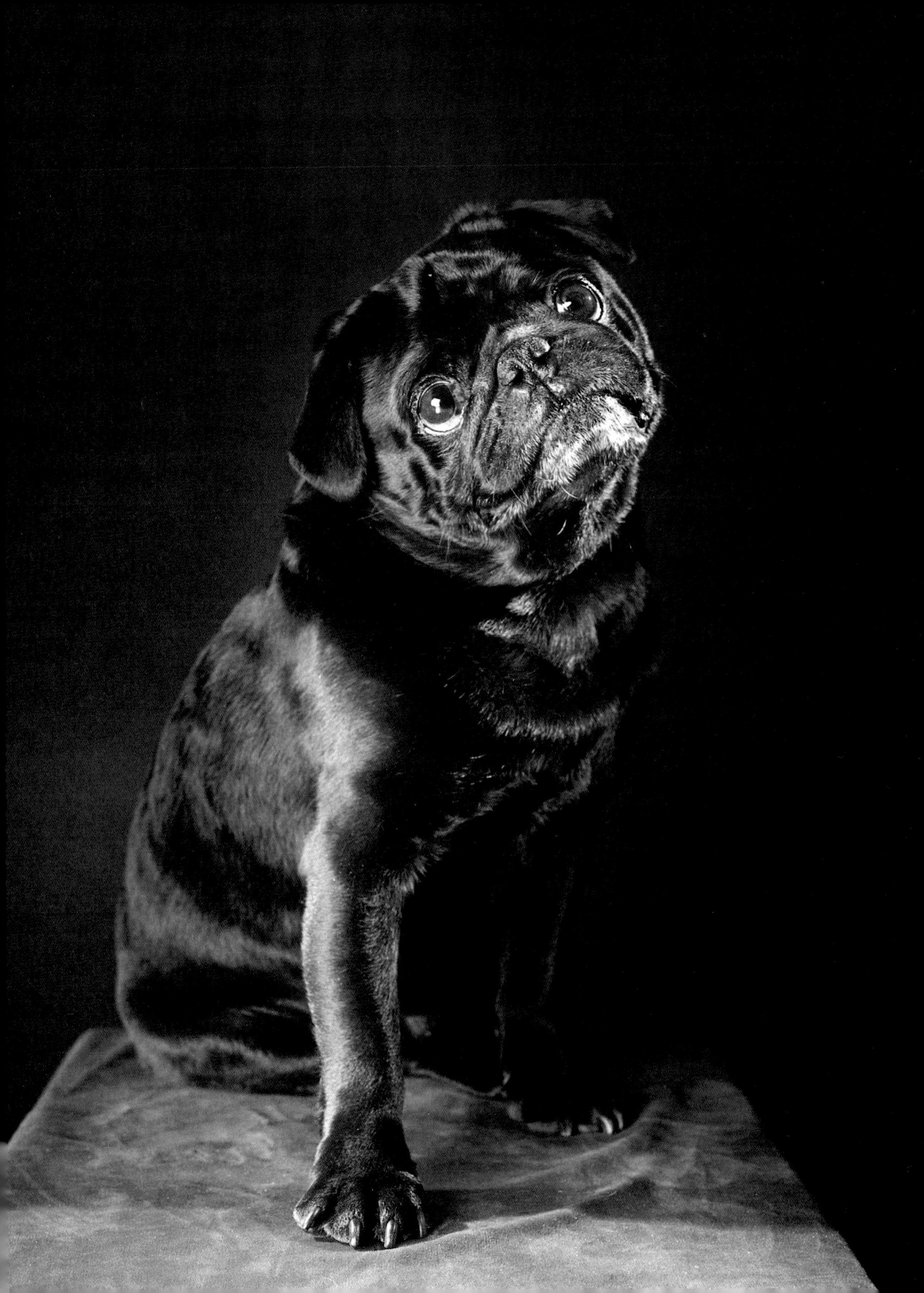

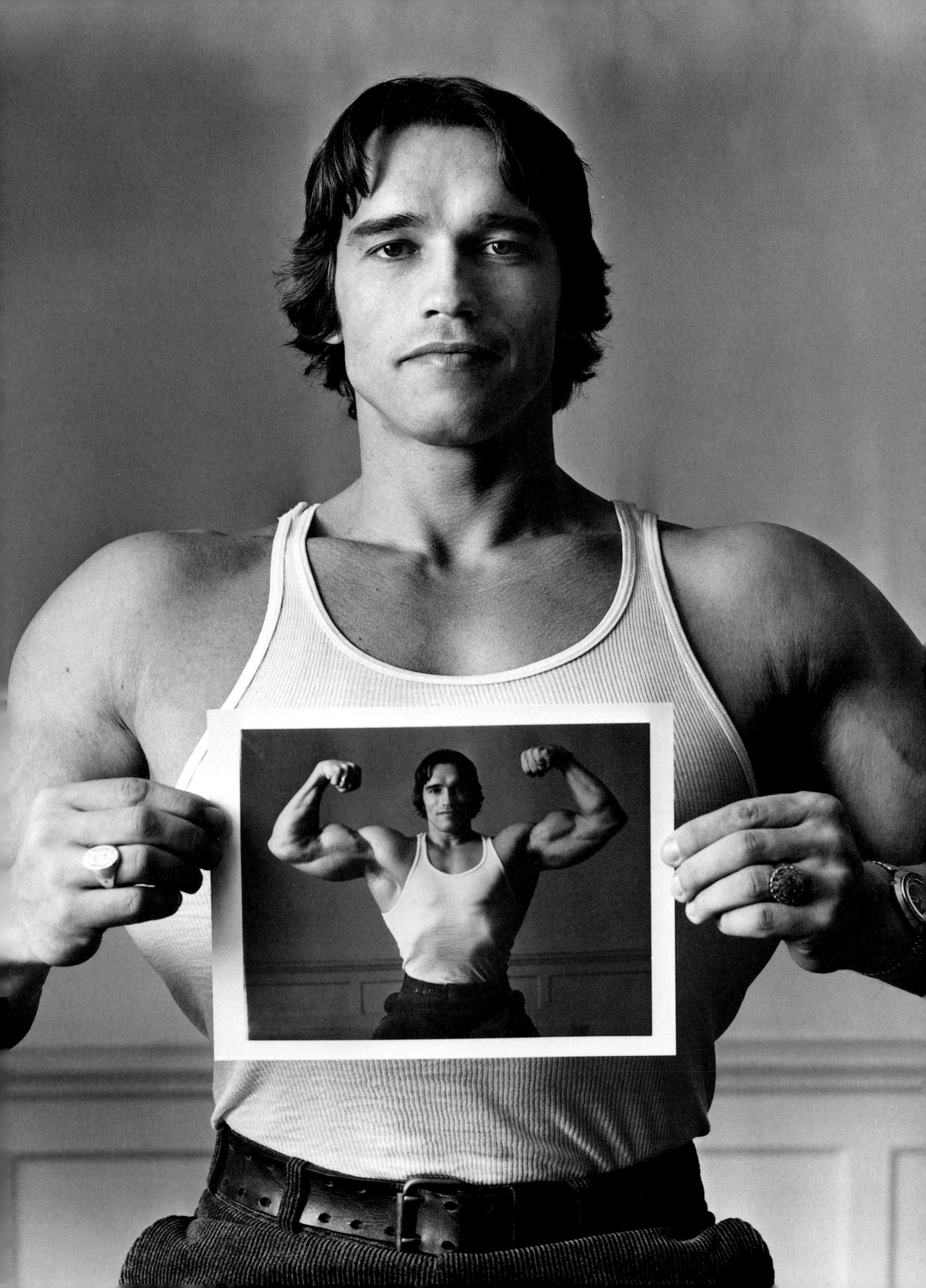

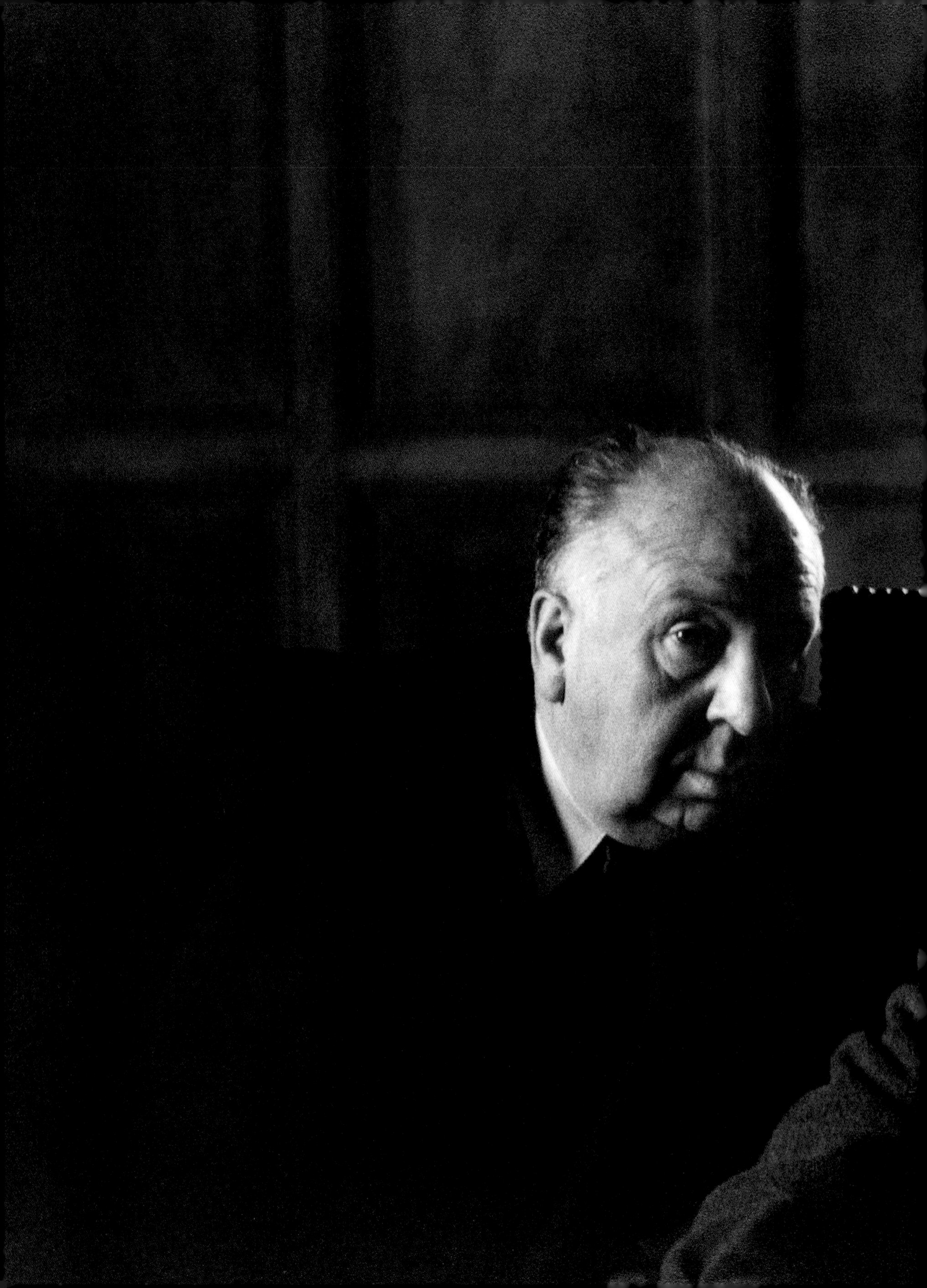

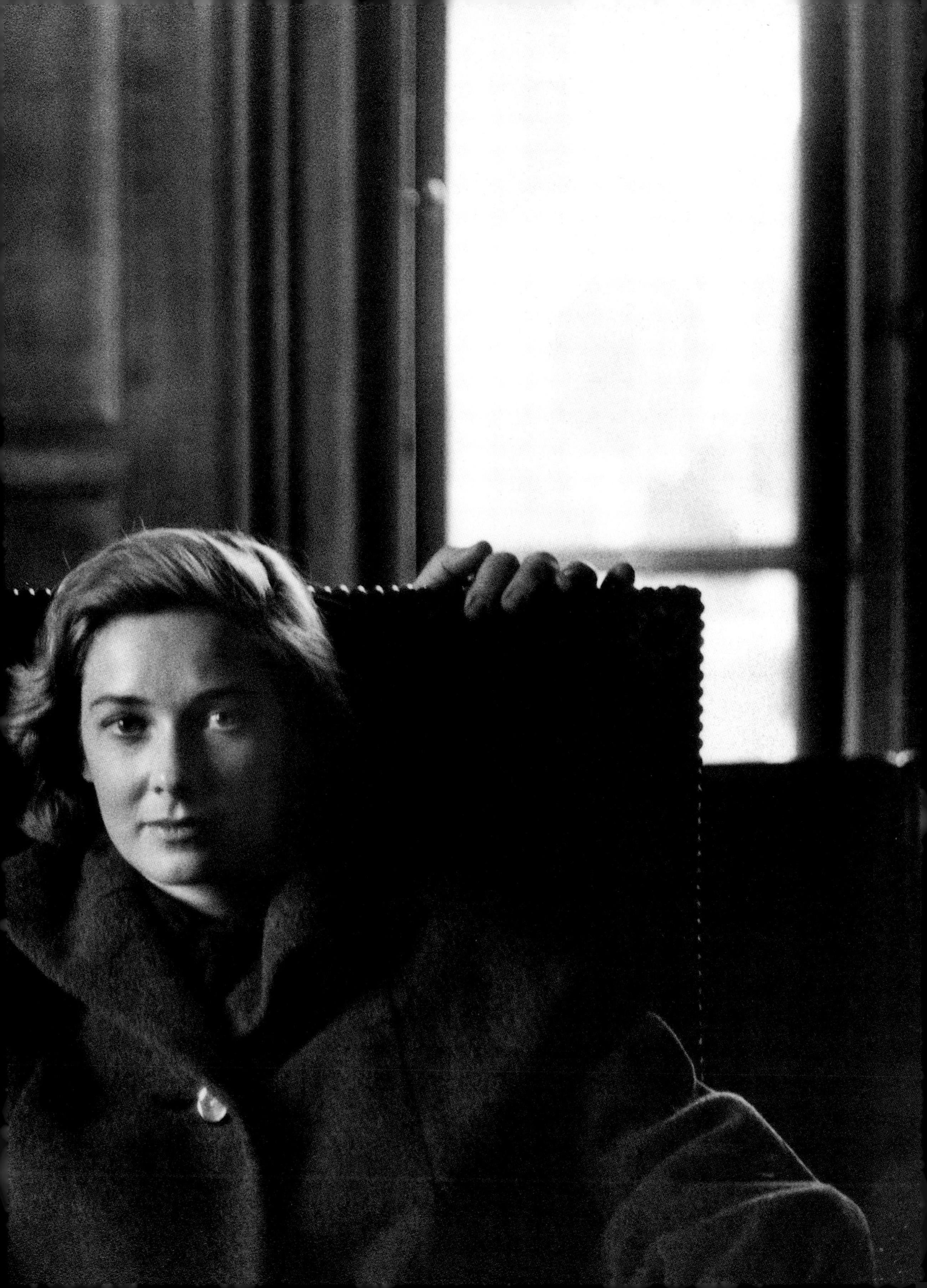

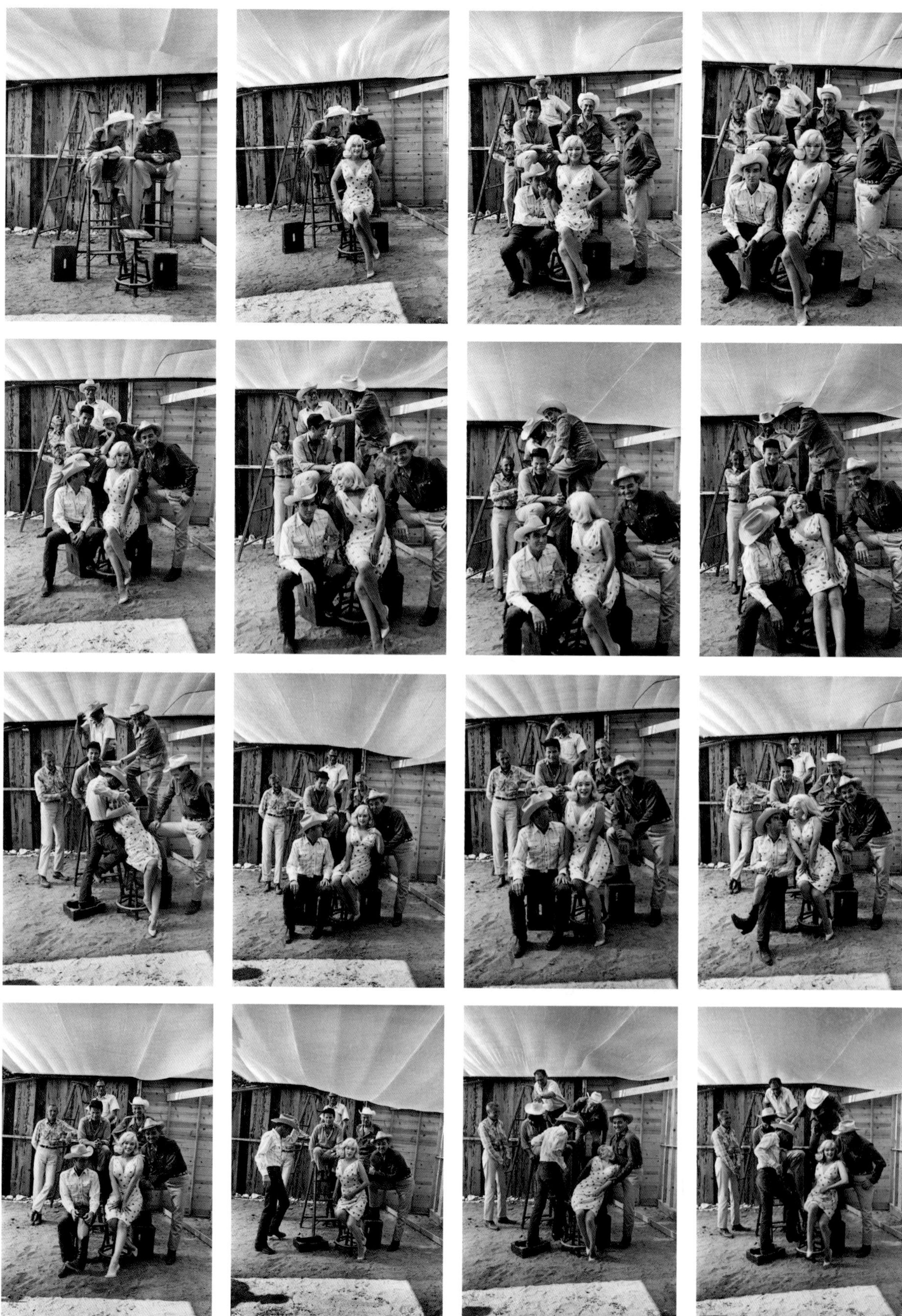

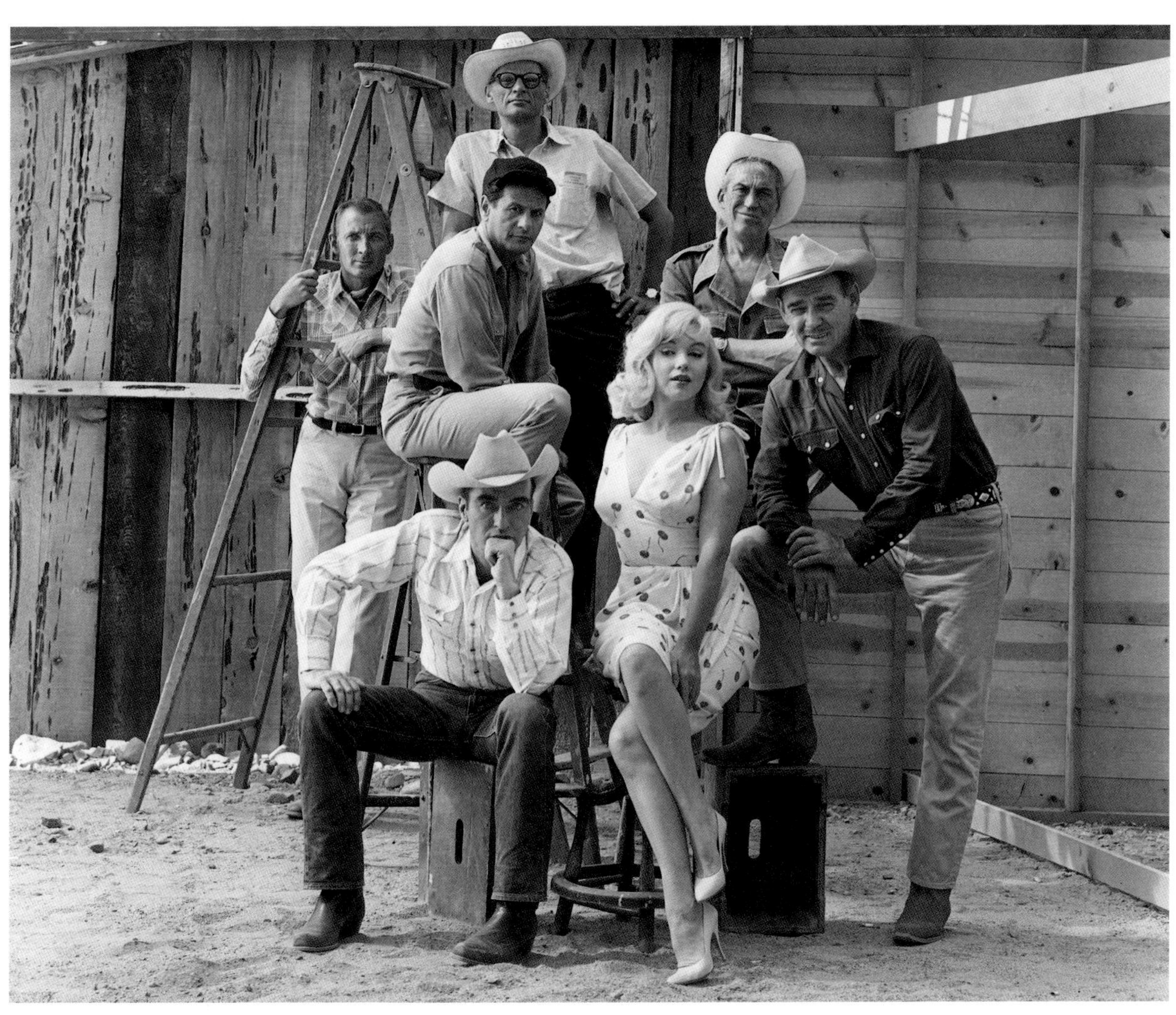

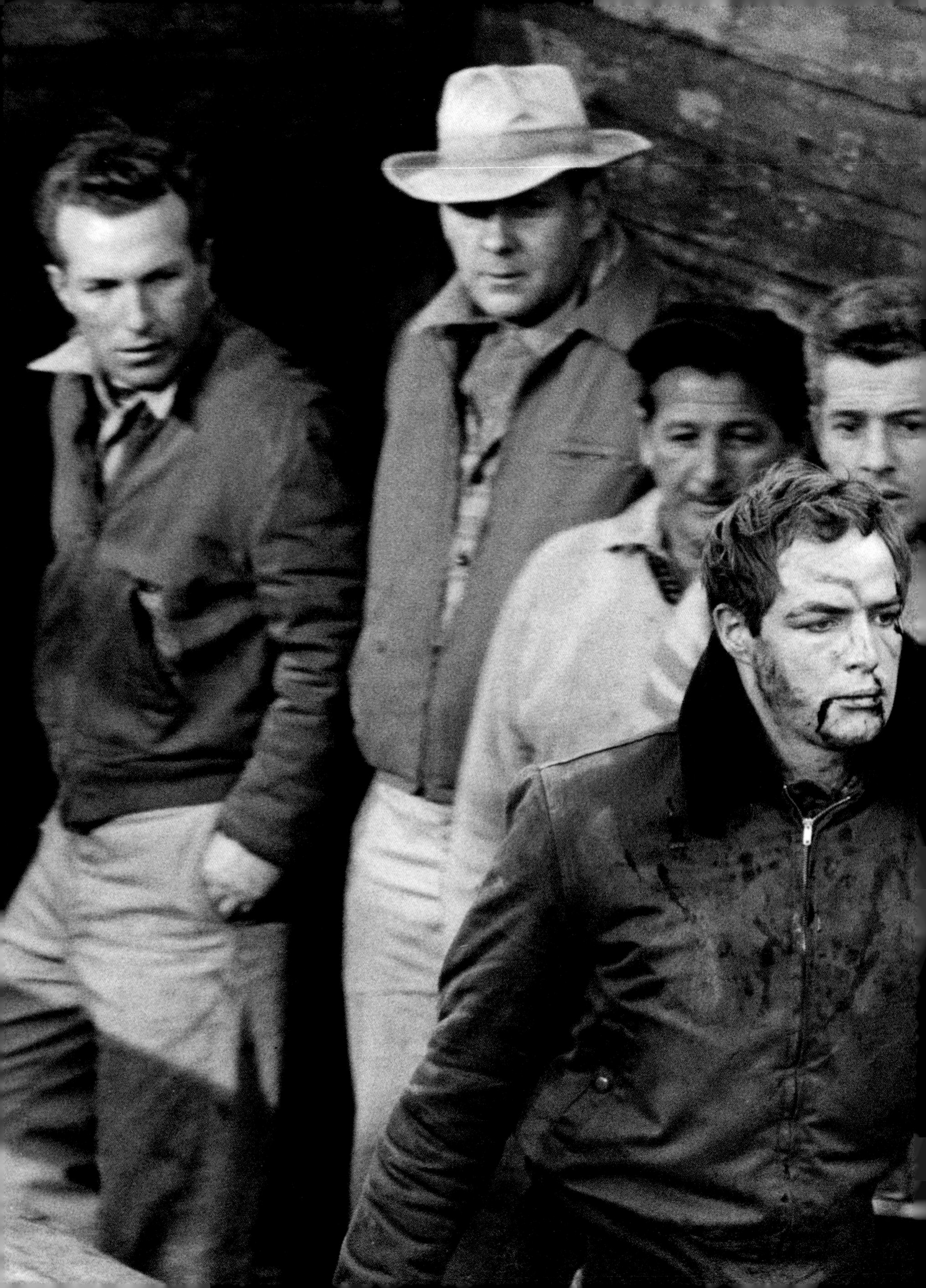

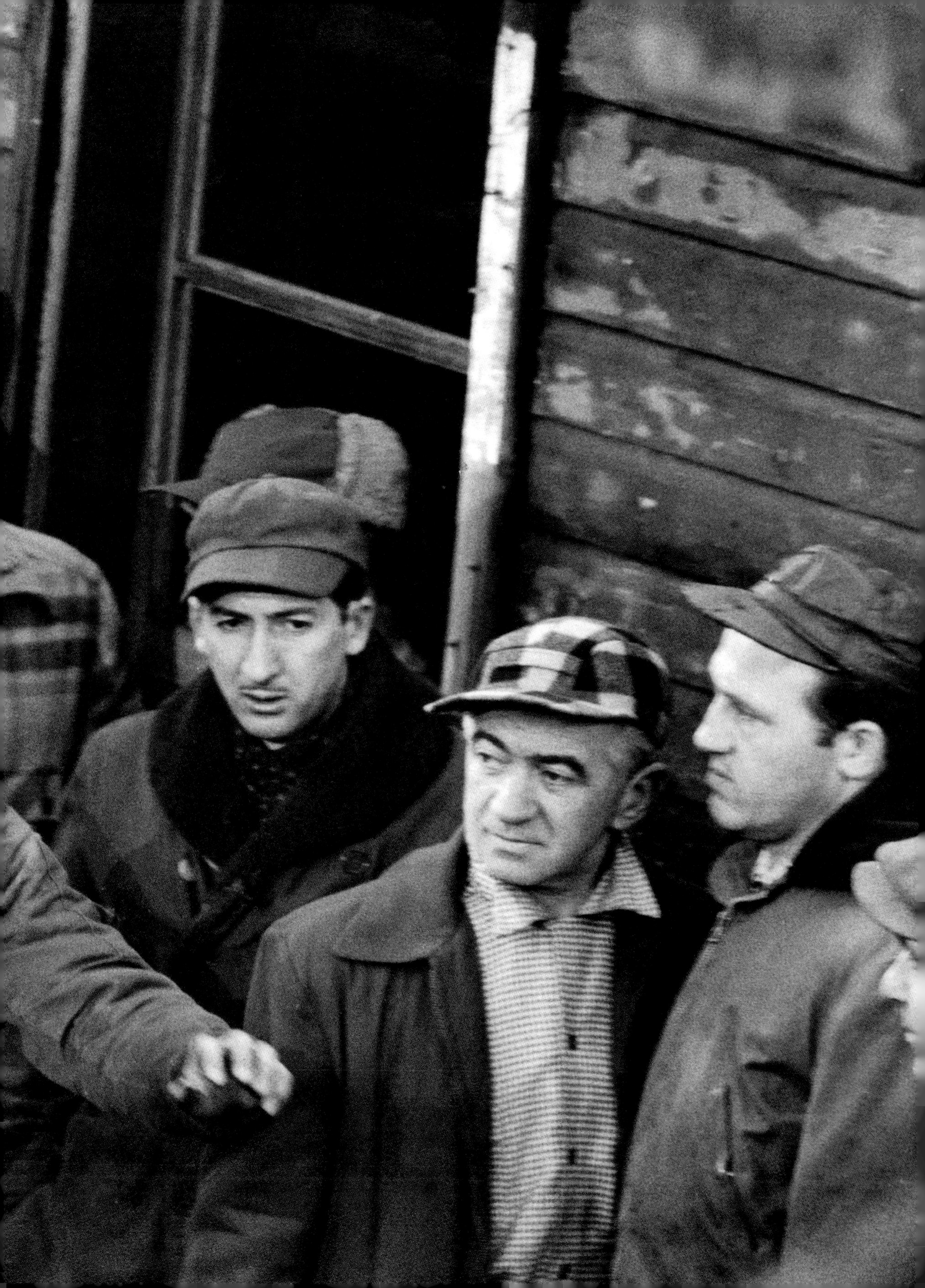

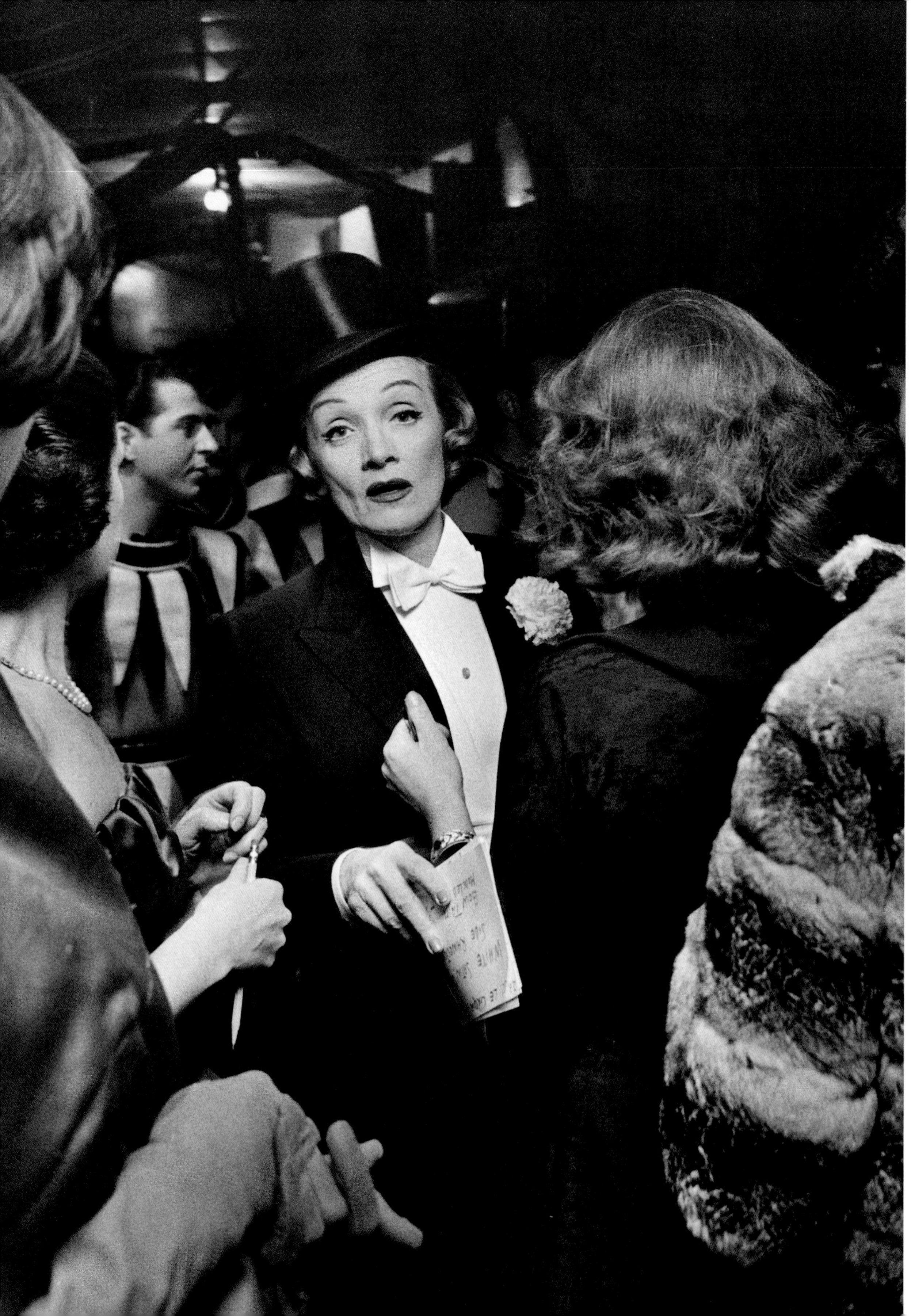

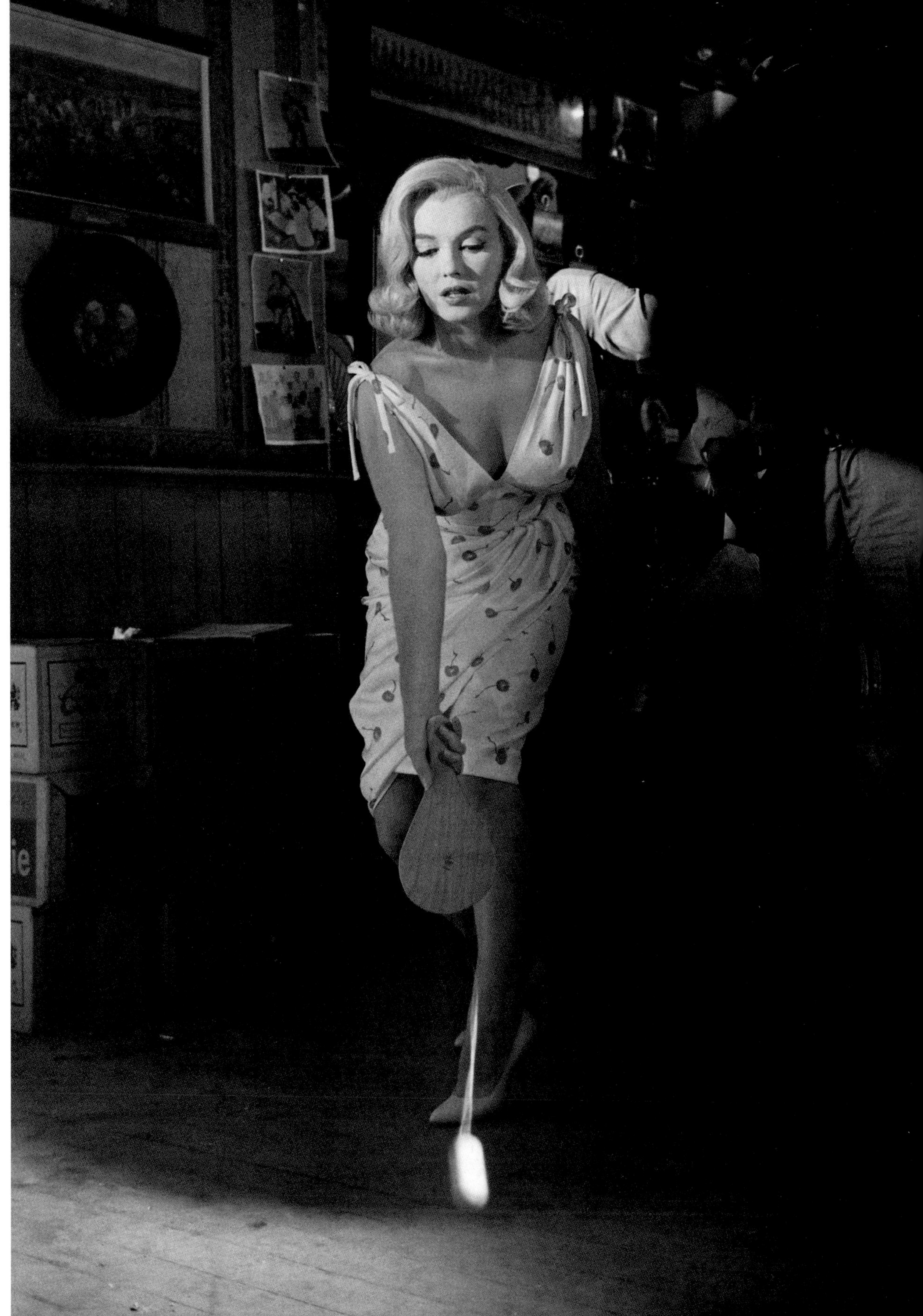

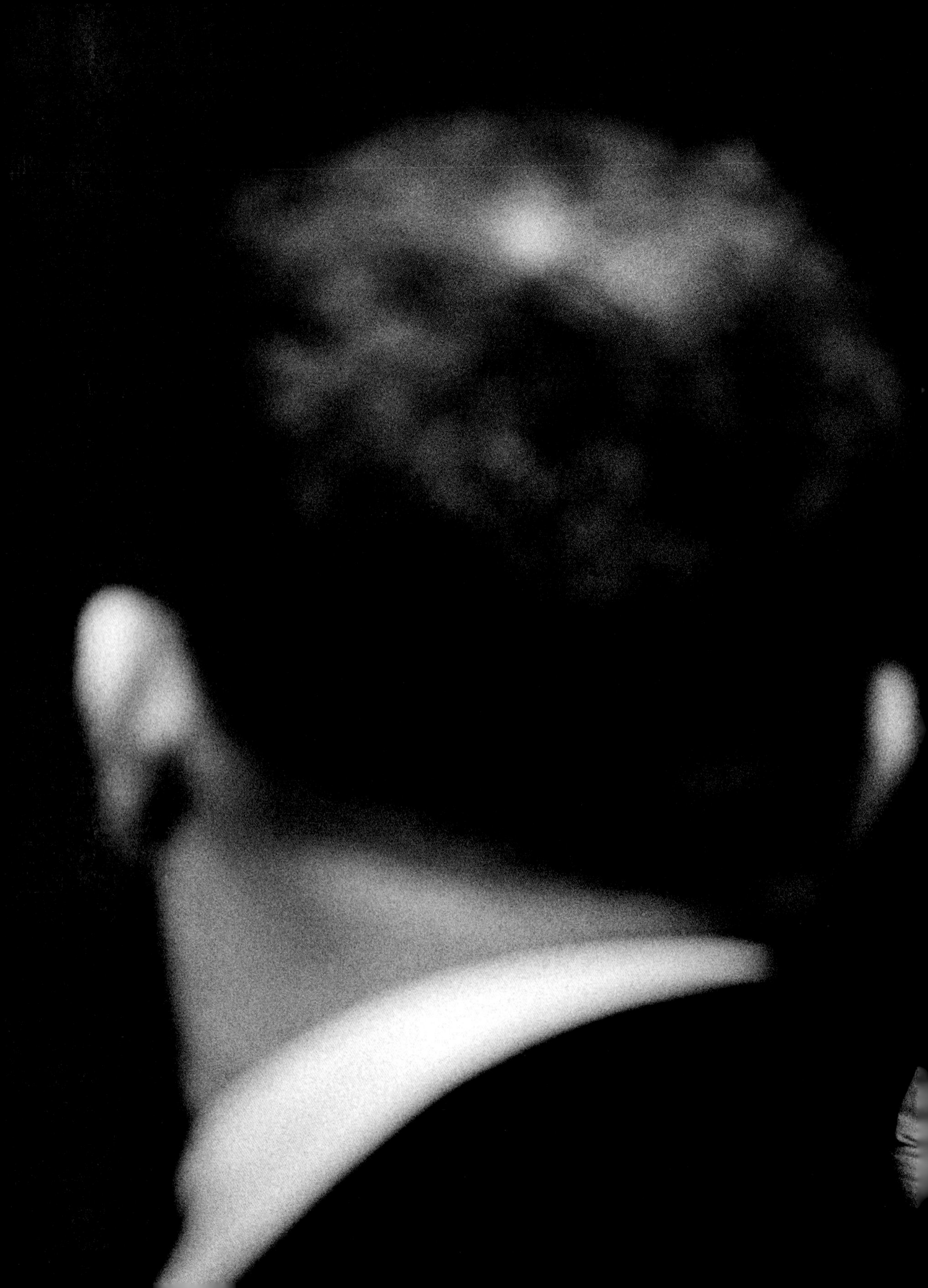

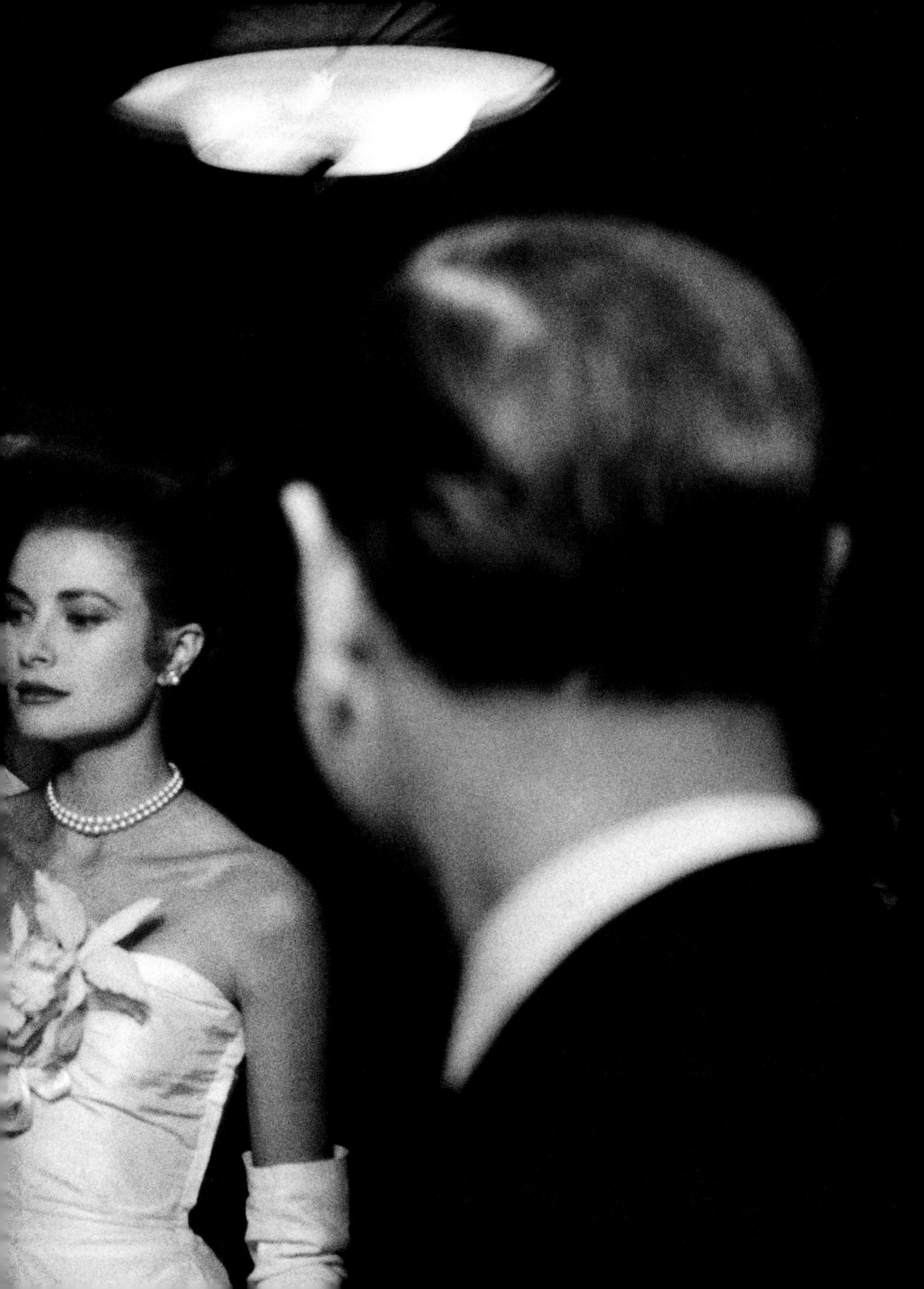

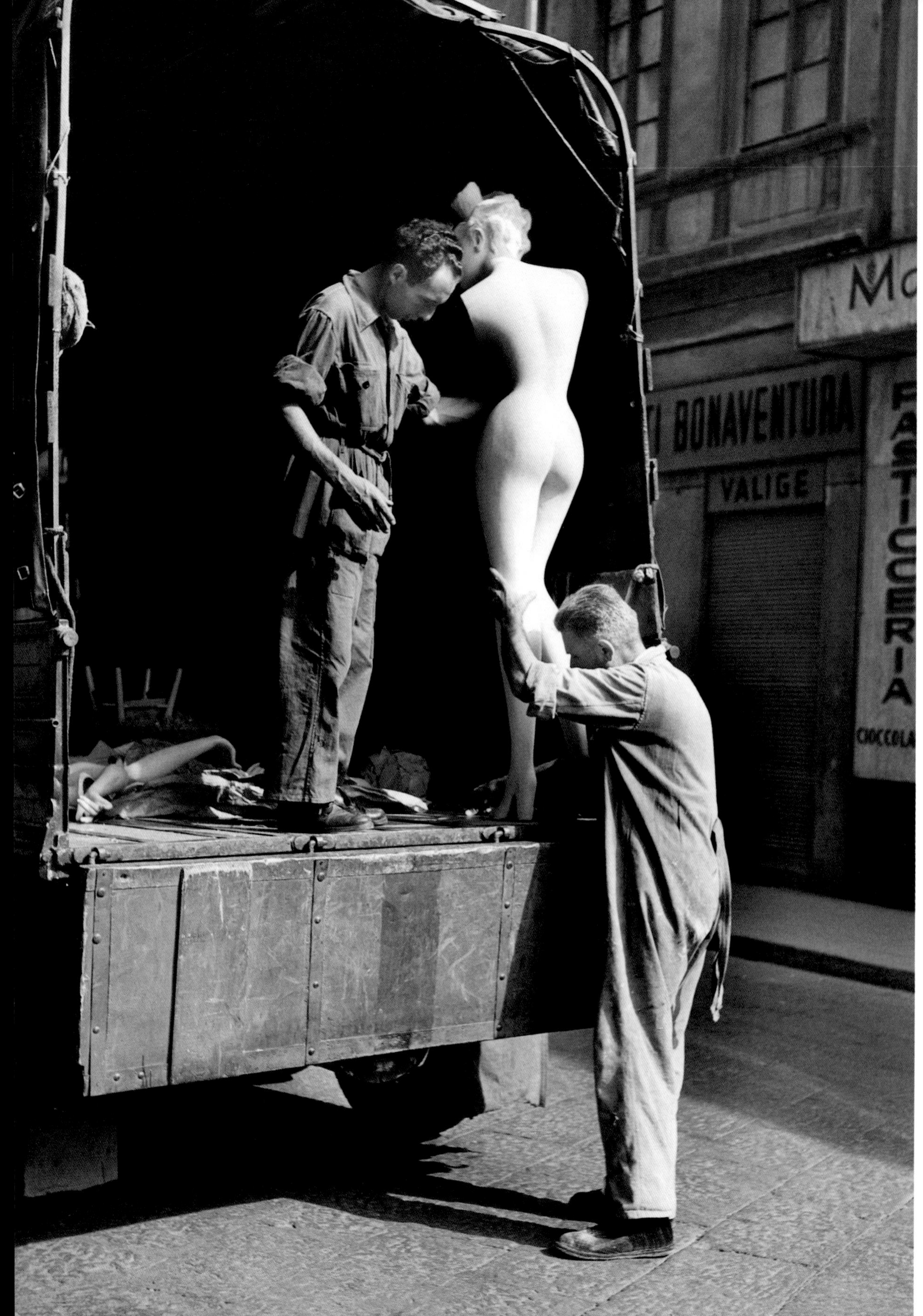

Mo
BONAVENTURA
VALIGE
PASTICCERIA
CIOCCOLA

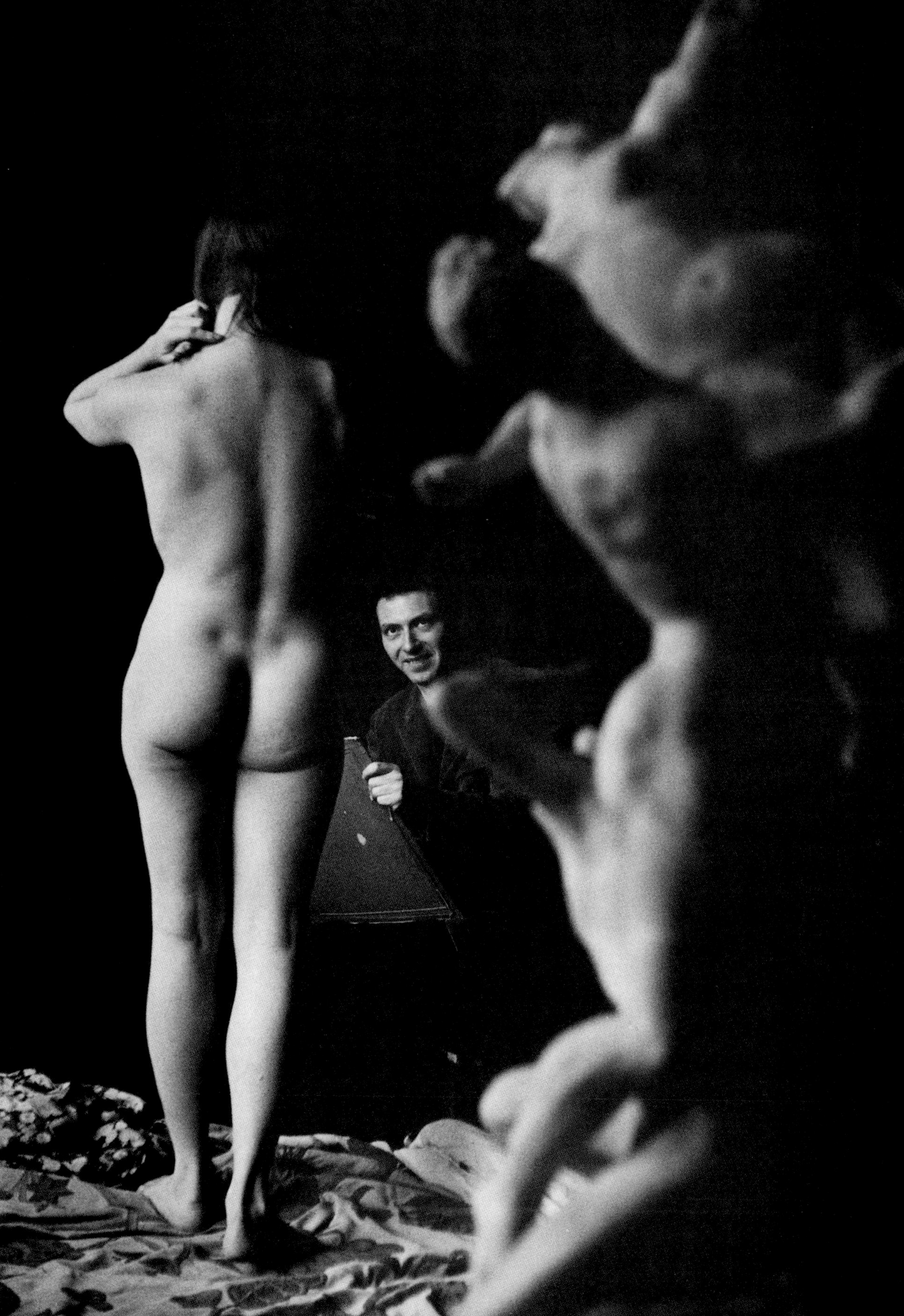

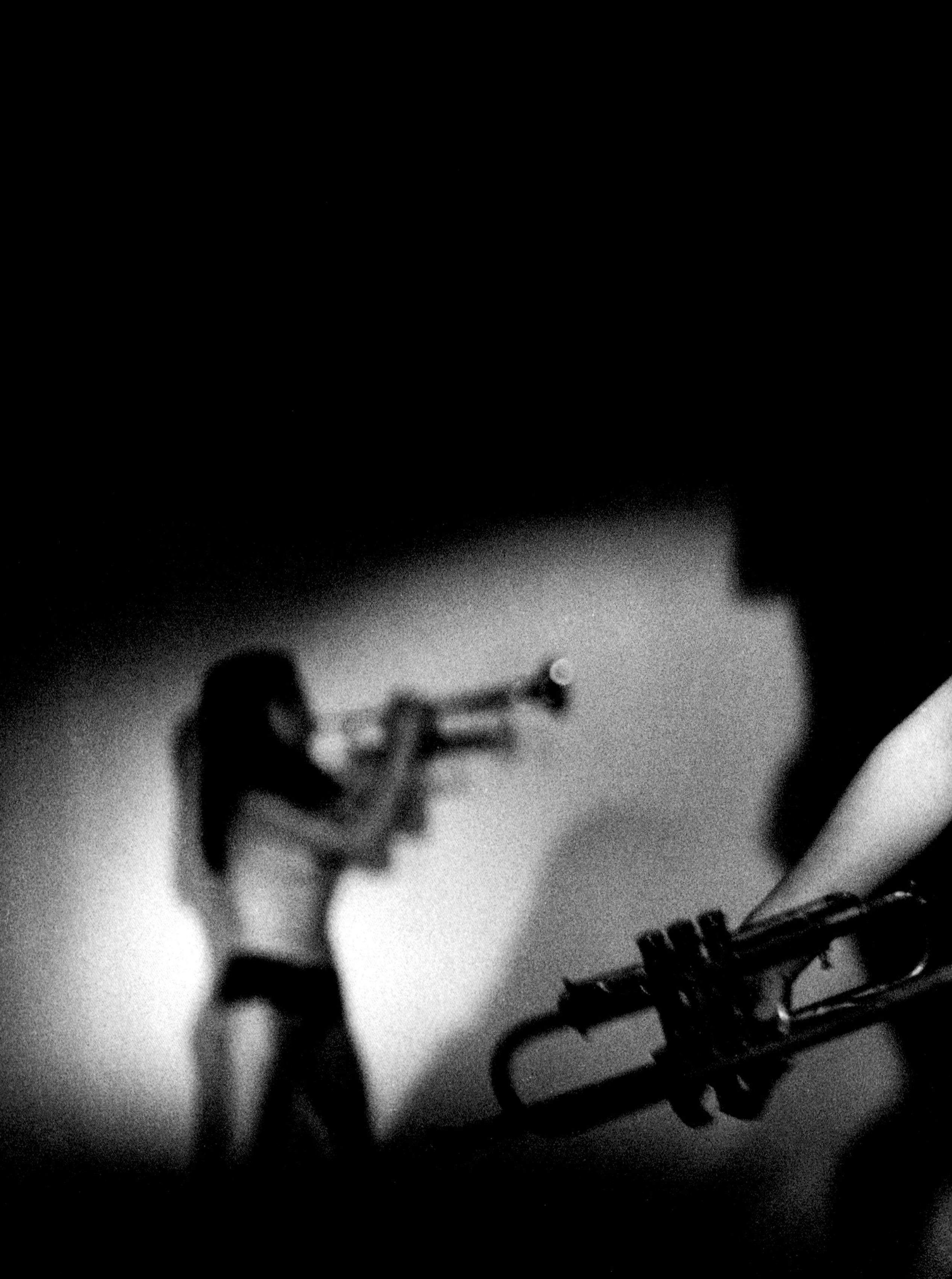

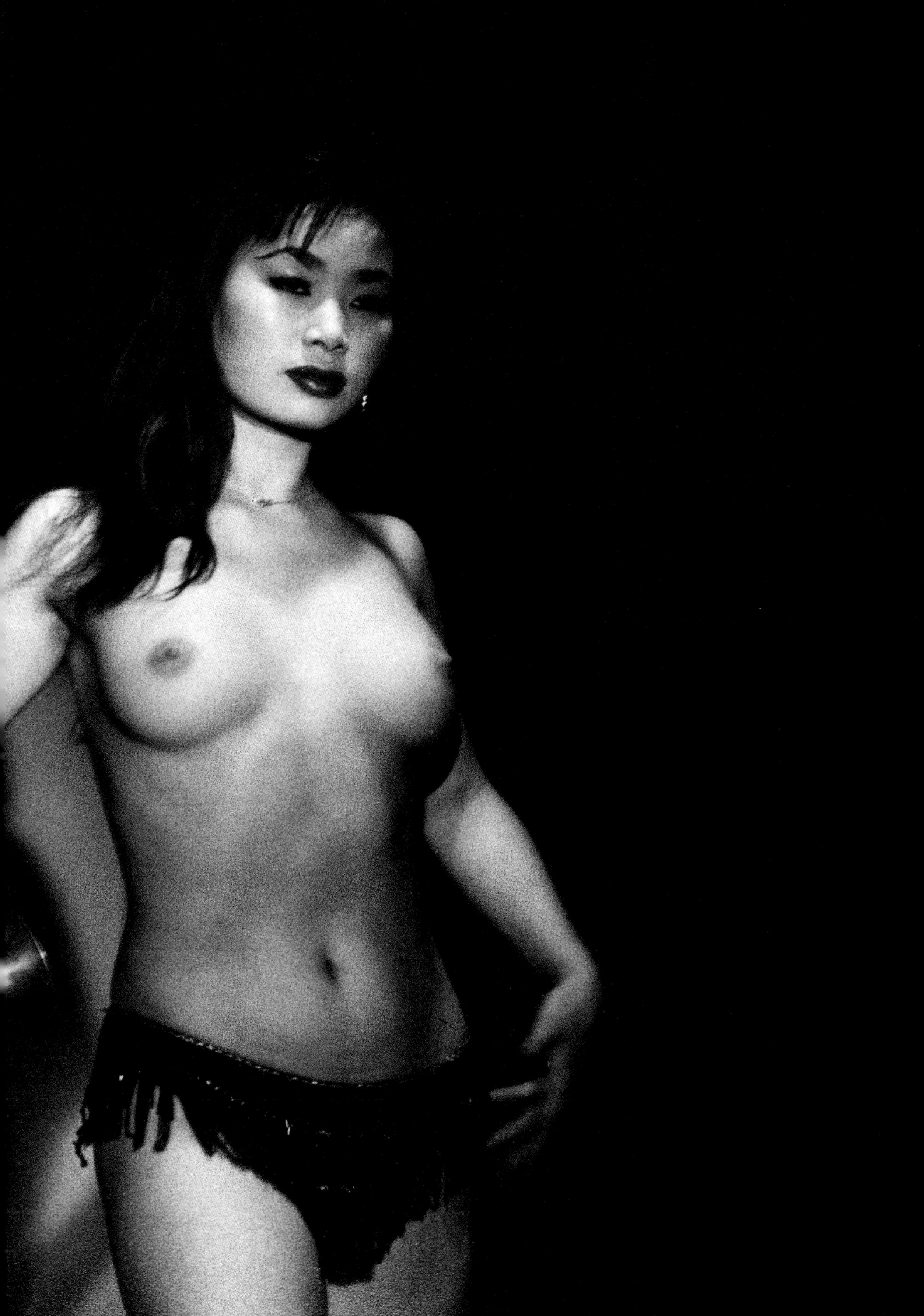

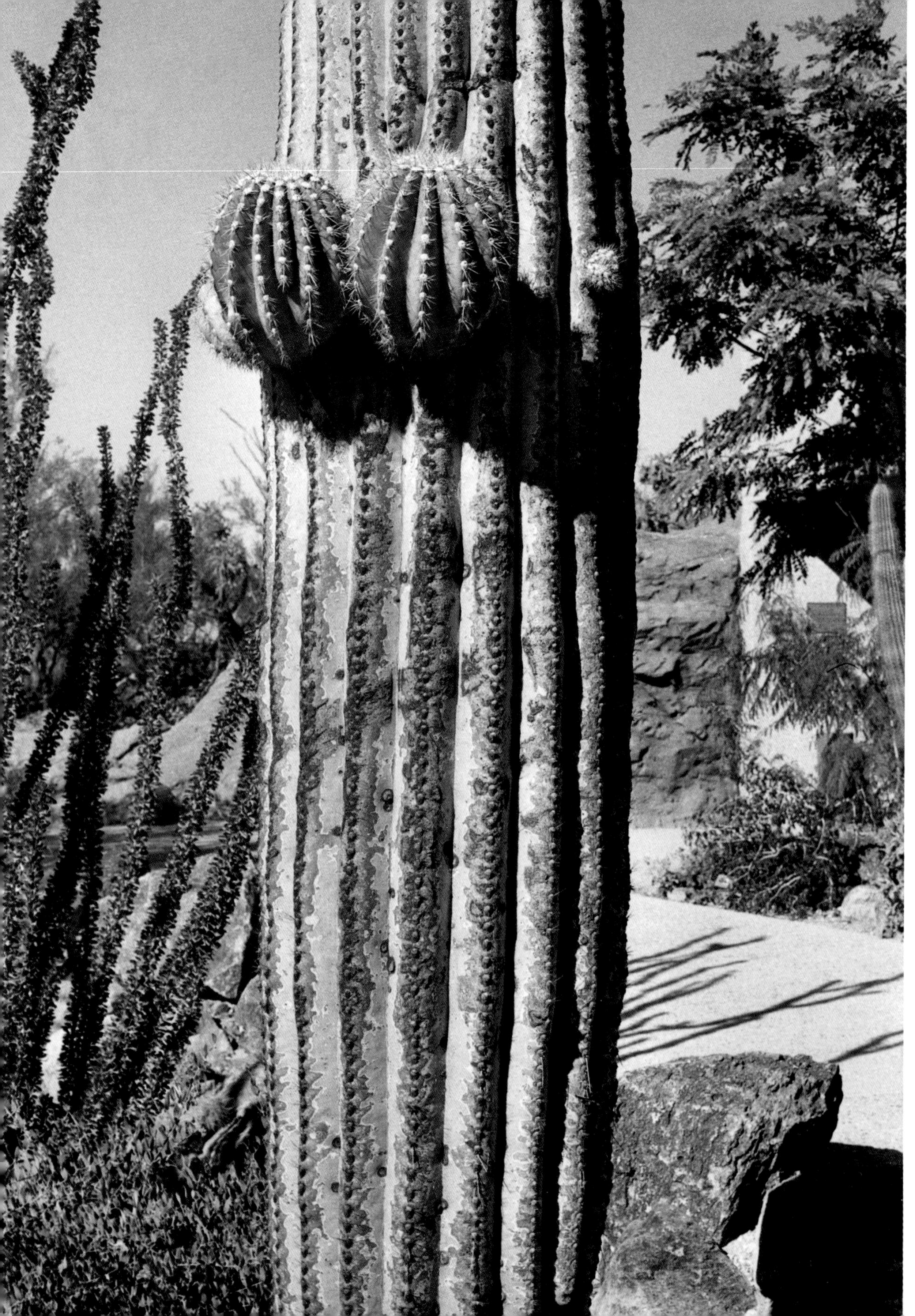

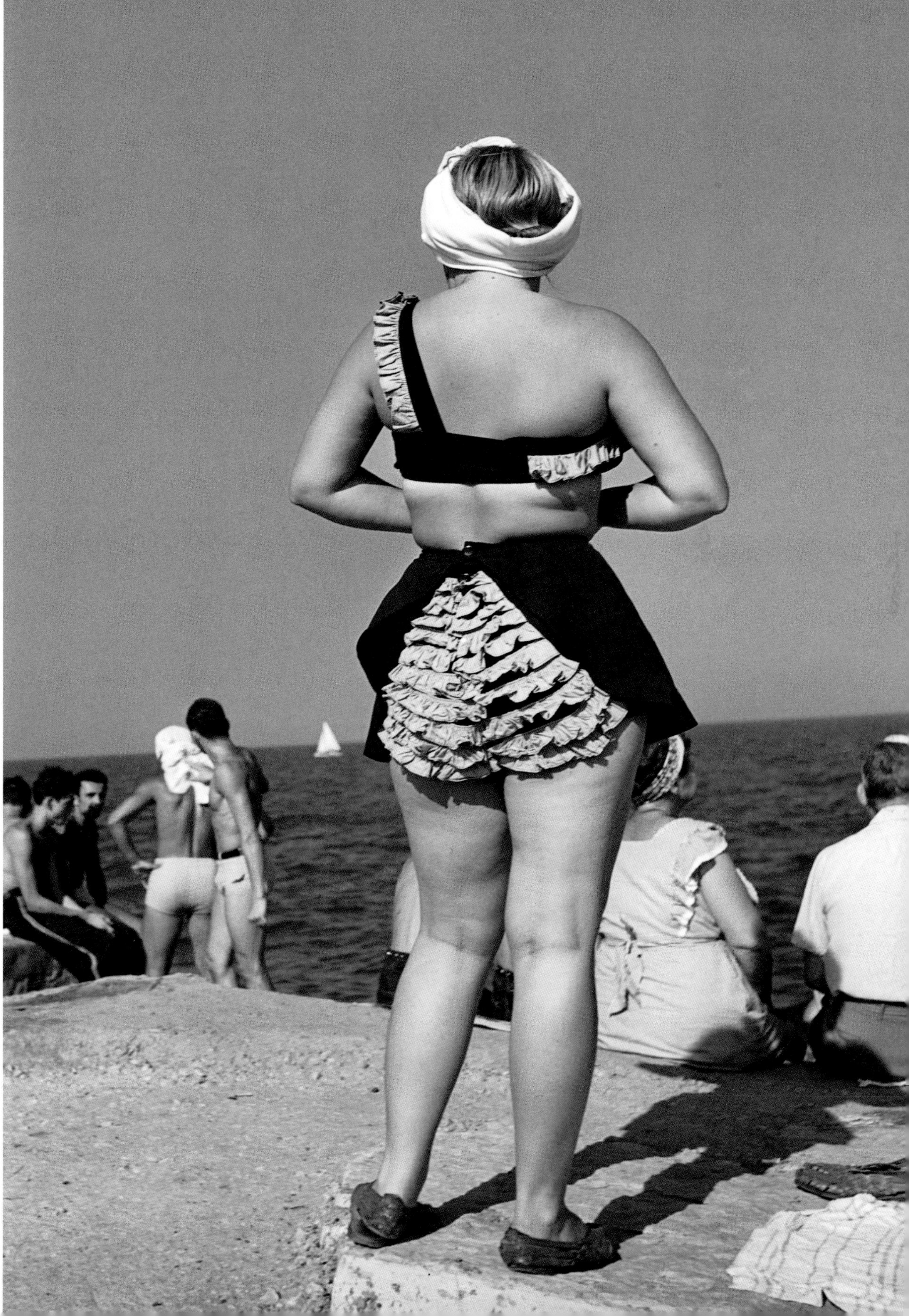

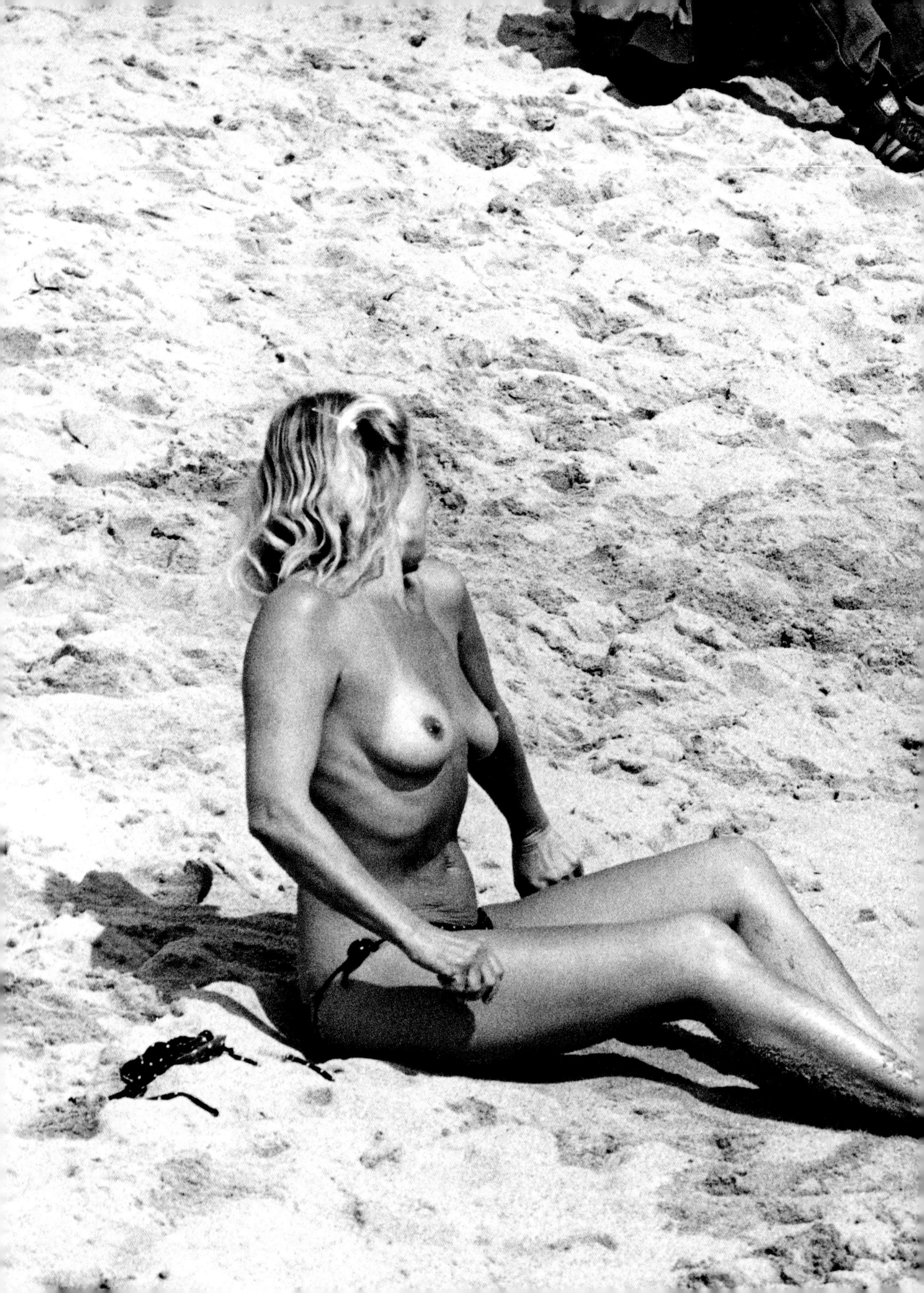

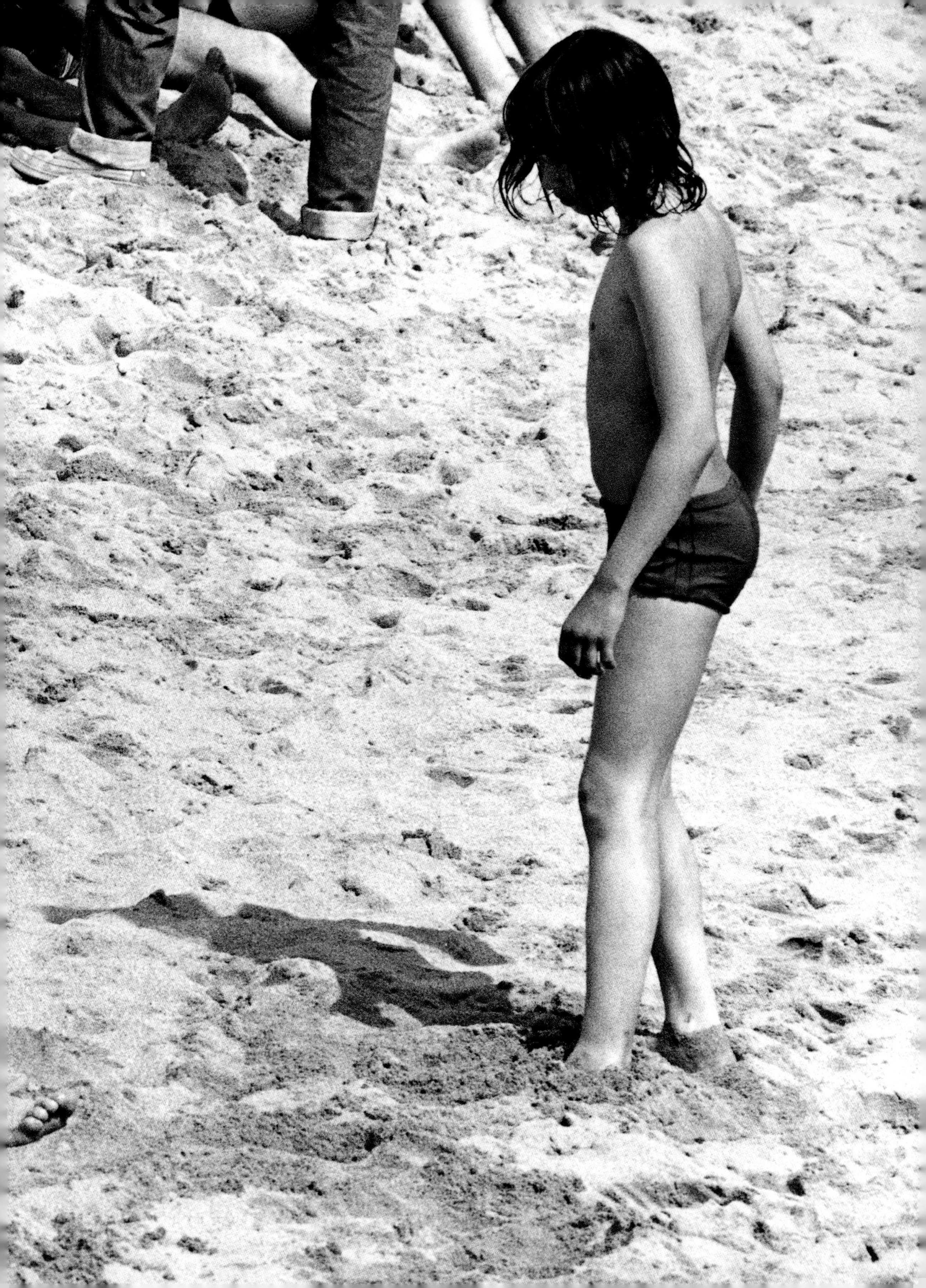

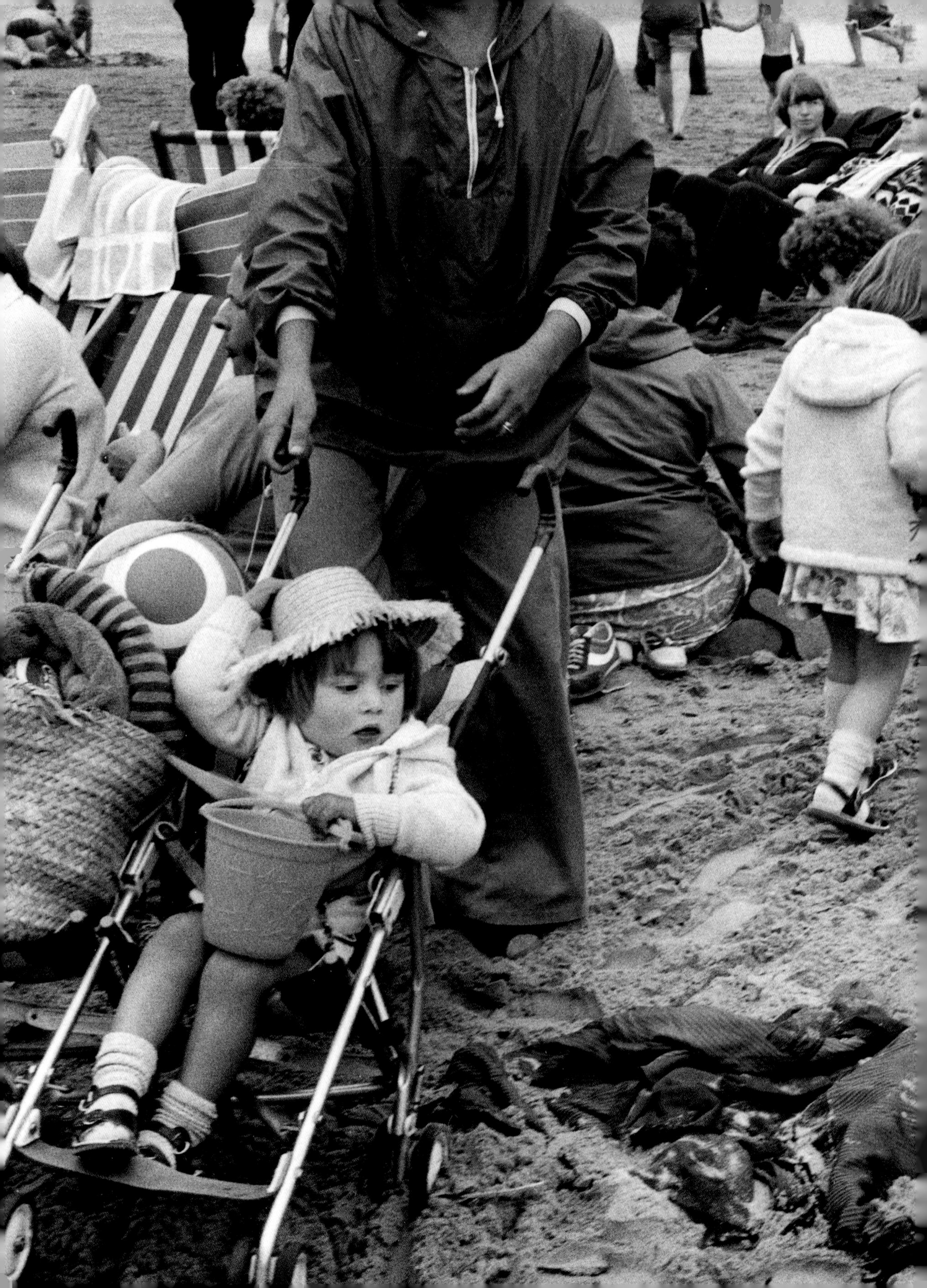

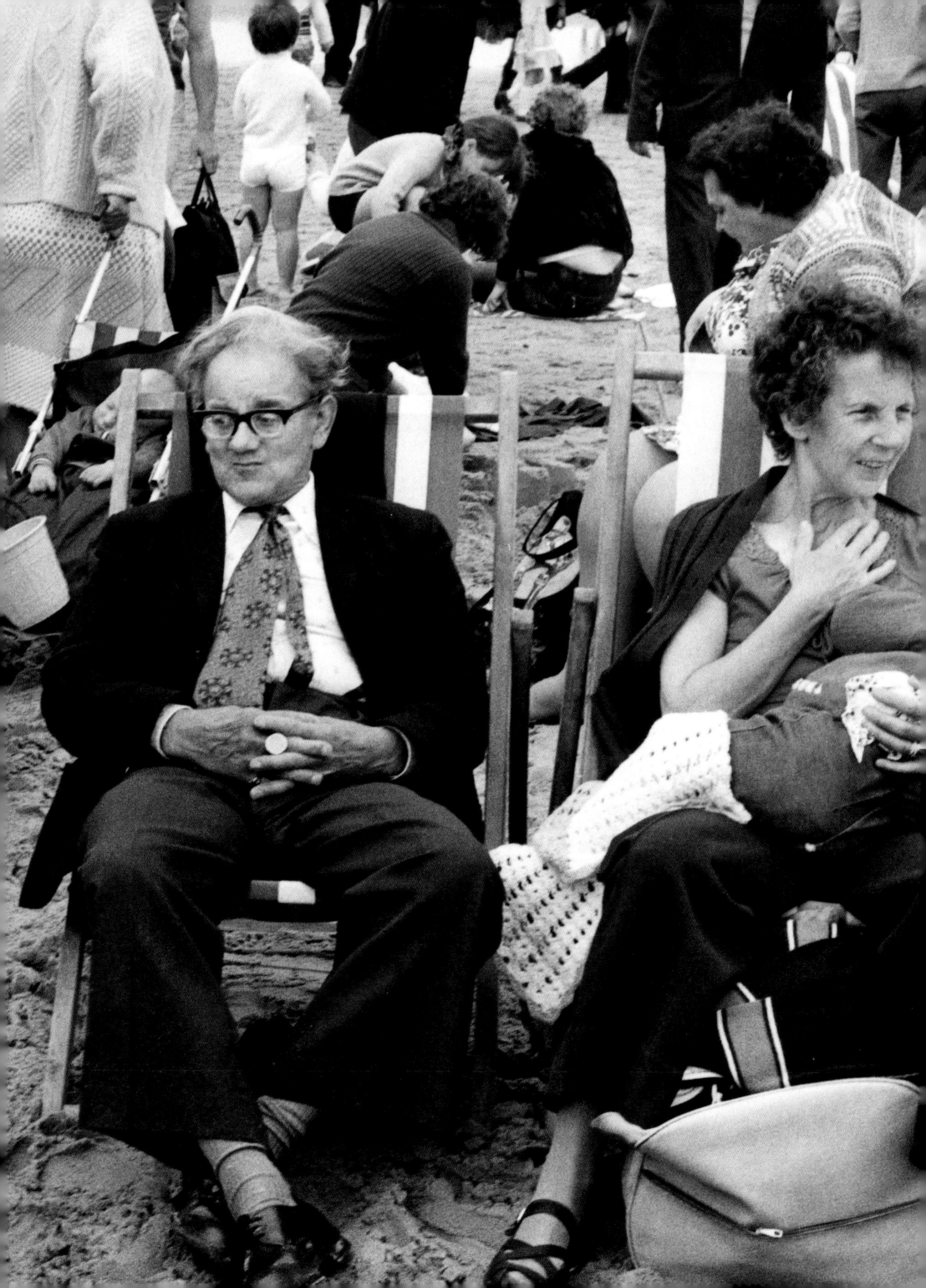

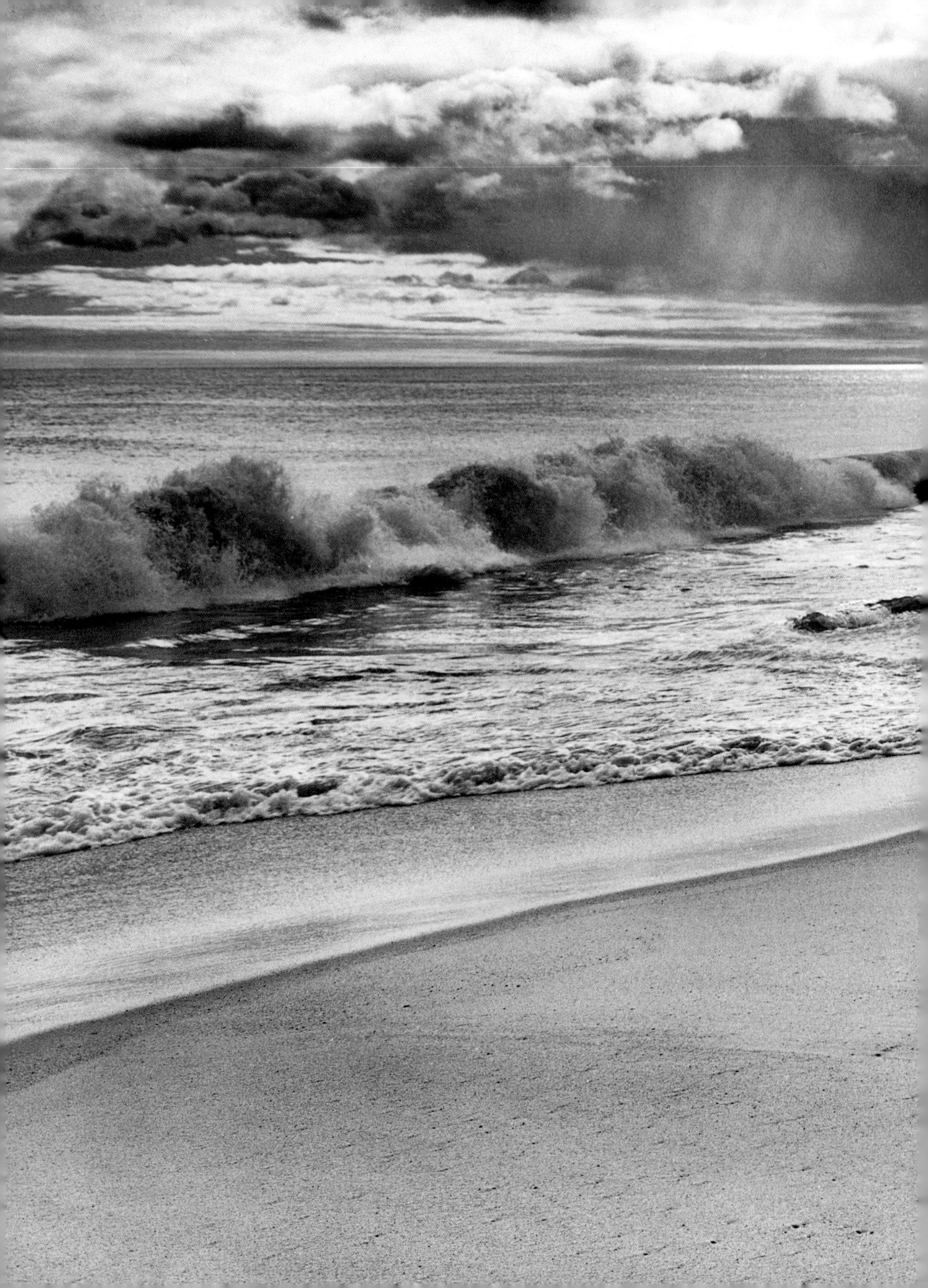

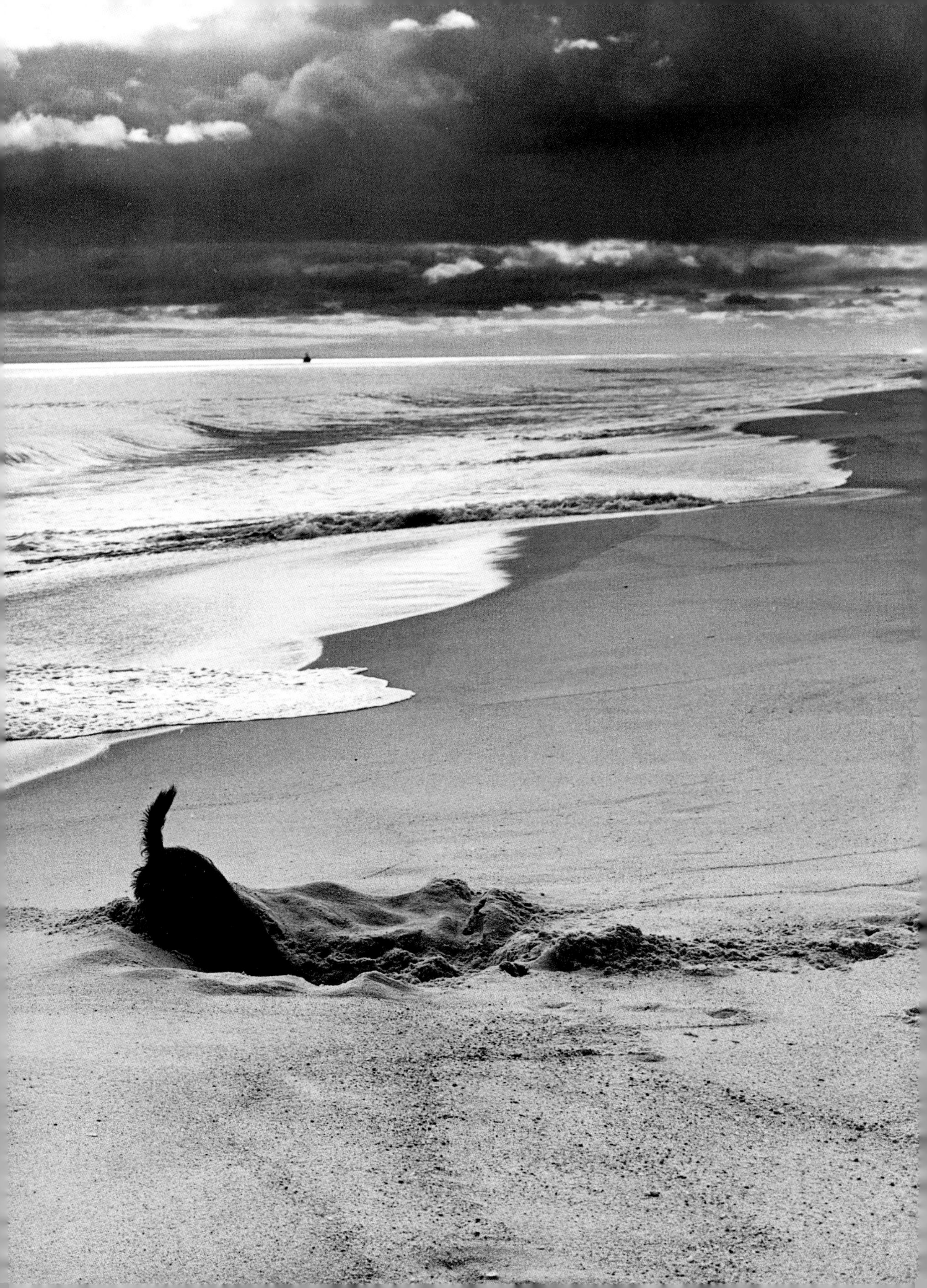

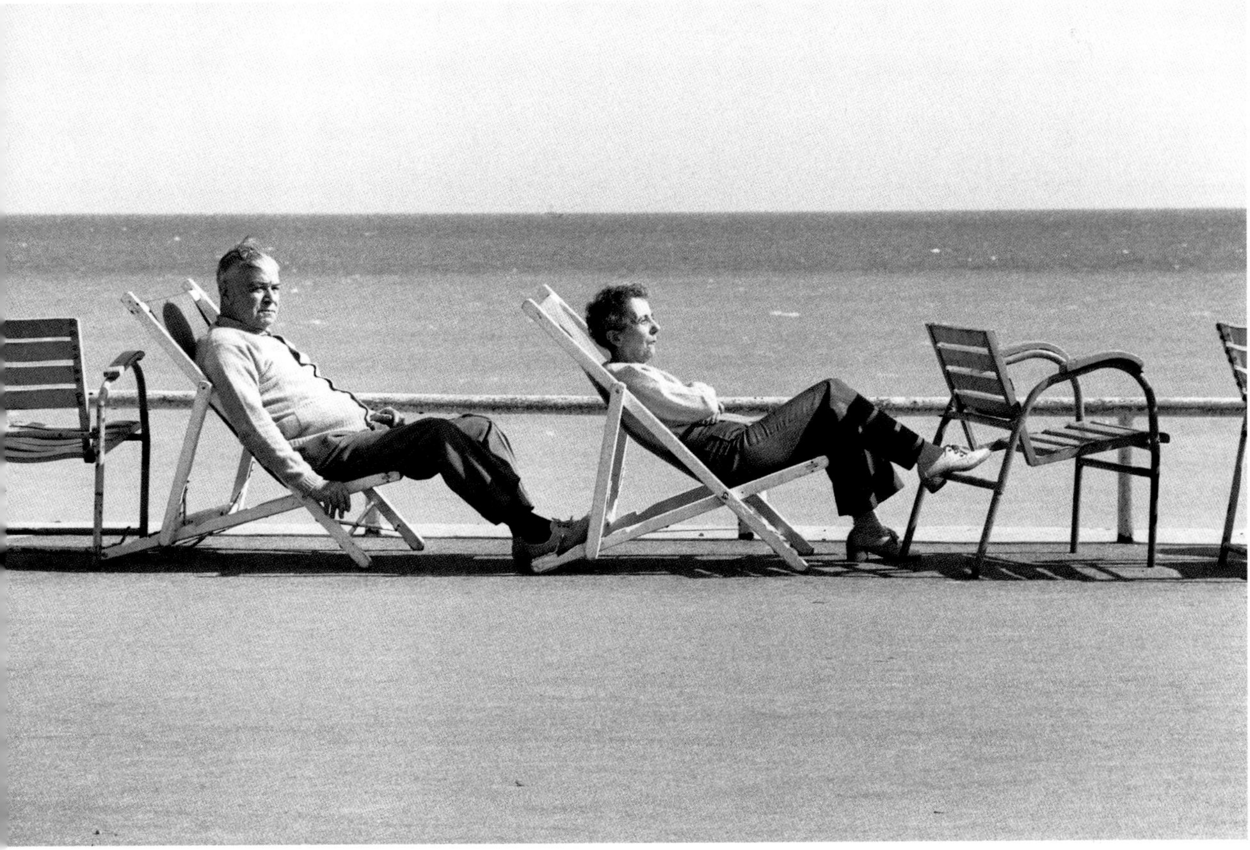

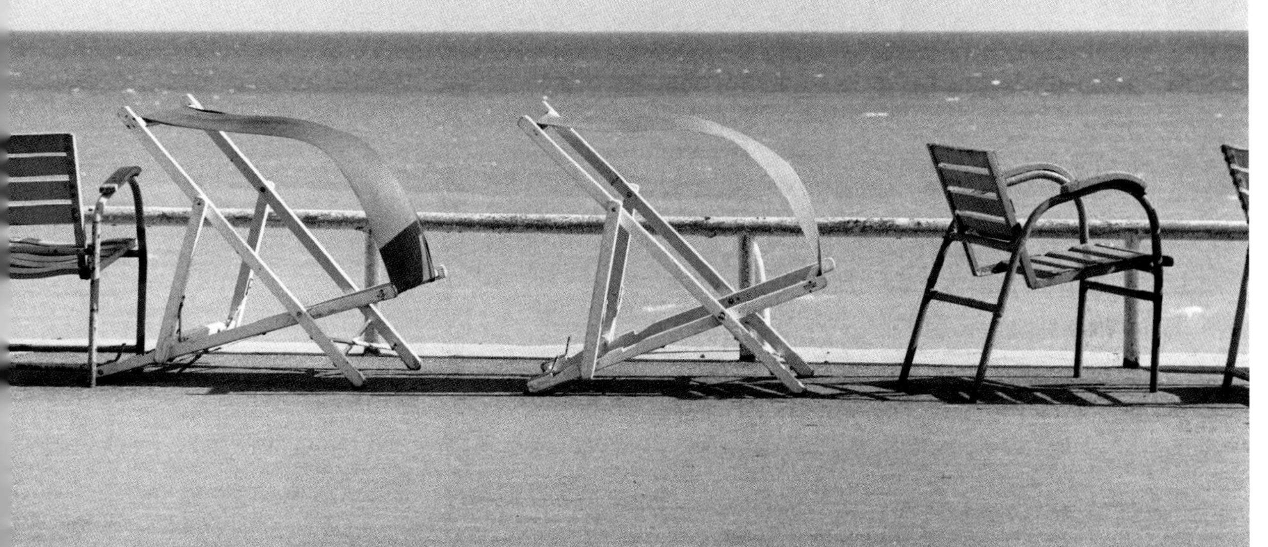

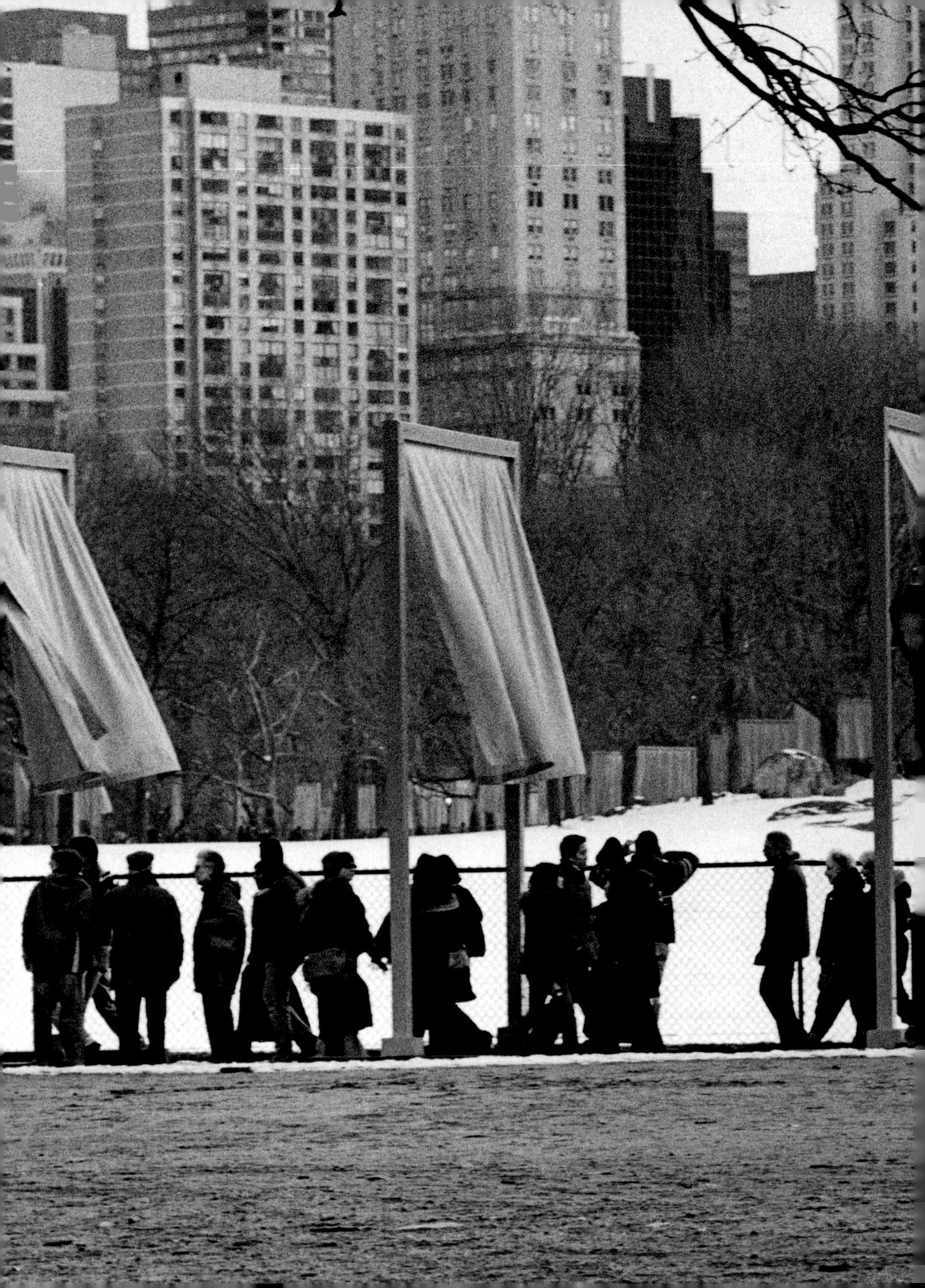

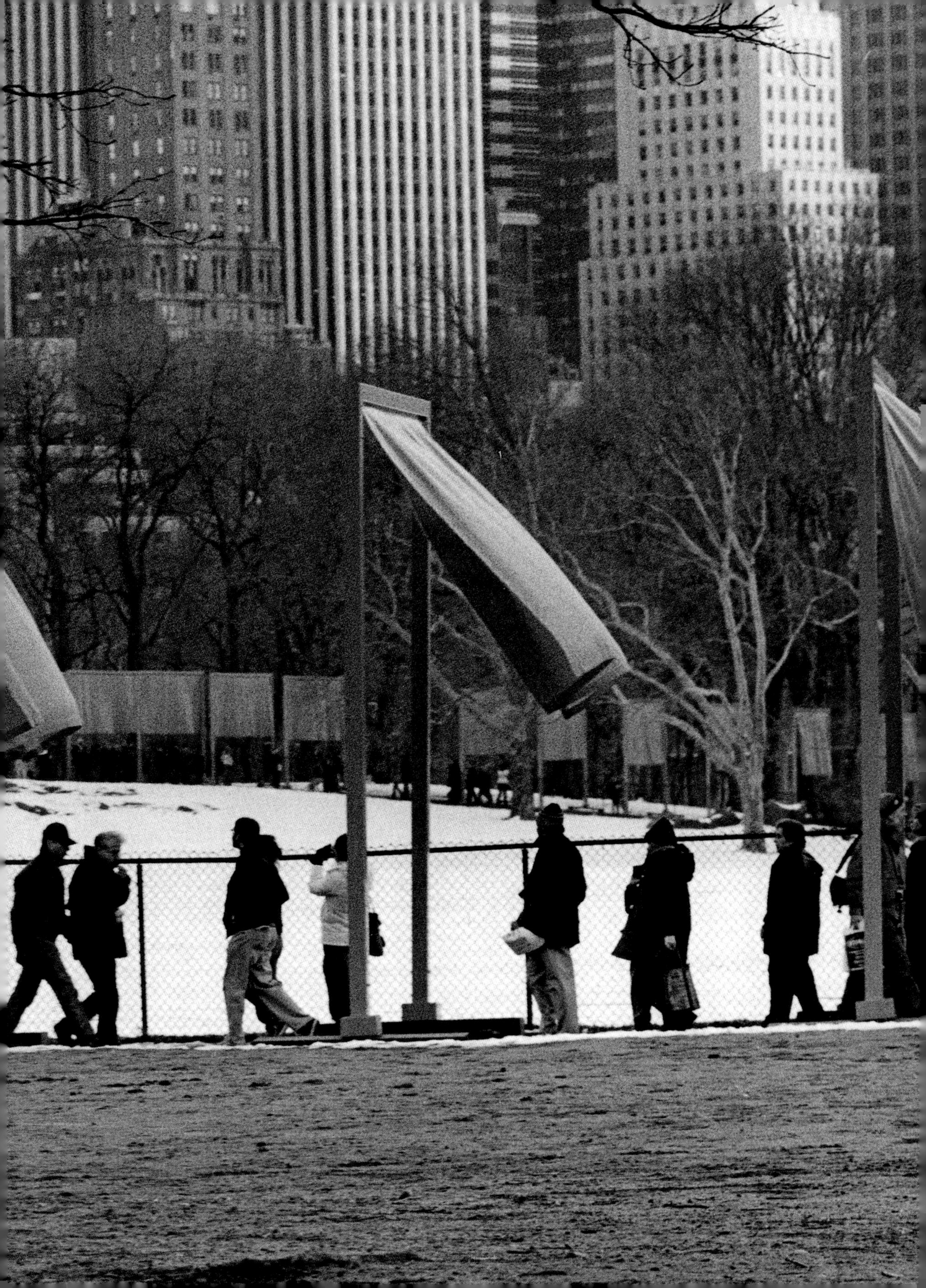

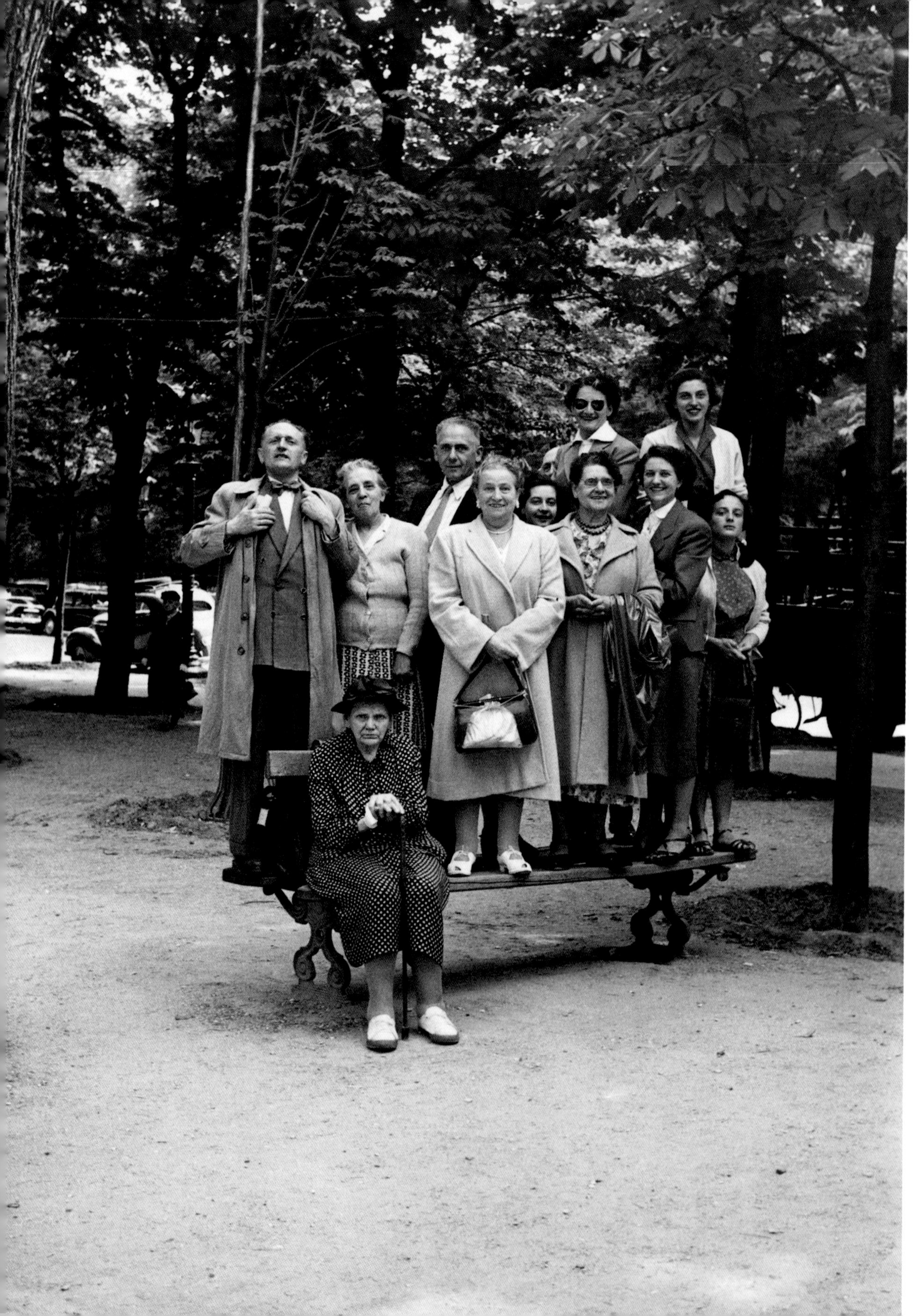

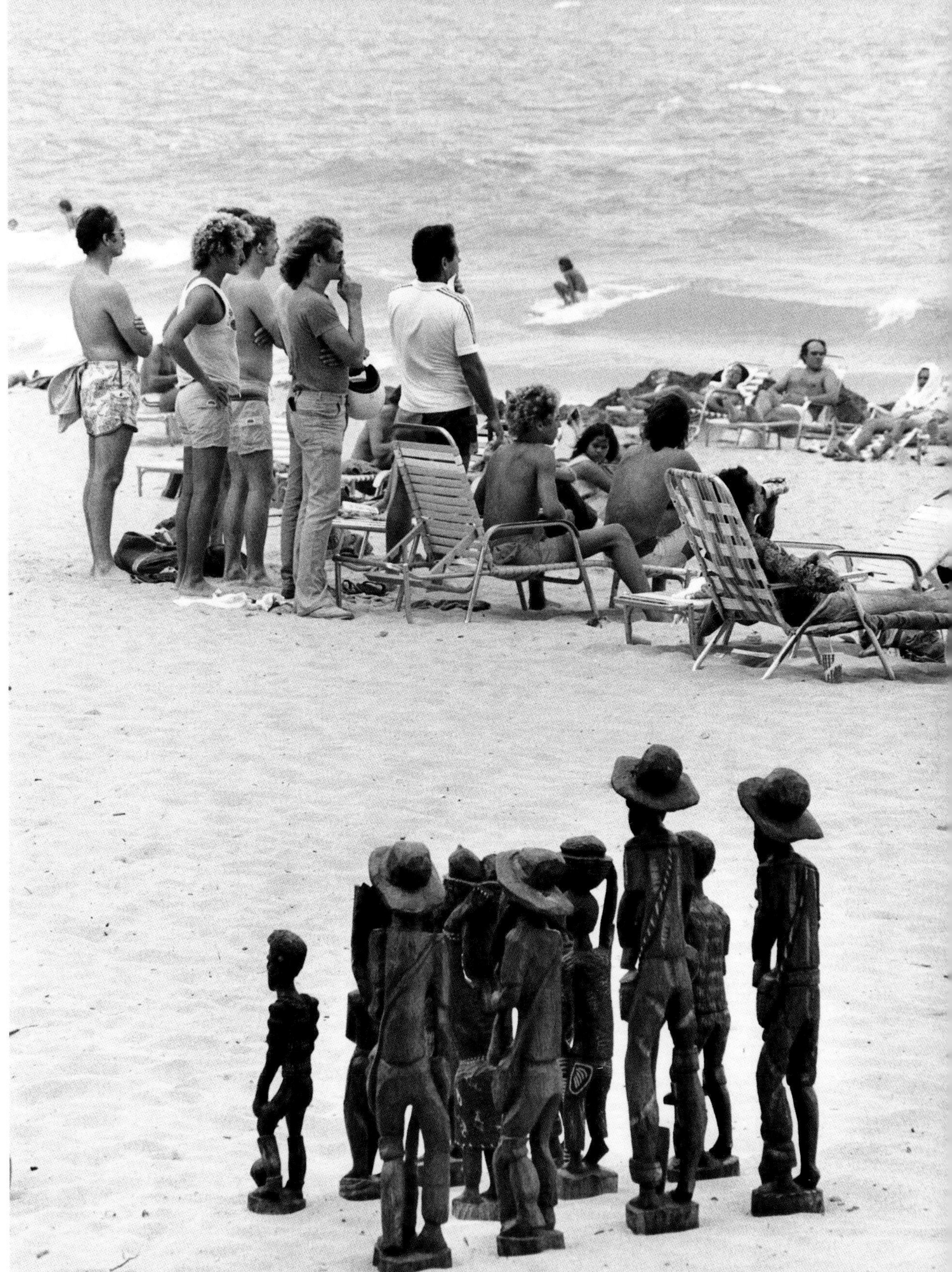

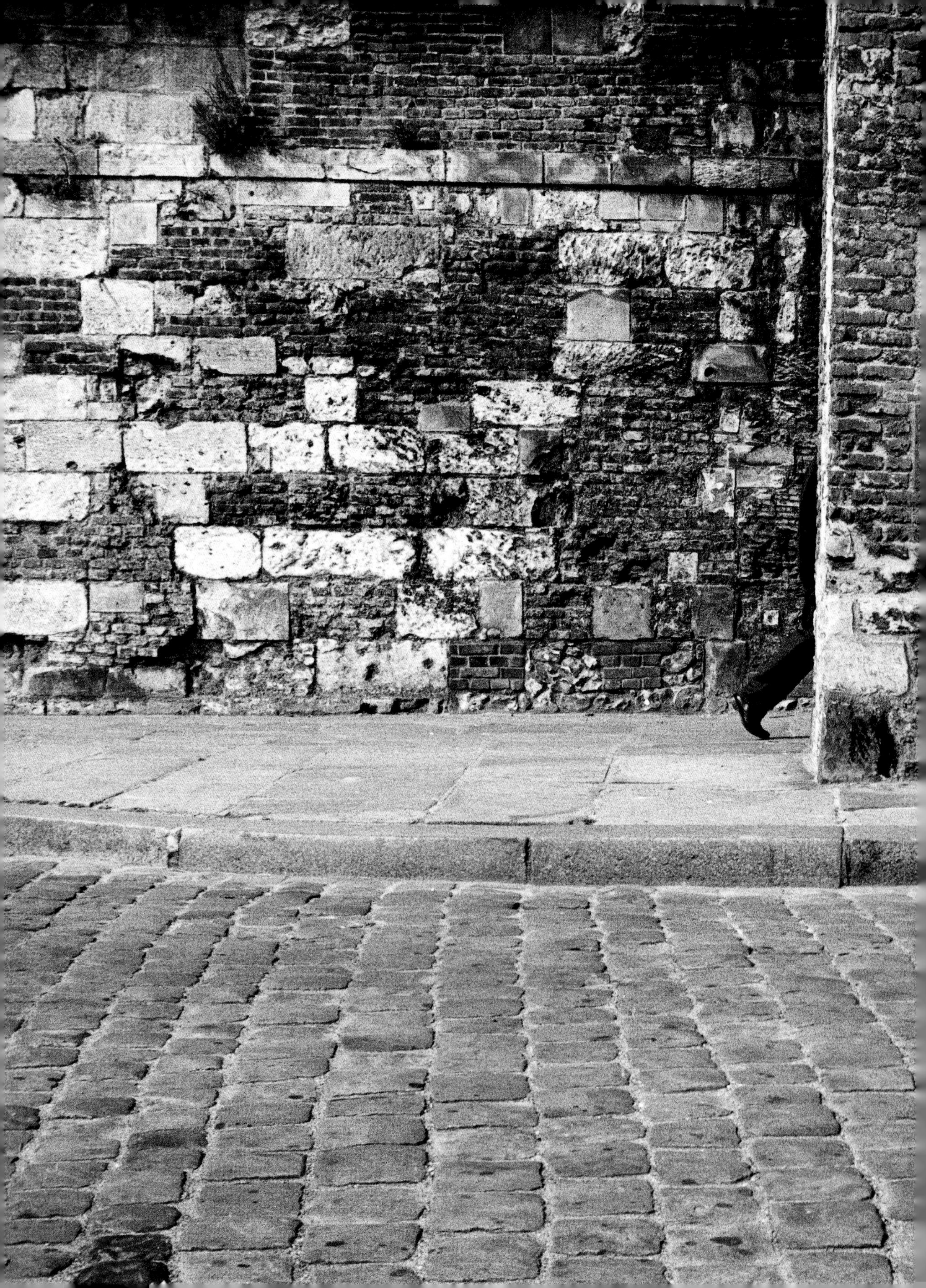

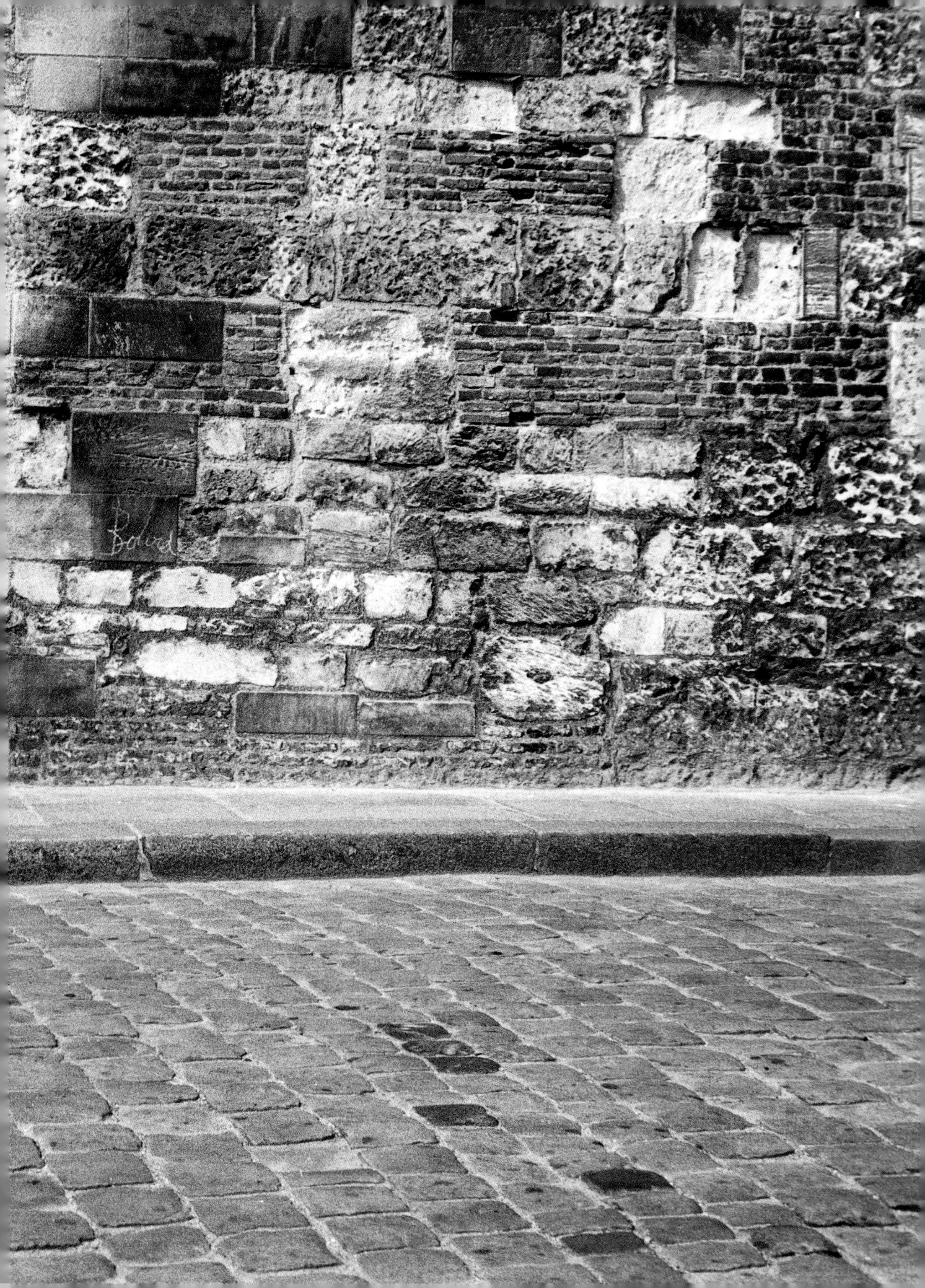

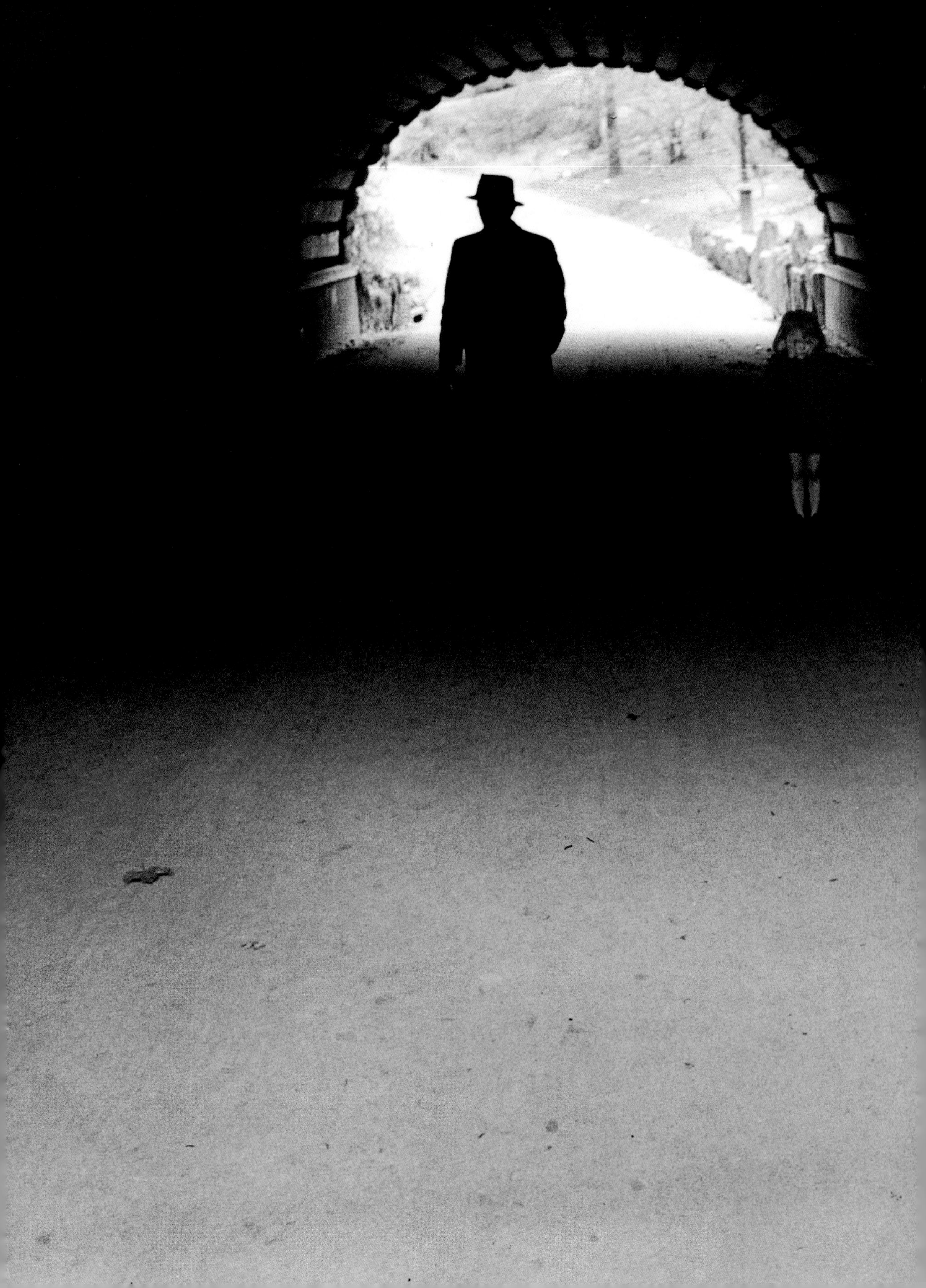

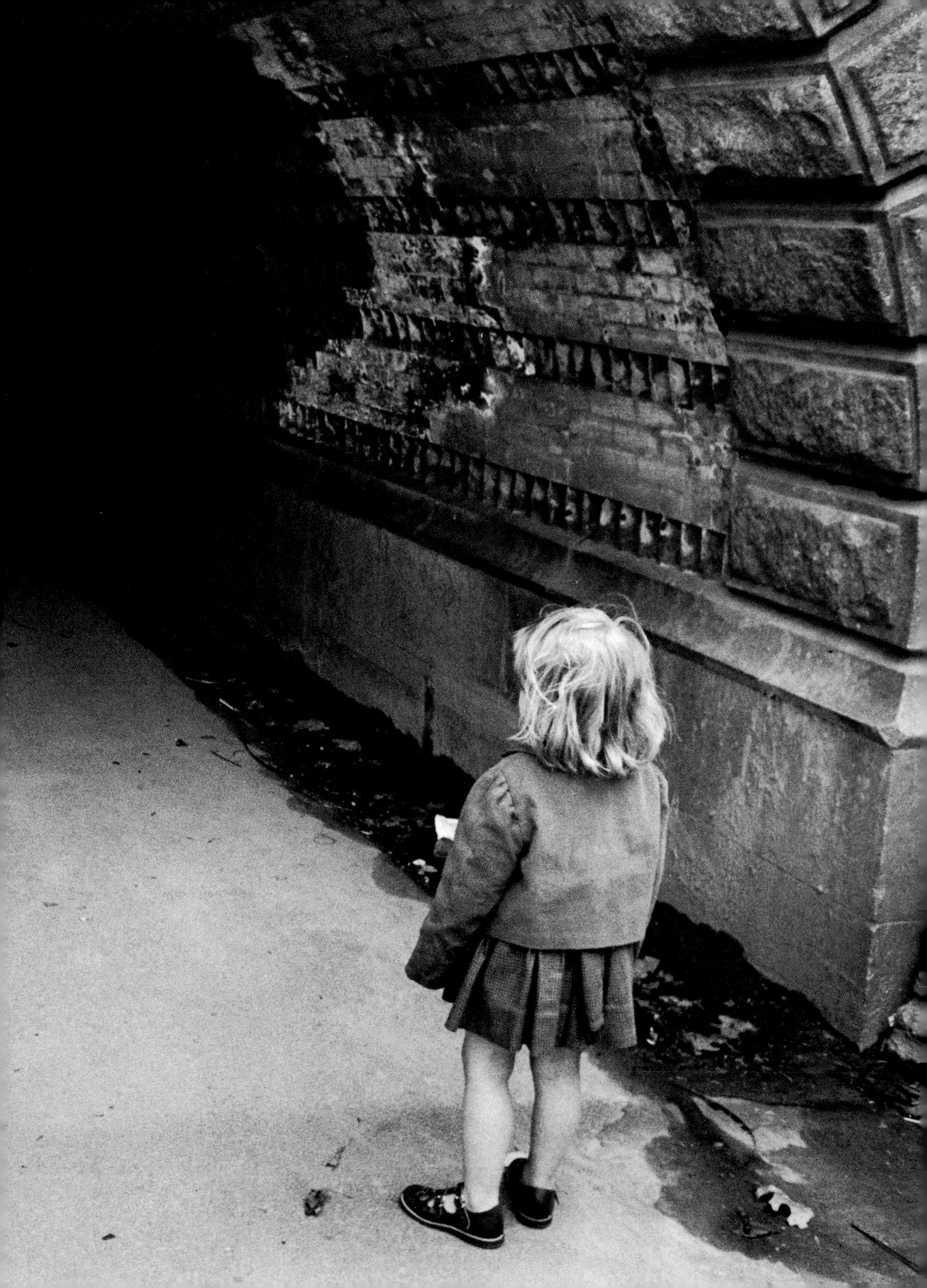

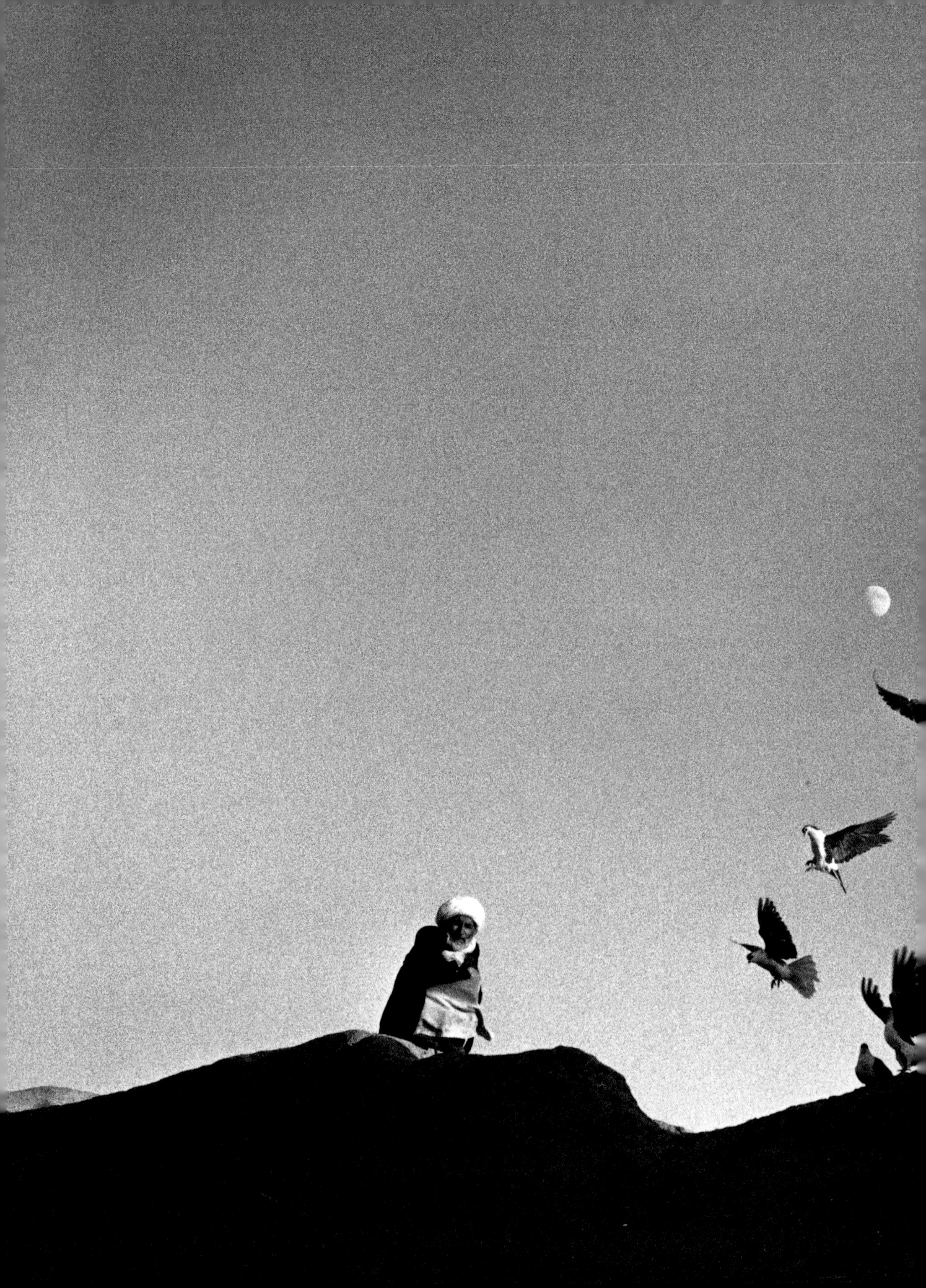

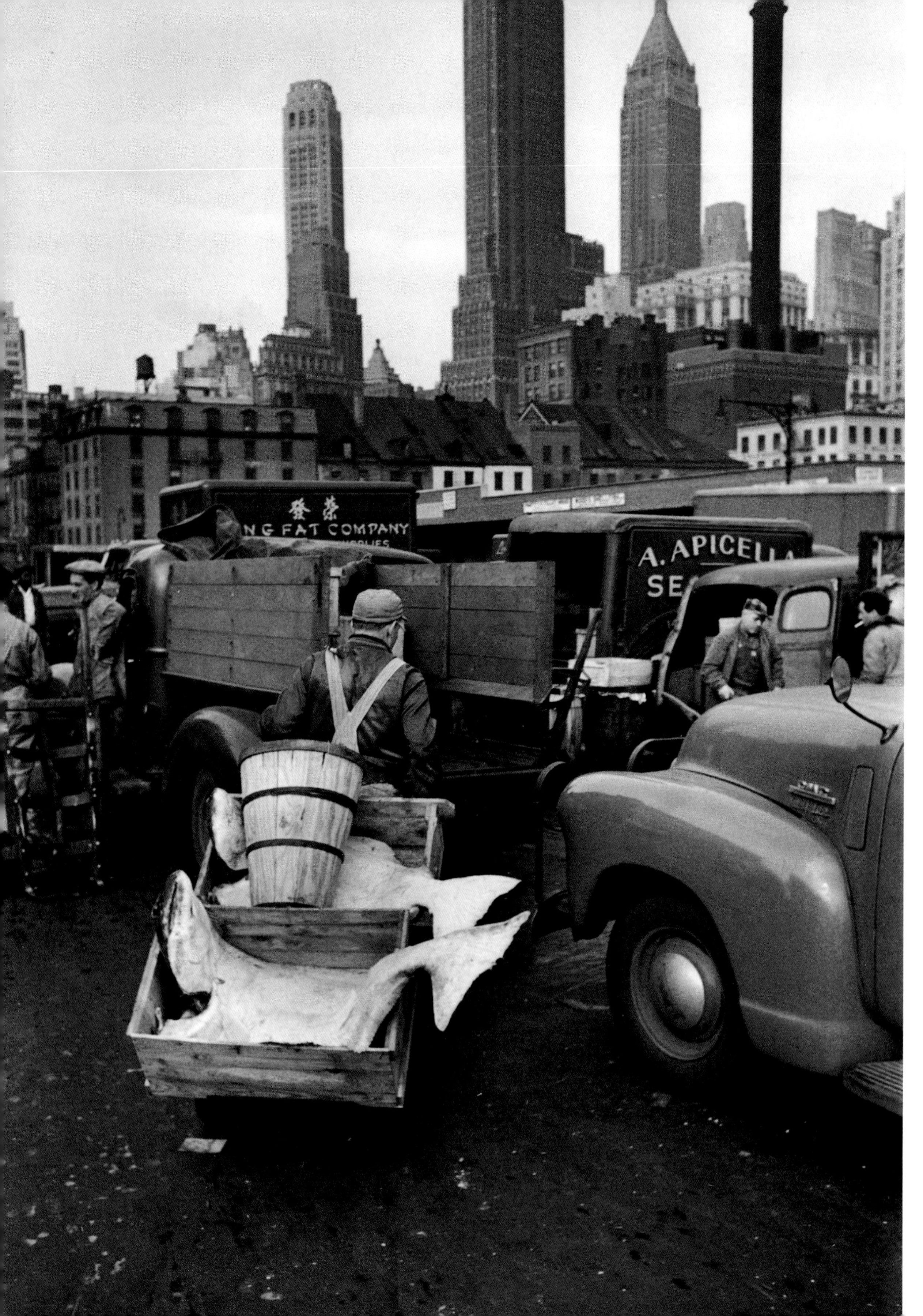
榮發
NG FAT COMPANY
SUPPLIES
A. APICELLA
SE

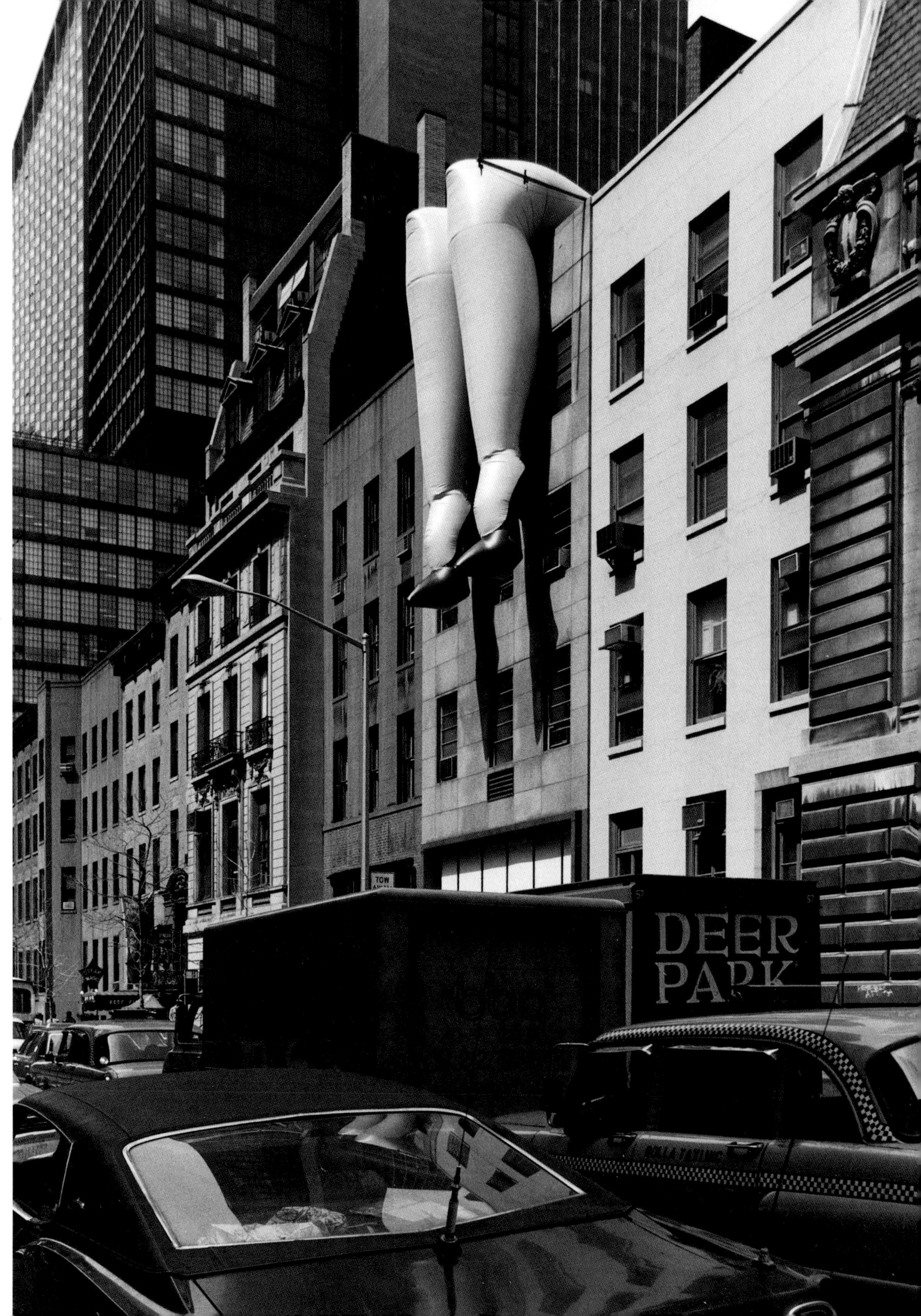

DEER
PARK
TOW

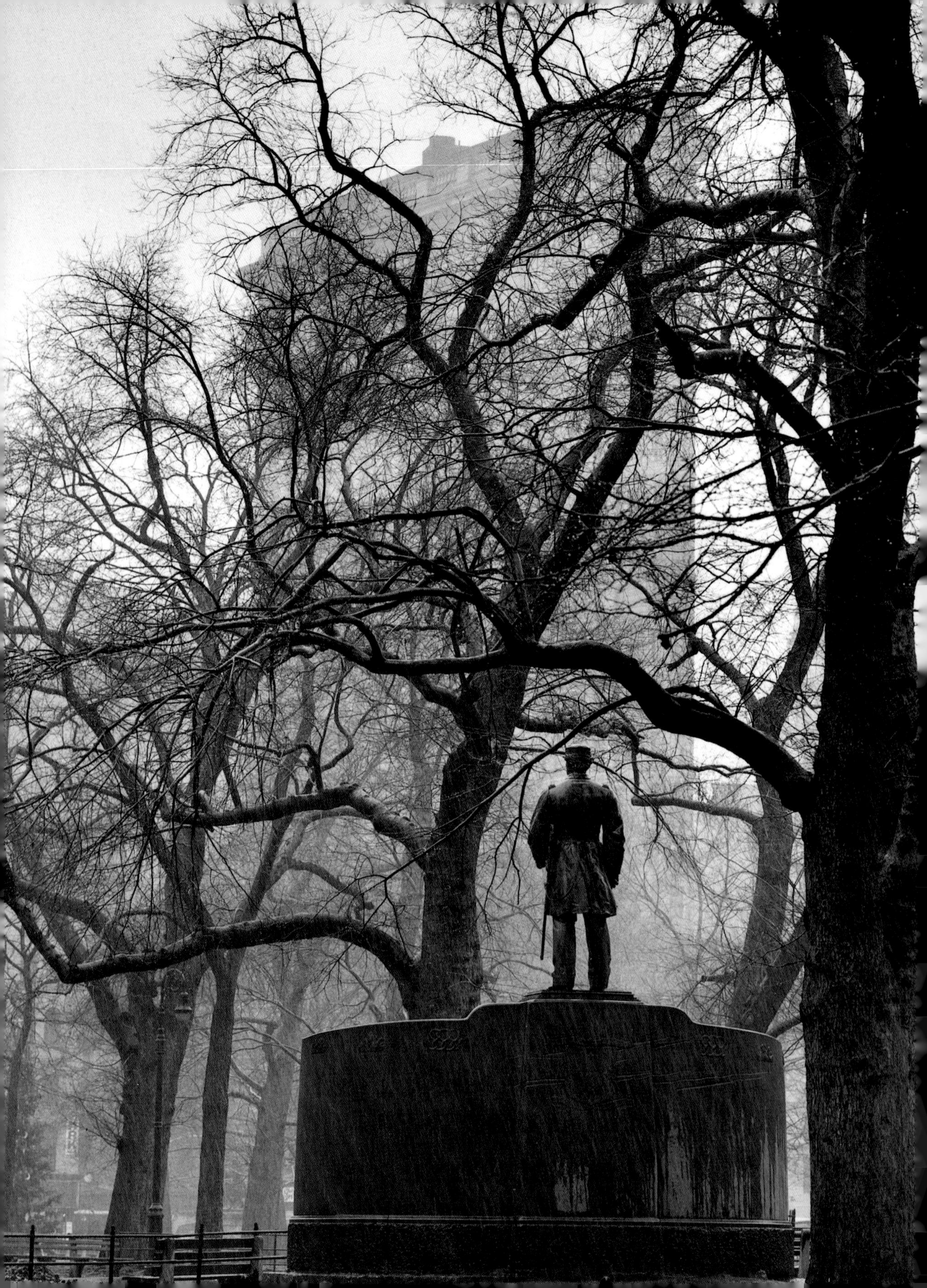

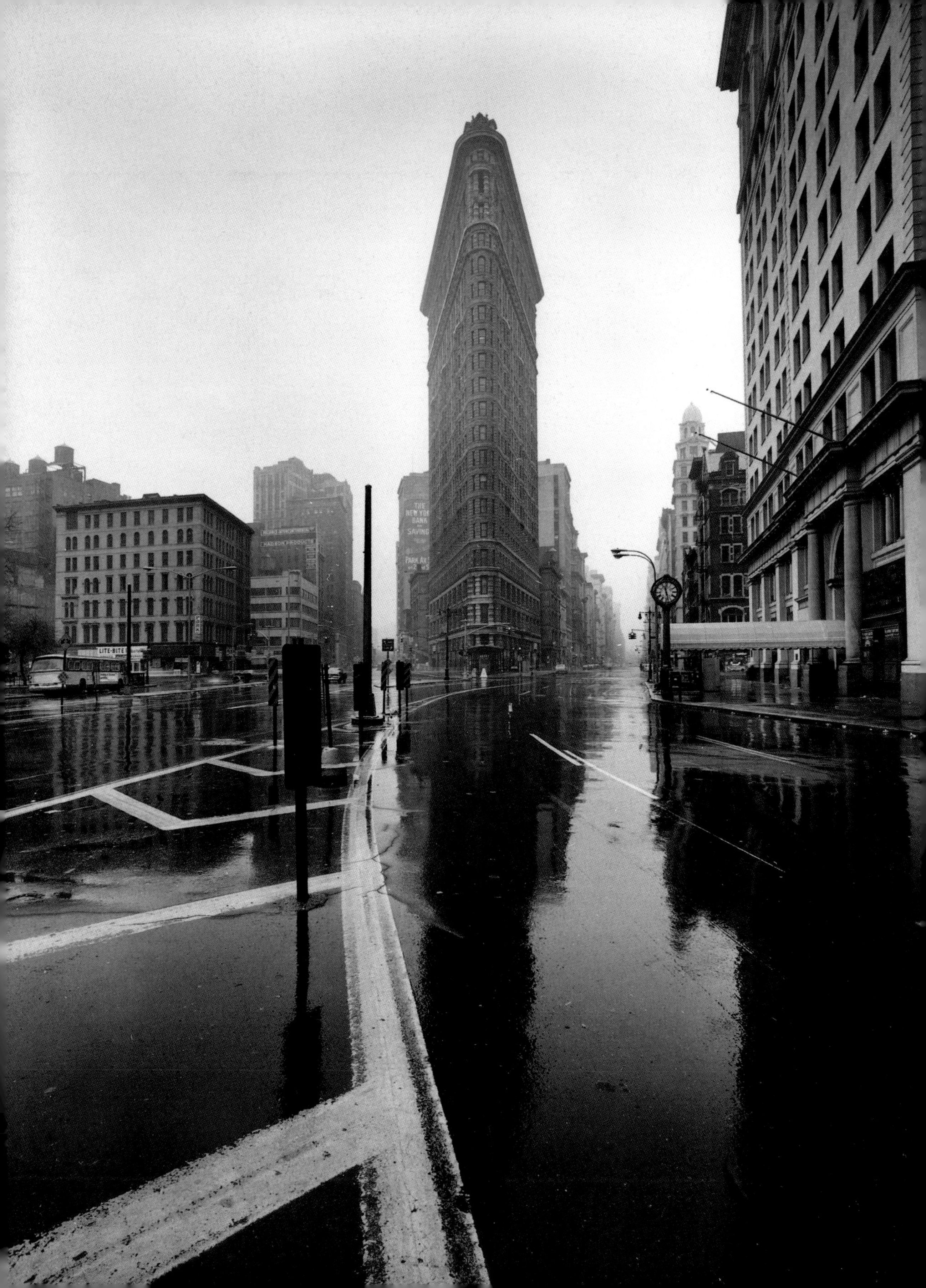

THE
NEW YORK
BANK
for
SAVING
PARK AV.
at 2 nd S.
LITE-BITE

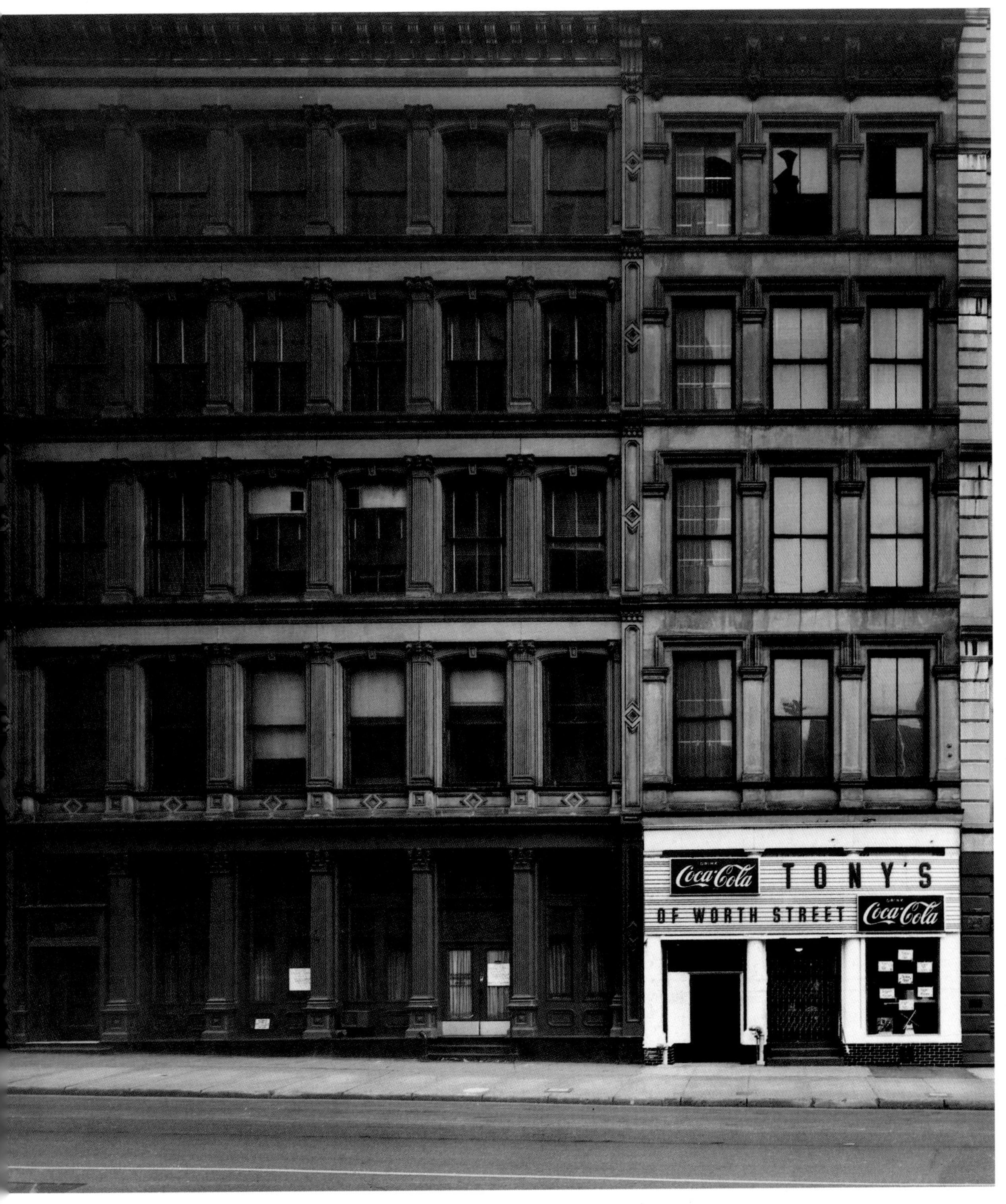

DRINK Coca-Cola
TONY'S
OF WORTH STREET
DRINK Coca-Cola

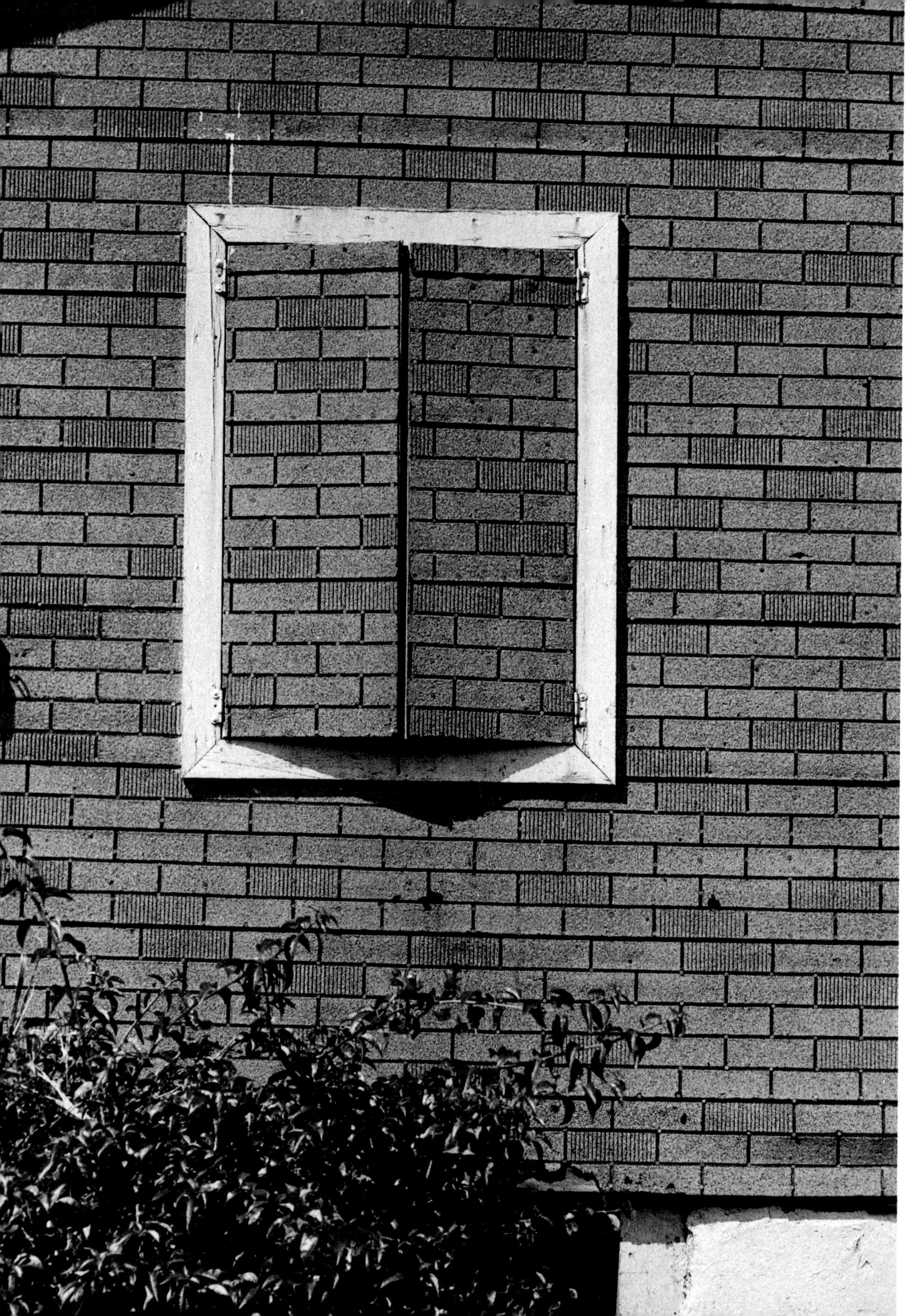

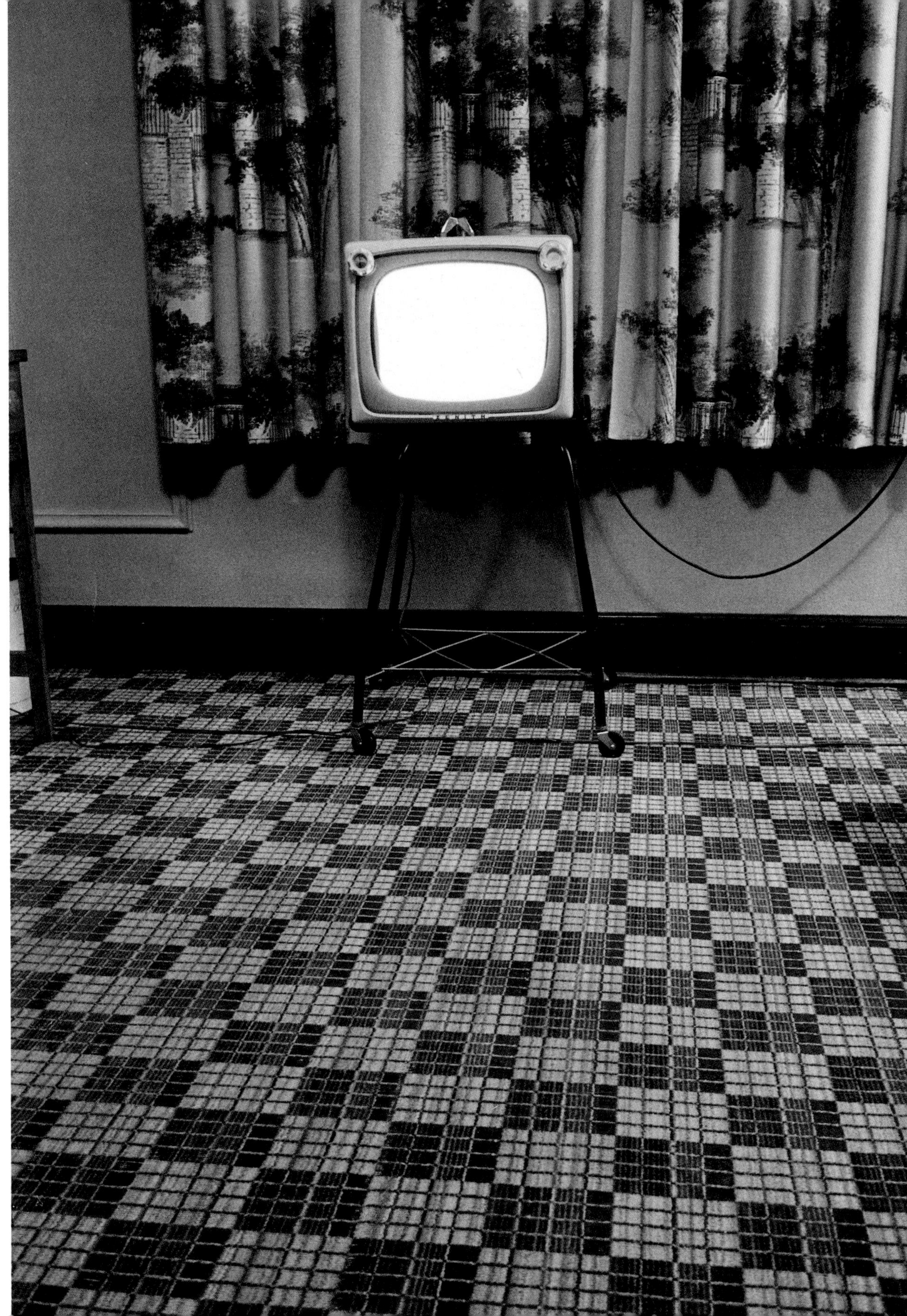

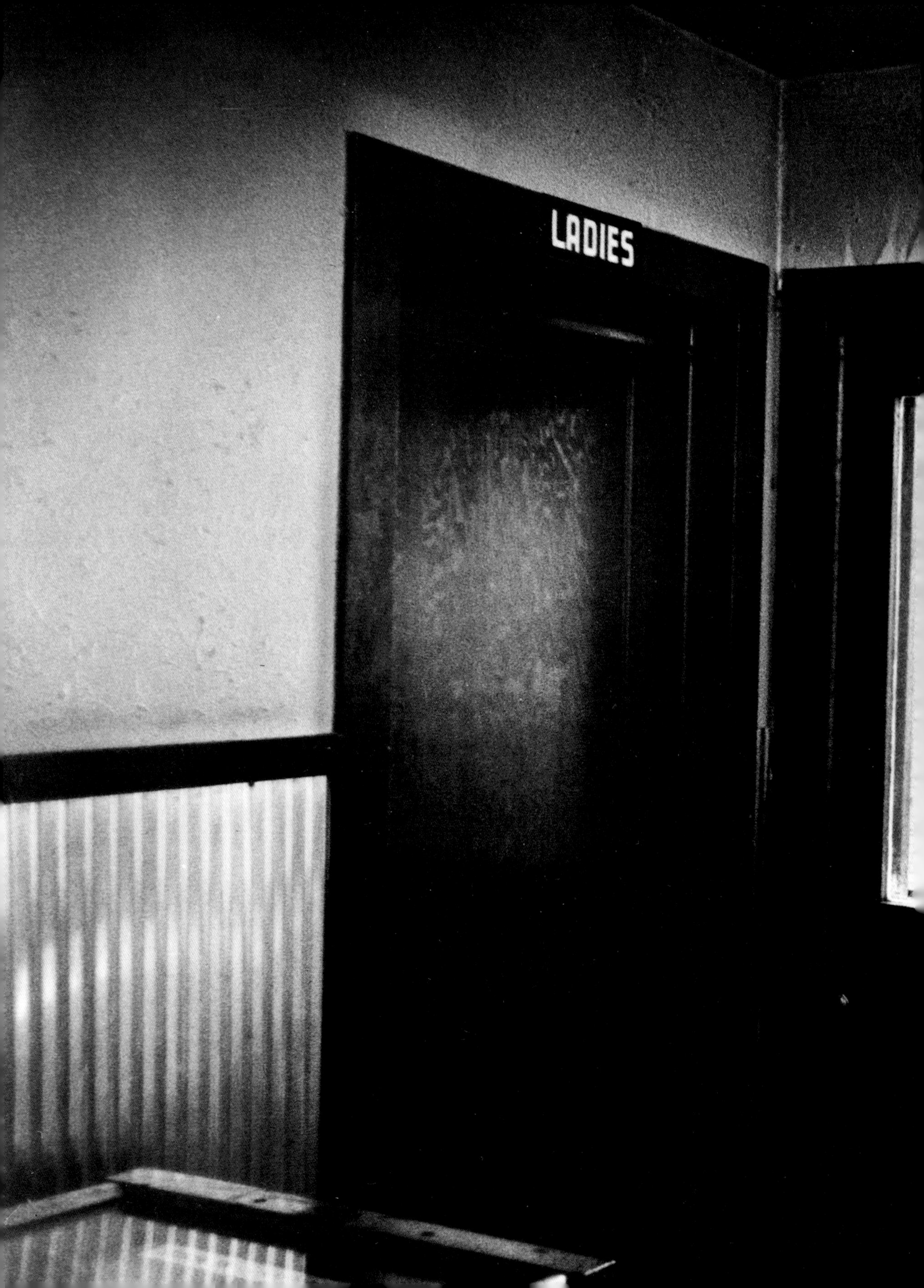

LADIES

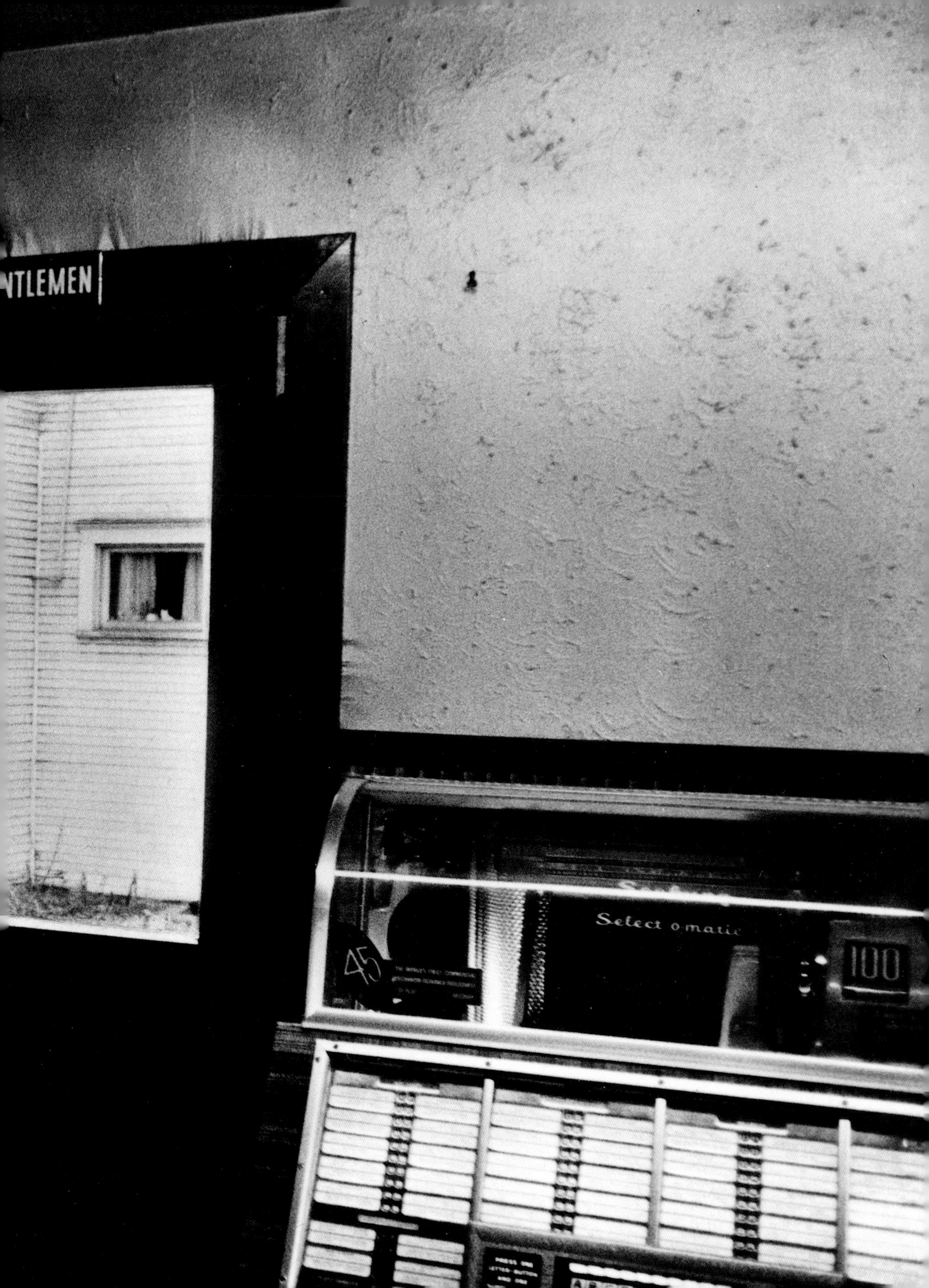
NTLEMEN
Select-o-matic
45
100

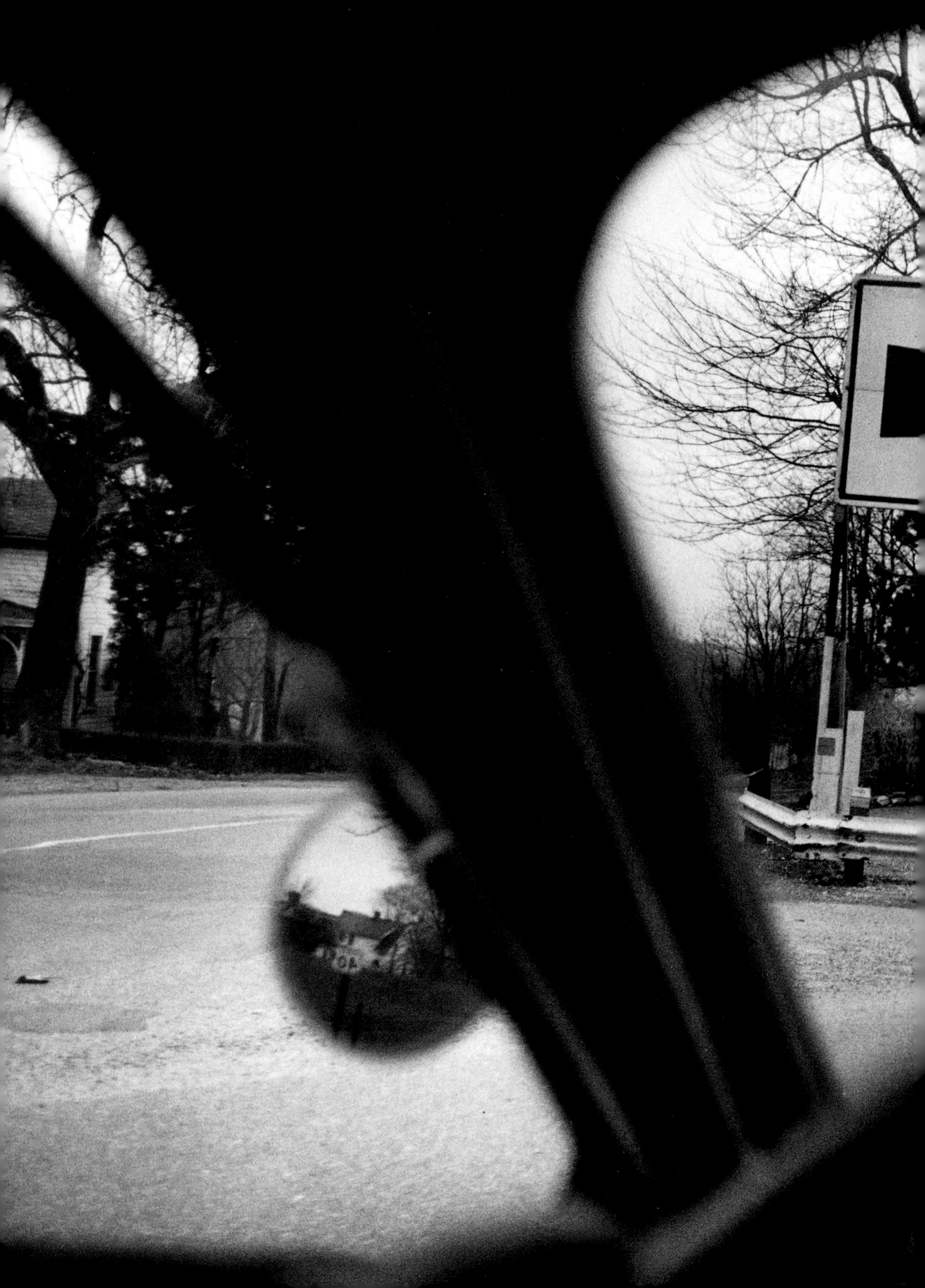

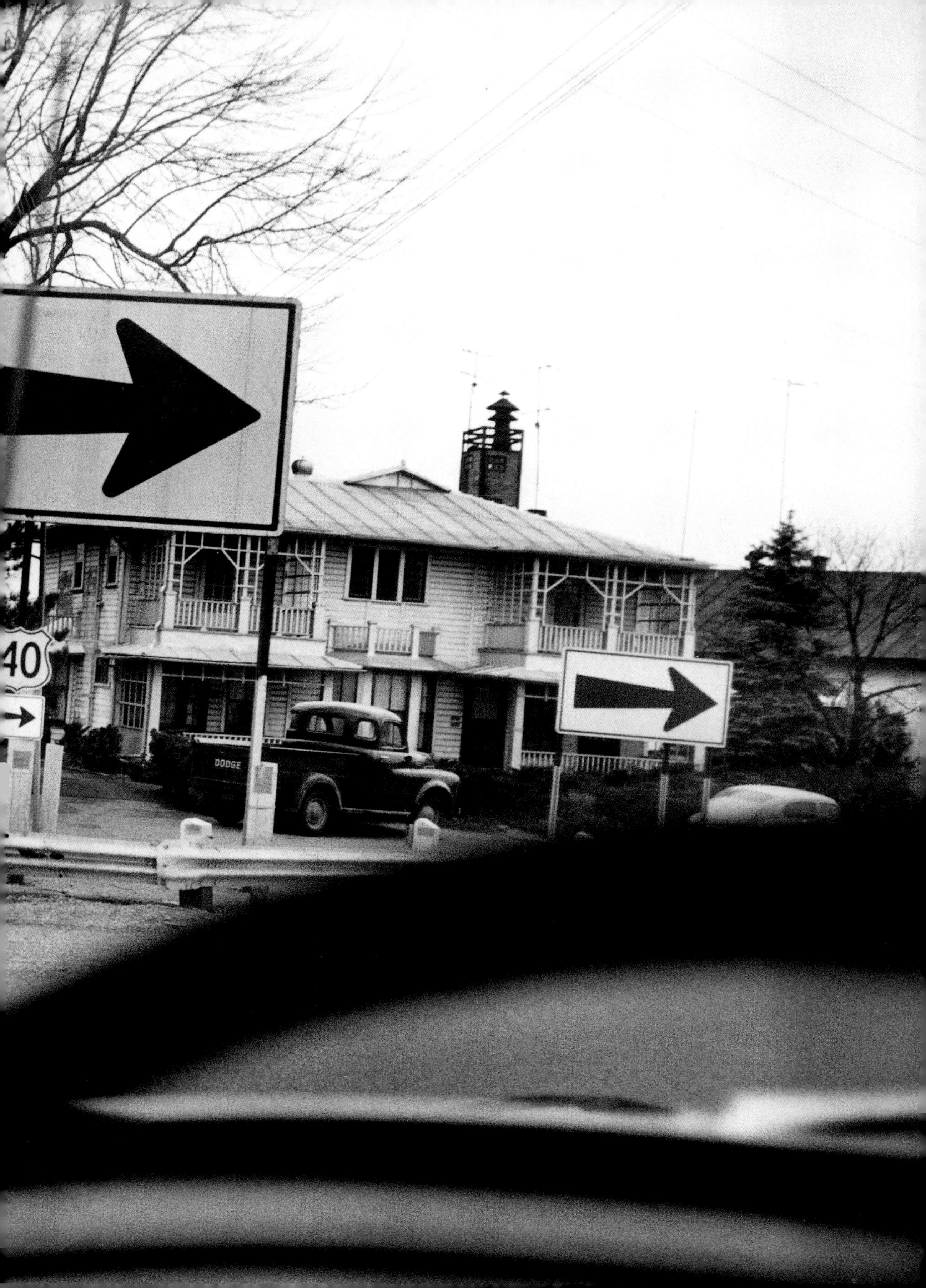

40
DODGE

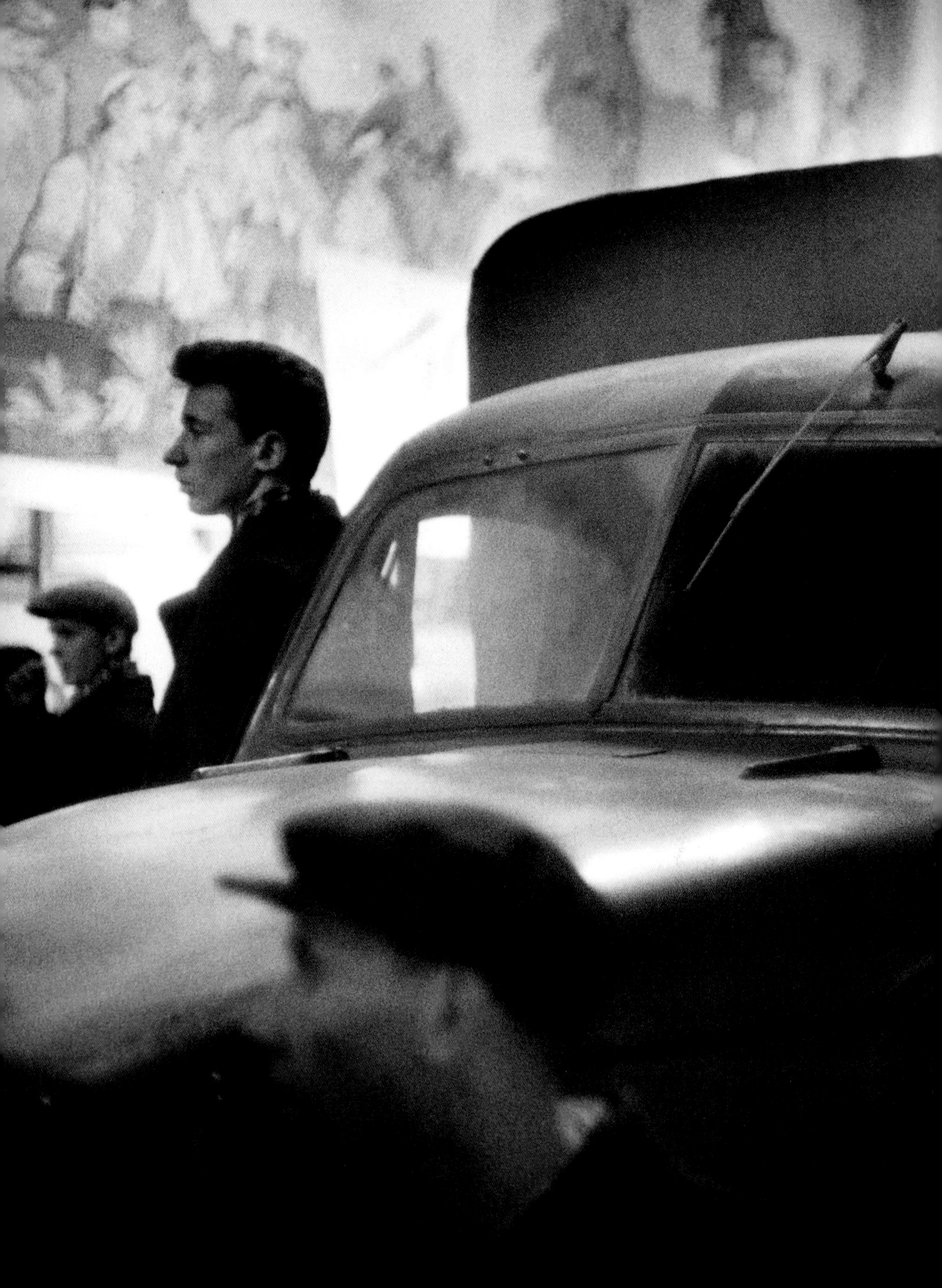

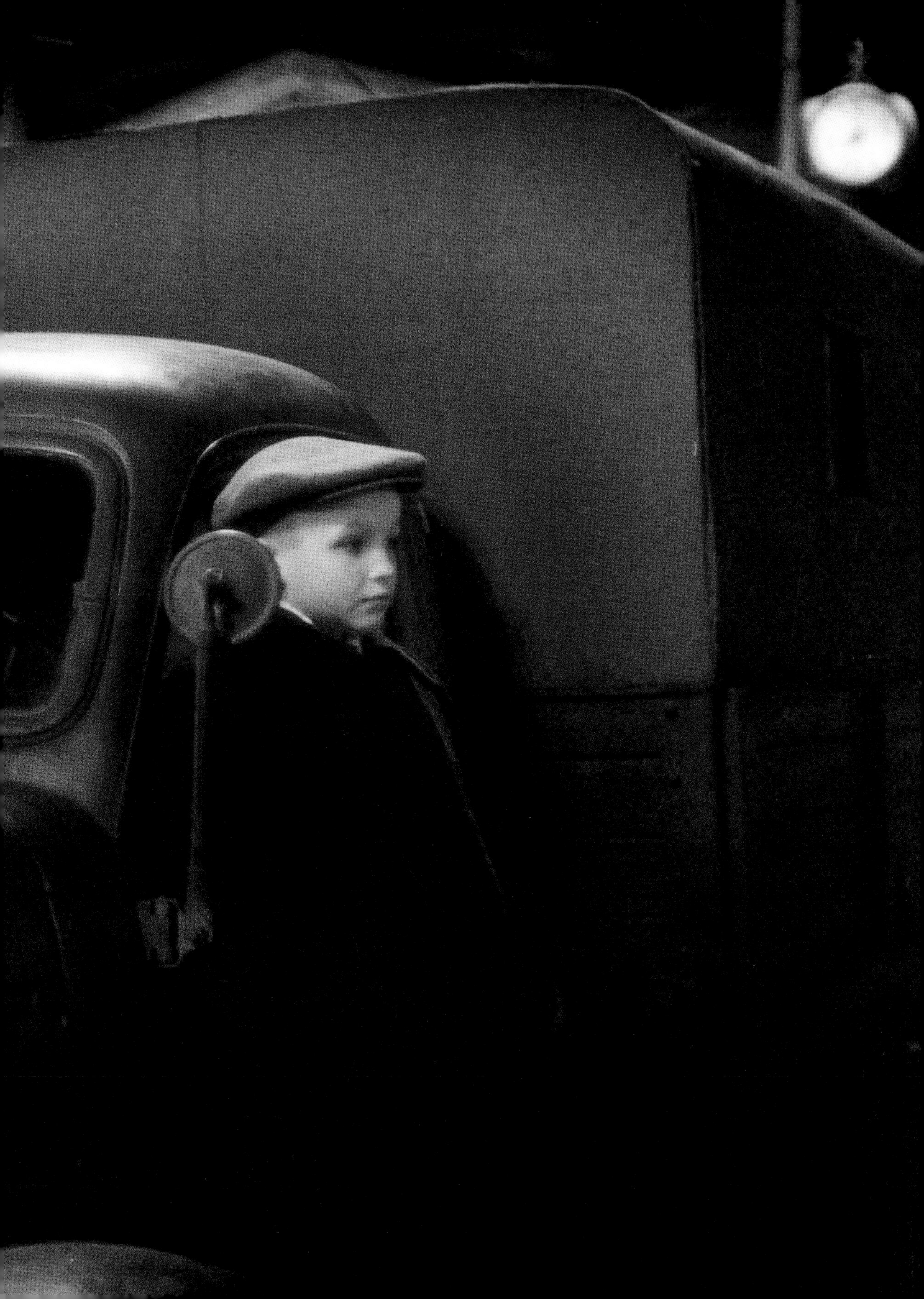

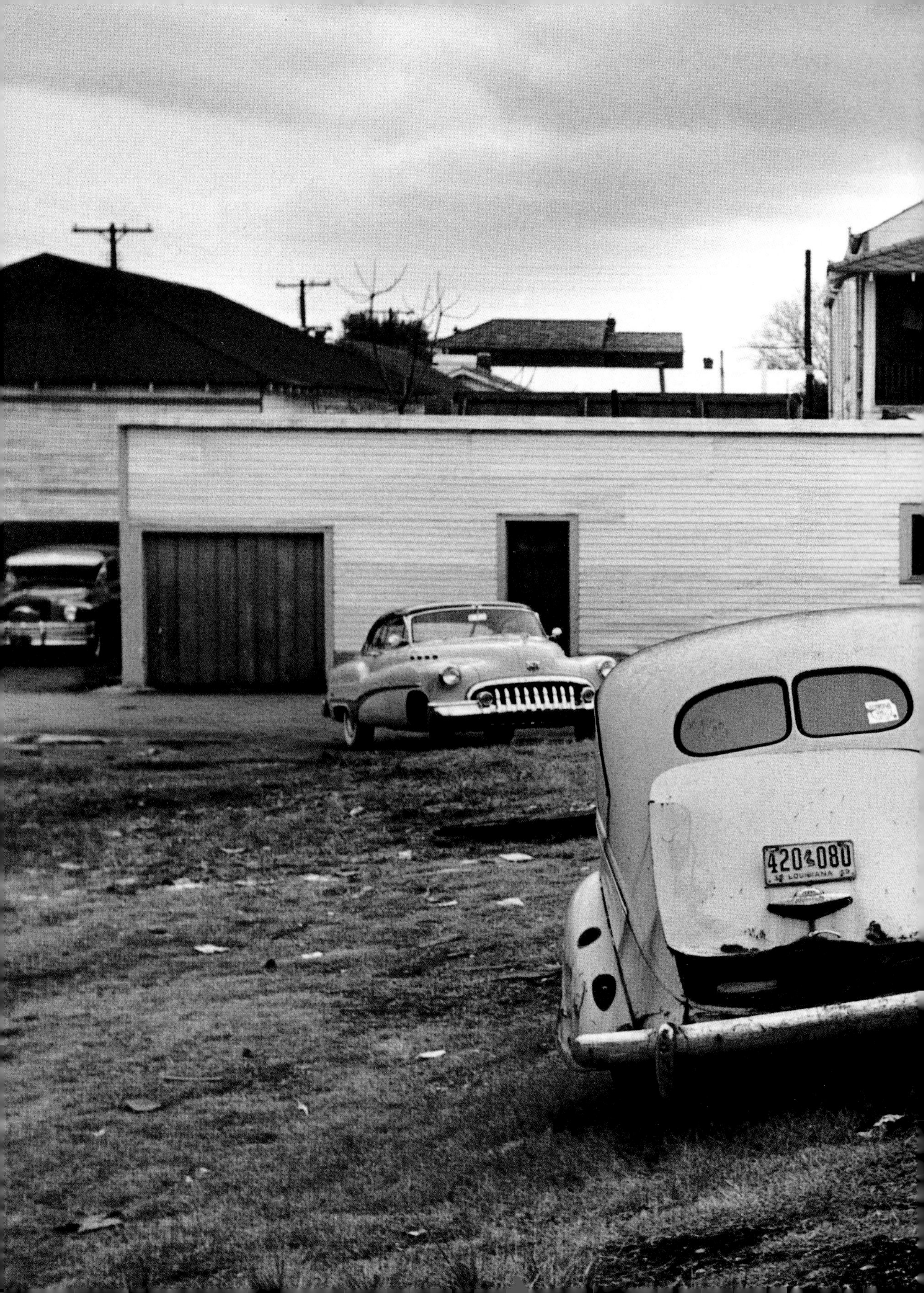

420 080
LOUISIANA

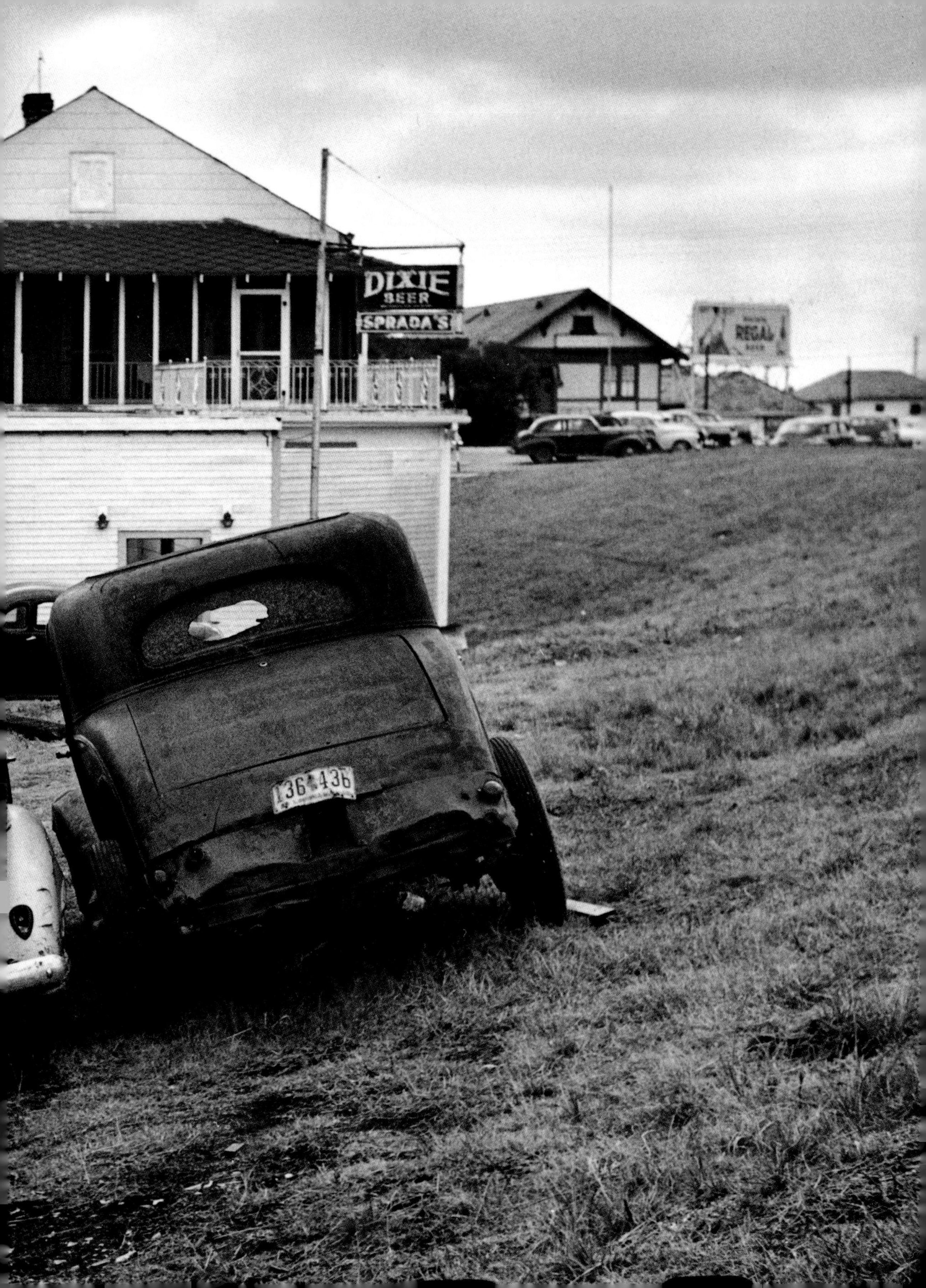

DIXIE
BEER
SPRADA'S
REGAL
136 436

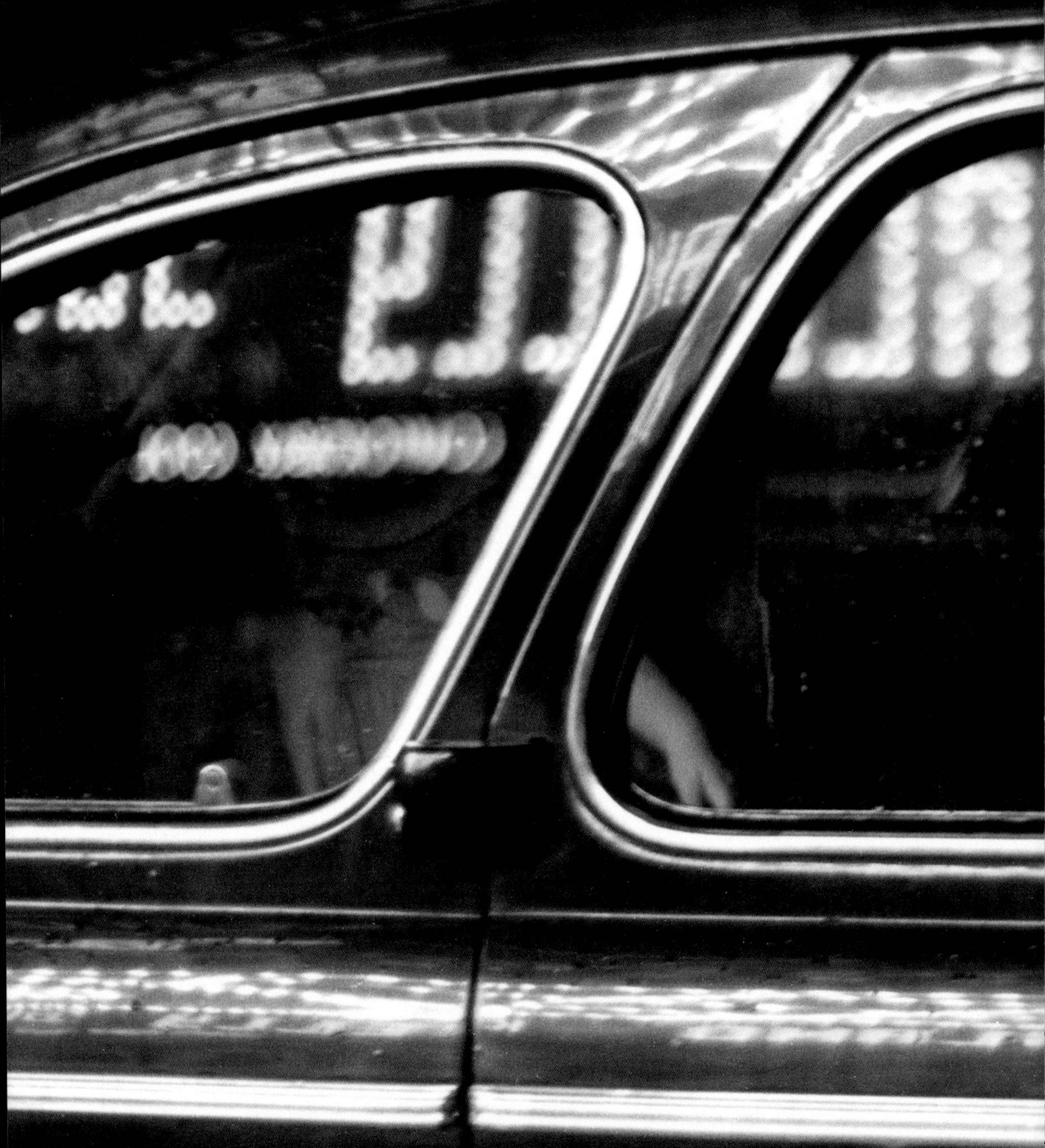

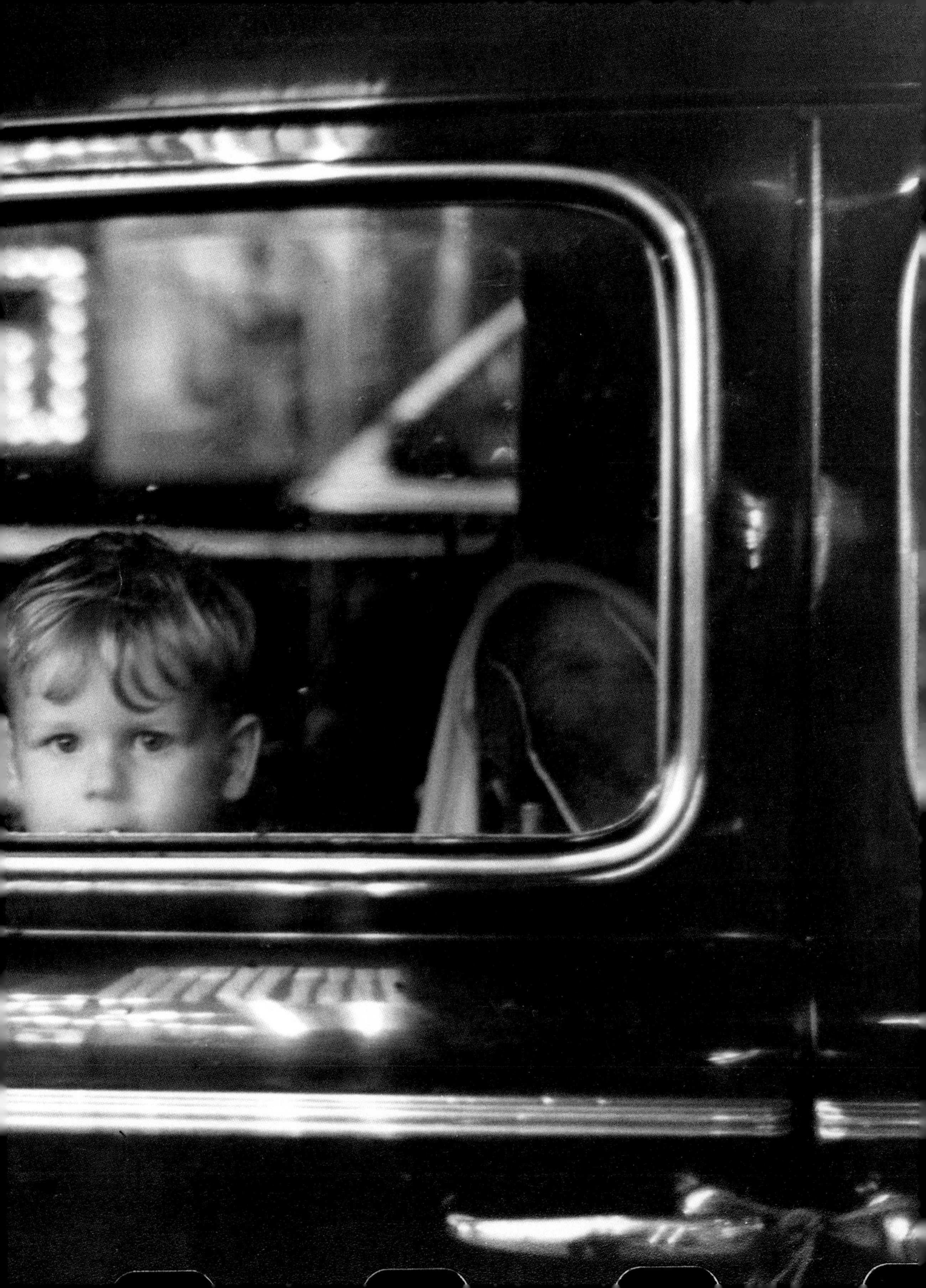

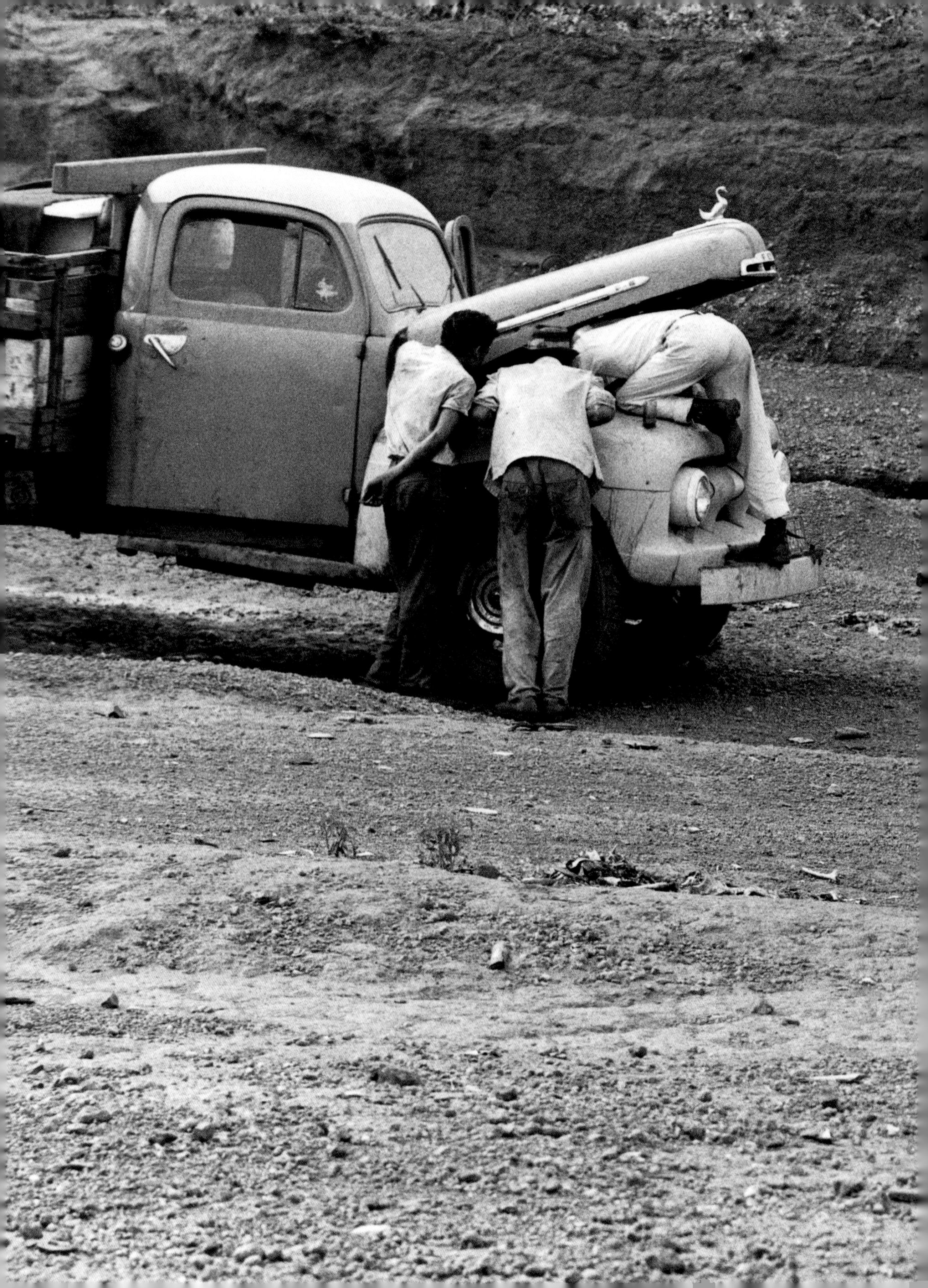

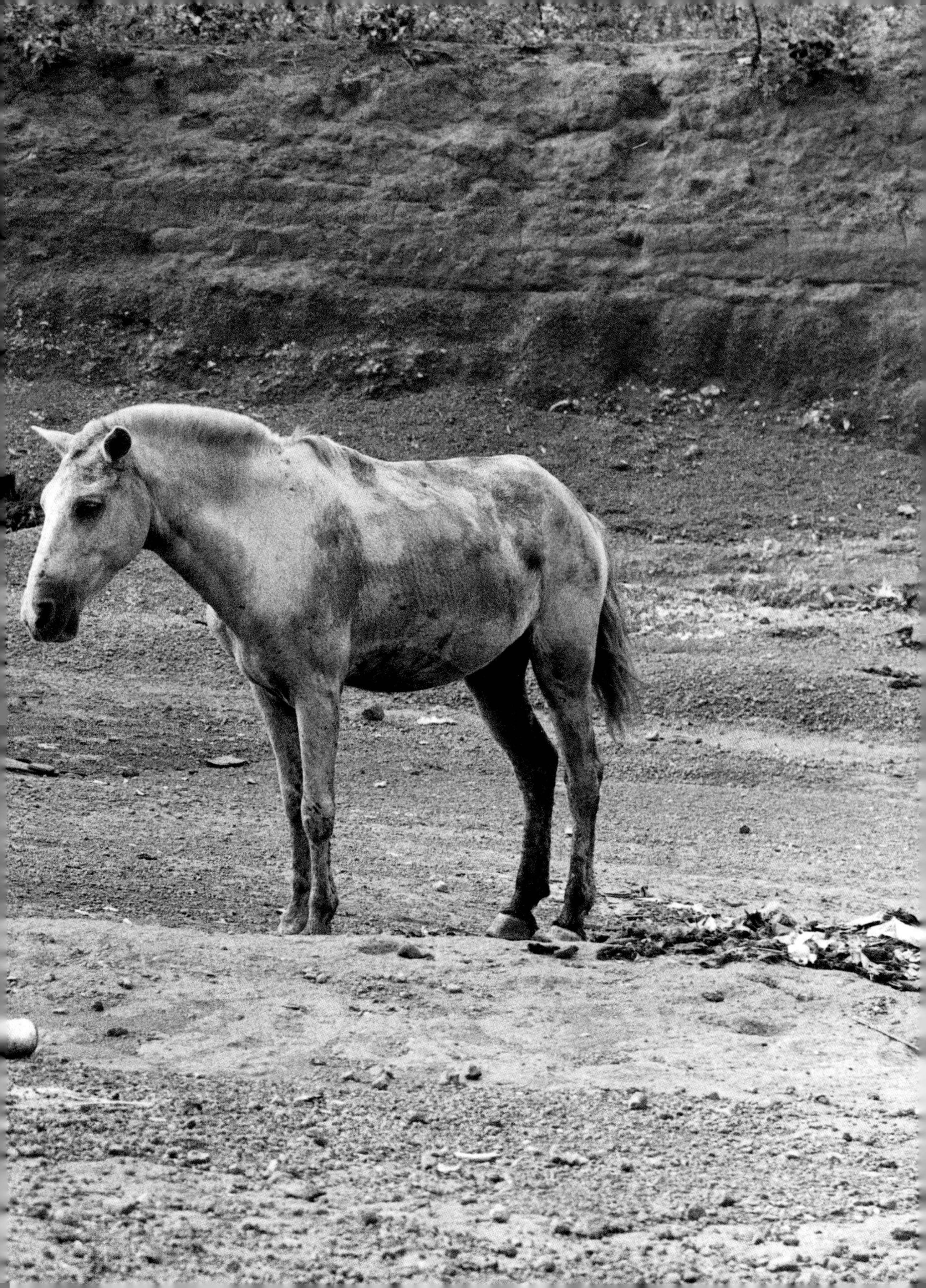

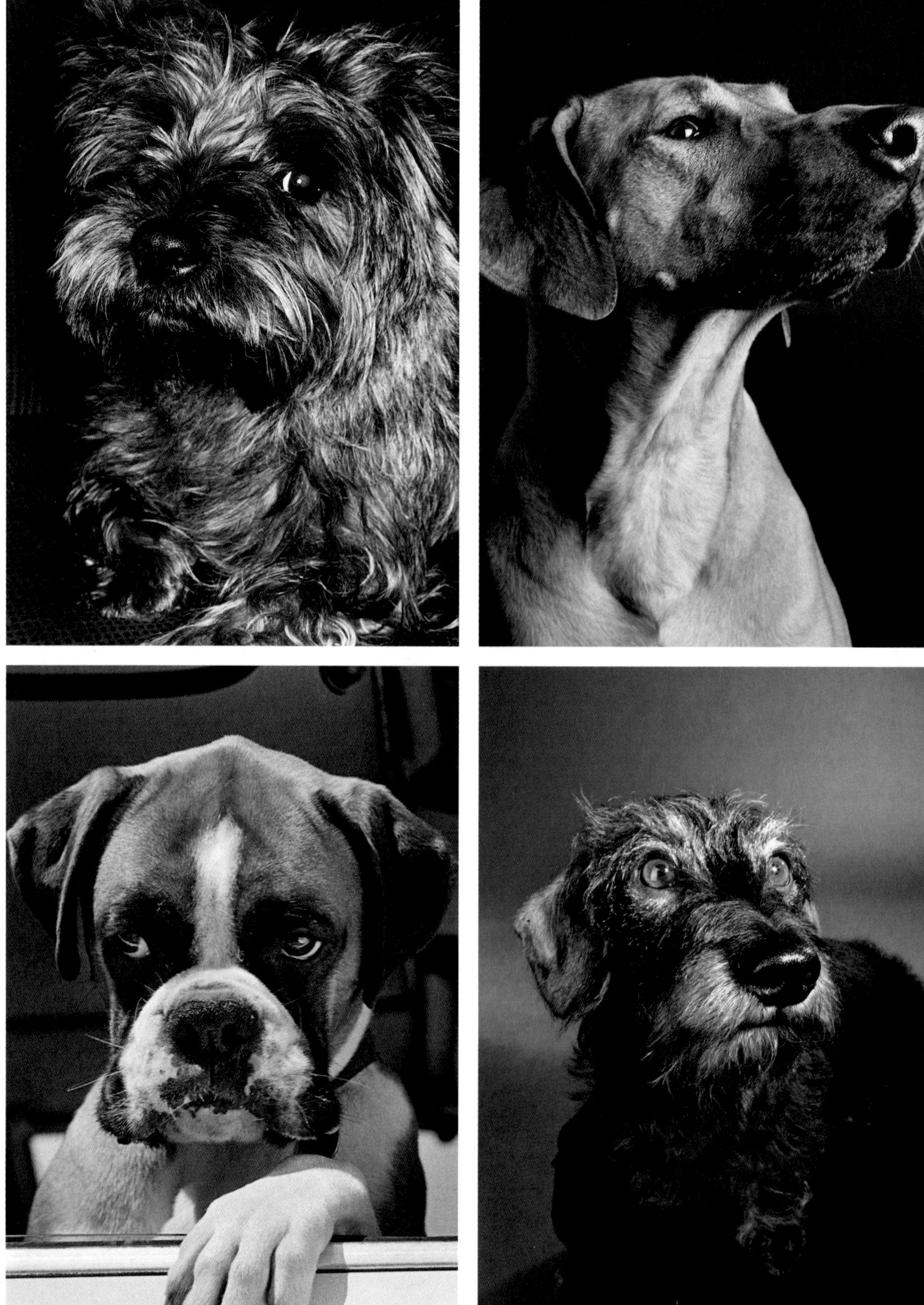

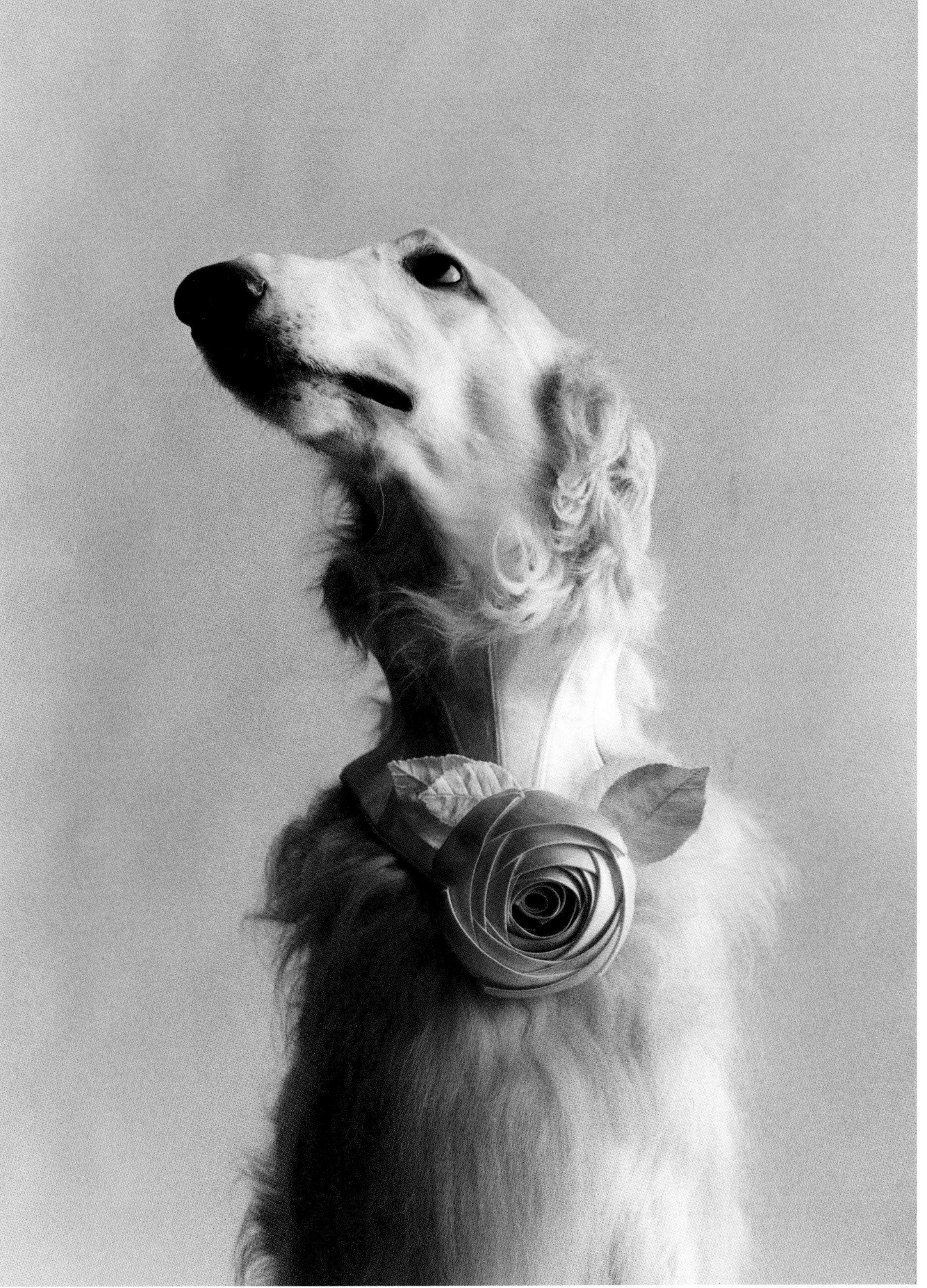

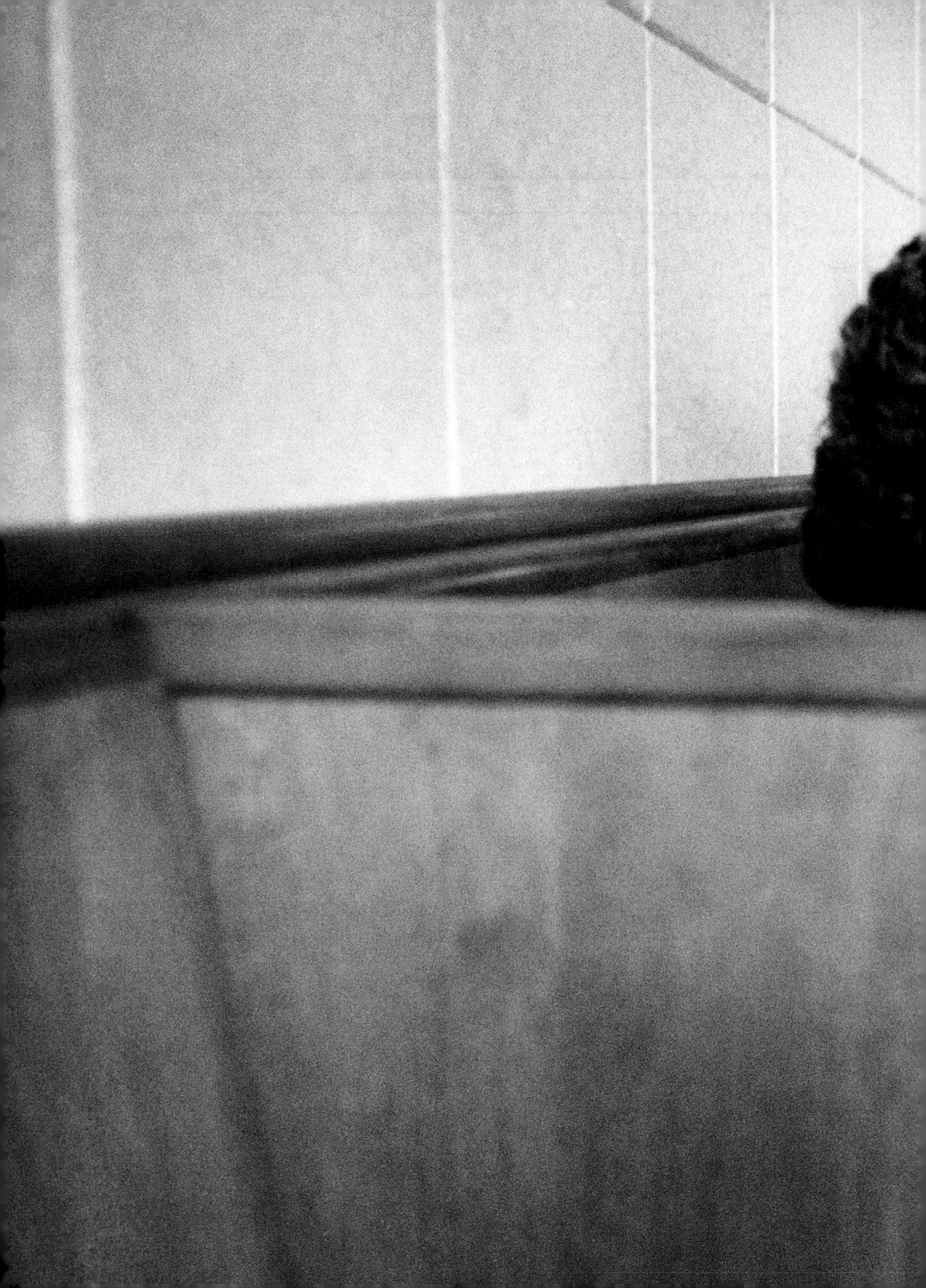

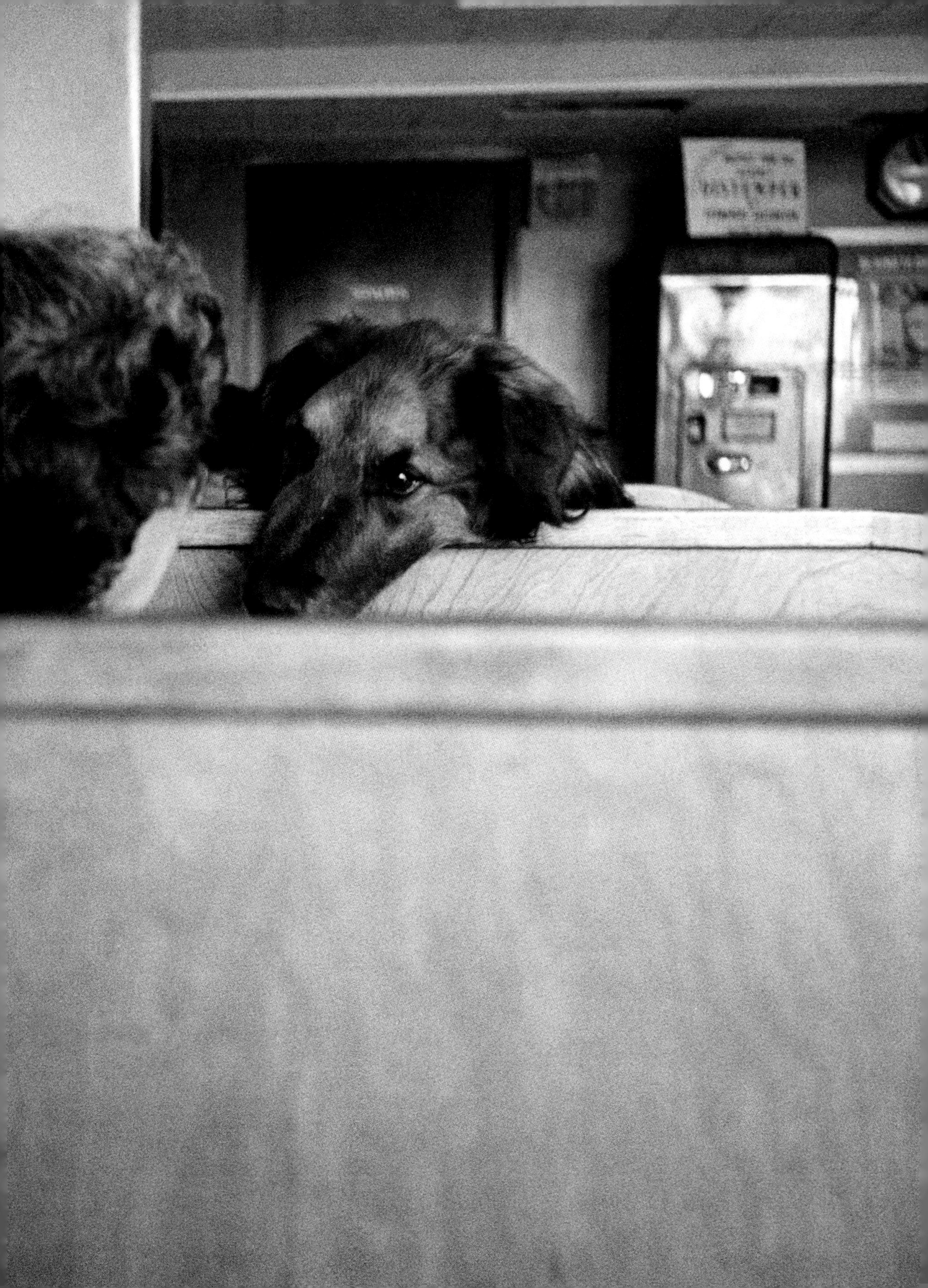

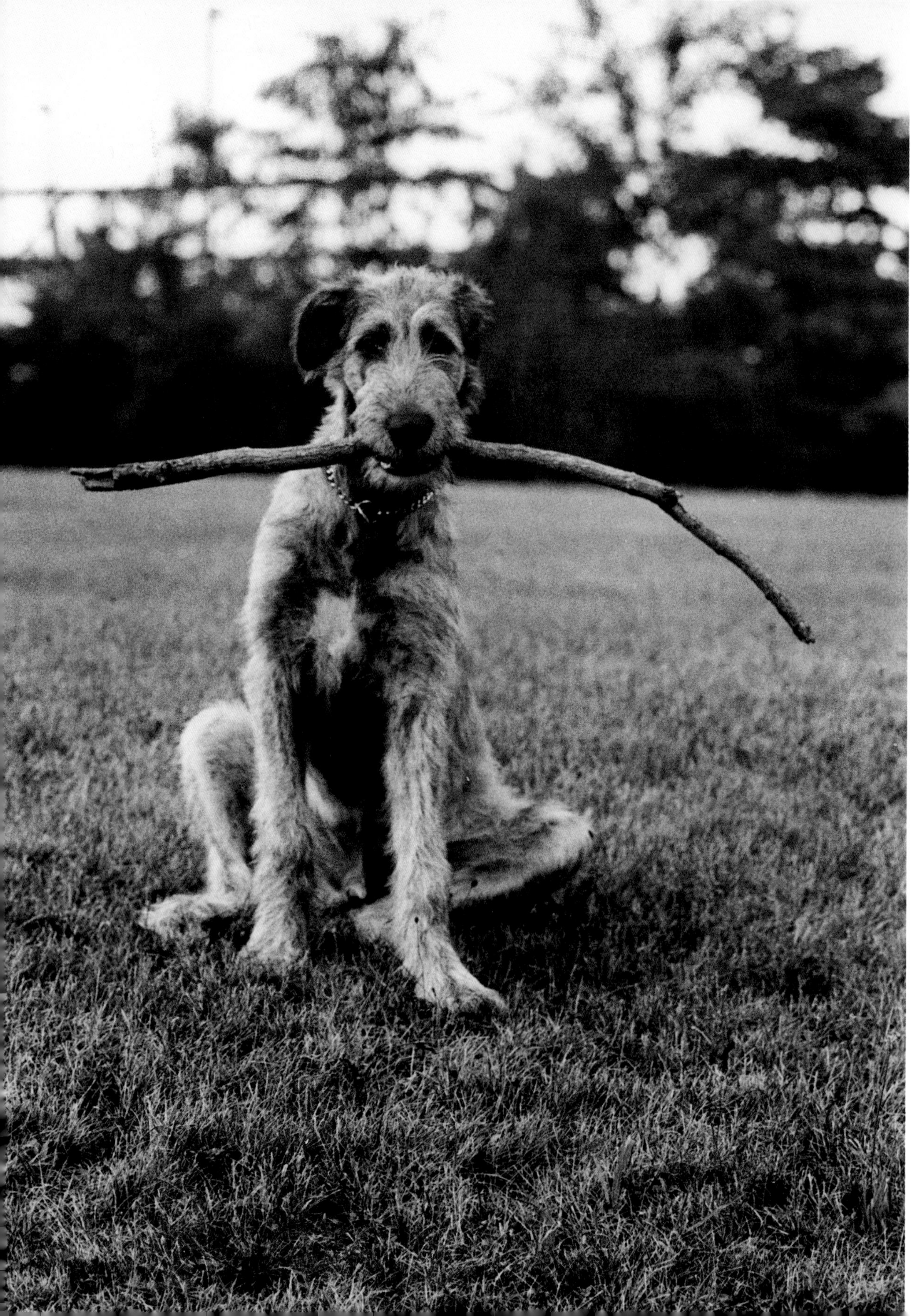

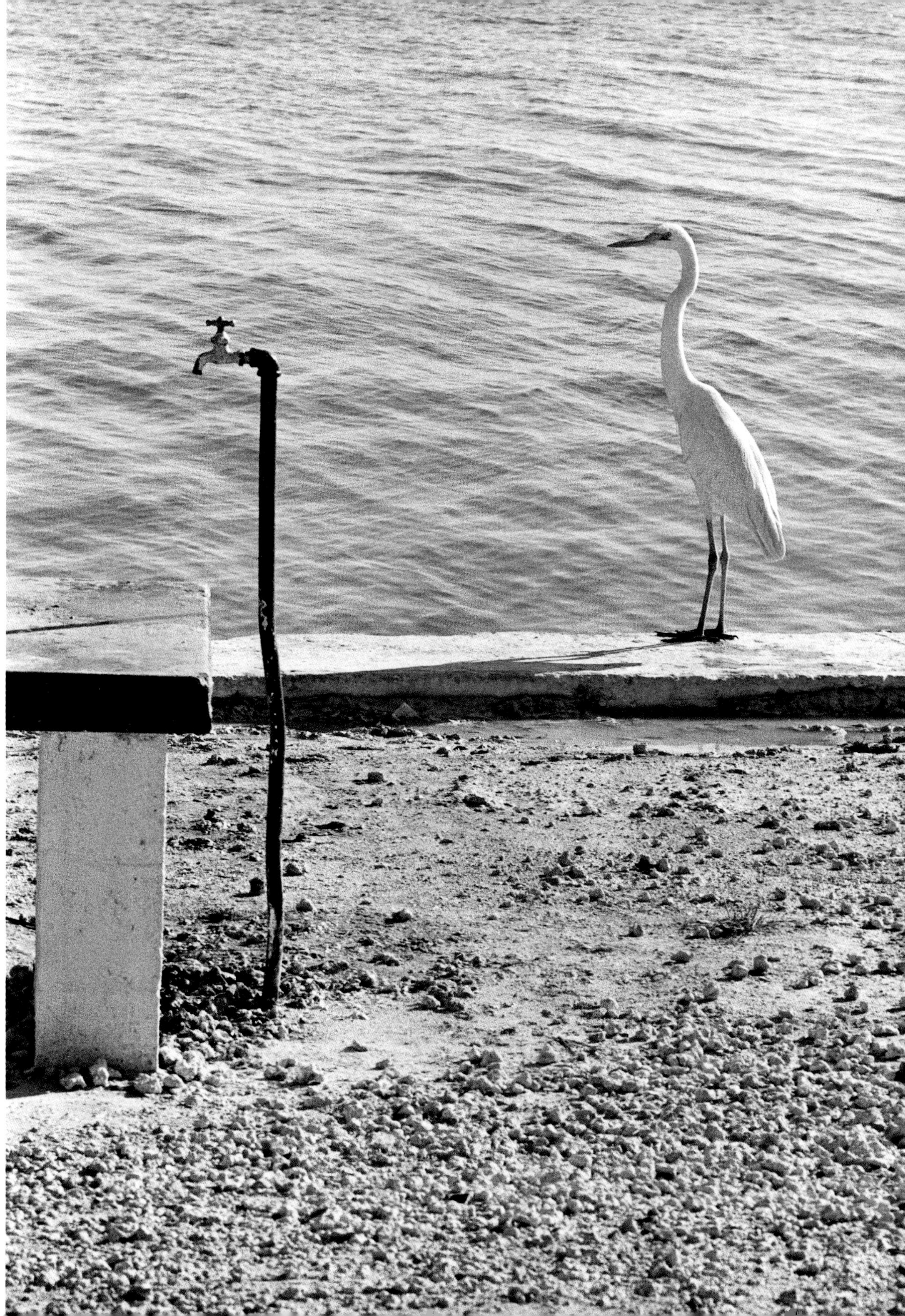

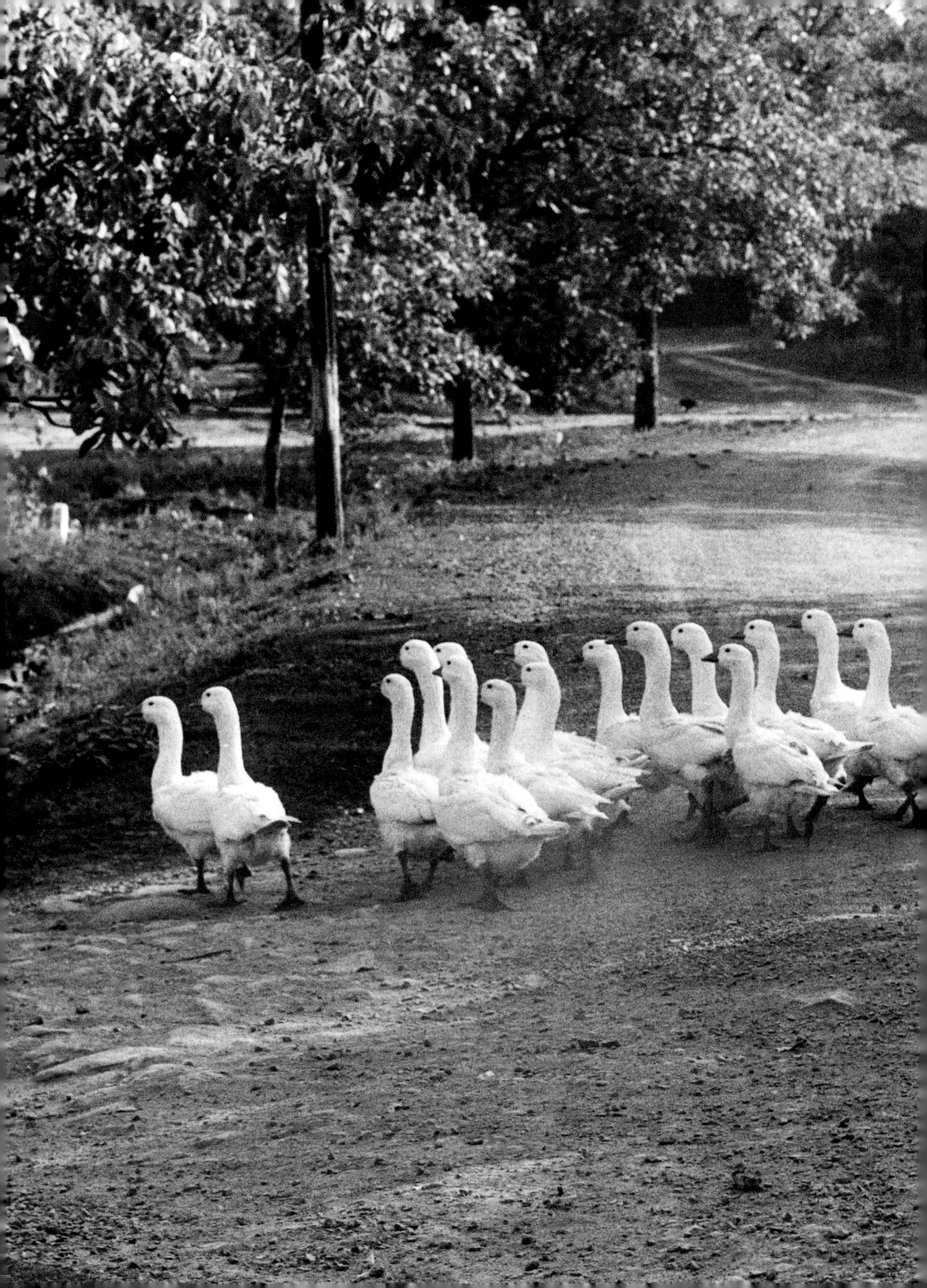

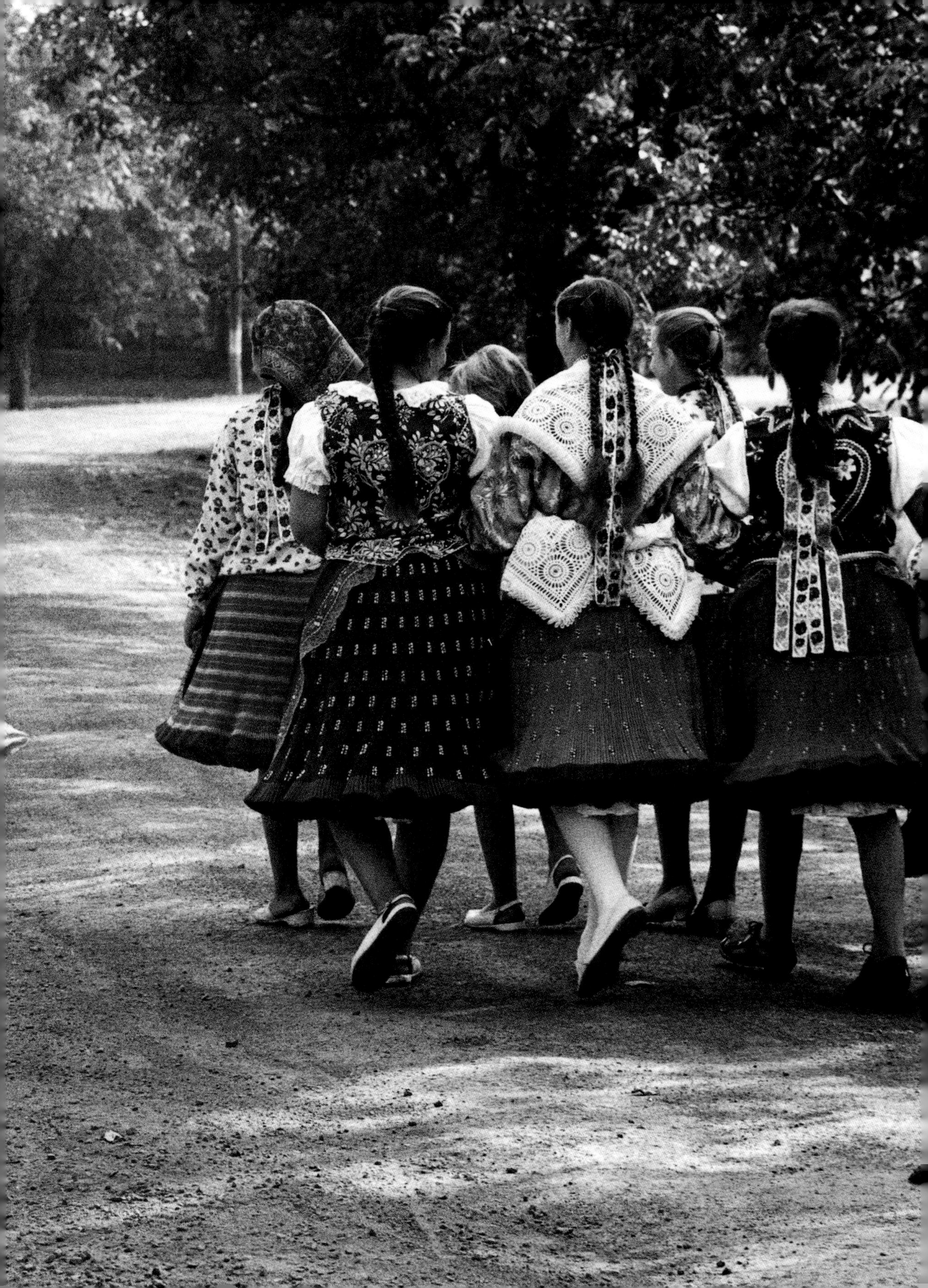

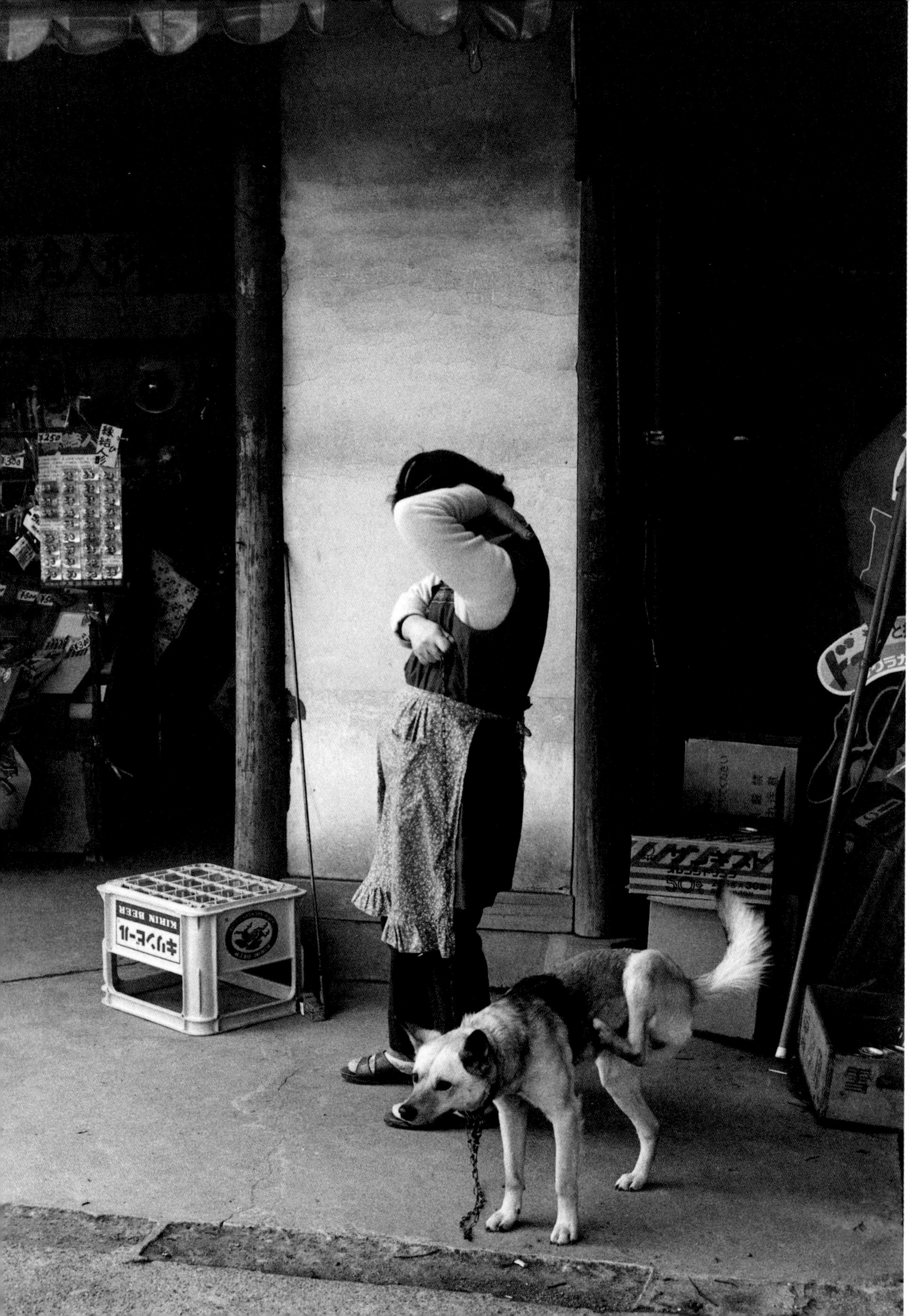

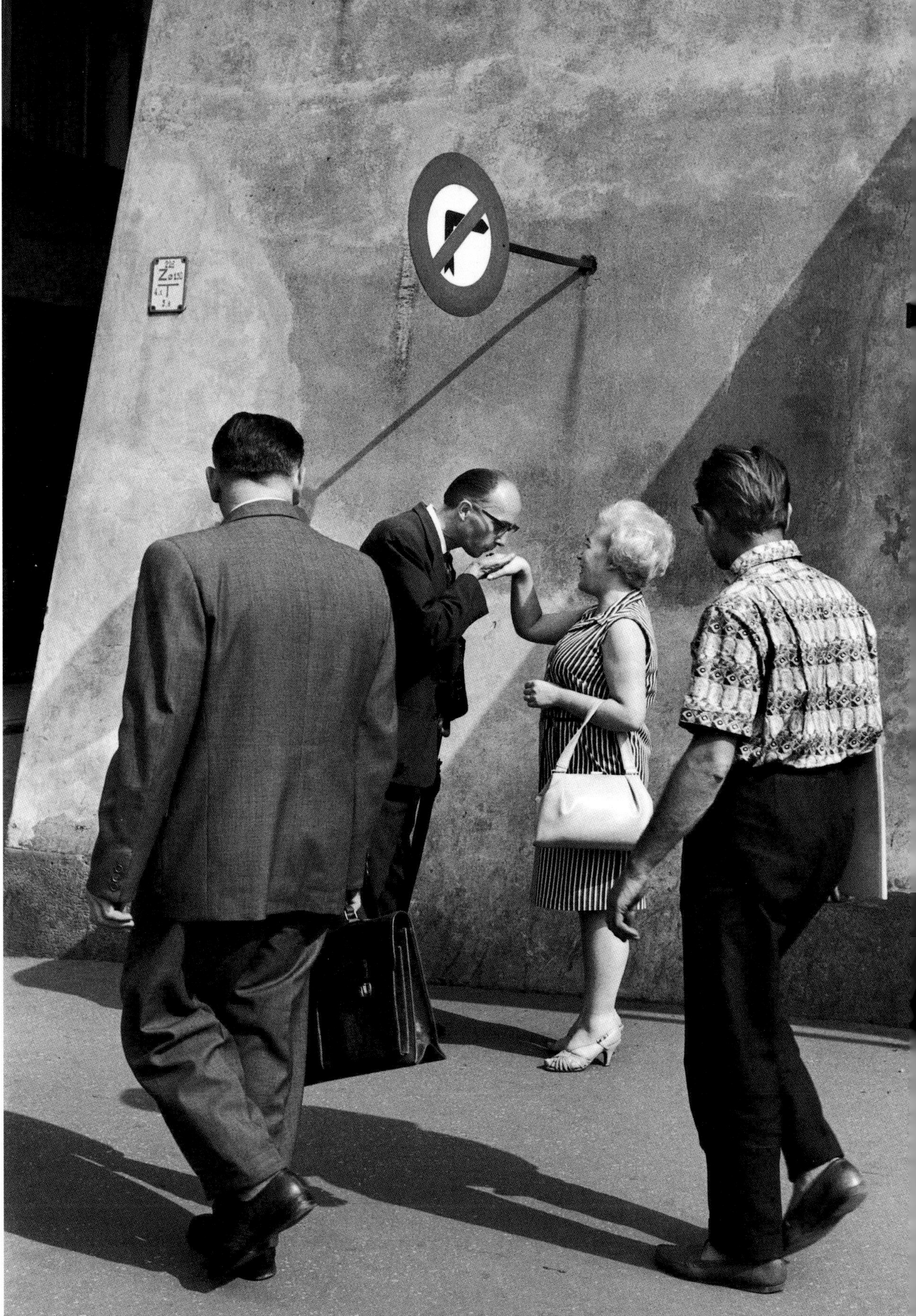

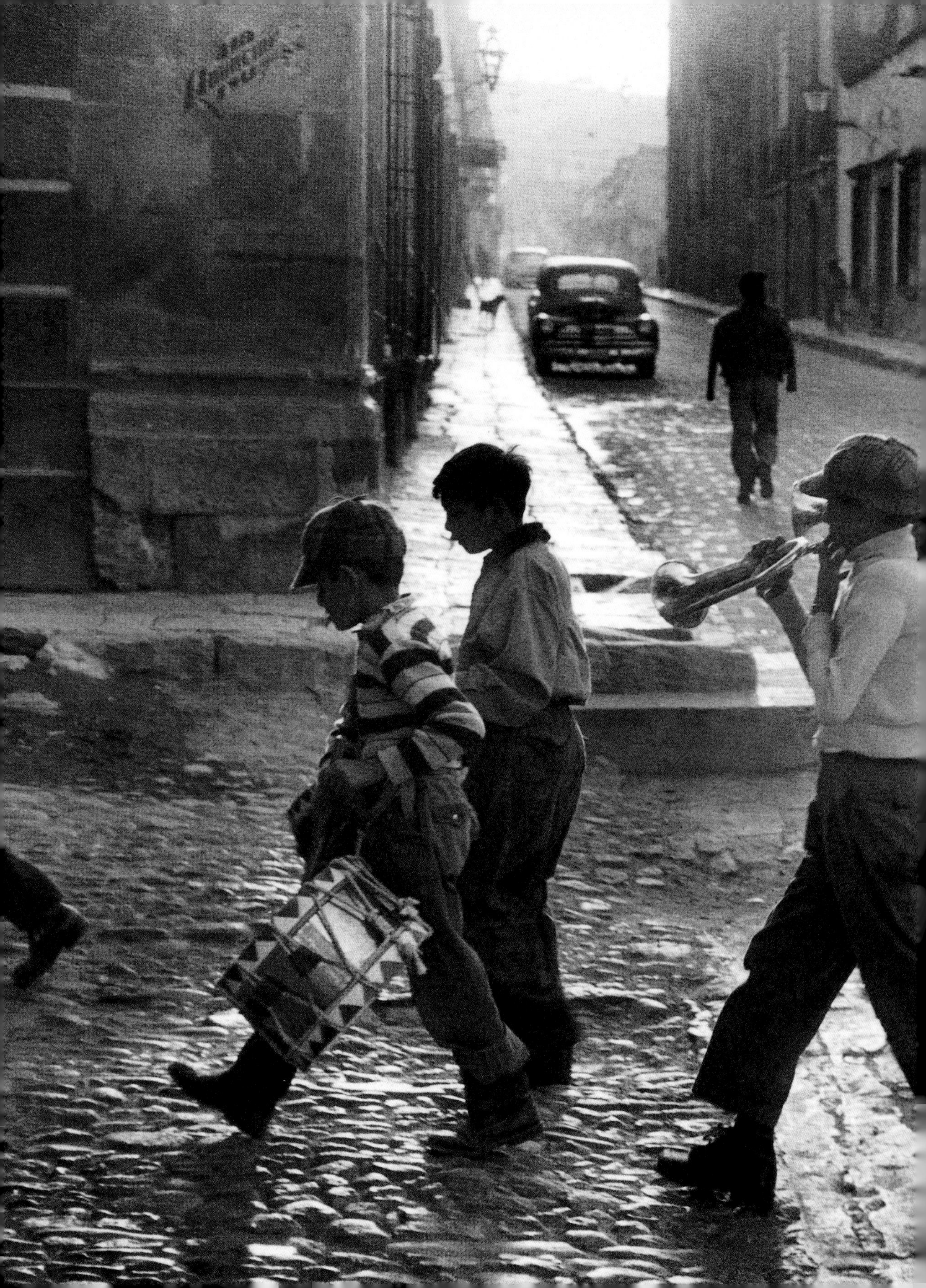

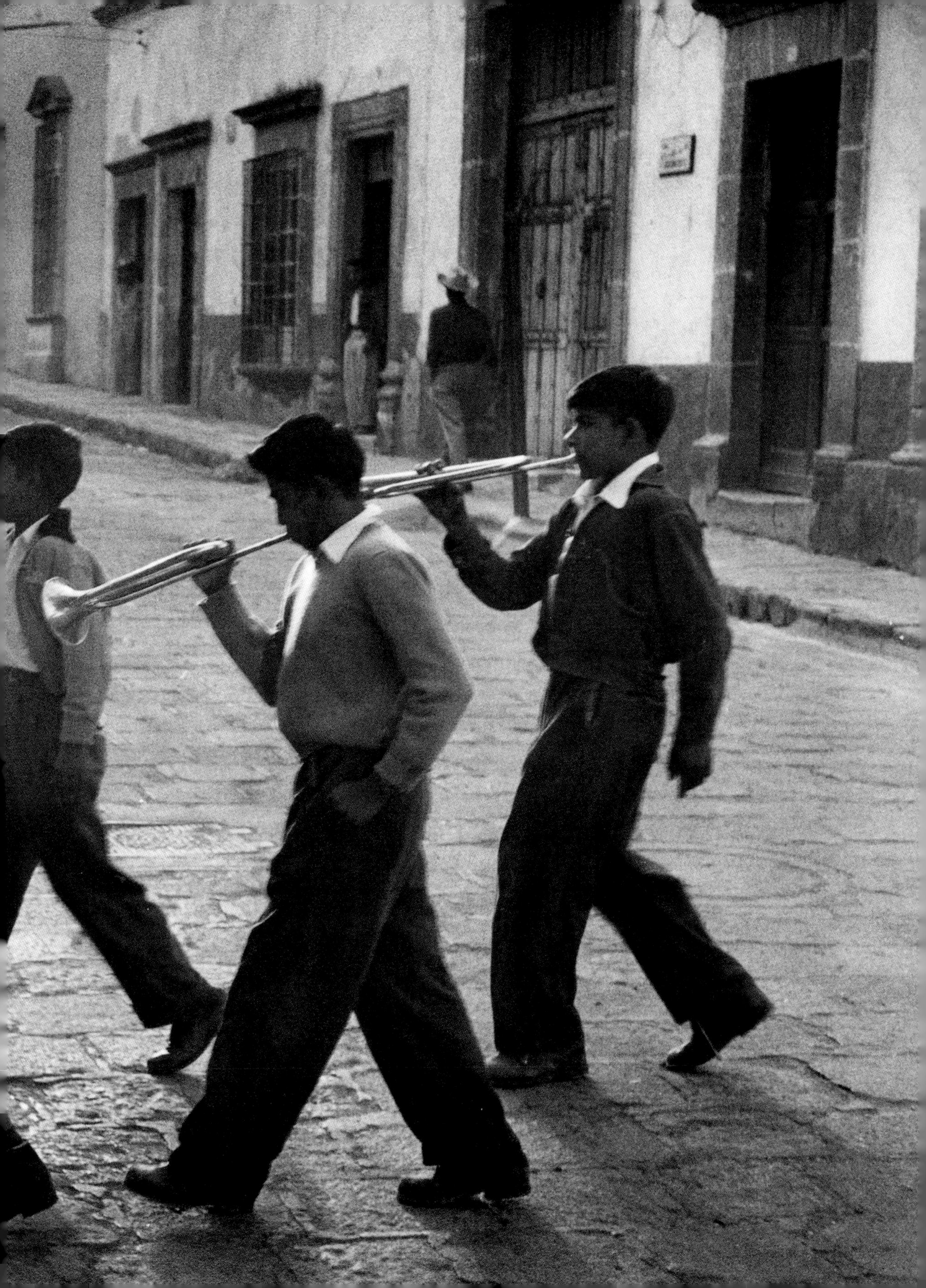

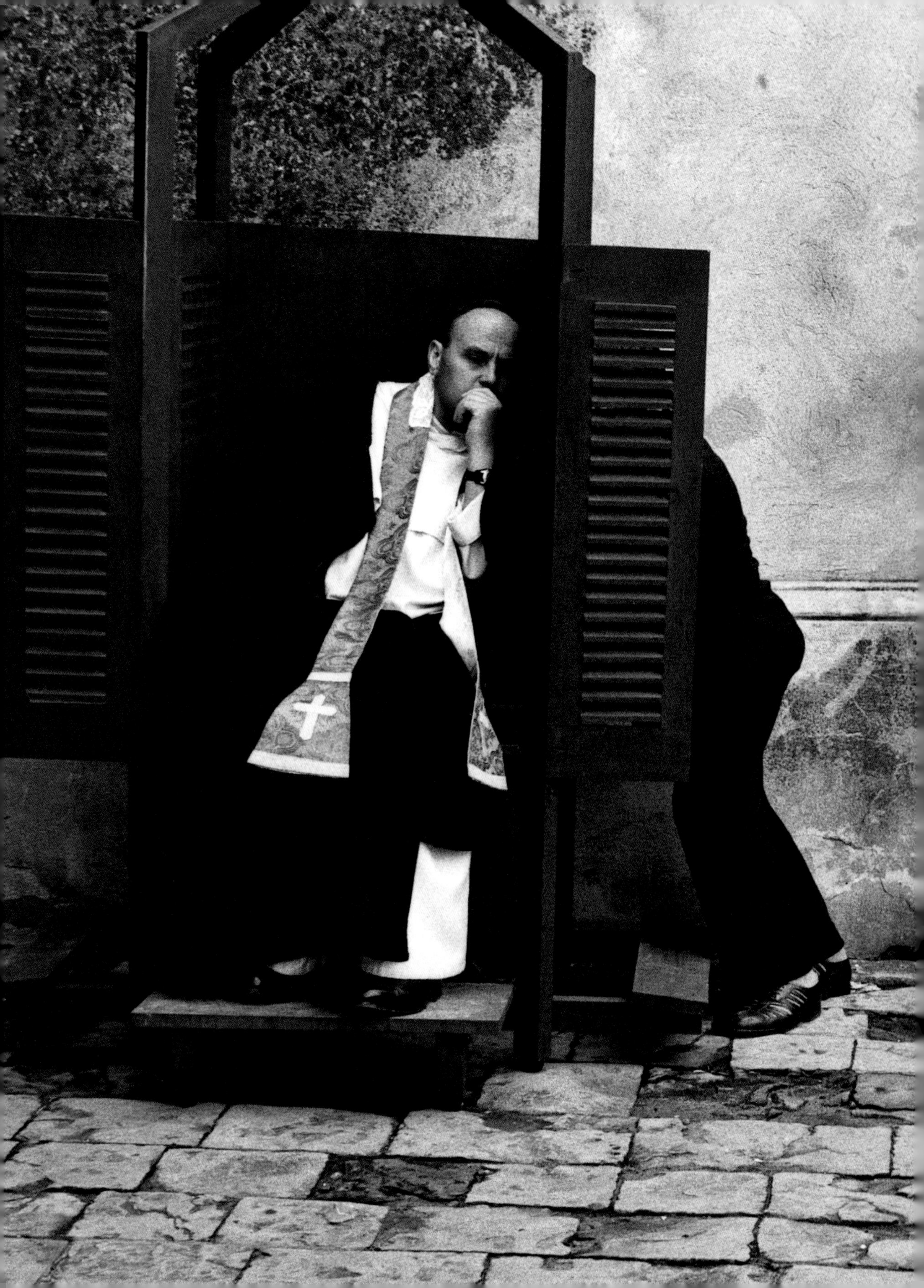

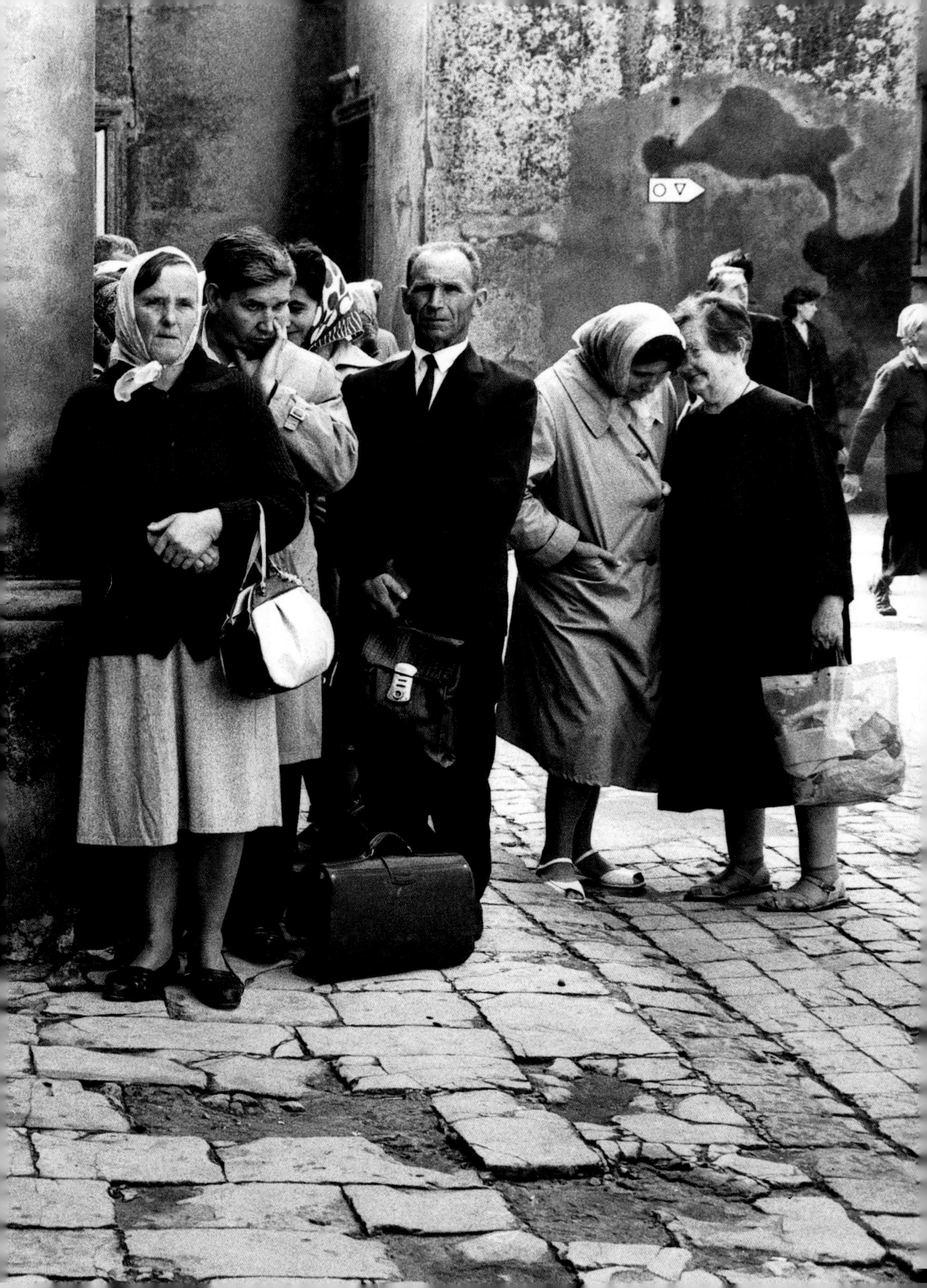

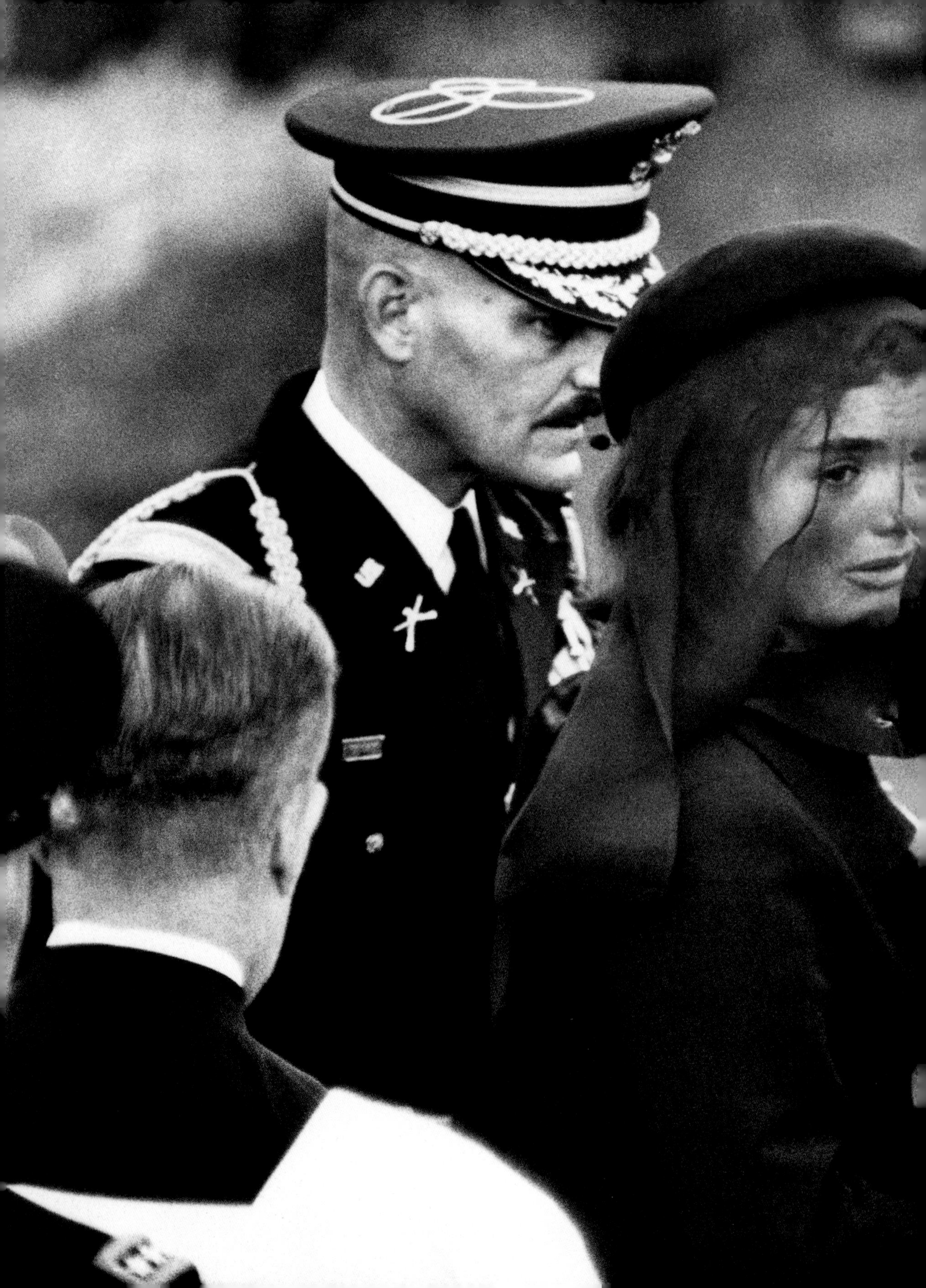

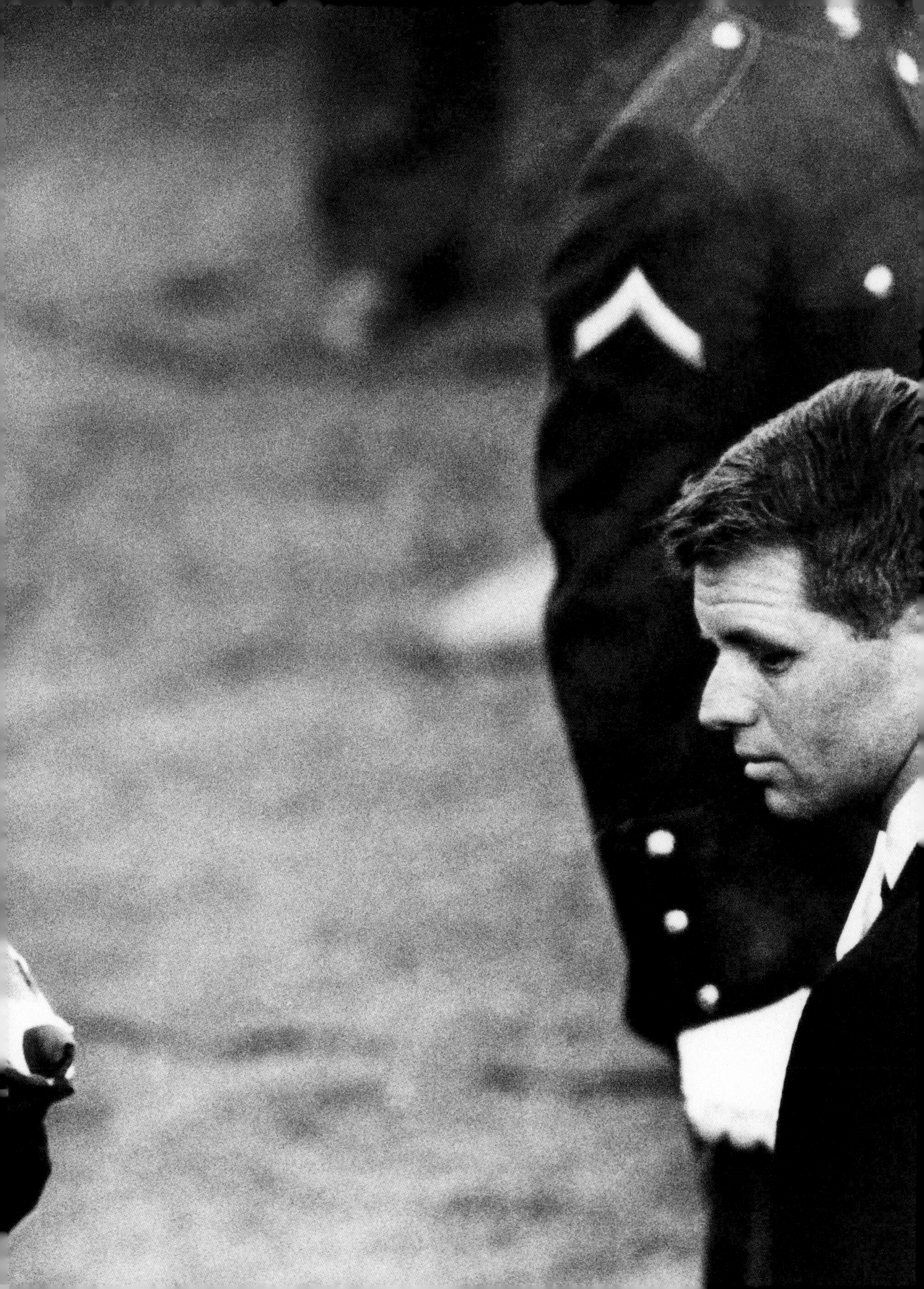

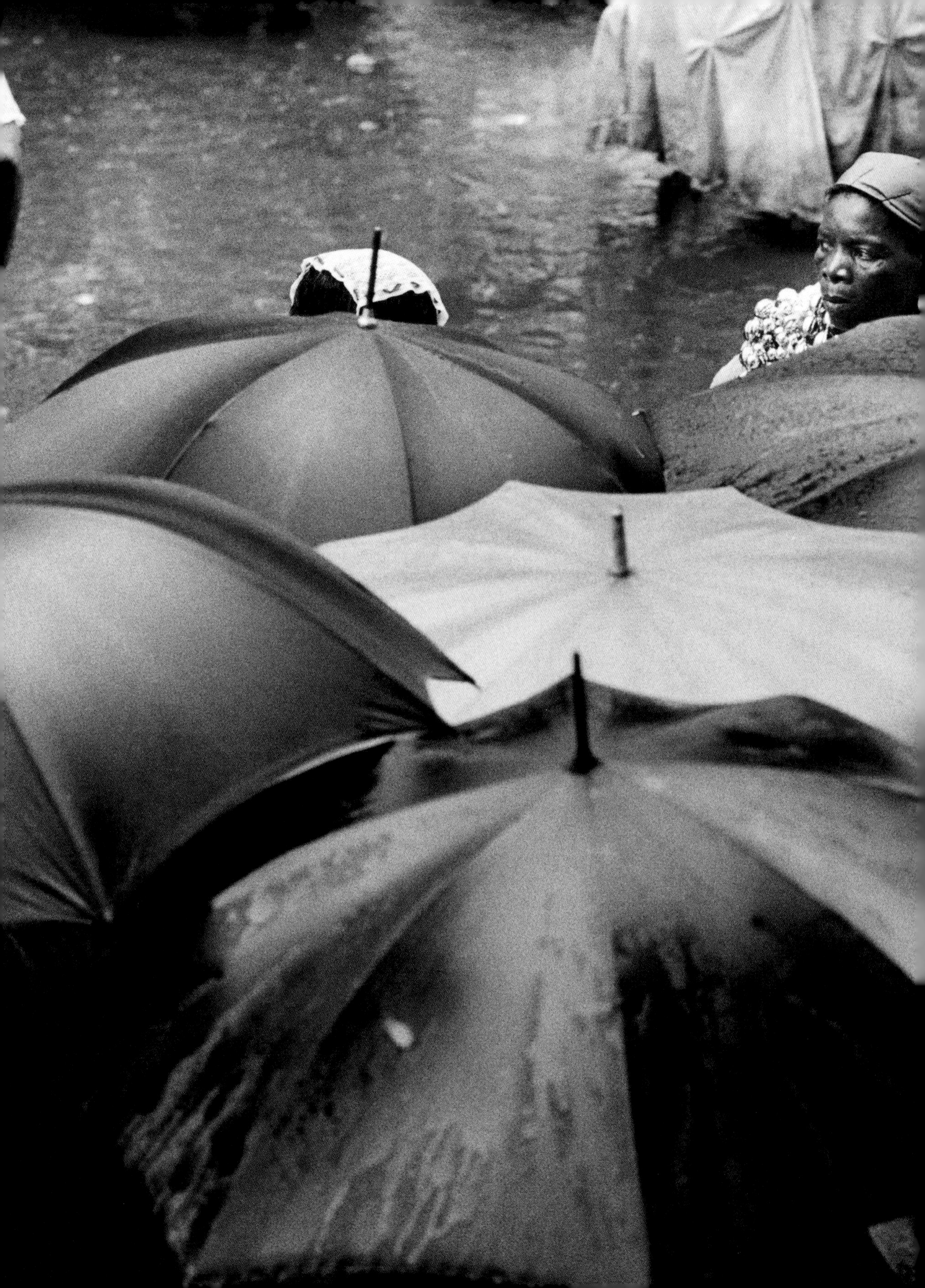

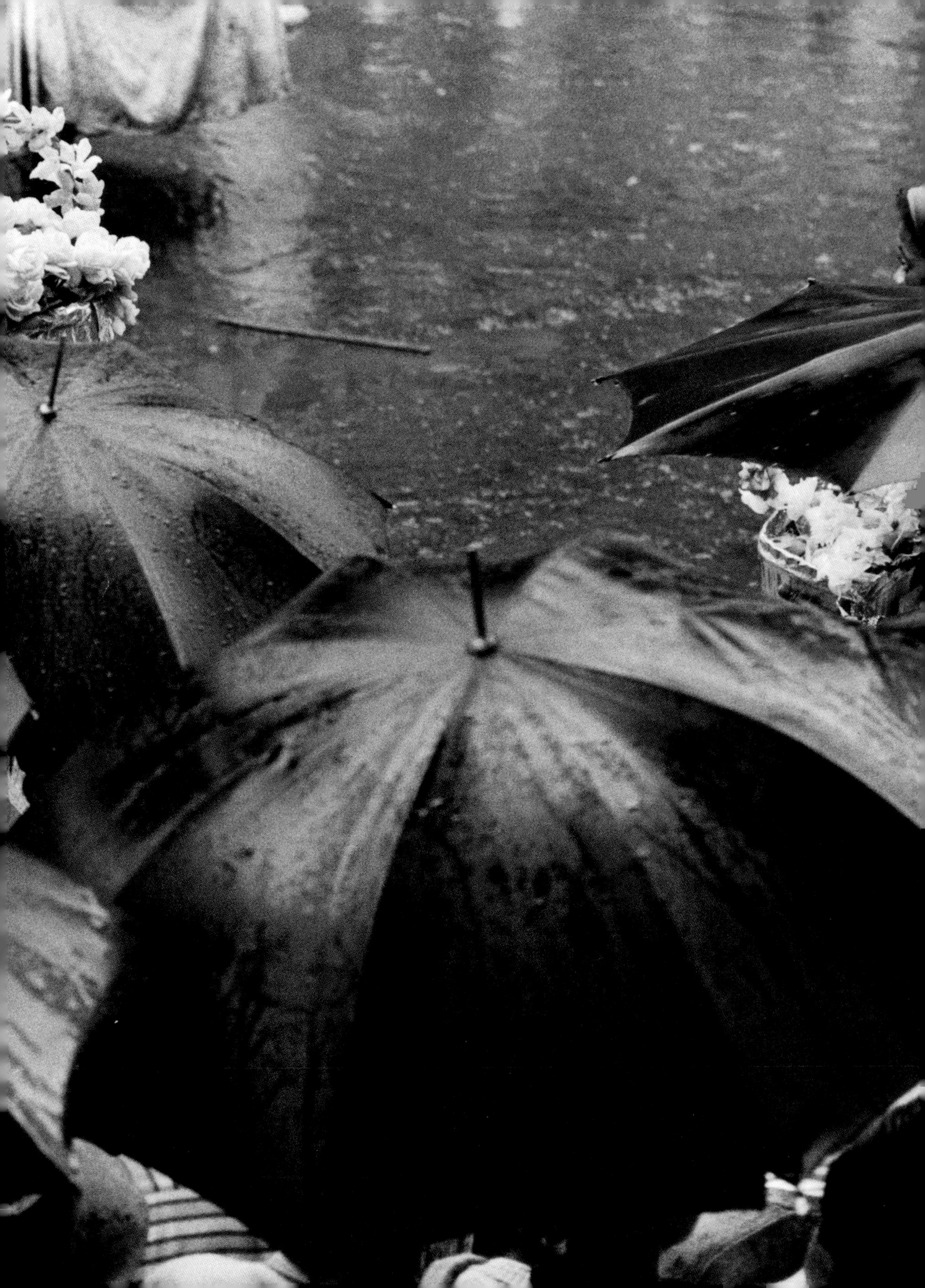

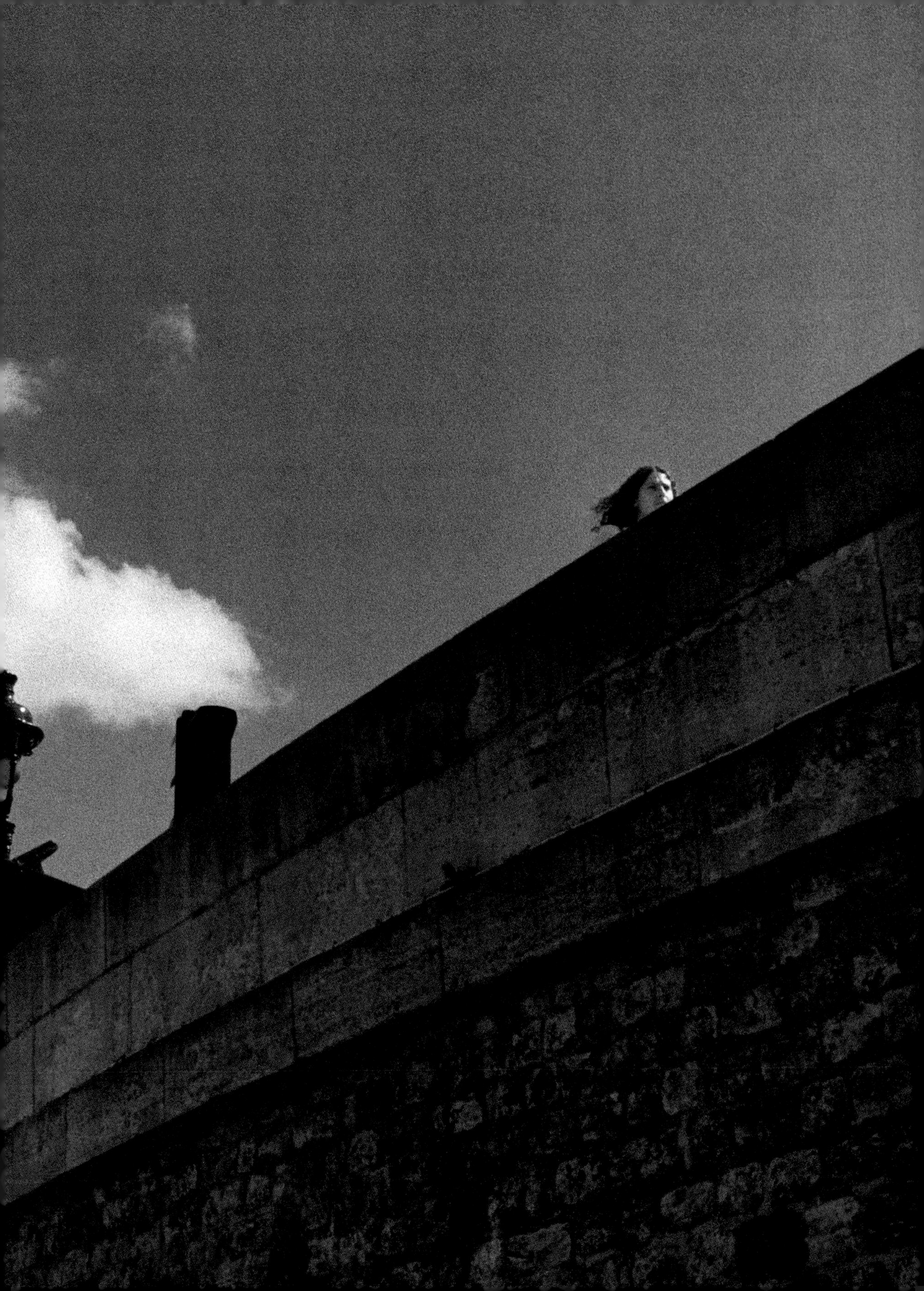

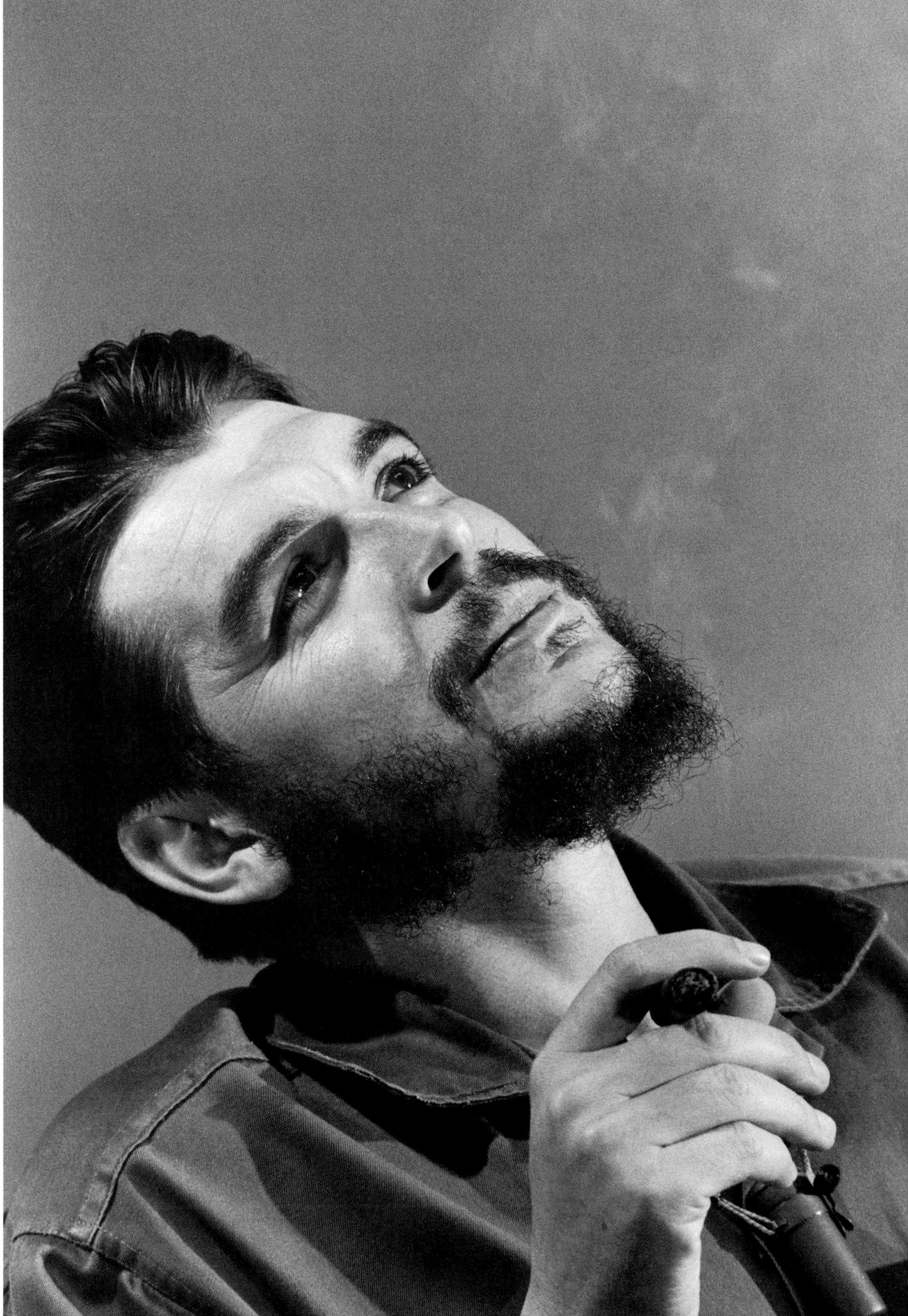

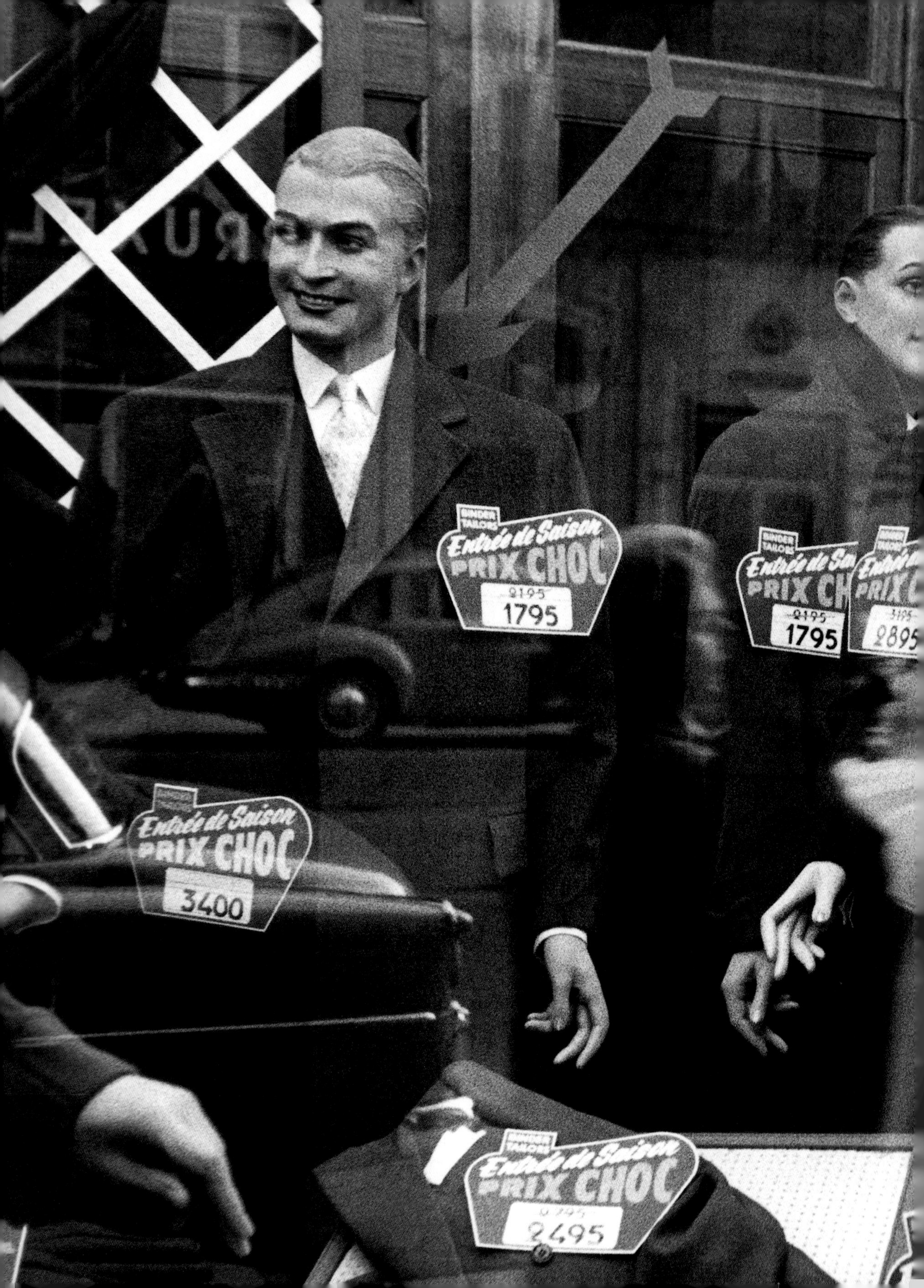
RUE
BINDER TAILORS
Entrée de Saison
PRIX CHOC
2195
1795
BINDER TAILORS
Entrée de Sai
PRIX CH
2195
1795
Entré
2195
2895
Entrée de Saison
PRIX CHOC
3400
BINDER TAILORS
Entrée de Saison
PRIX CHOC
2795
2495

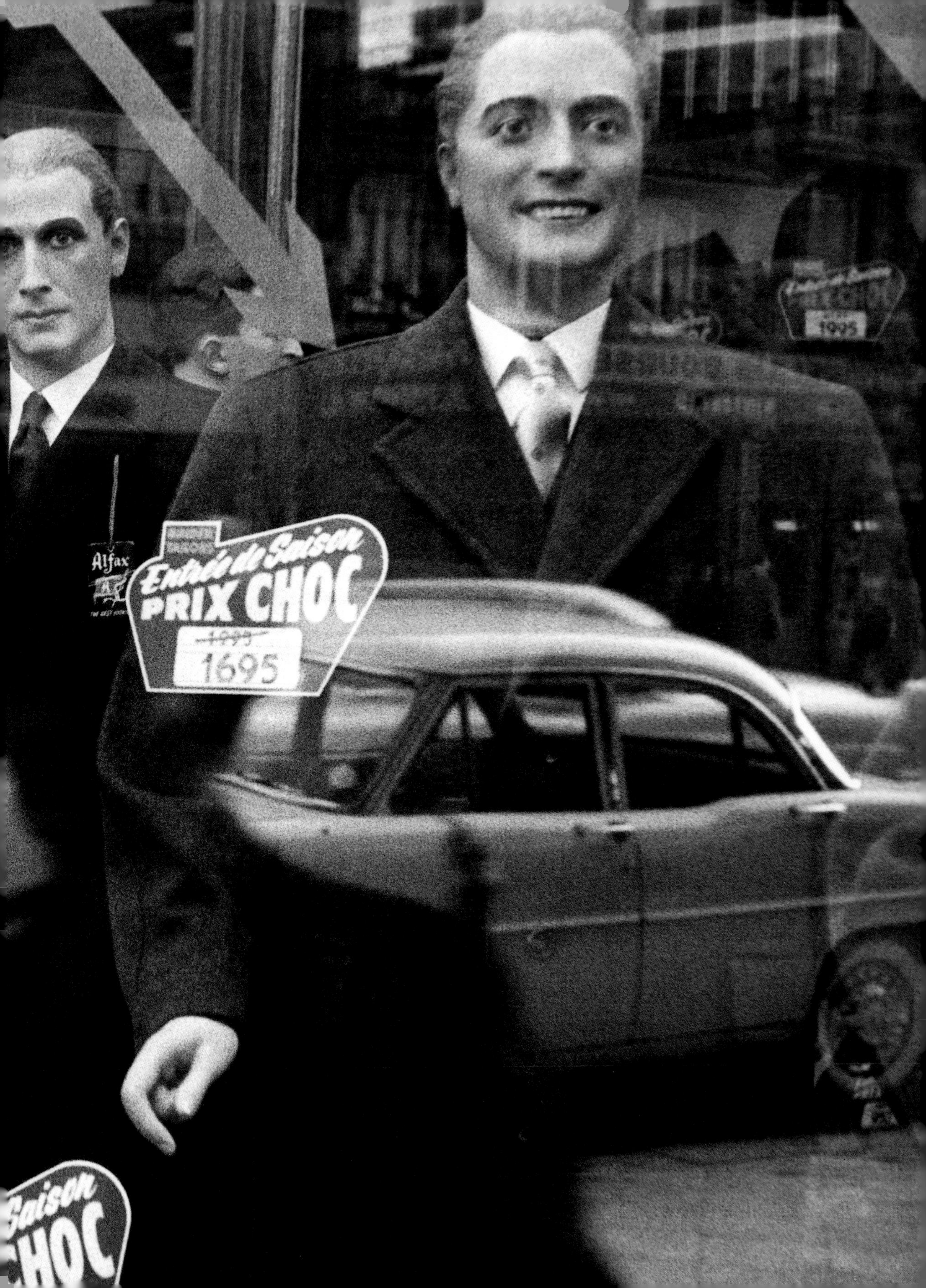
Alfax
Entrée de Saison
PRIX CHOC
1695
Entrée de Saison
PRIX CHOC
1995
Saison
CHOC

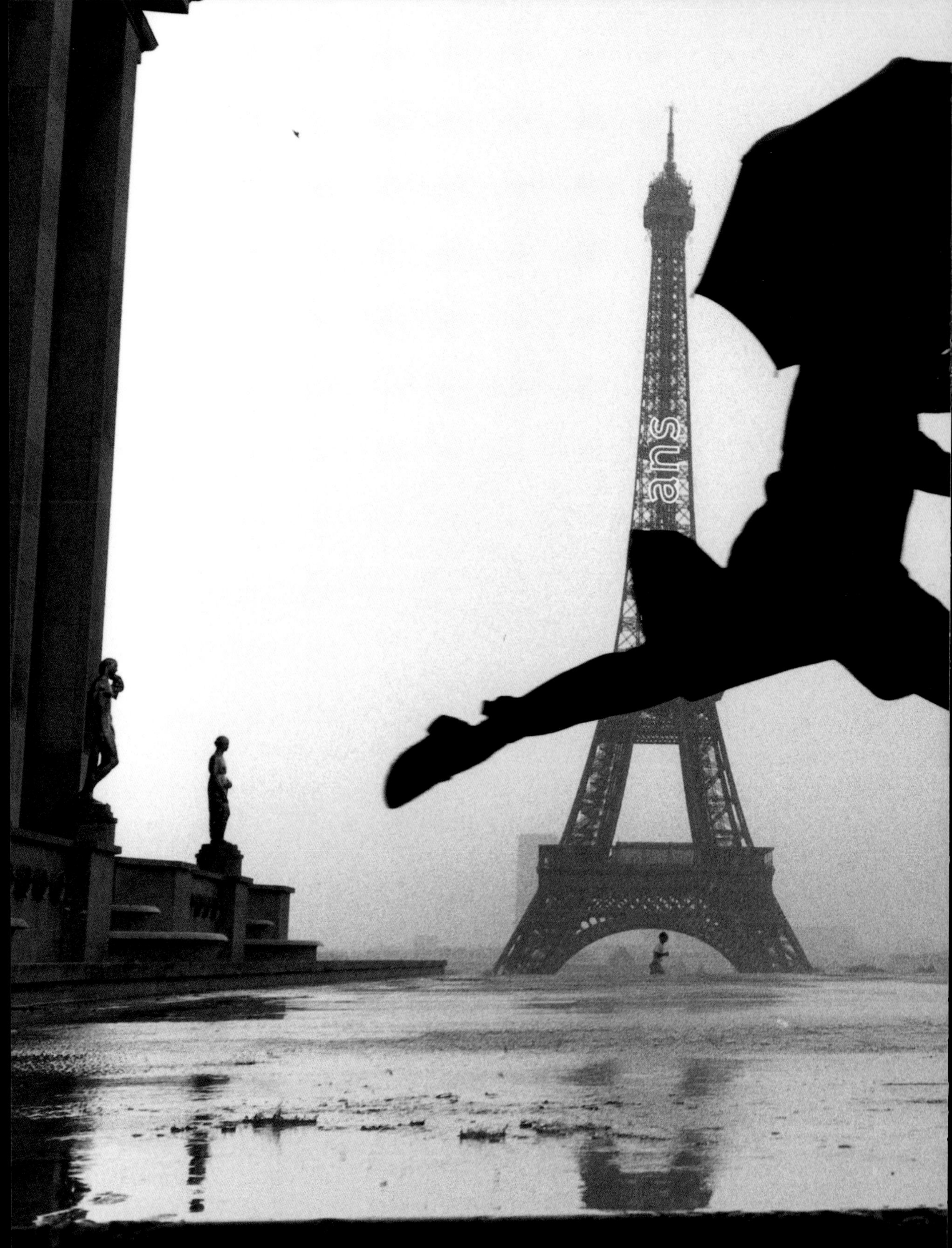
sans

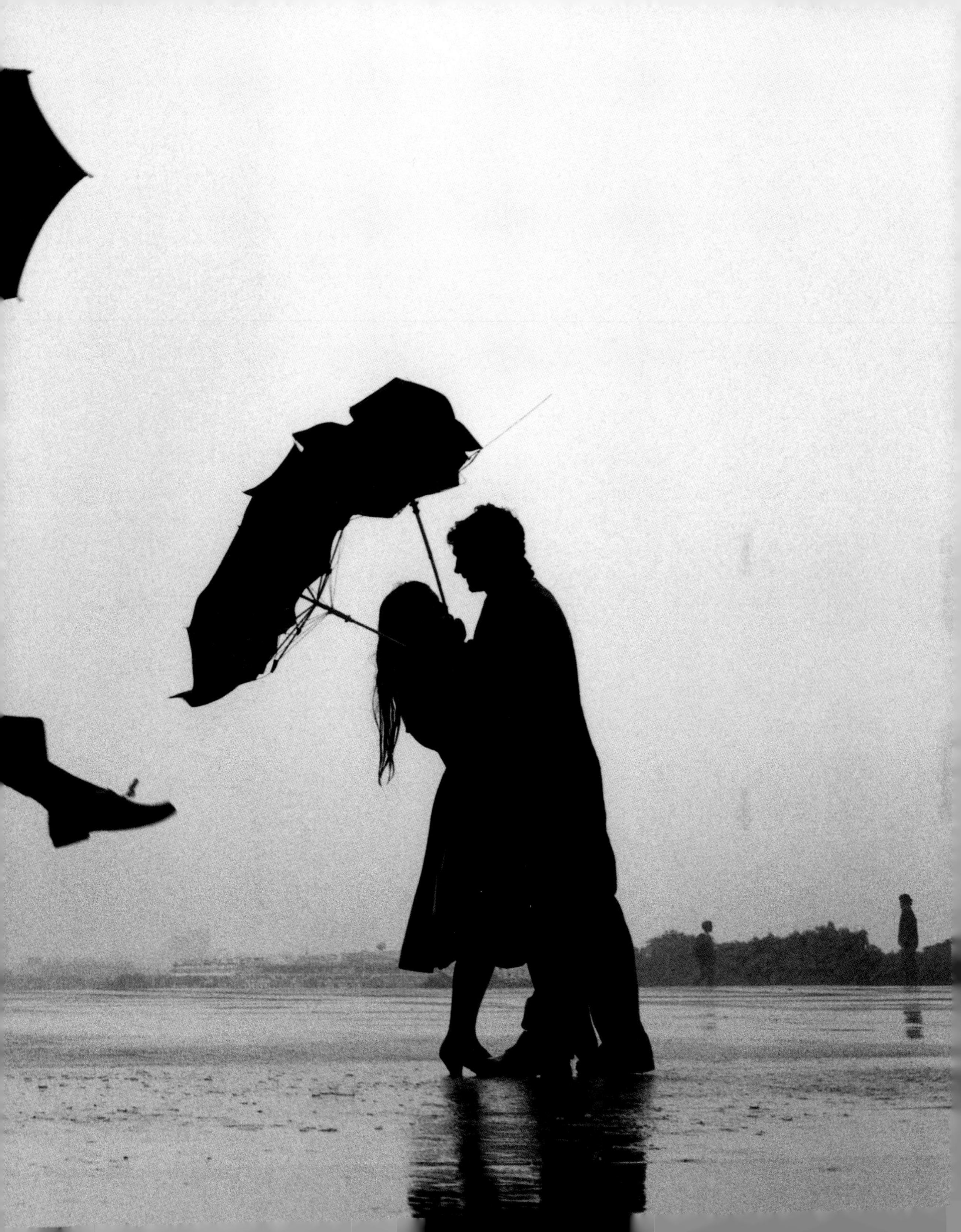

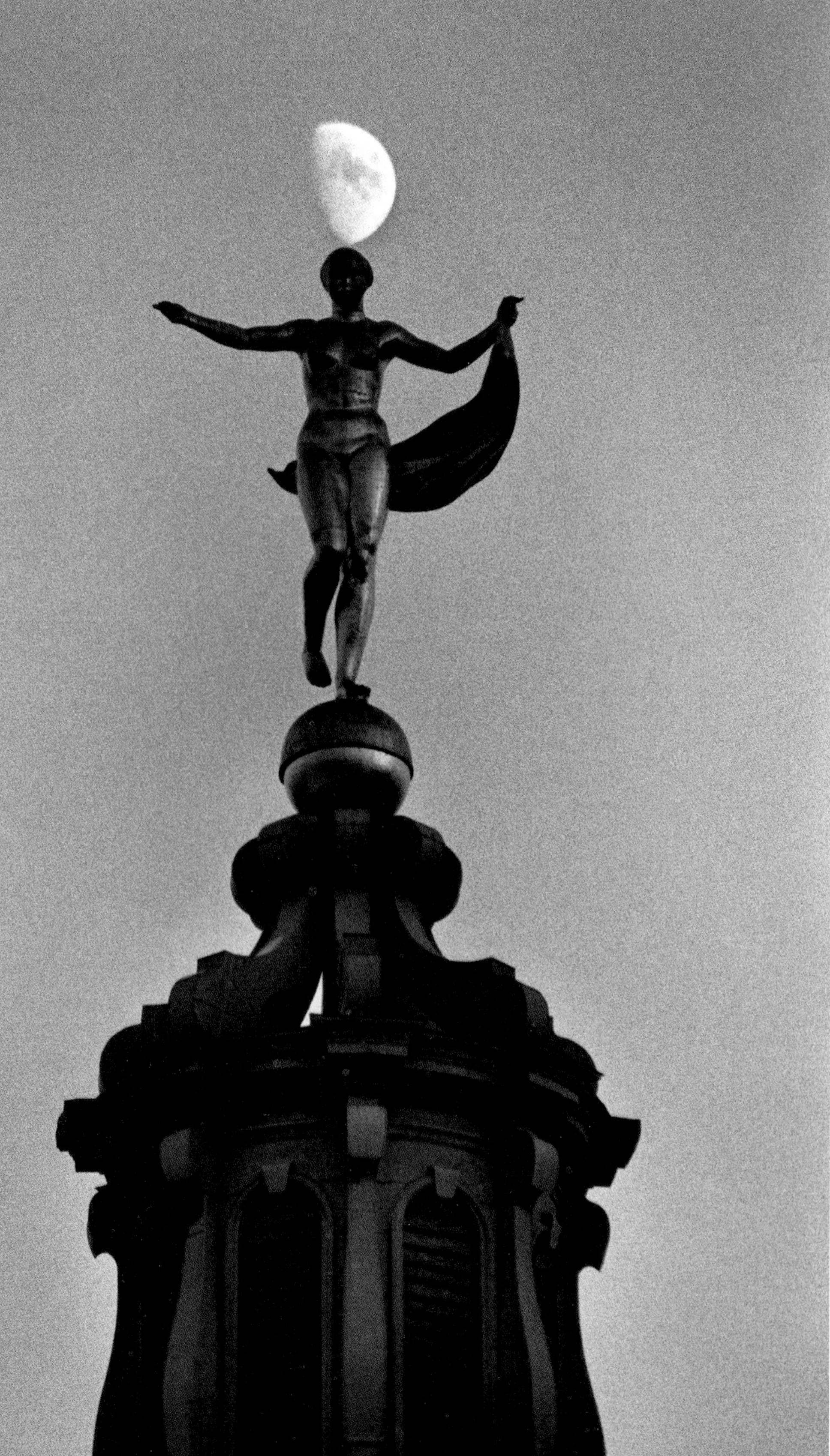

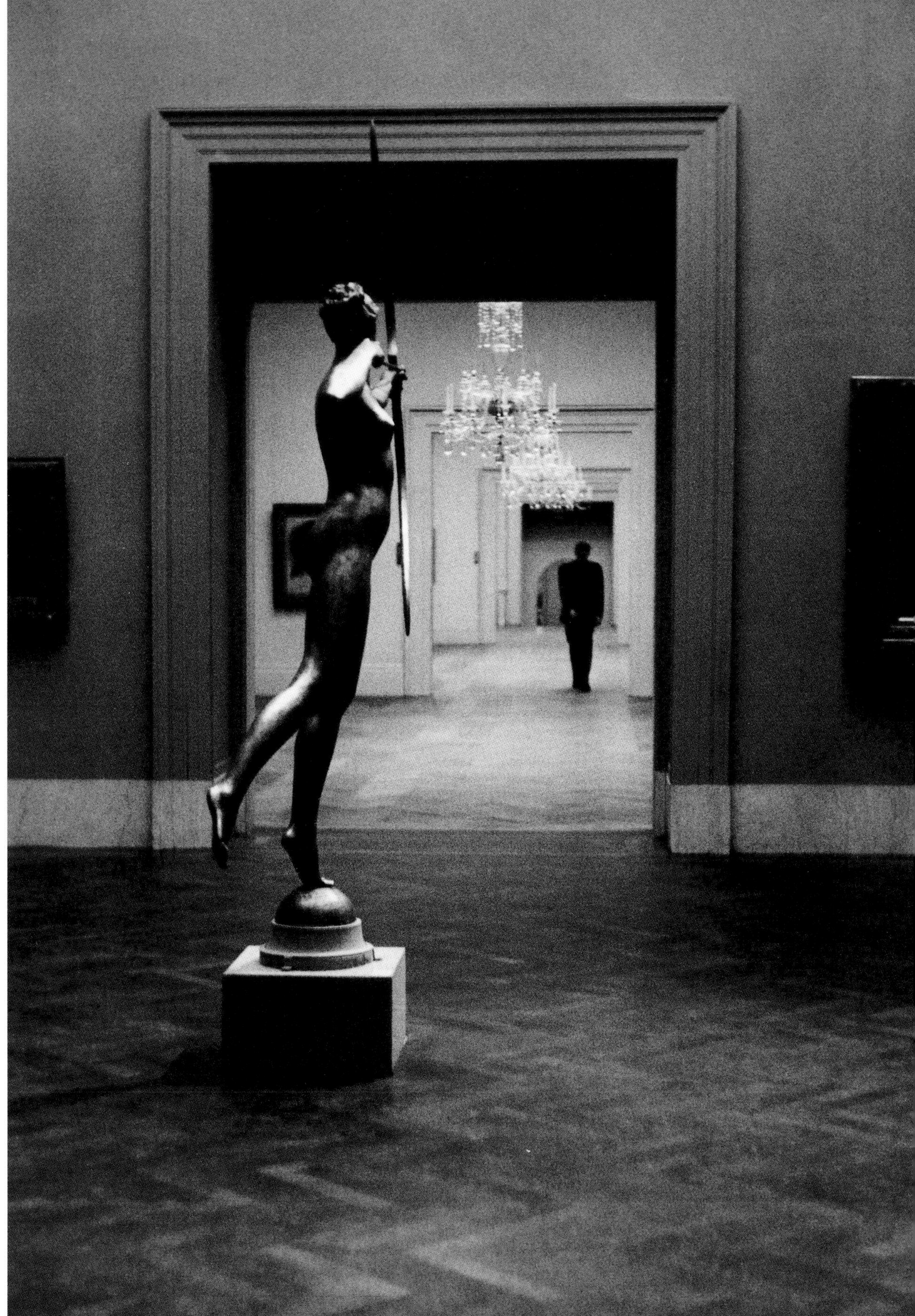

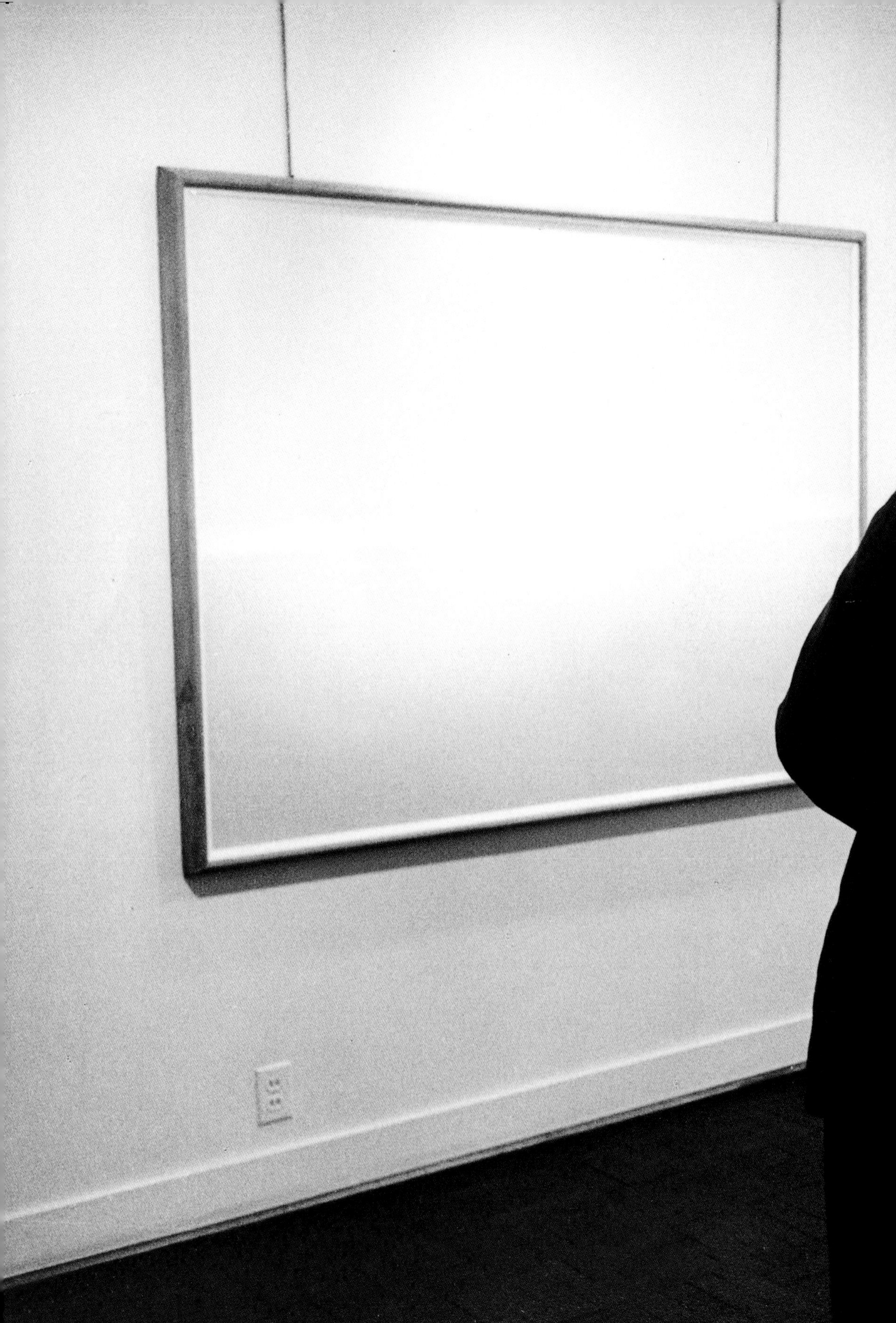

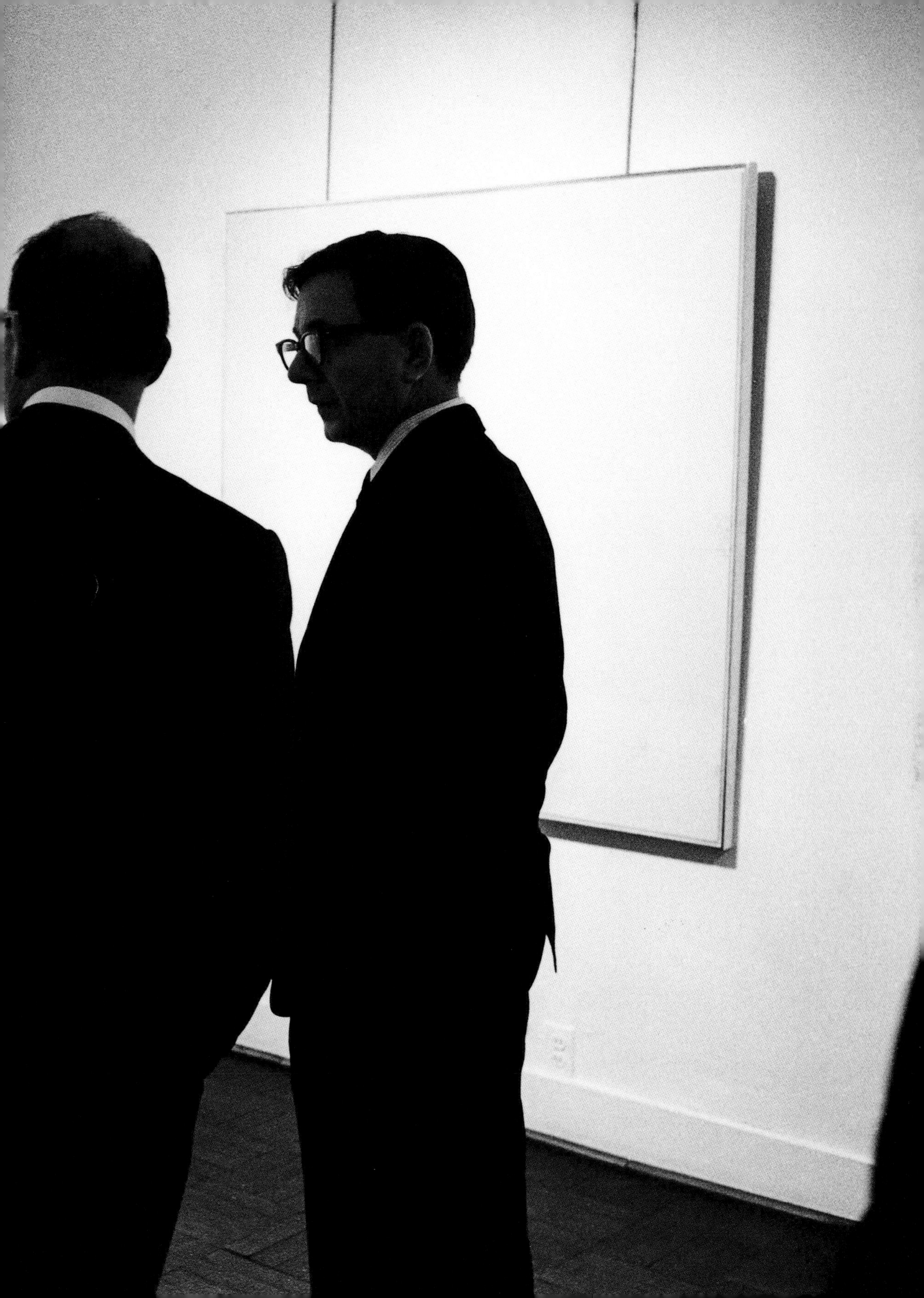

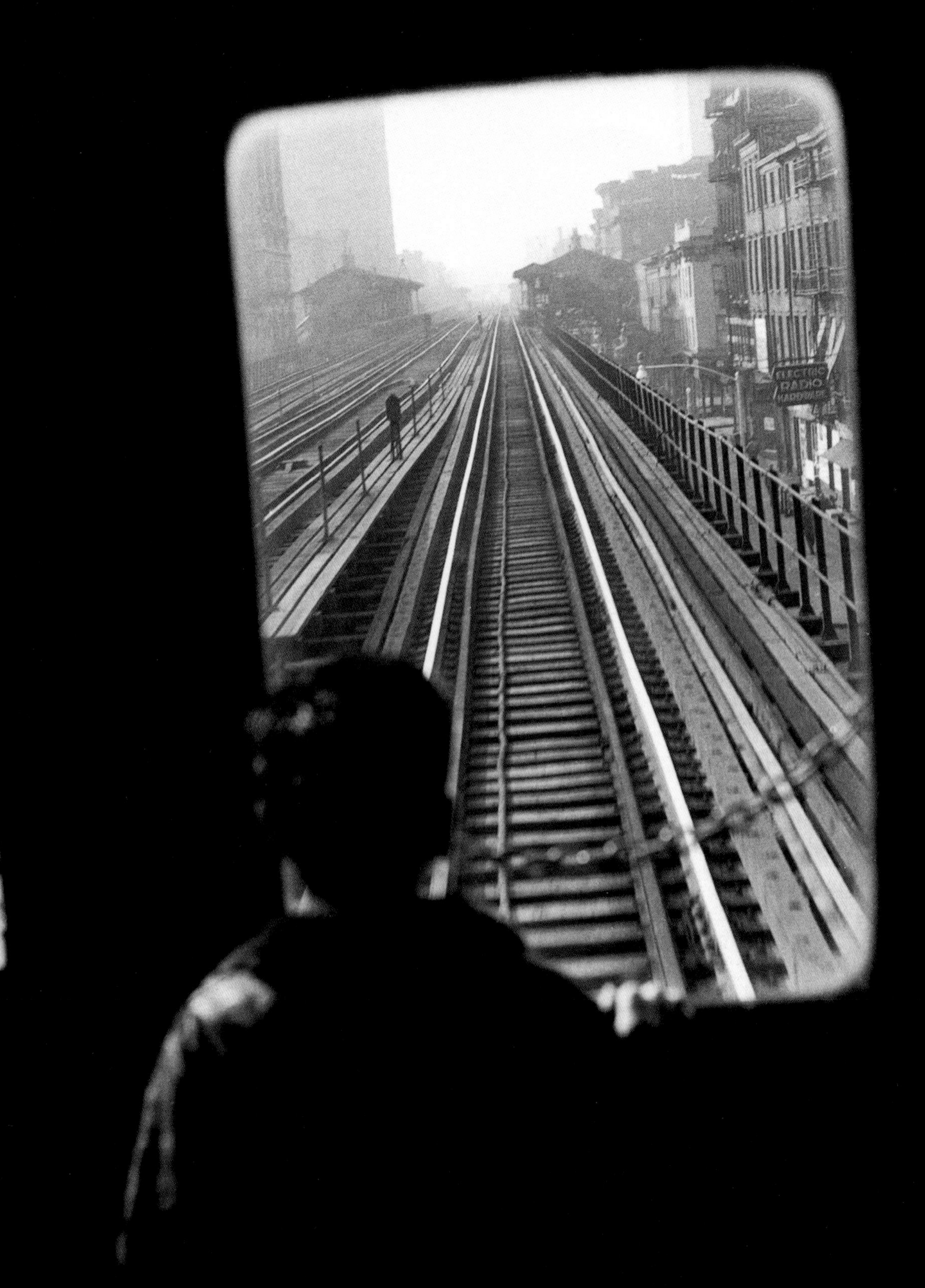

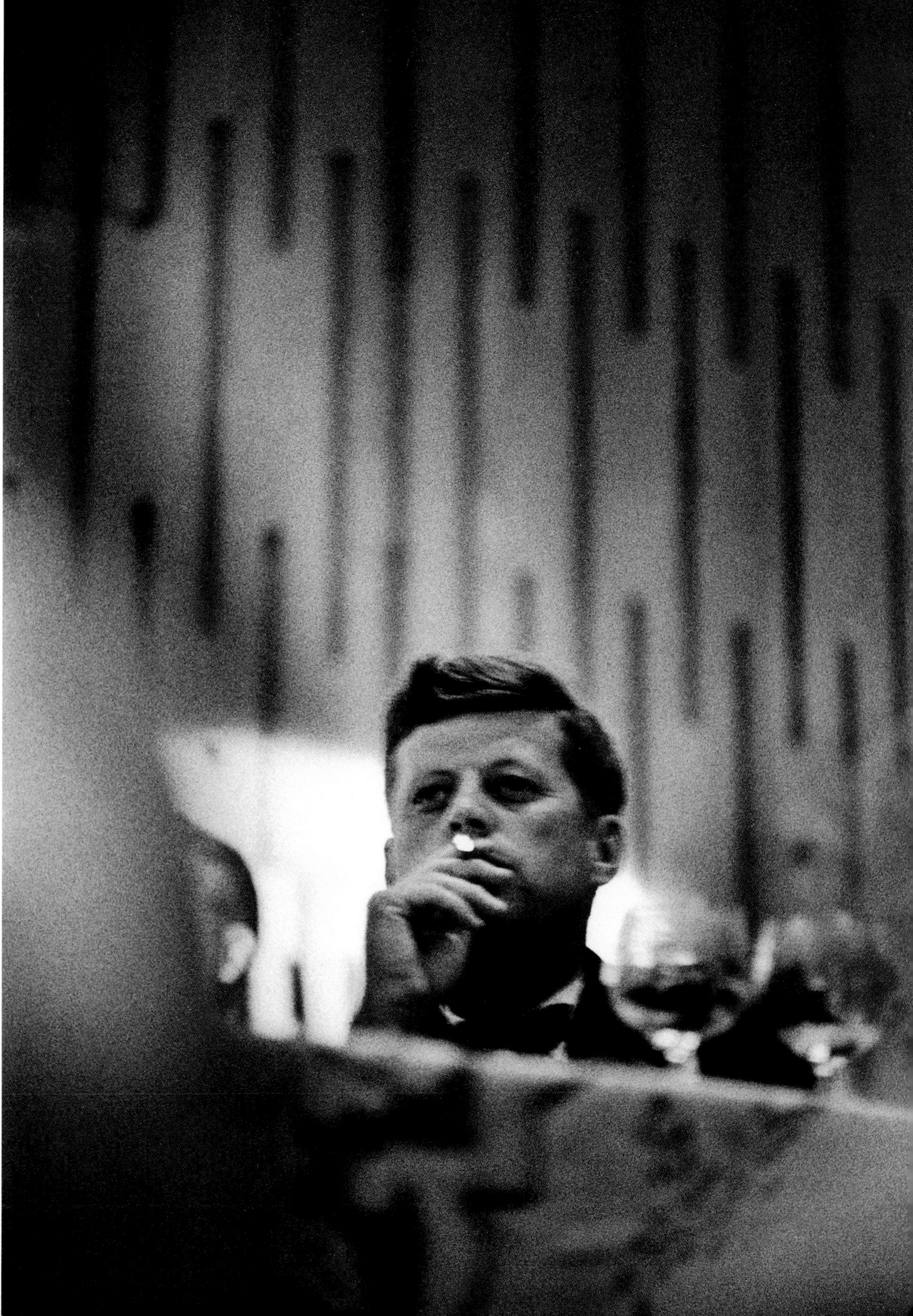

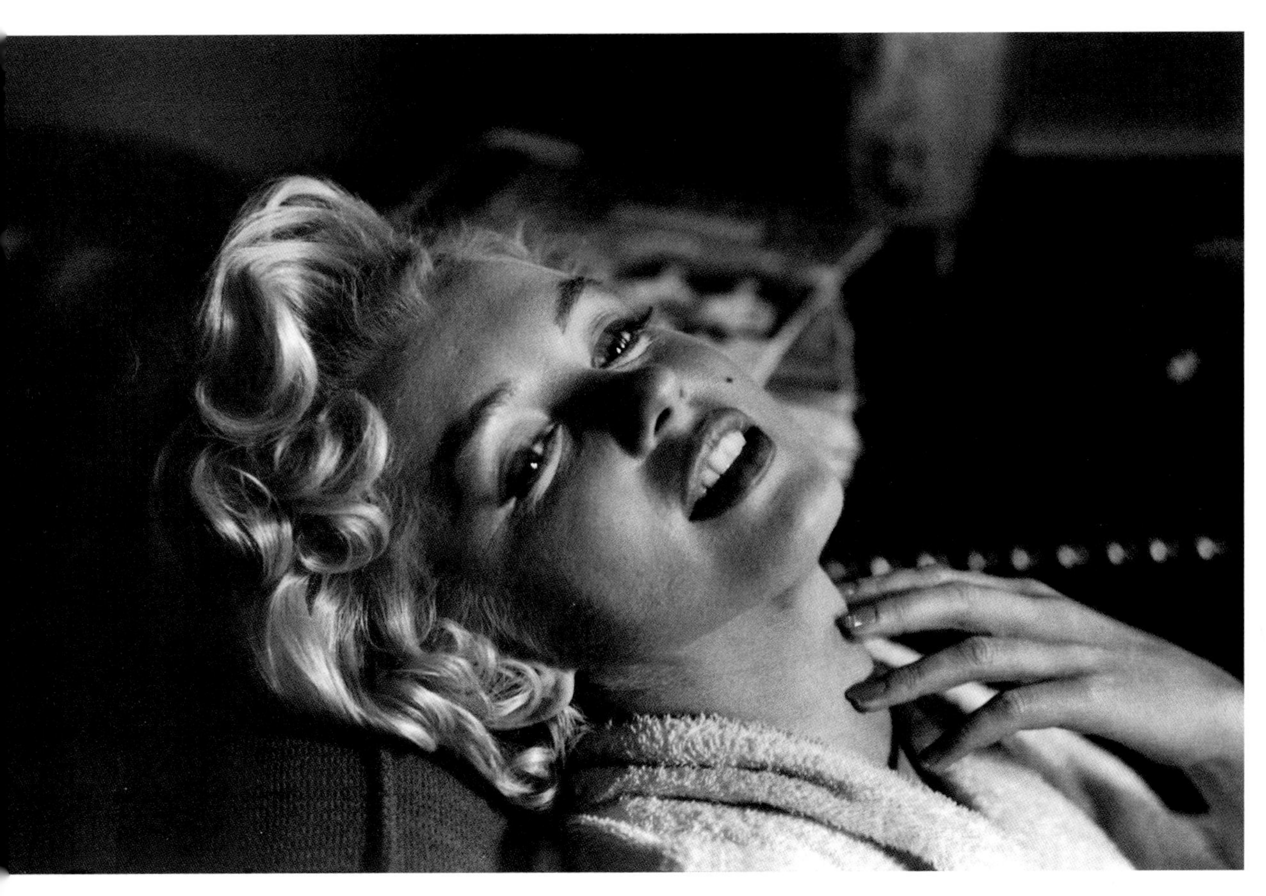

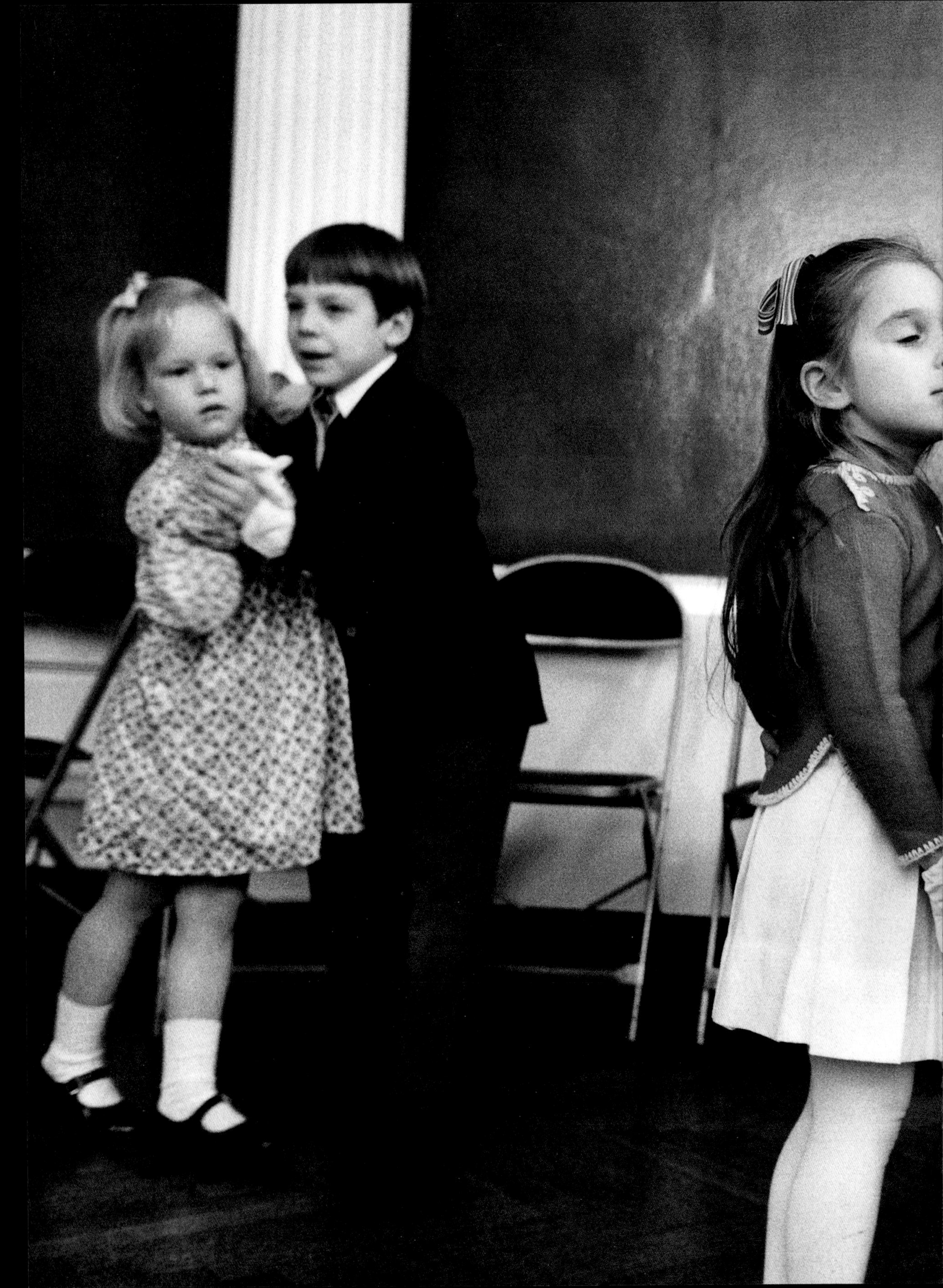

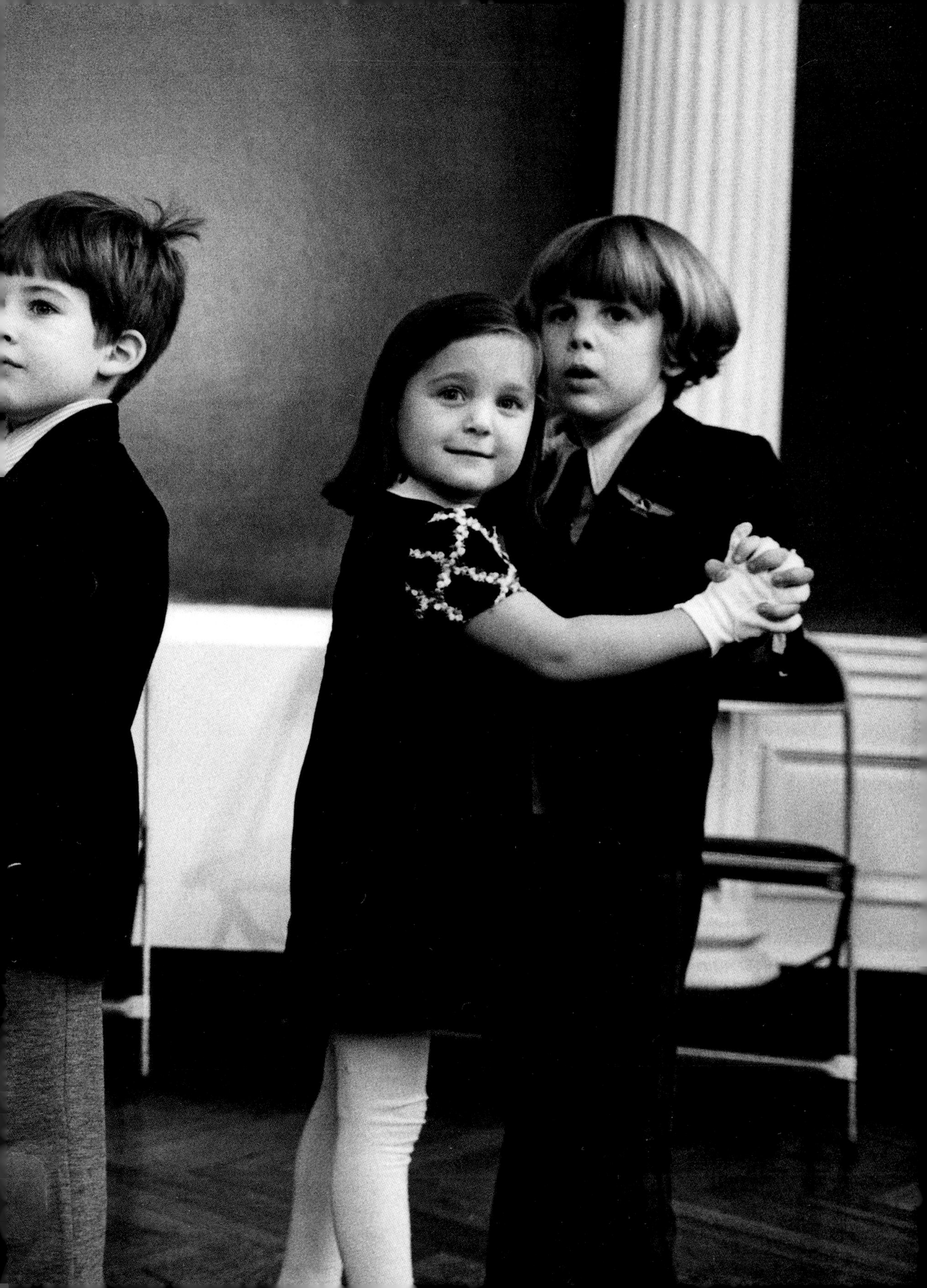

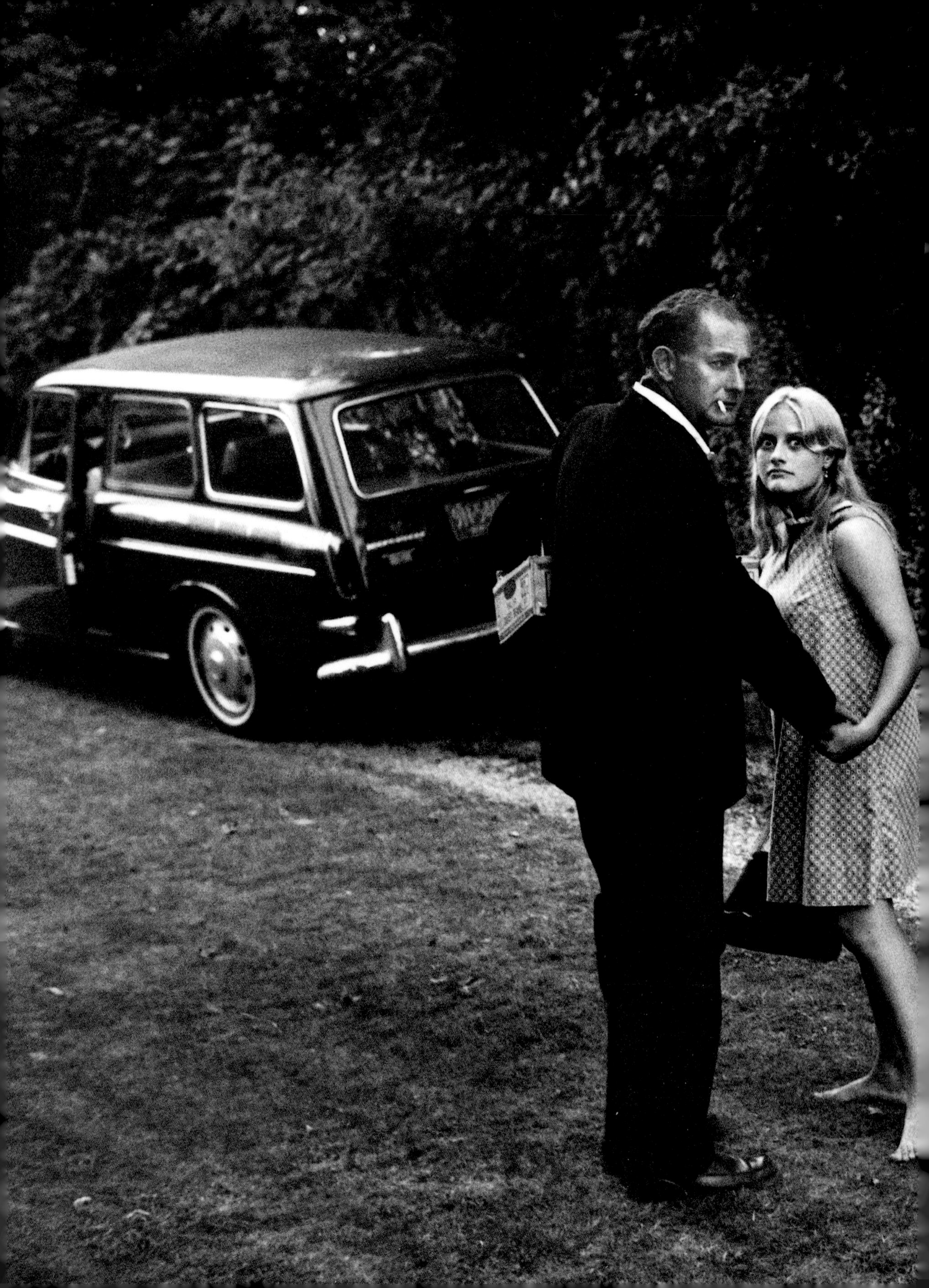

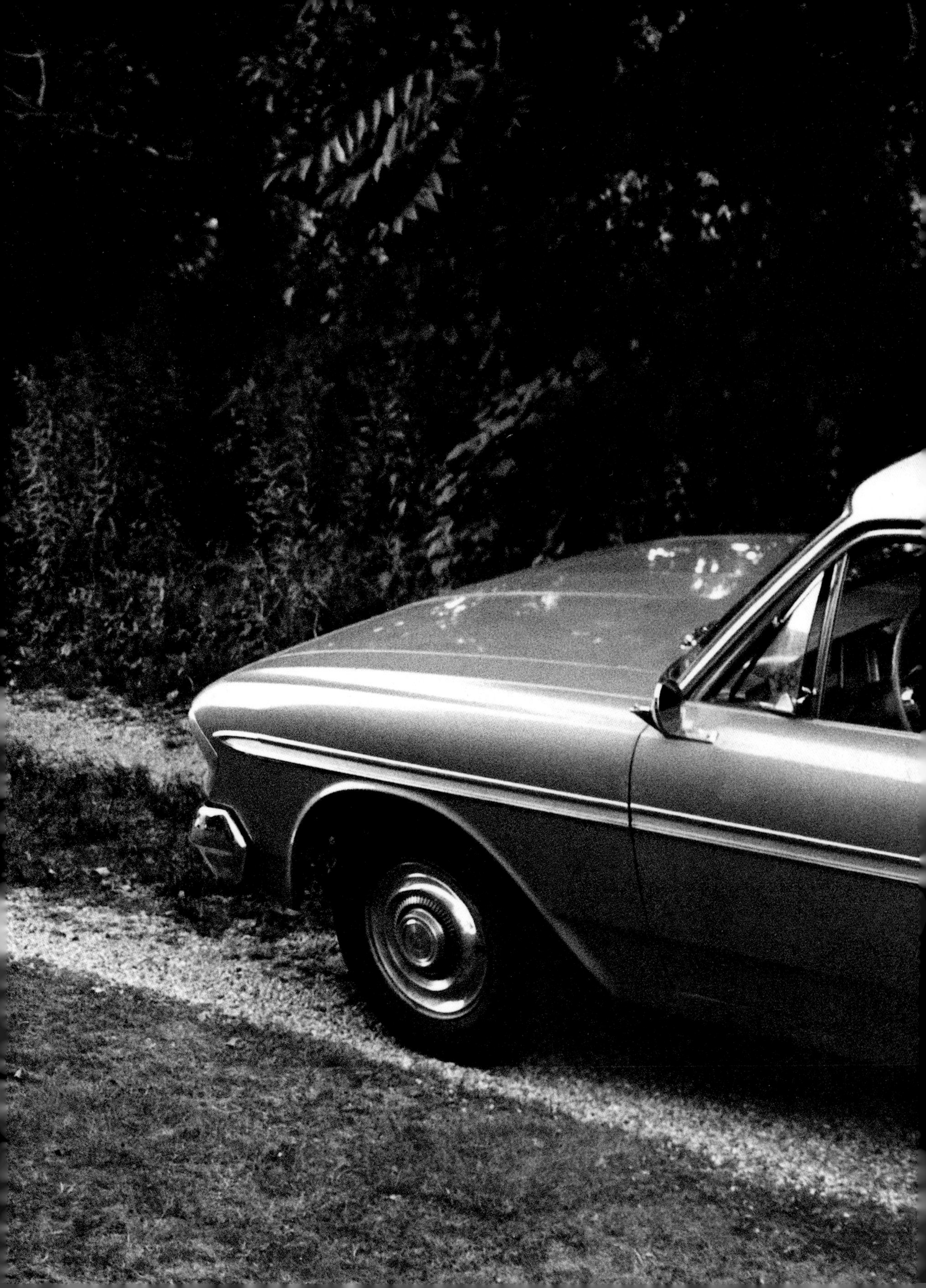

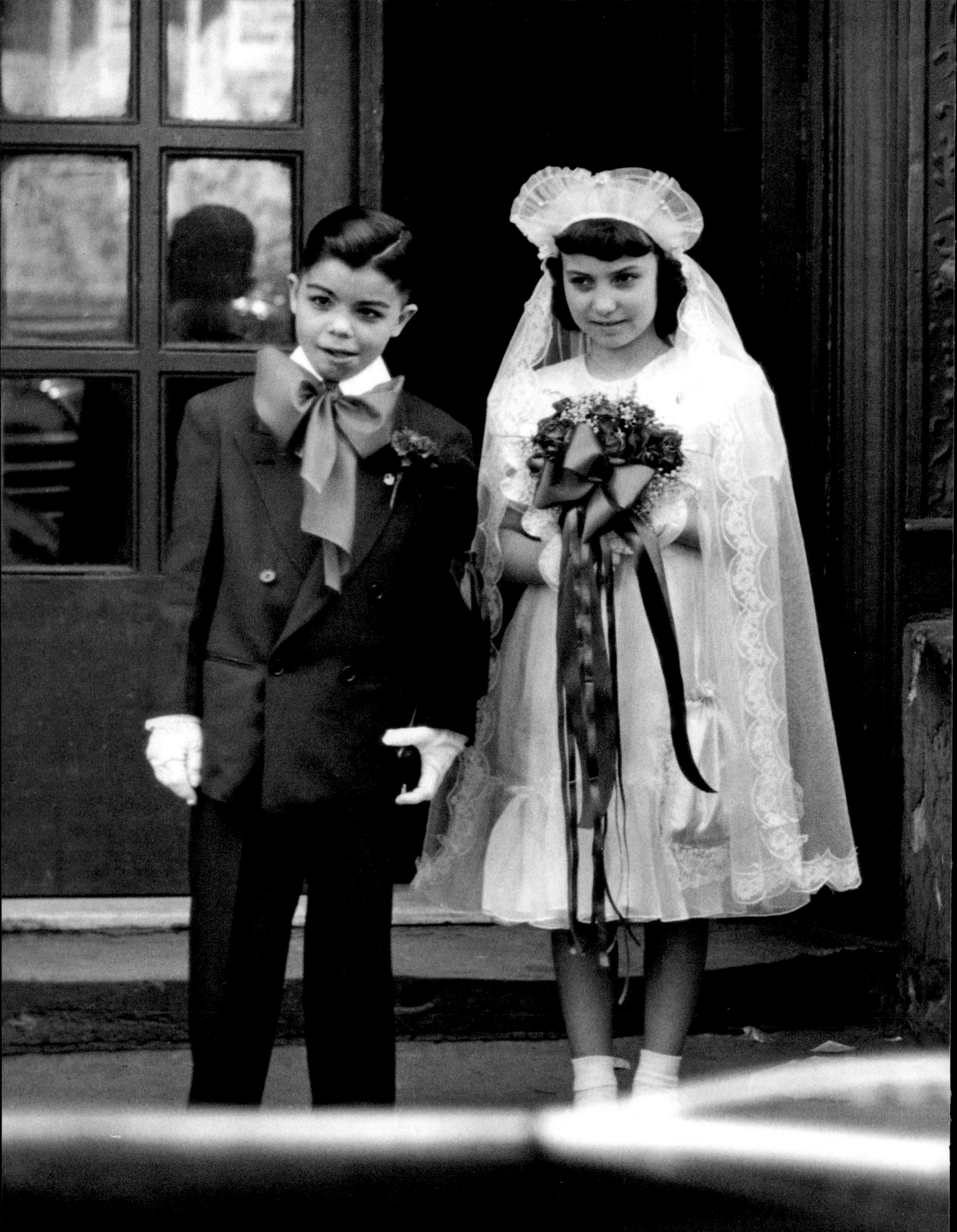

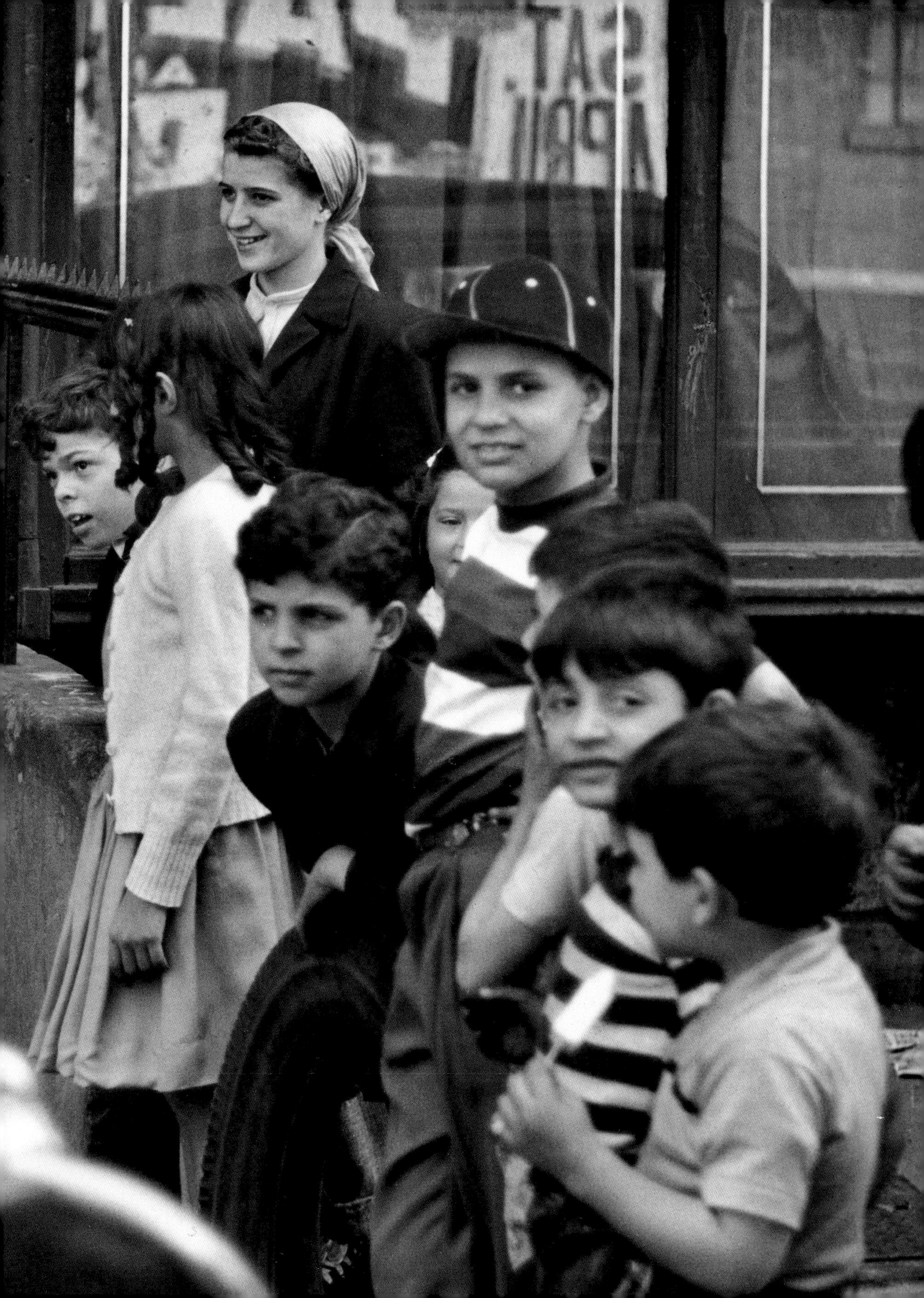

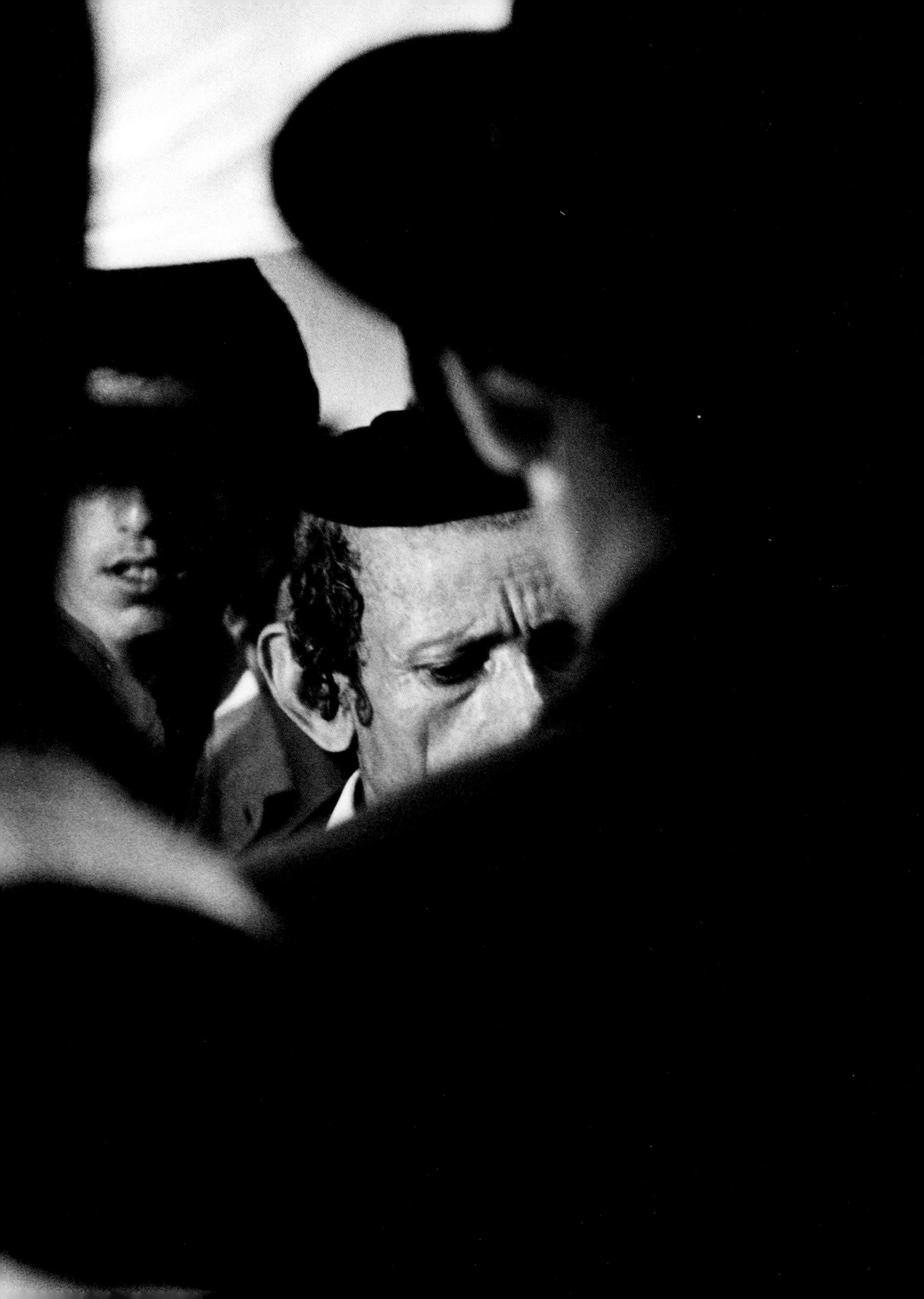

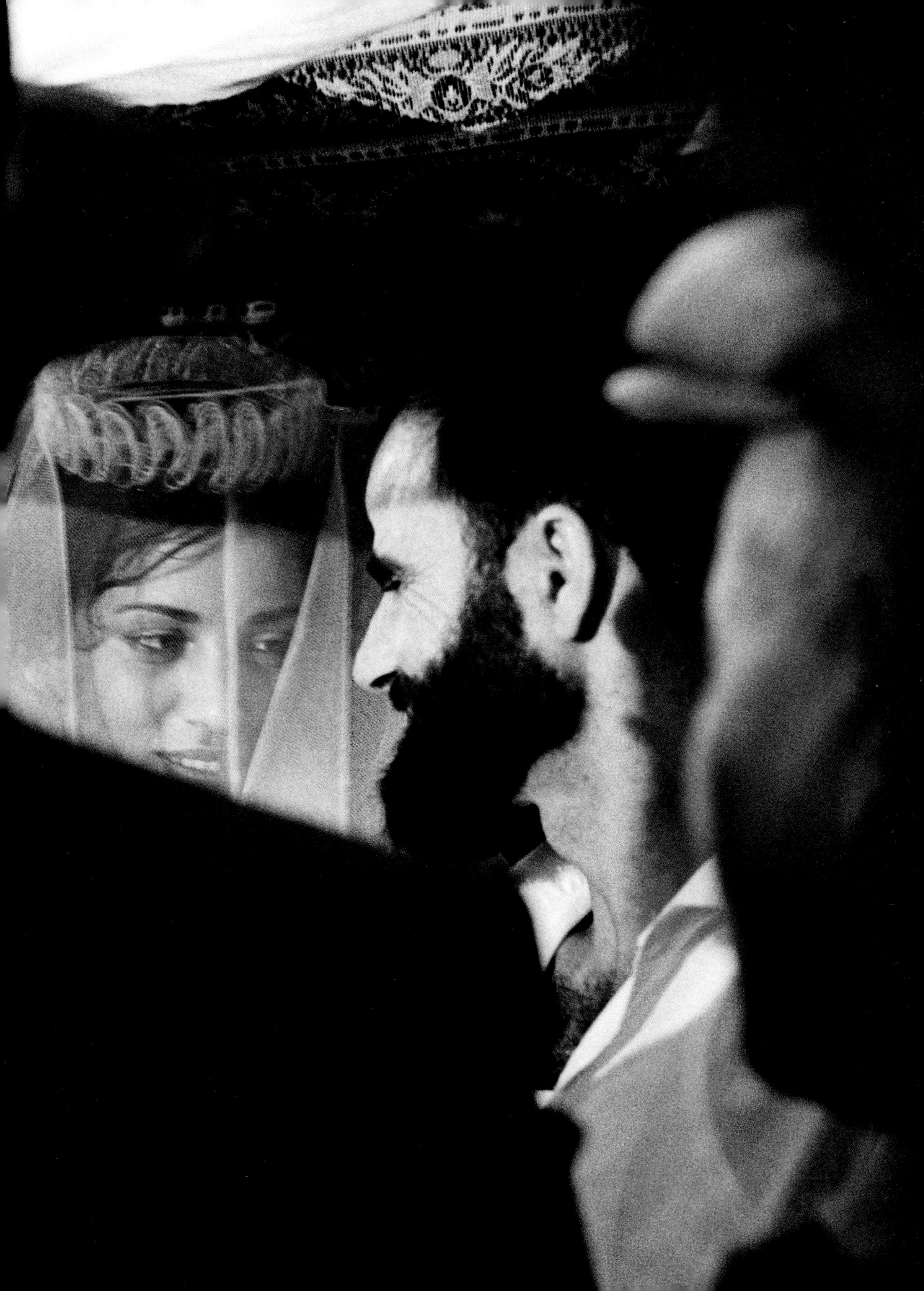

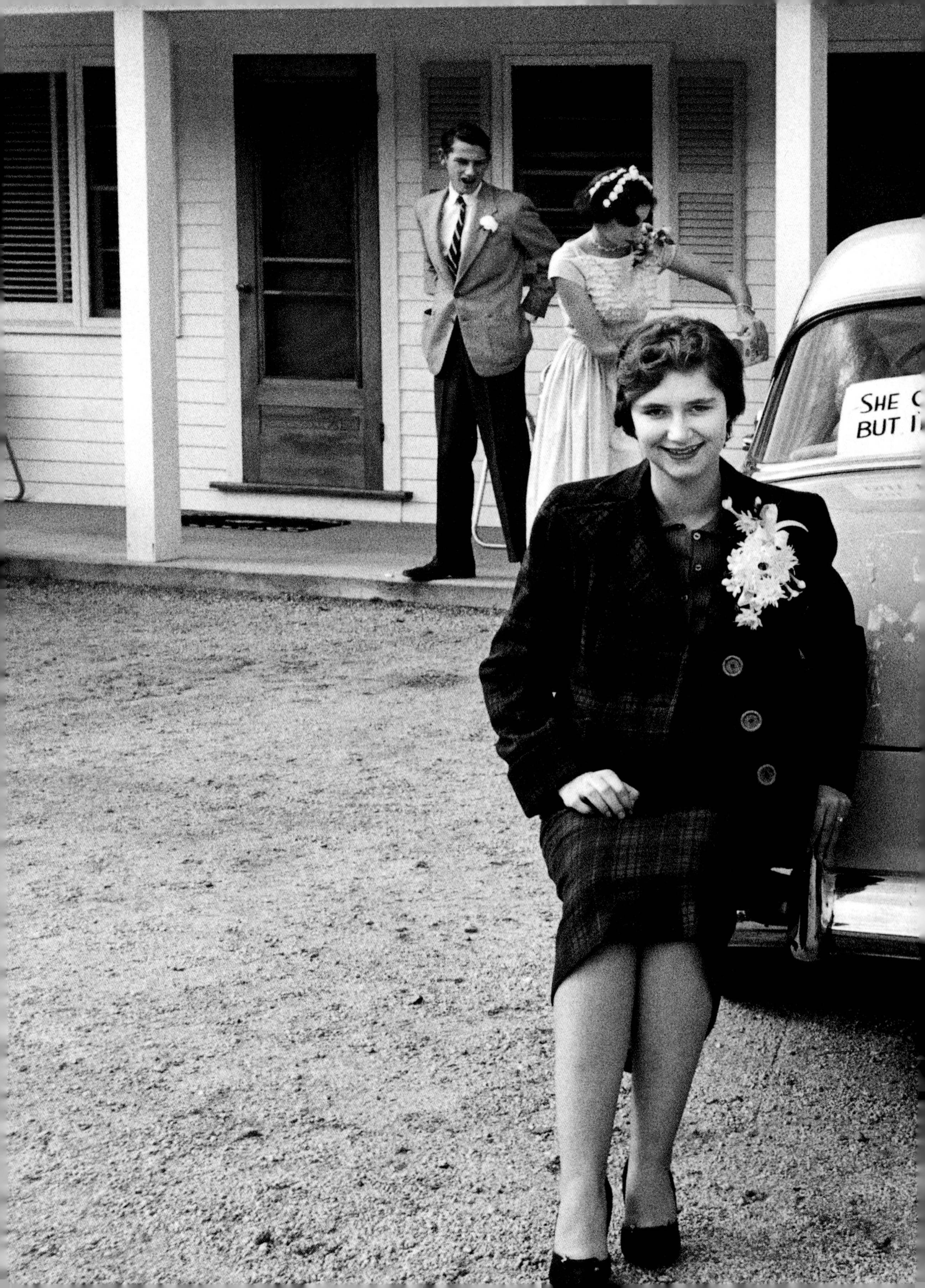

SHE C
BUT I

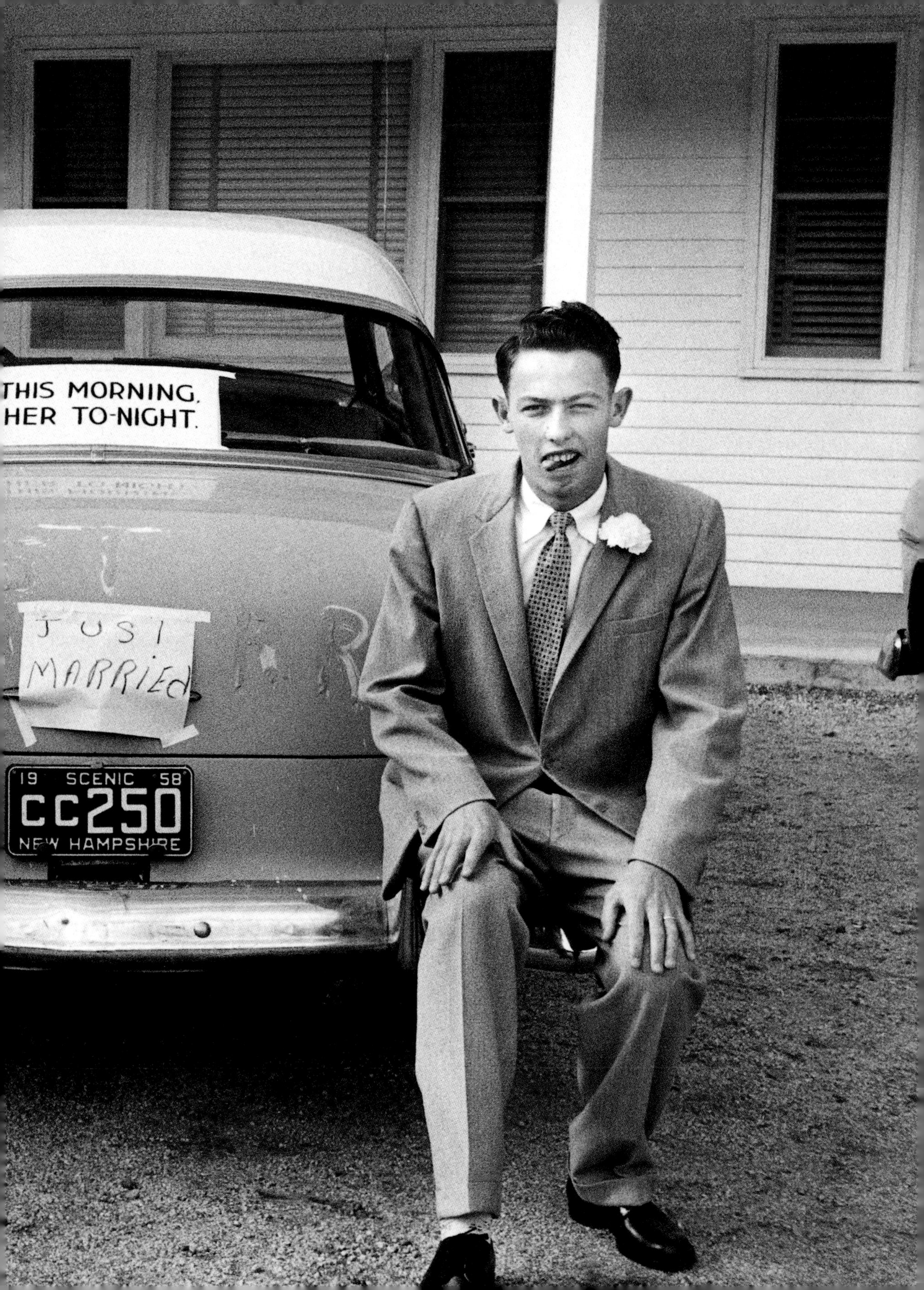
THIS MORNING,
HER TO-NIGHT.
JUST MARRIED
19 SCENIC 58
CC250
NEW HAMPSHIRE

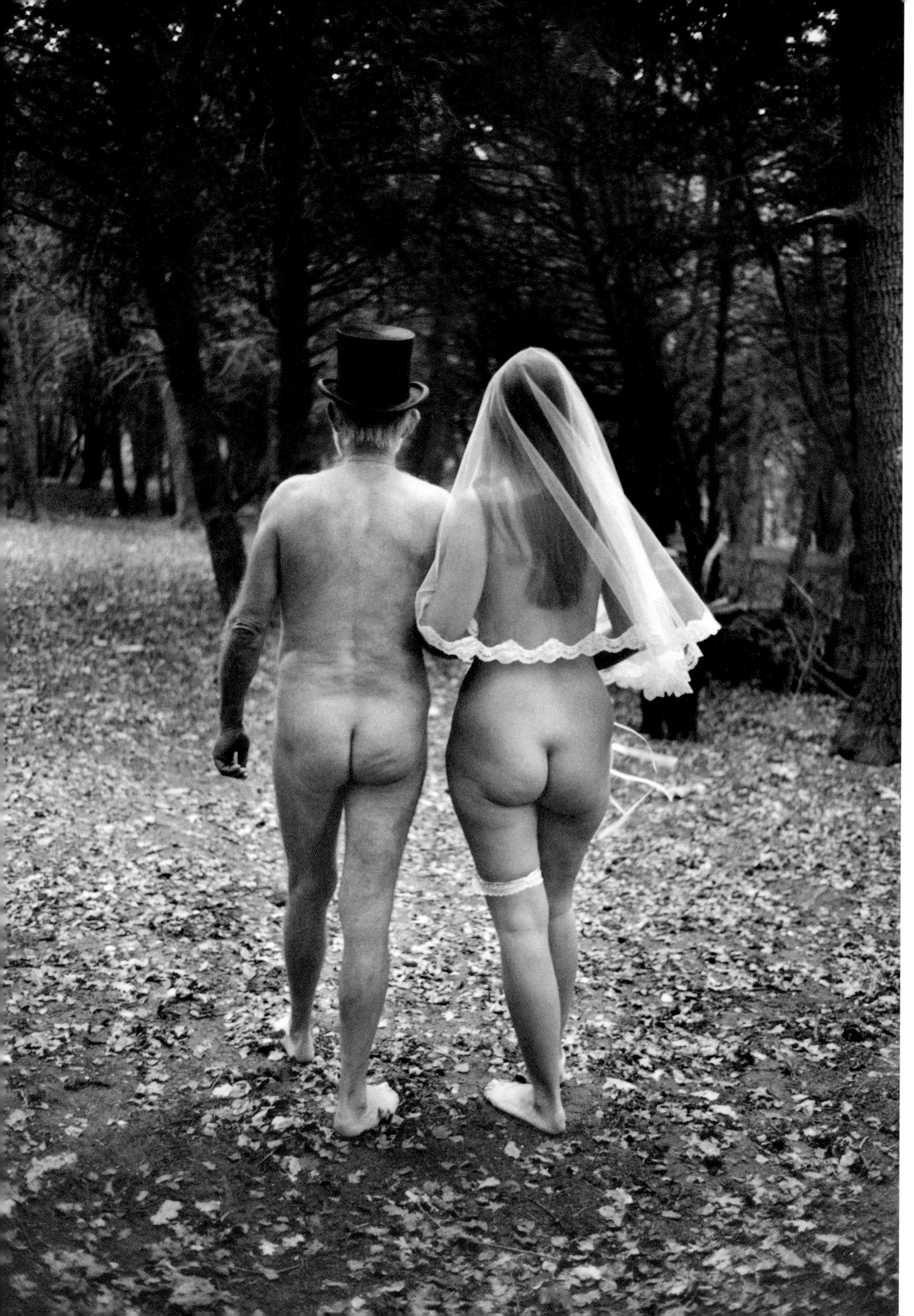

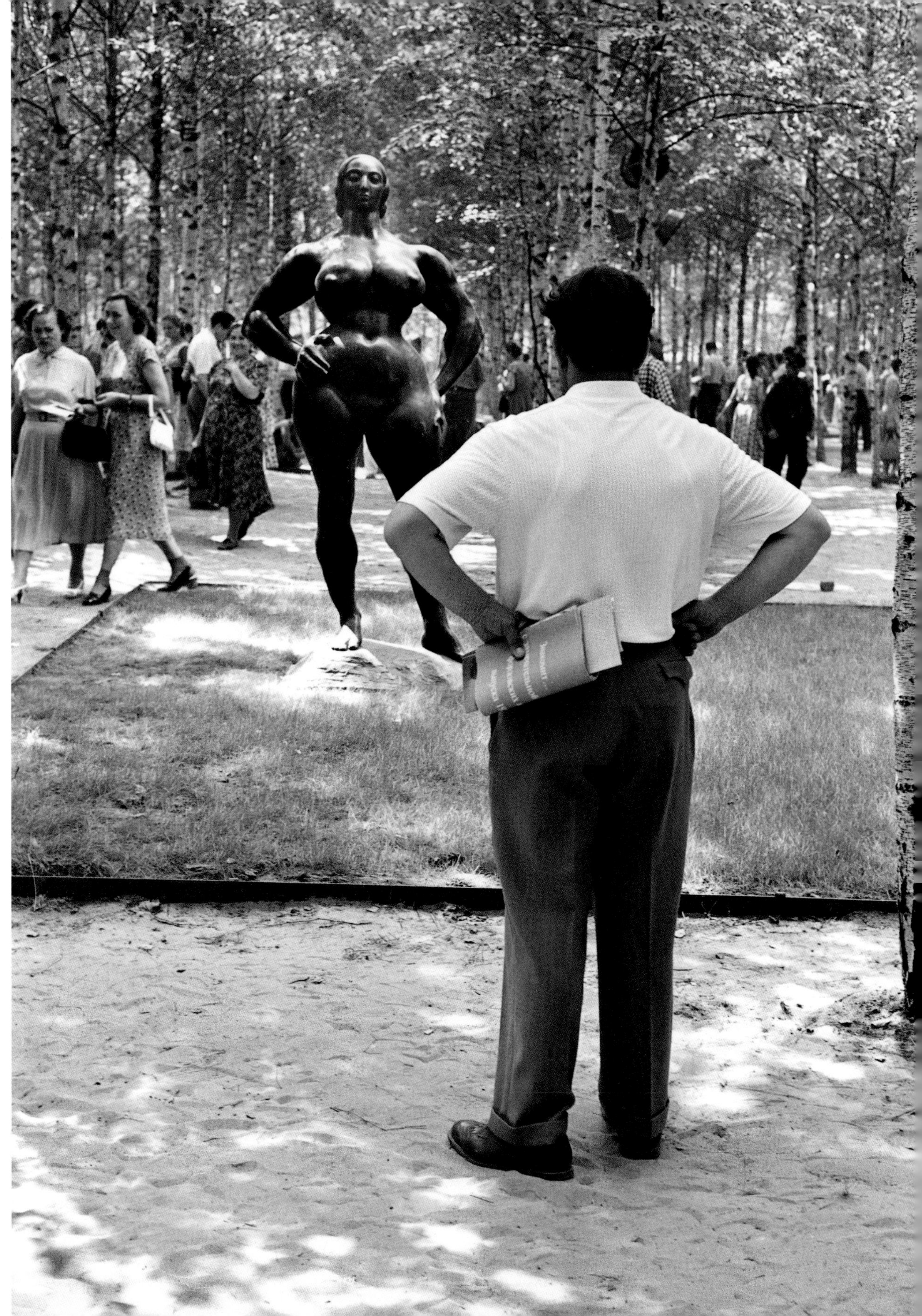

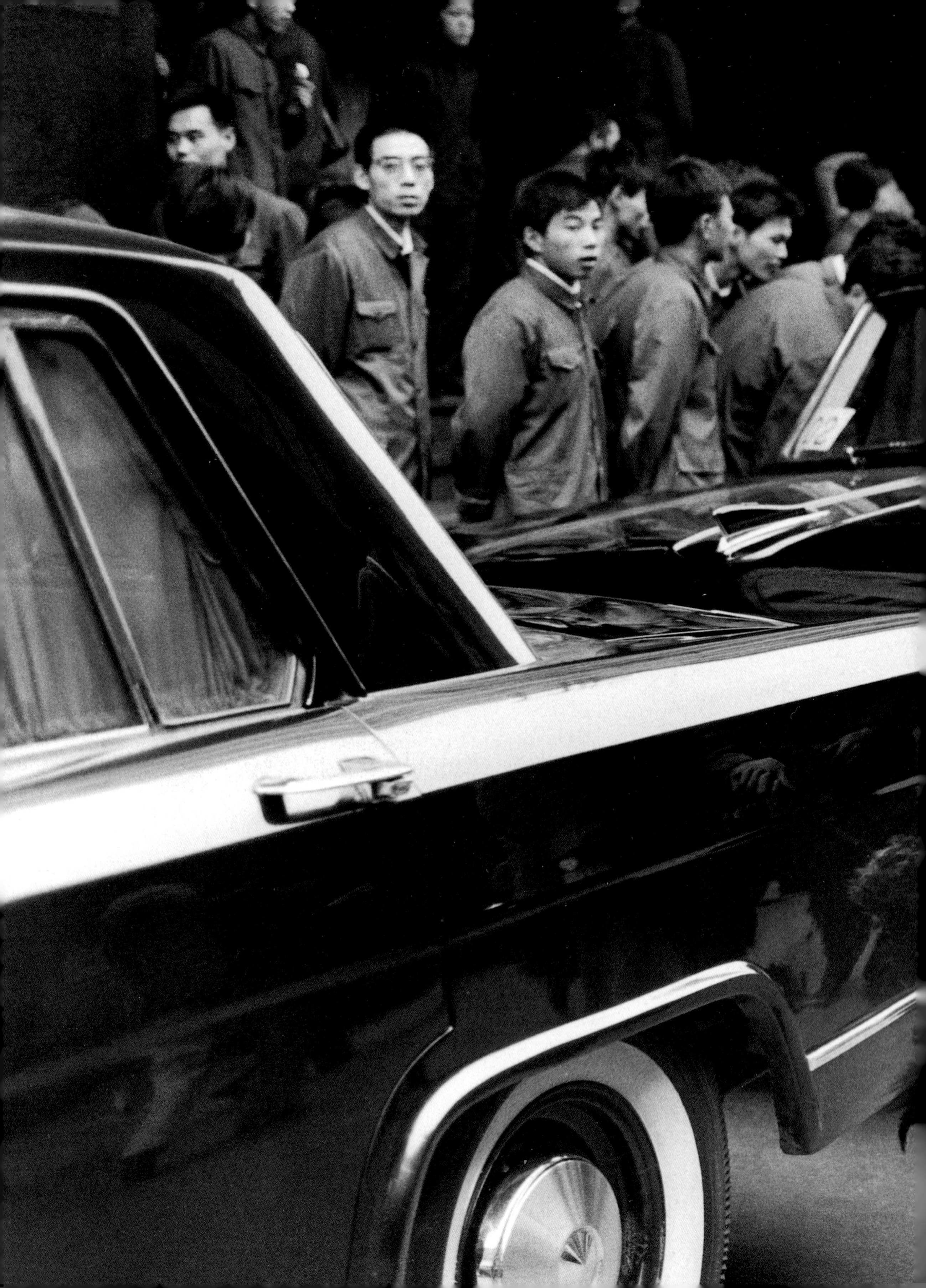

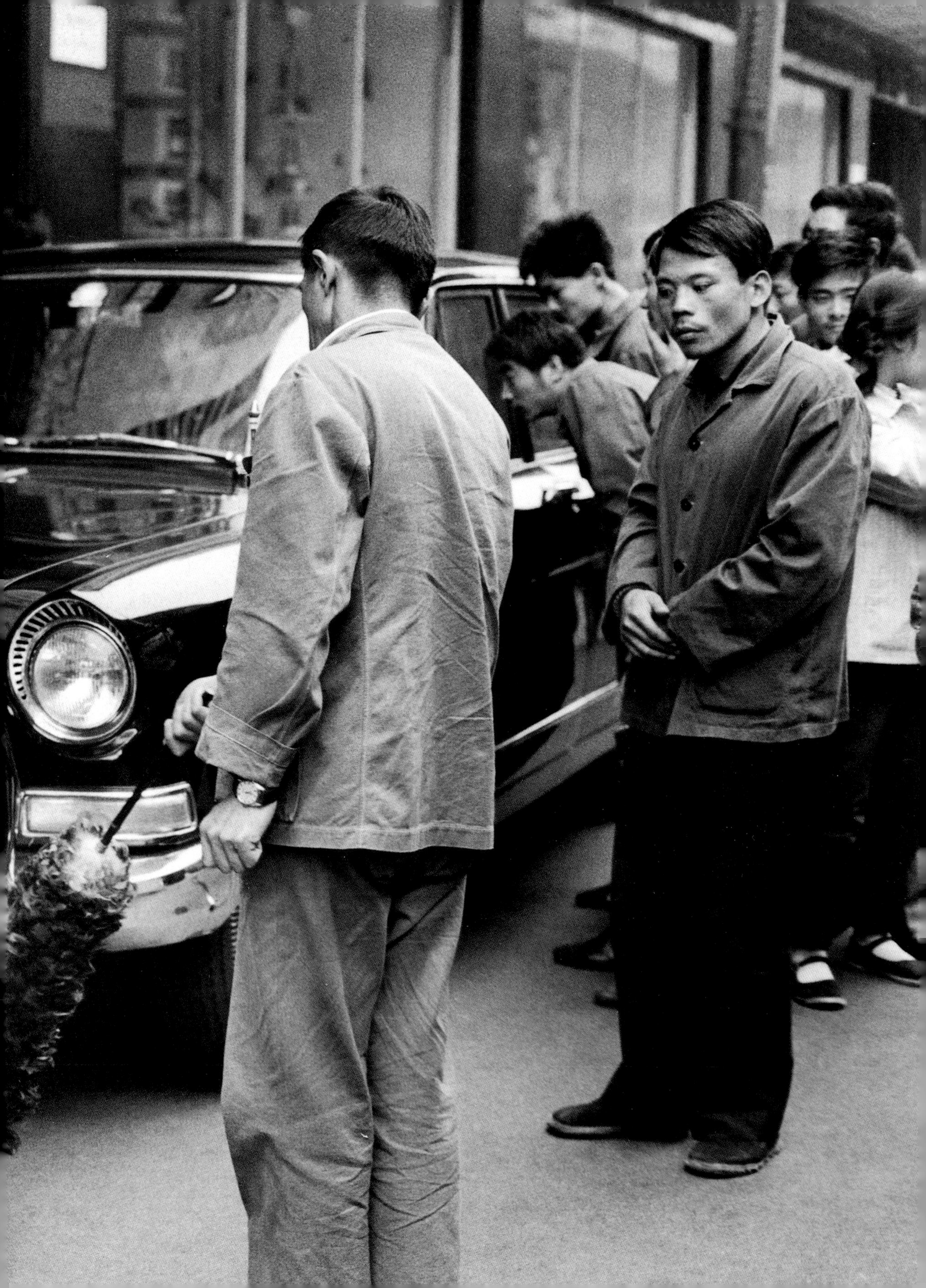

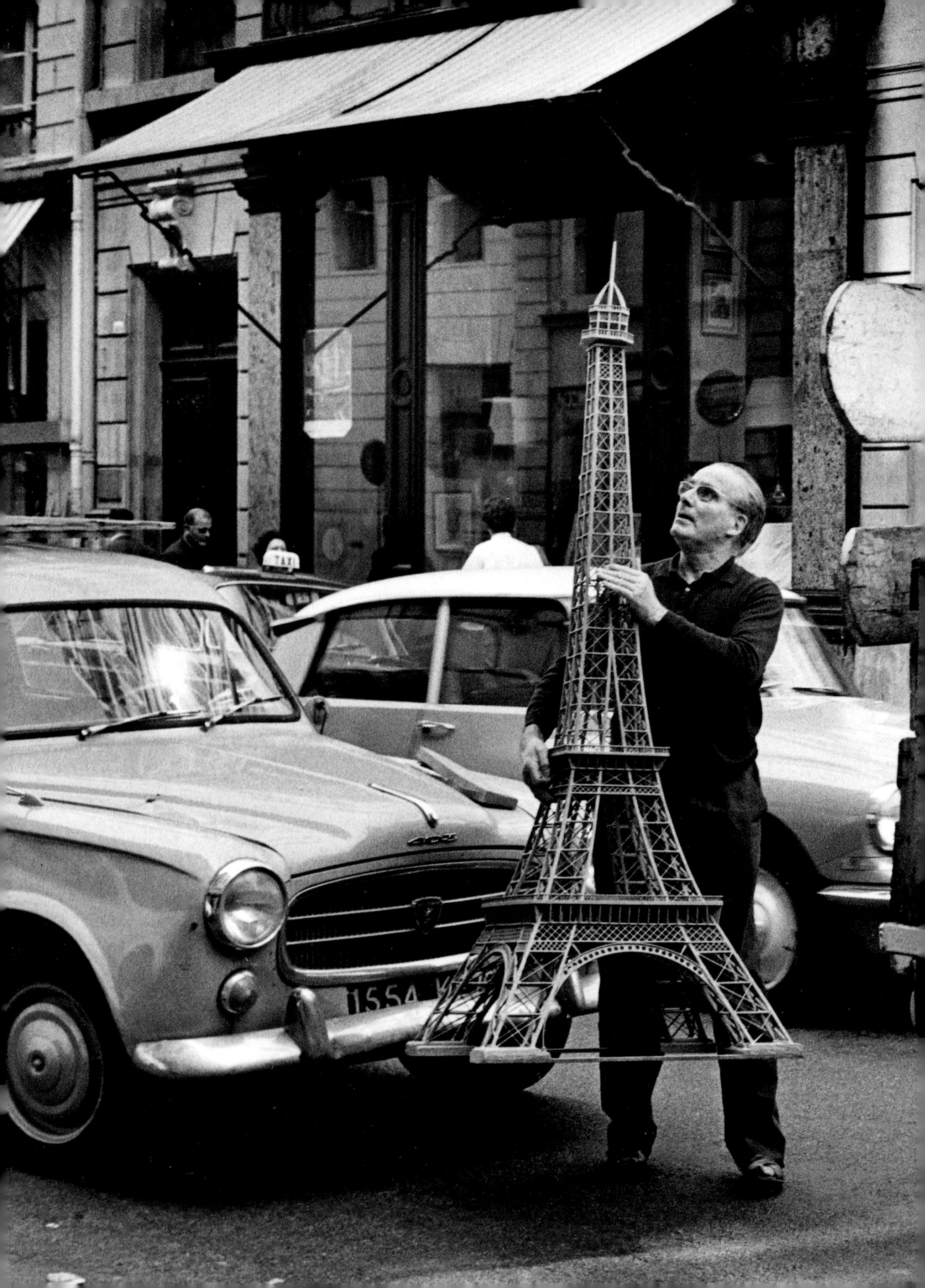

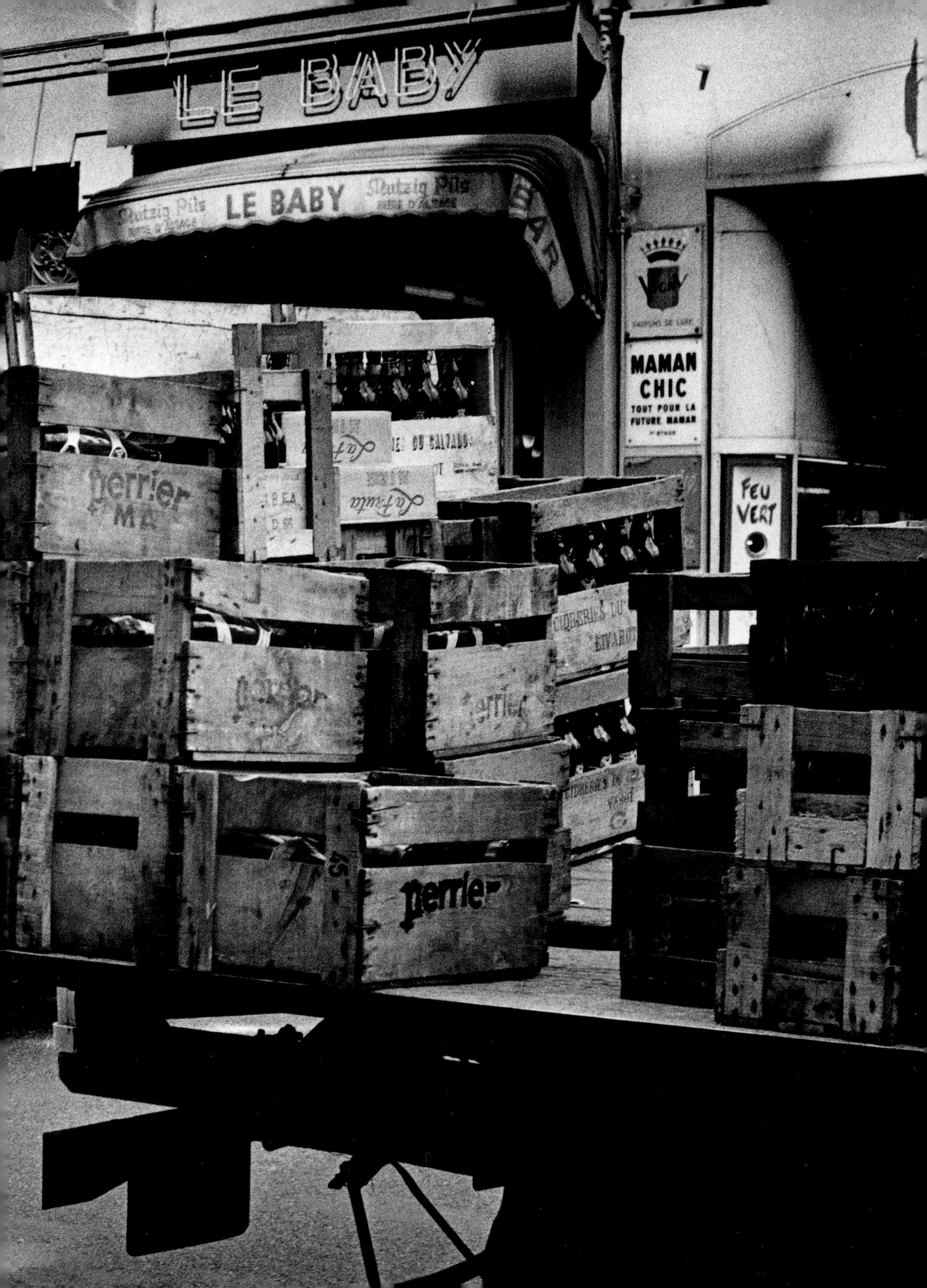

LE BABY
LE BABY
Mutzig Pils
MAMAN
CHIC
TOUT POUR LA
FUTURE MAMAN
FEU
VERT
Perrier
Perrier
Perrier
Perrier

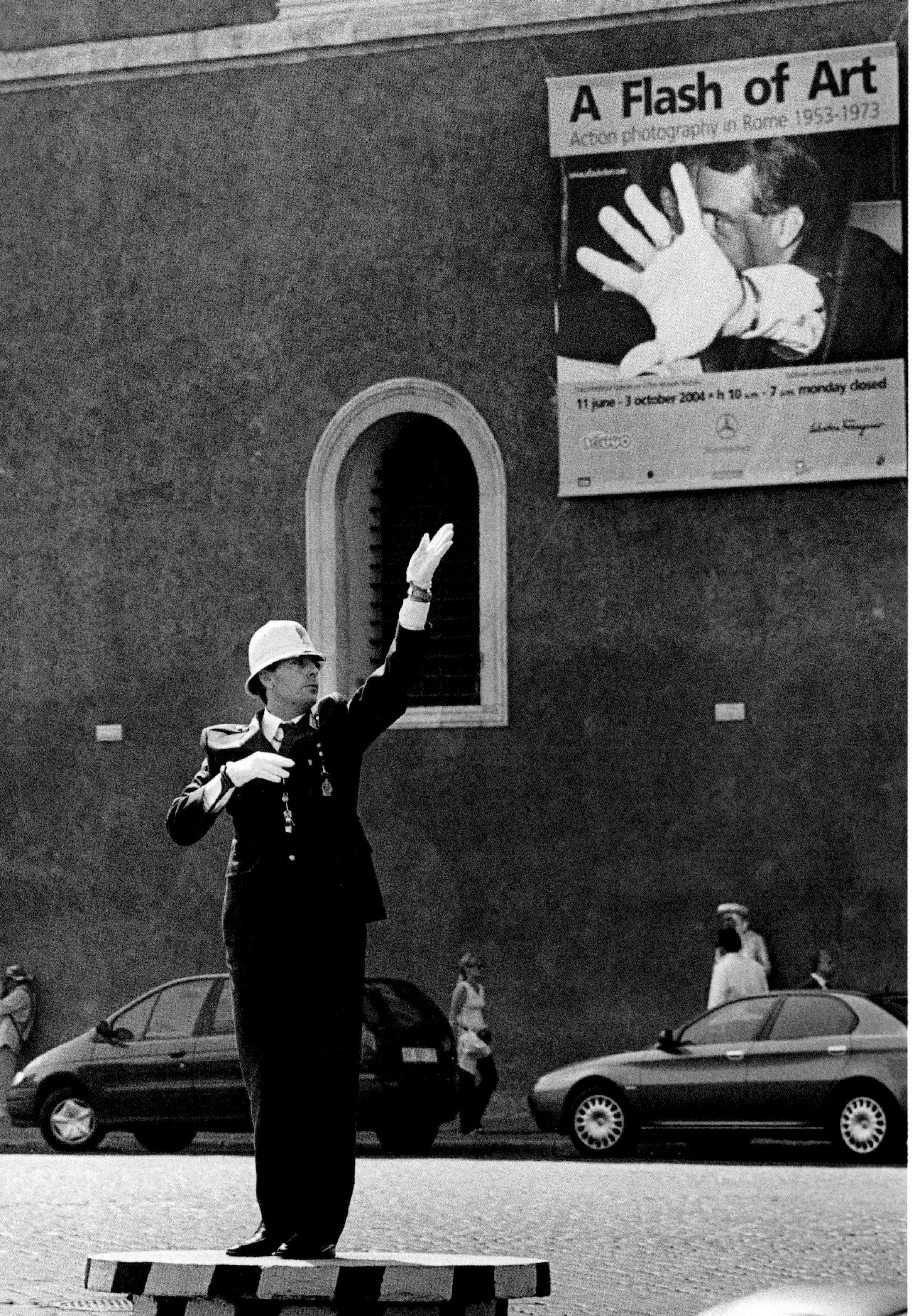
A Flash of Art
Action photography in Rome 1953-1973
11 june - 3 october 2004 • h 10 a.m. - 7 p.m. monday closed

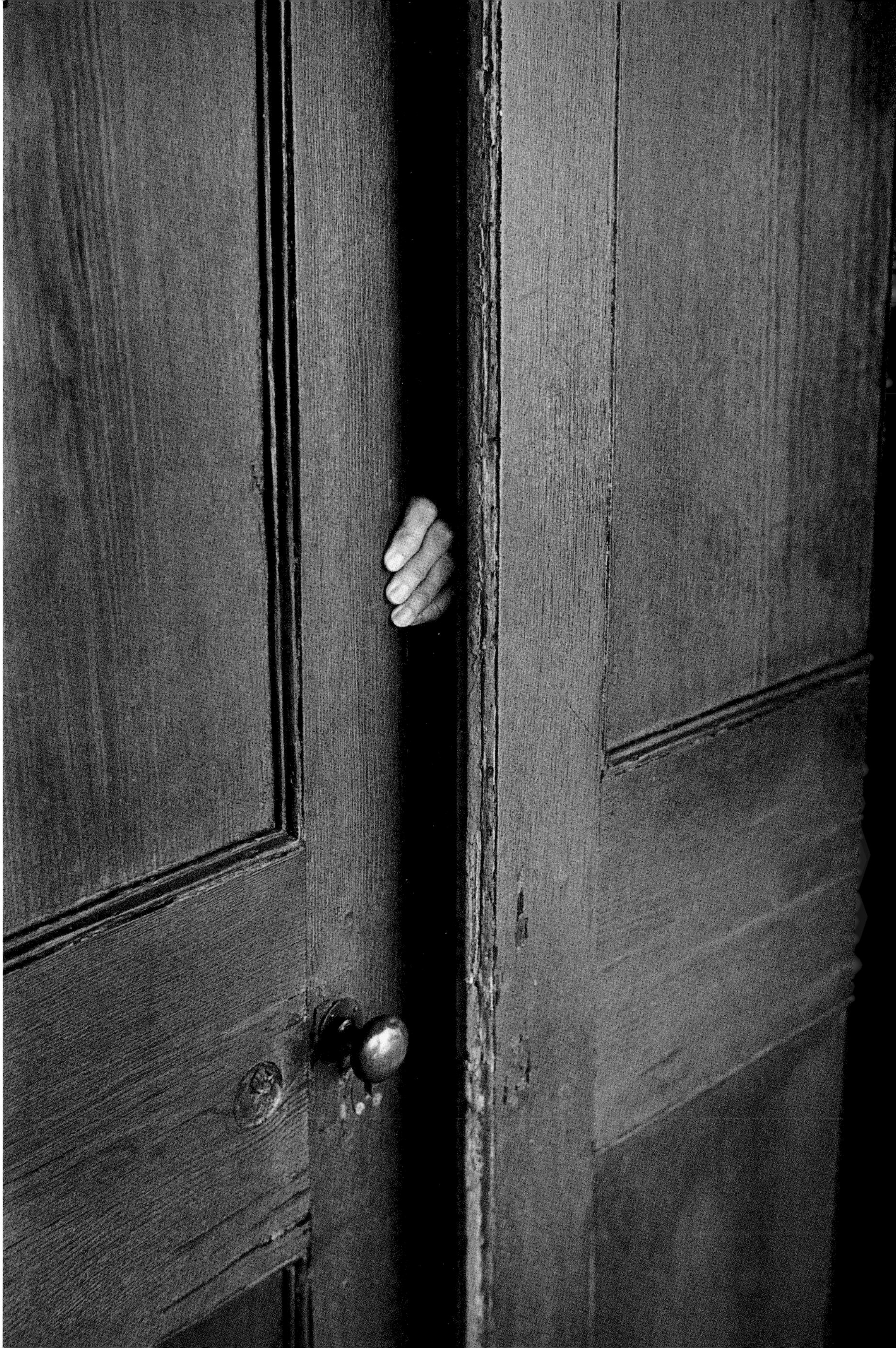

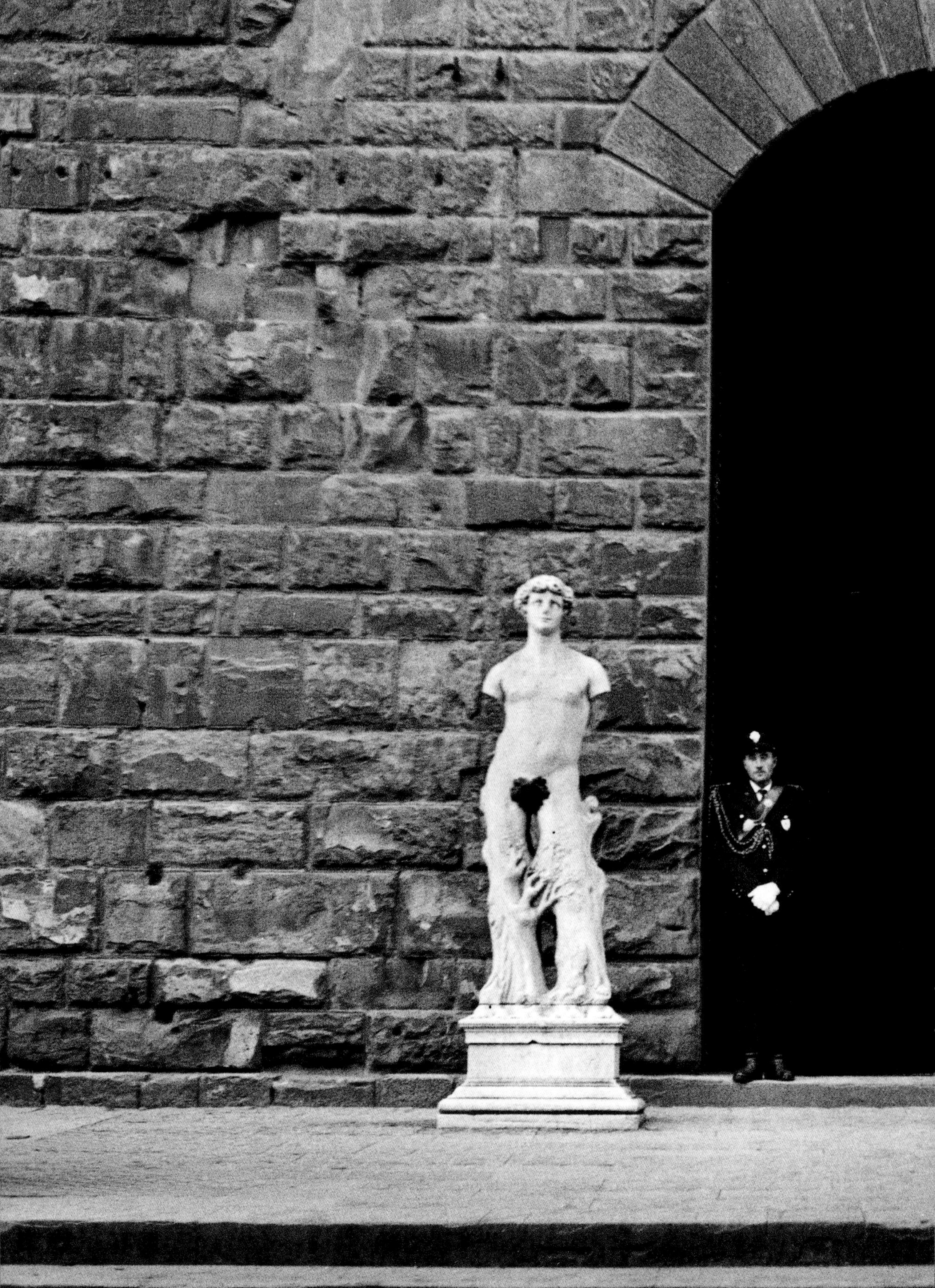

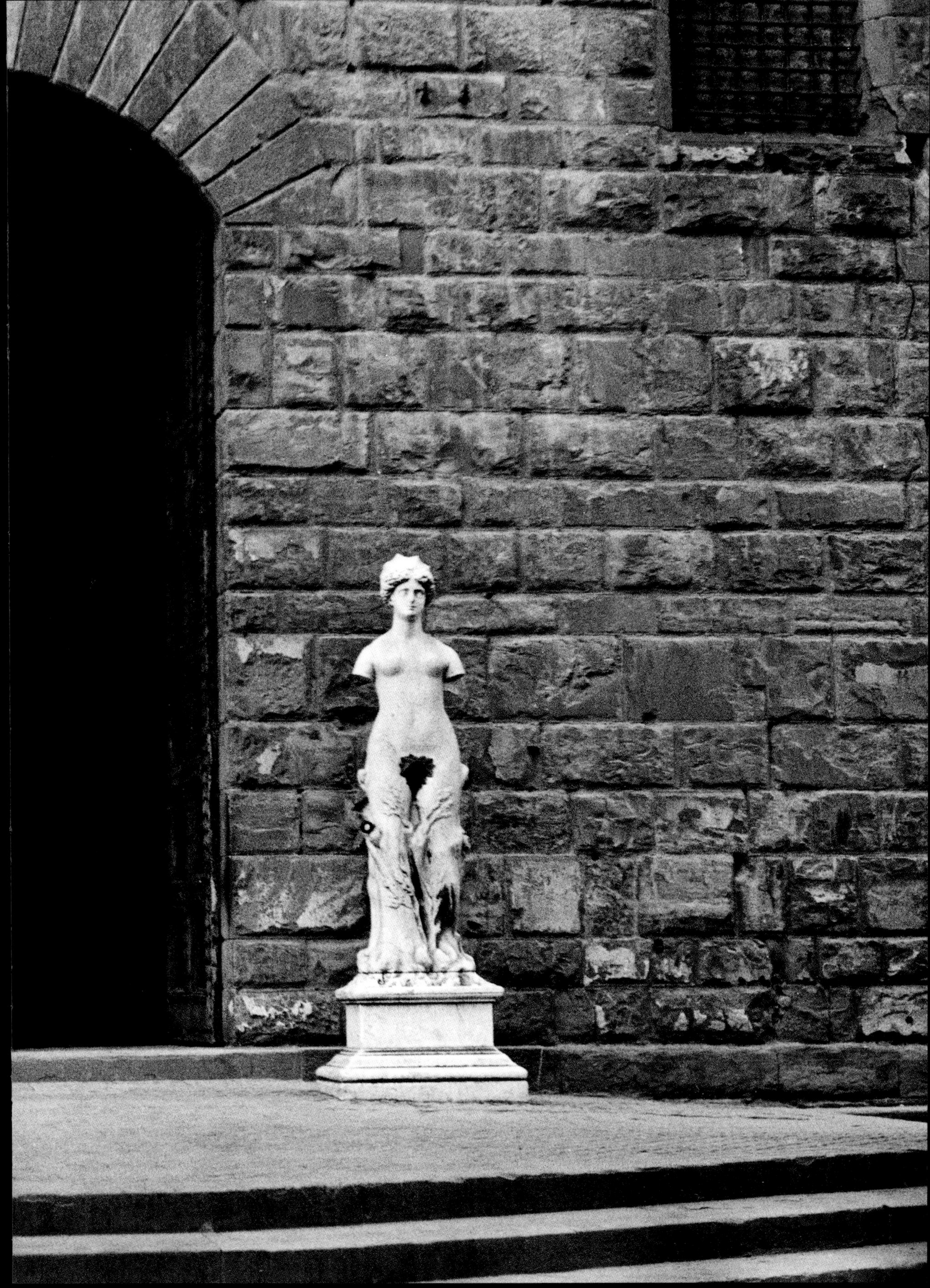

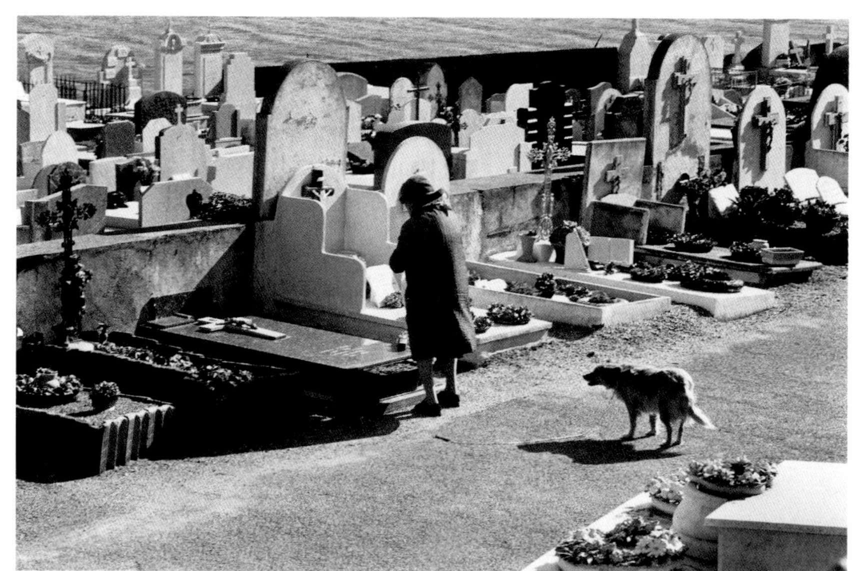

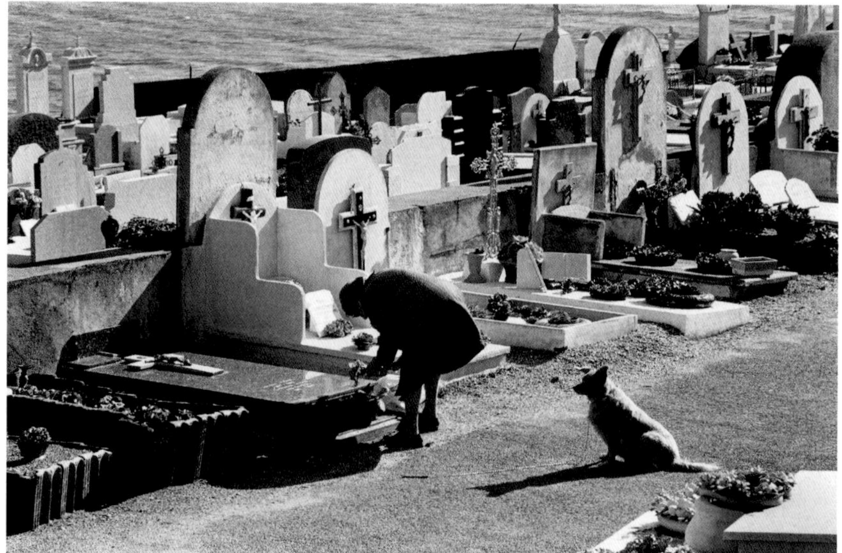

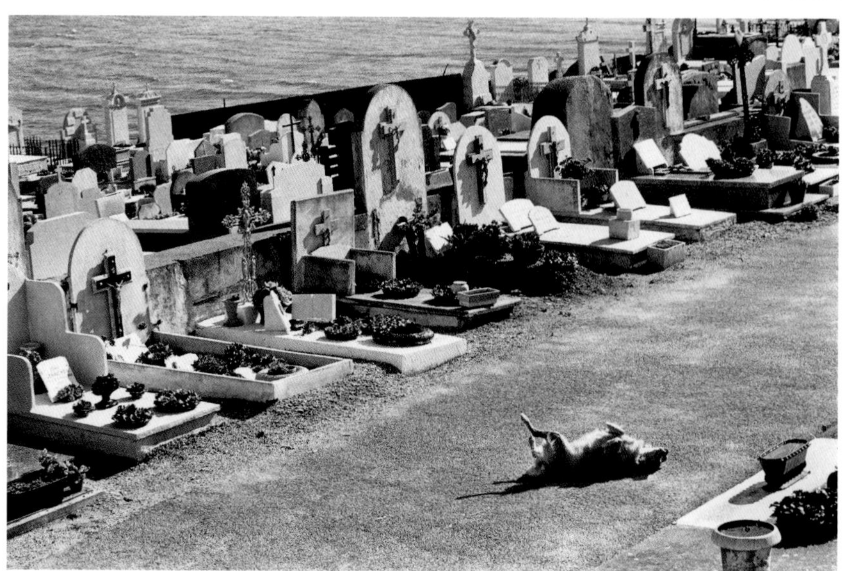

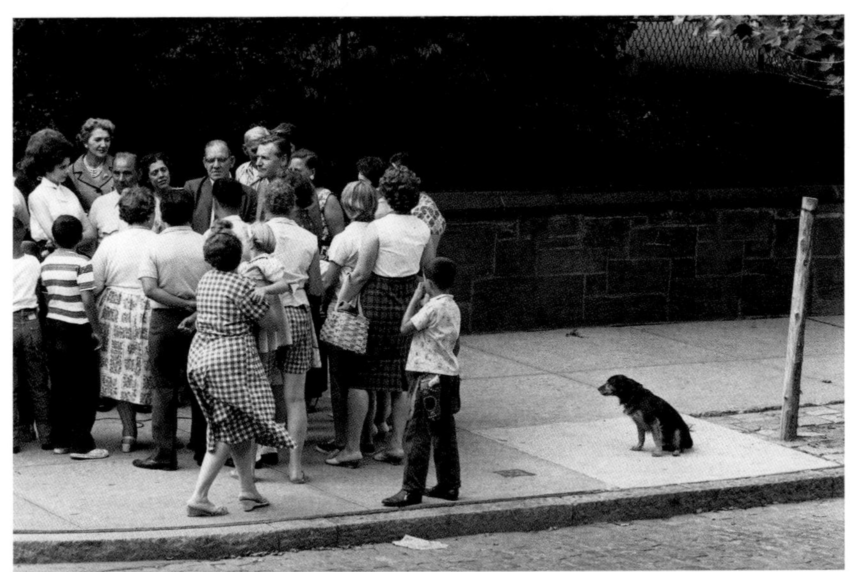

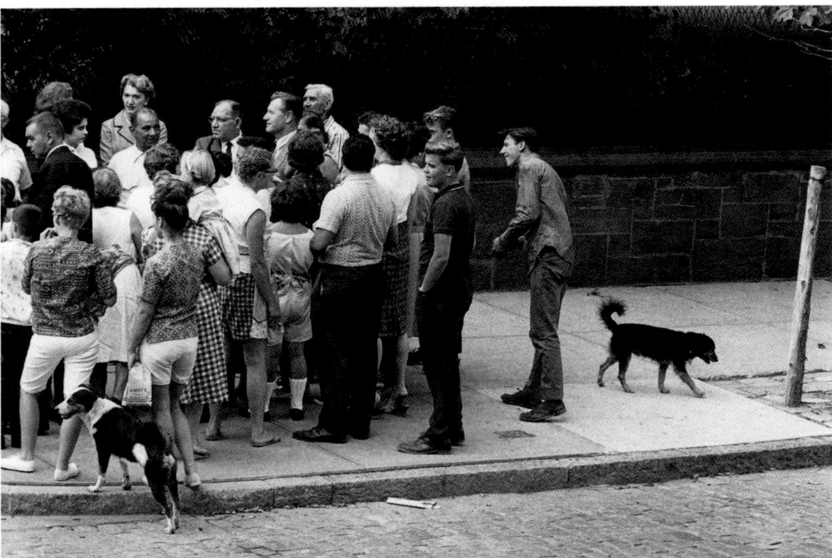

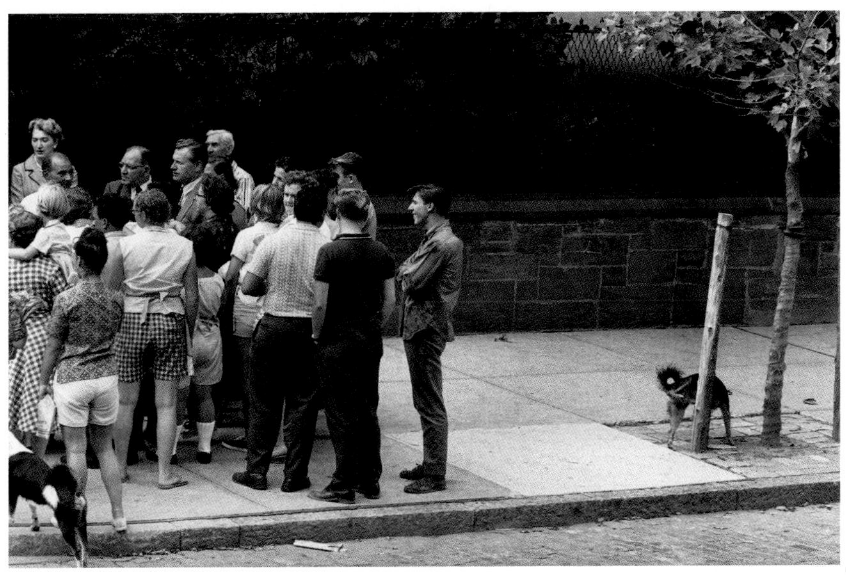

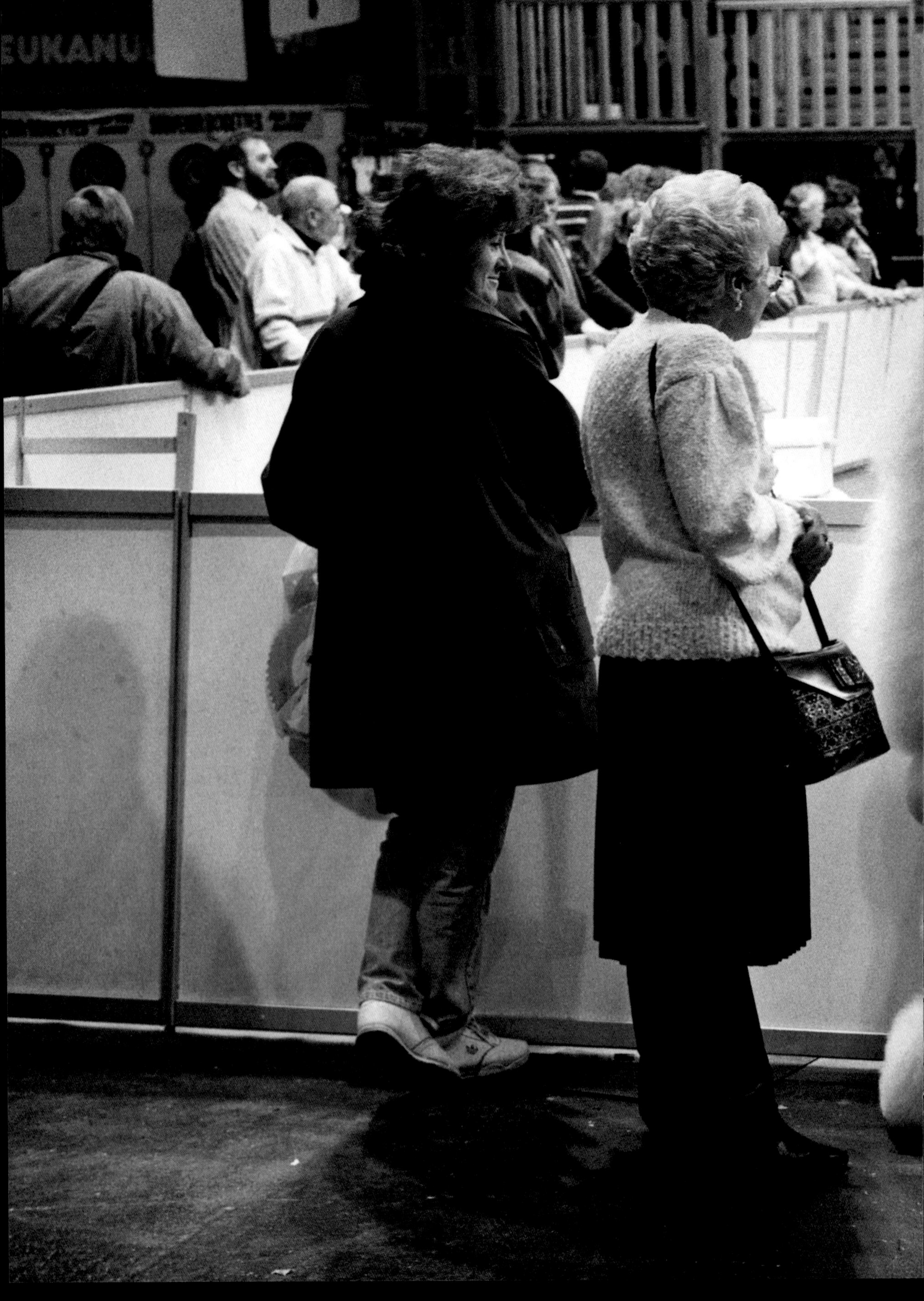

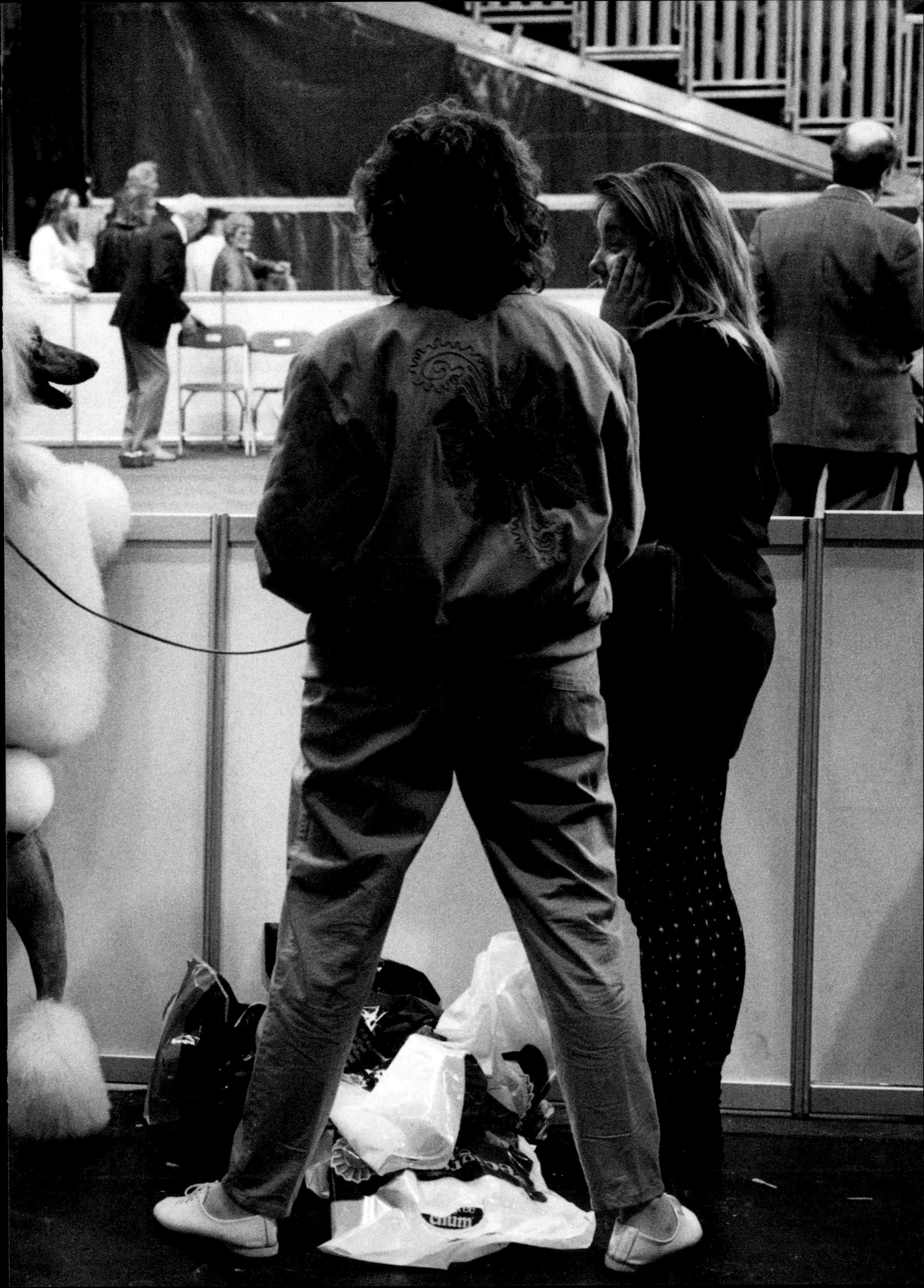

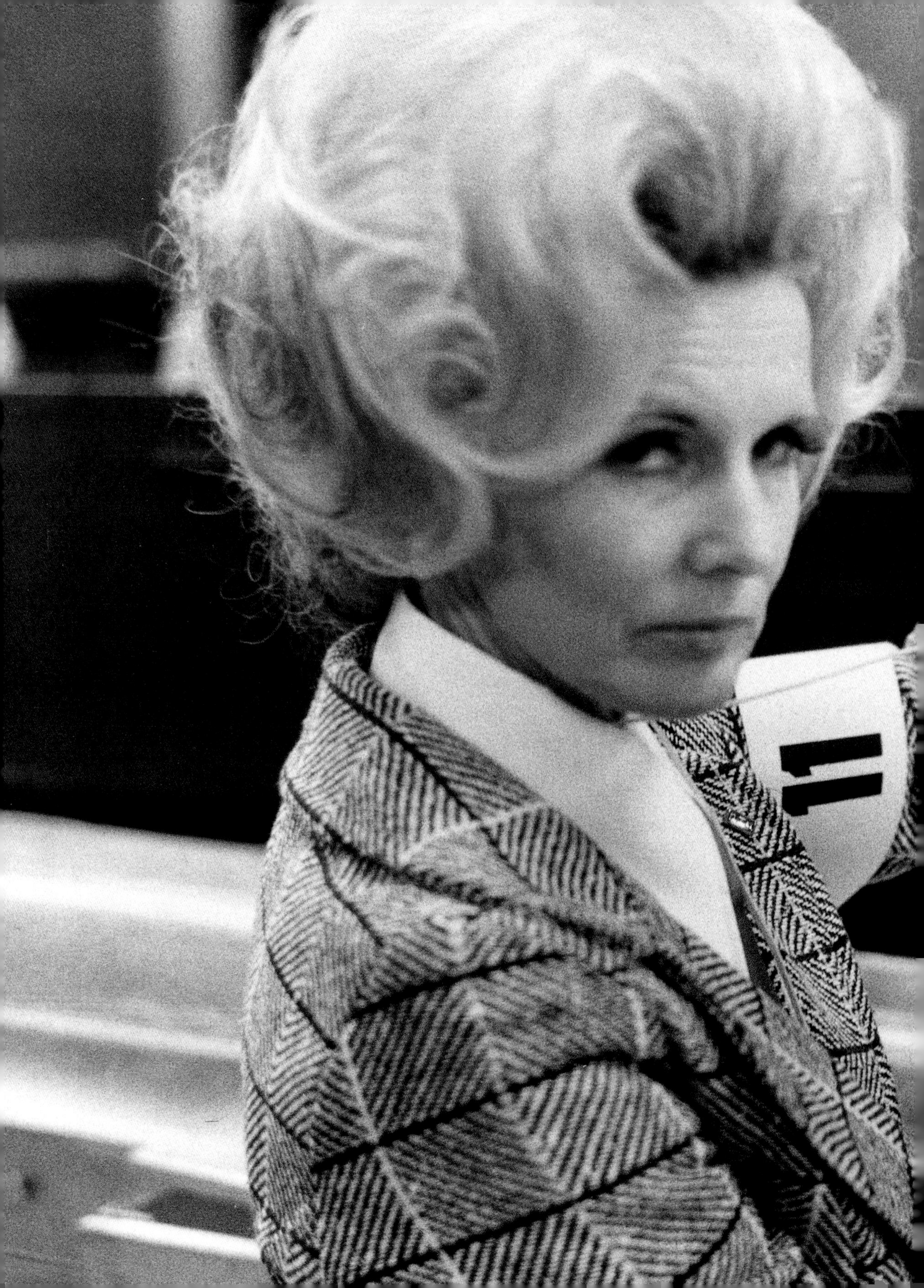

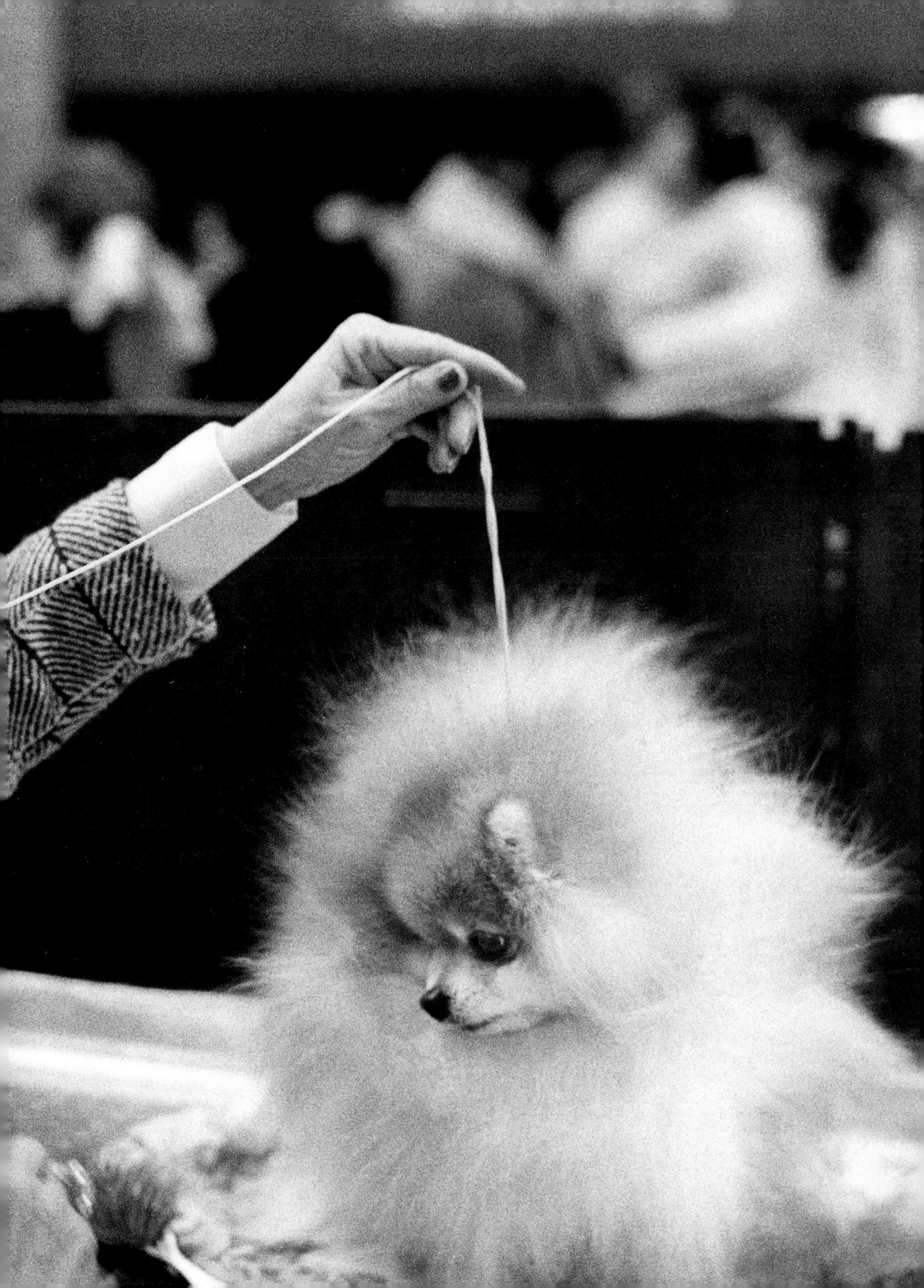

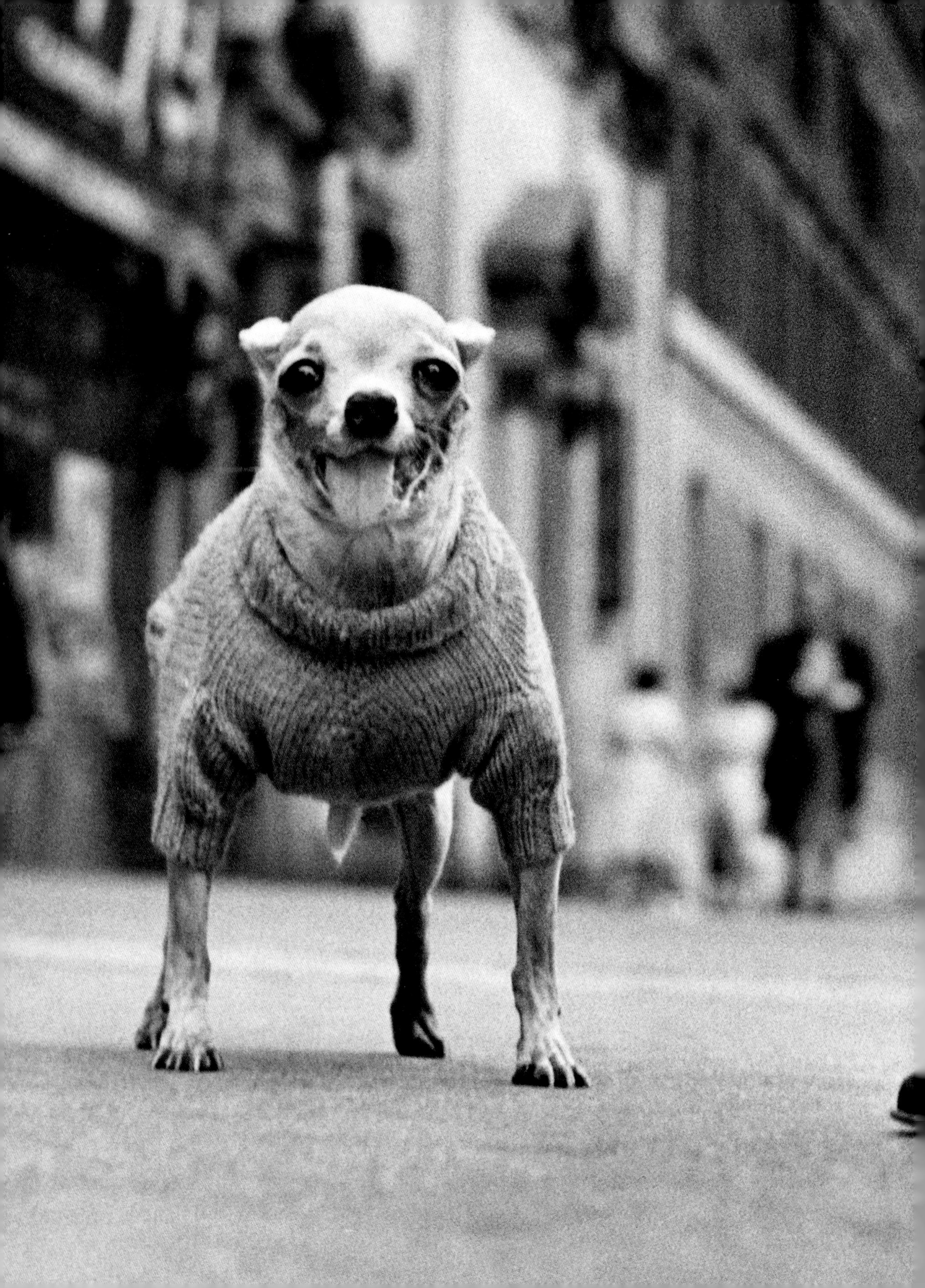

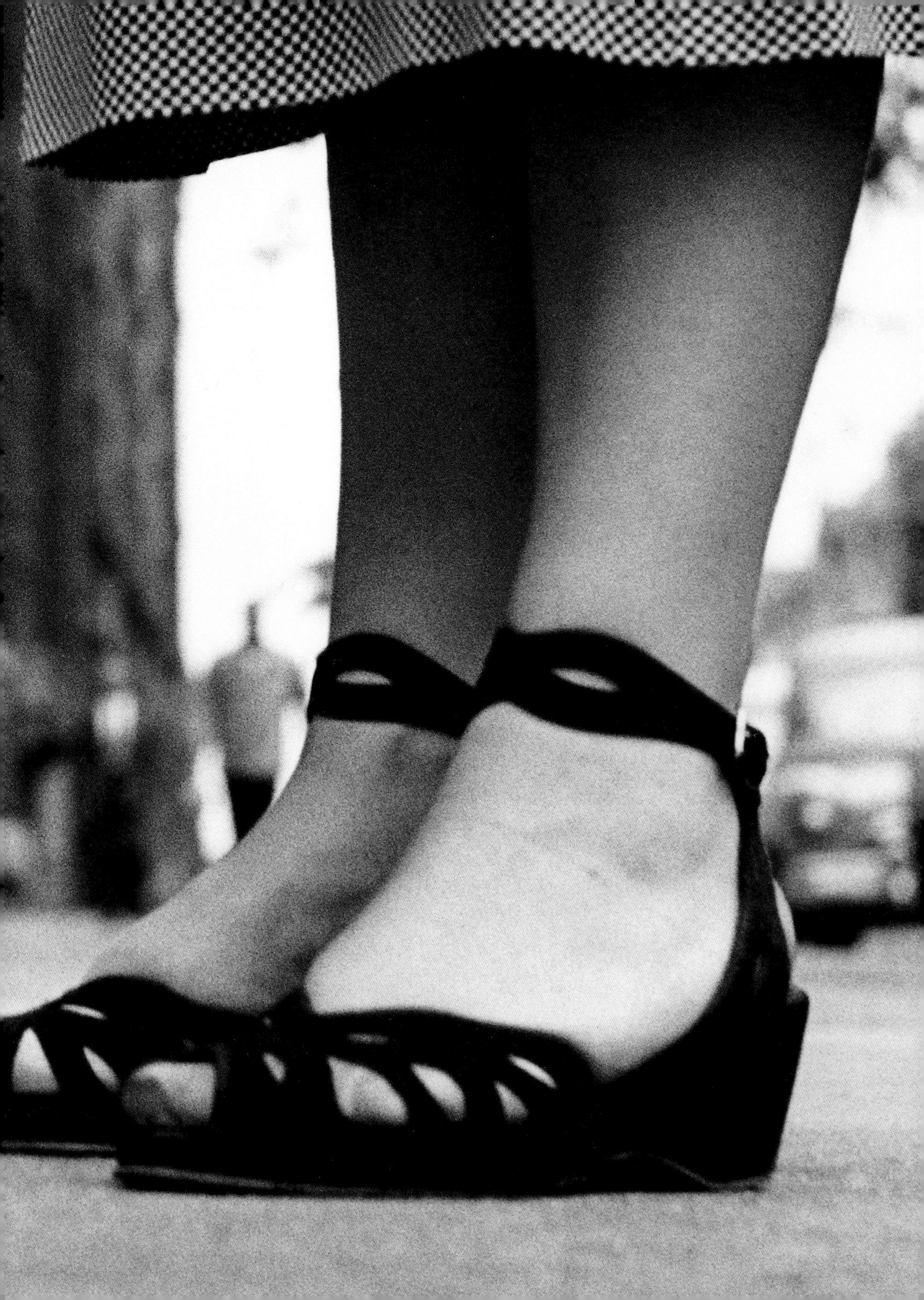

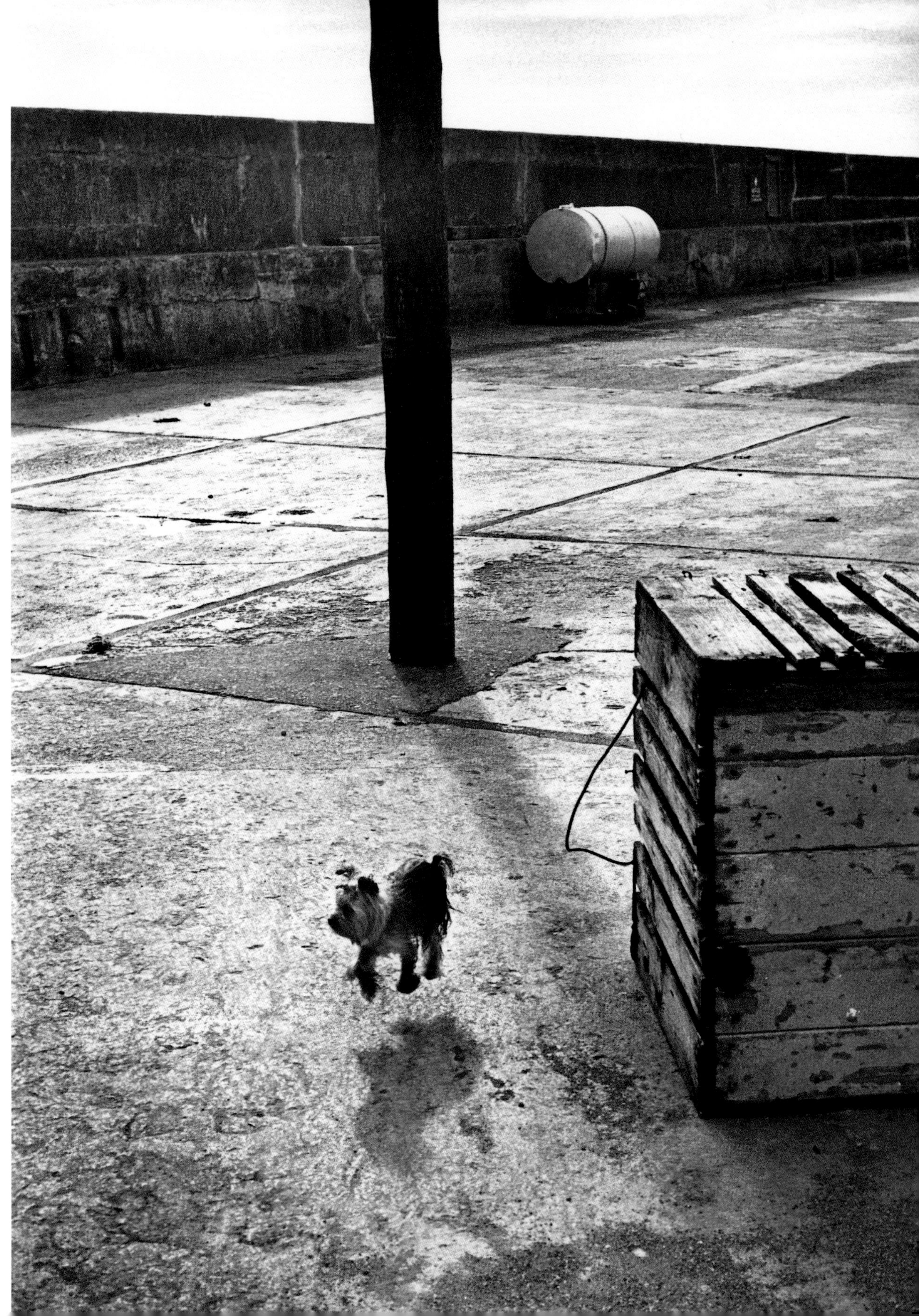

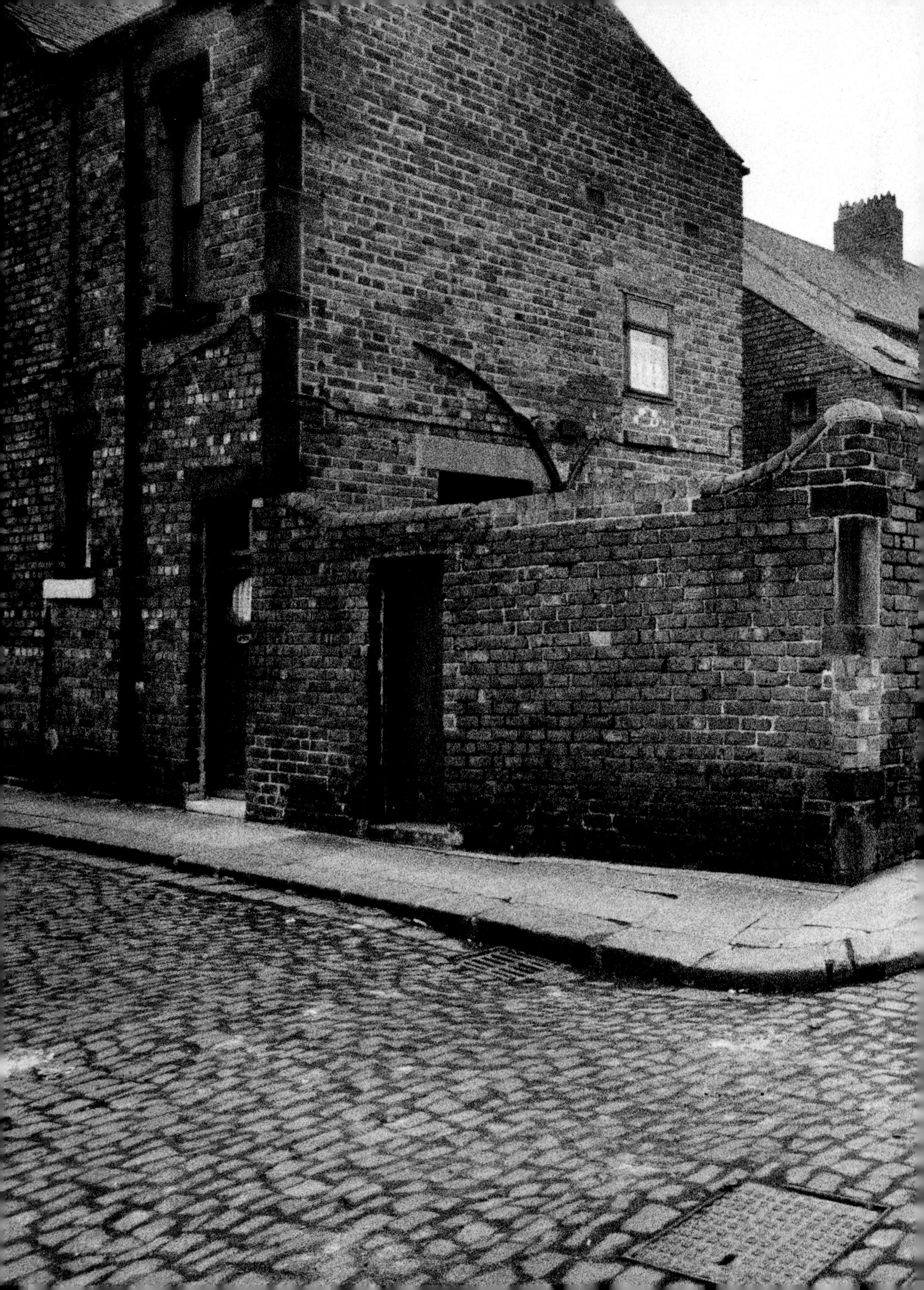

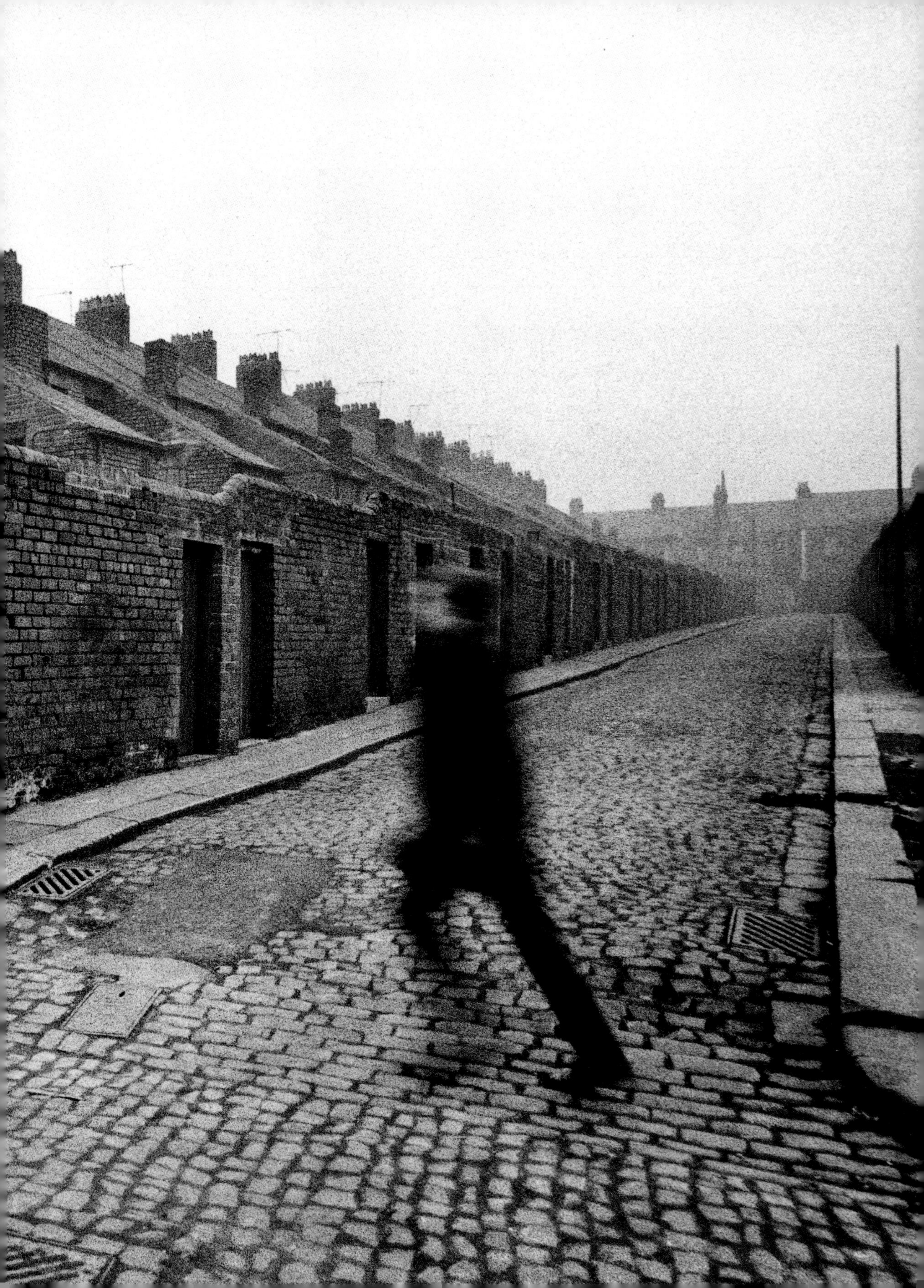

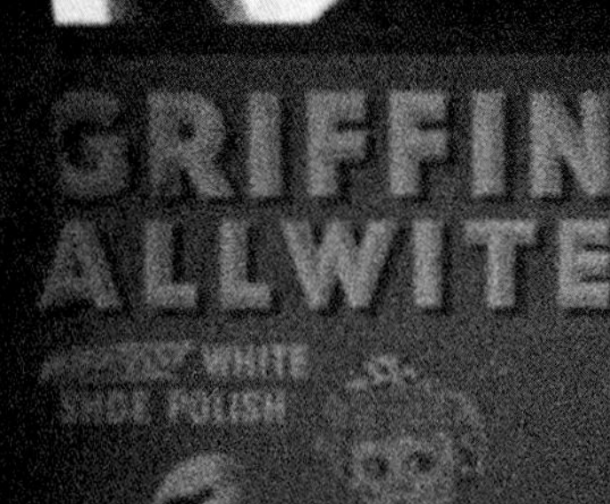
GRIFFIN
ALLWITE
WHITE
SHOE POLISH
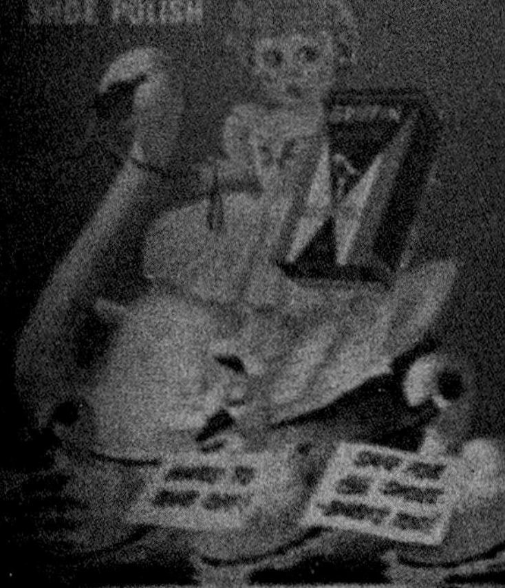

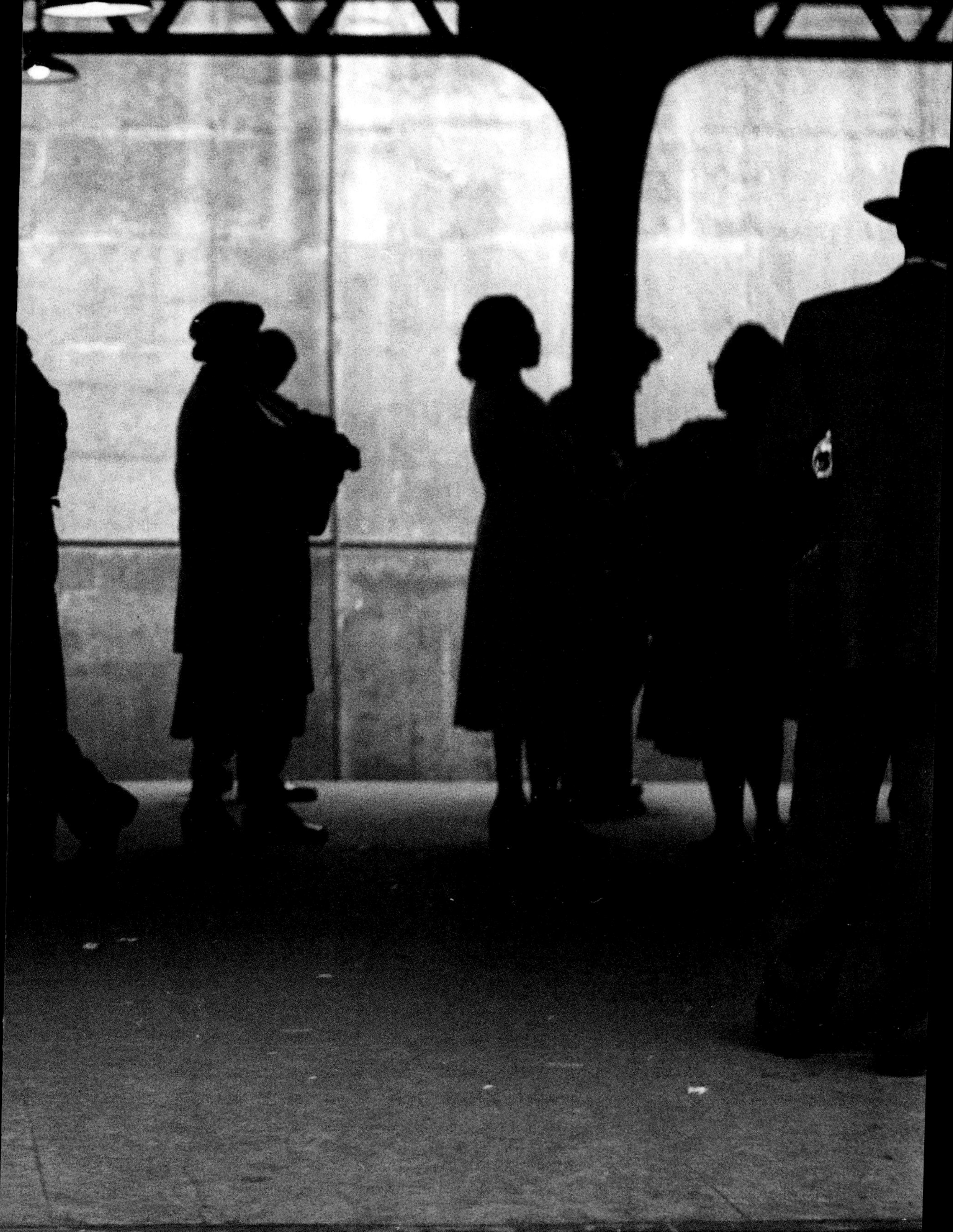

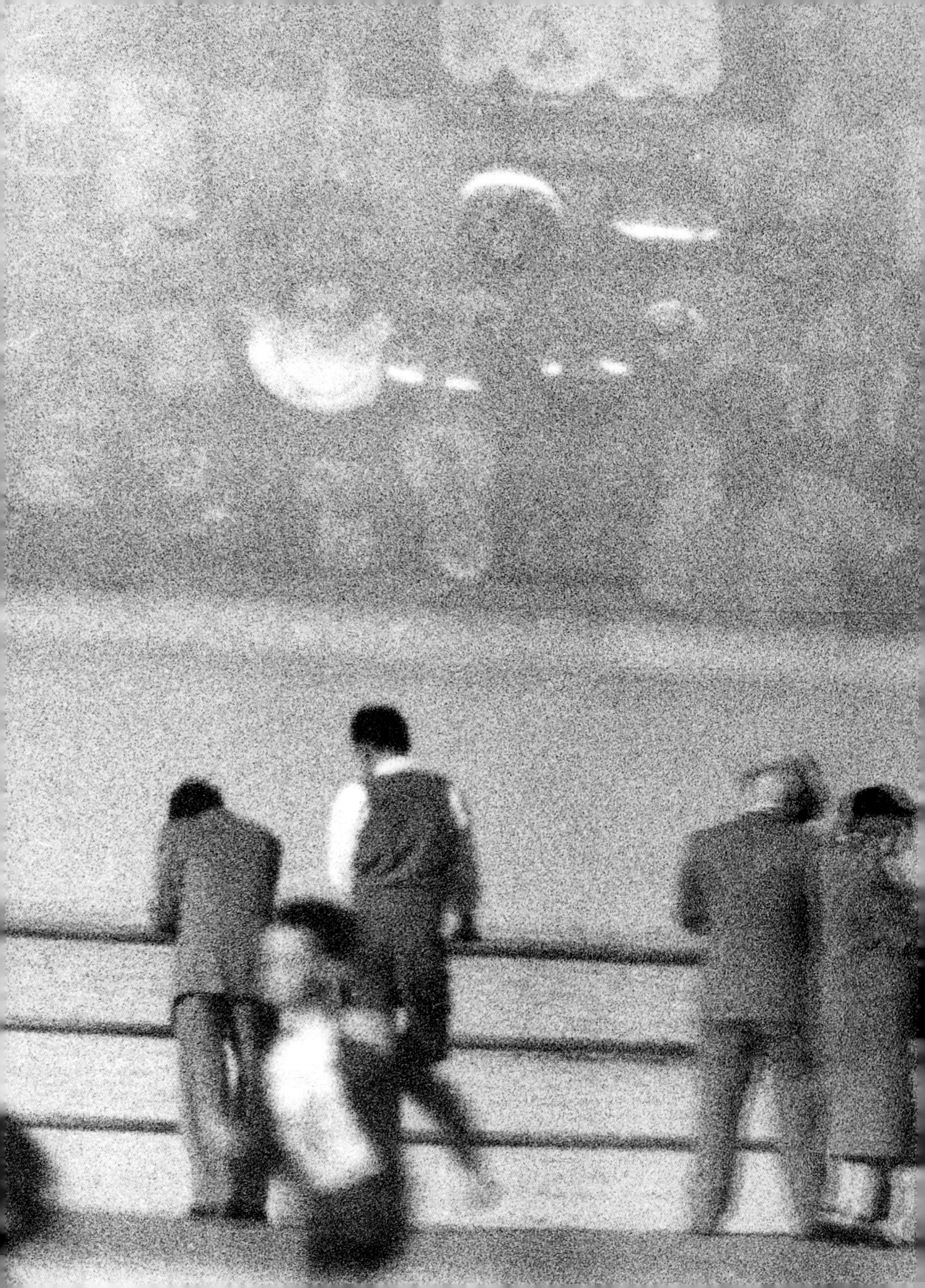

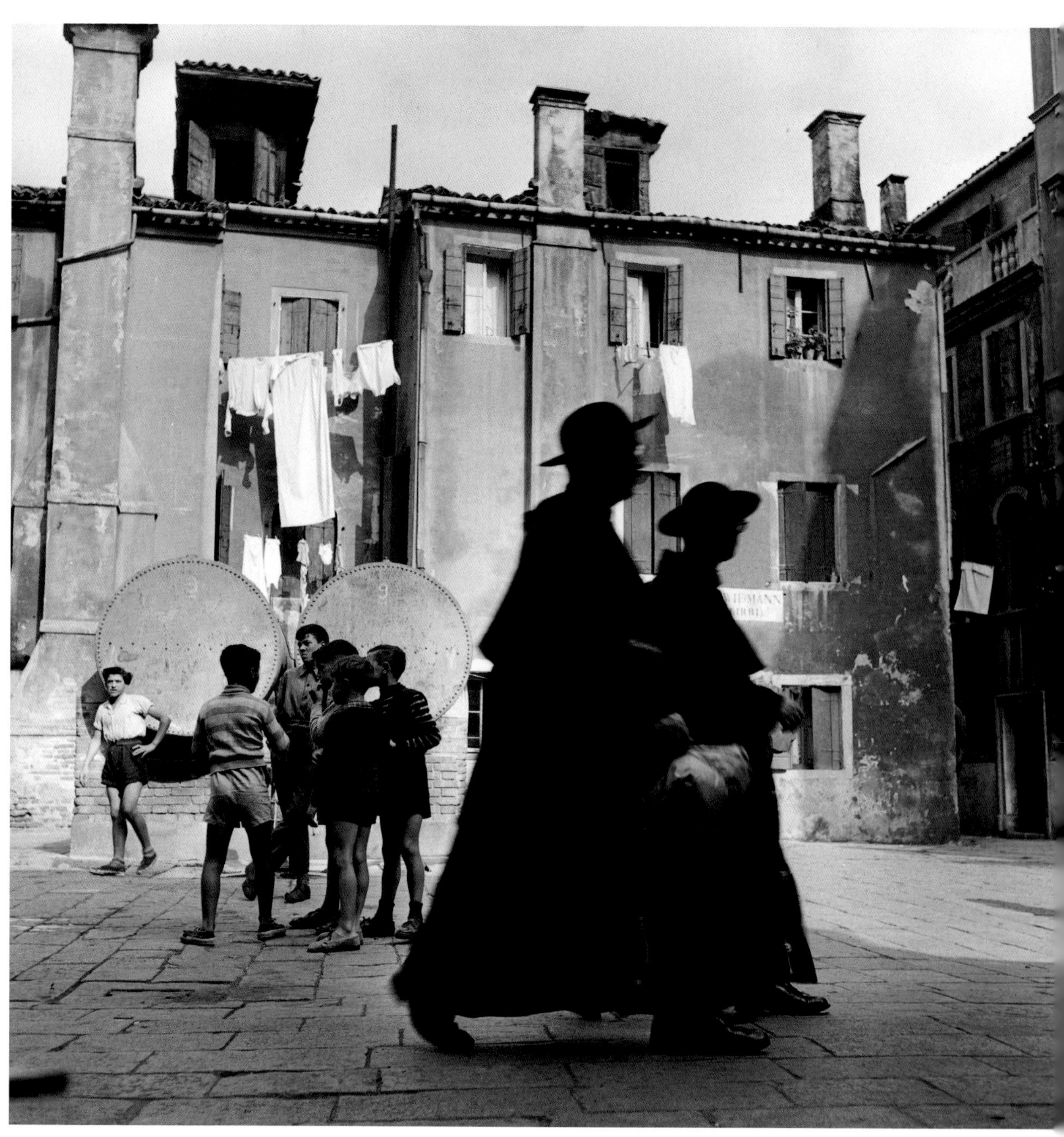

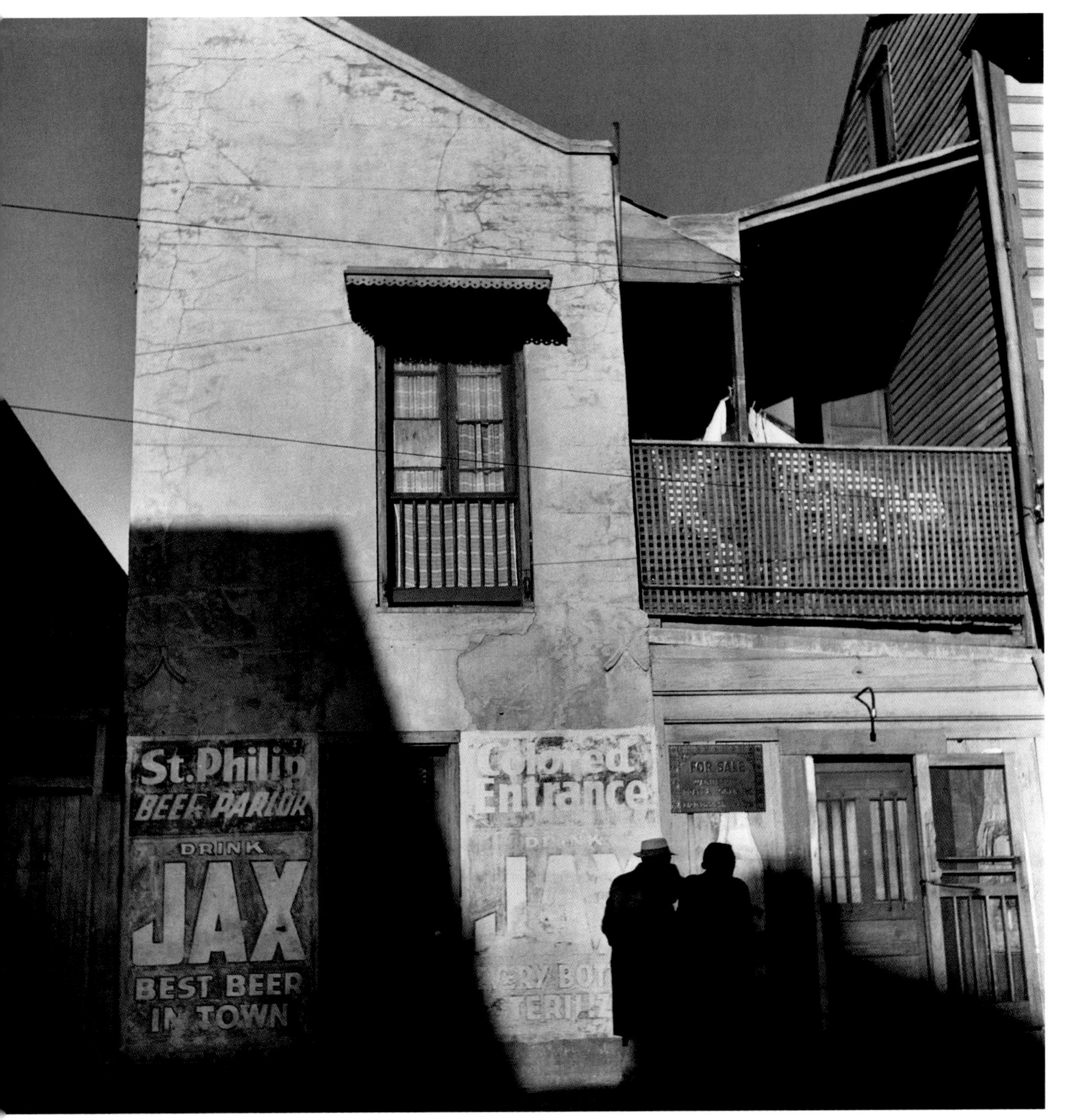

St. Philip
BEER PARLOR
DRINK
JAX
BEST BEER
IN TOWN
Colored Entrance
DRINK
JAX
FOR SALE

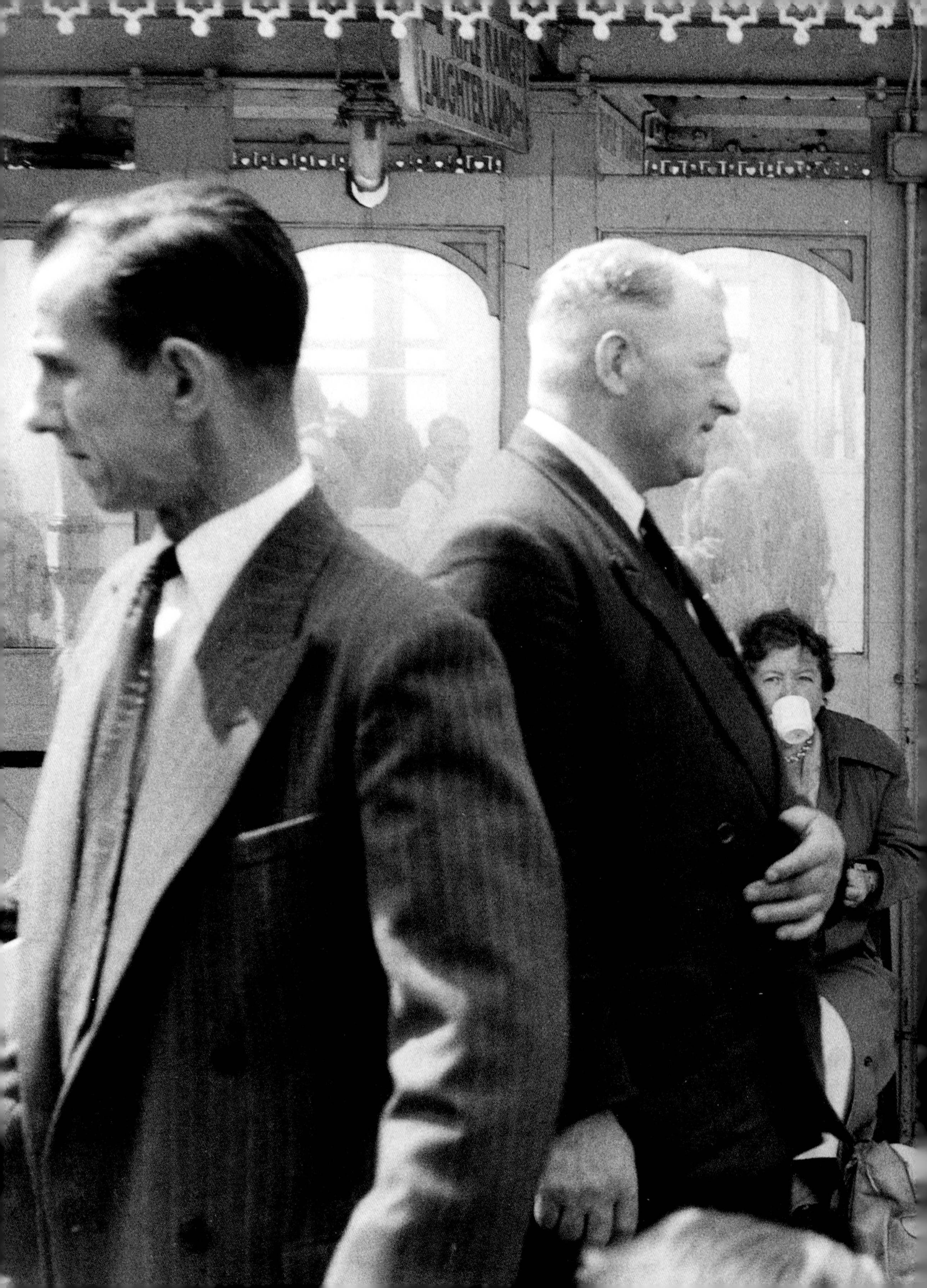

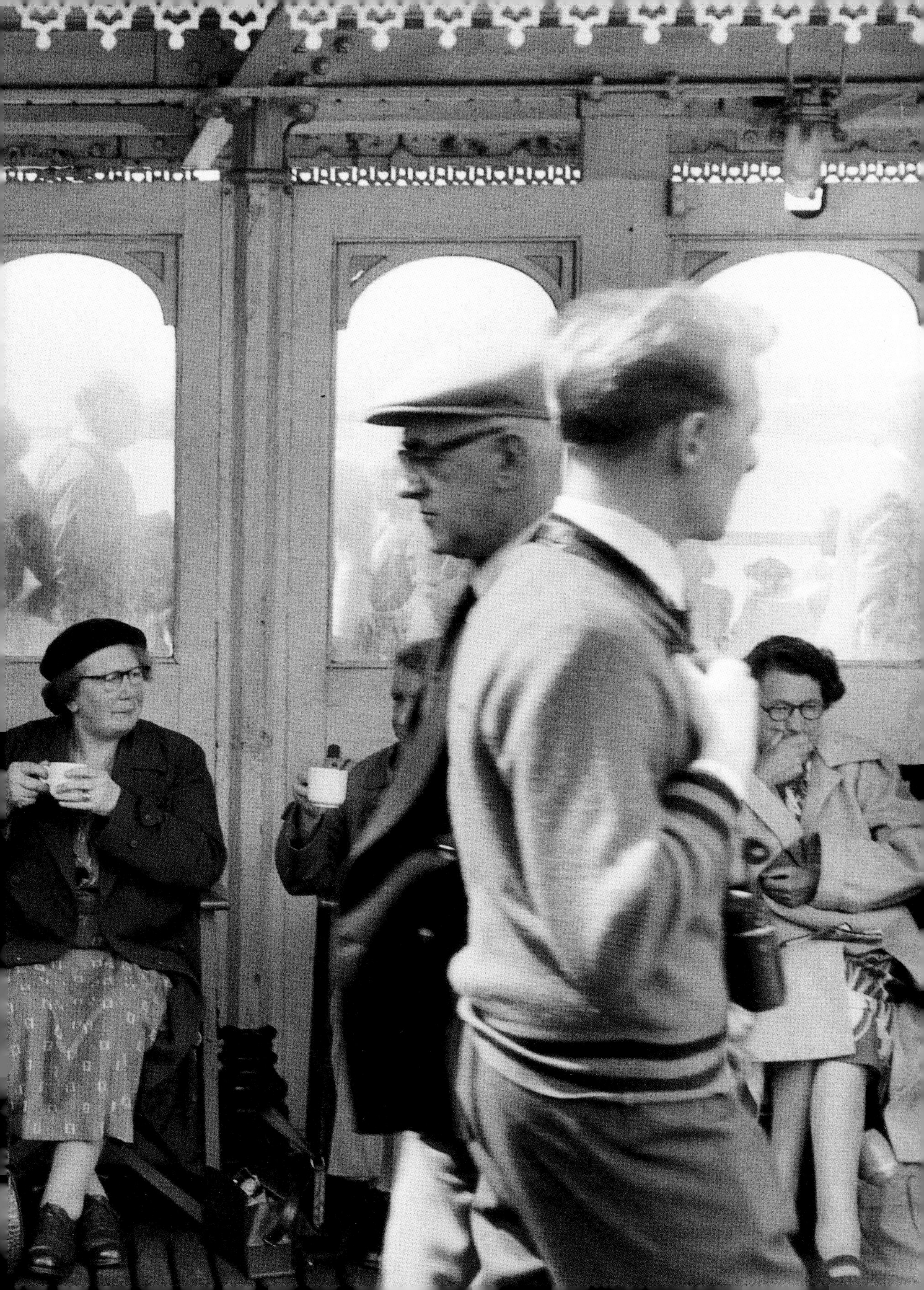

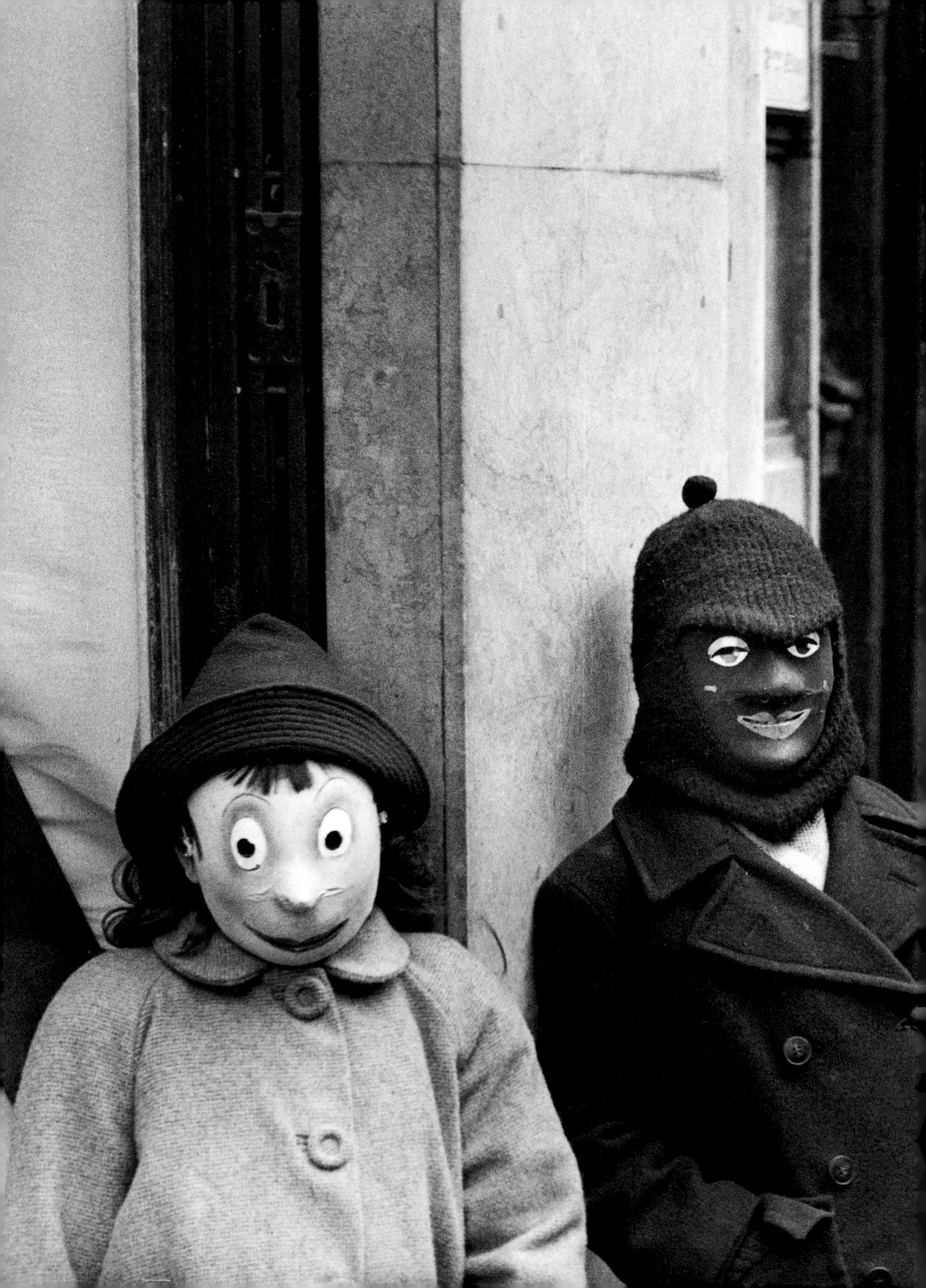

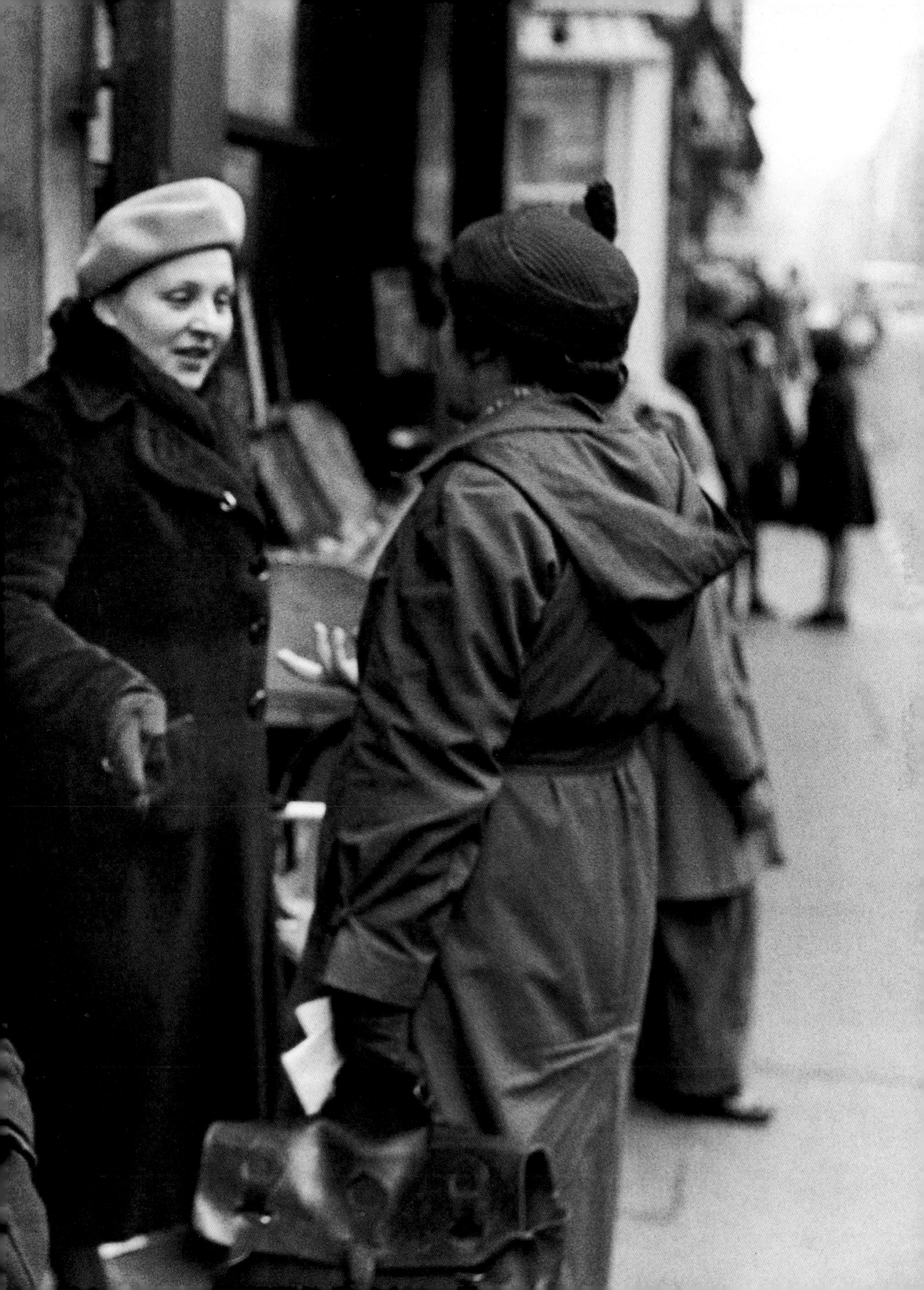

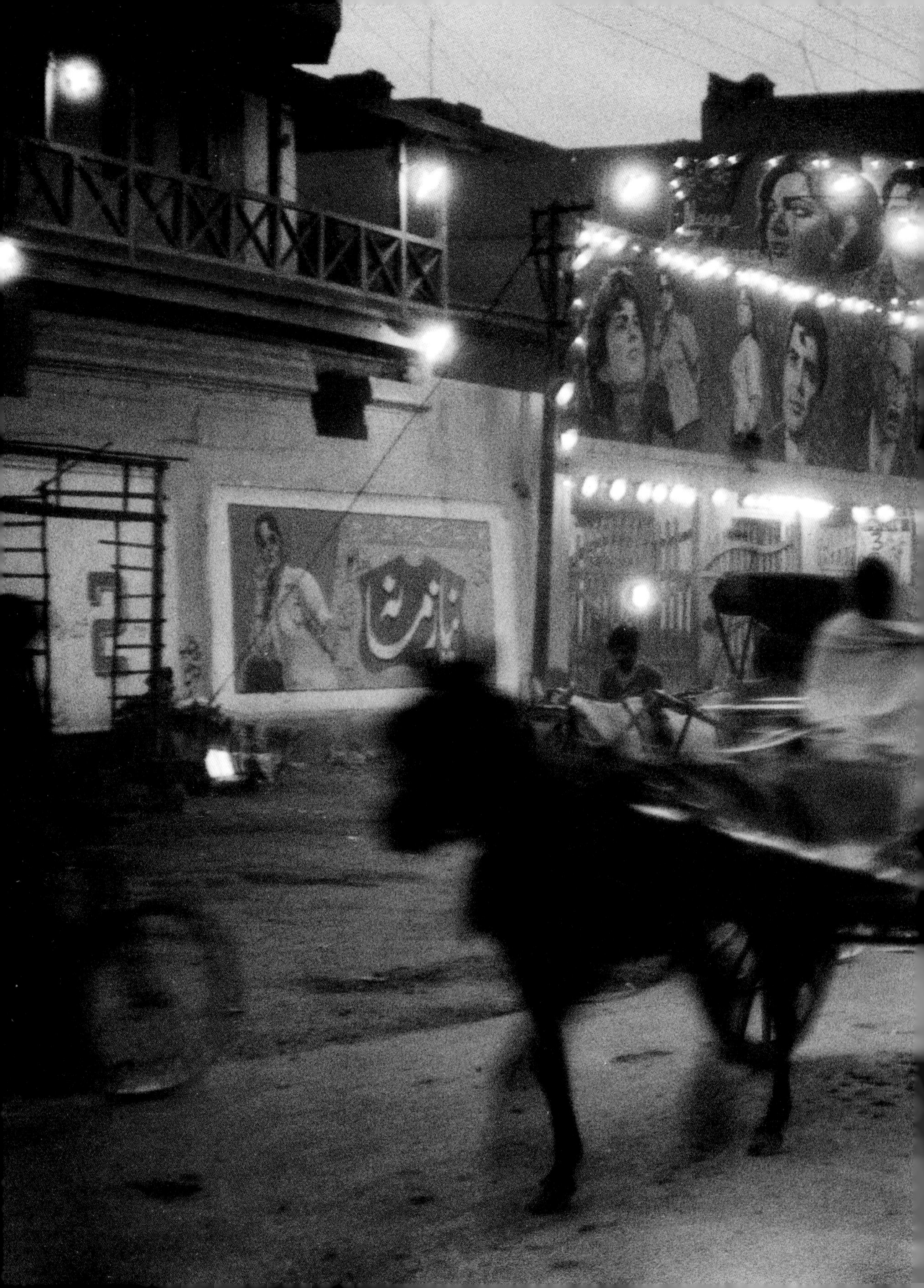

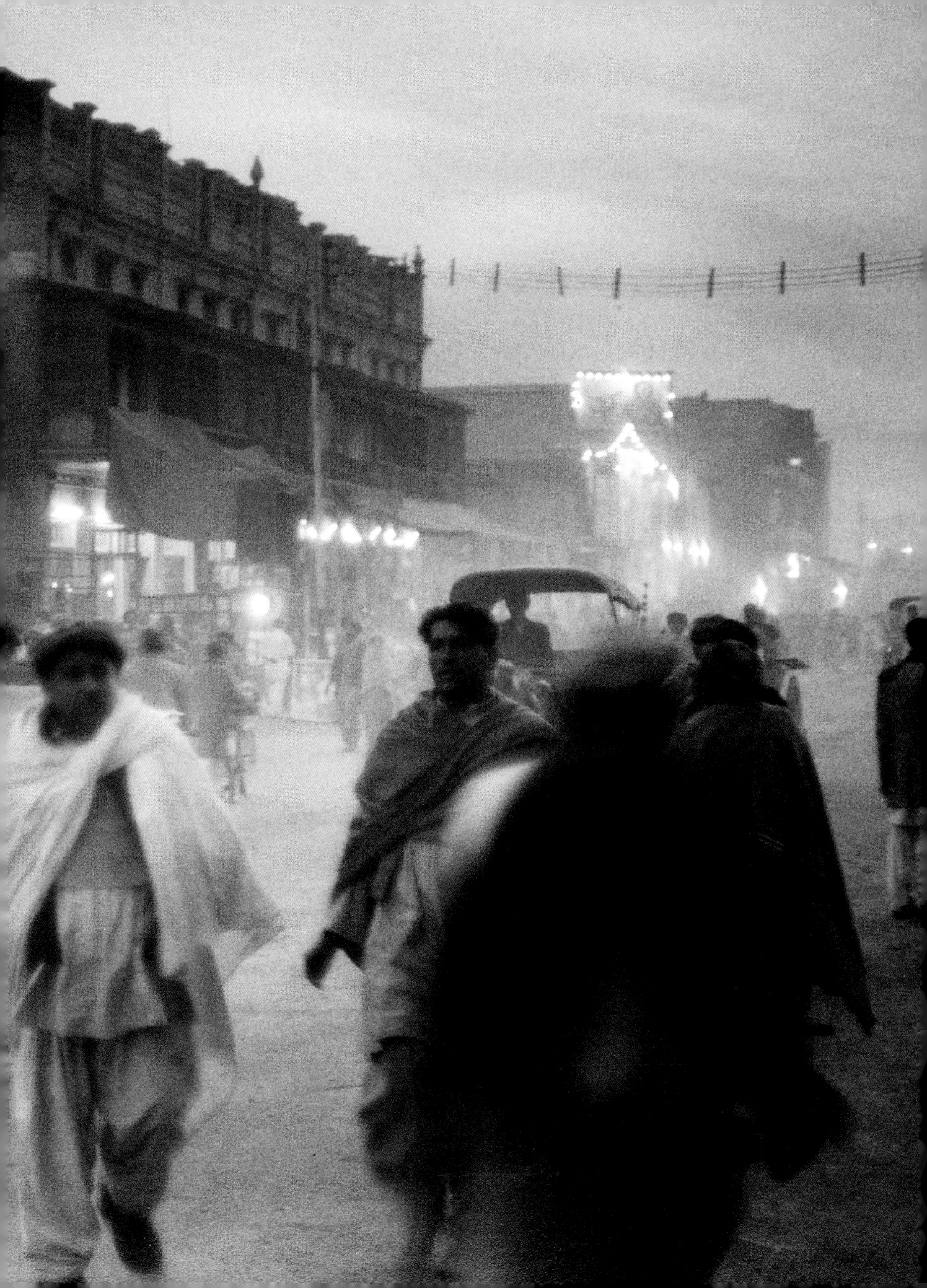

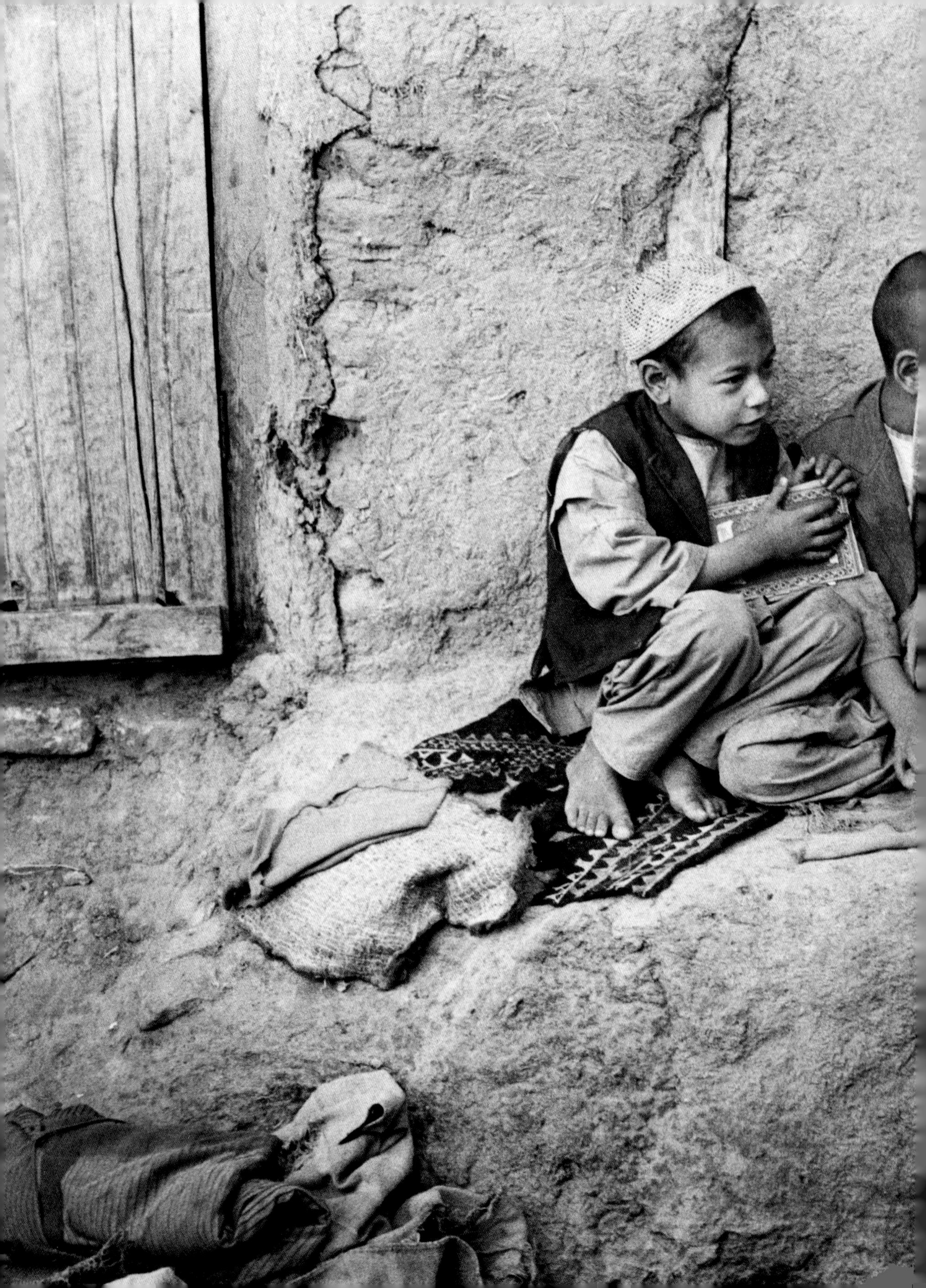

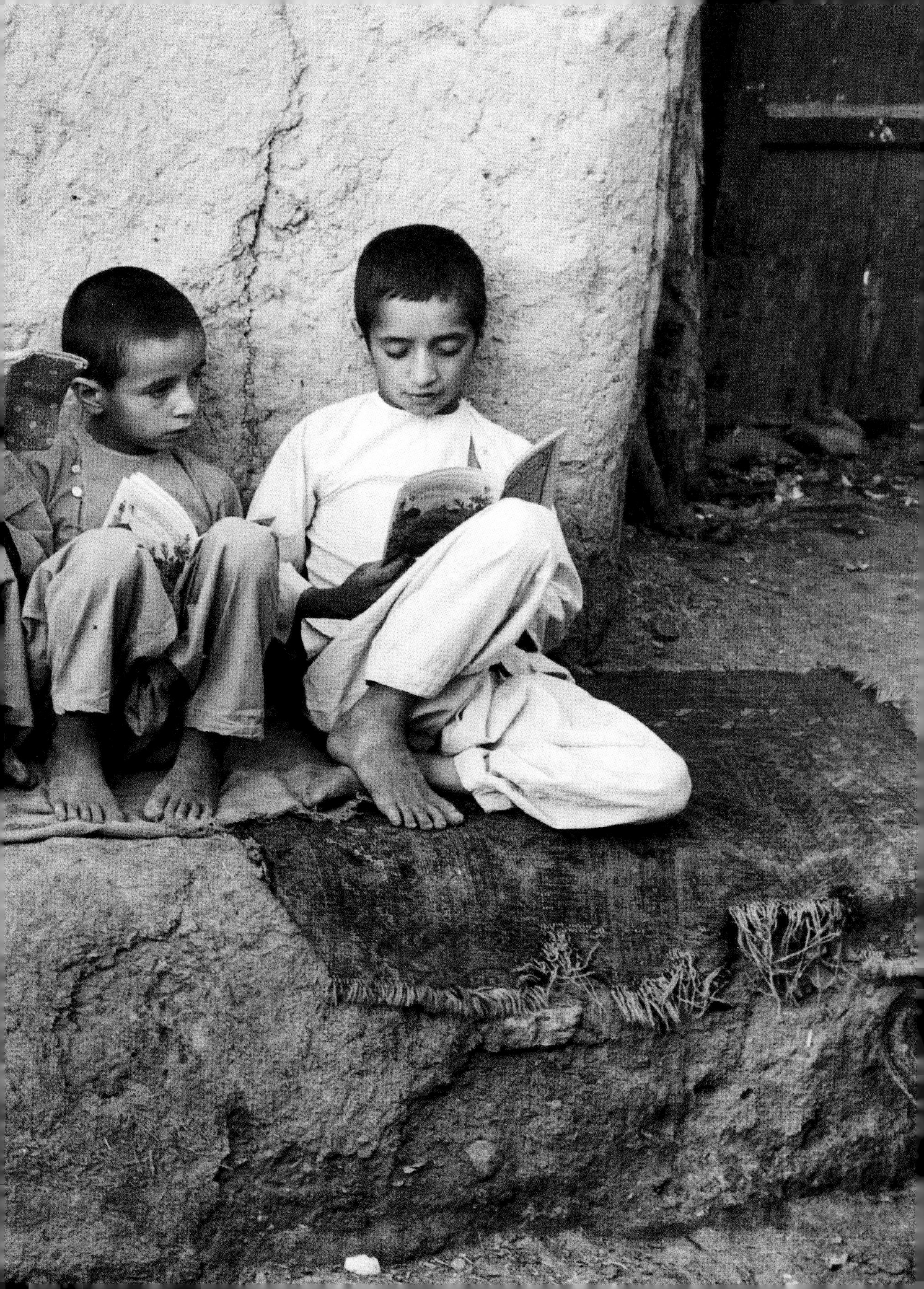

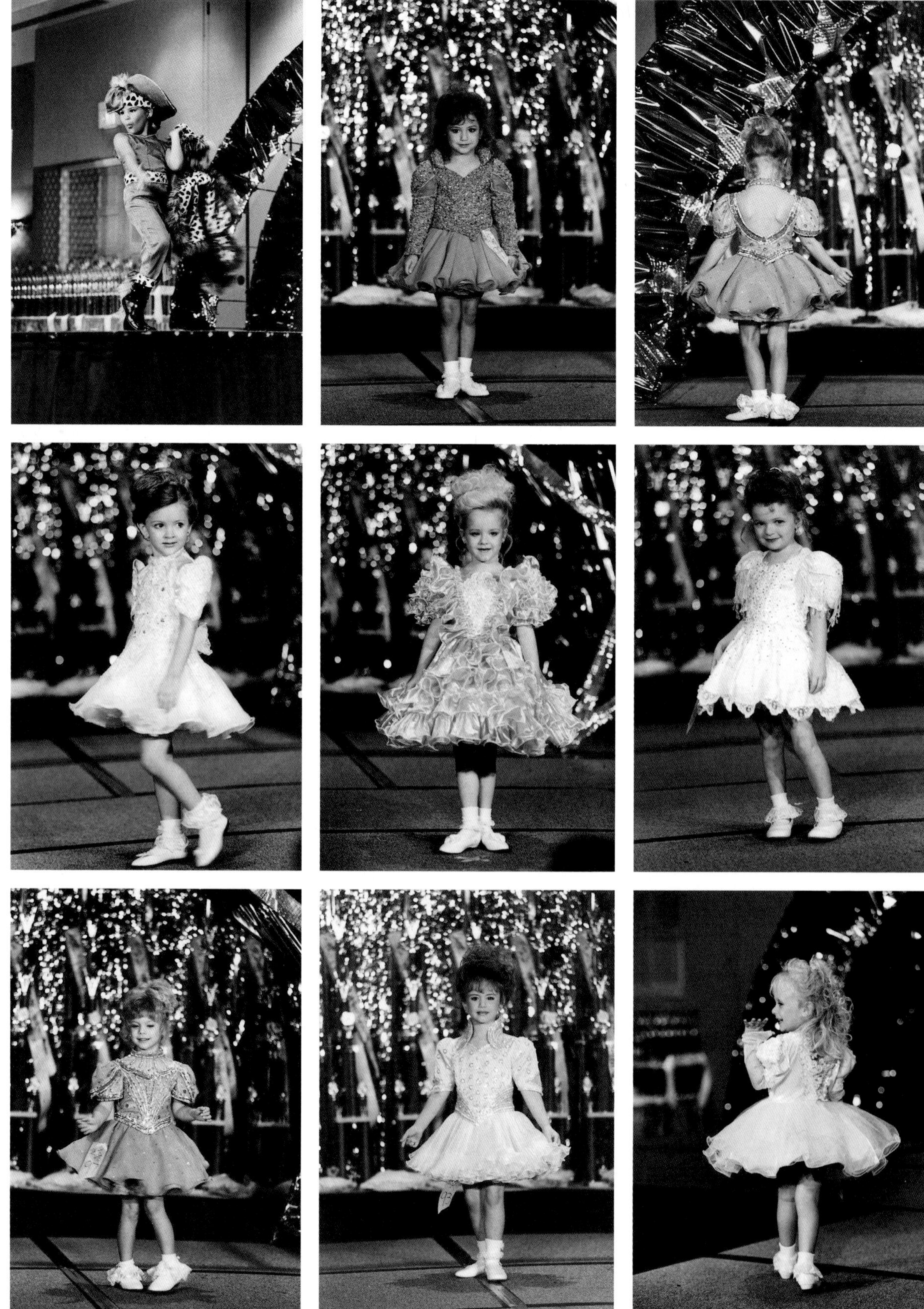

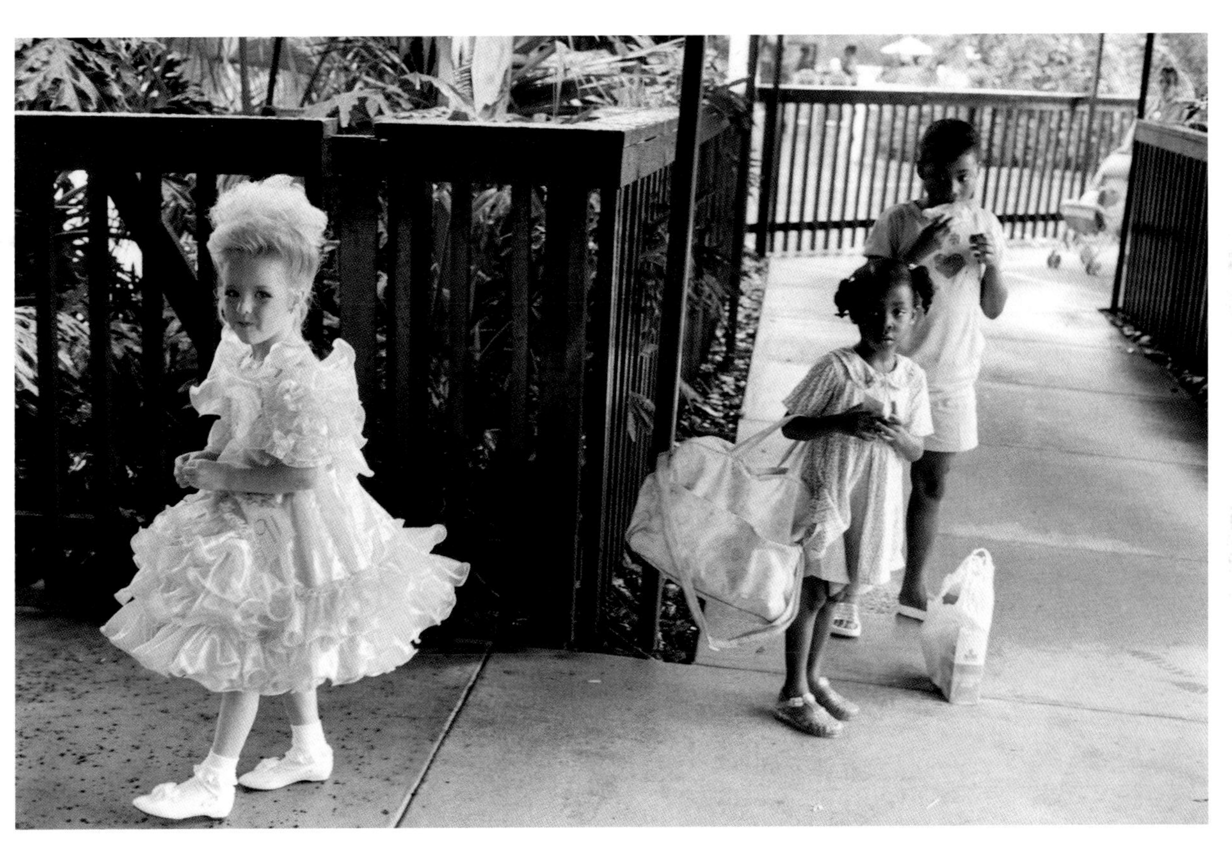

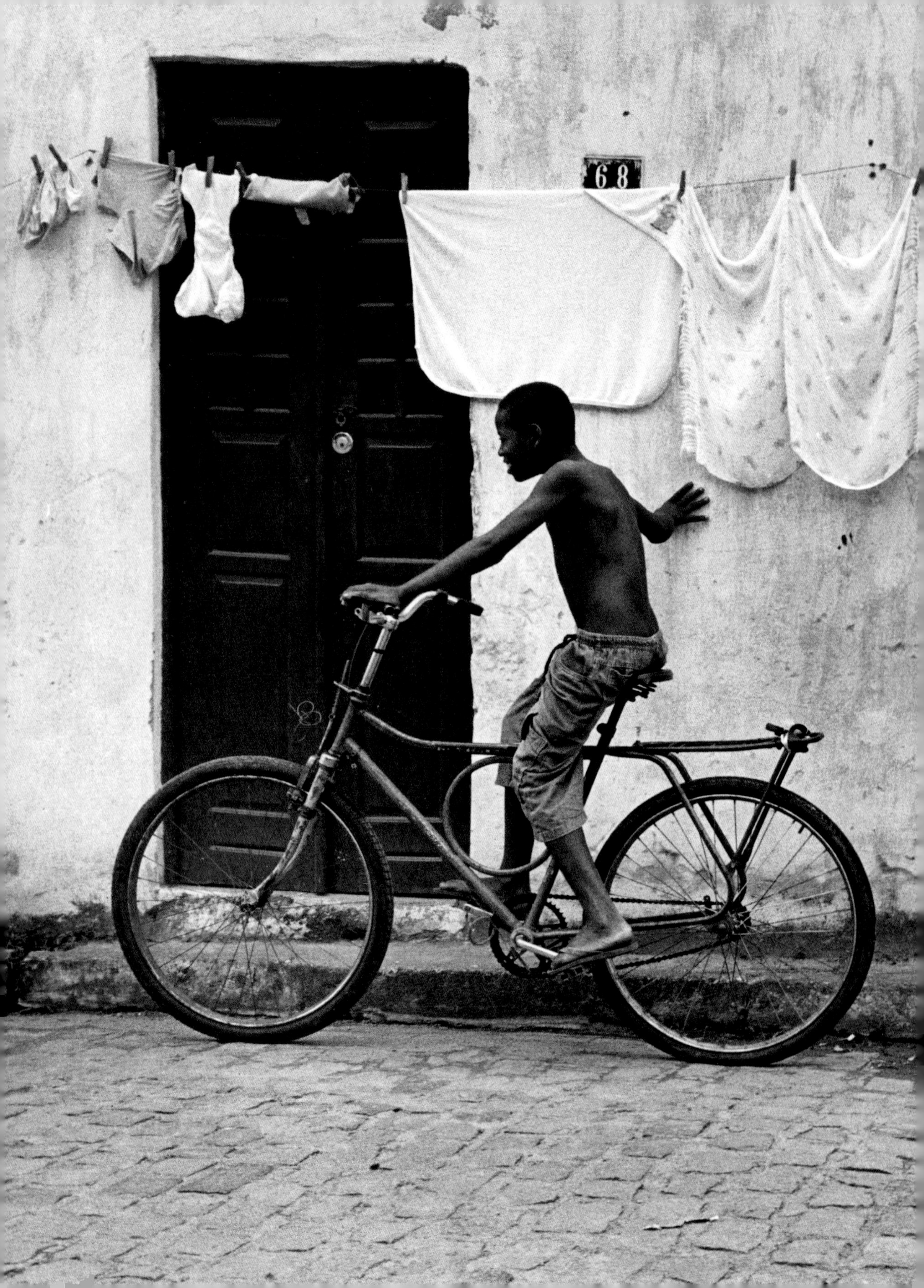

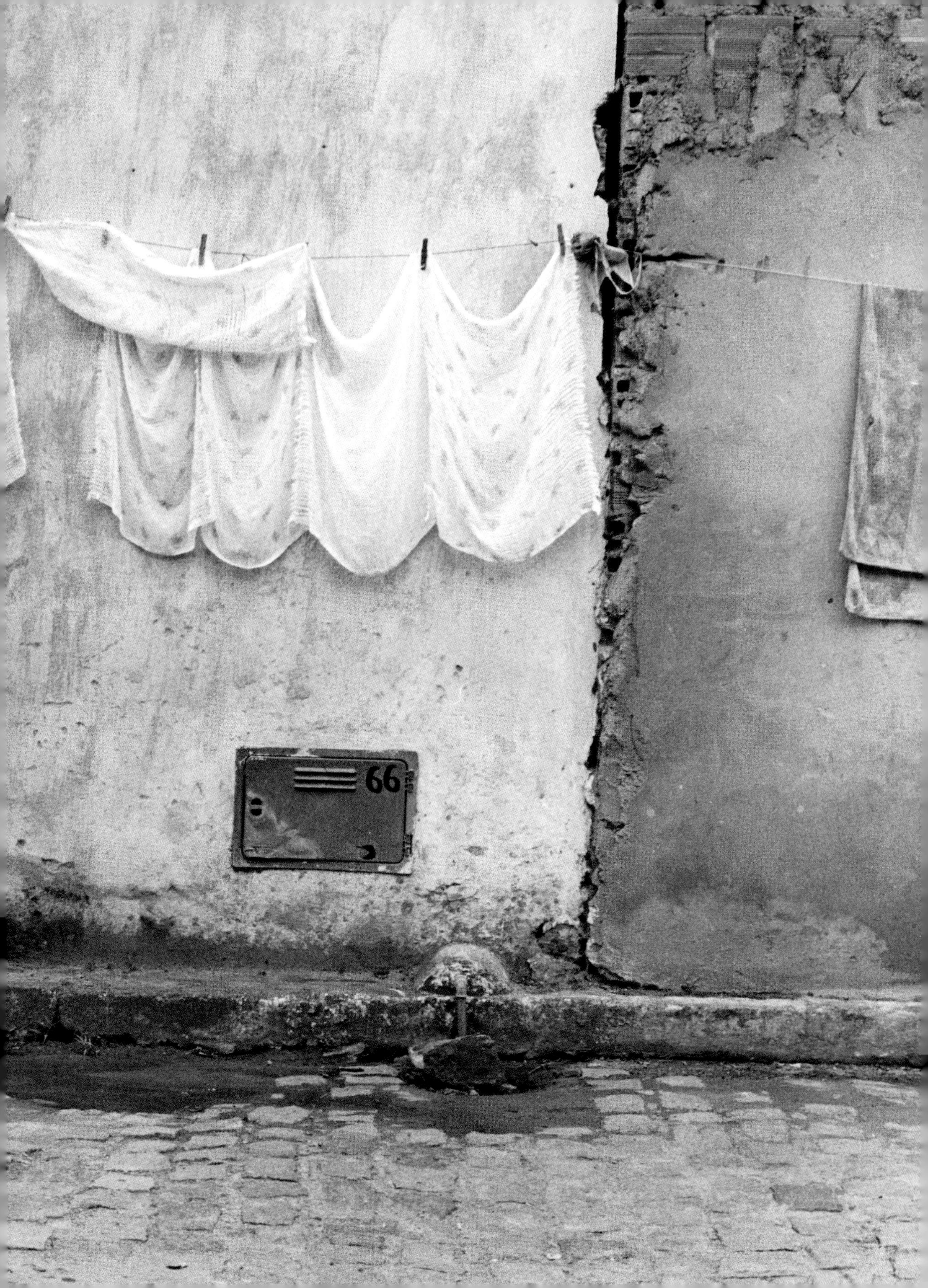

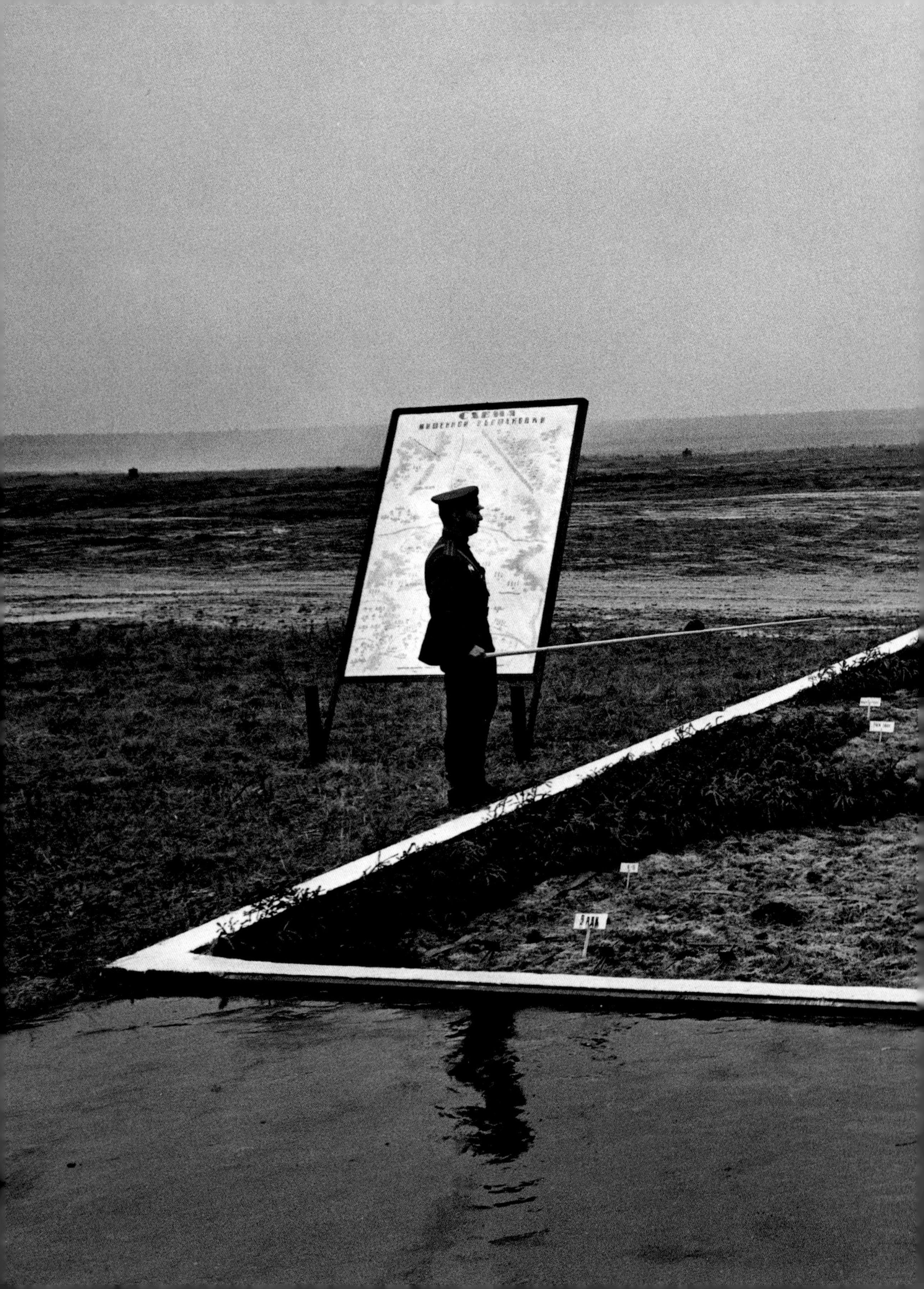

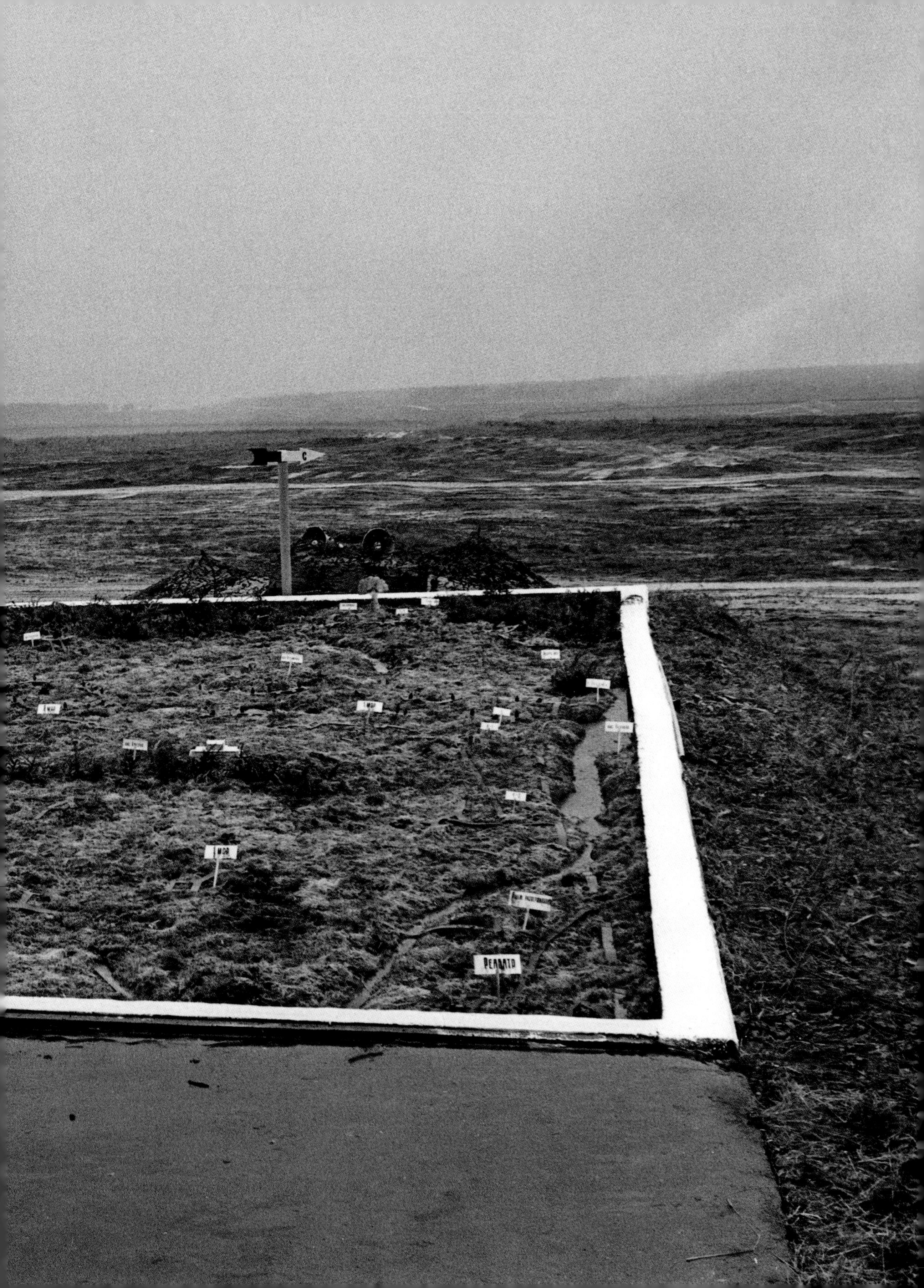

C

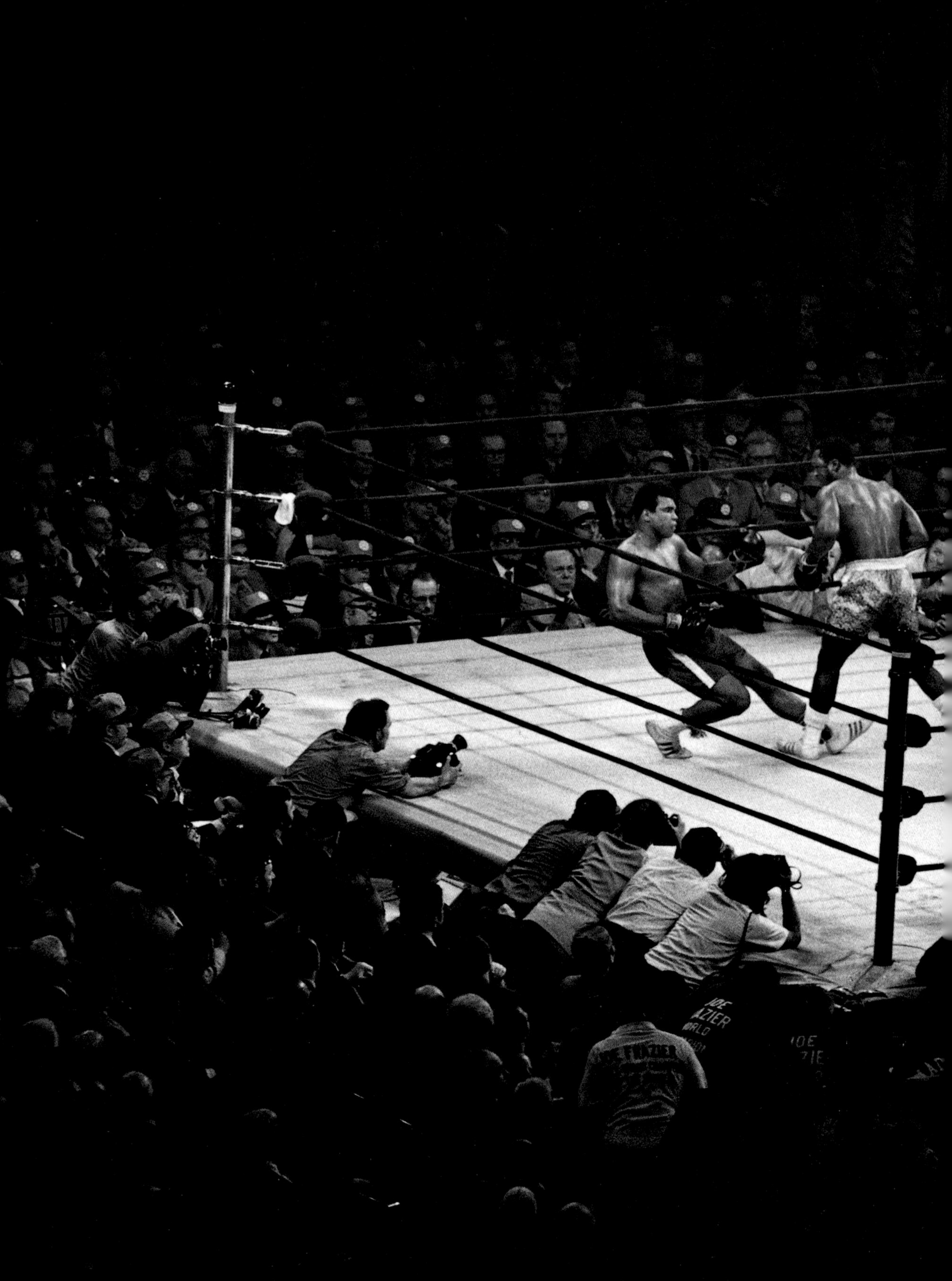

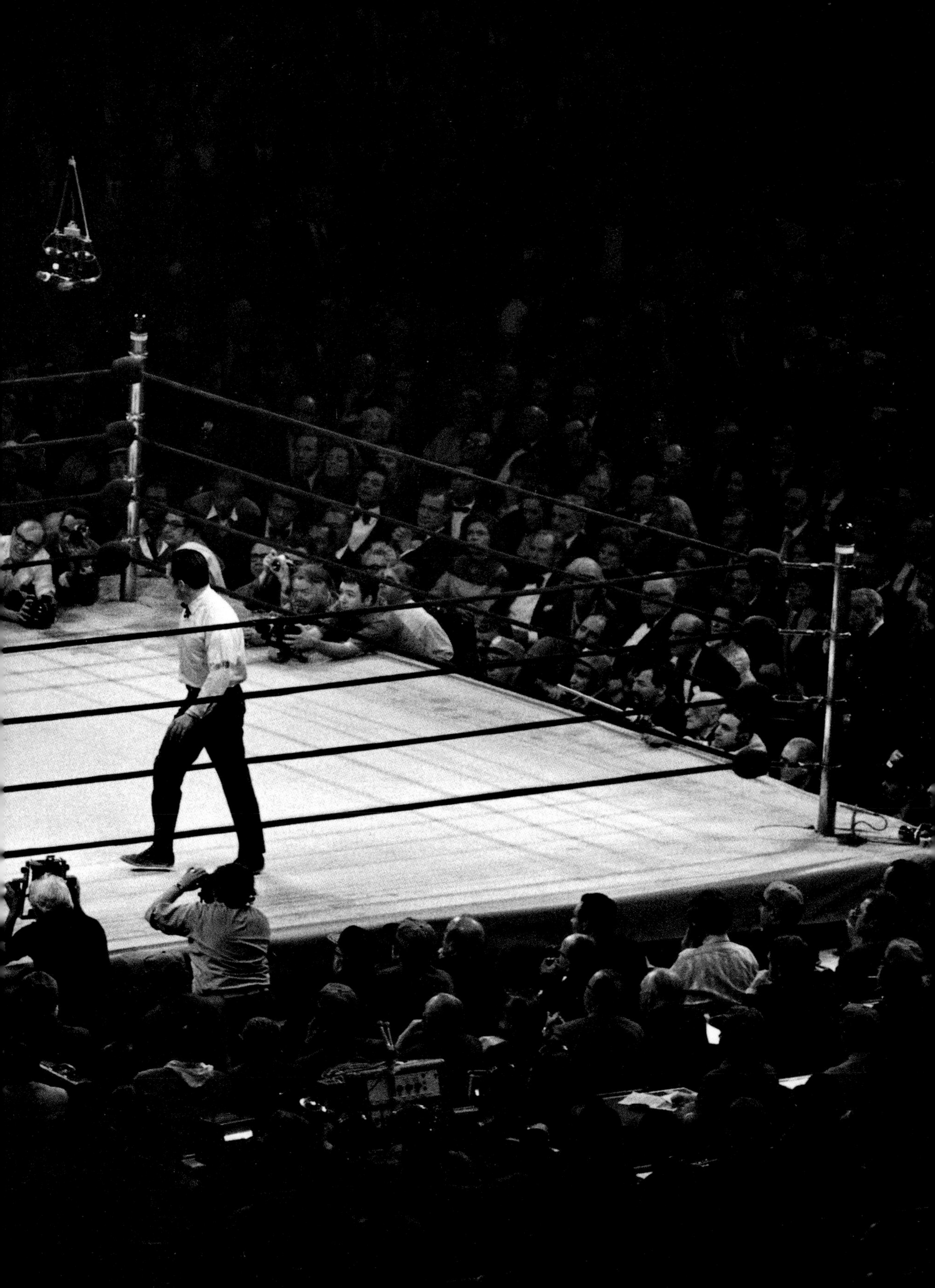

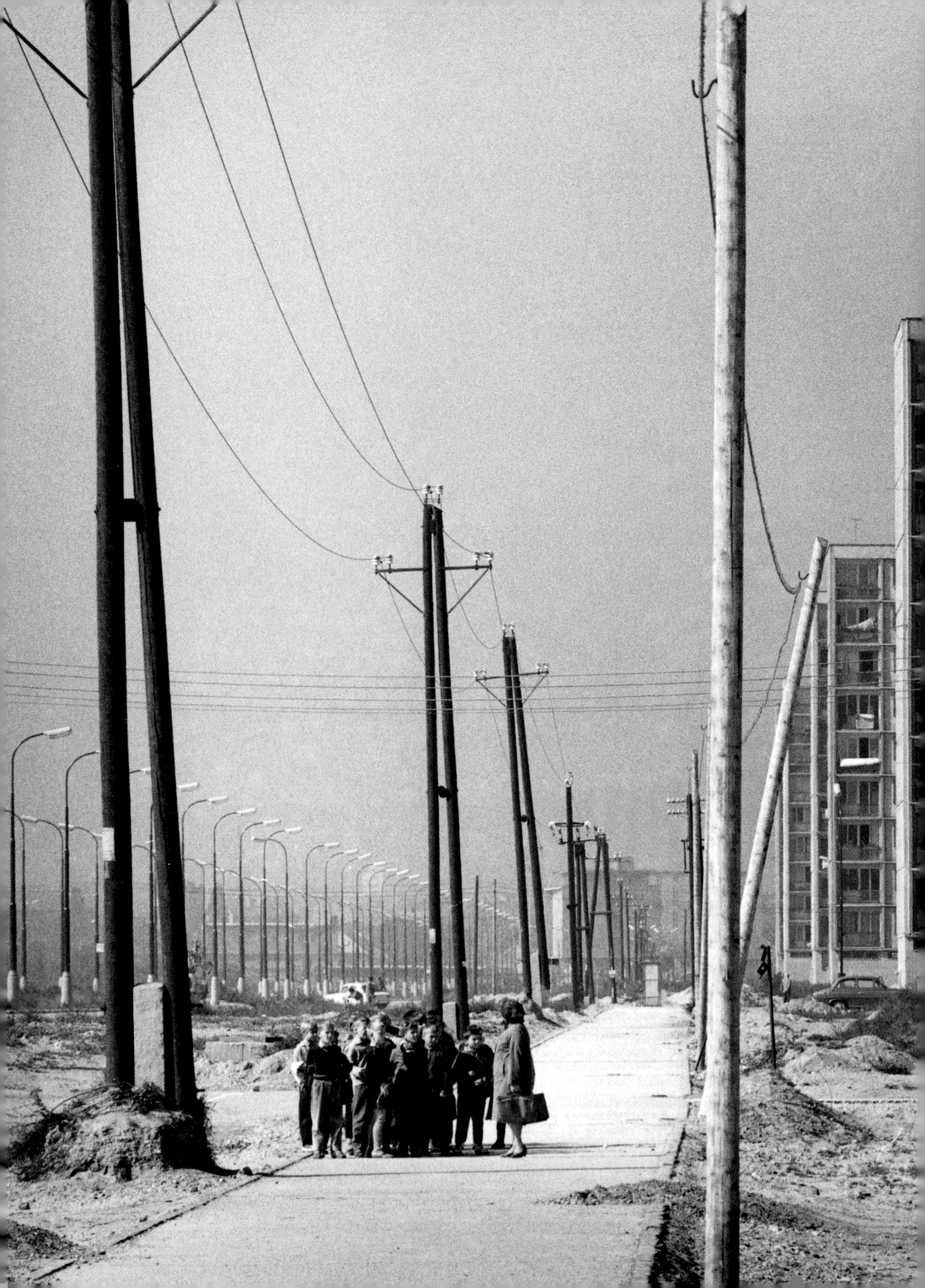

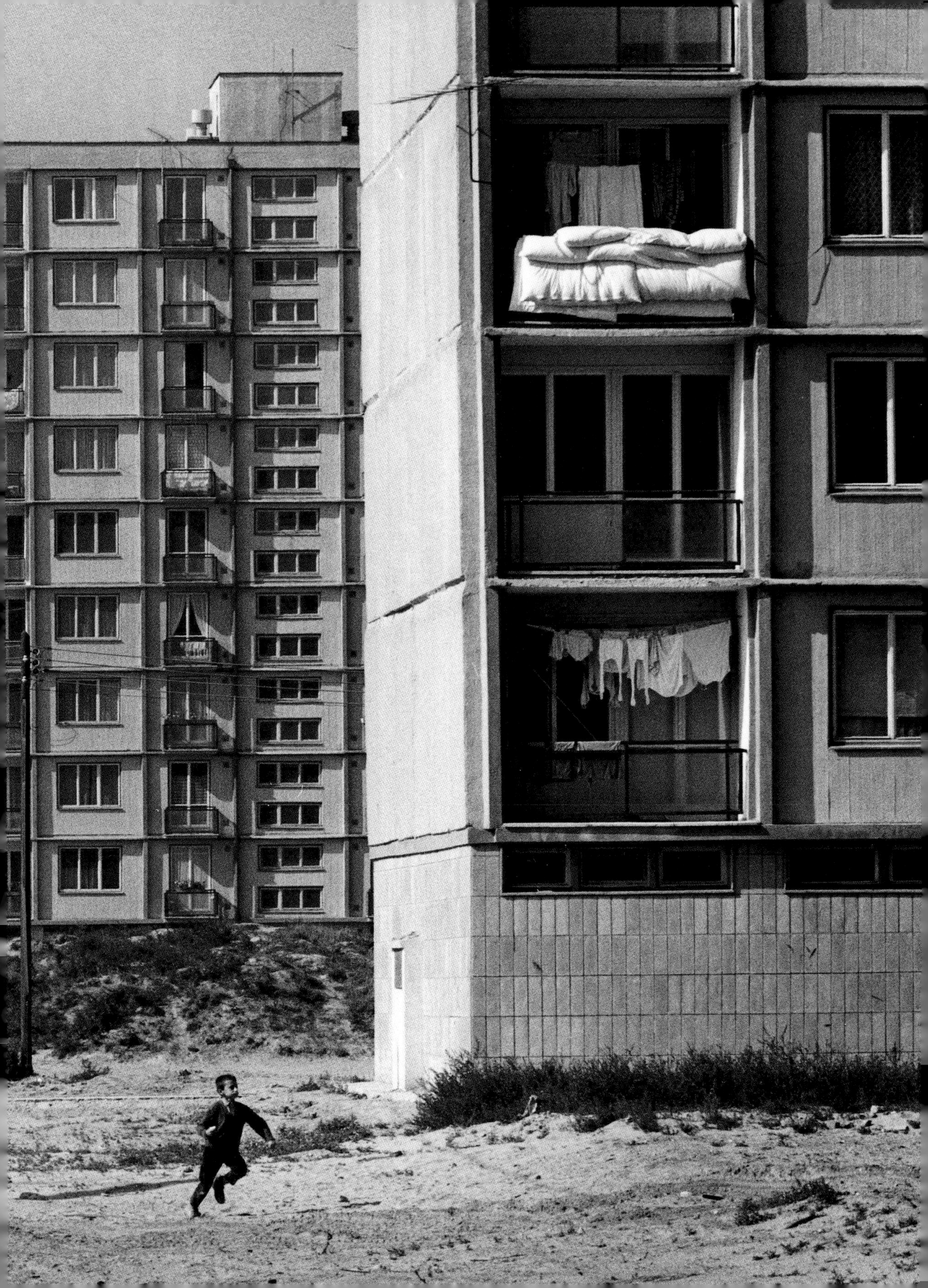

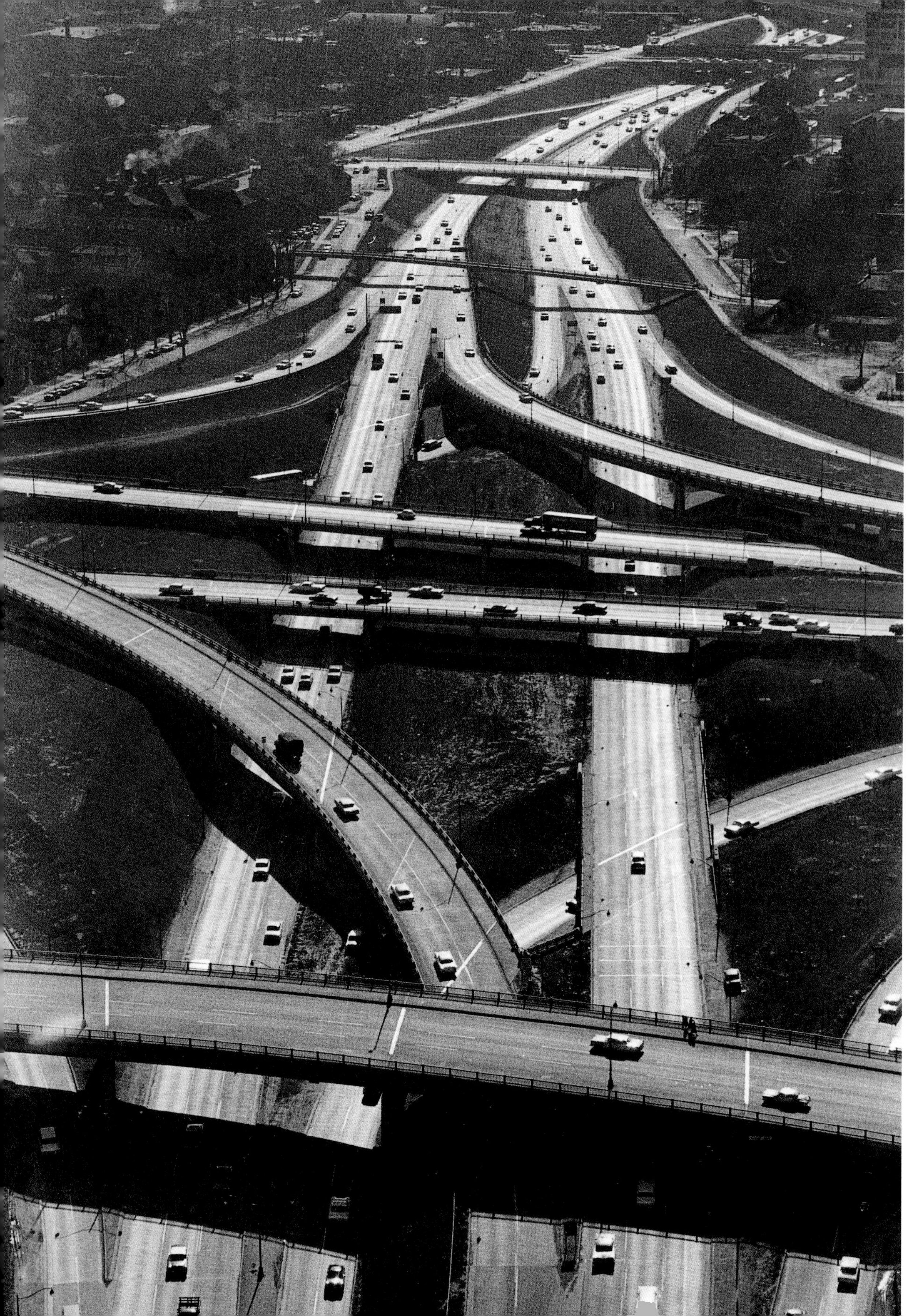

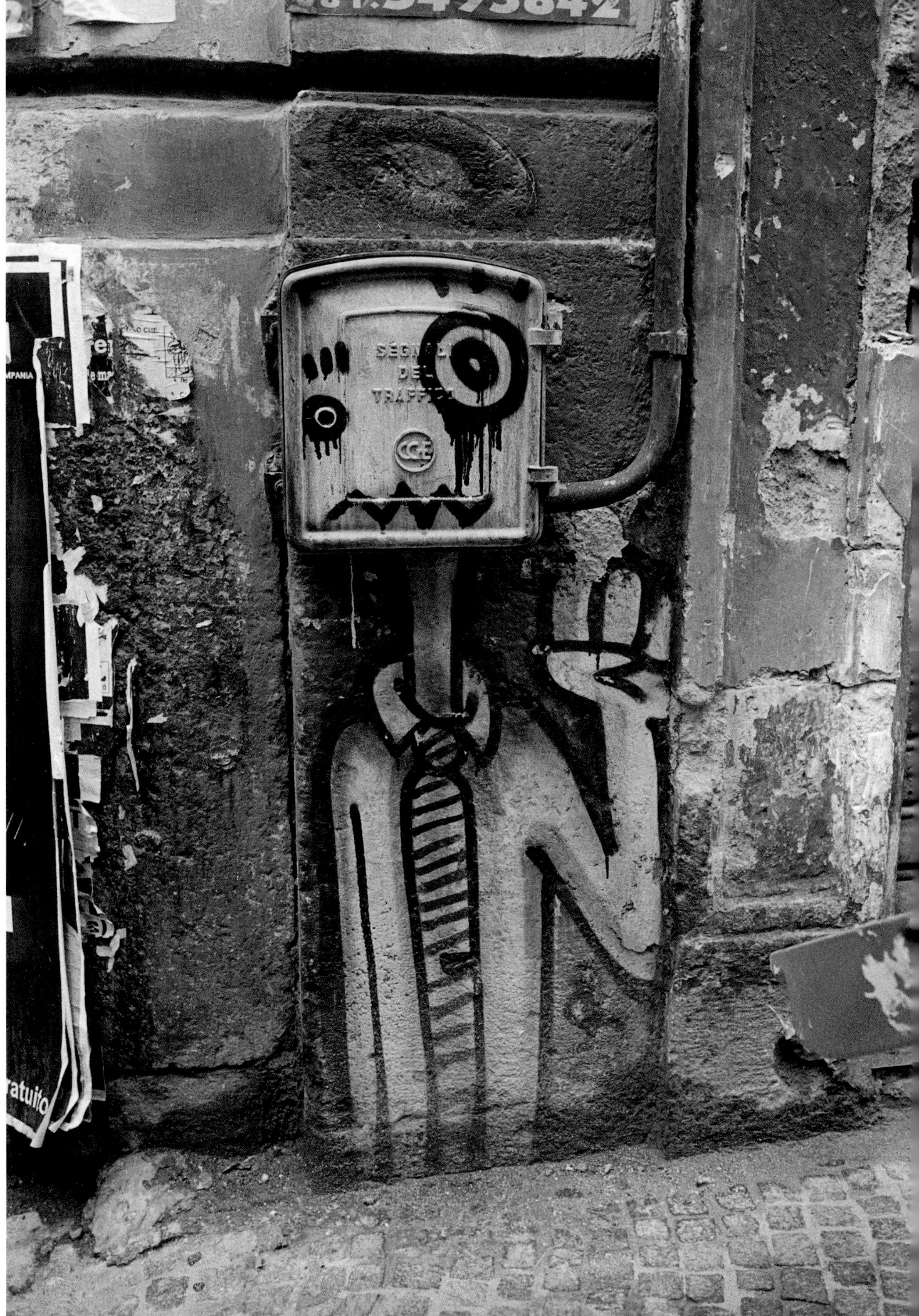
SEGNALI
DEL
TRAFFICO
CCE

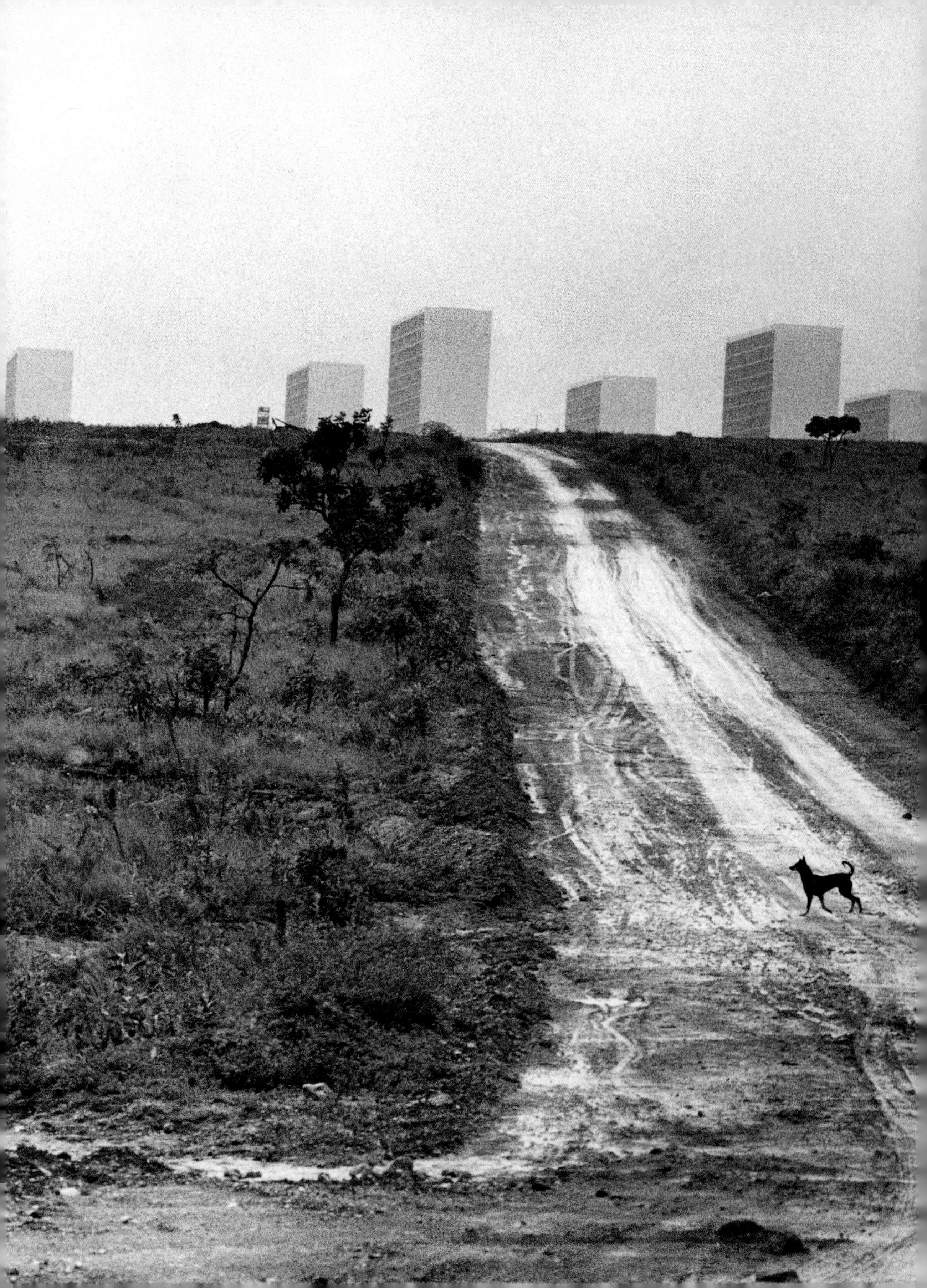

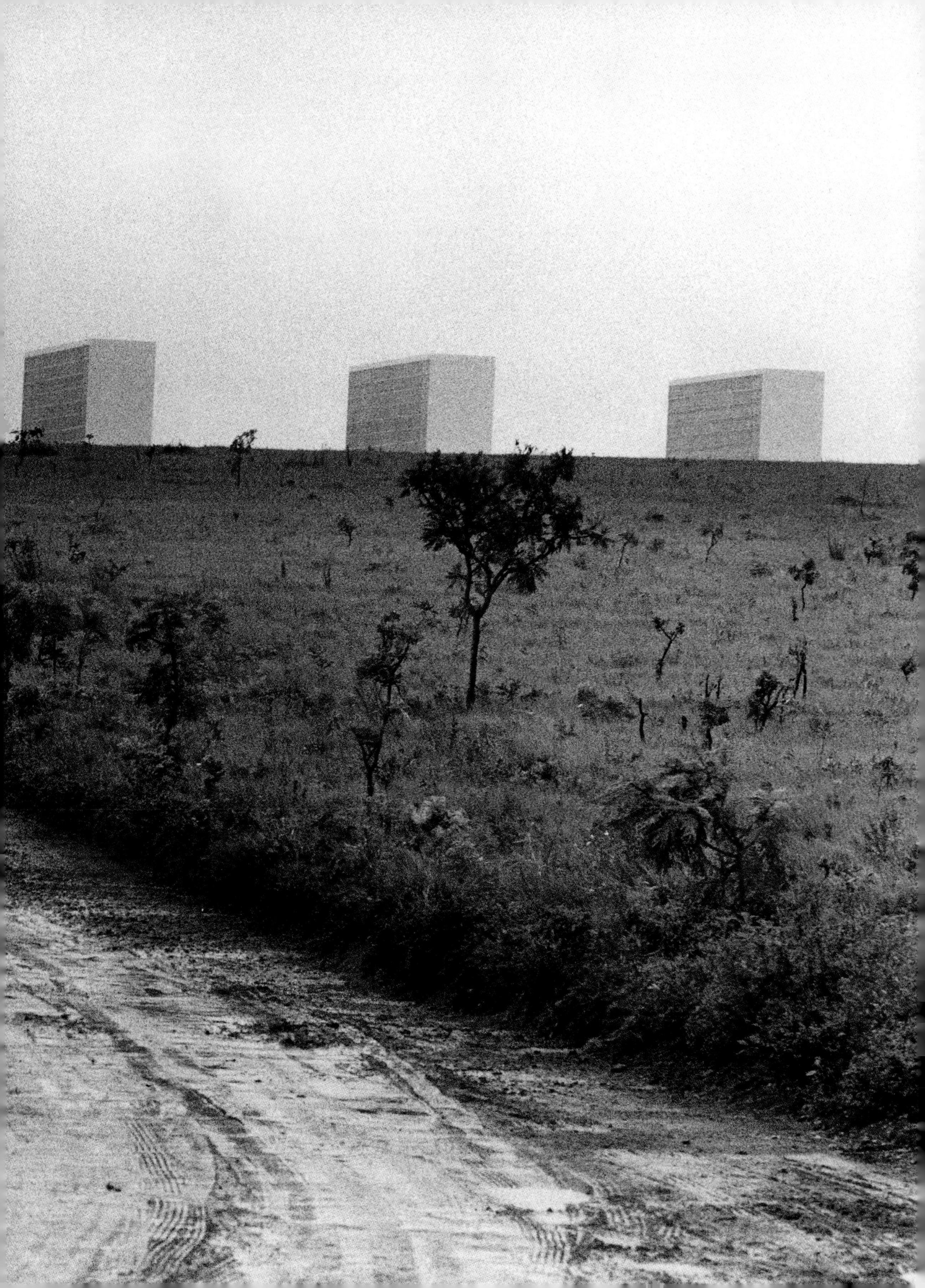

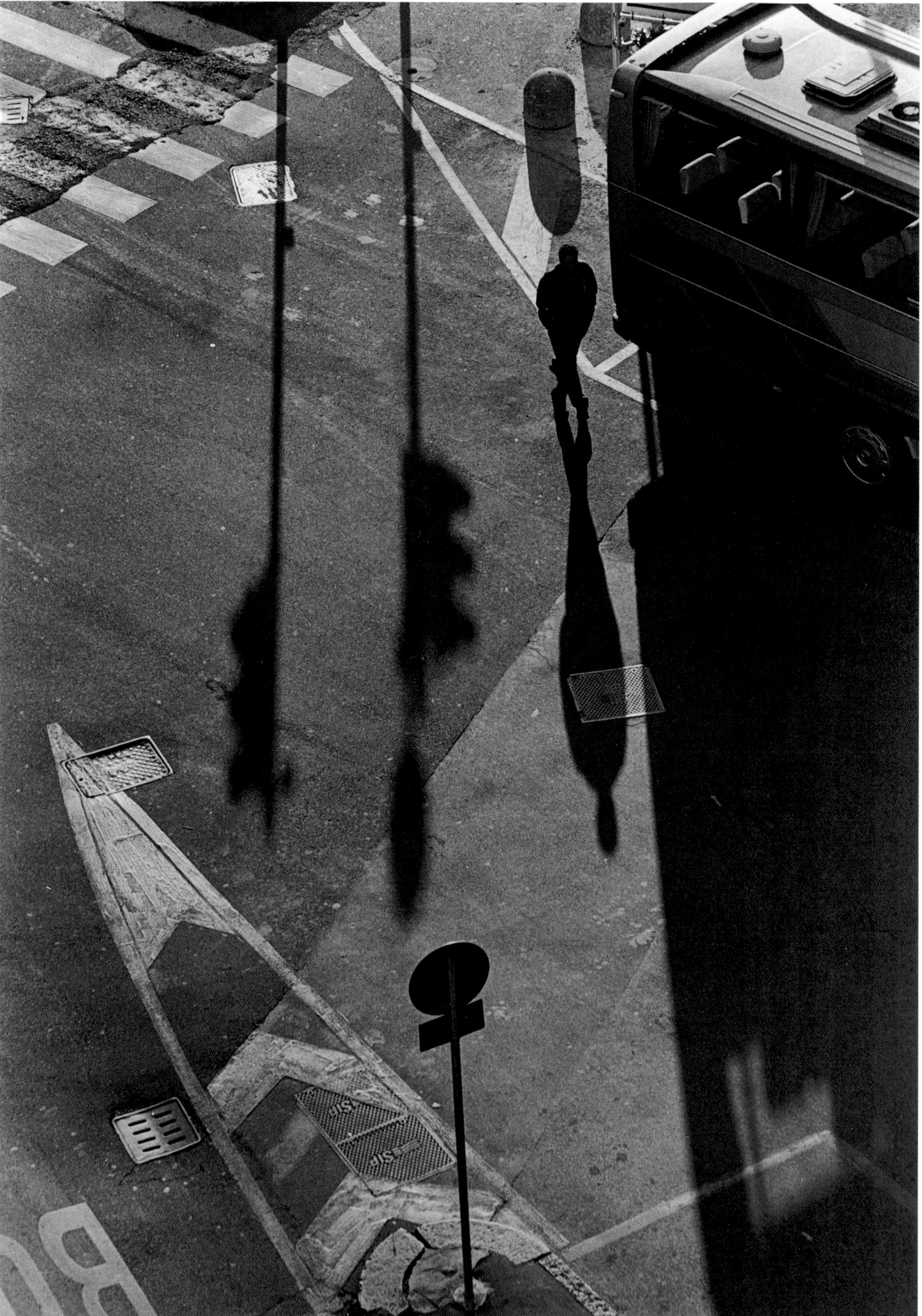

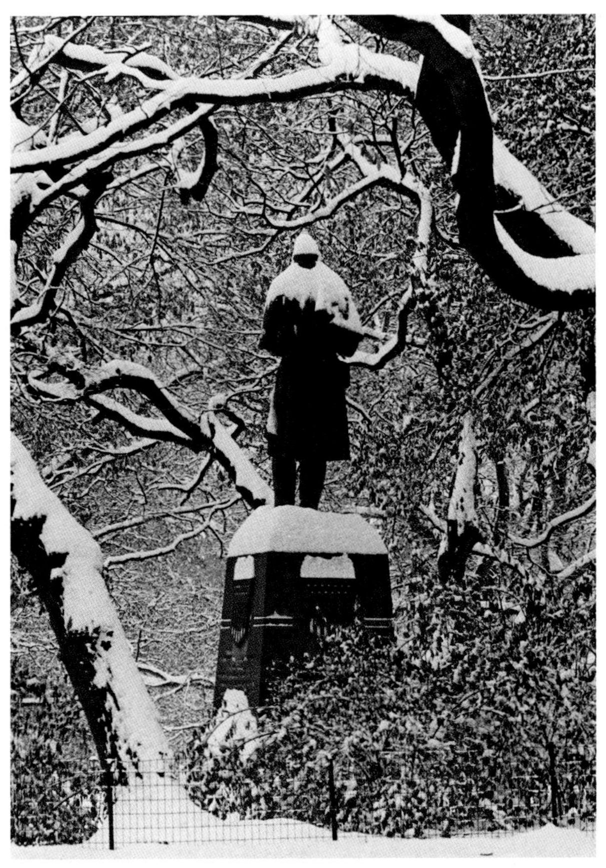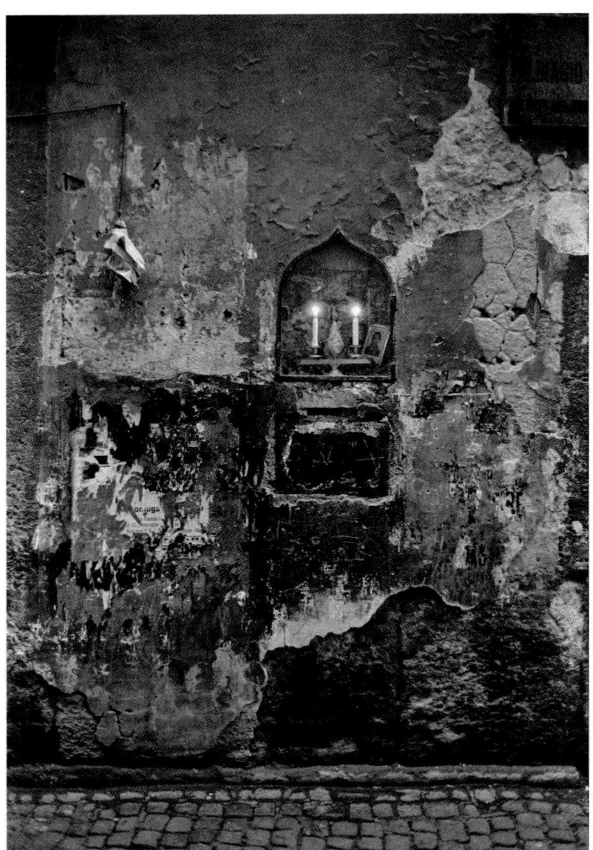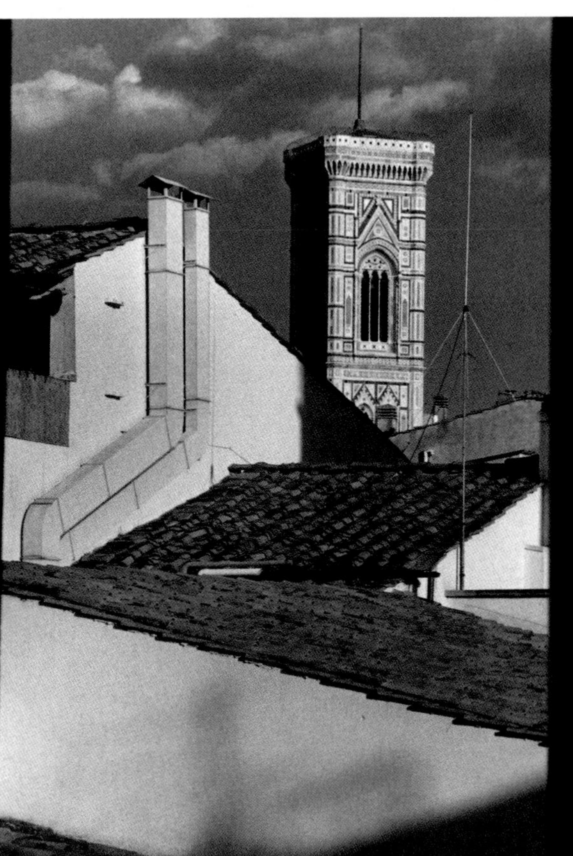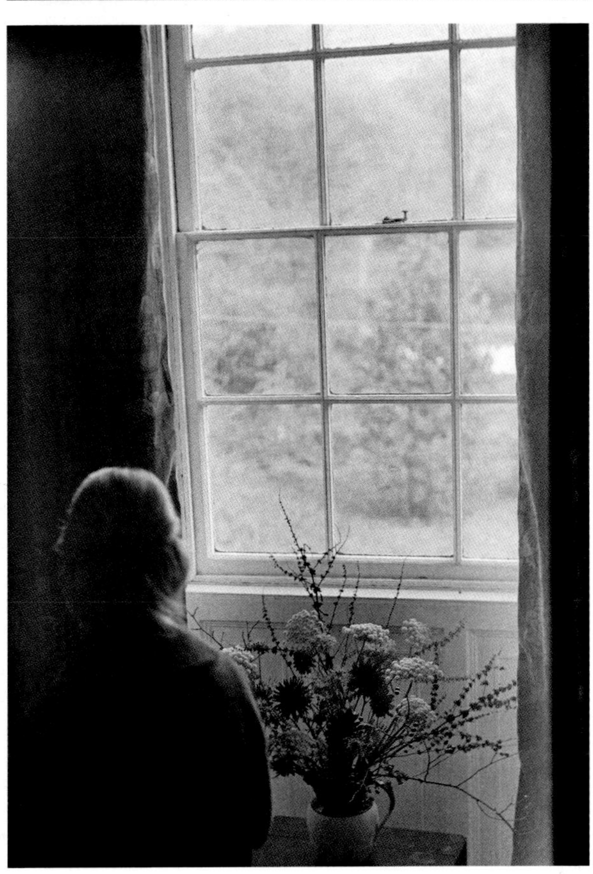

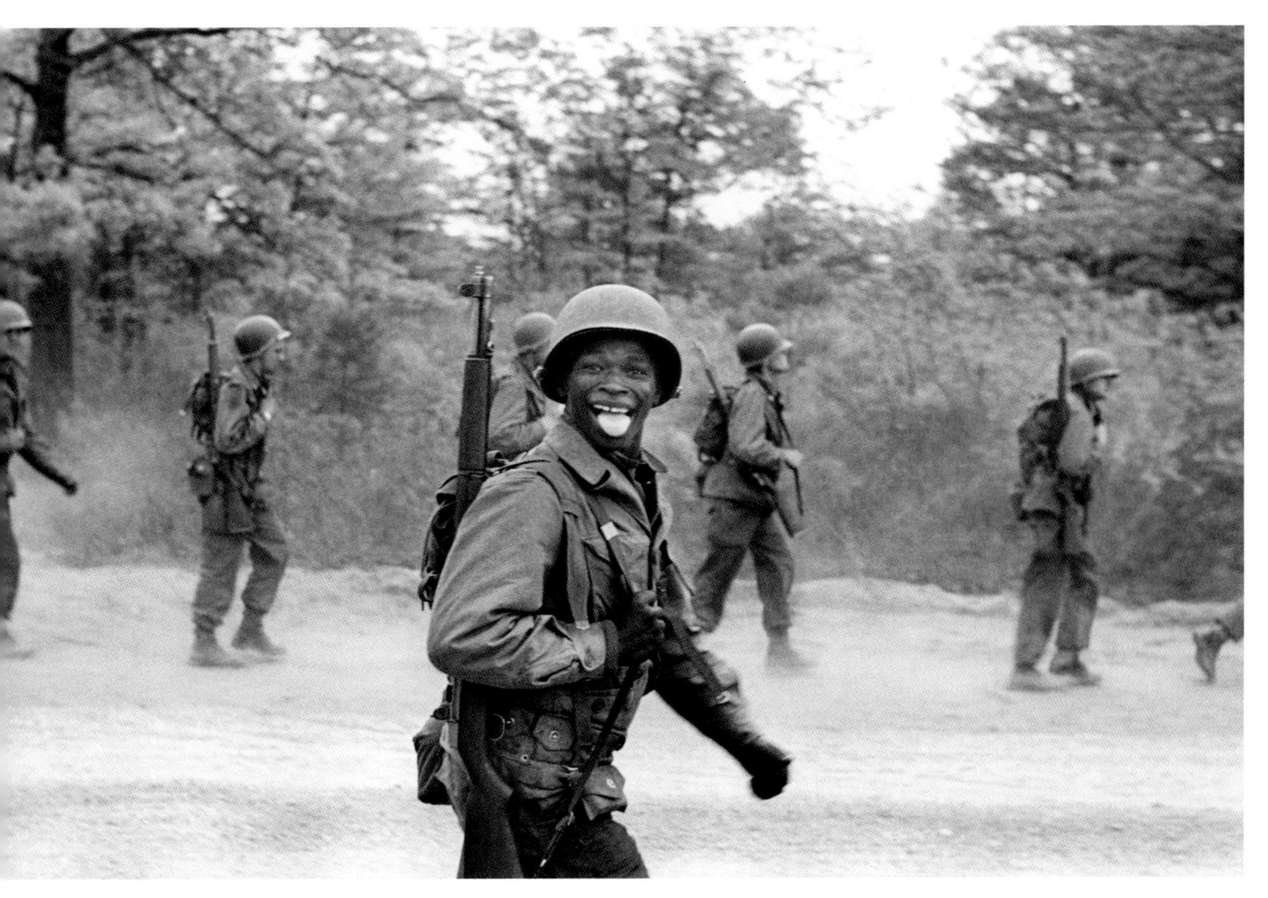

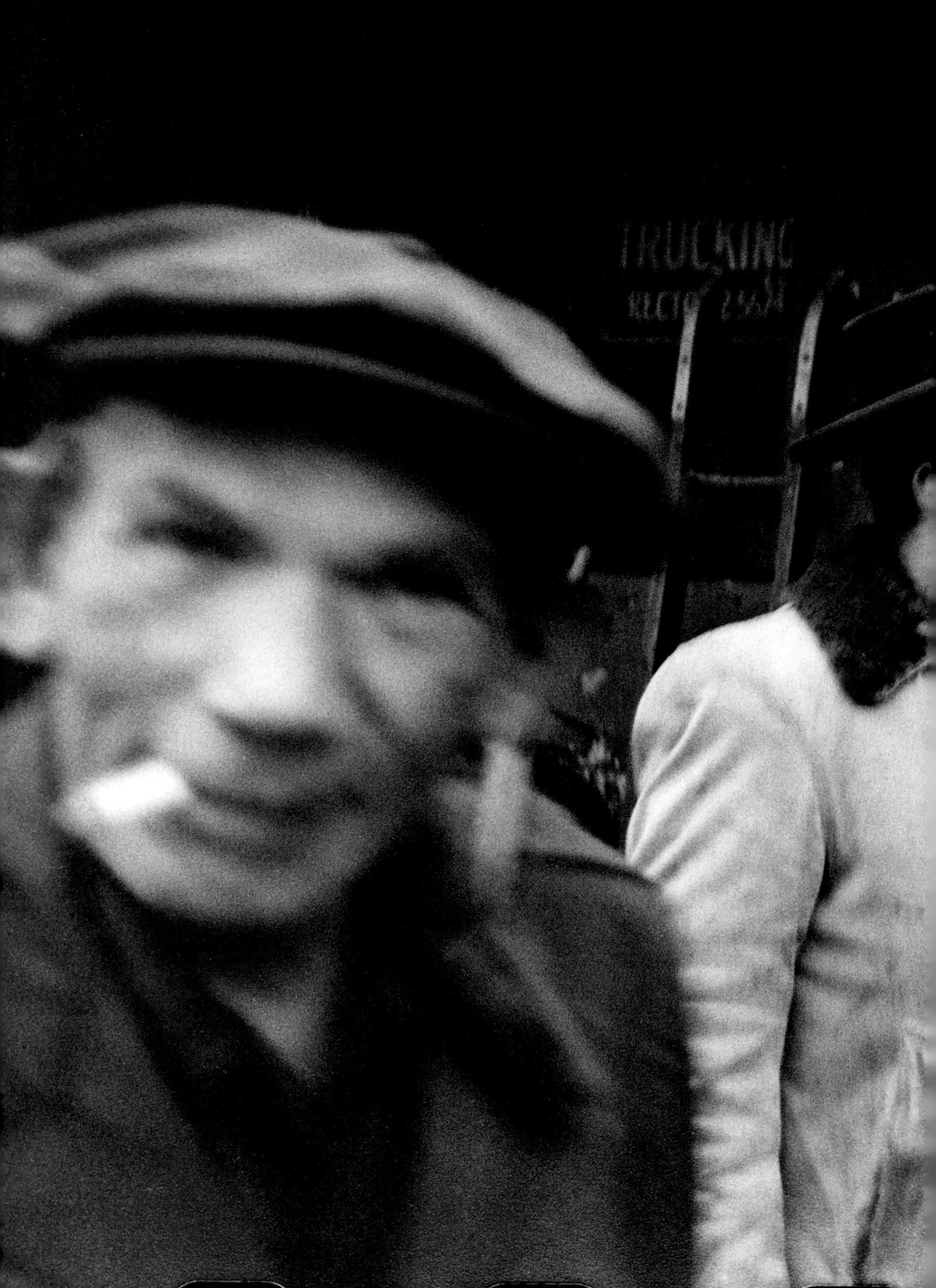
TRUCKING

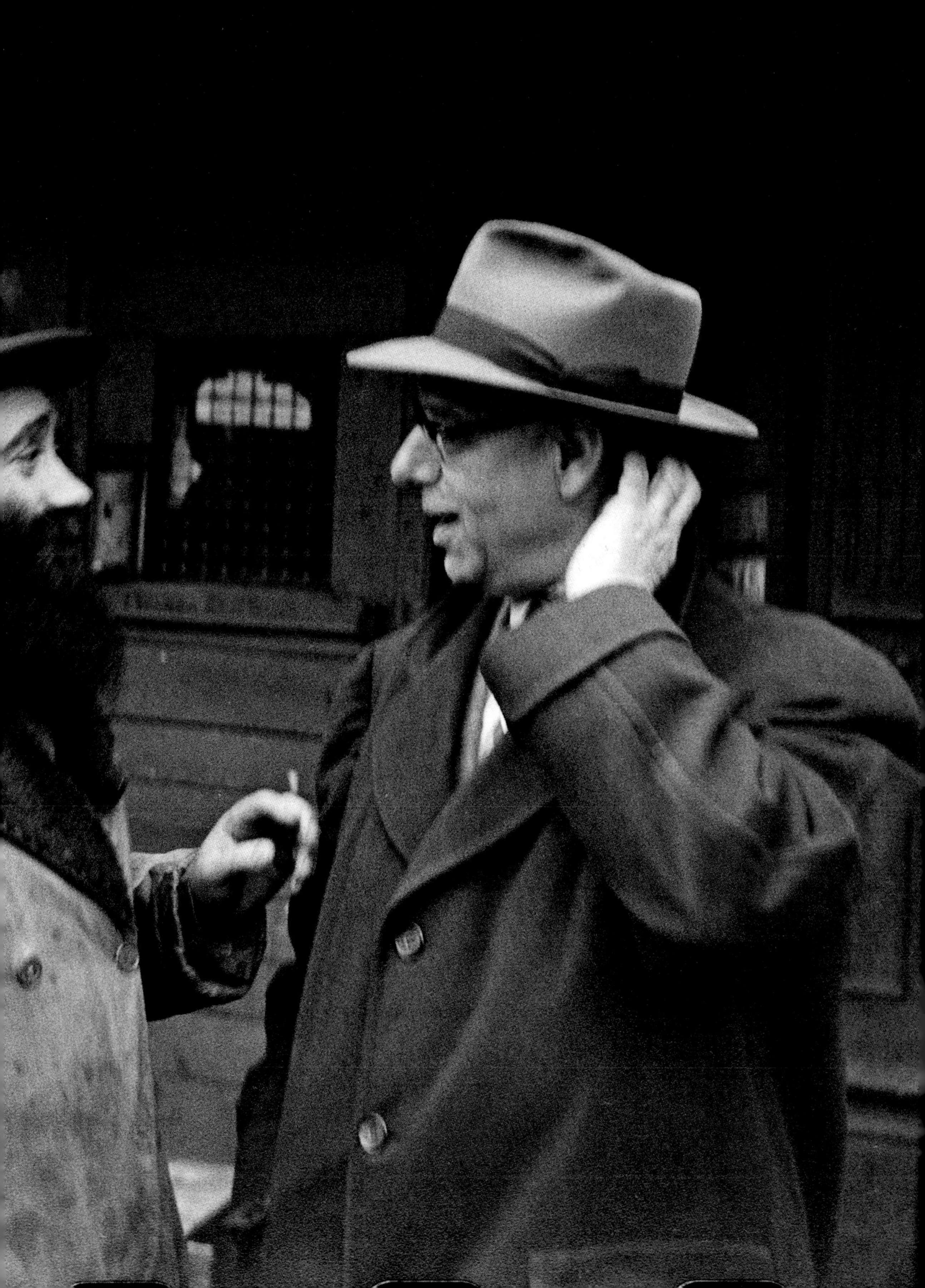

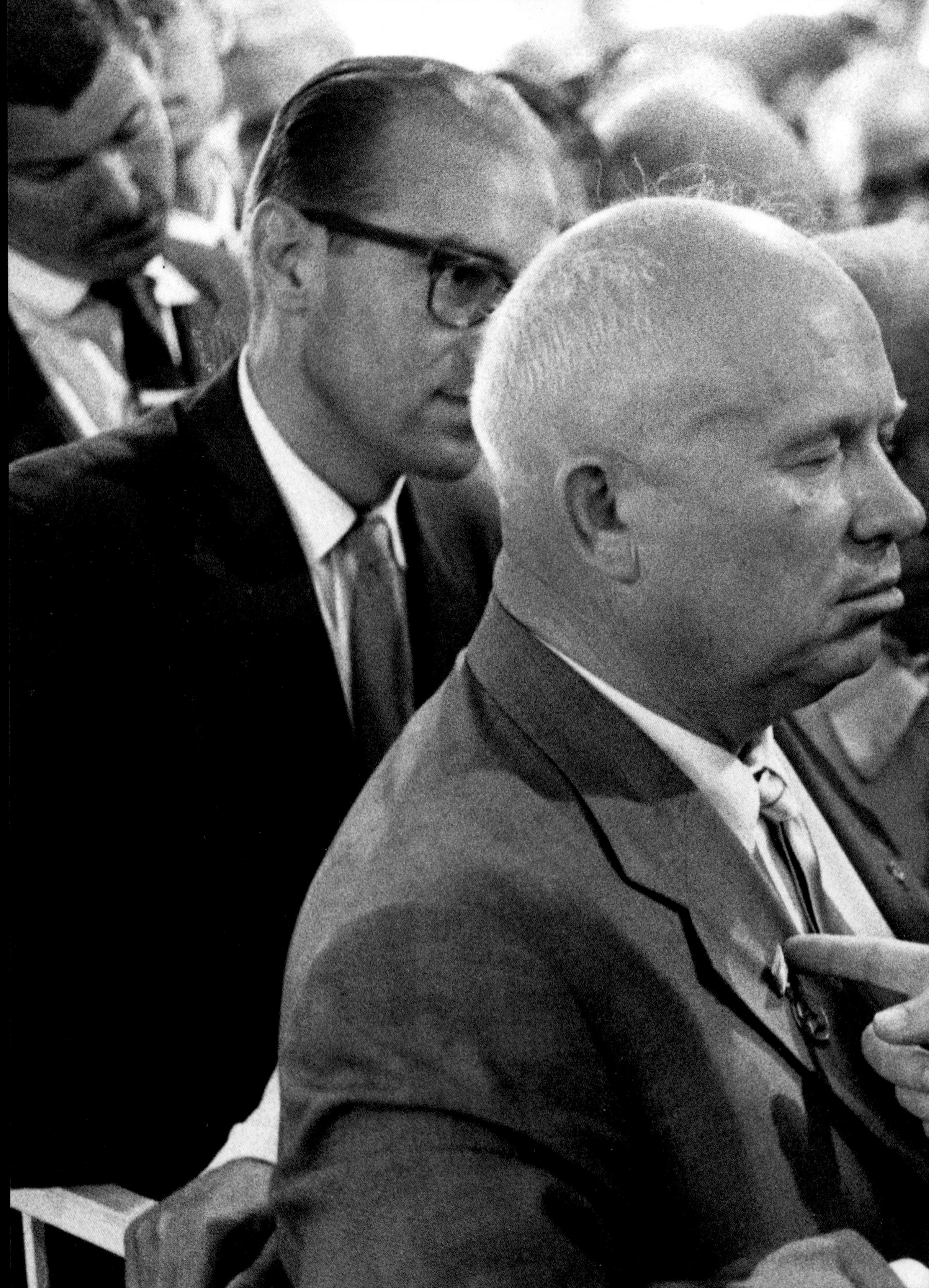

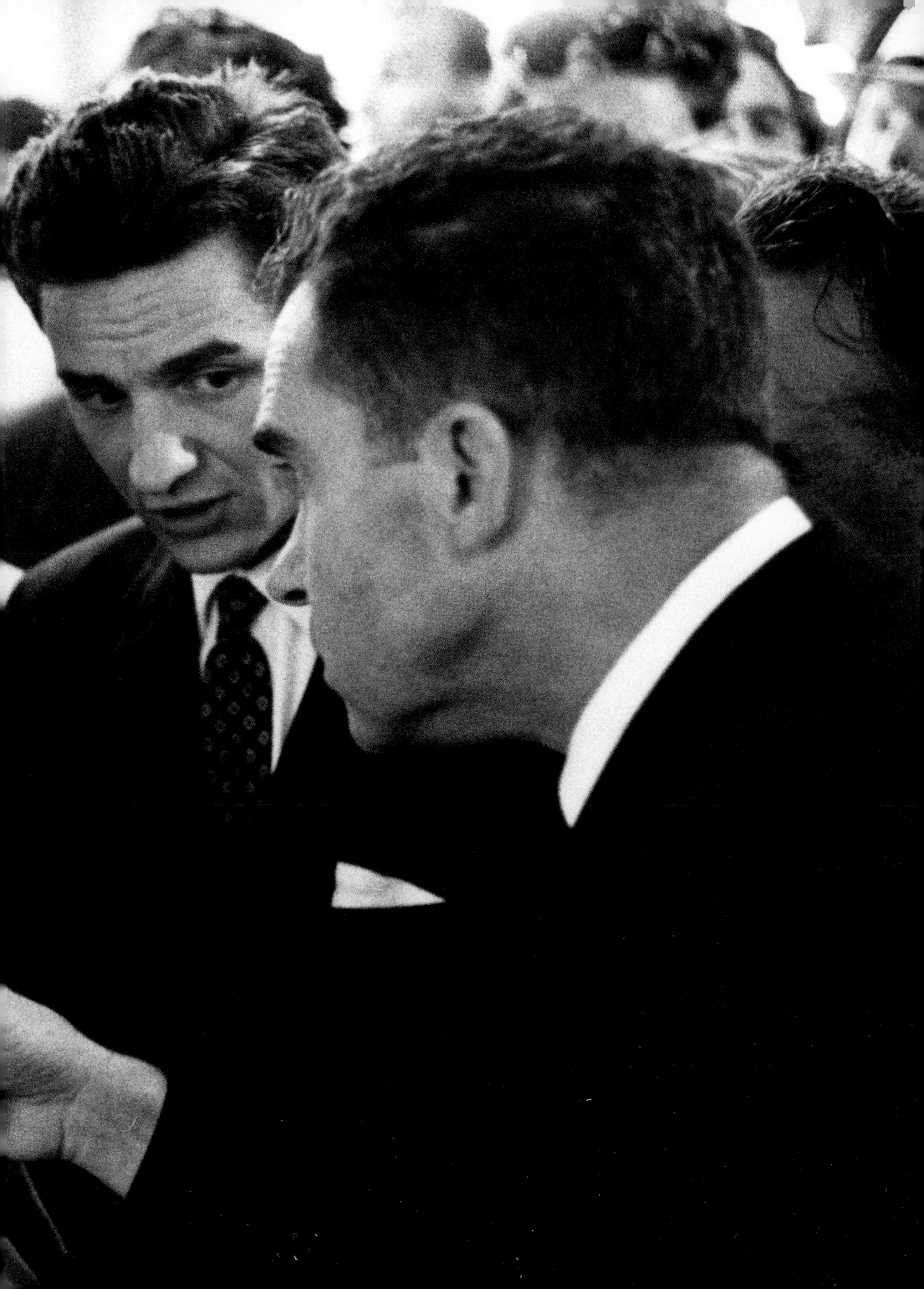

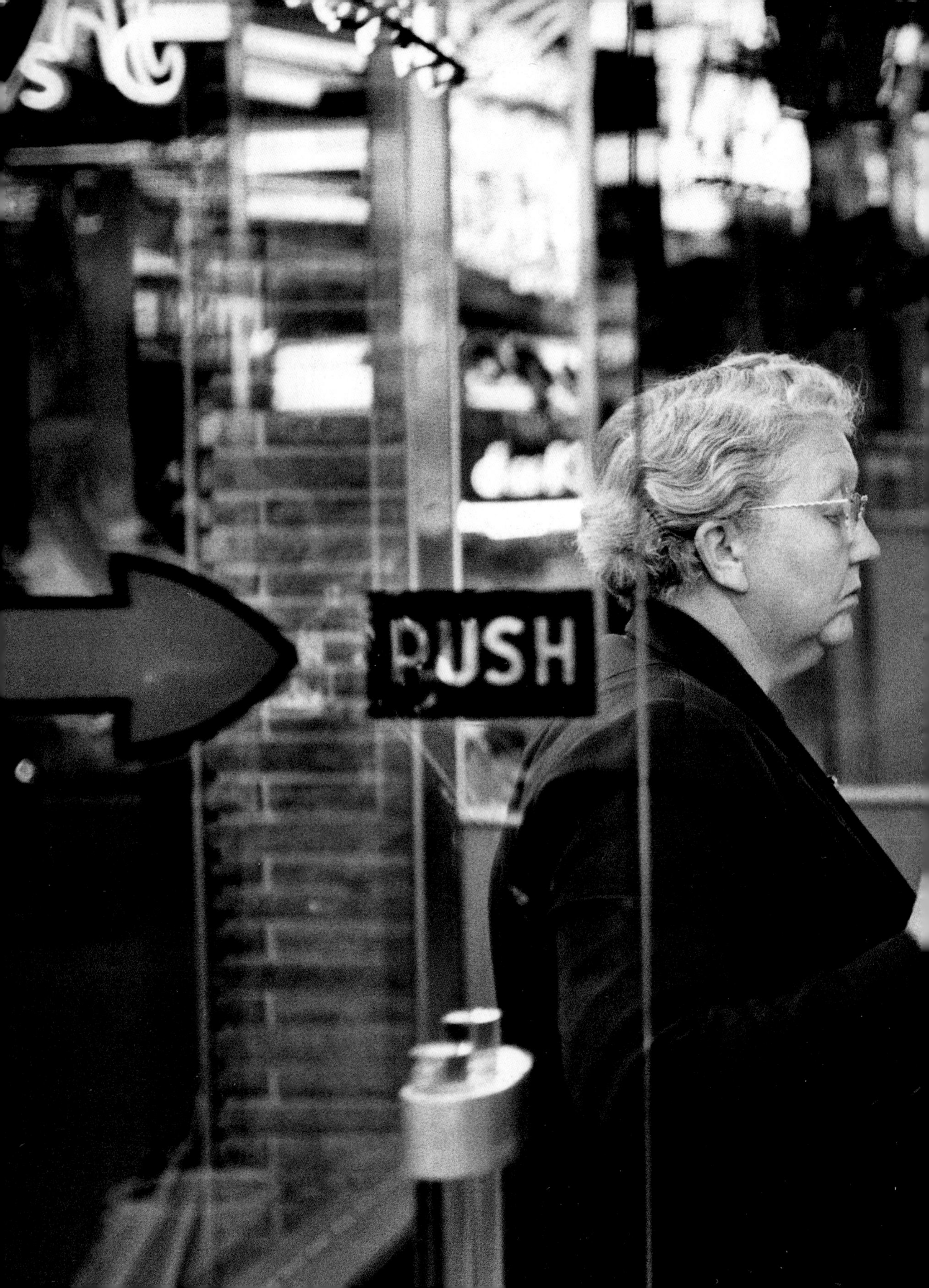

PUSH

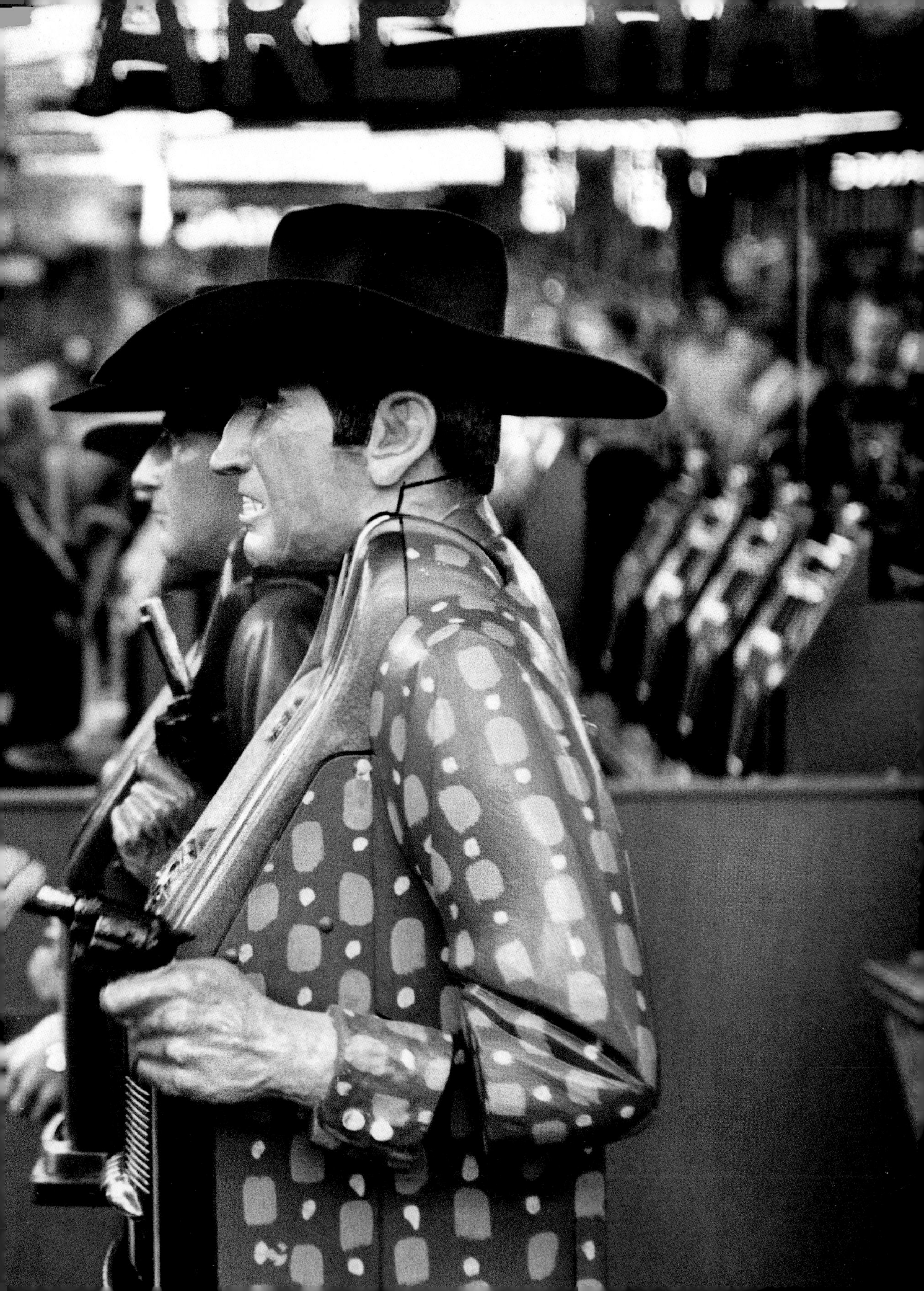

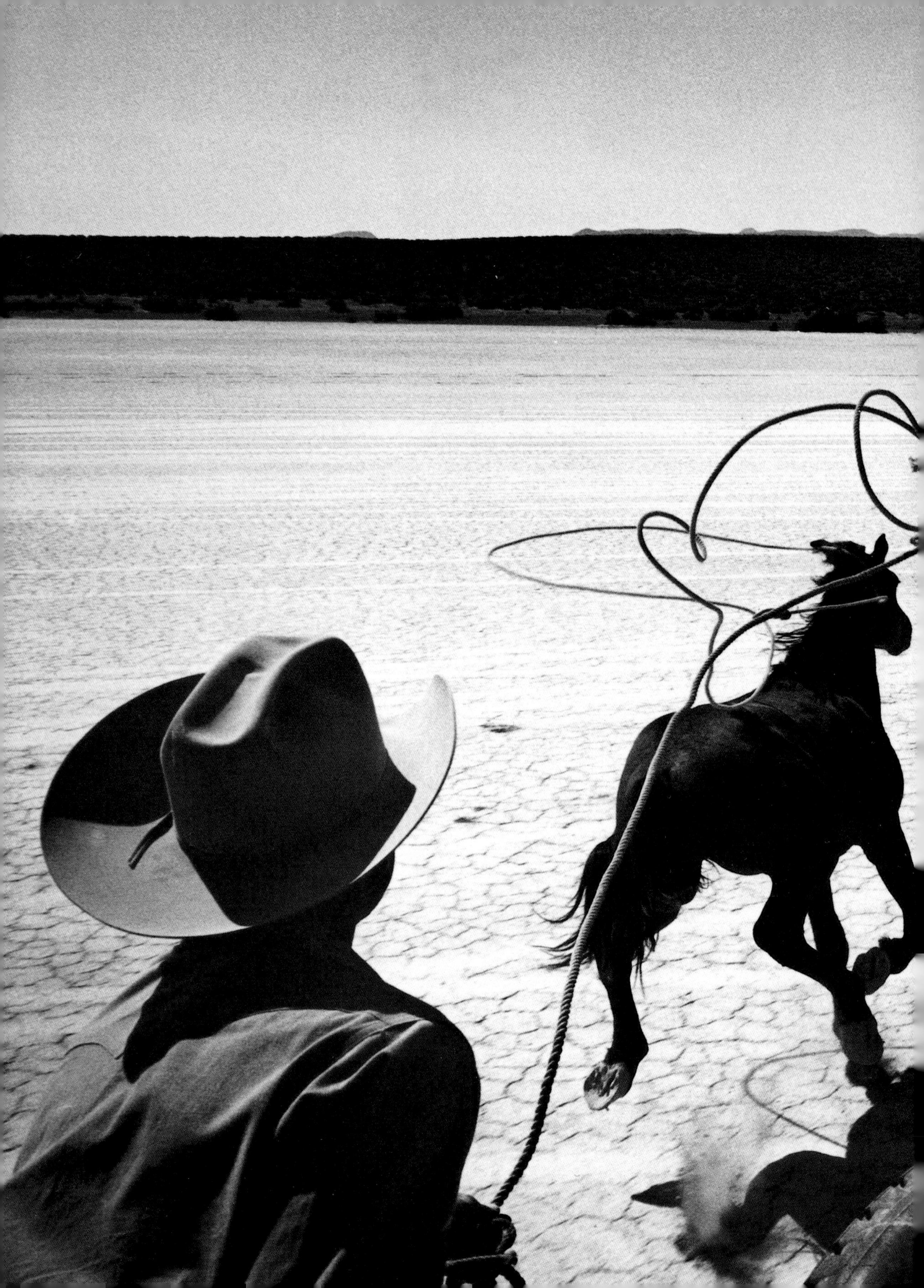

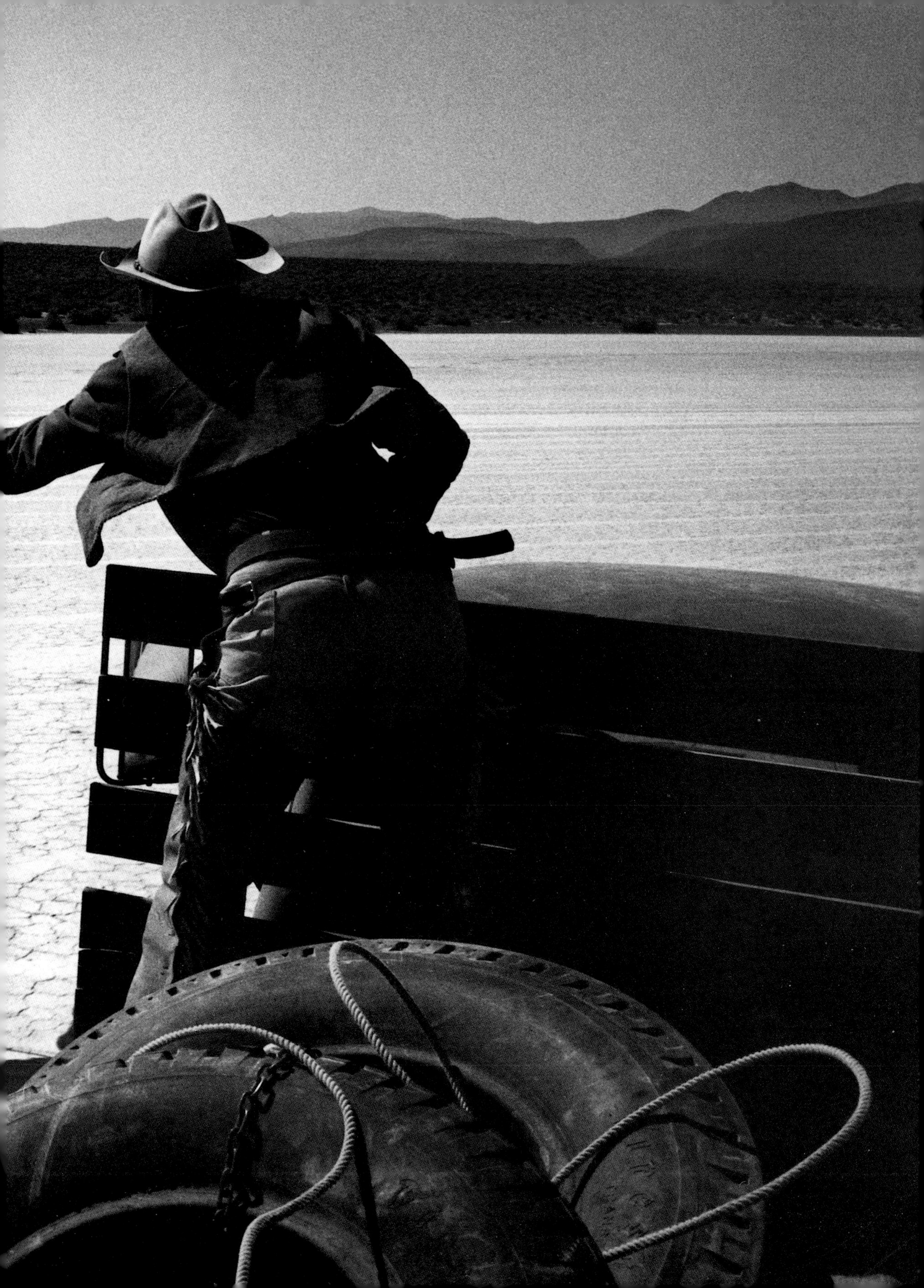

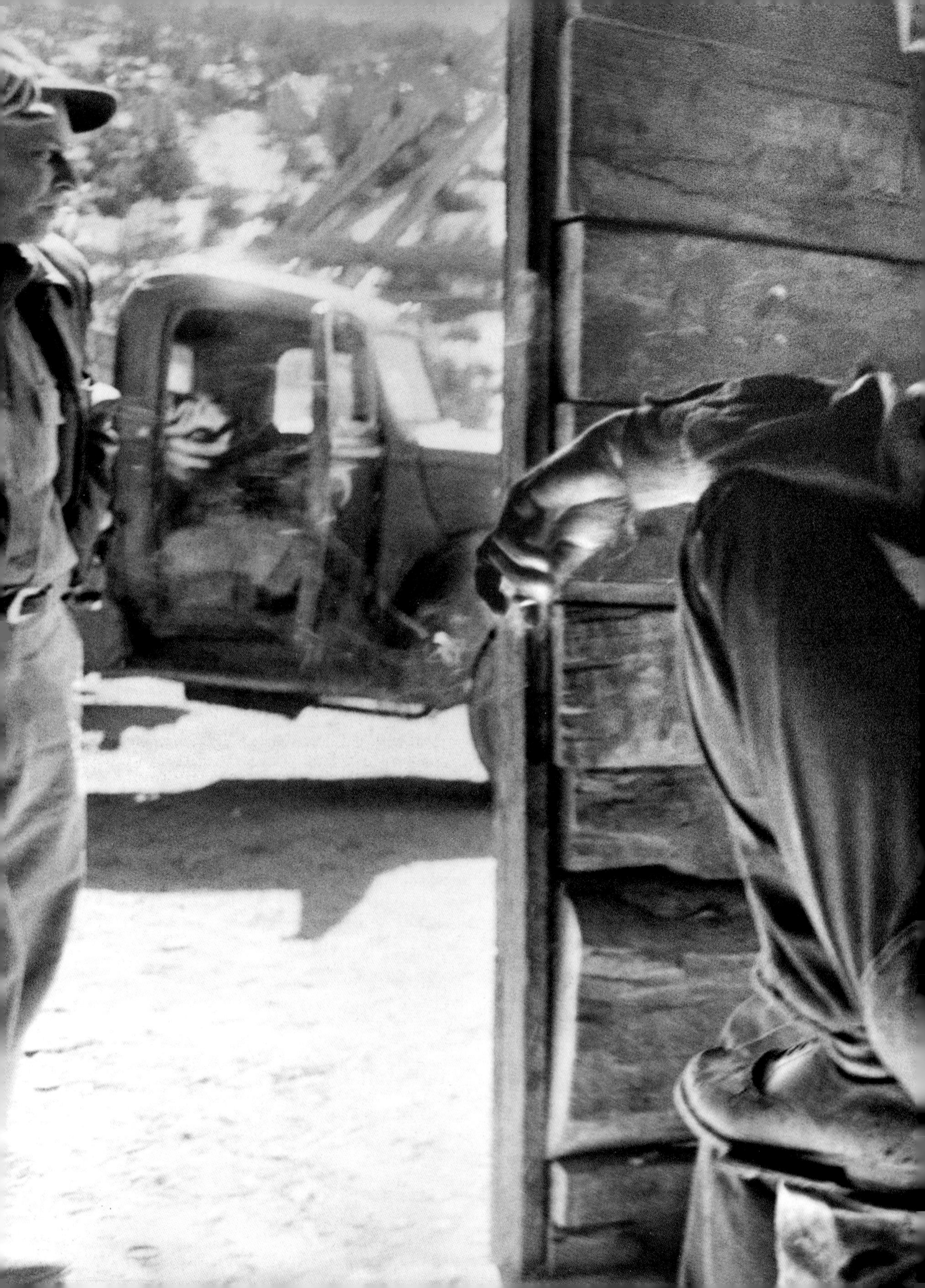

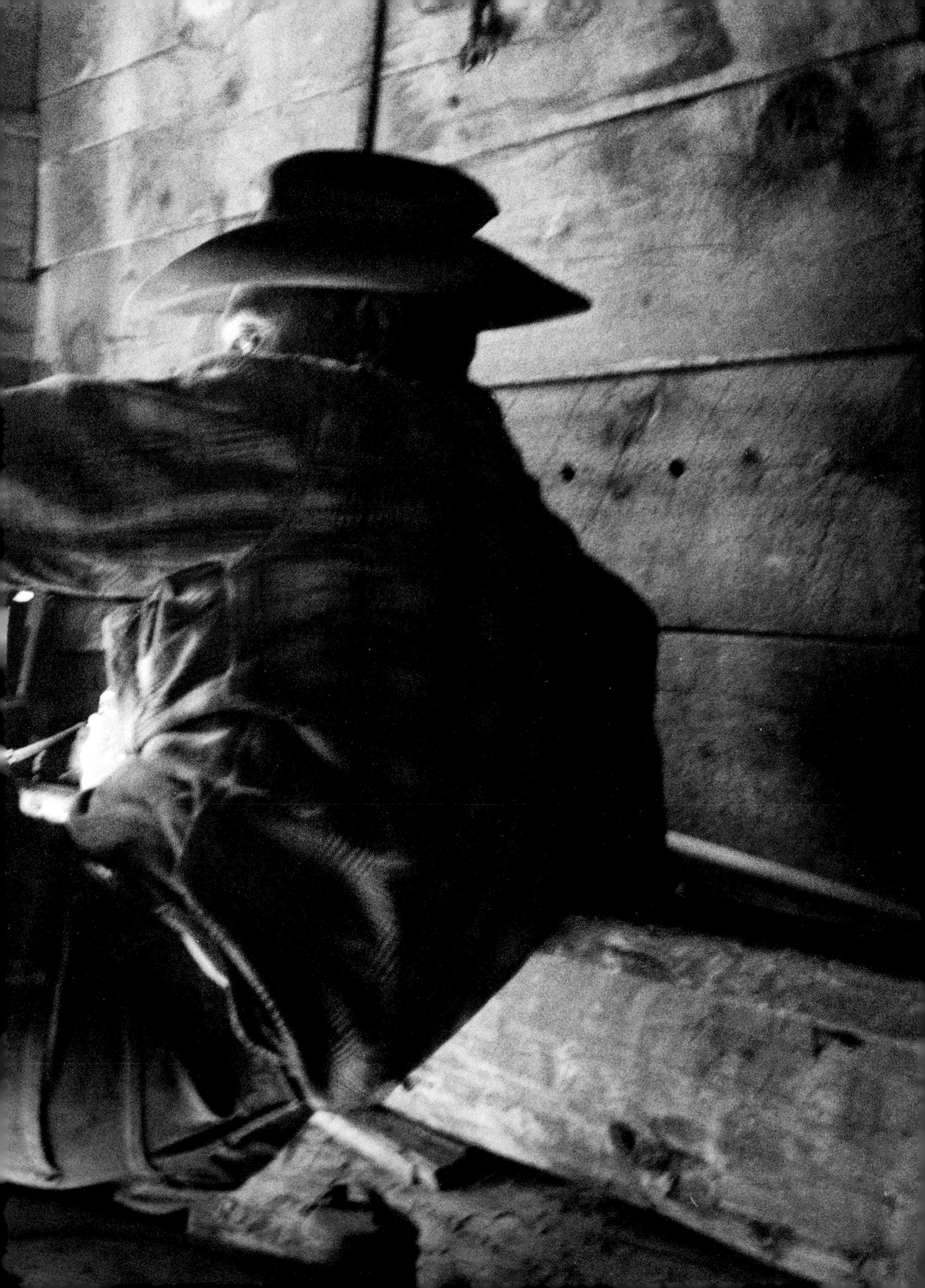

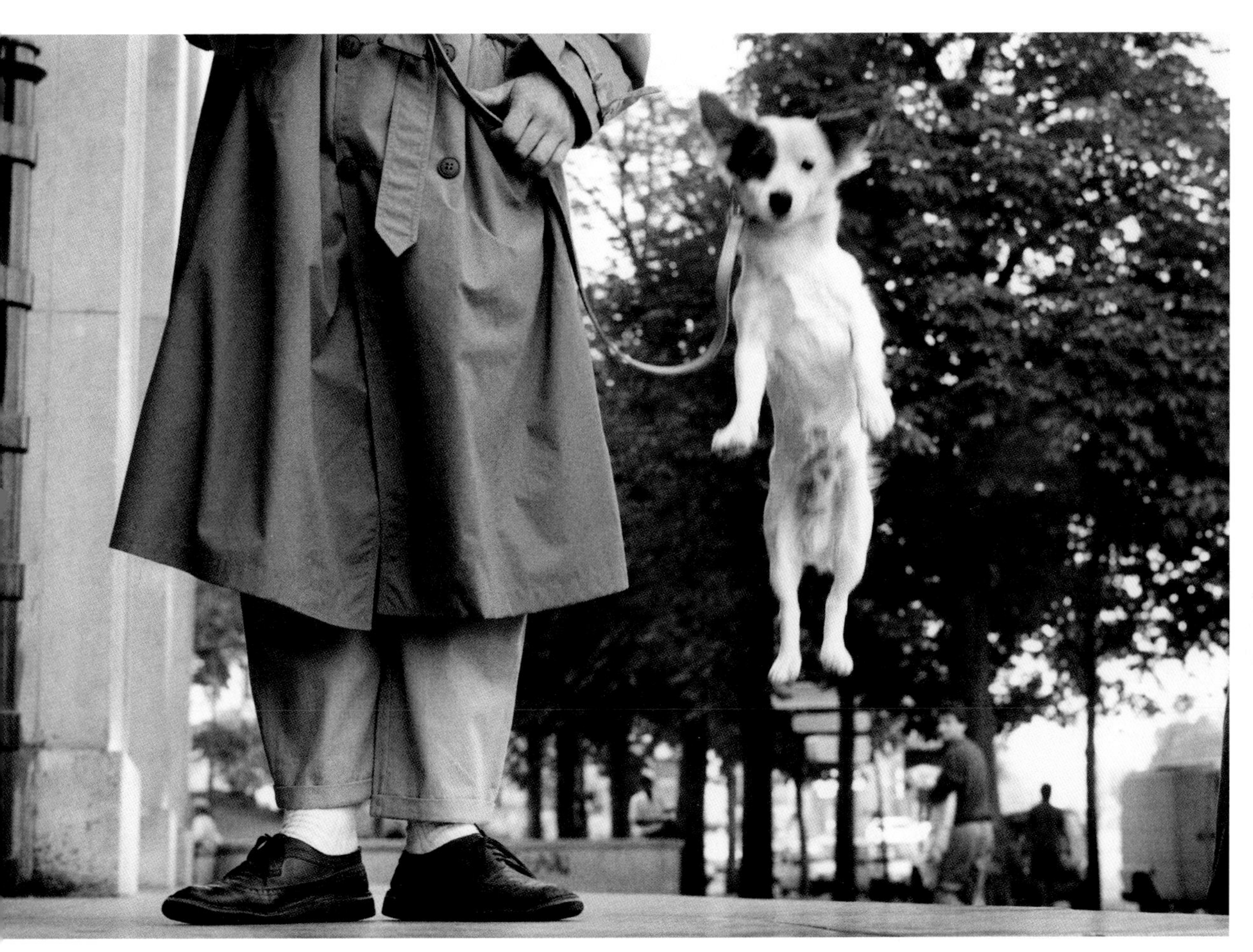

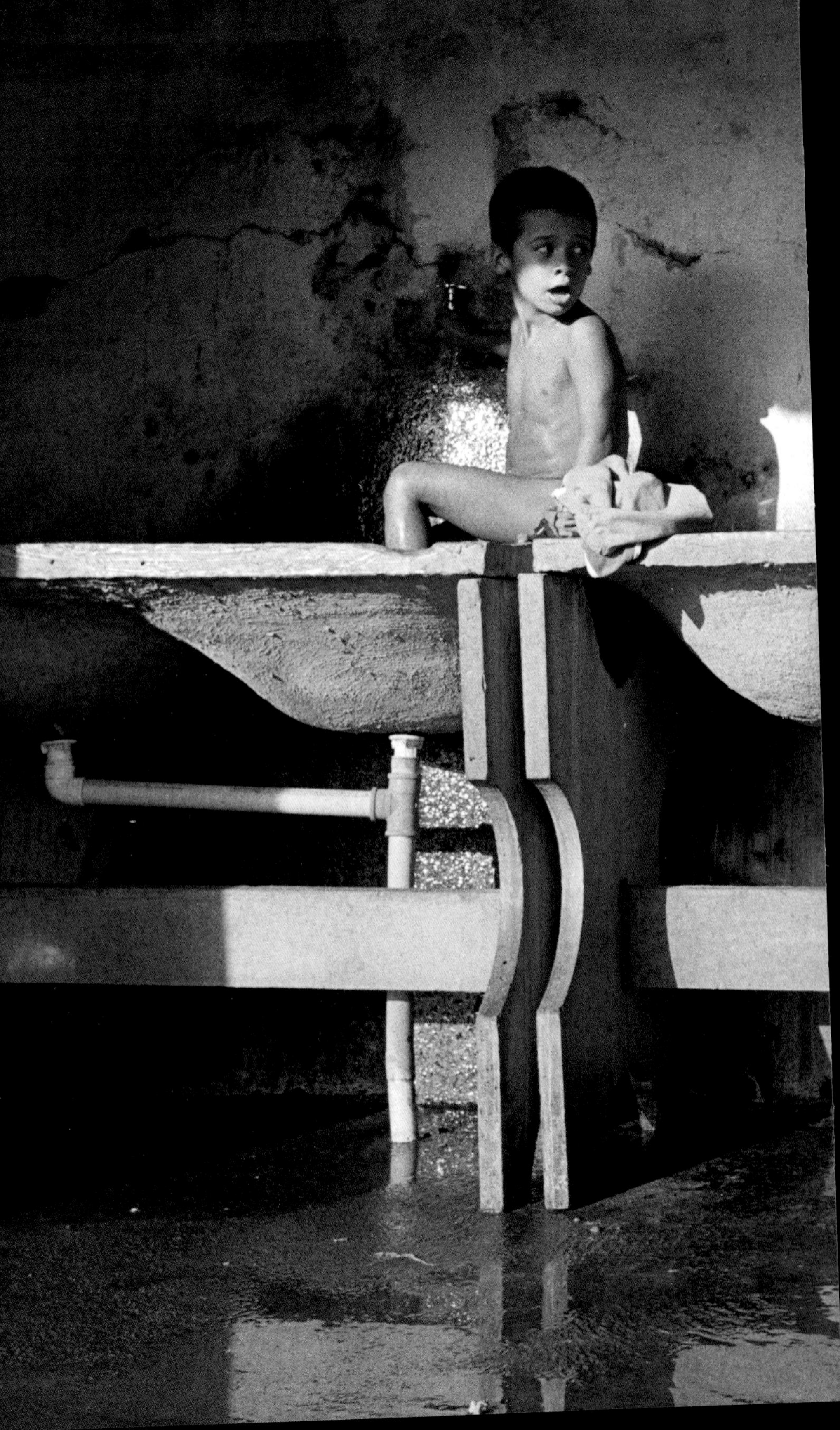

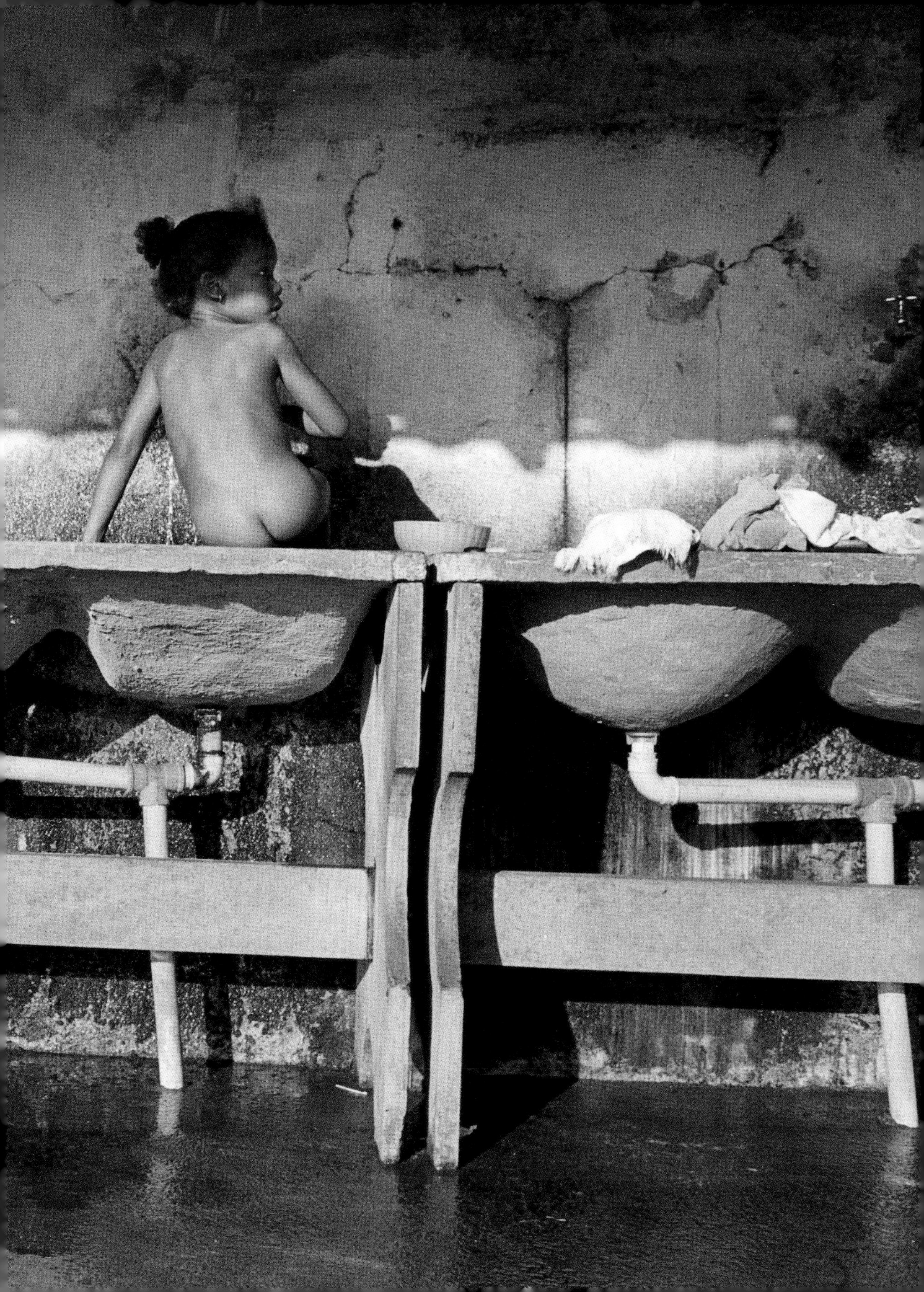

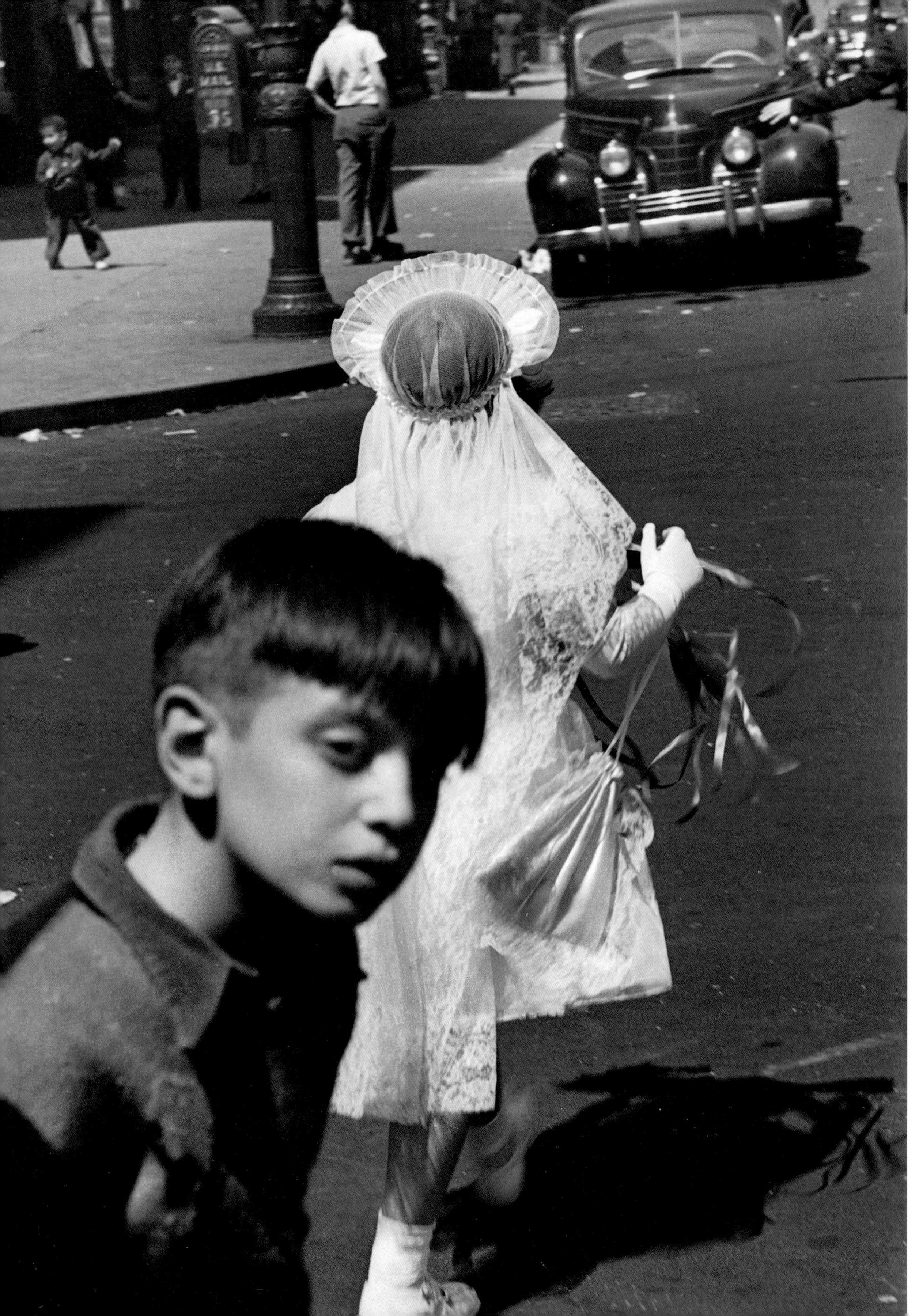

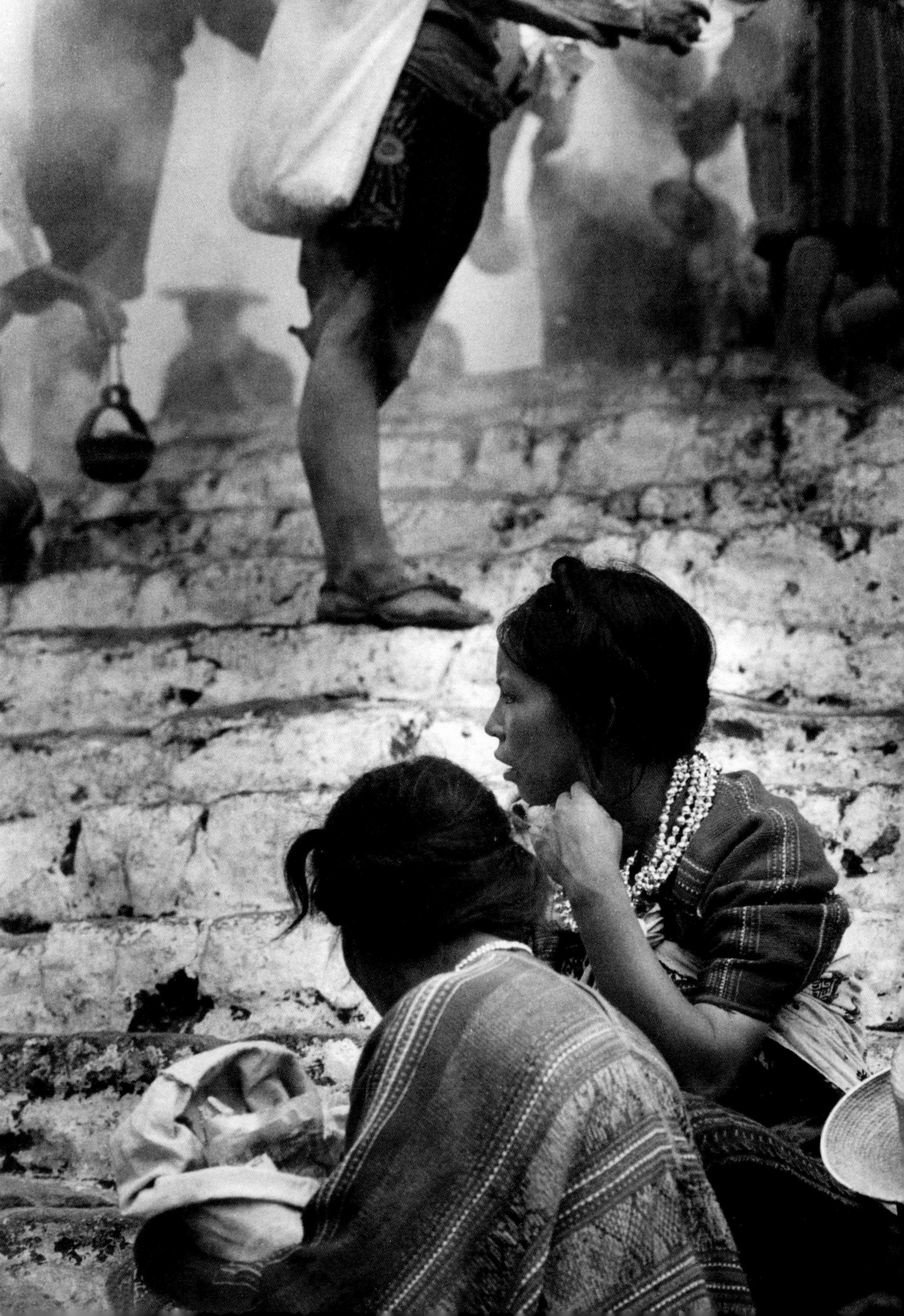

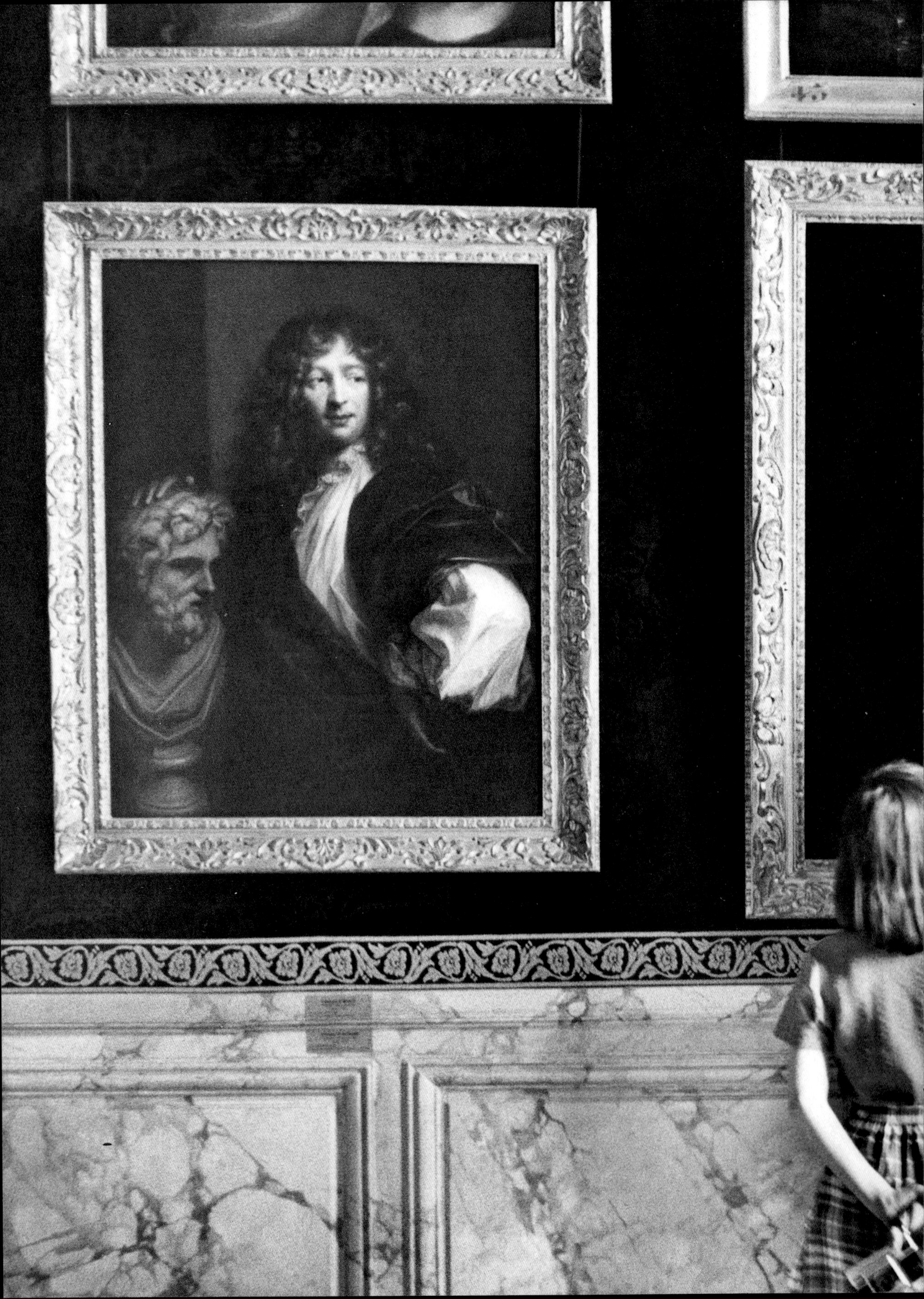

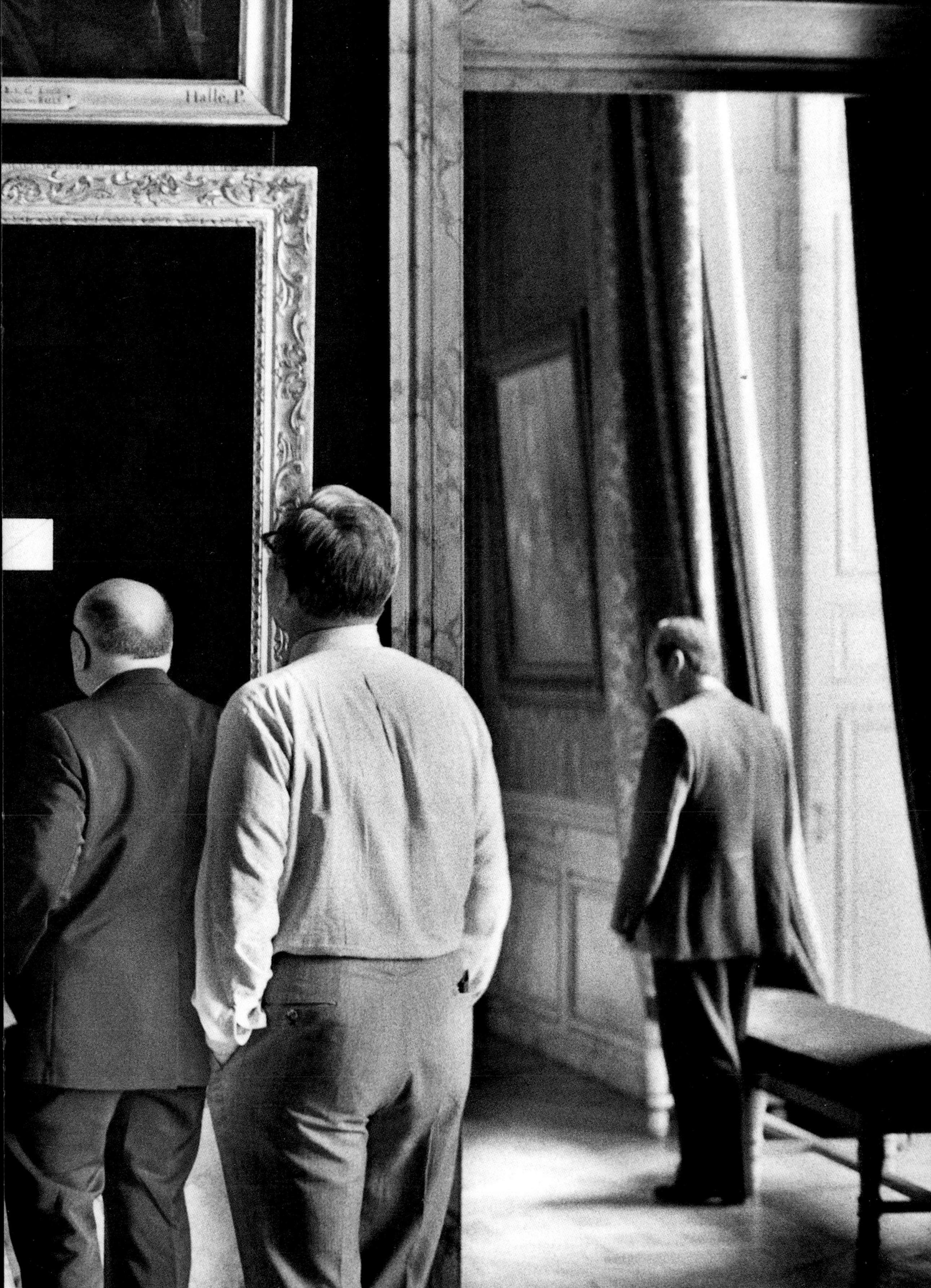

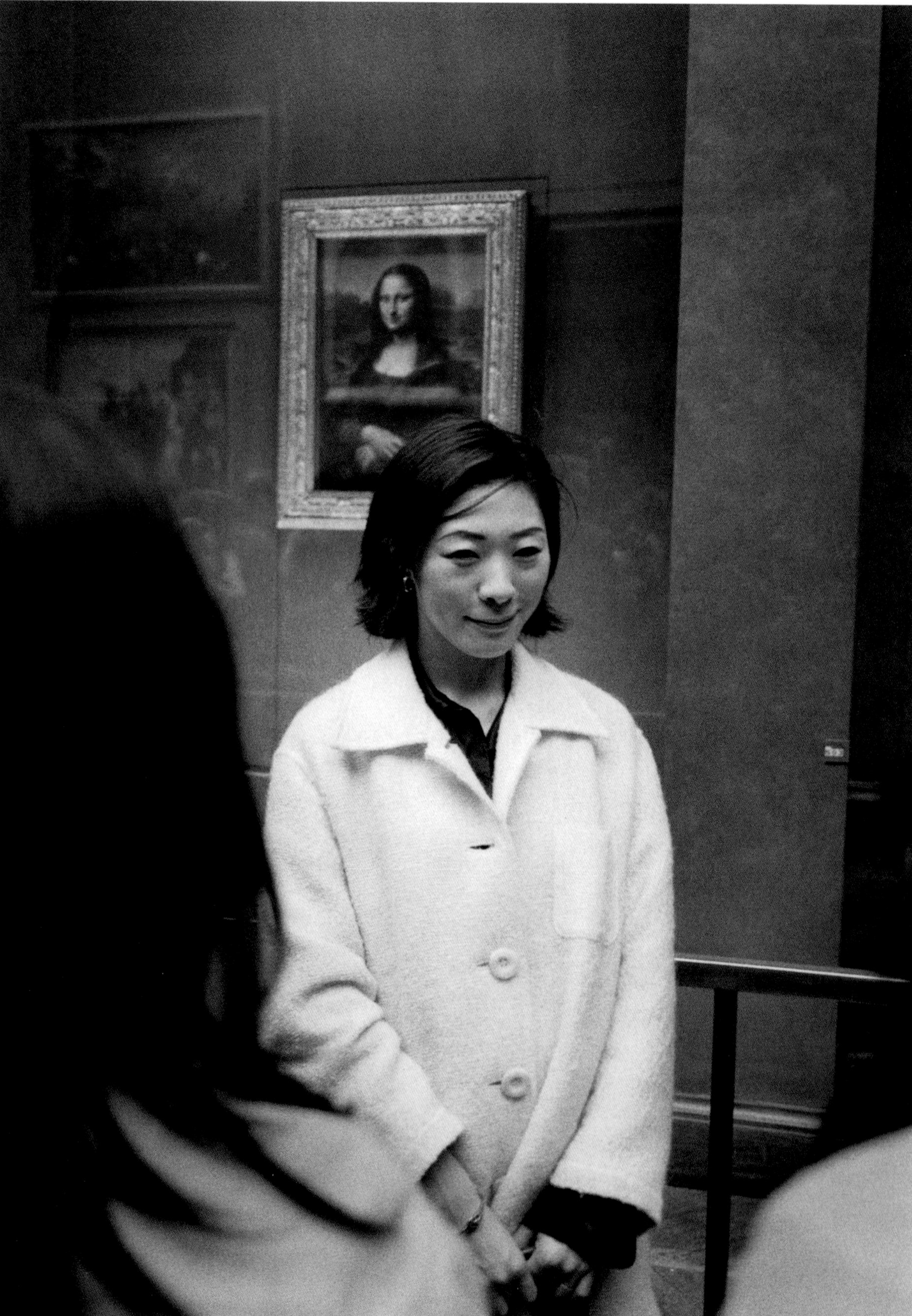

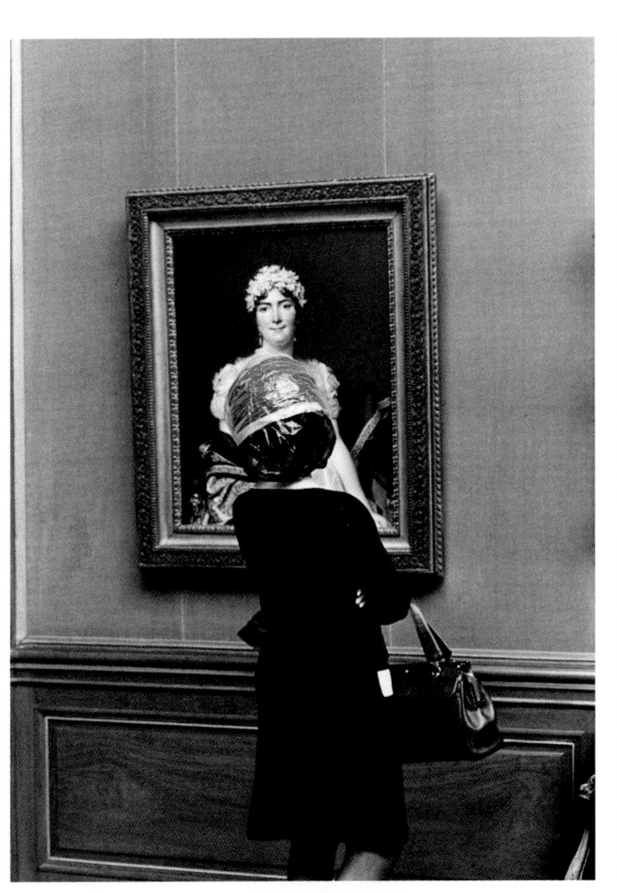
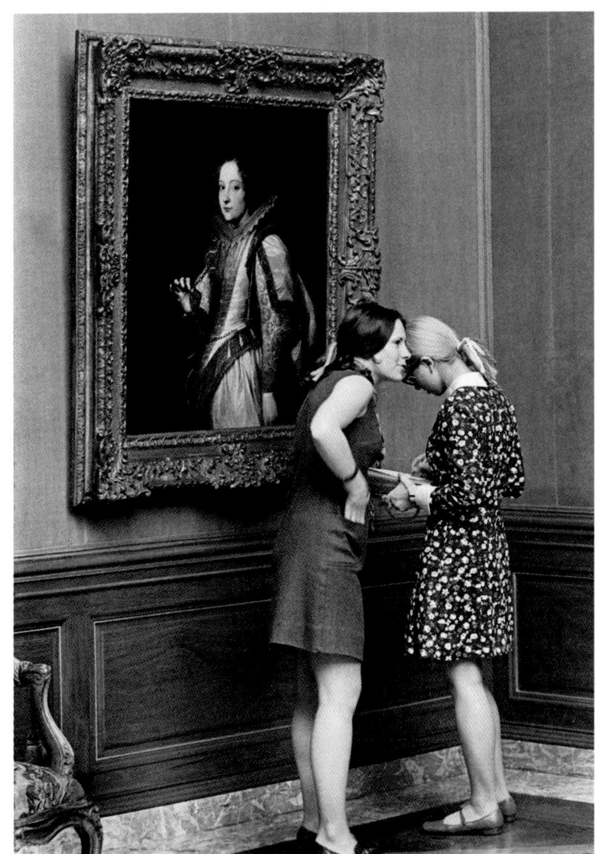
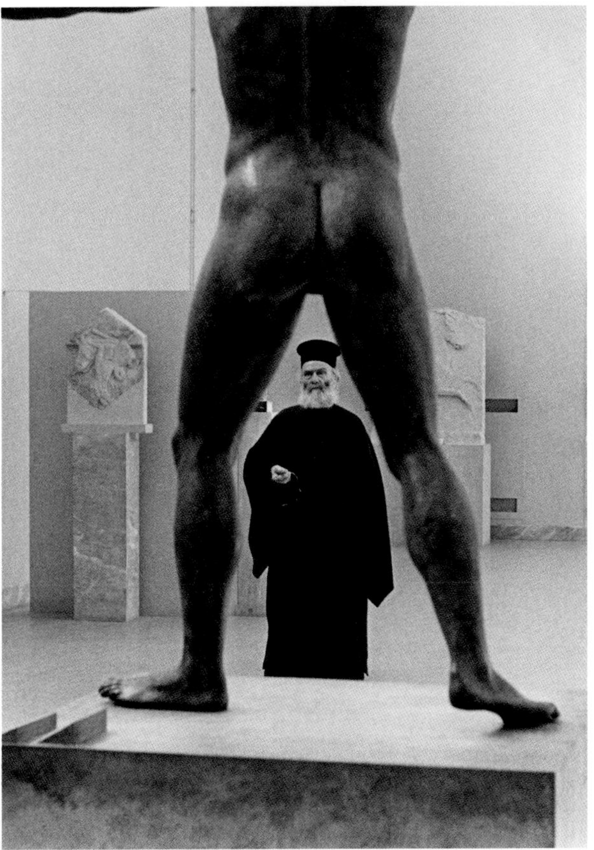
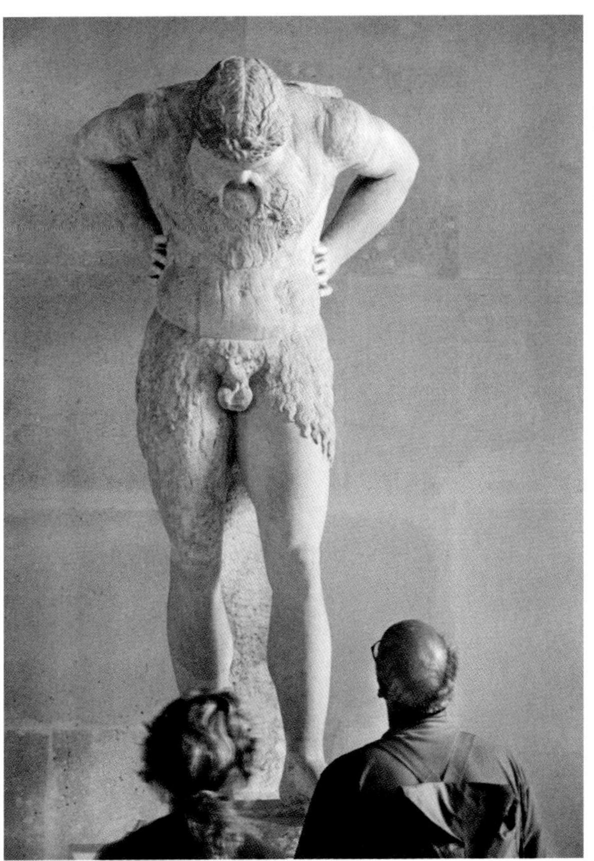

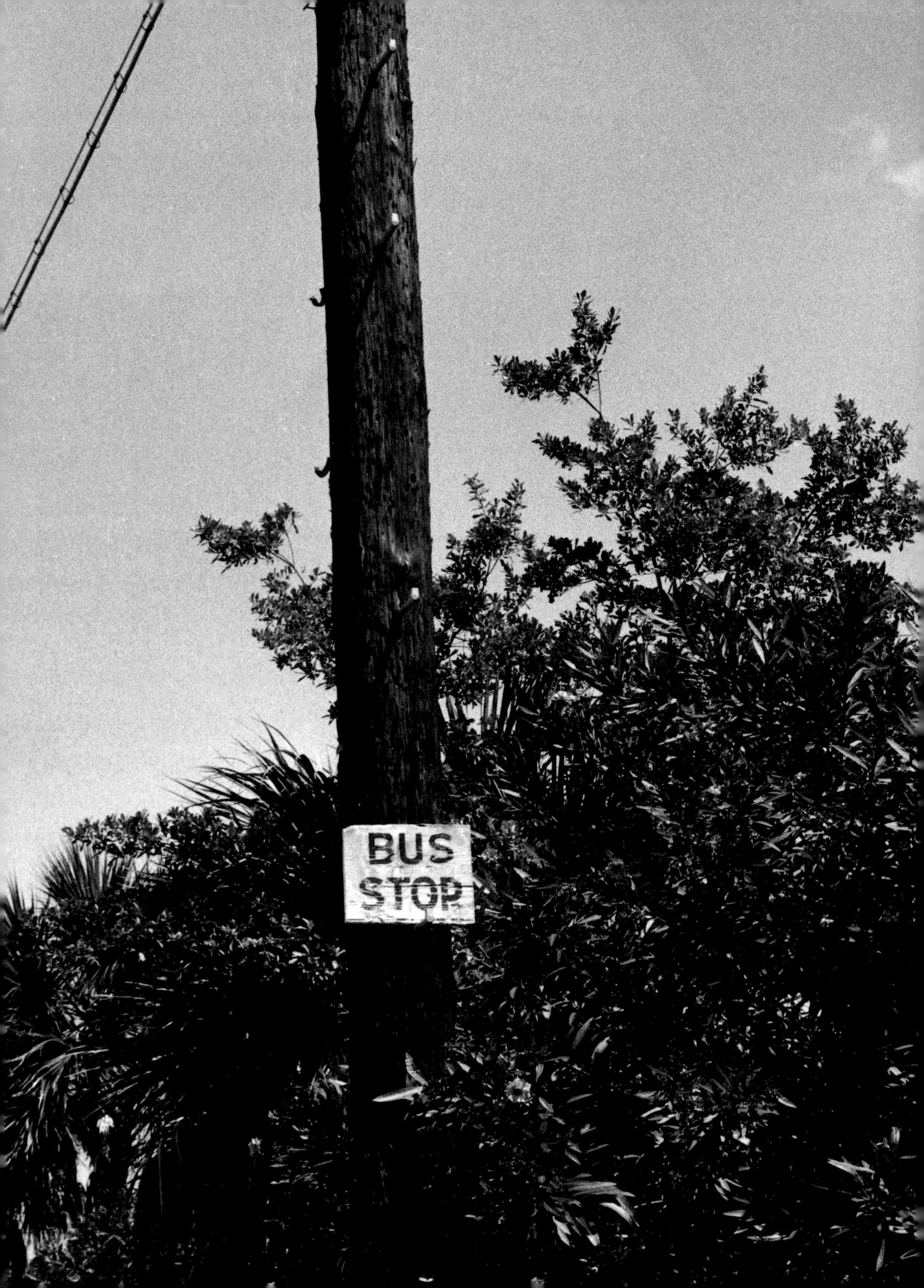
BUS
STOP

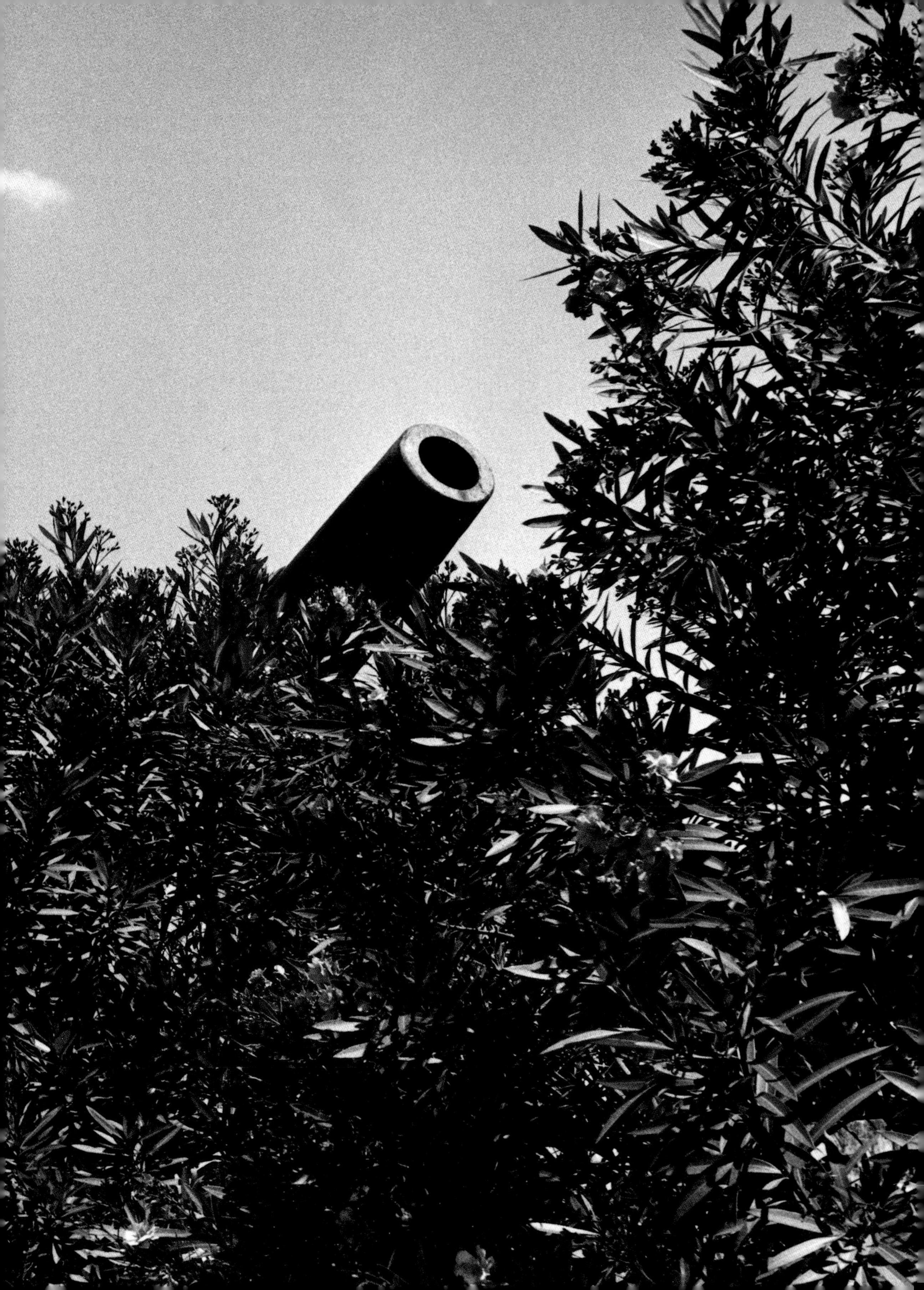

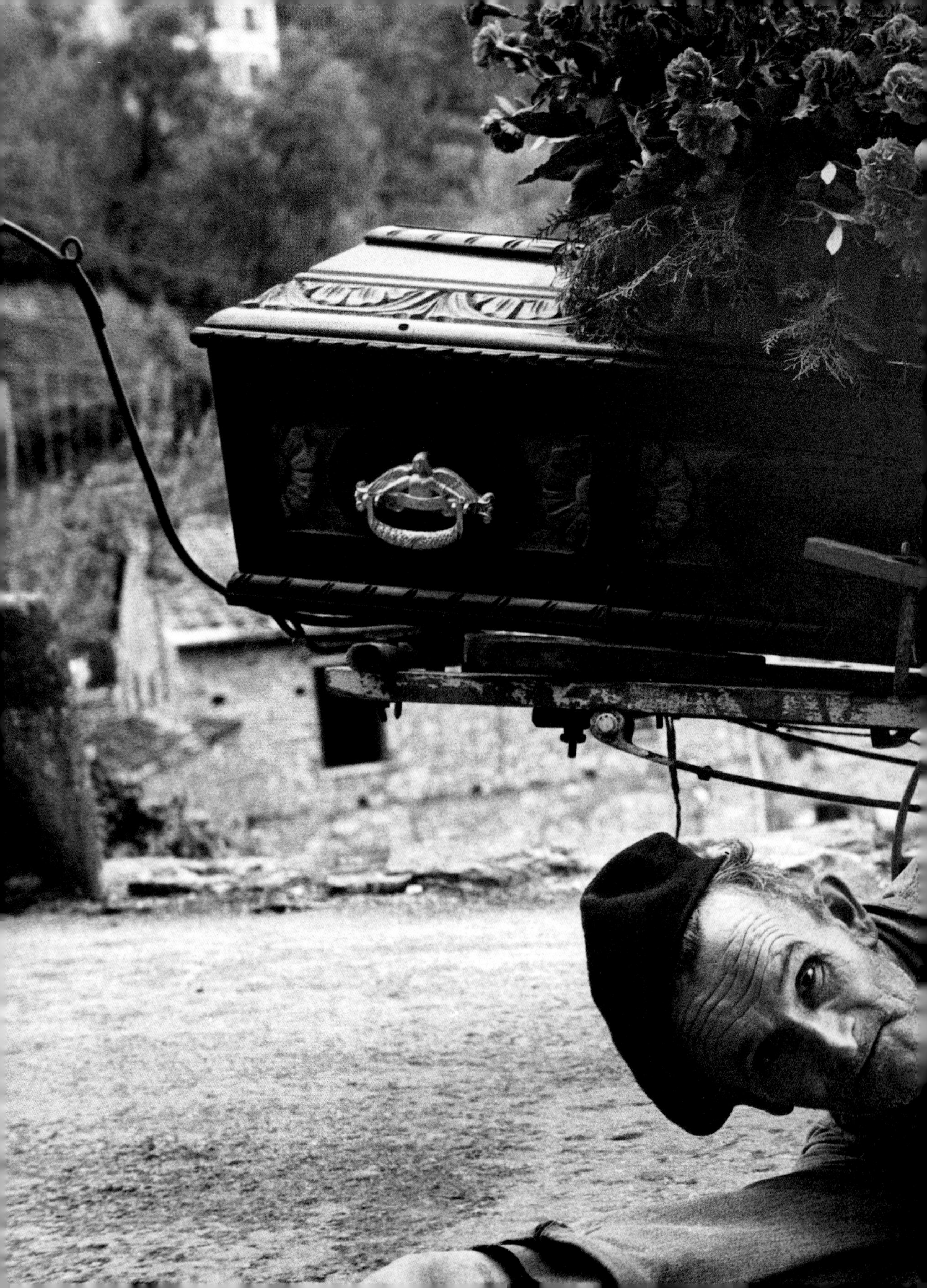

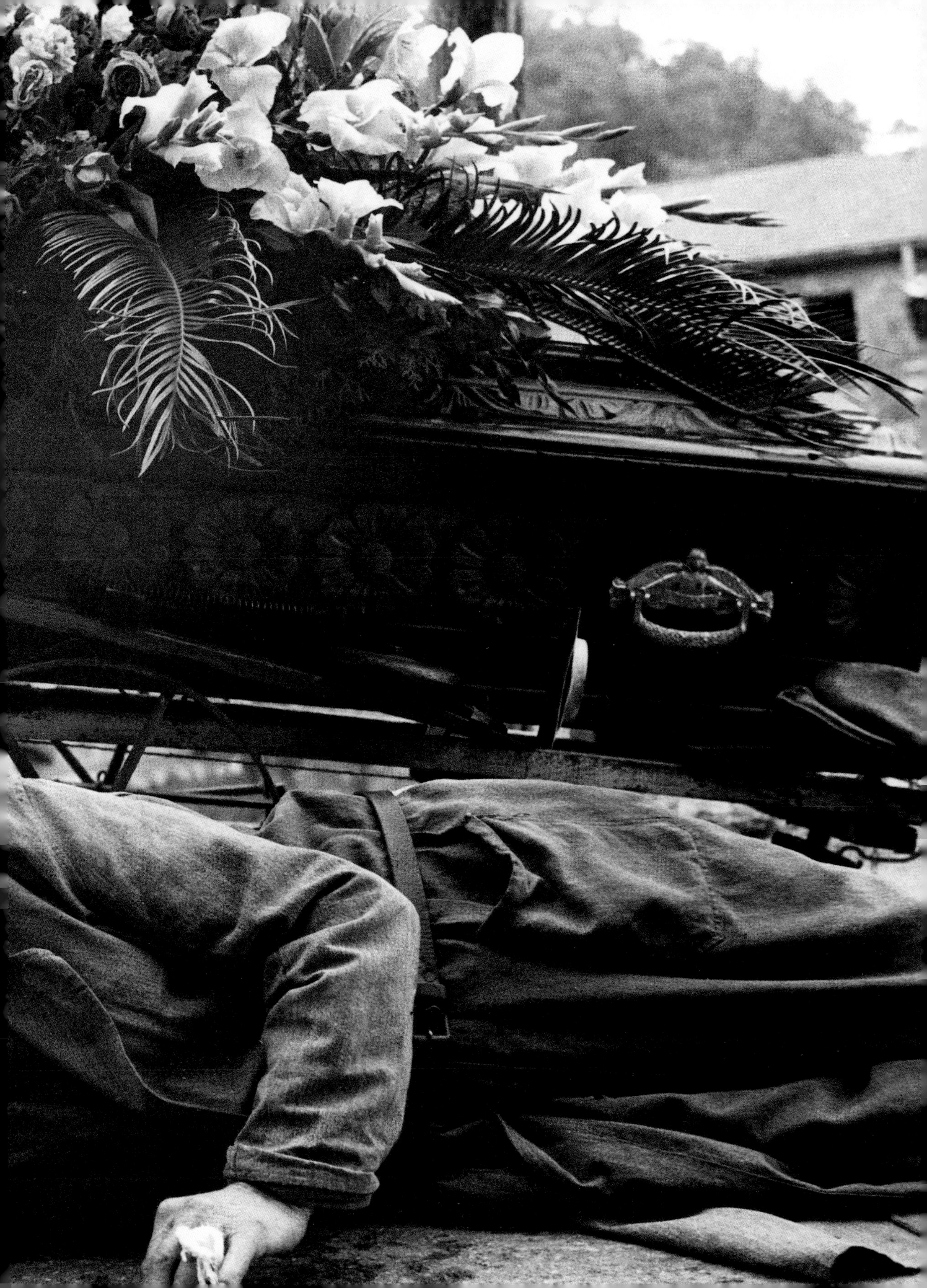

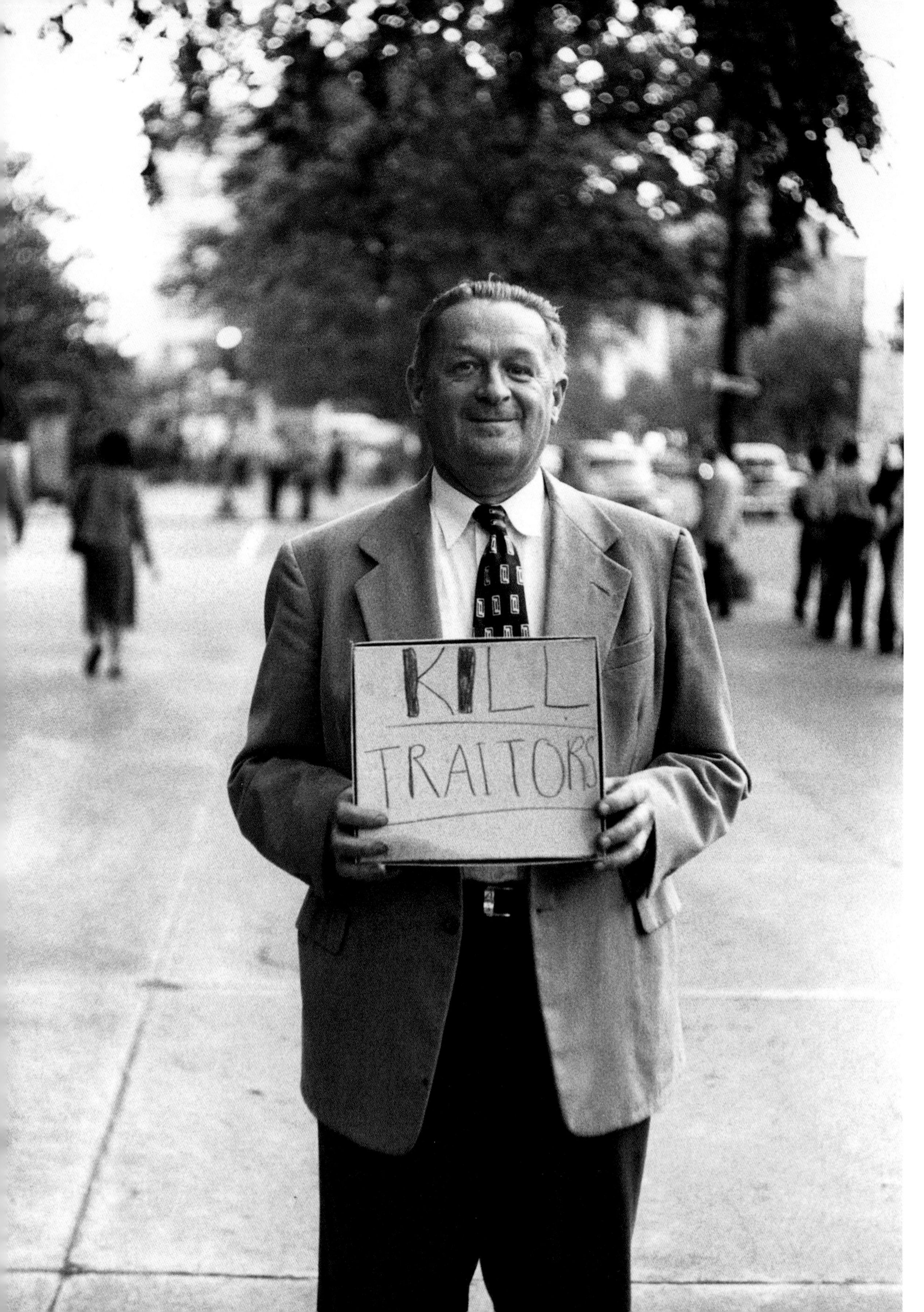

KILL
TRAITORS

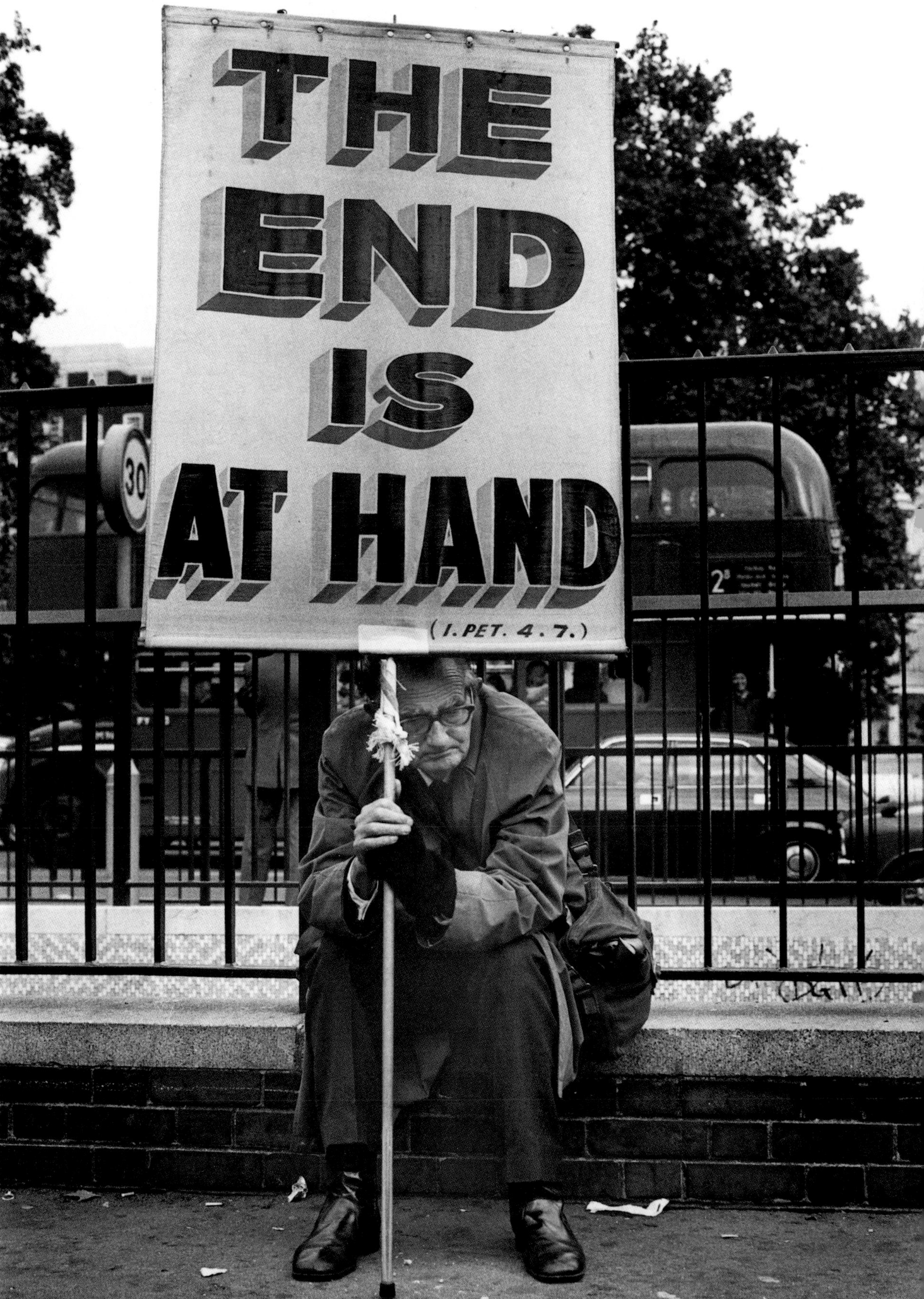

THE
END
IS
AT HAND
(I. PET. 4. 7.)
30
2B

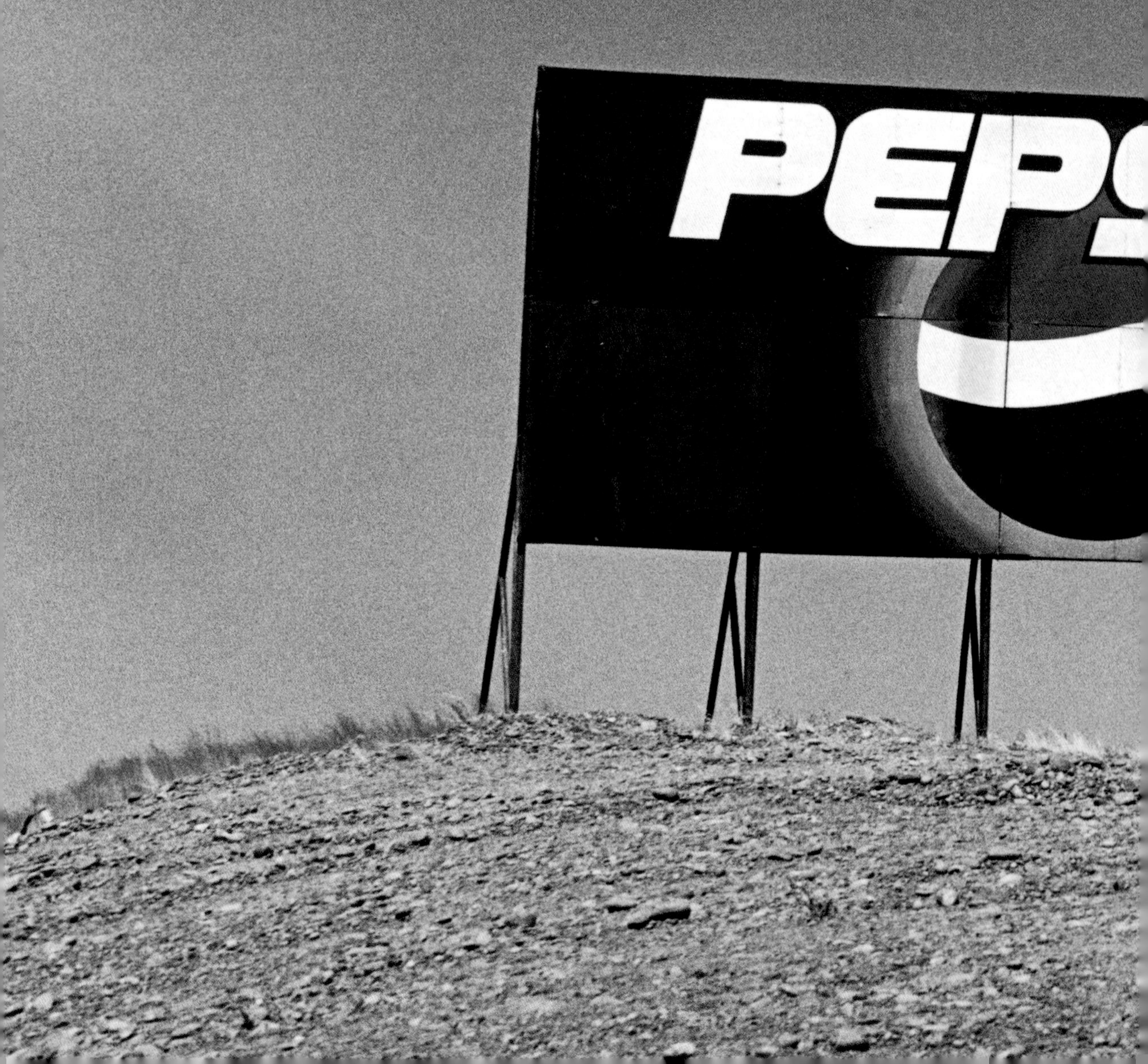
PEPS

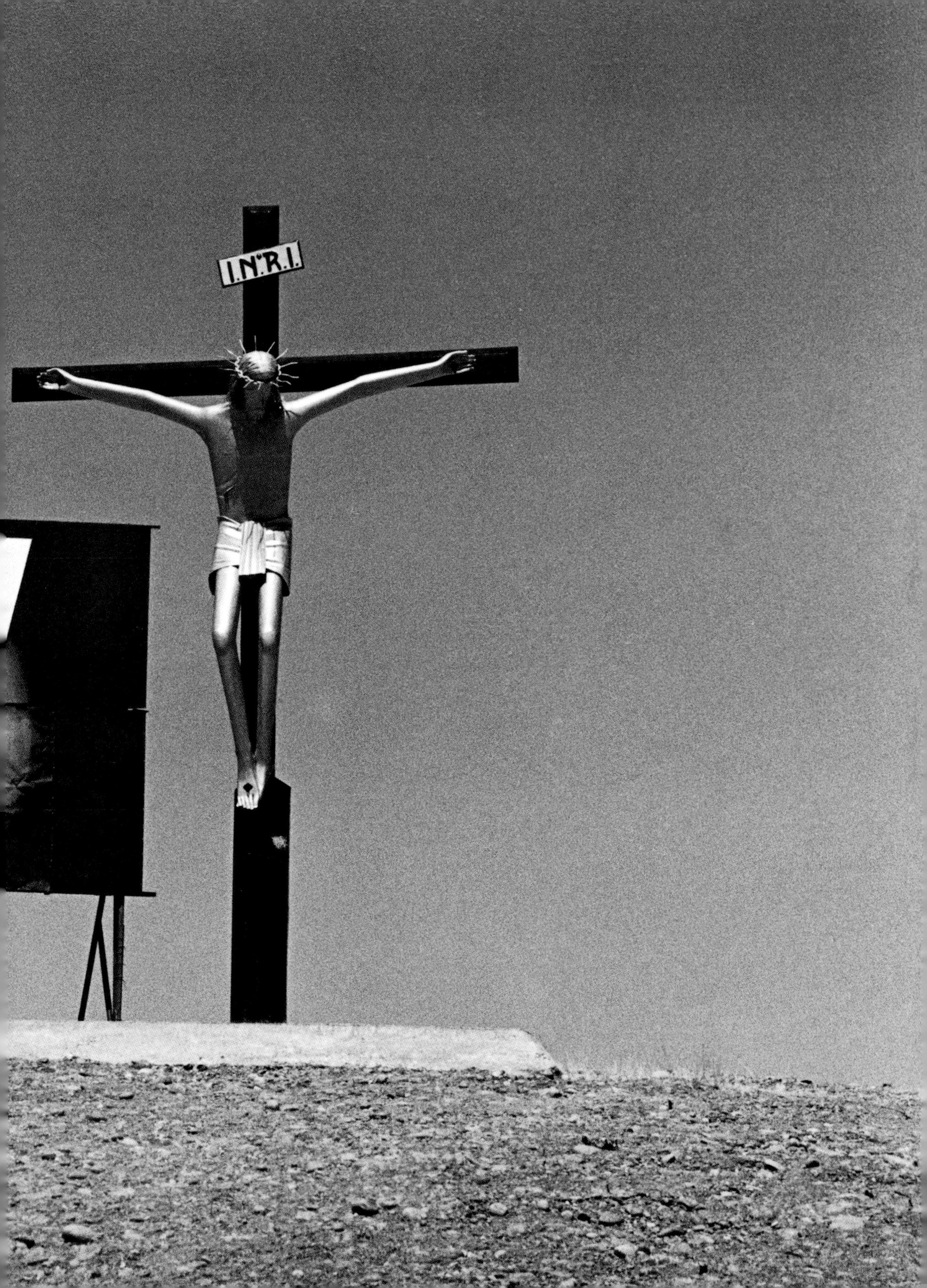

I.N.R.I.

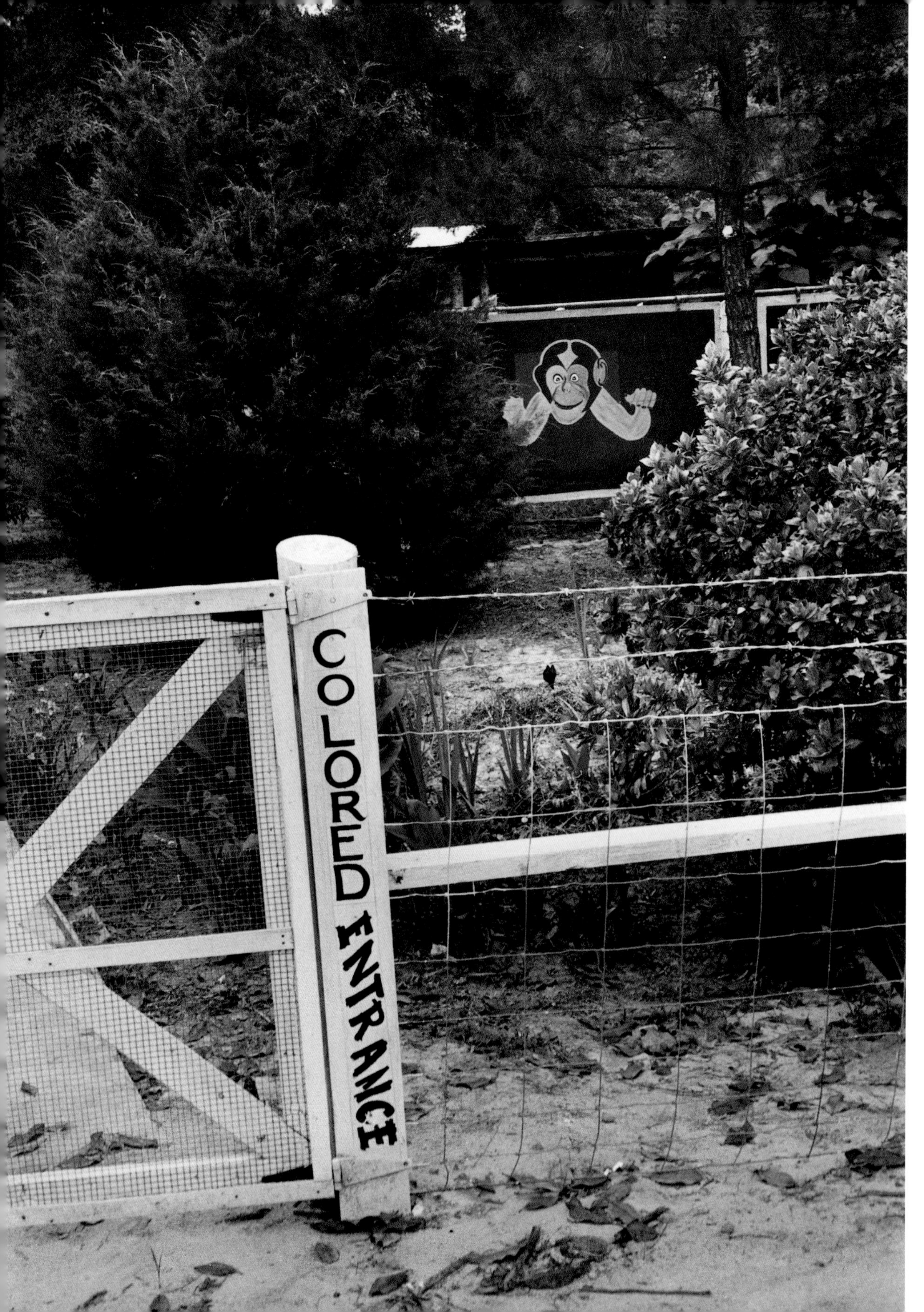

COLORED ENTRANCE

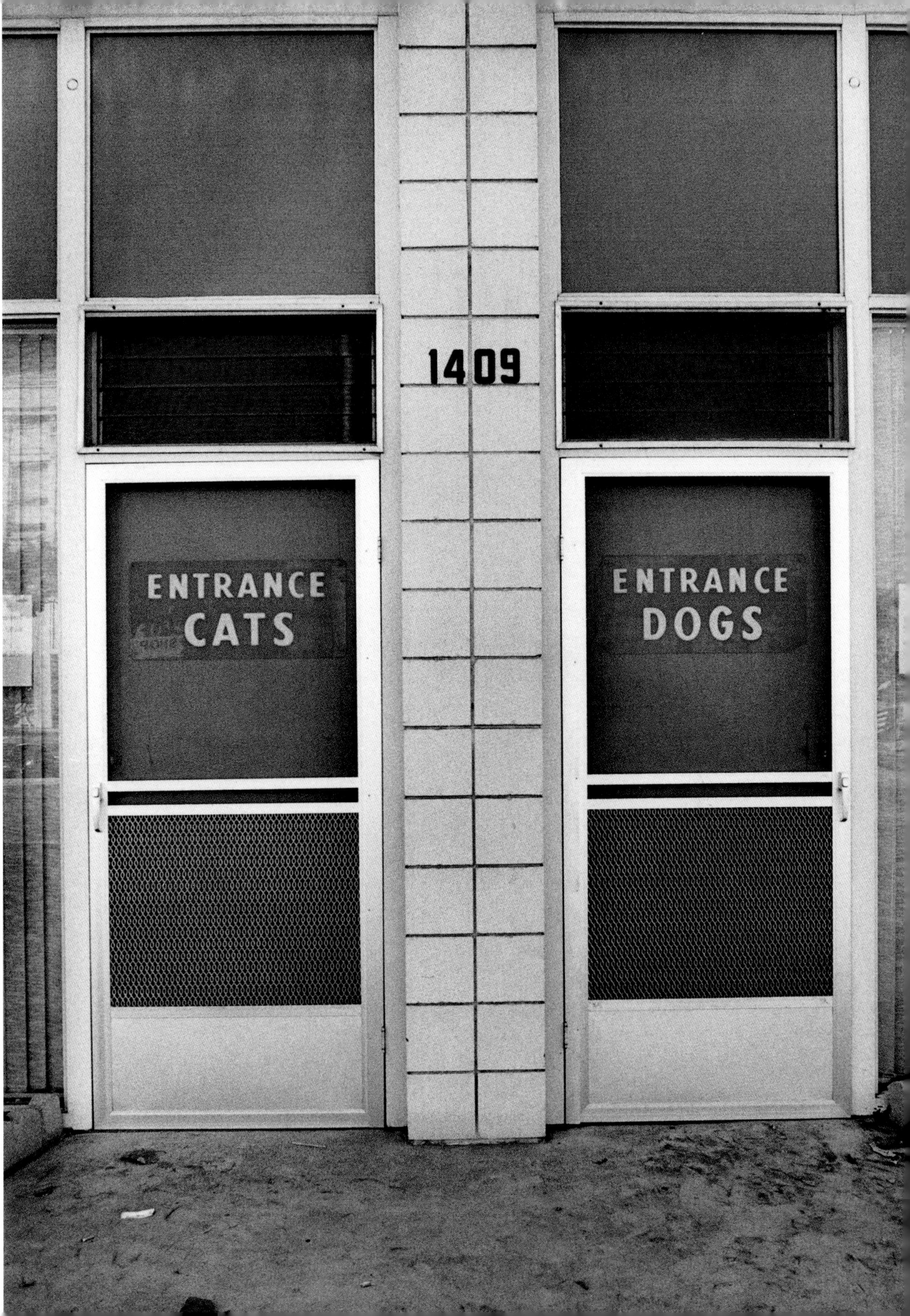

1409
ENTRANCE
CATS
ENTRANCE
DOGS

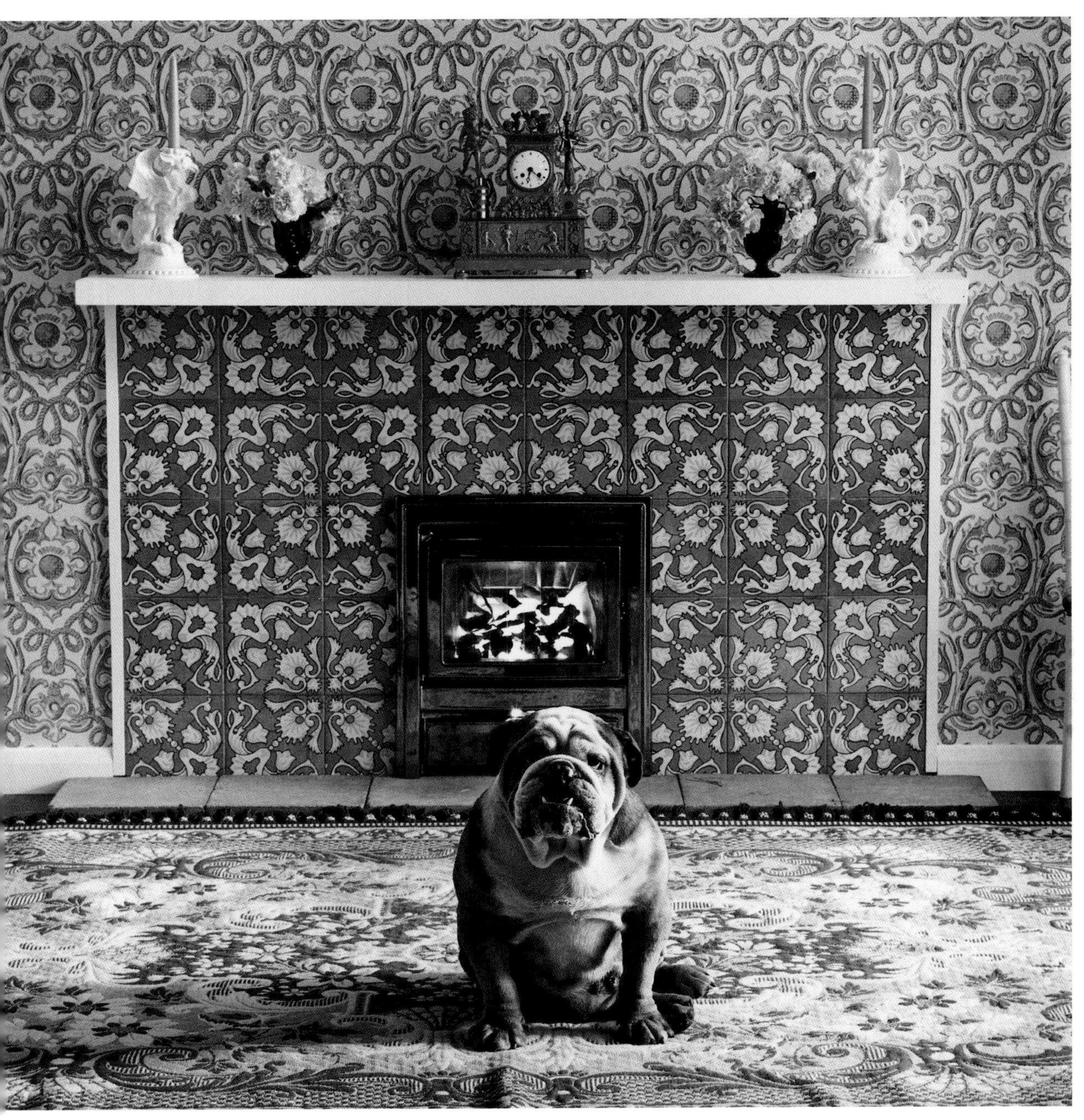

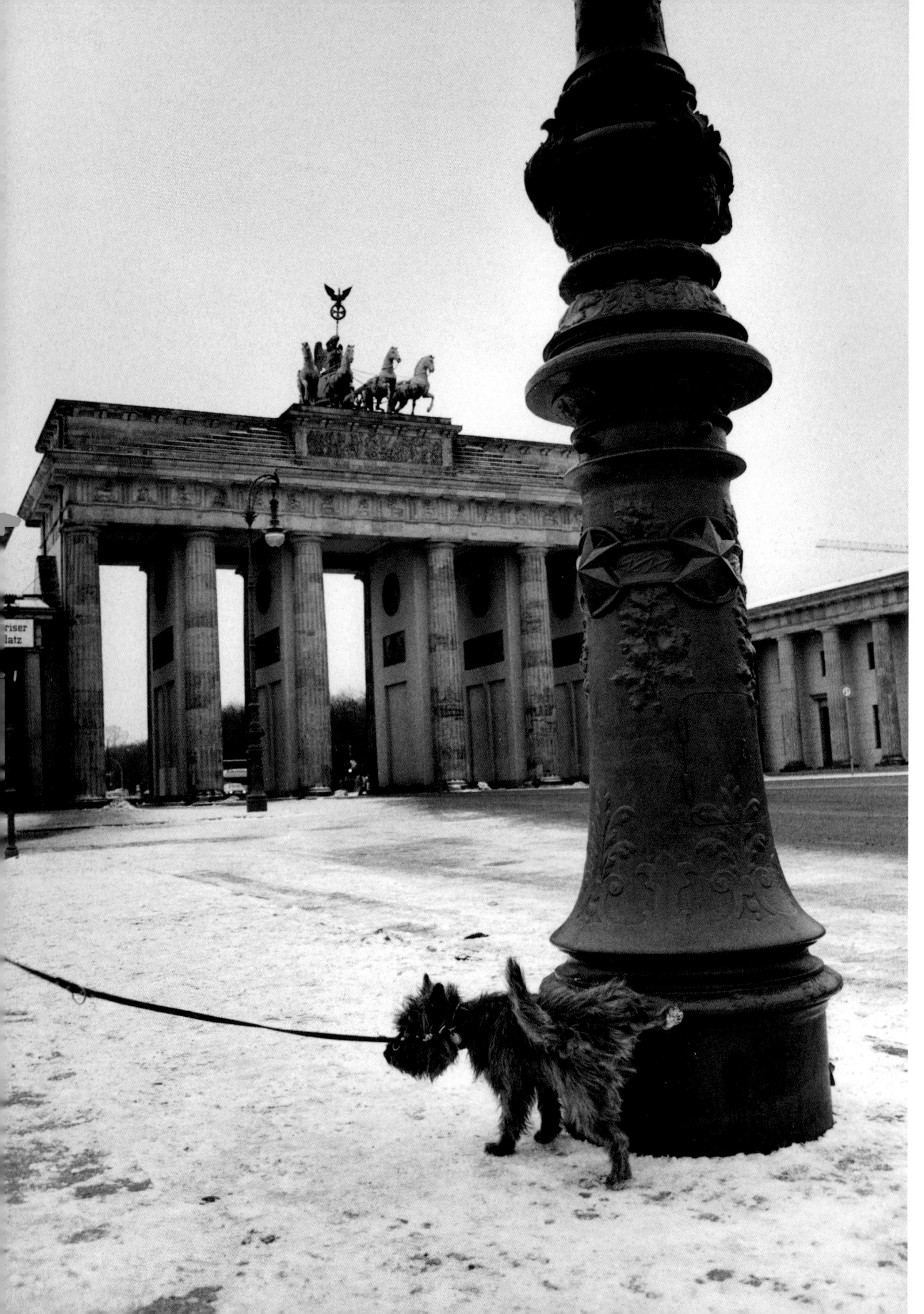
riser
latz

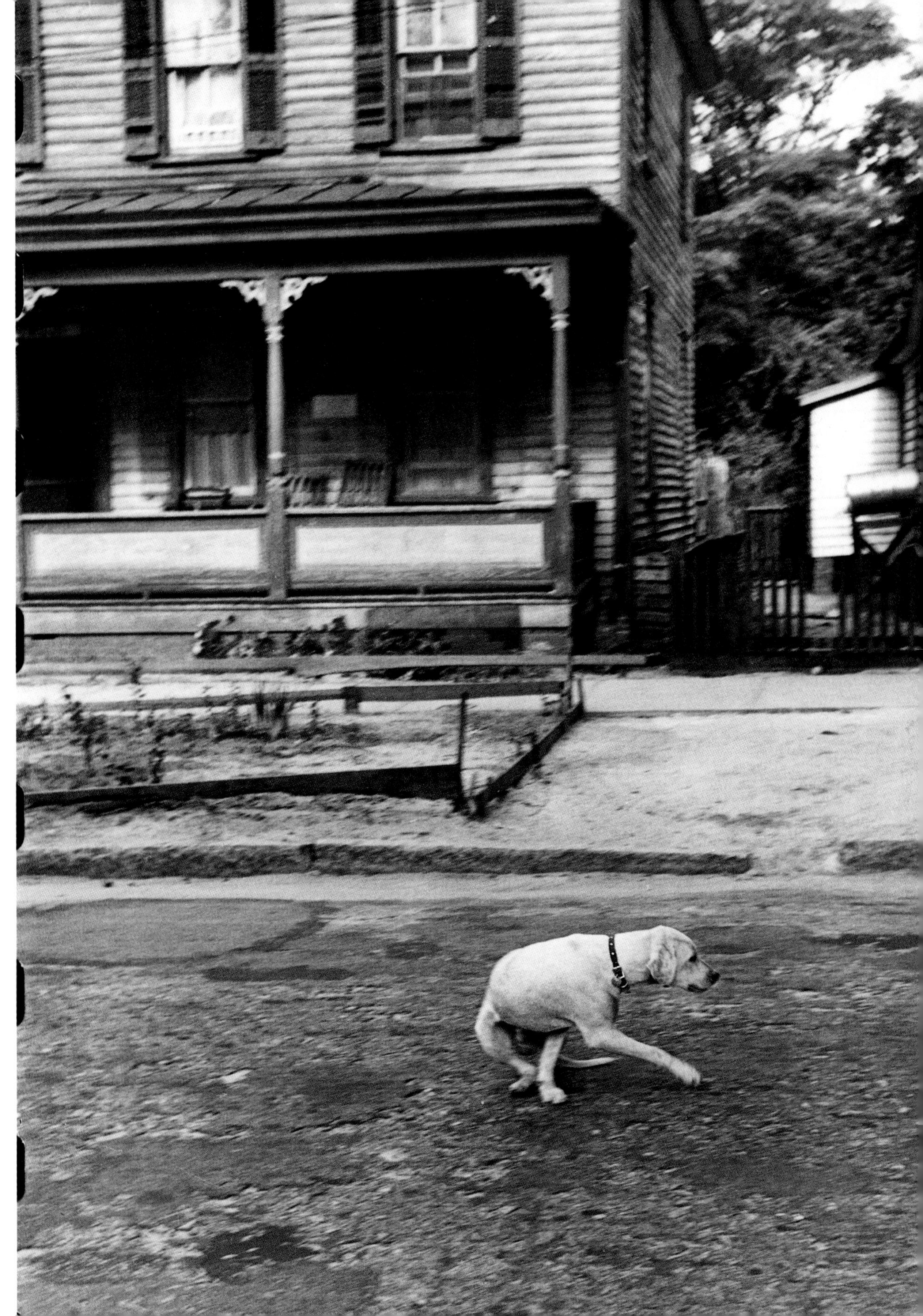

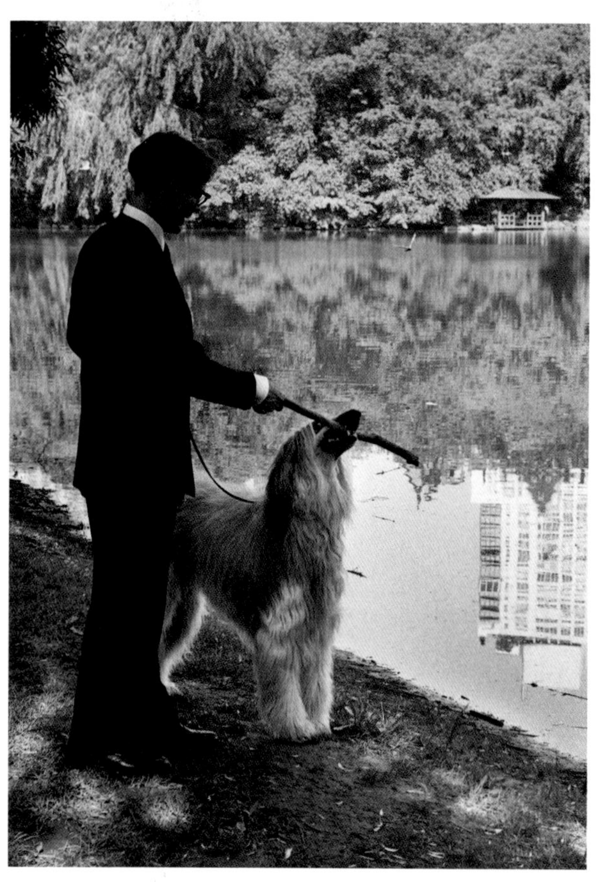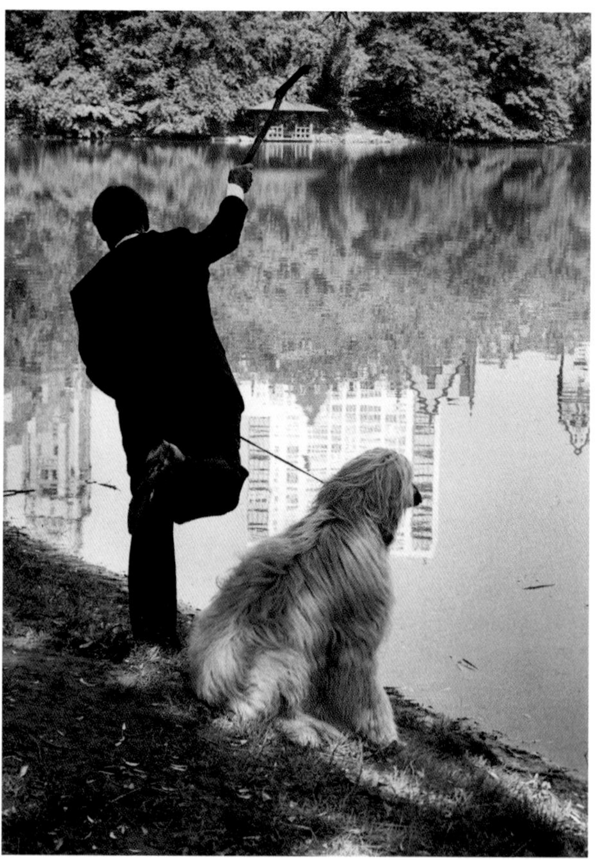

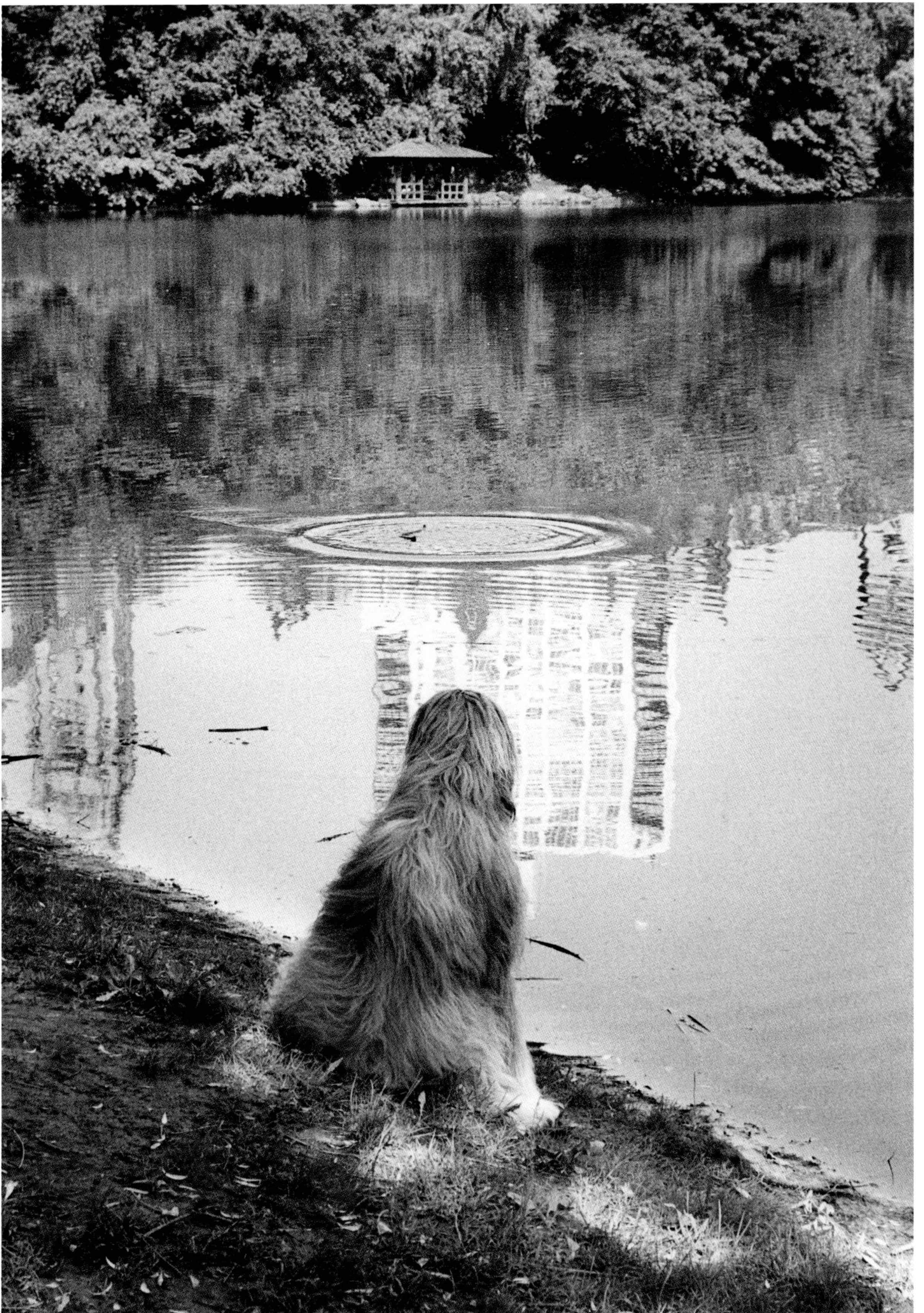

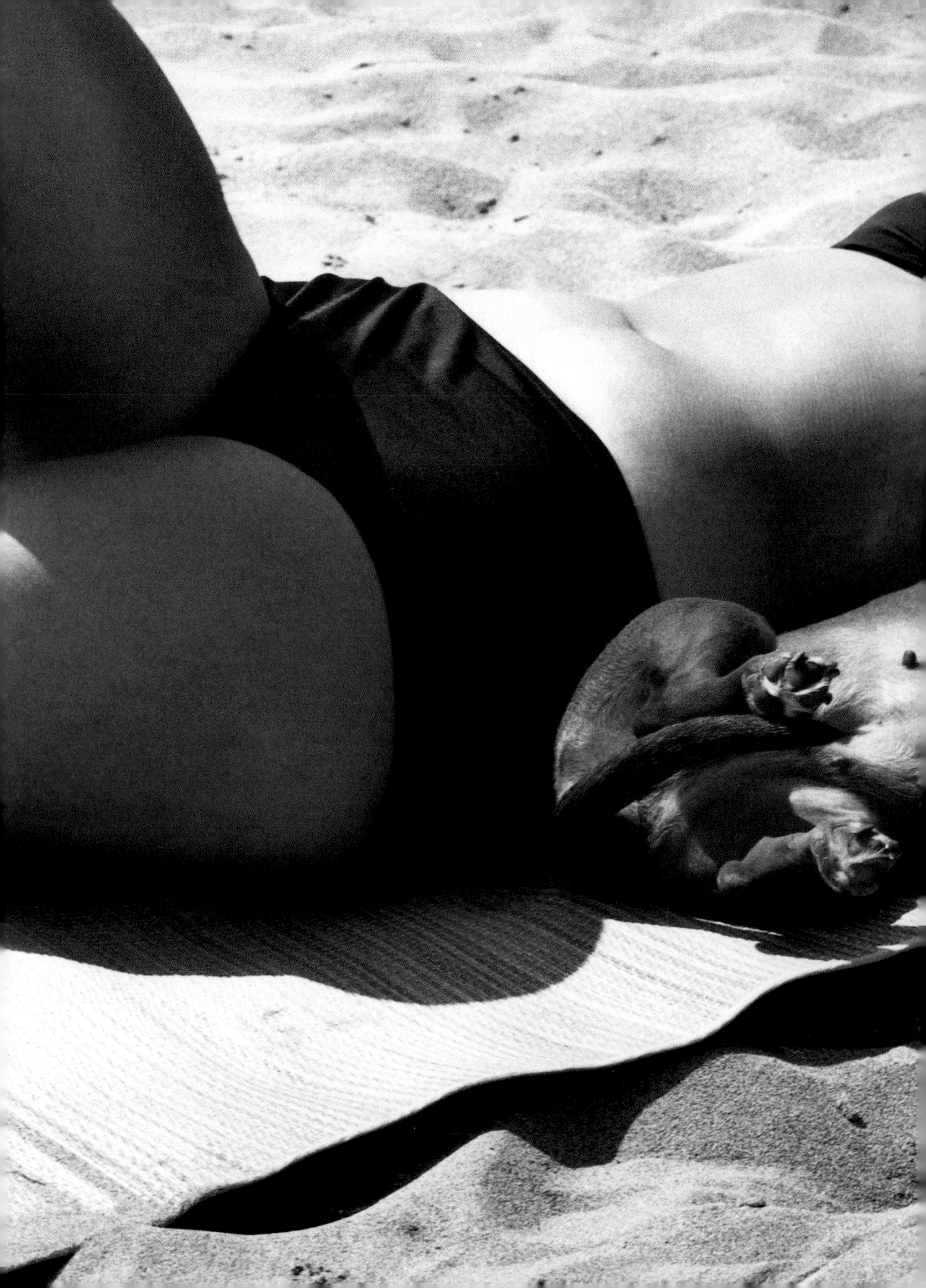

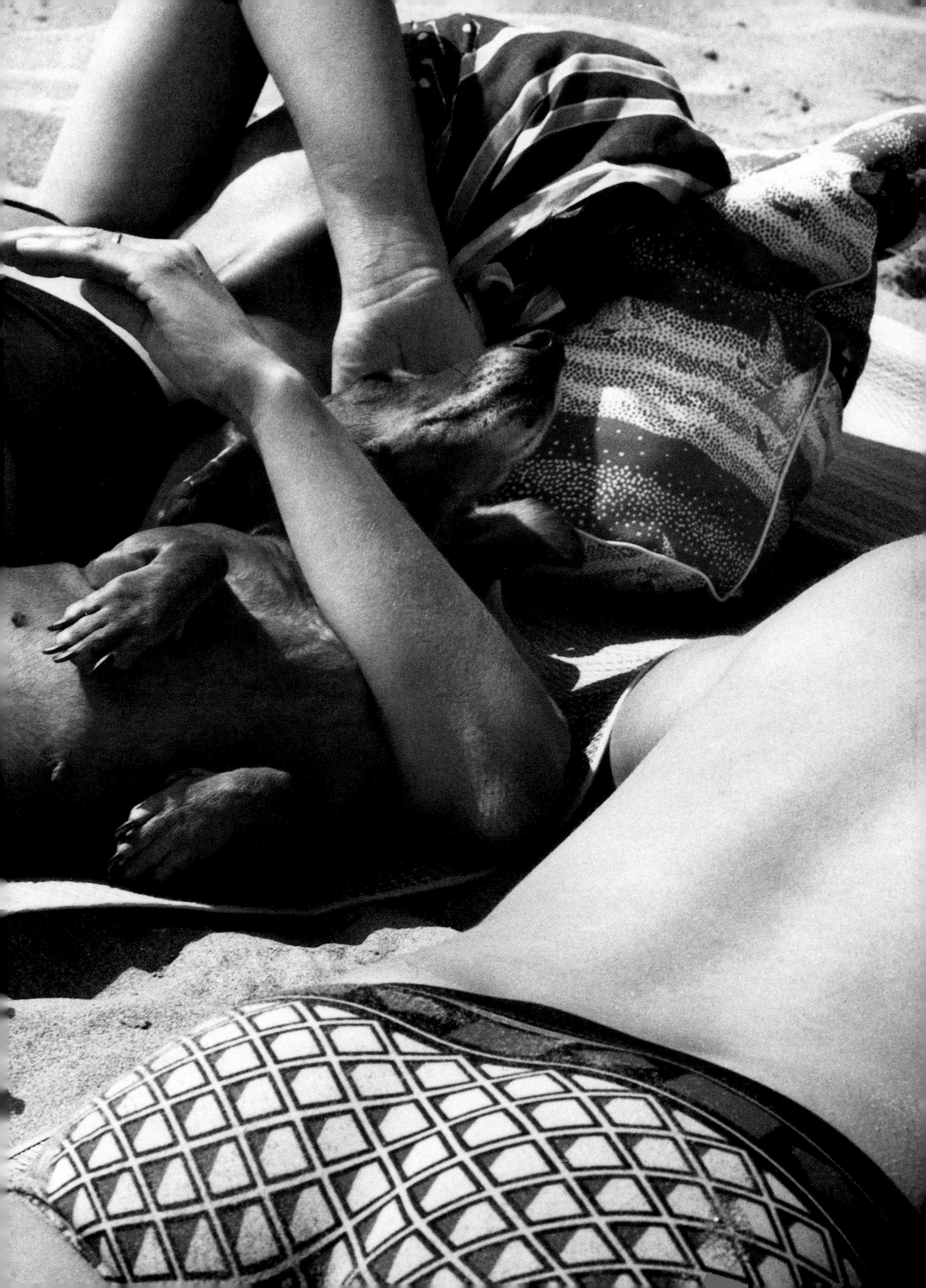

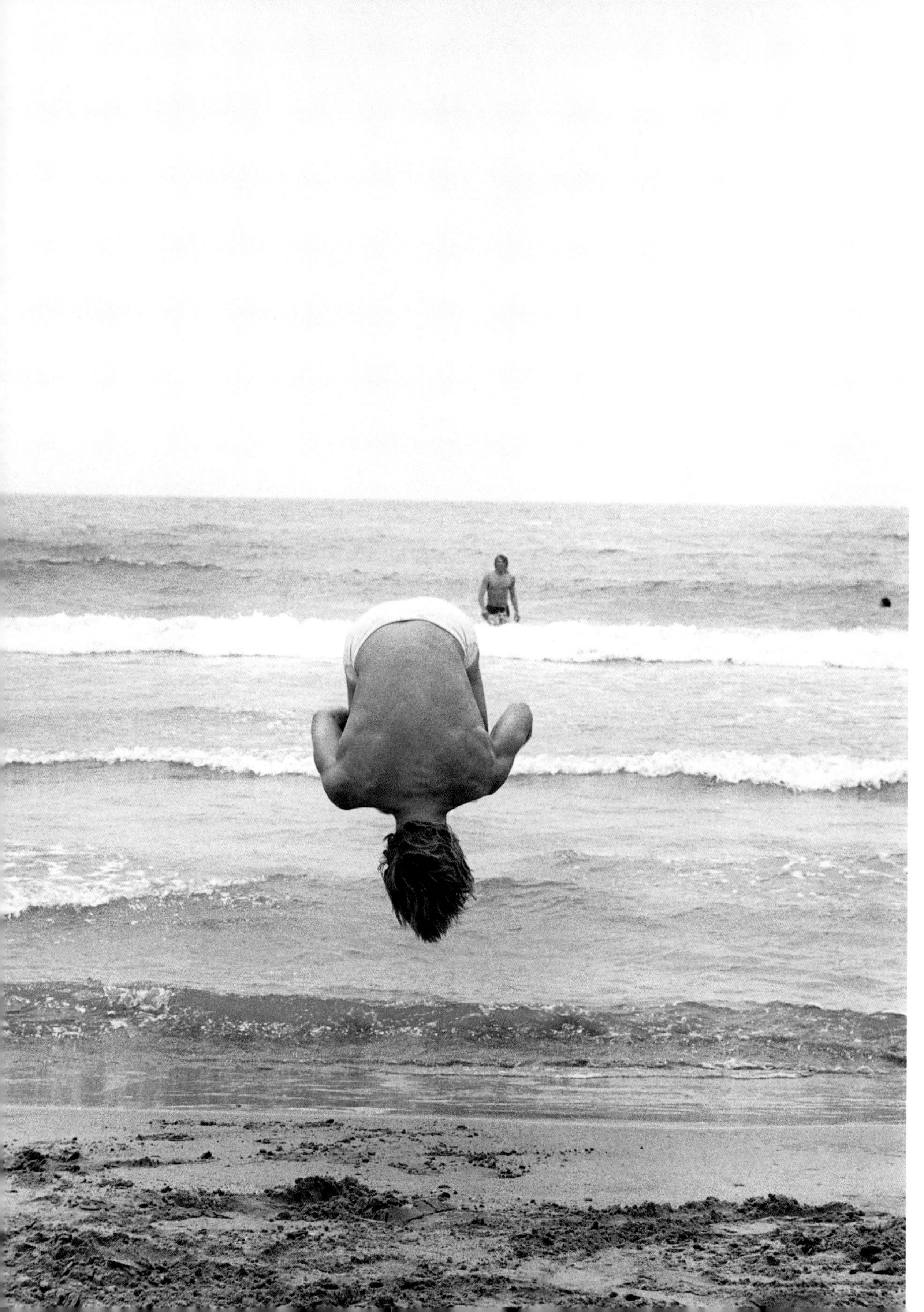

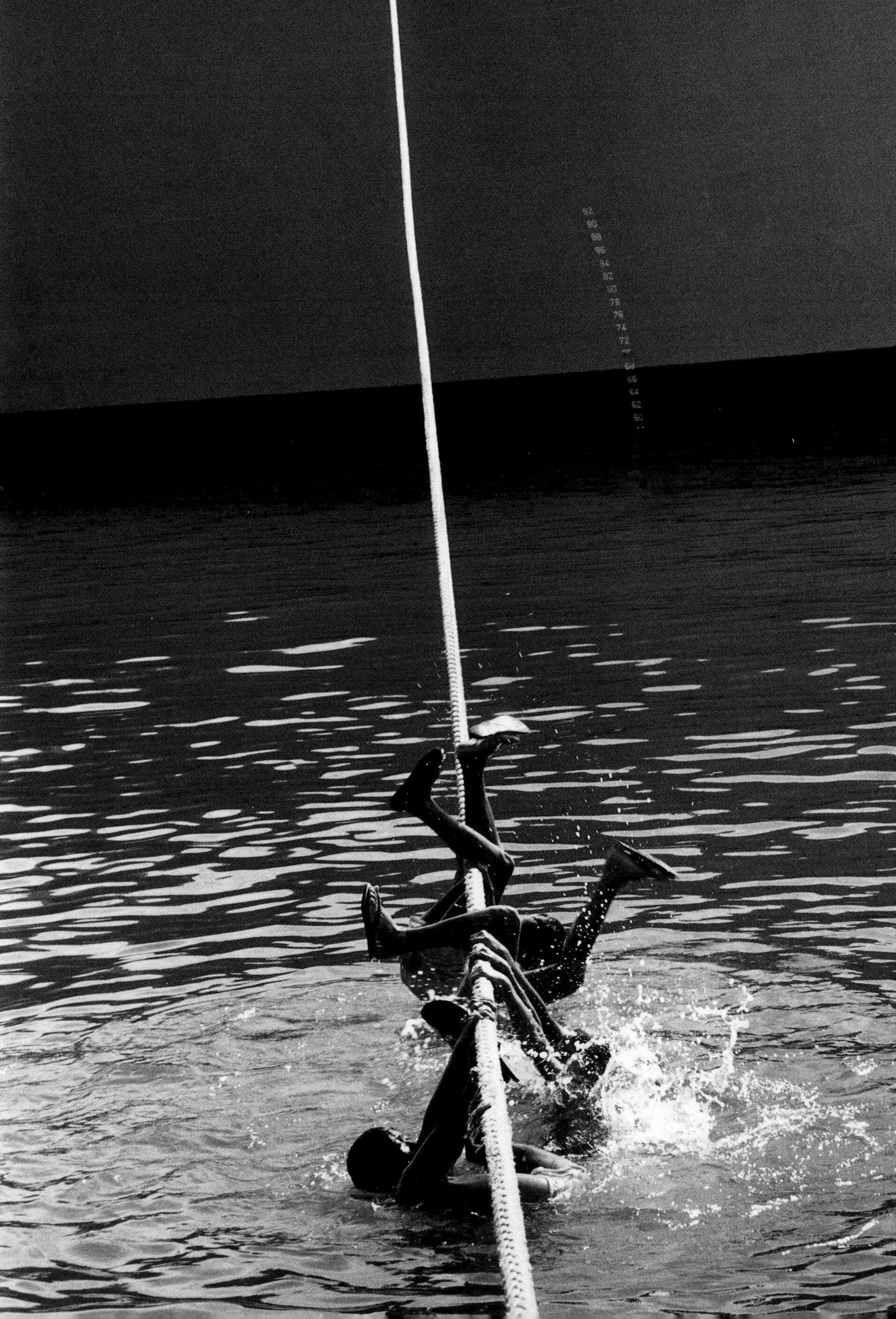

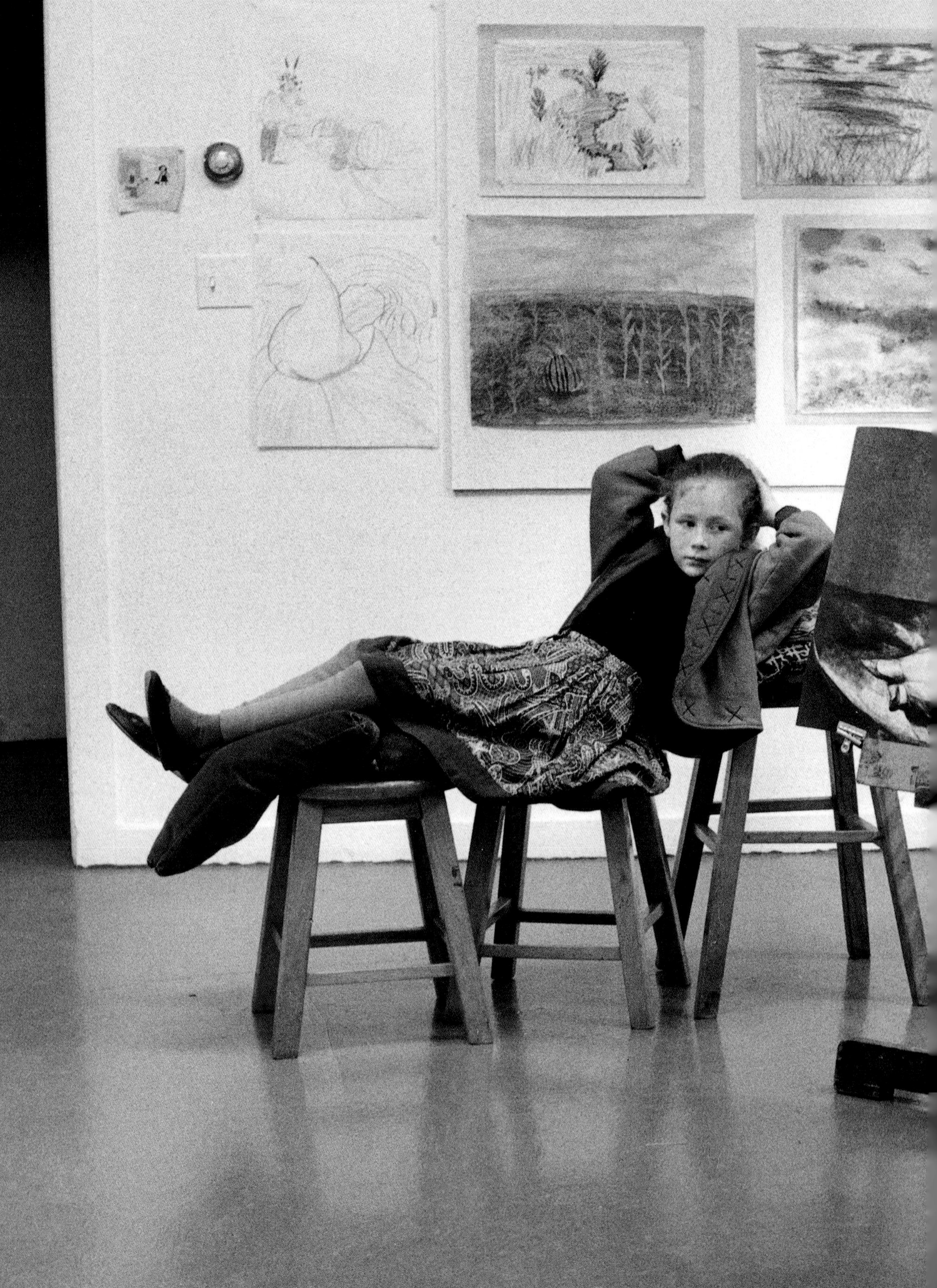

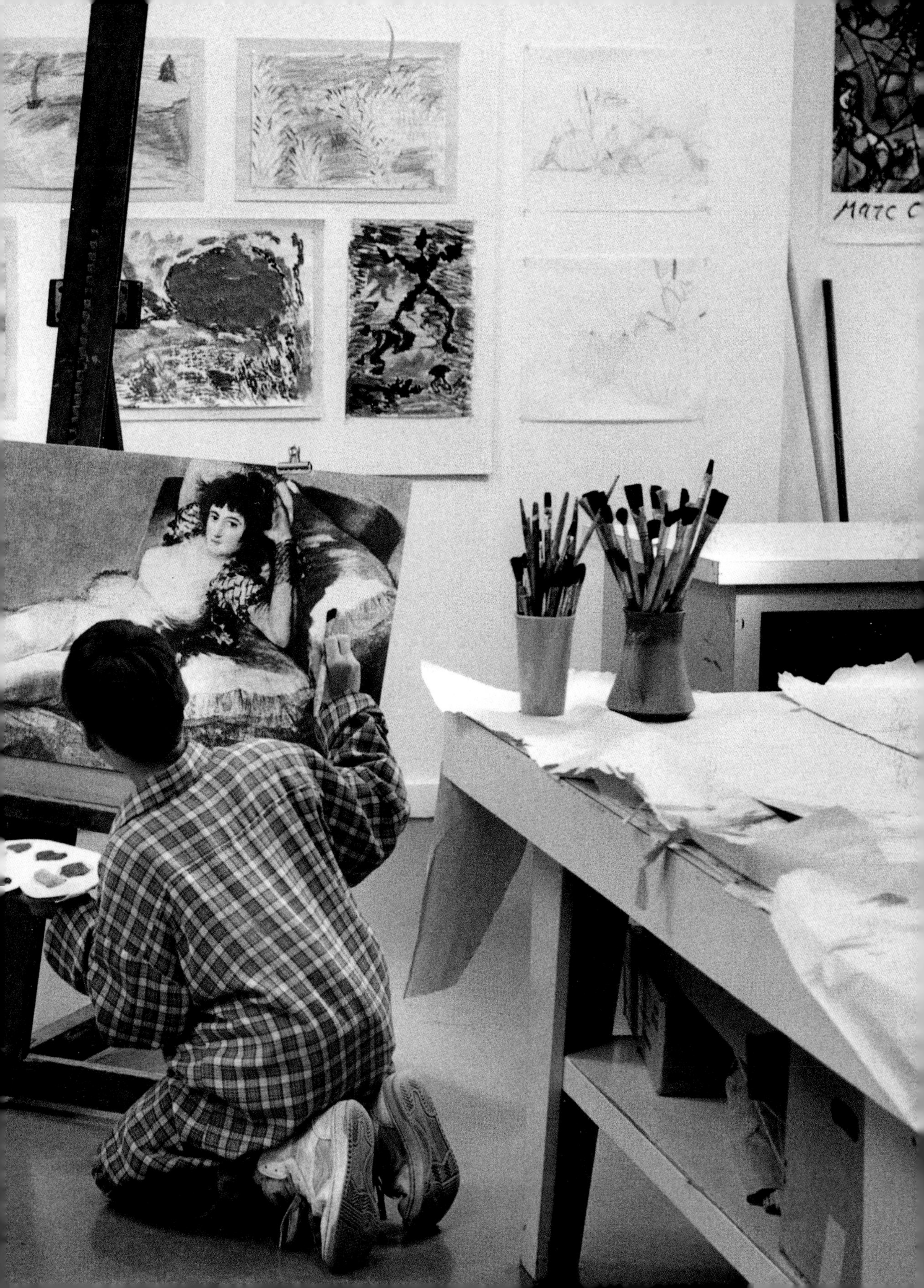

MArC C

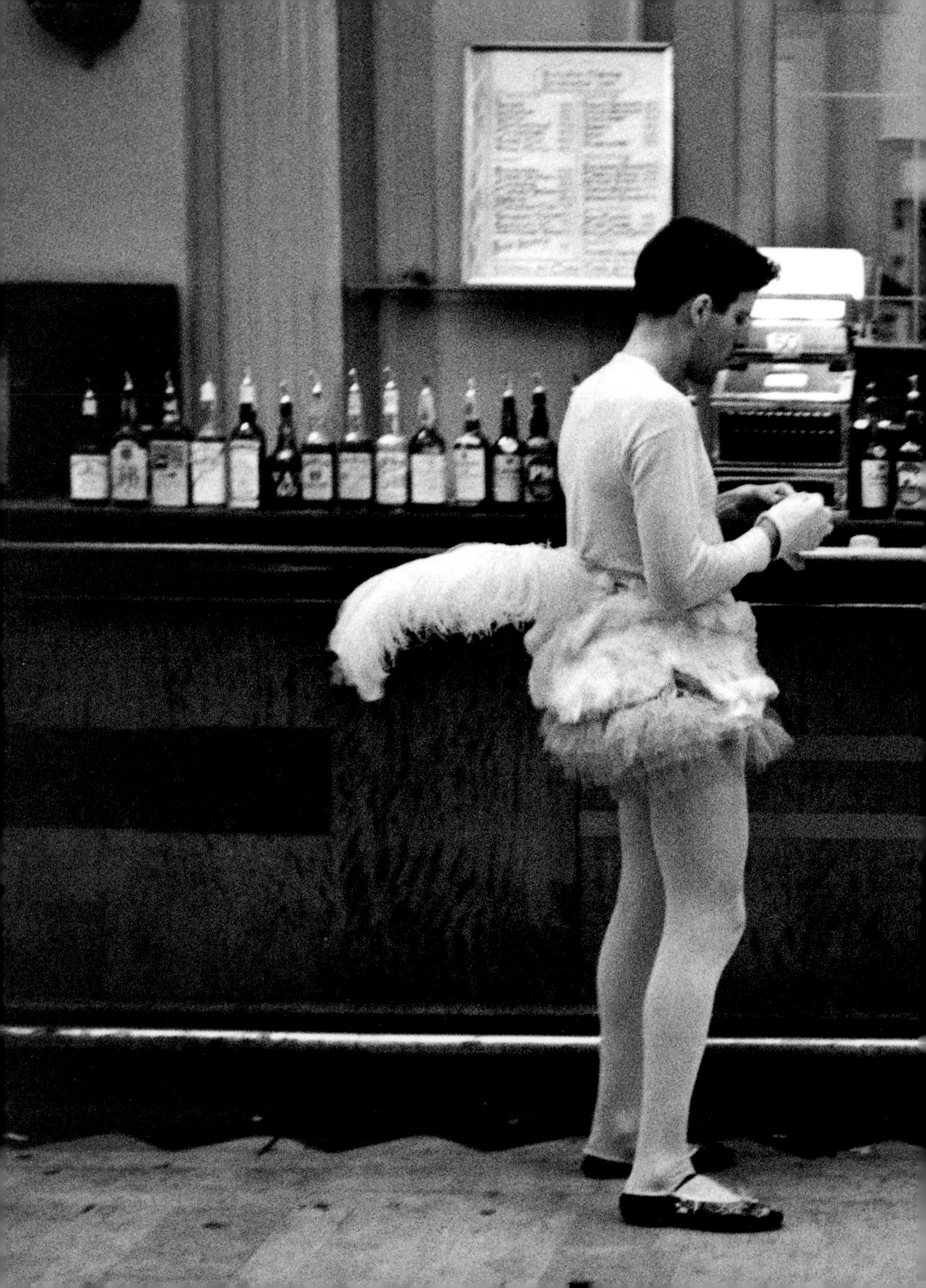

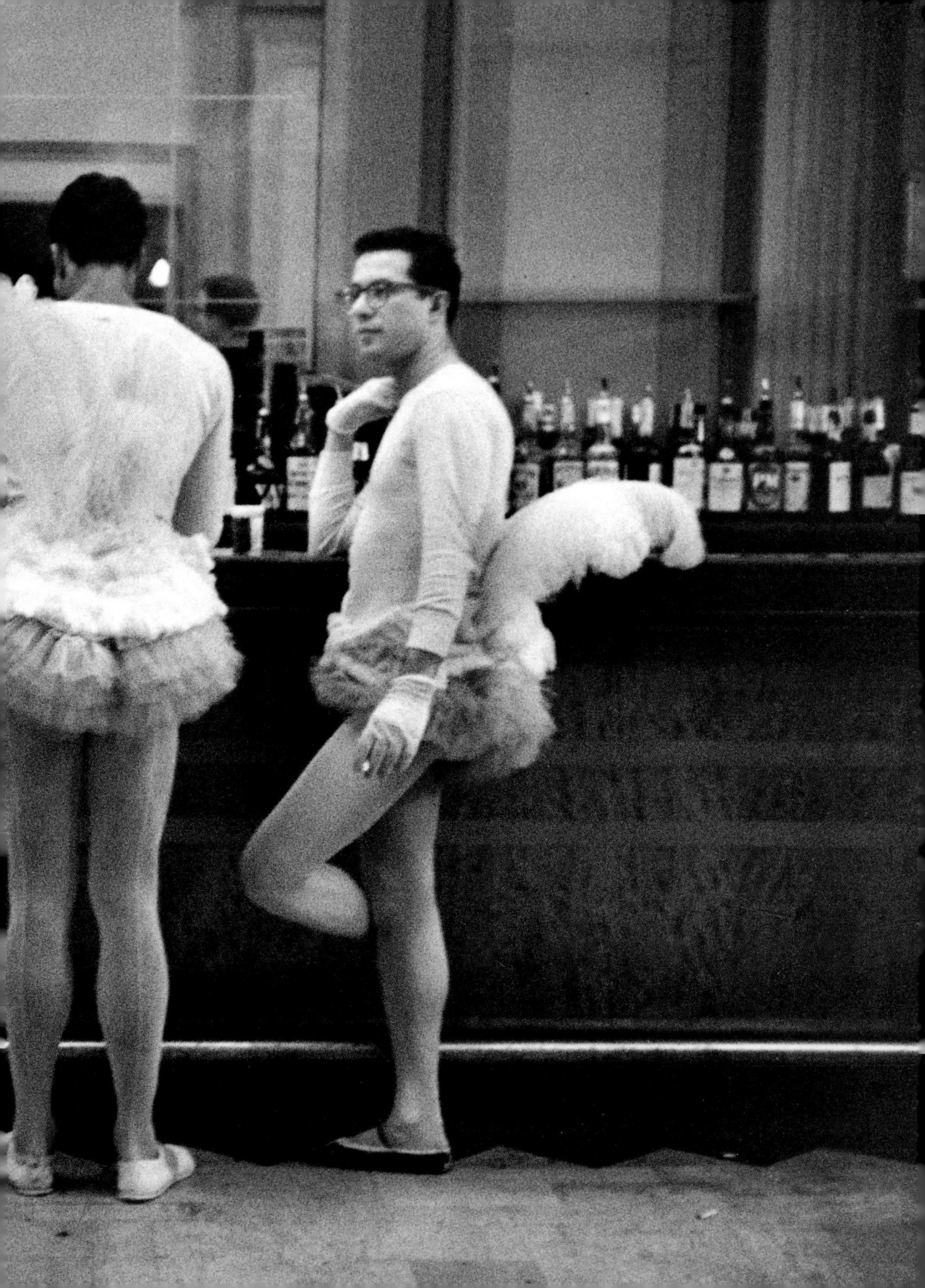

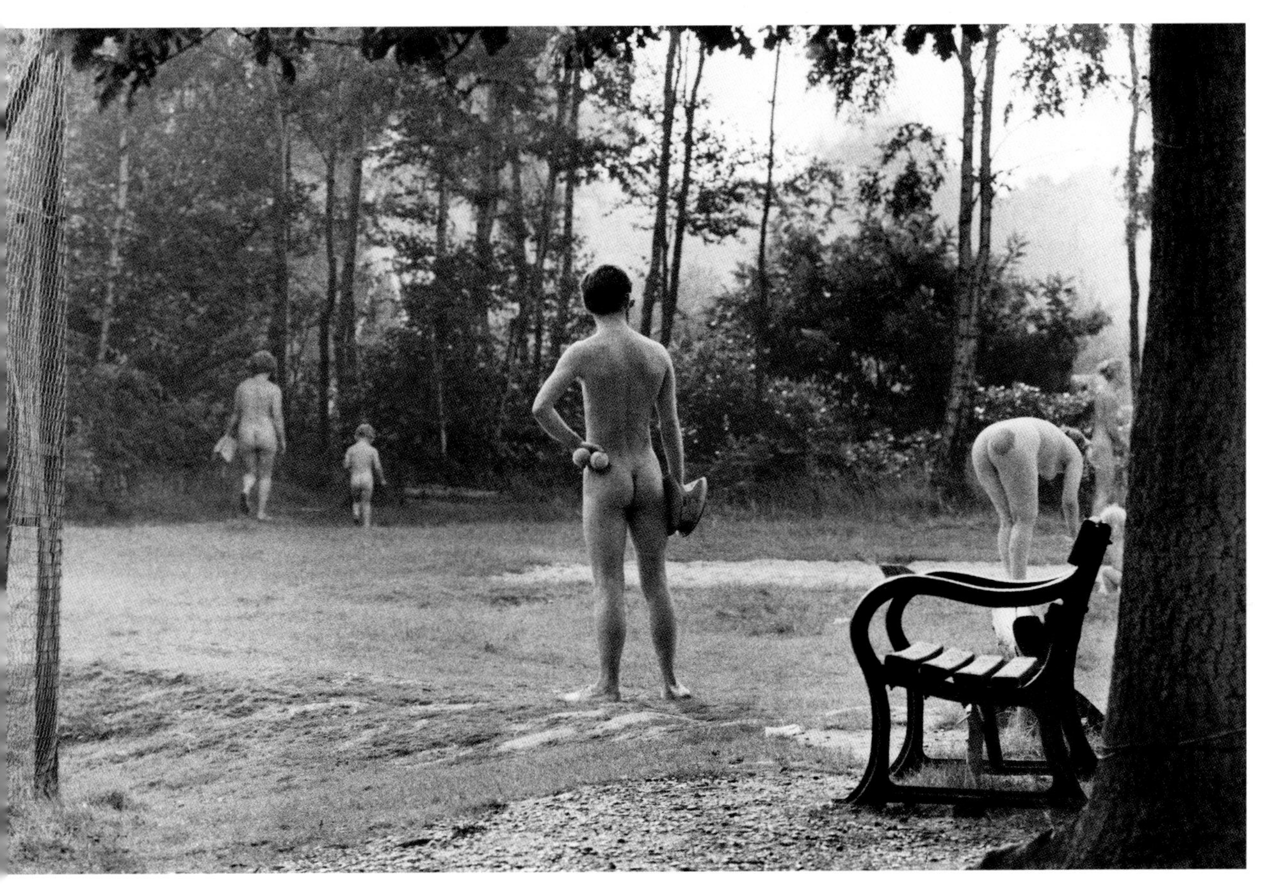

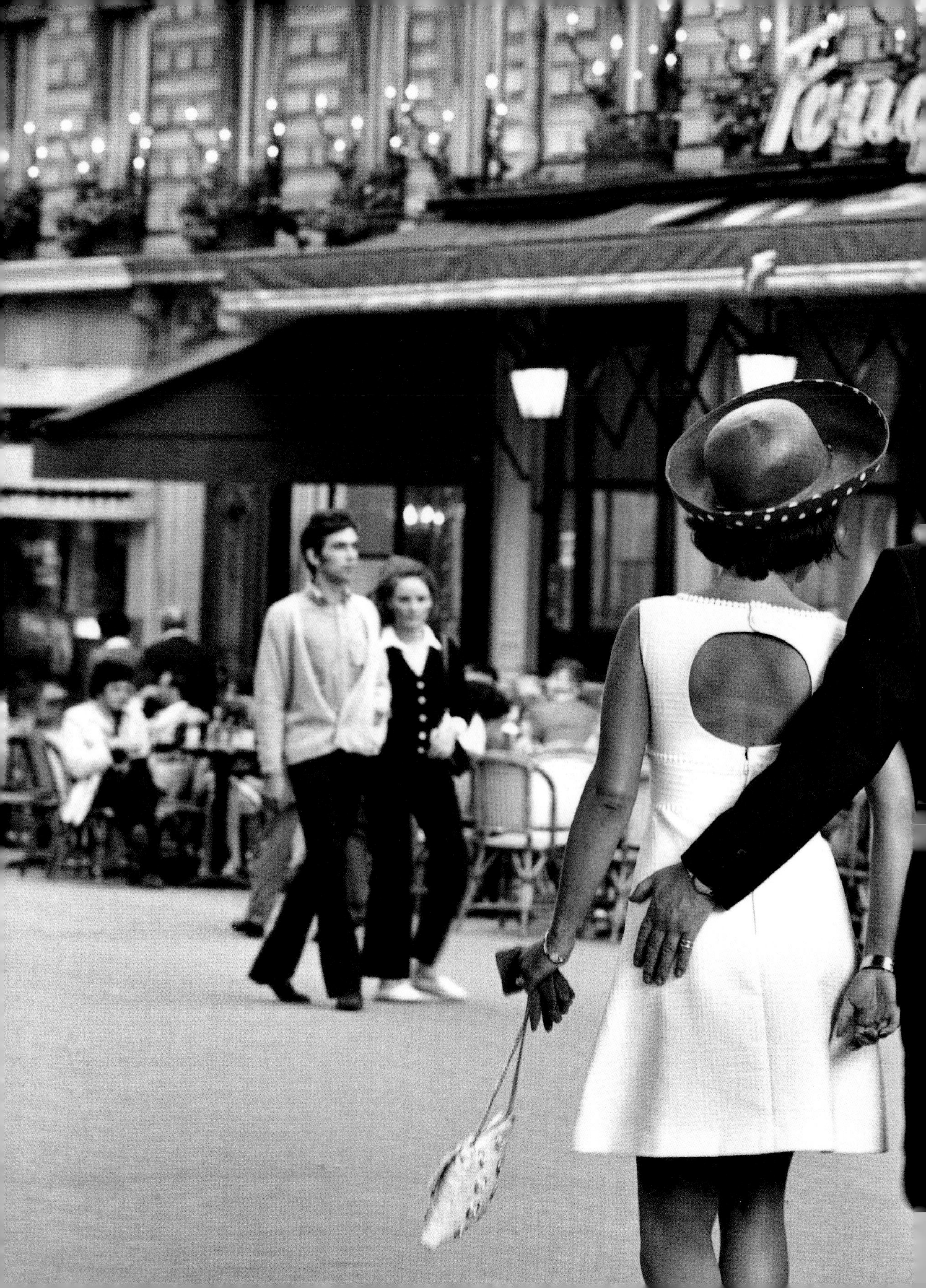

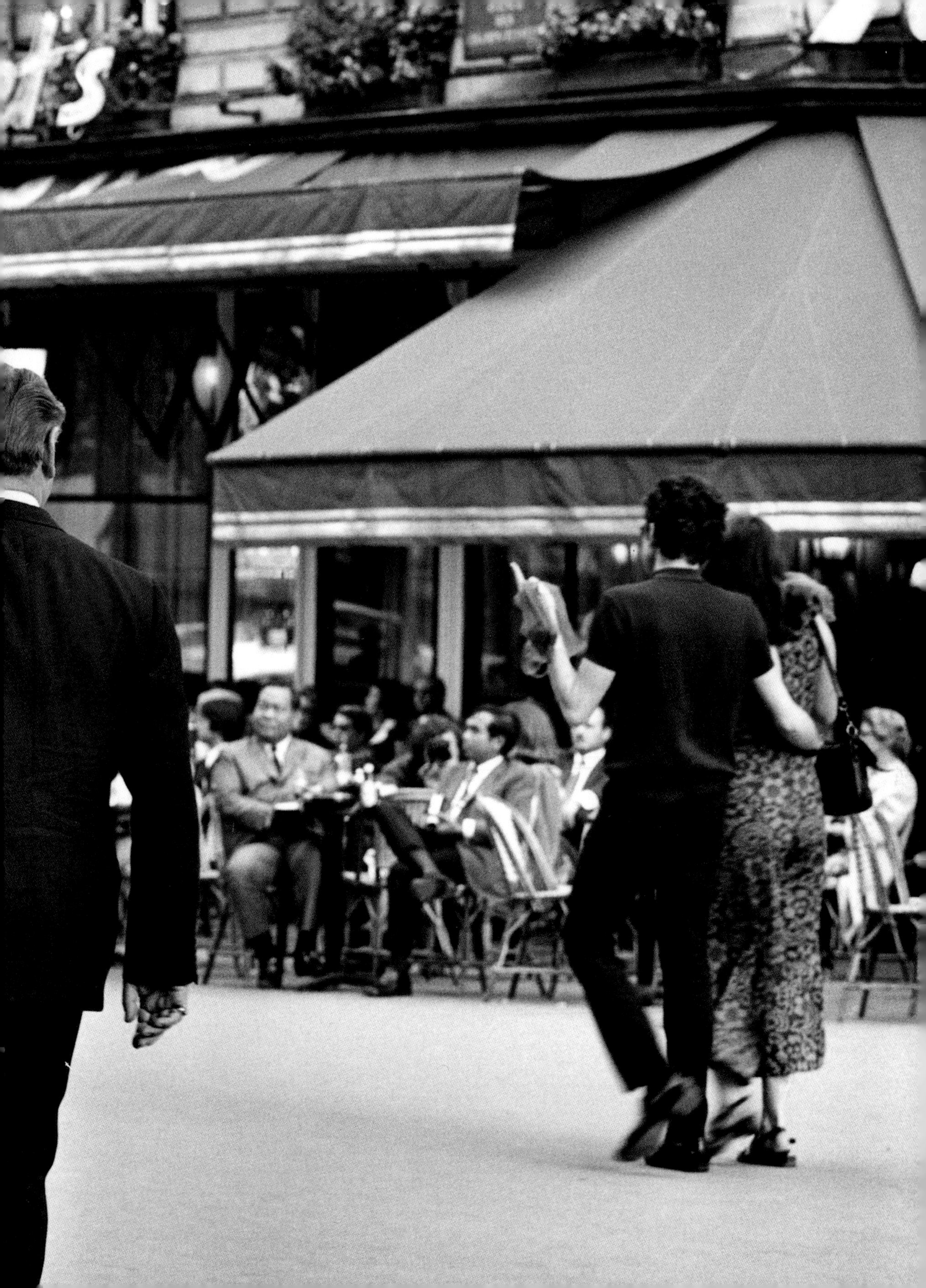

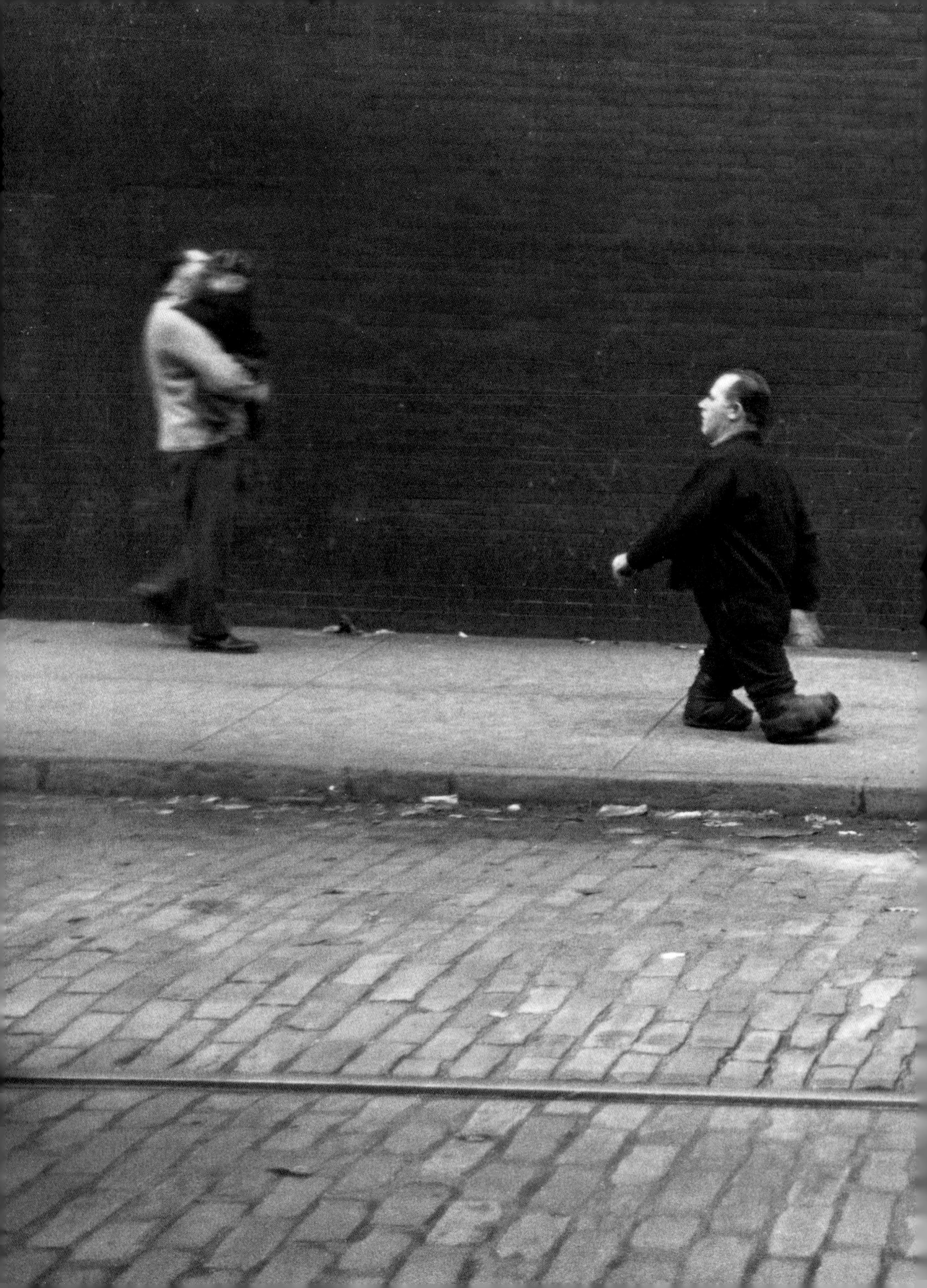

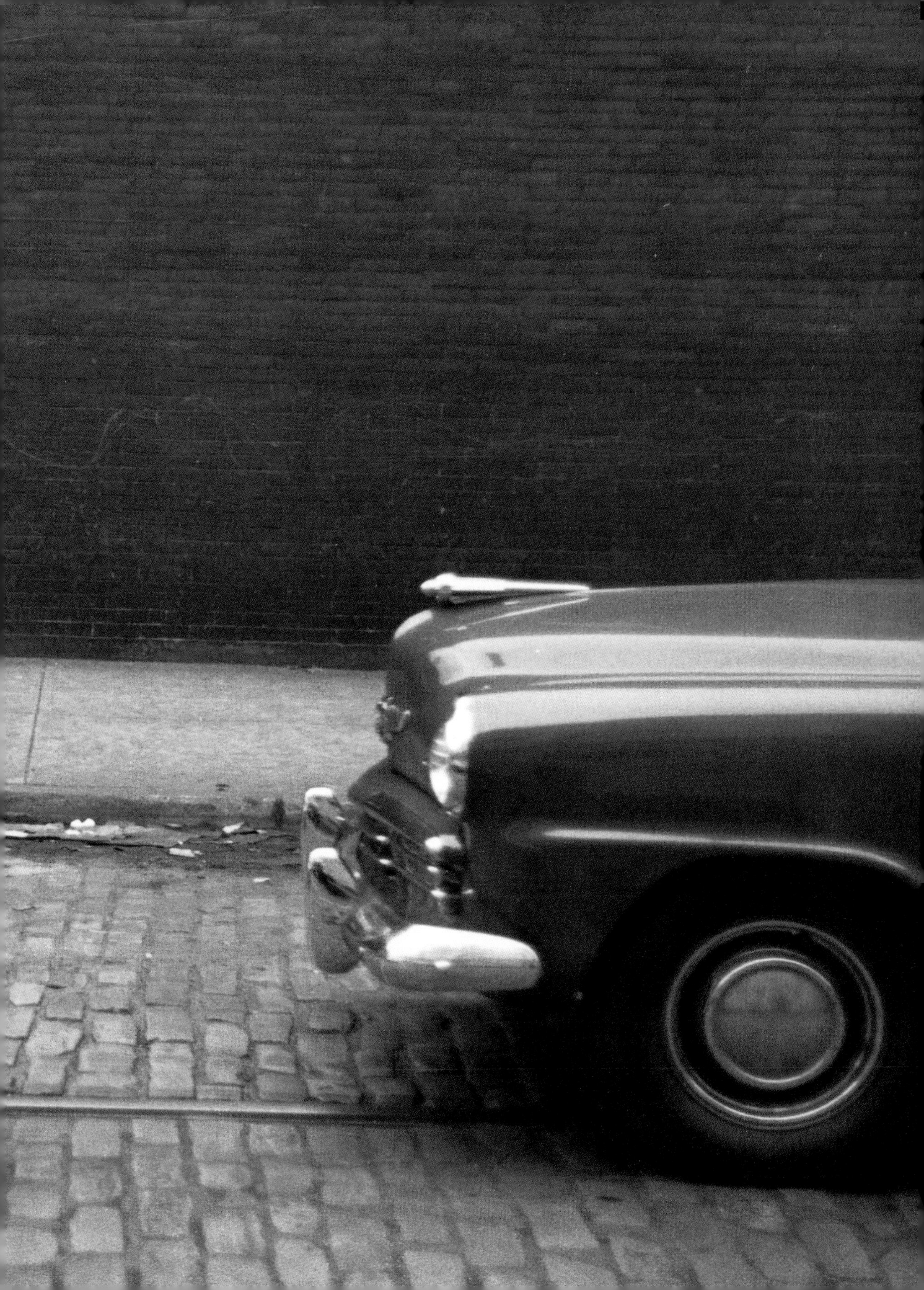

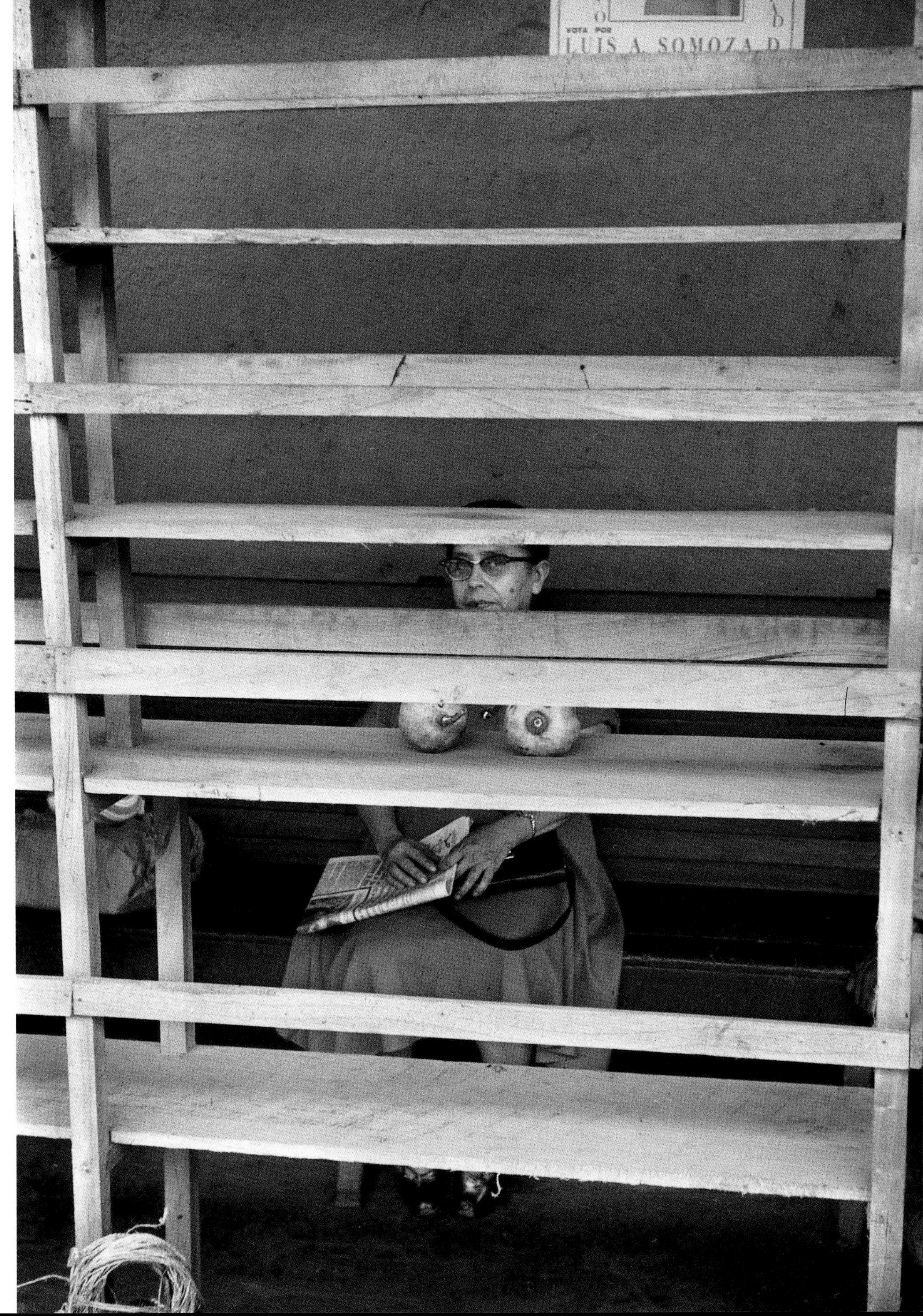

S
O
D
VOTA POR
LUIS A. SOMOZA D.

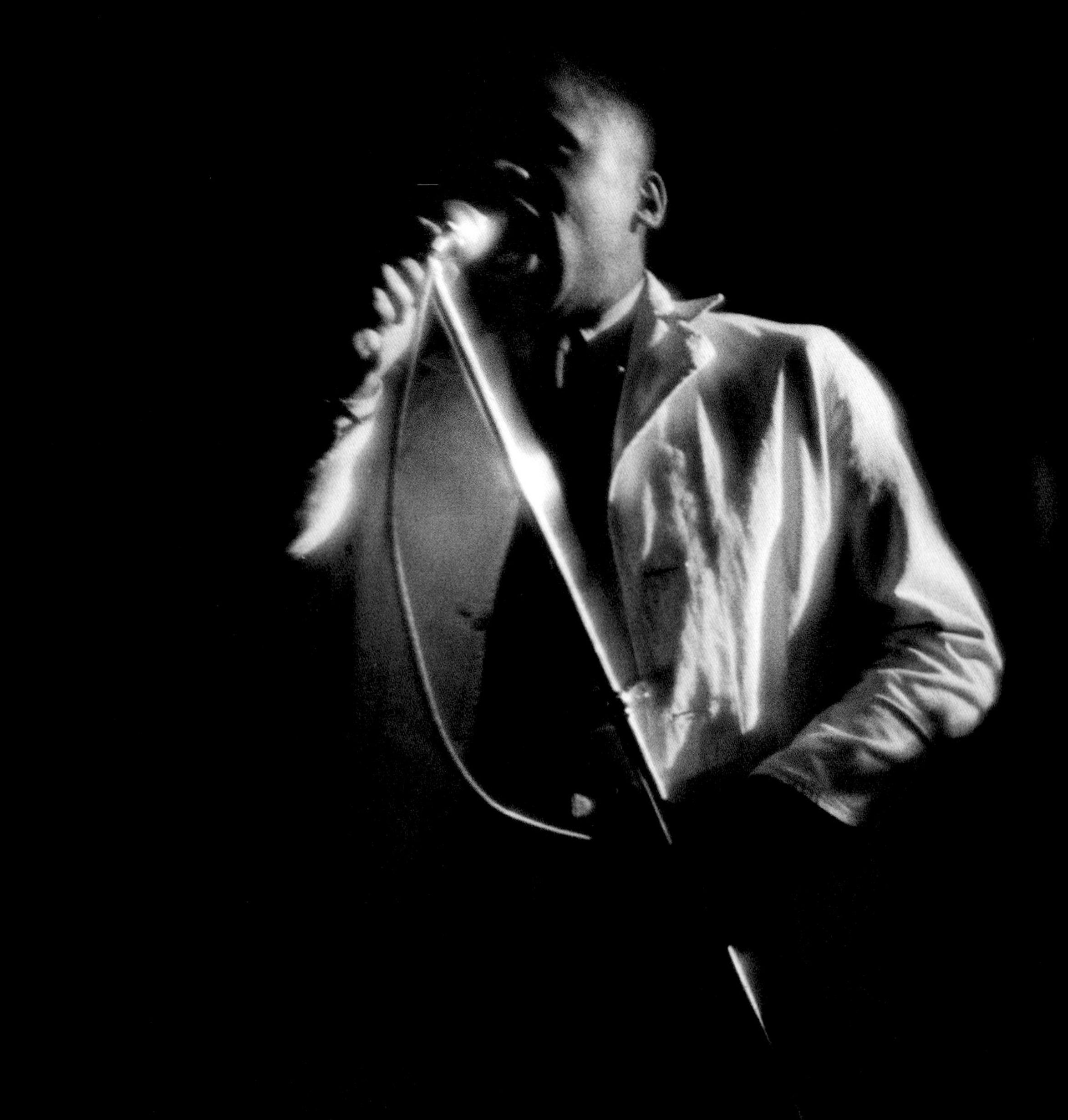

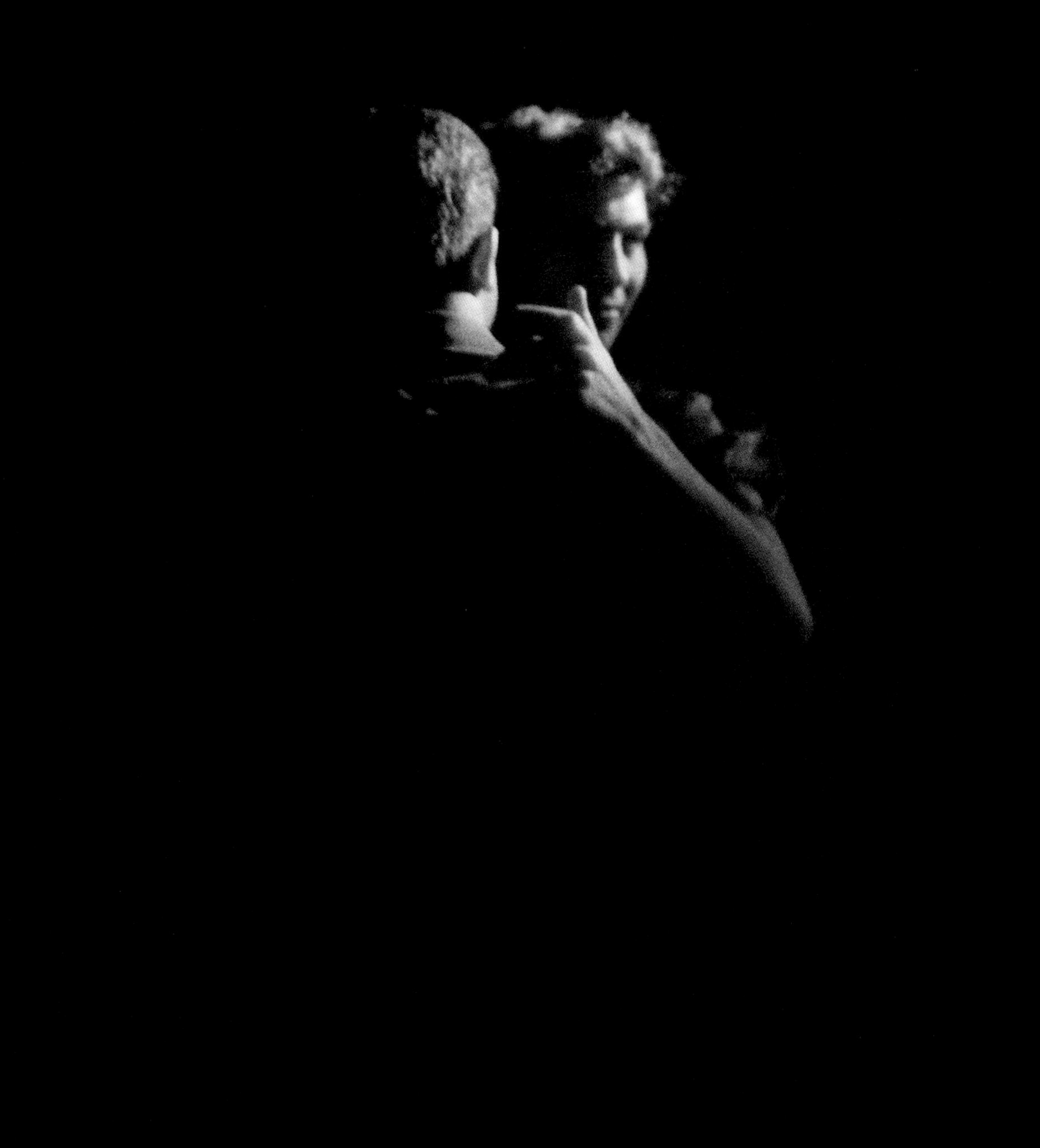

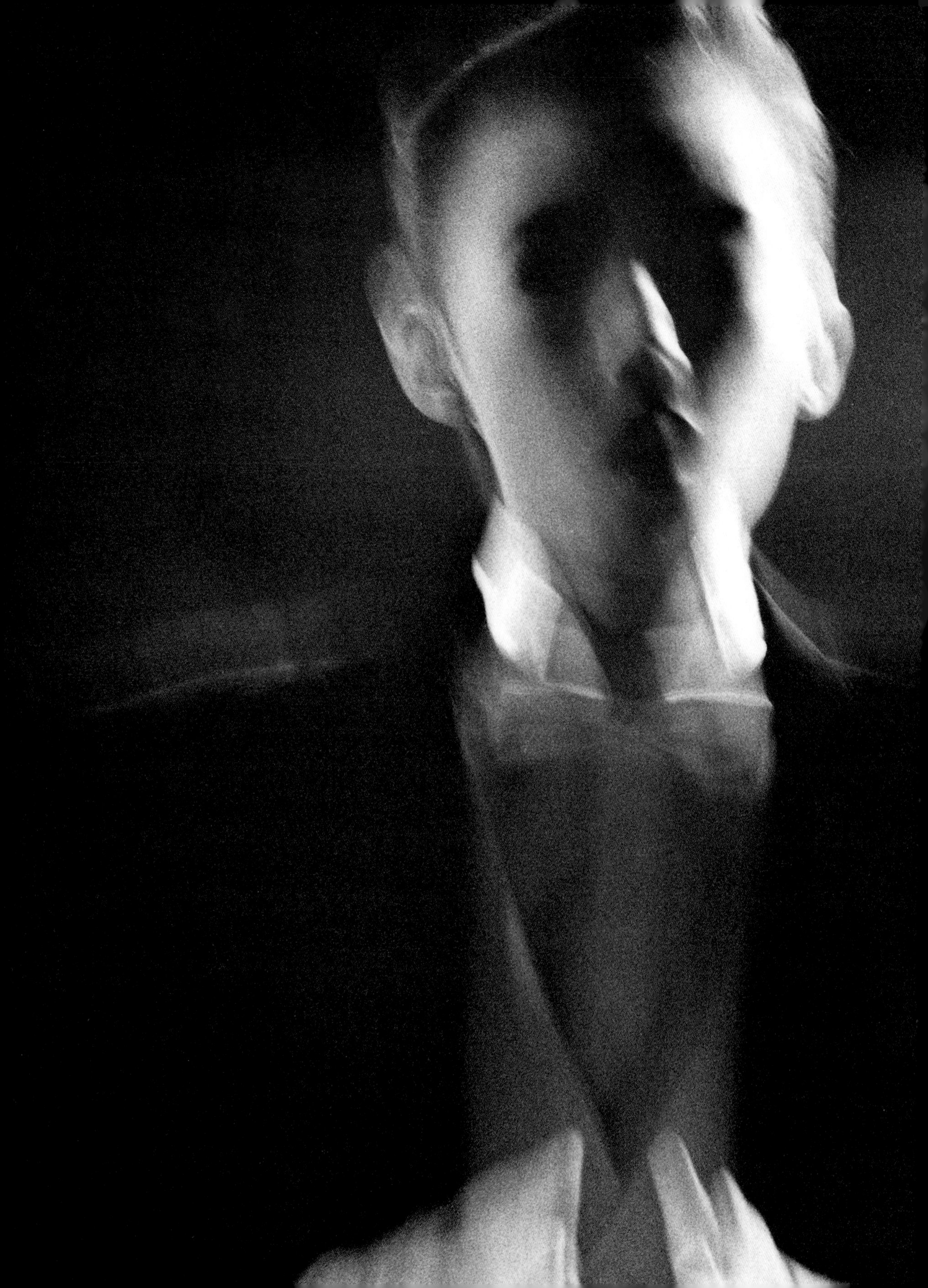

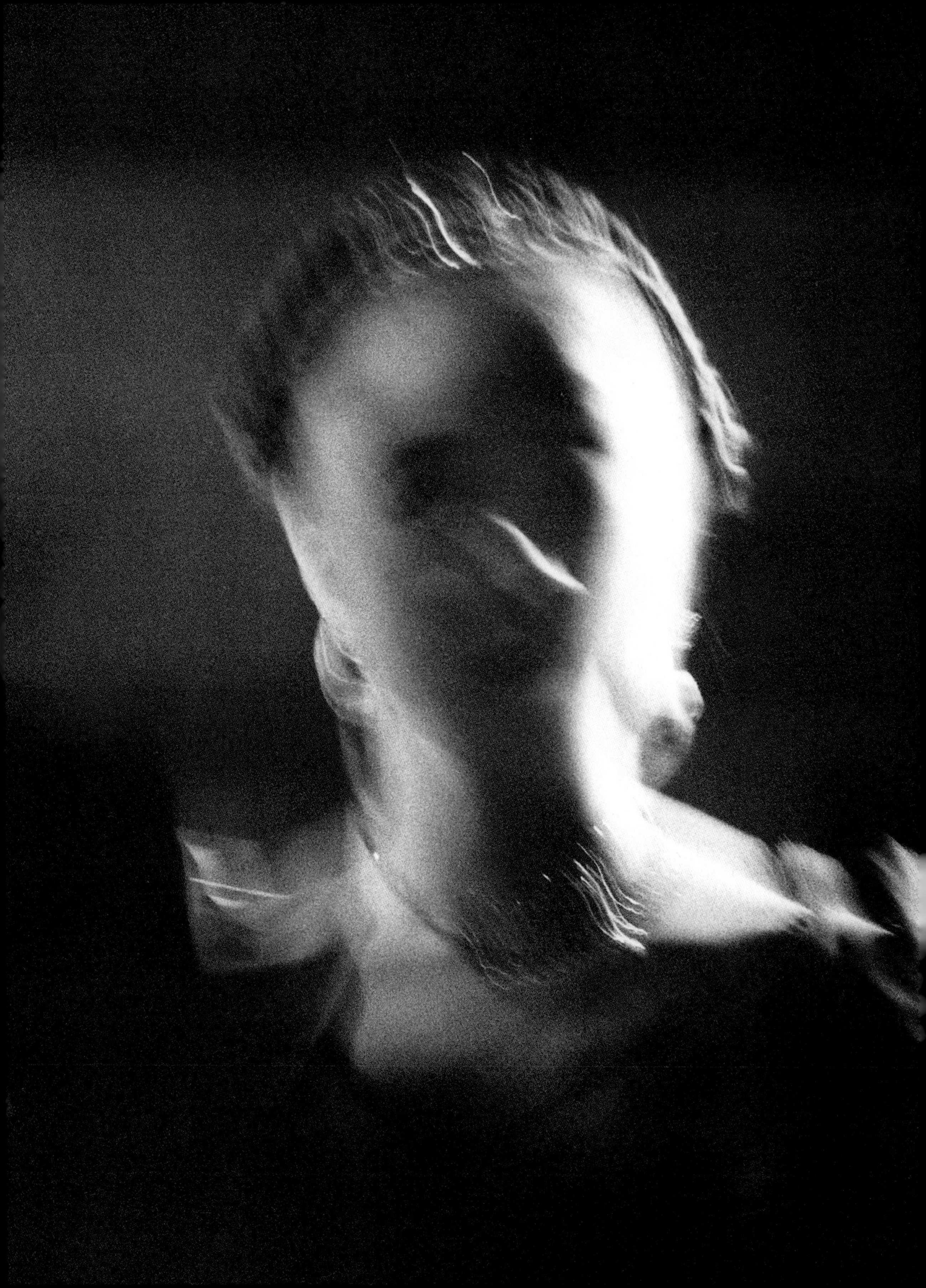

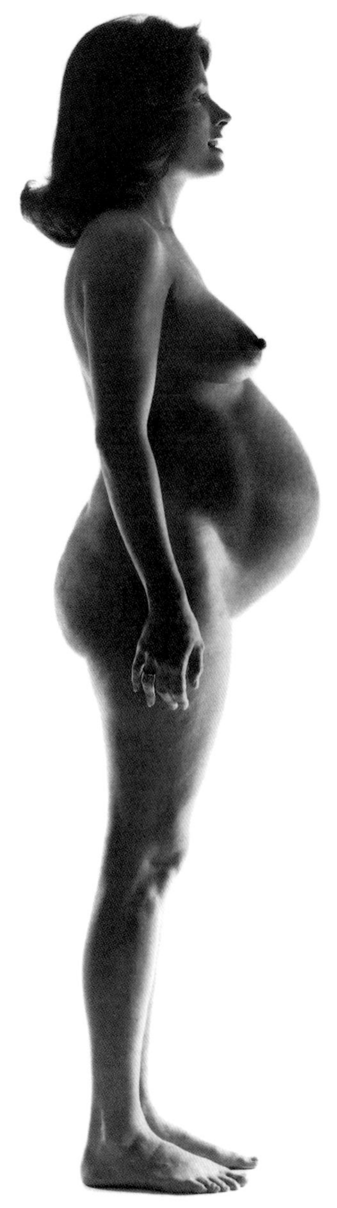

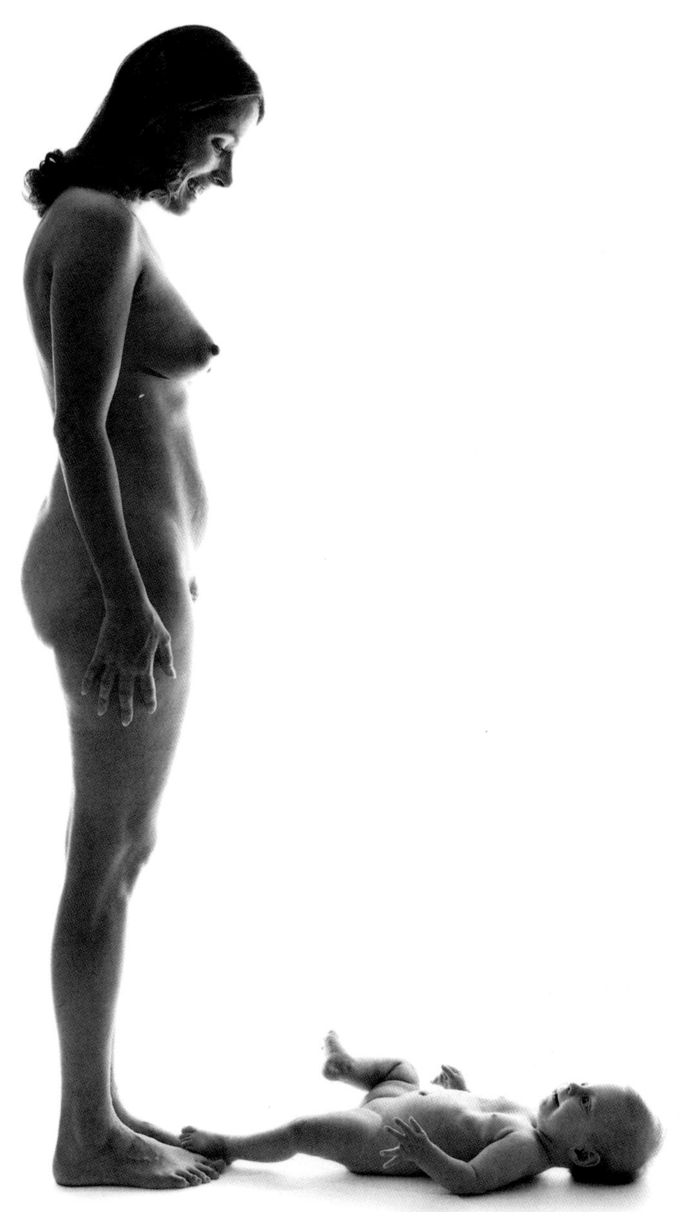

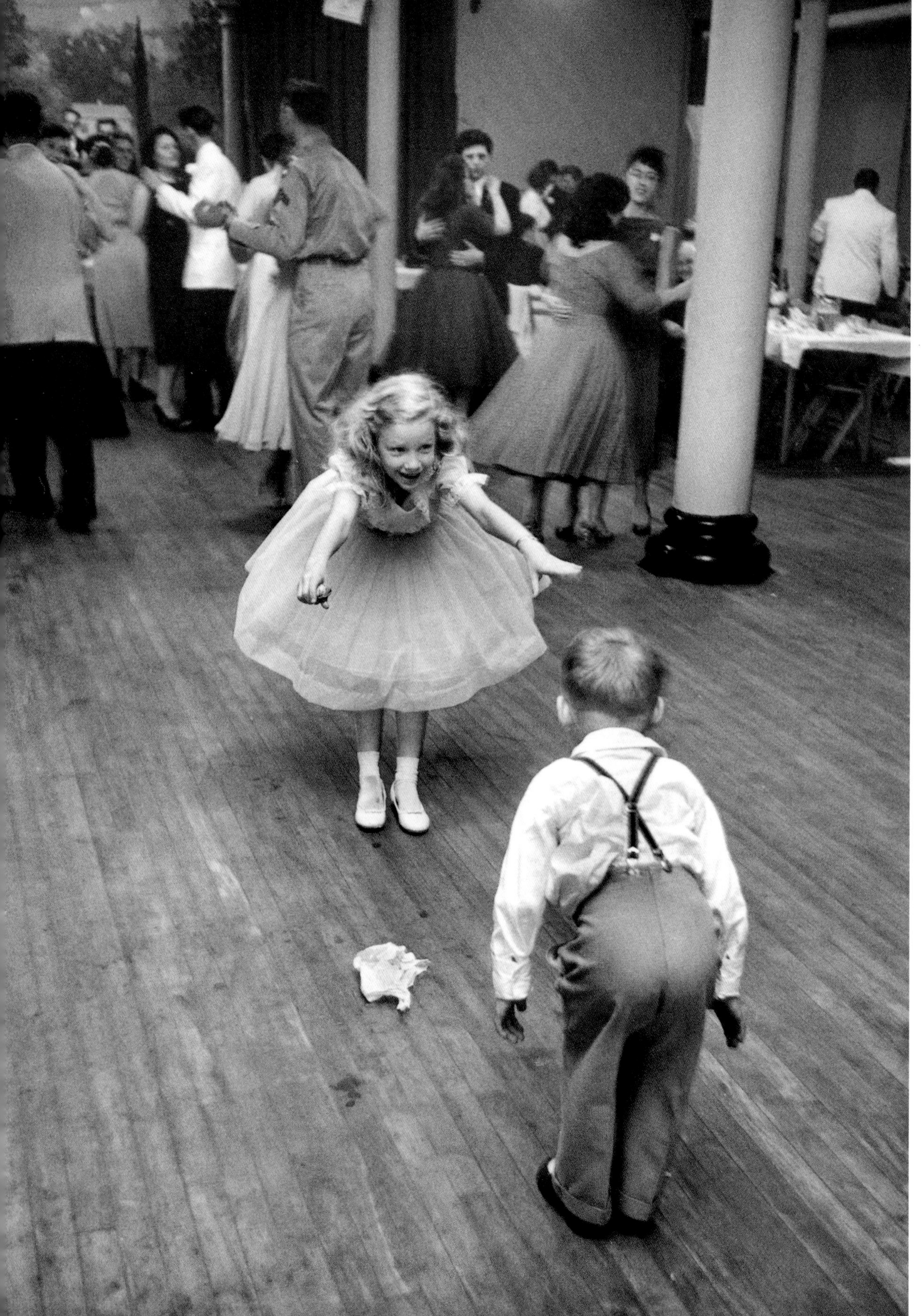

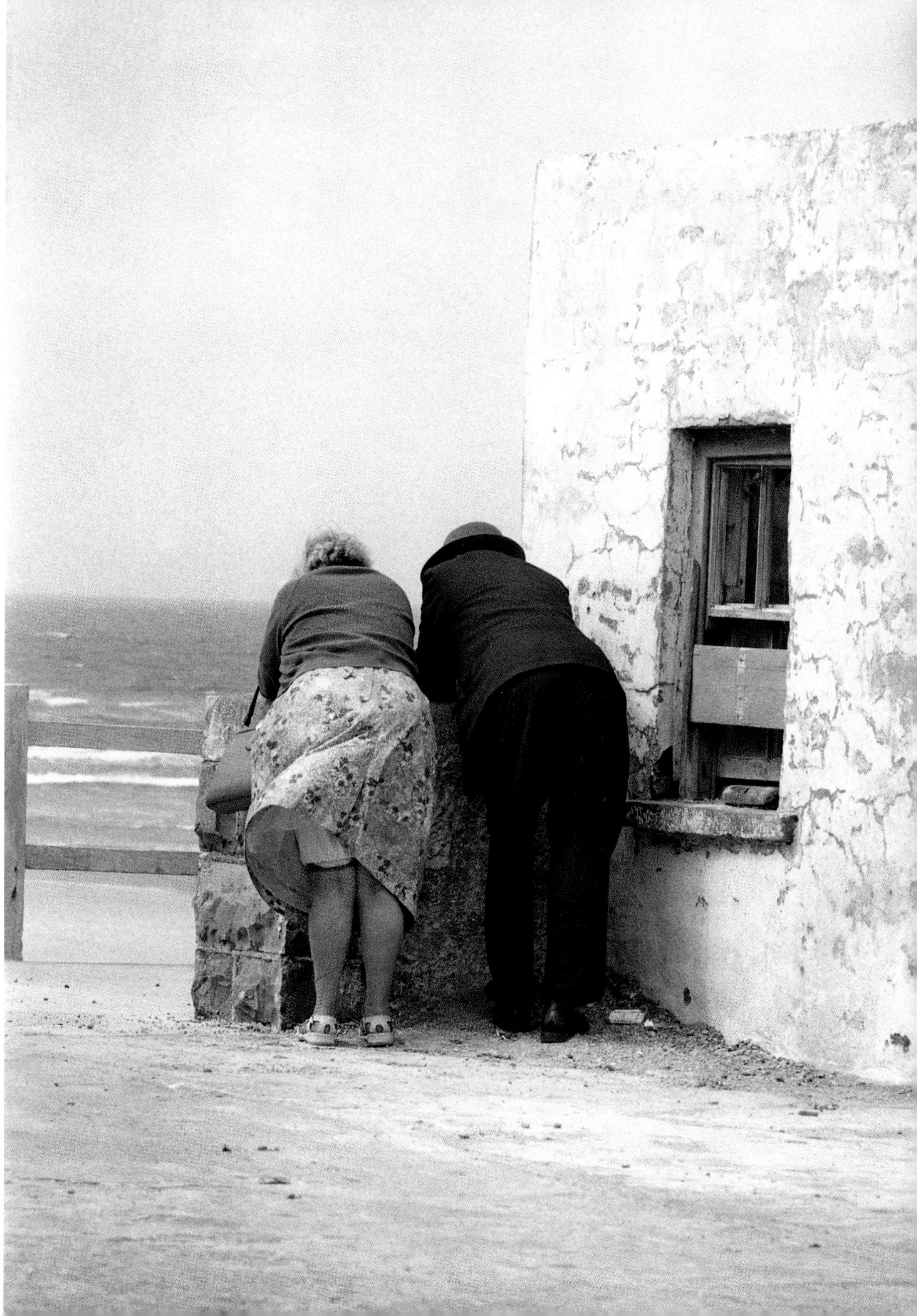

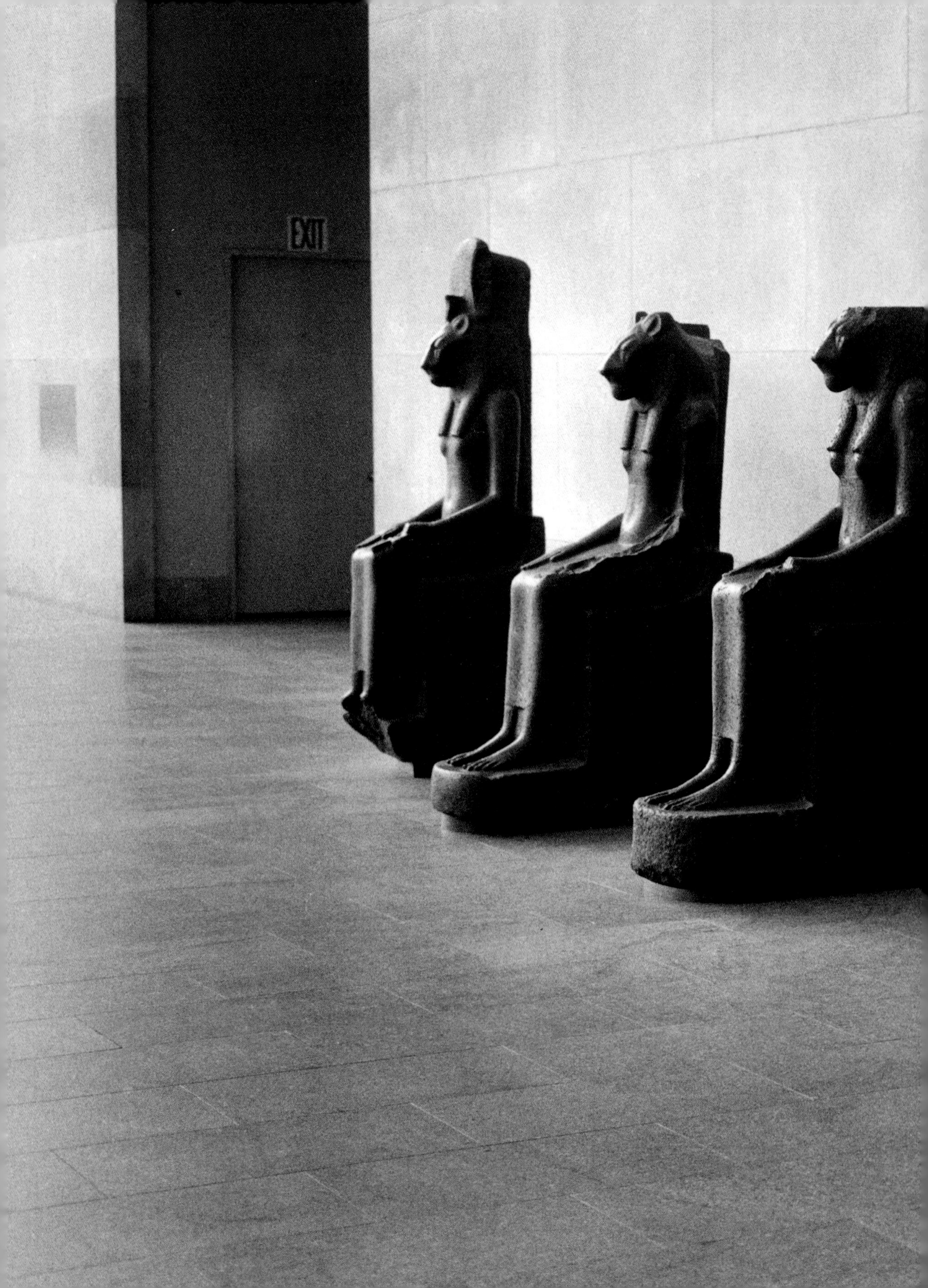
EXIT

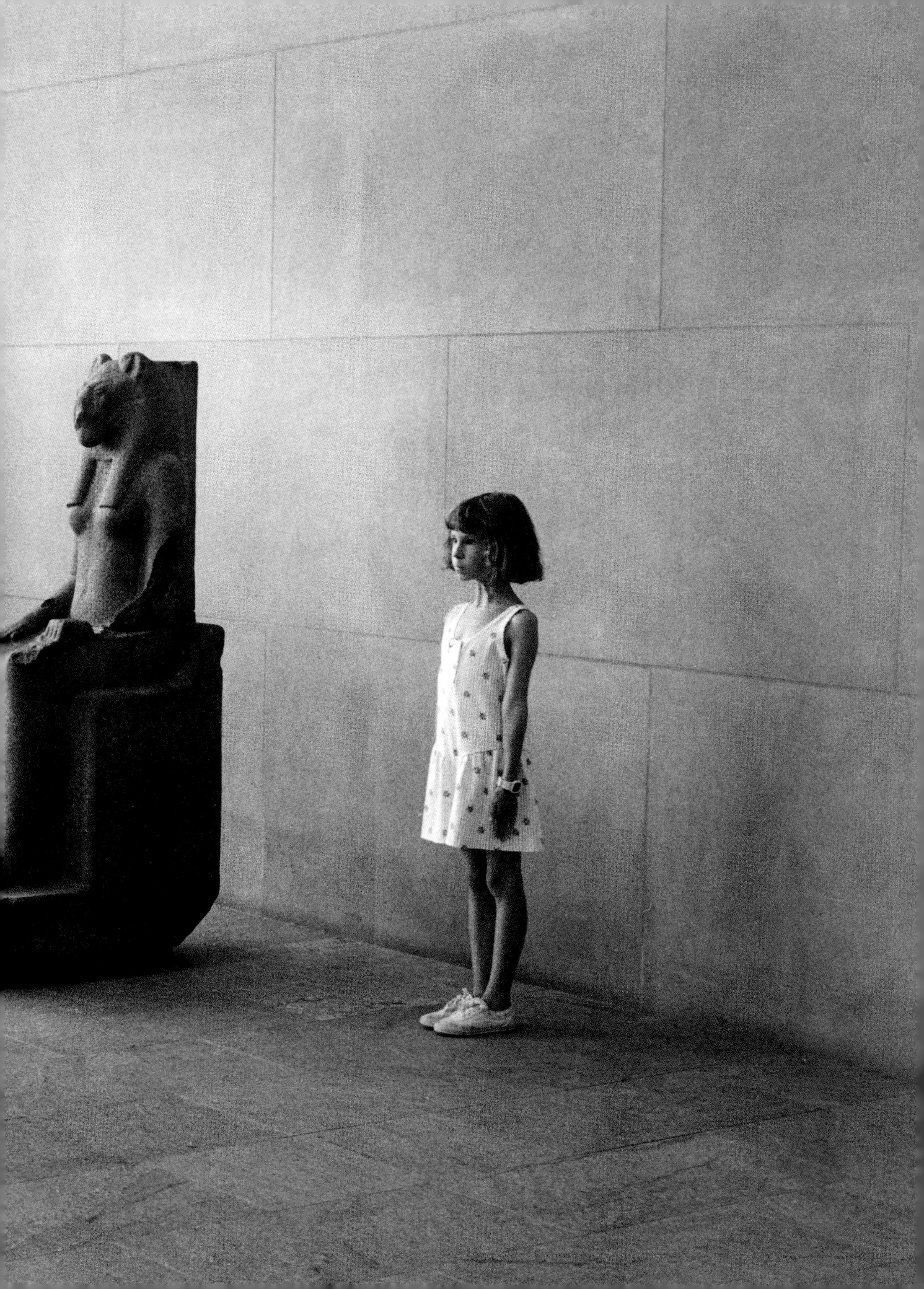

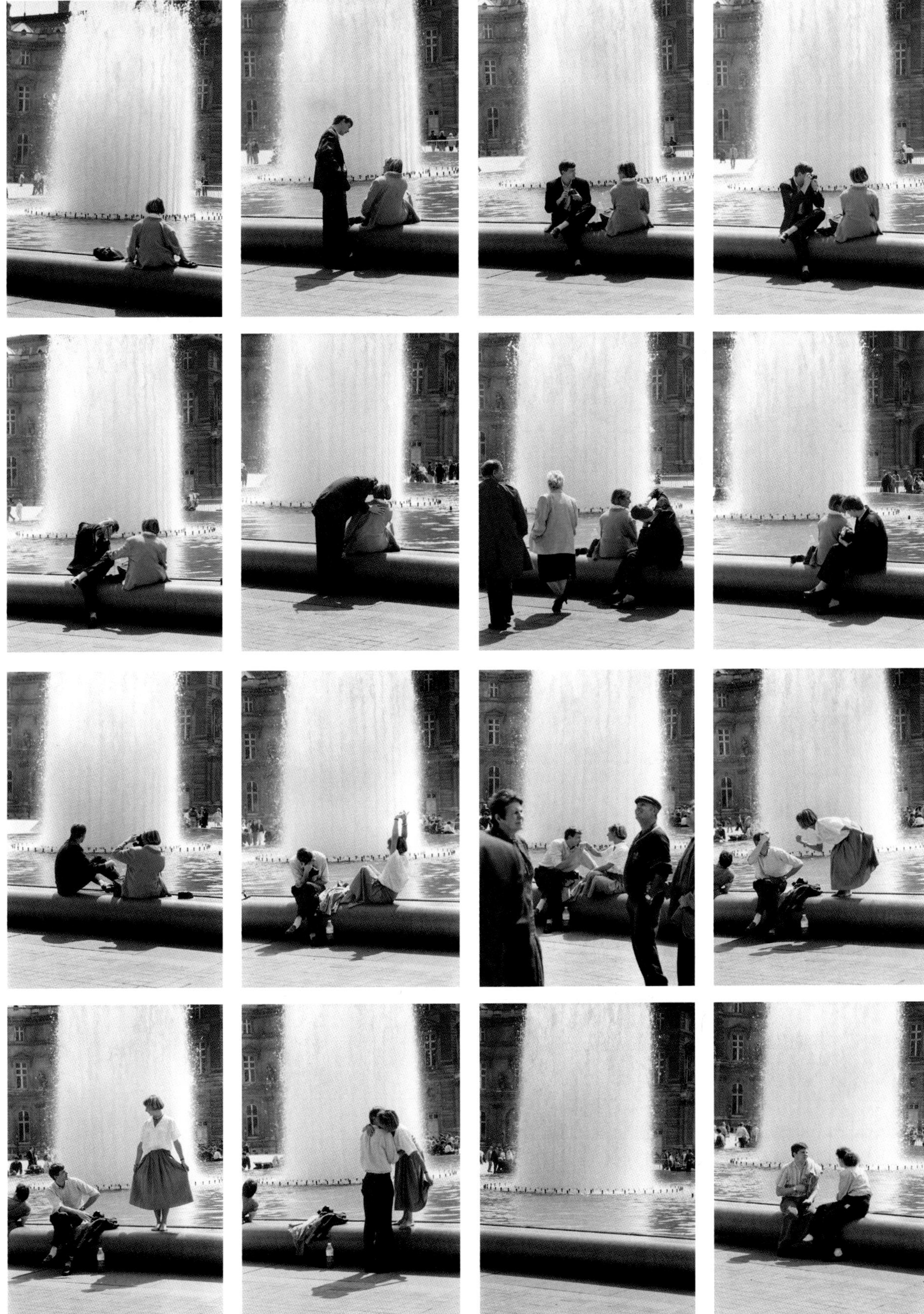

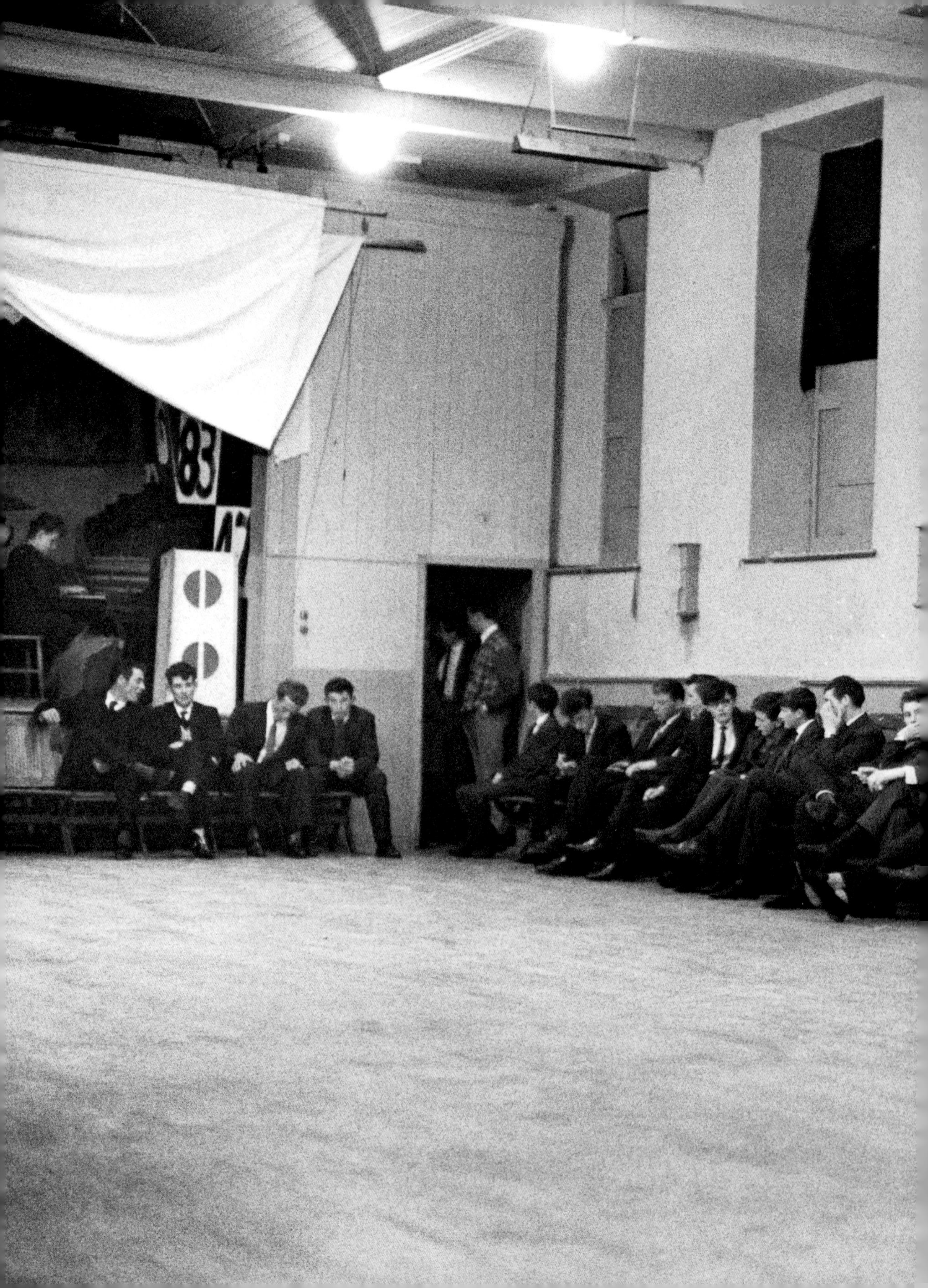

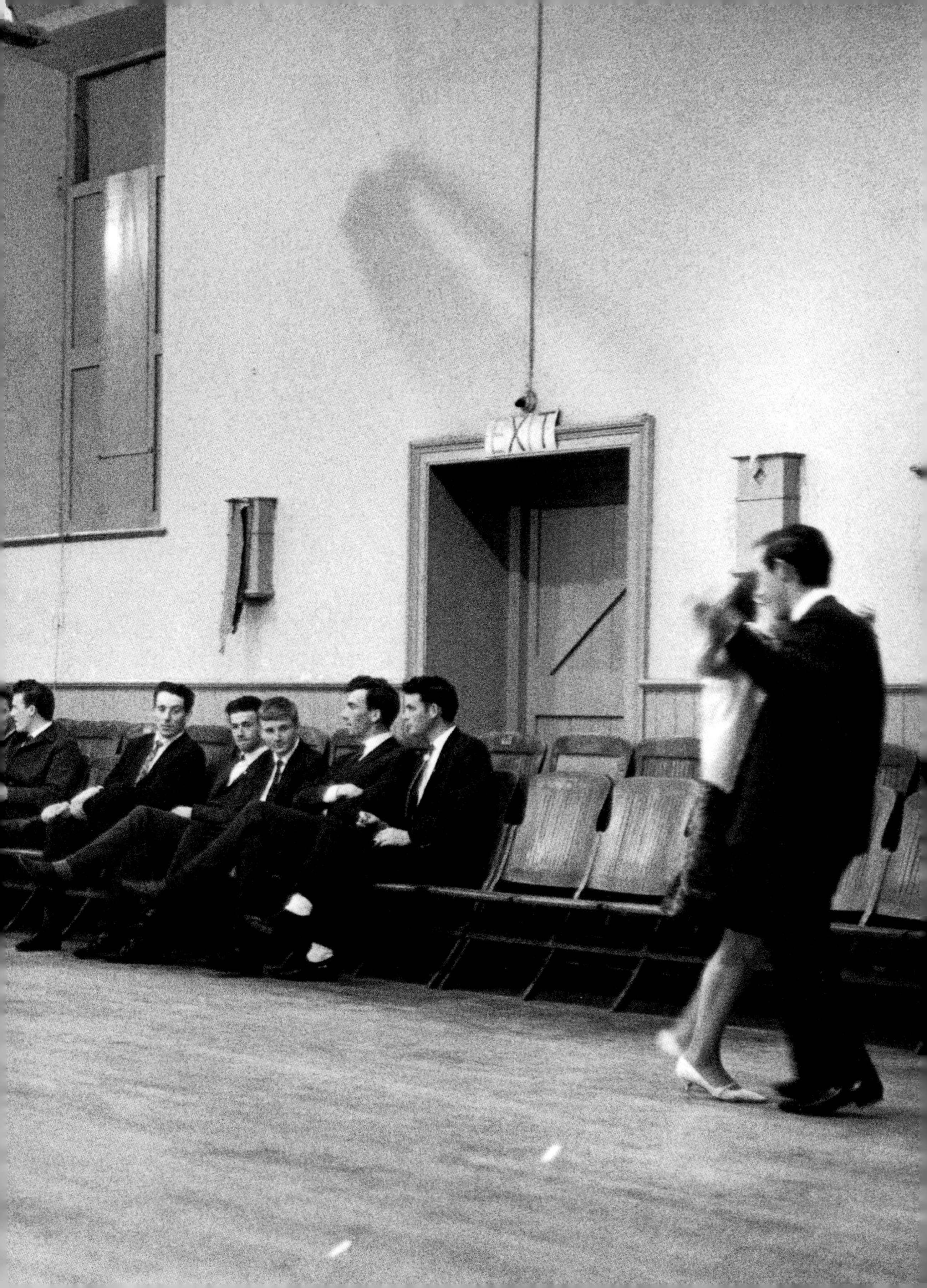

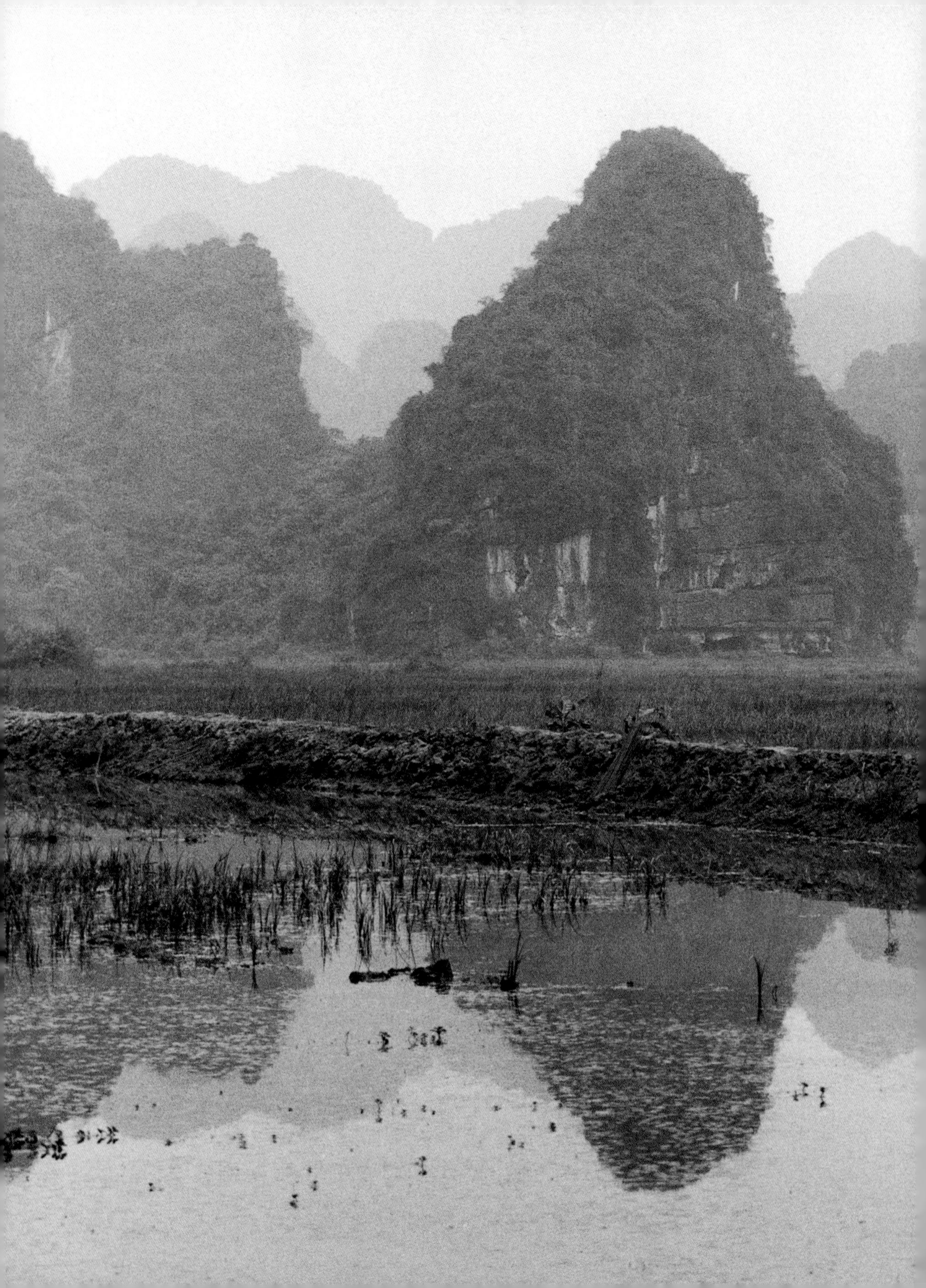

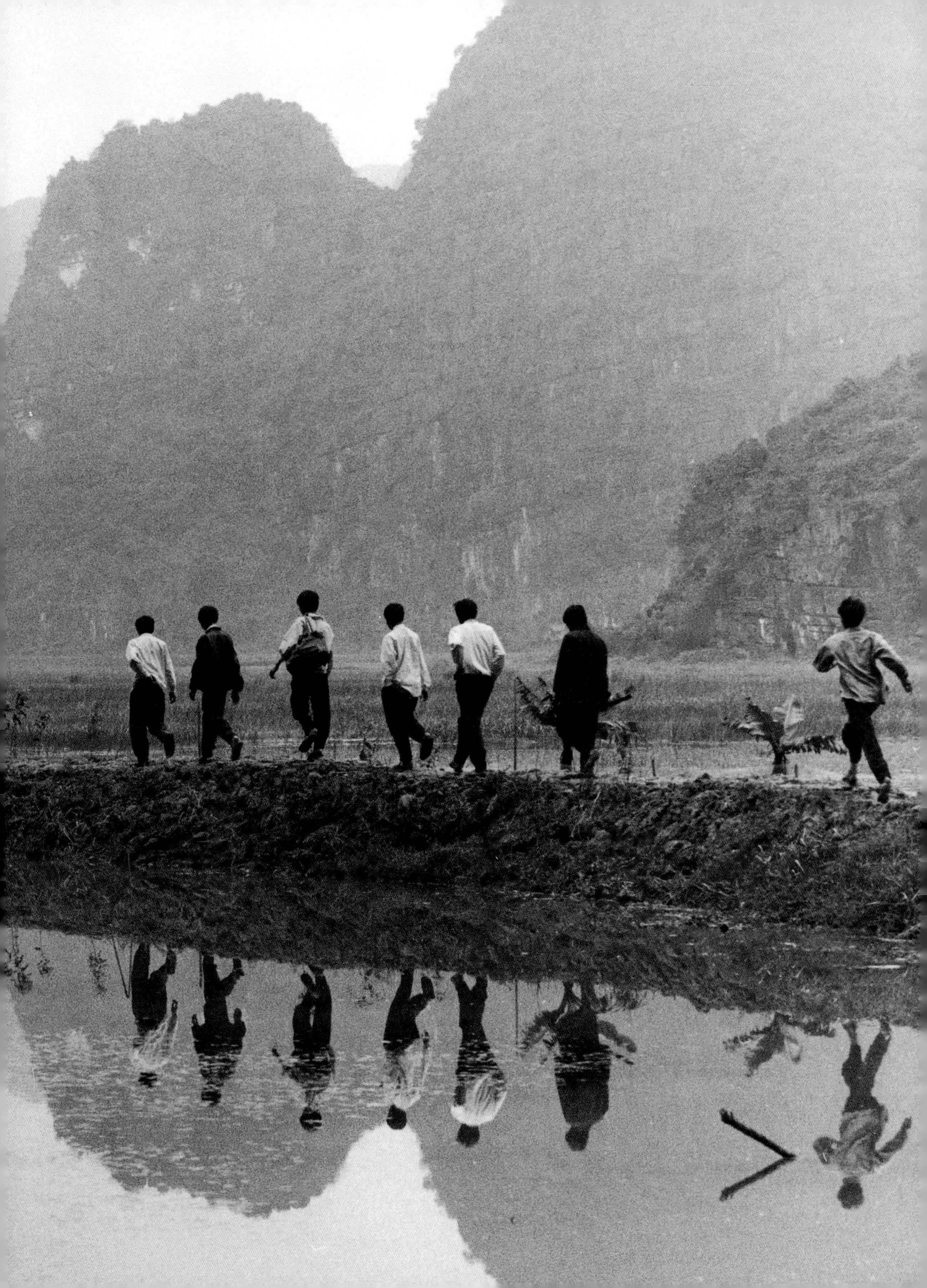

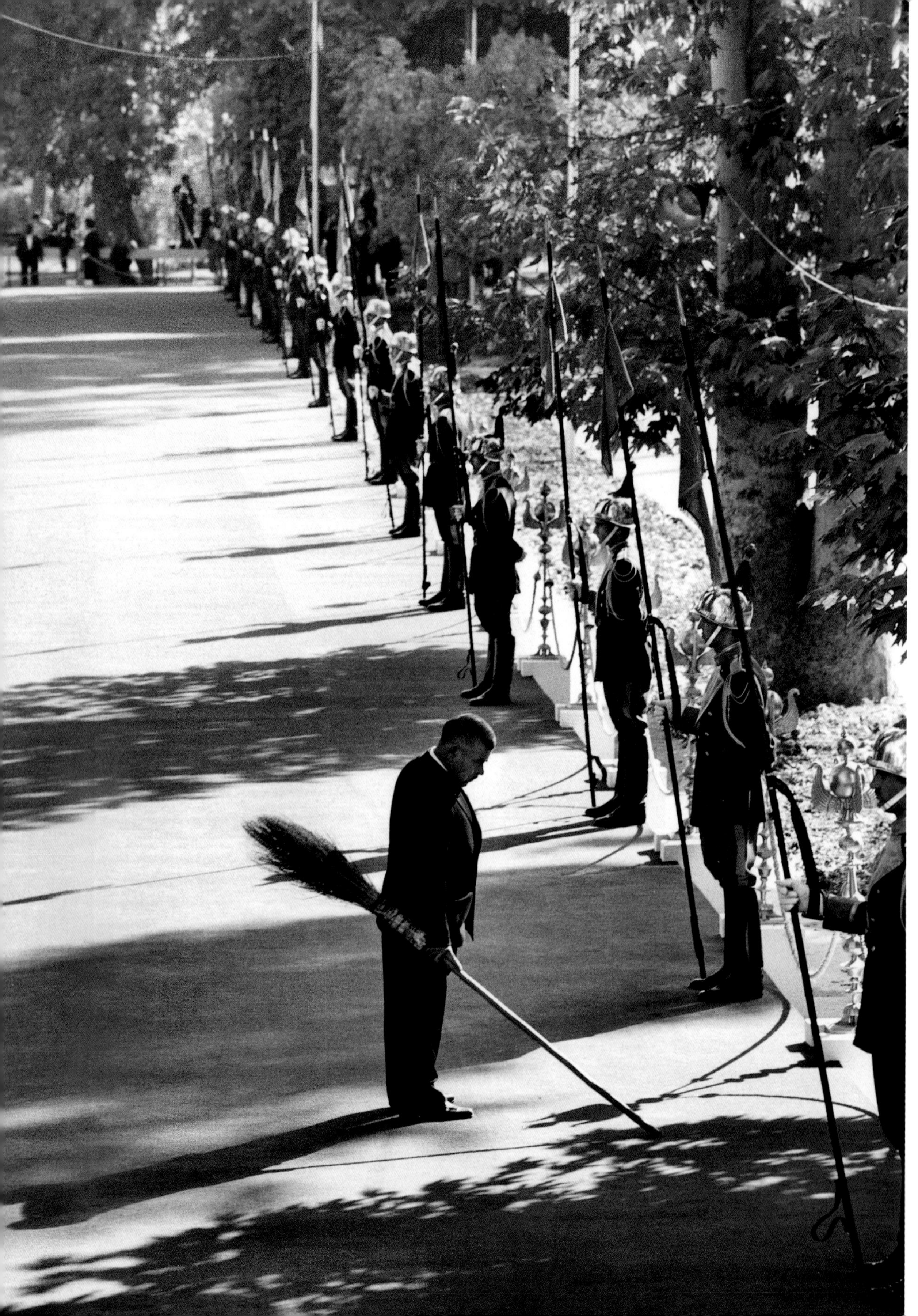

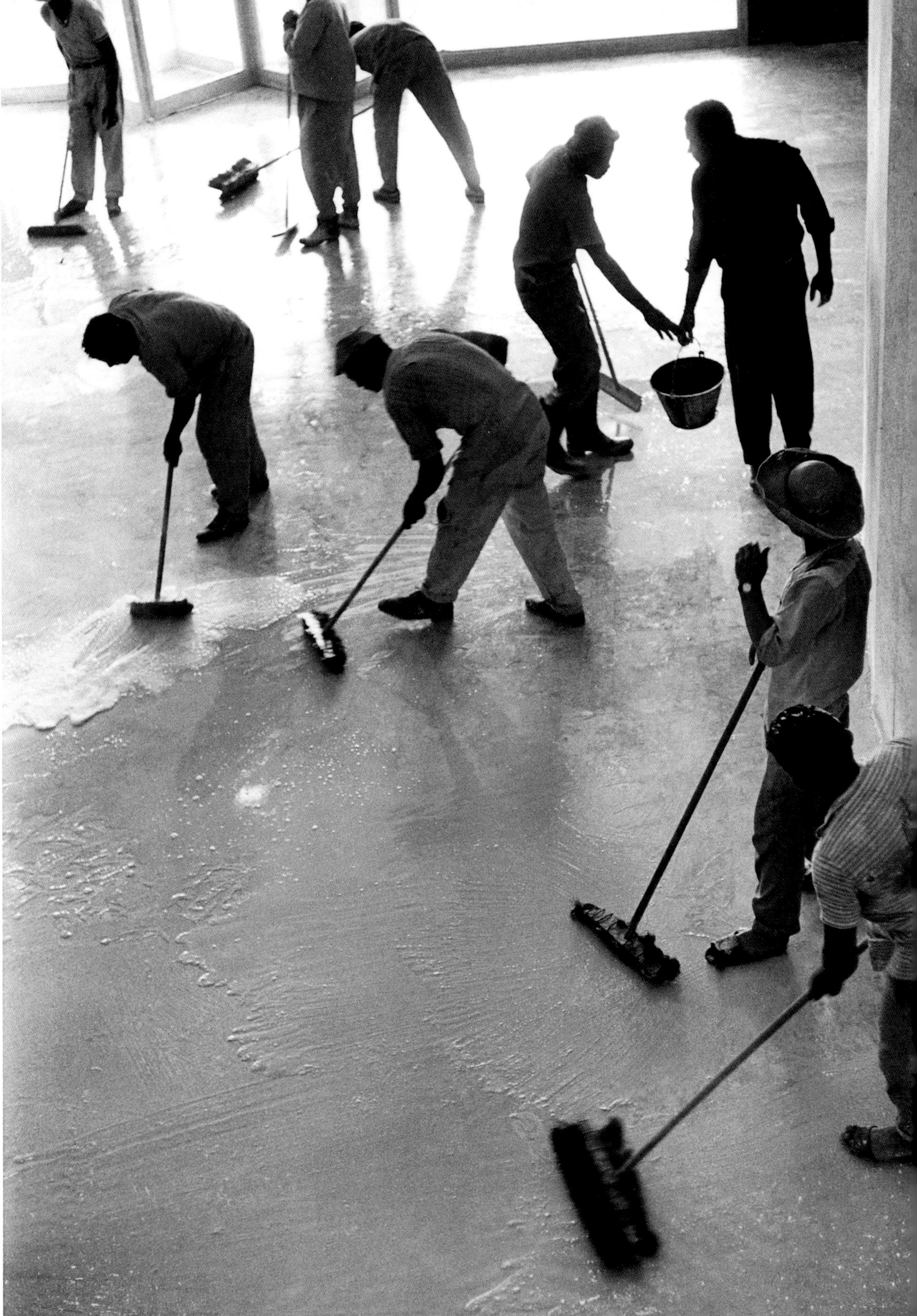

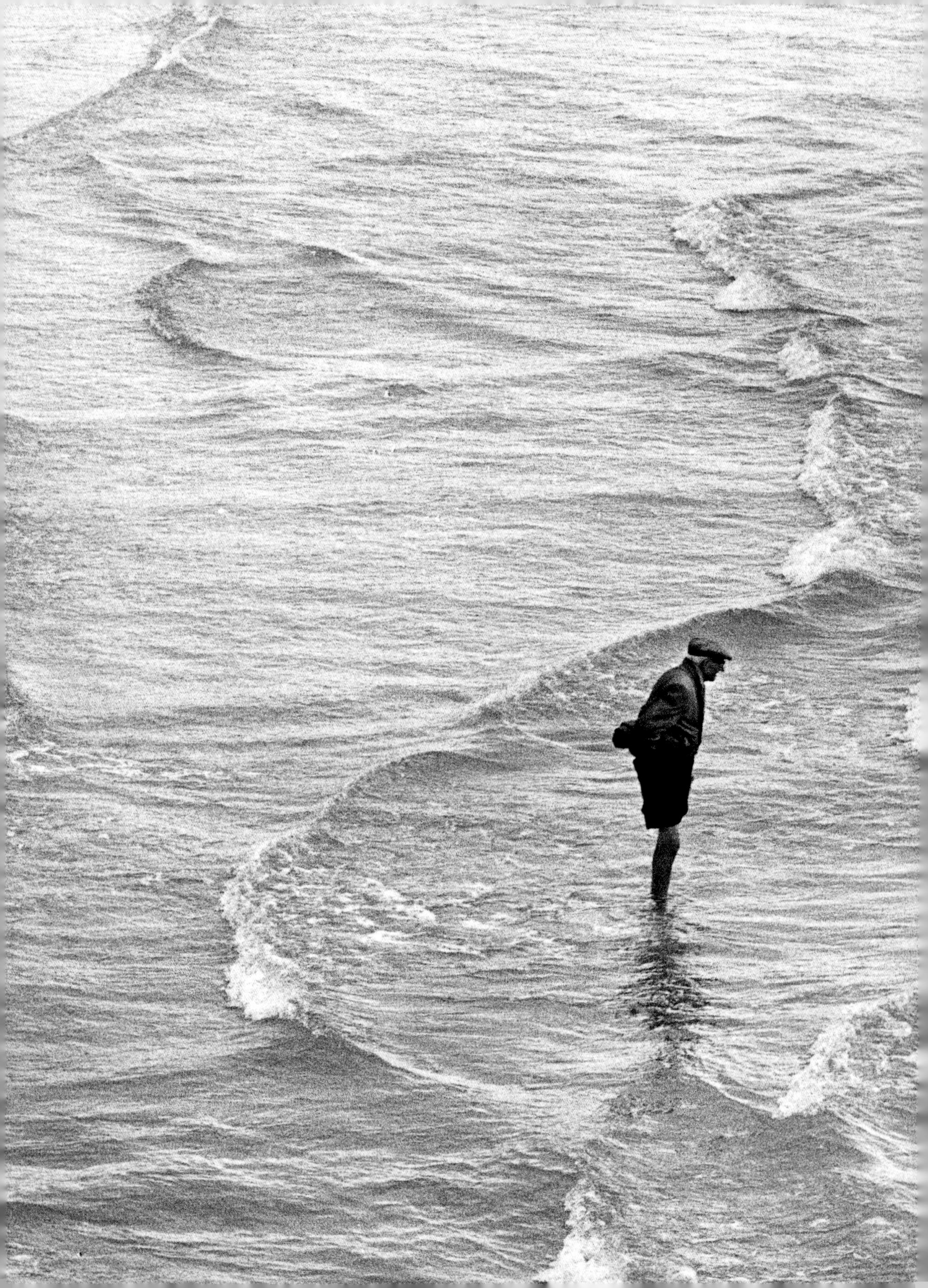

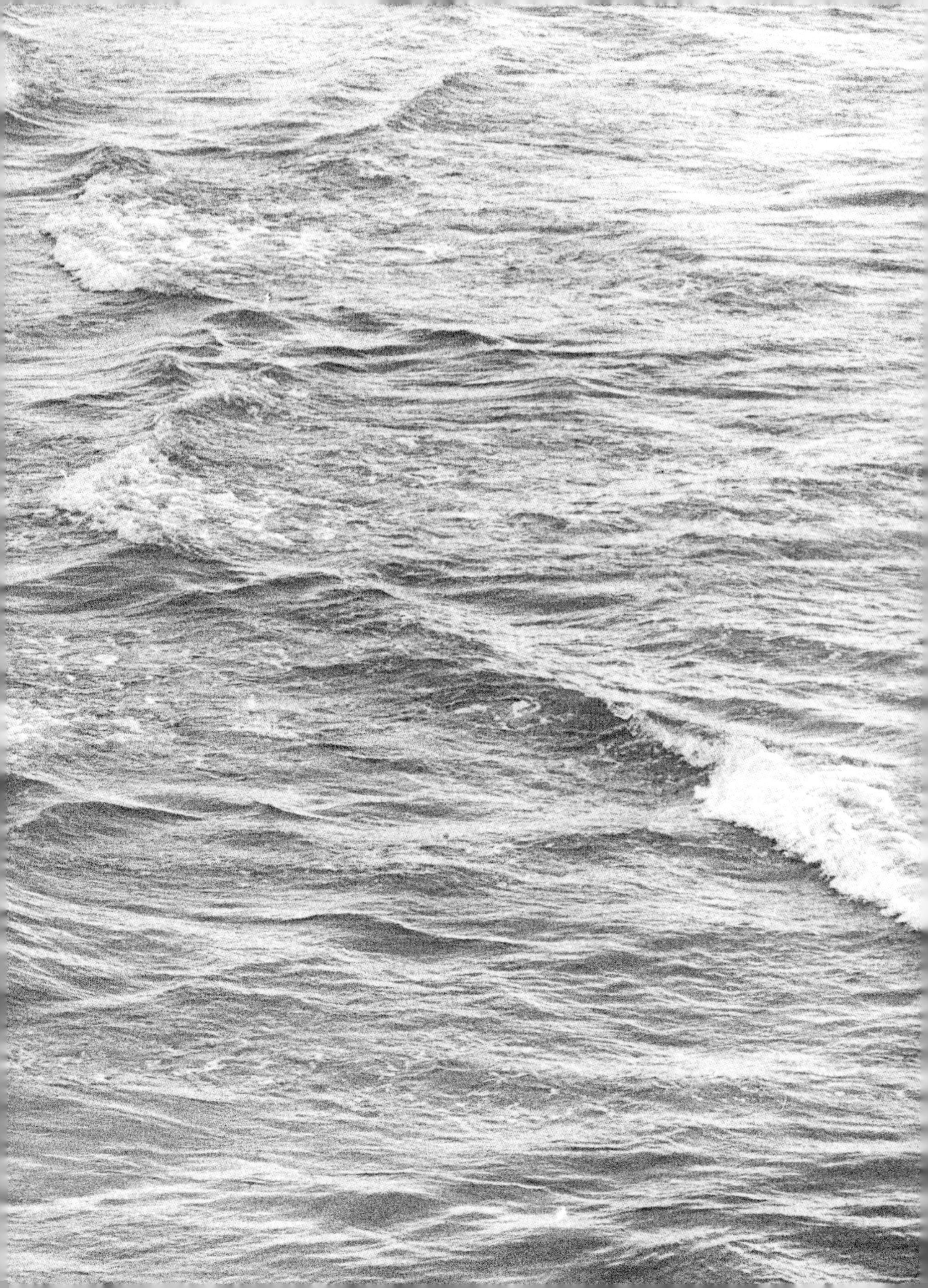

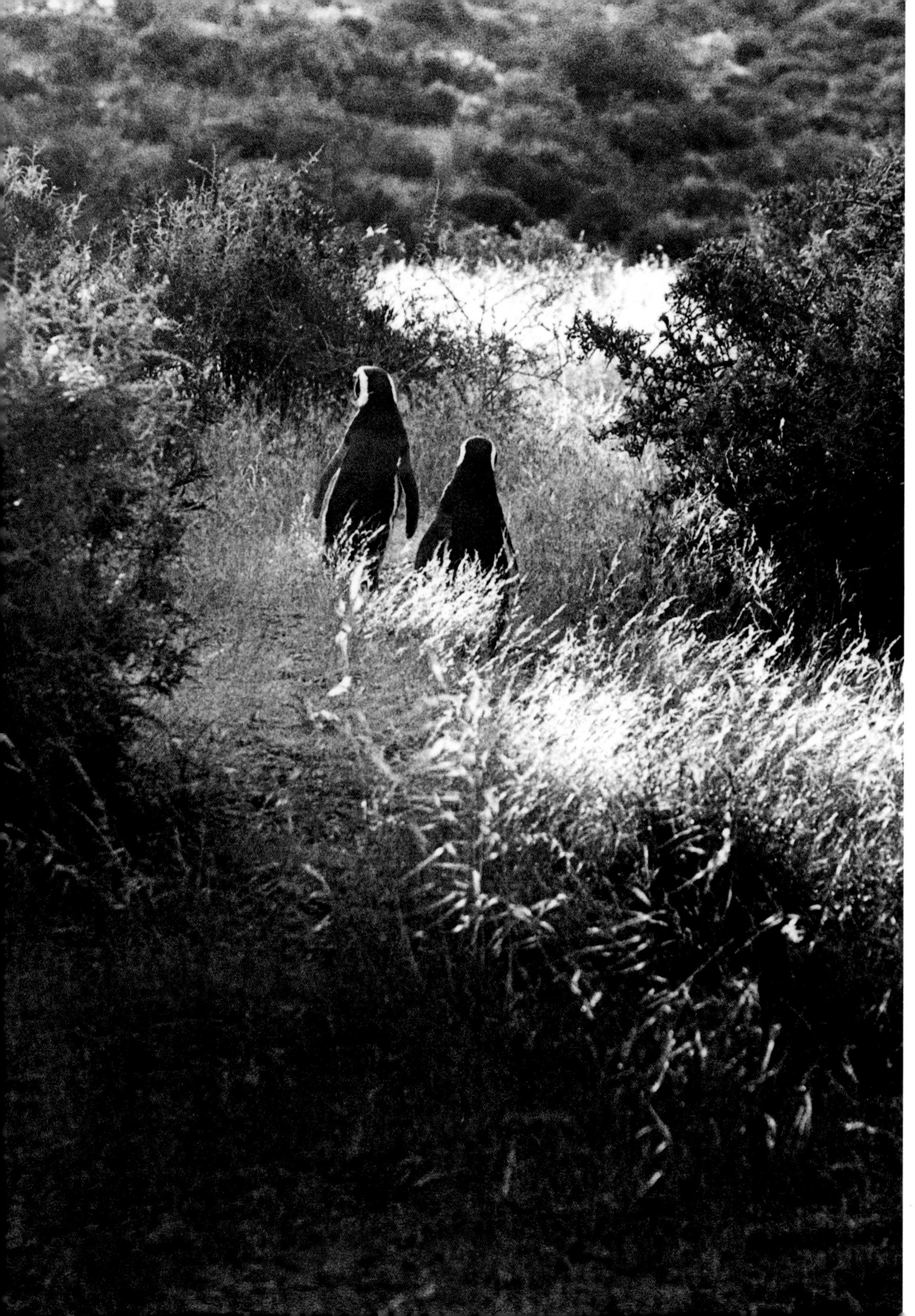

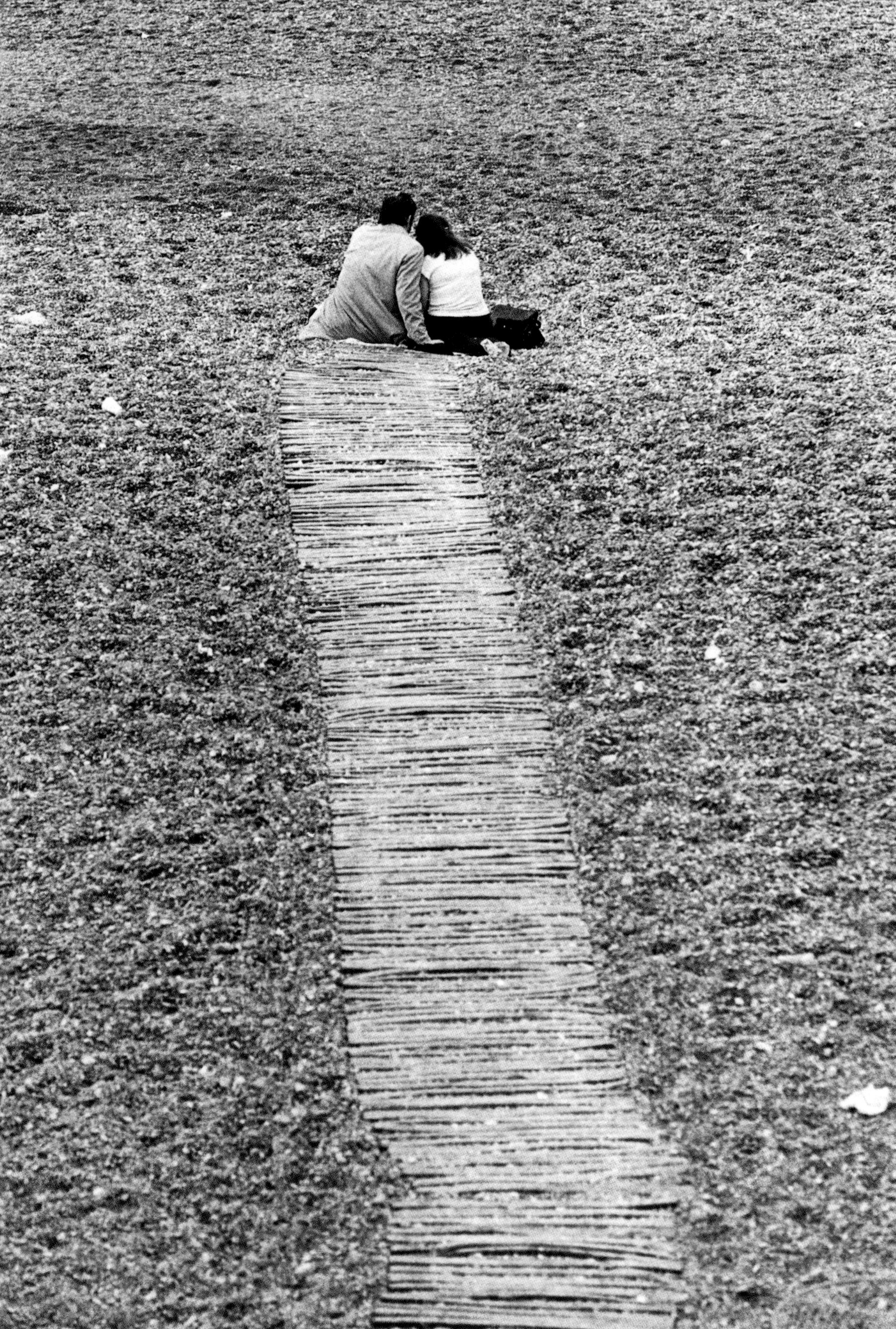

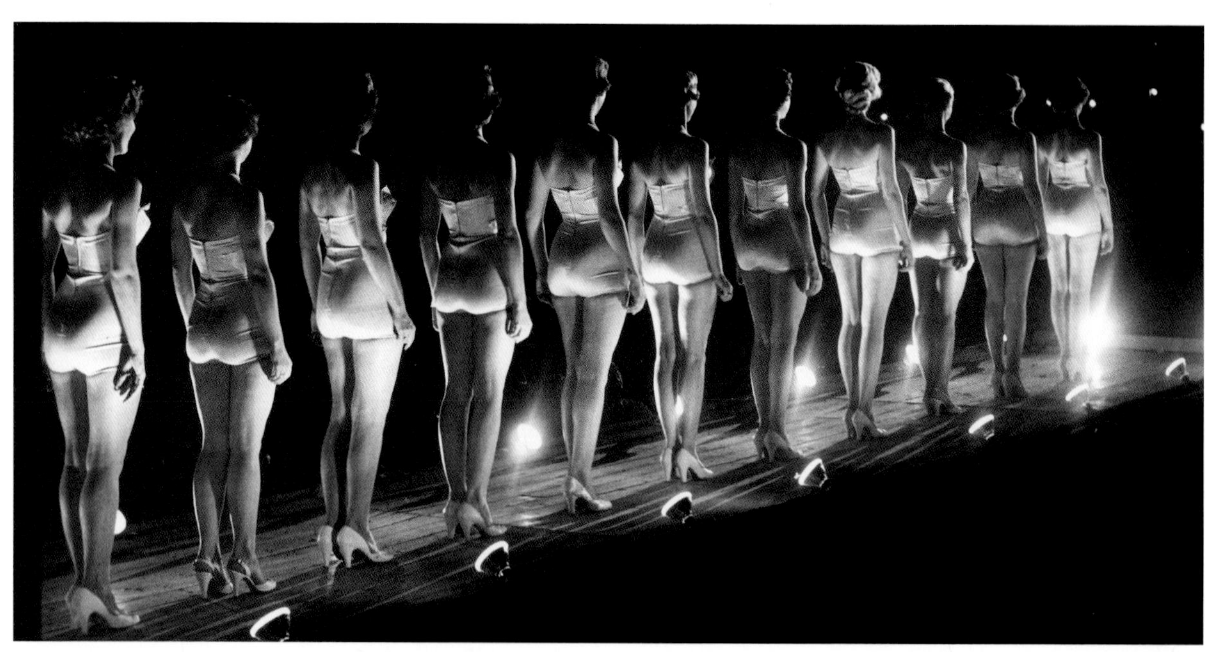

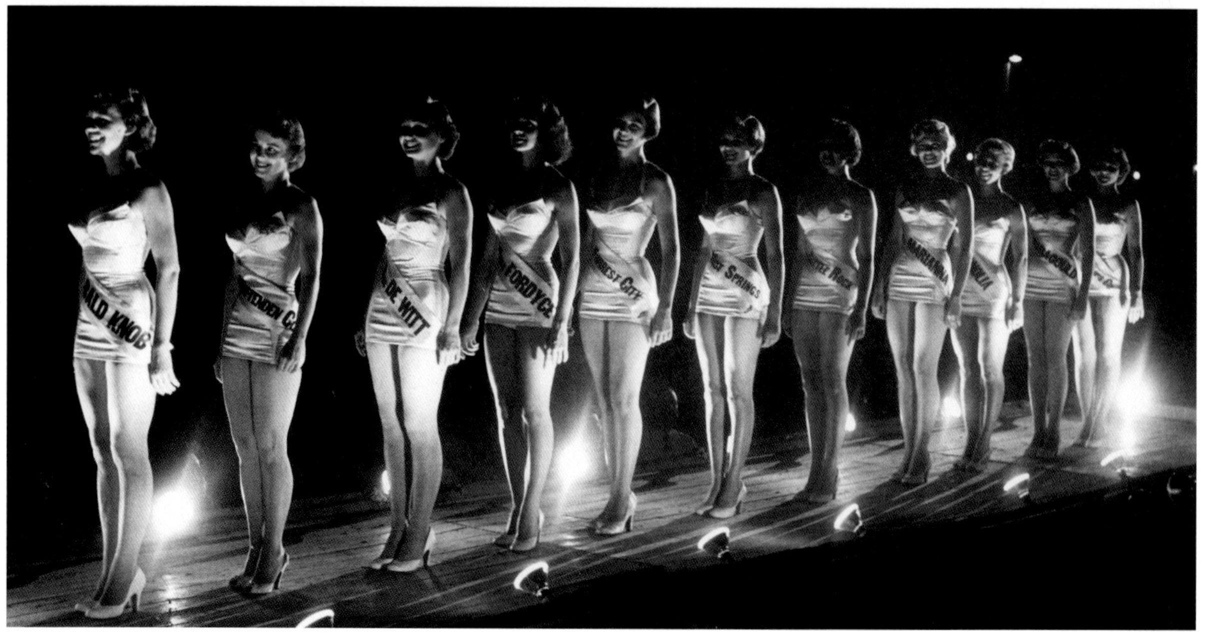

BALD KNOB
FORREST CITY
DE WITT
FORDYCE
FOREST CITY
HOT SPRINGS
LITTLE ROCK
MARIANNA

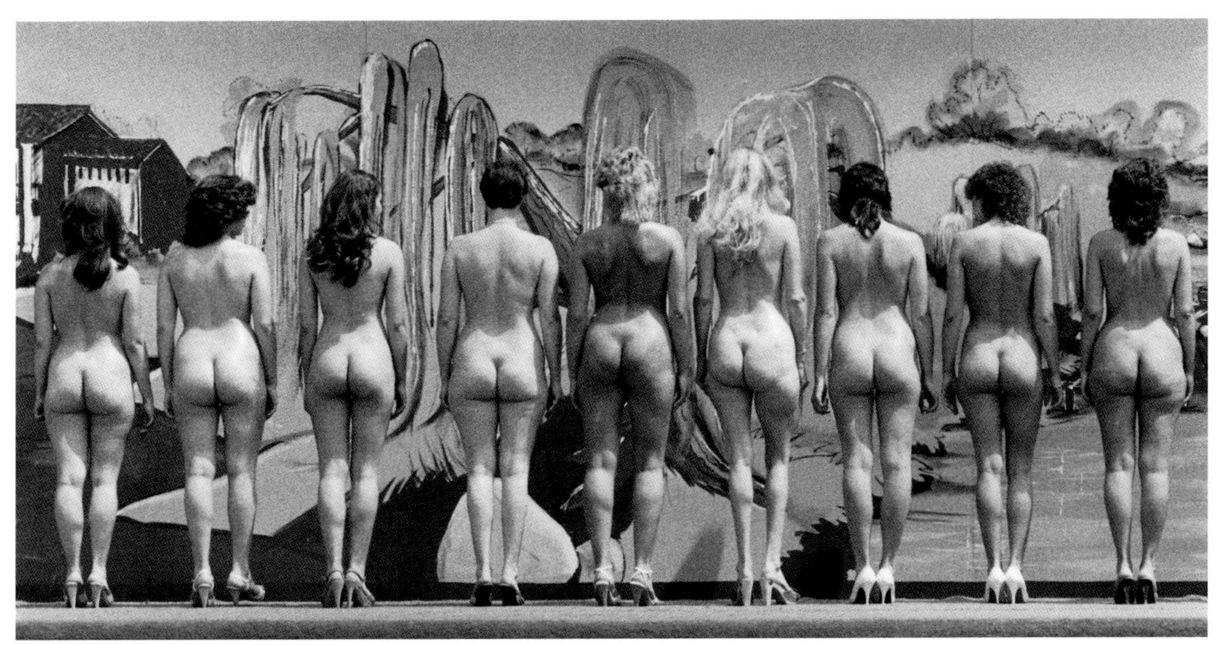

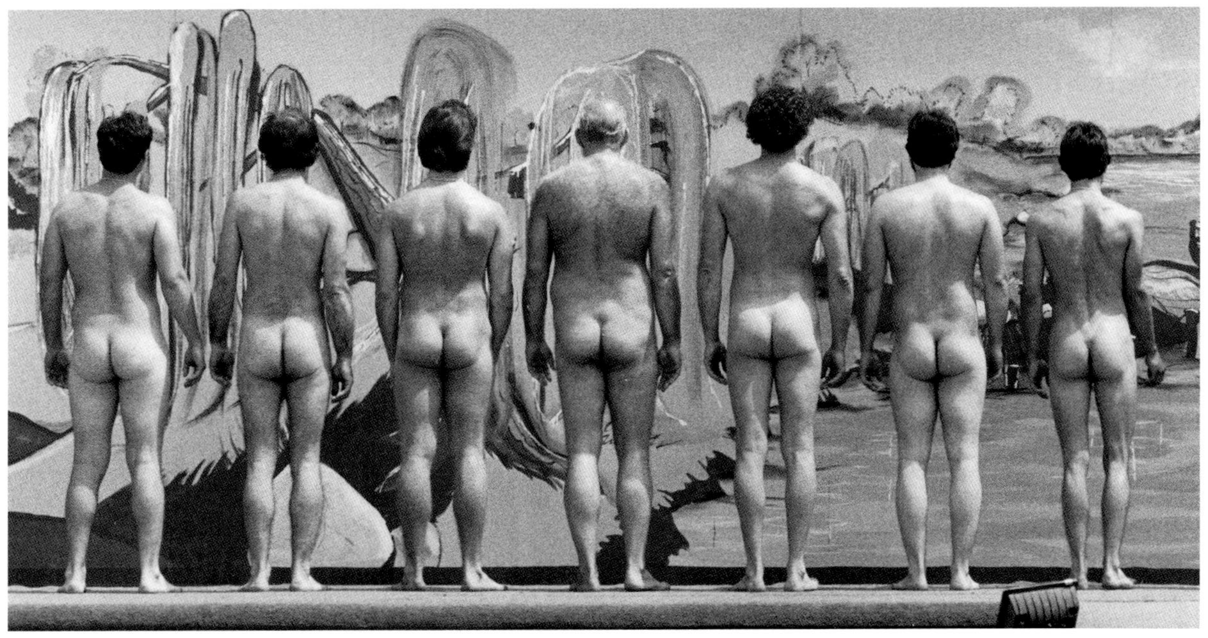

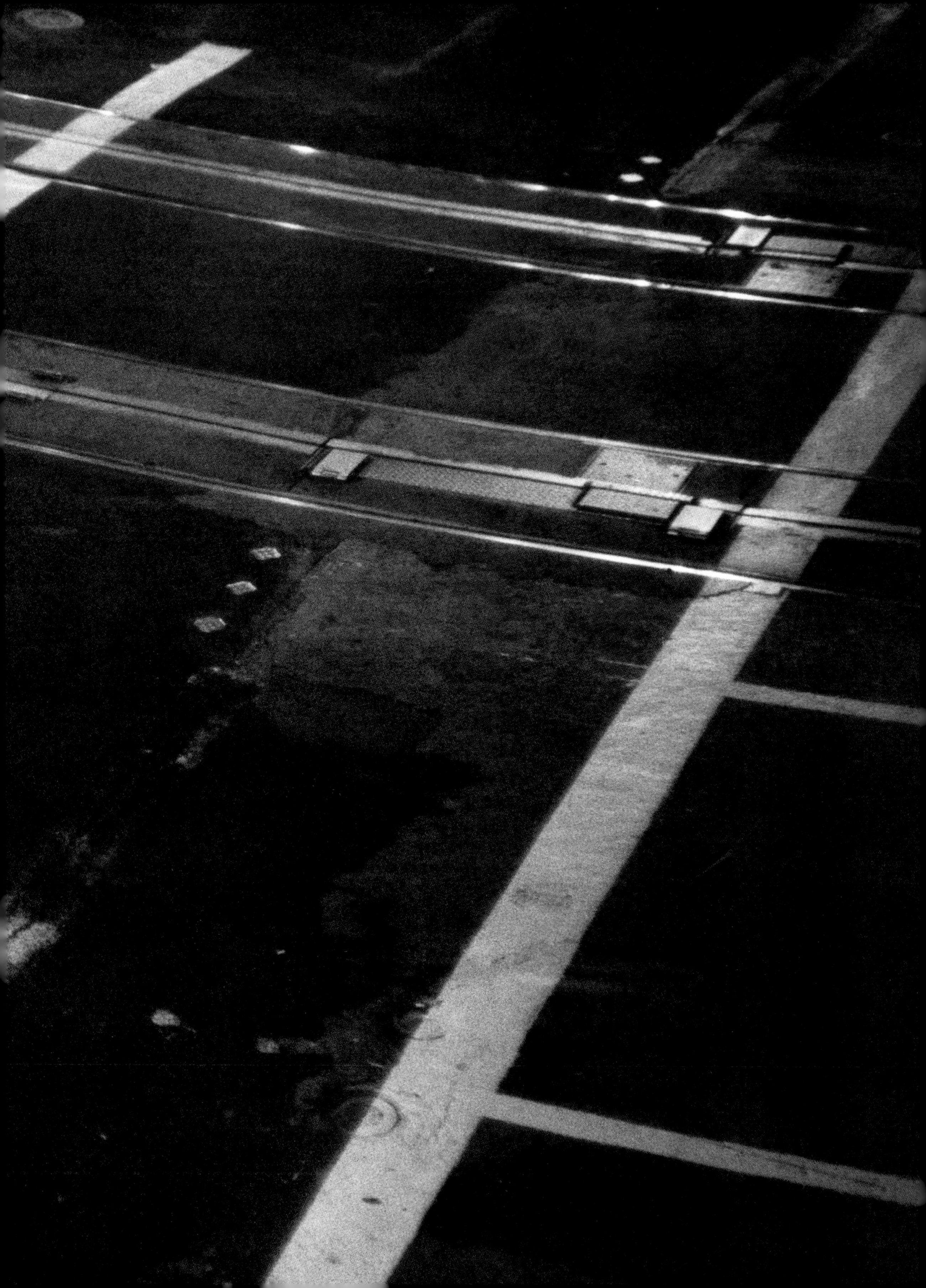

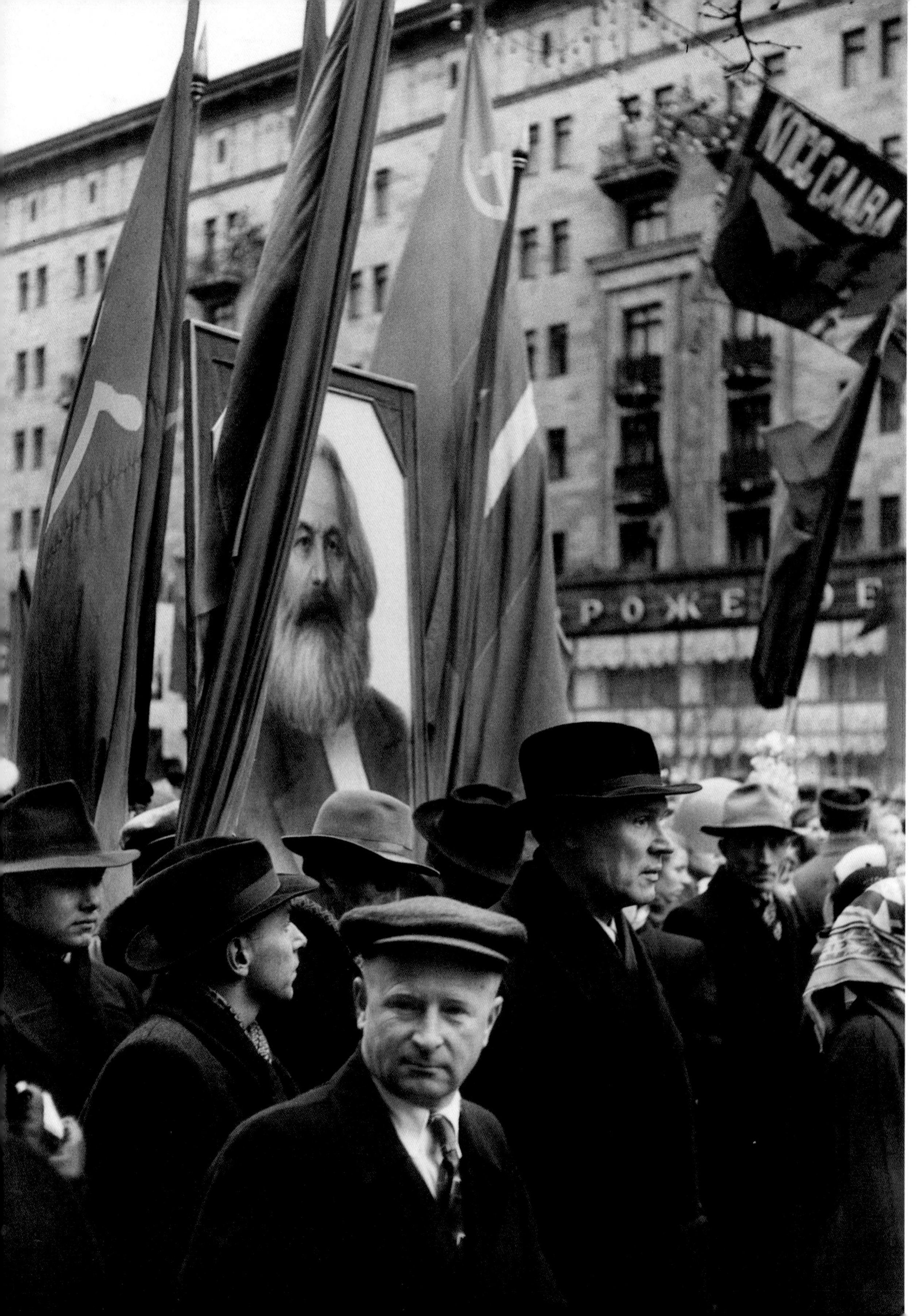

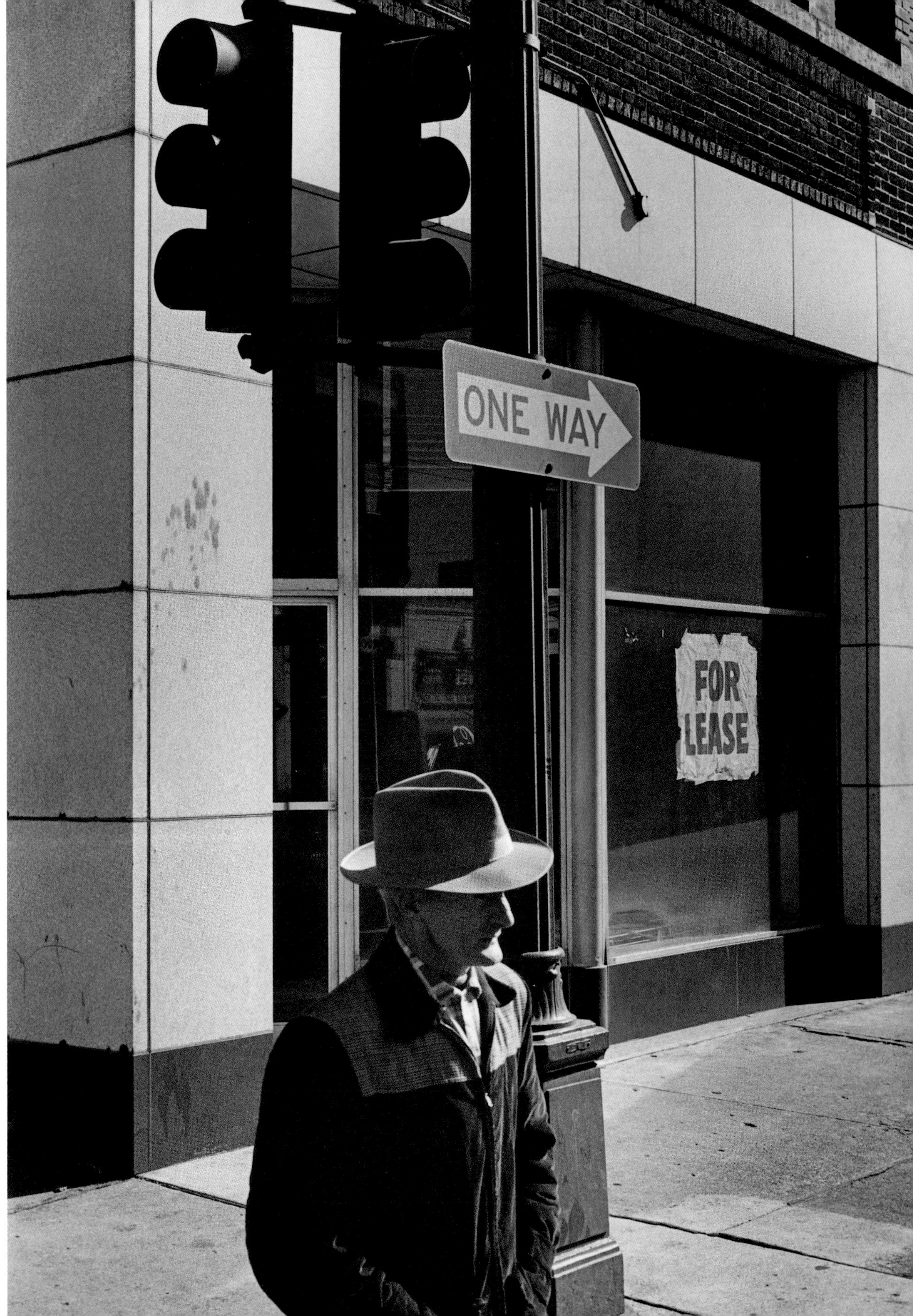

ONE WAY
FOR LEASE

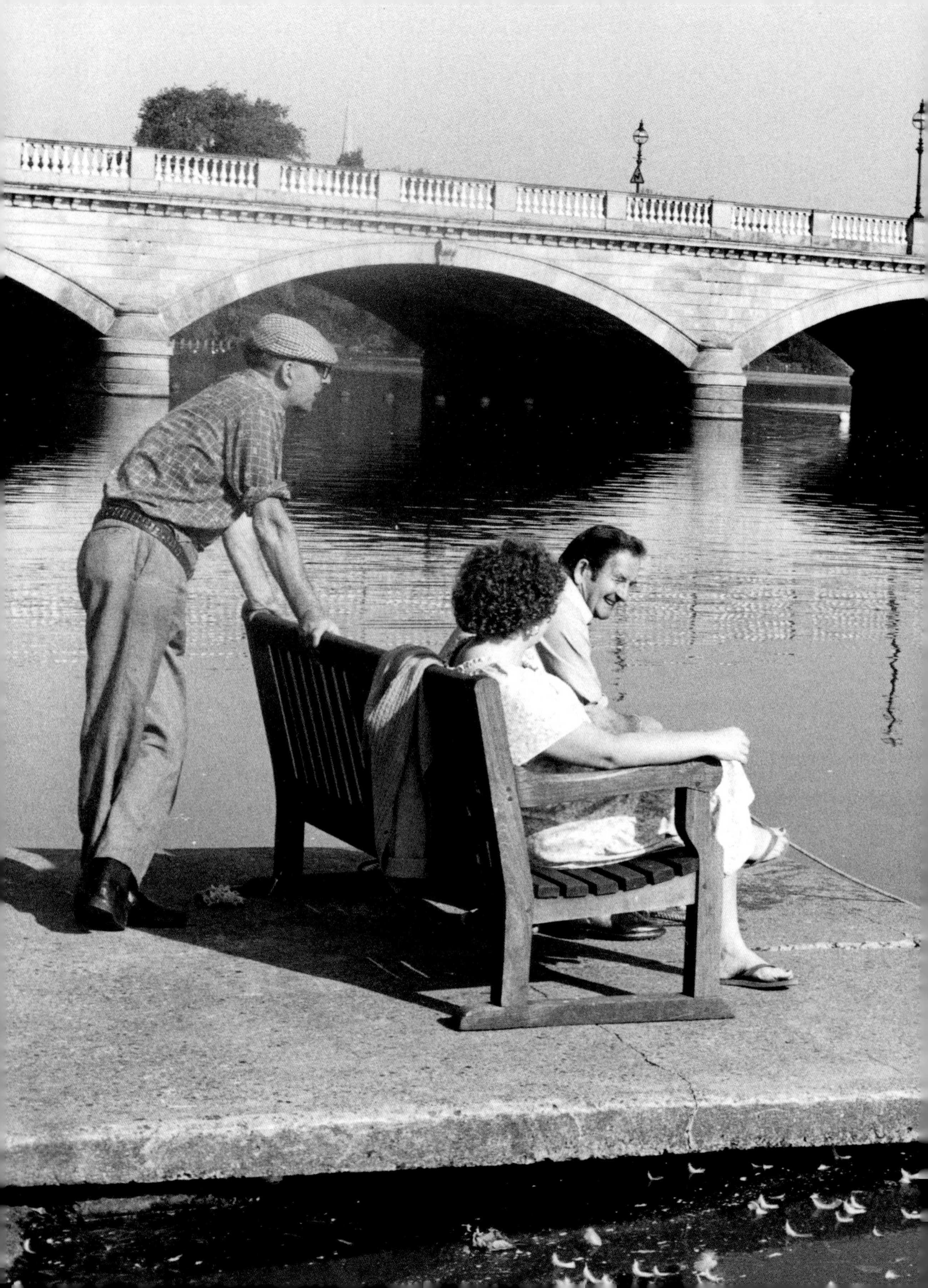

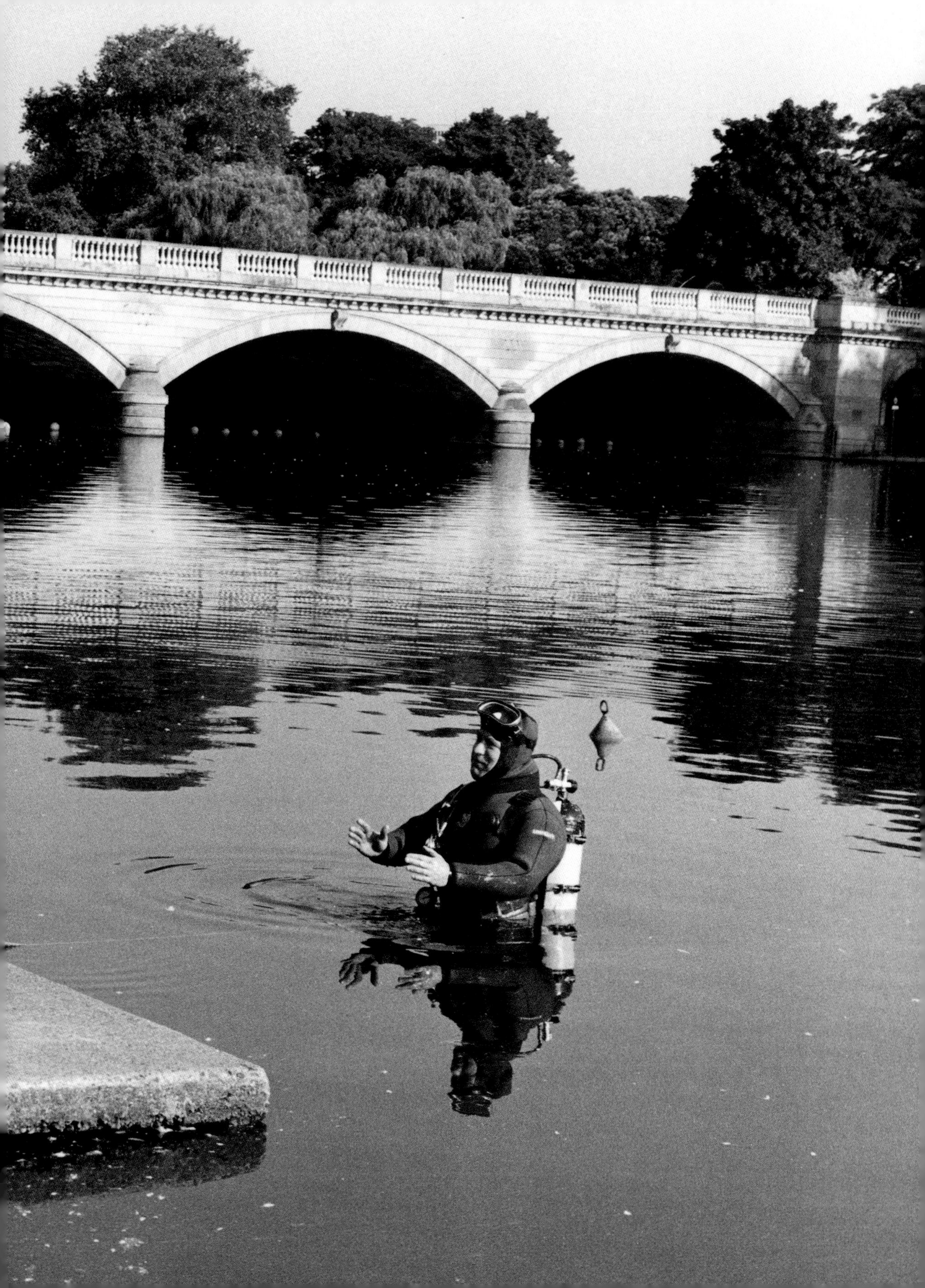

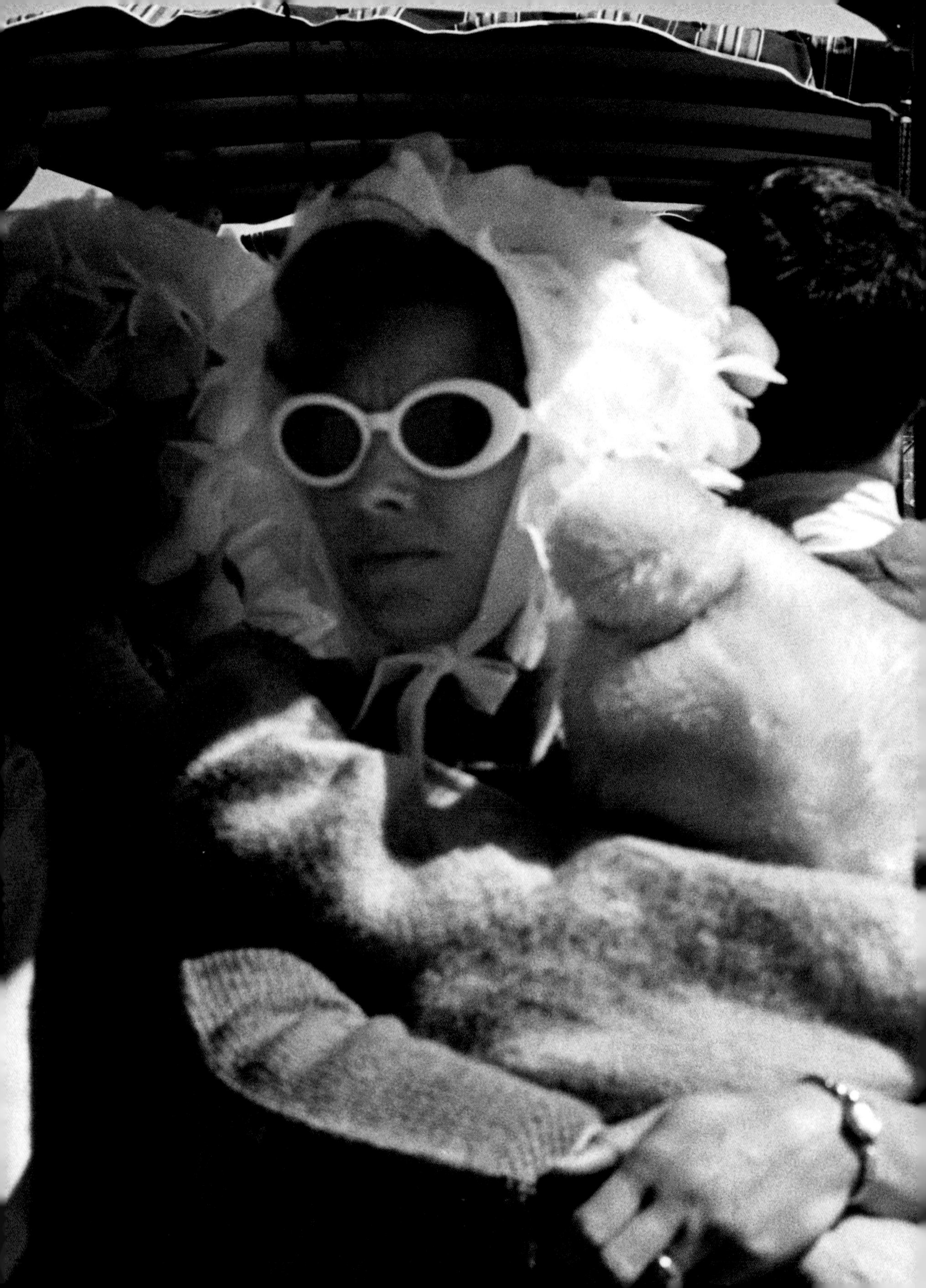

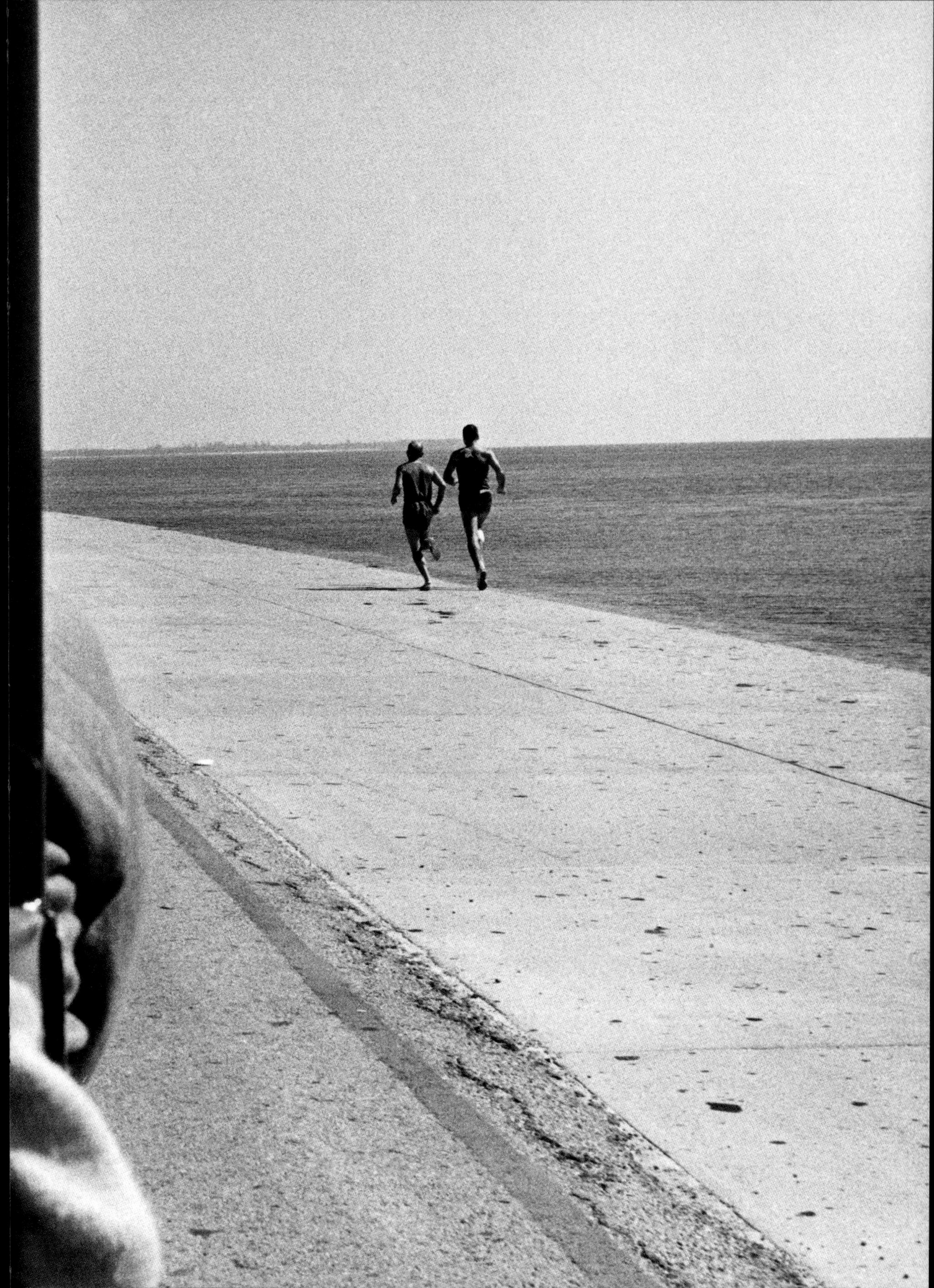

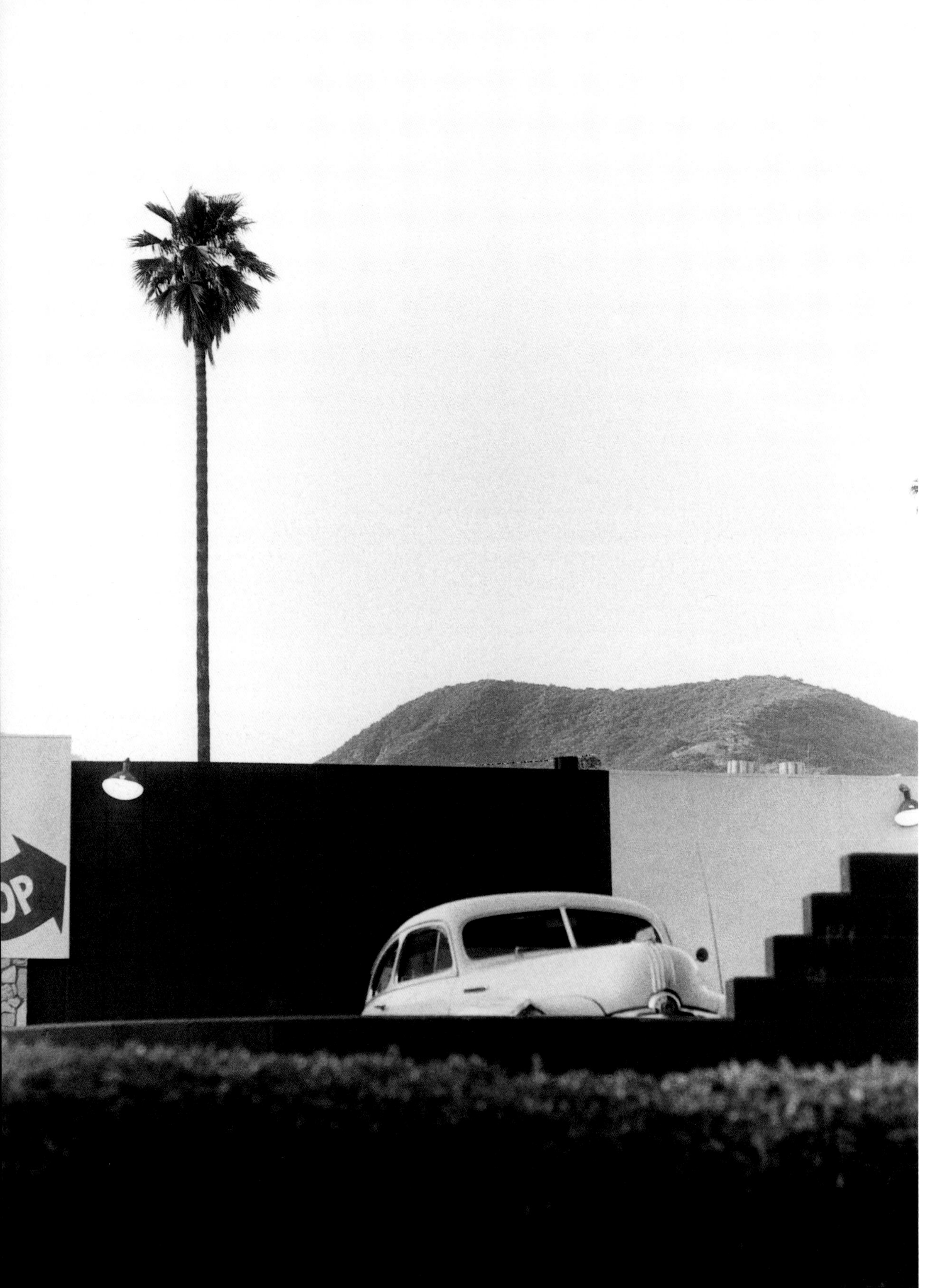

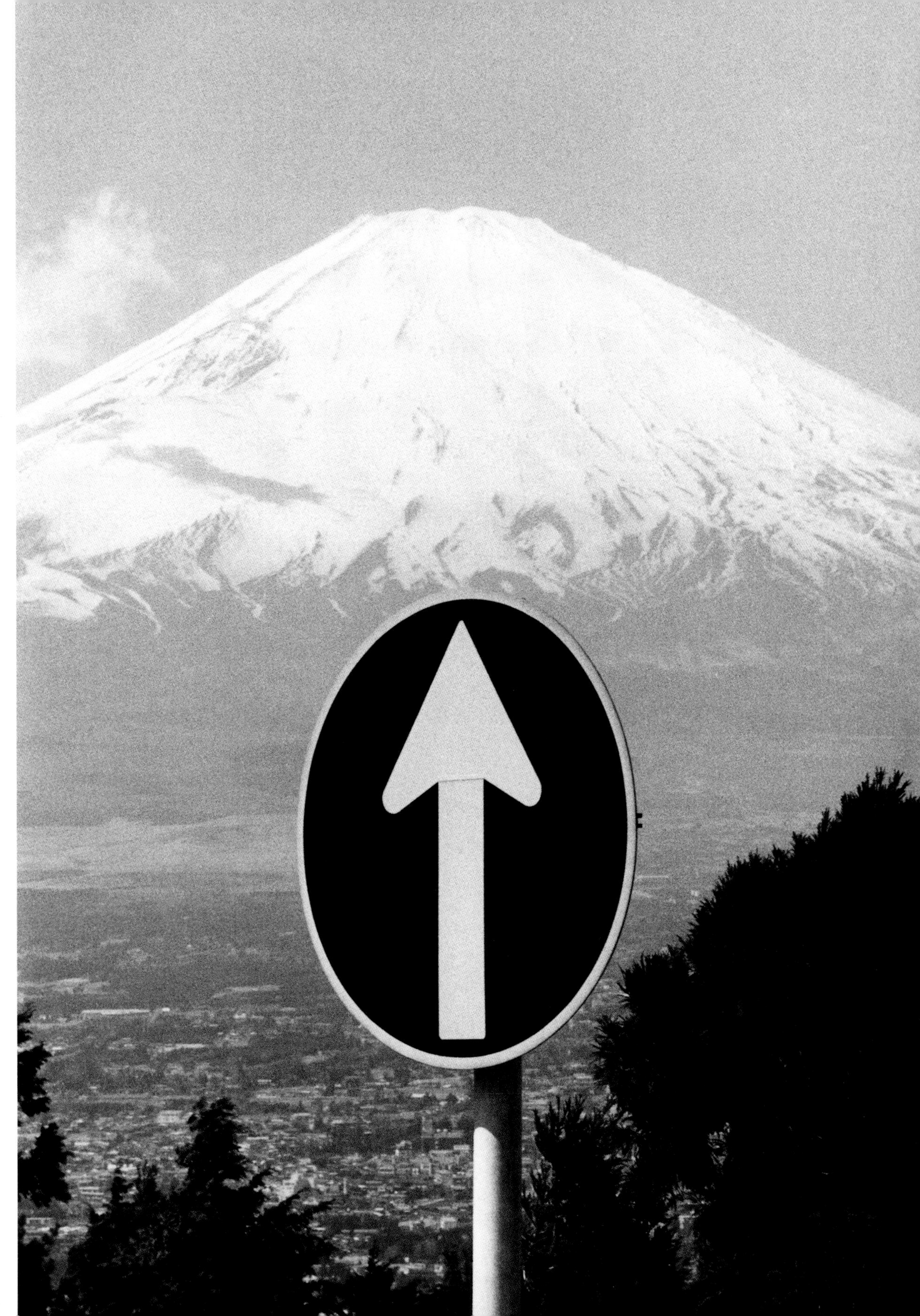

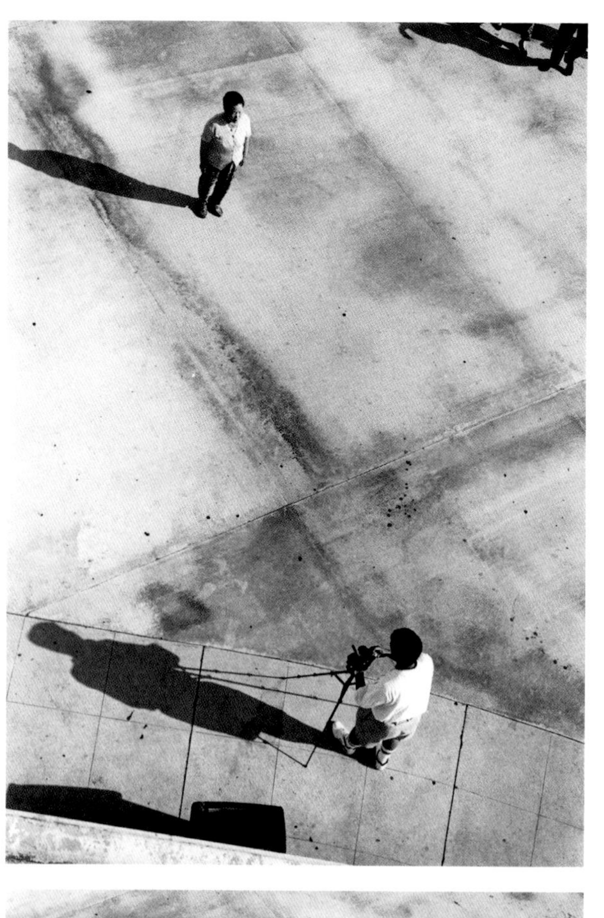
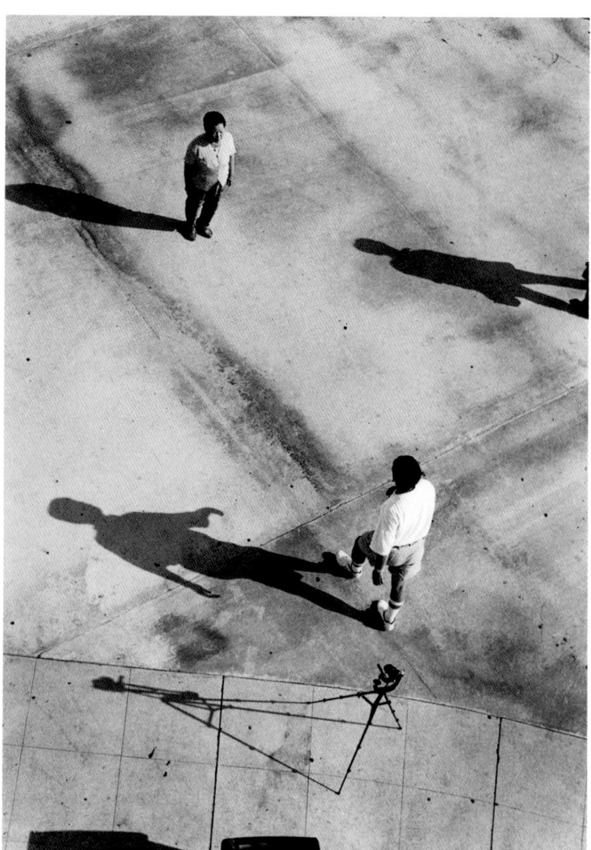
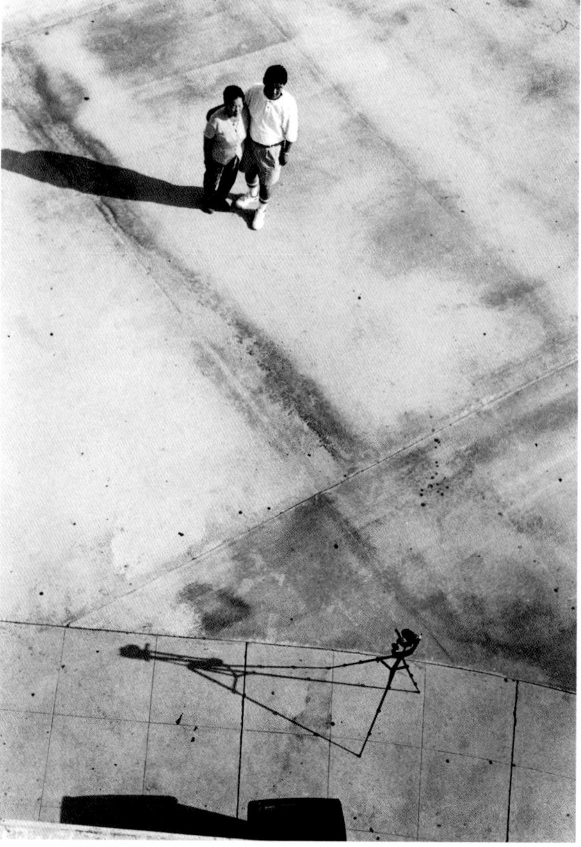
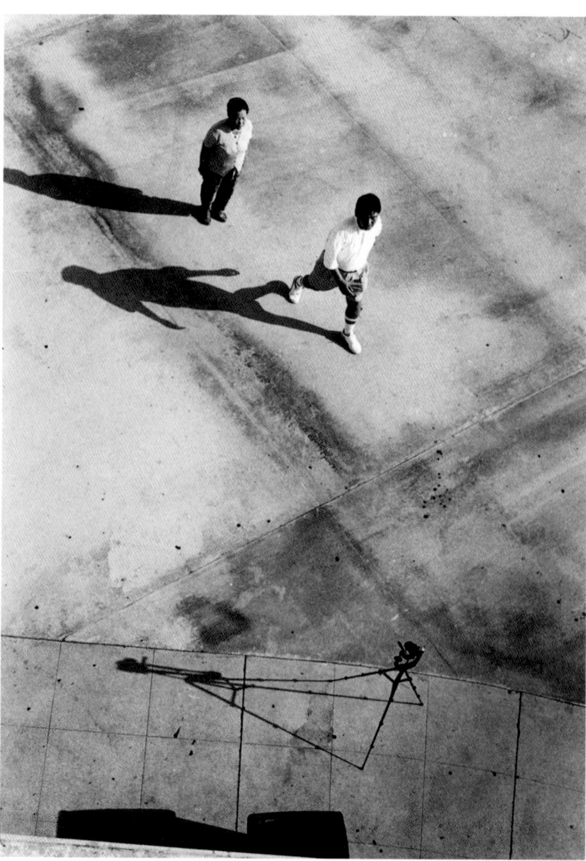

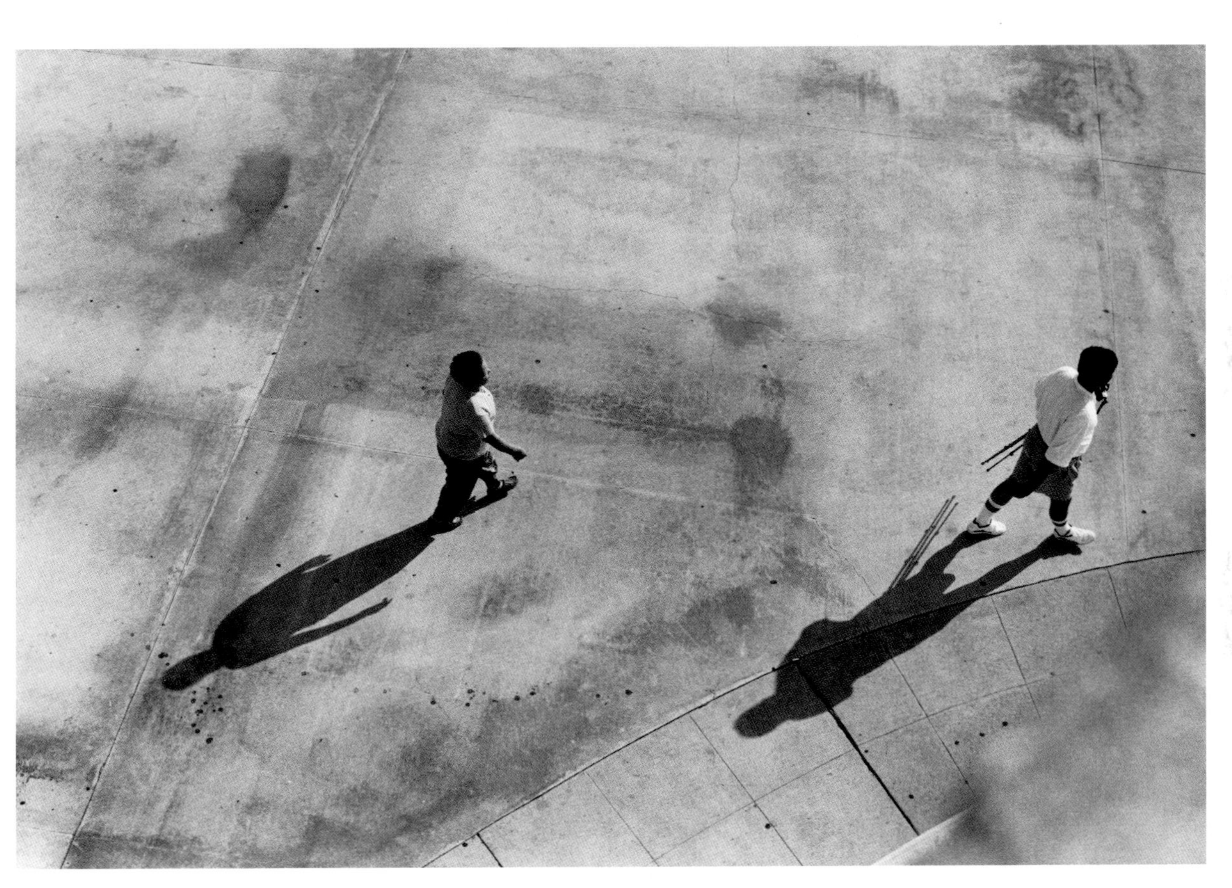

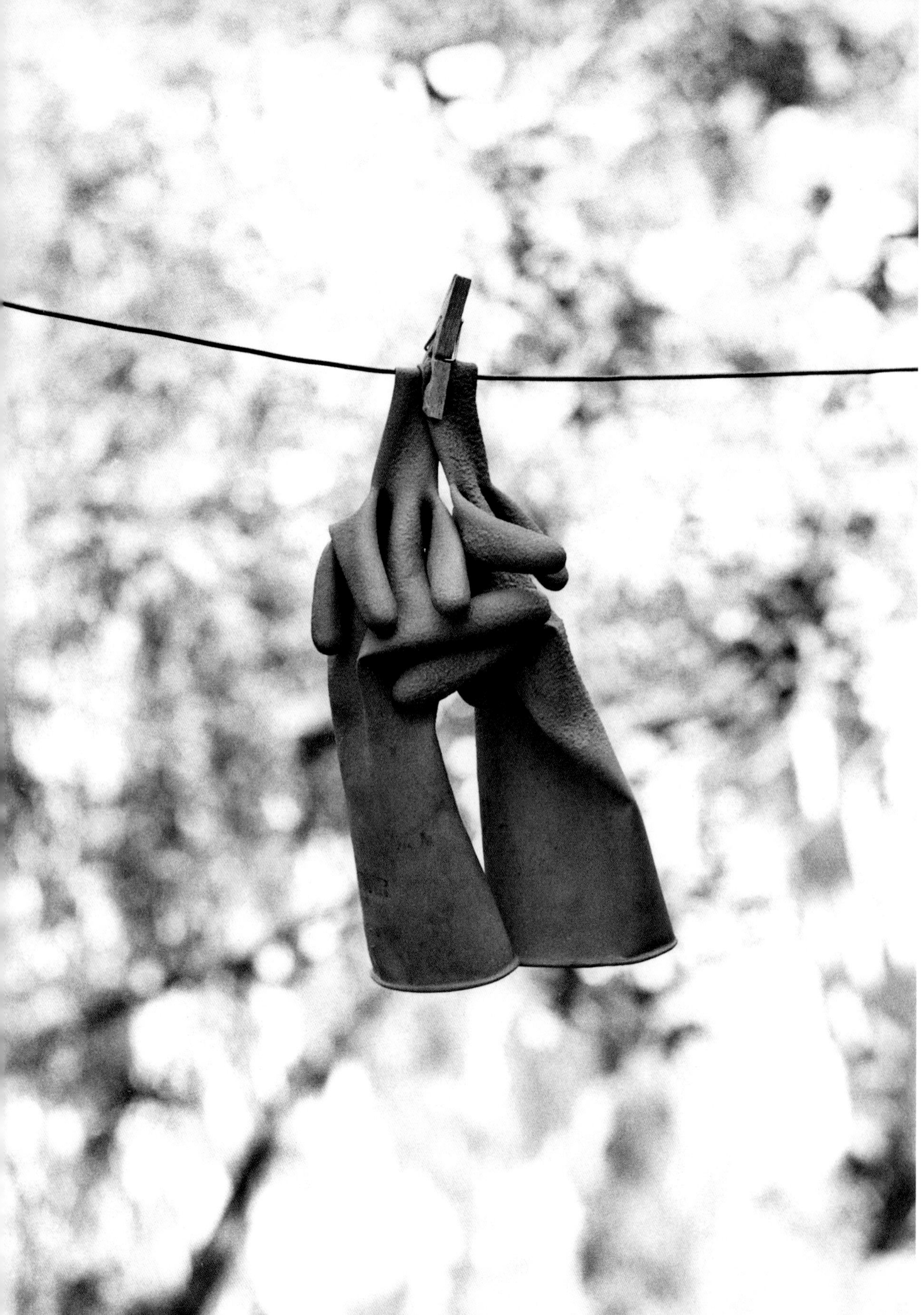

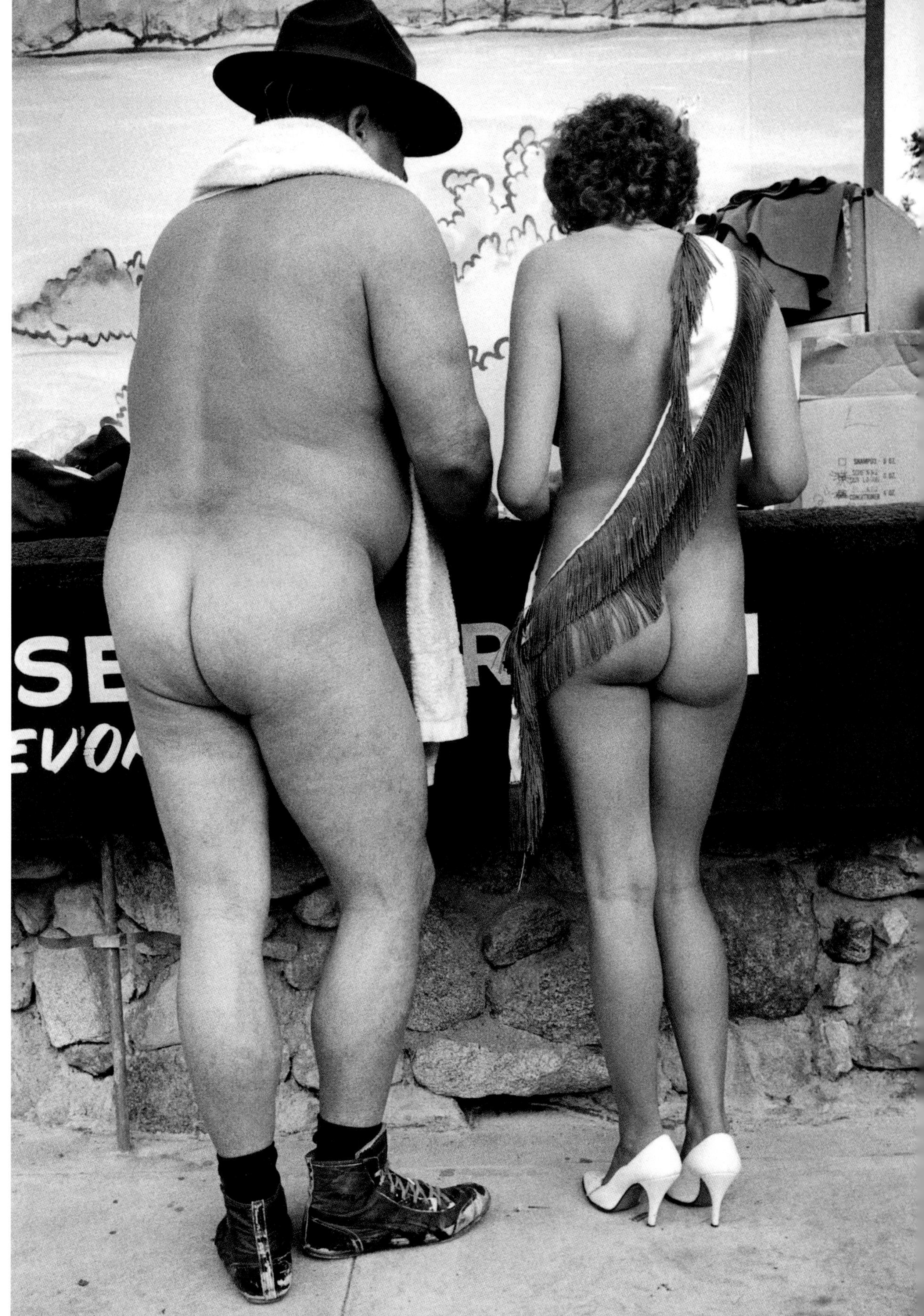

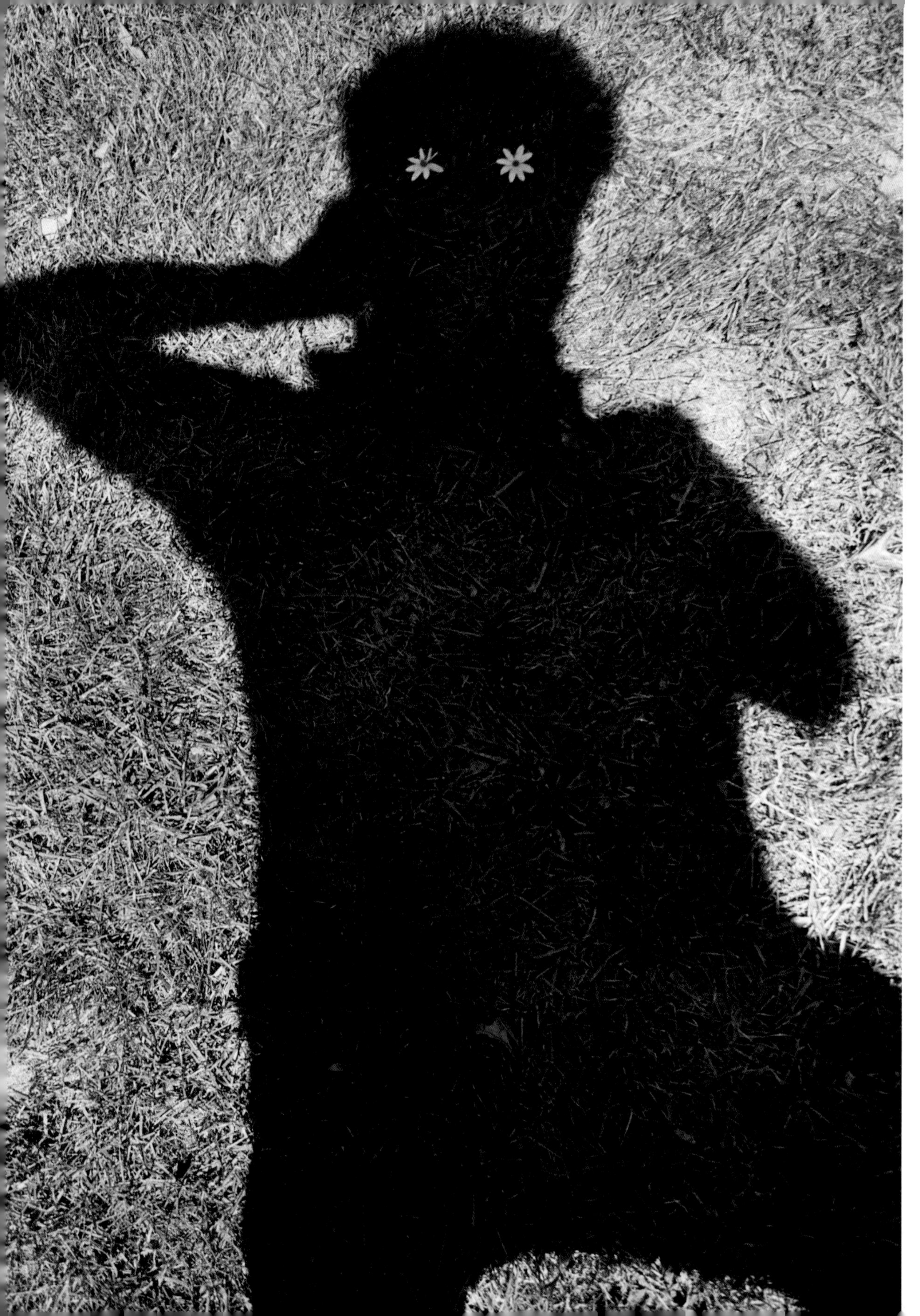

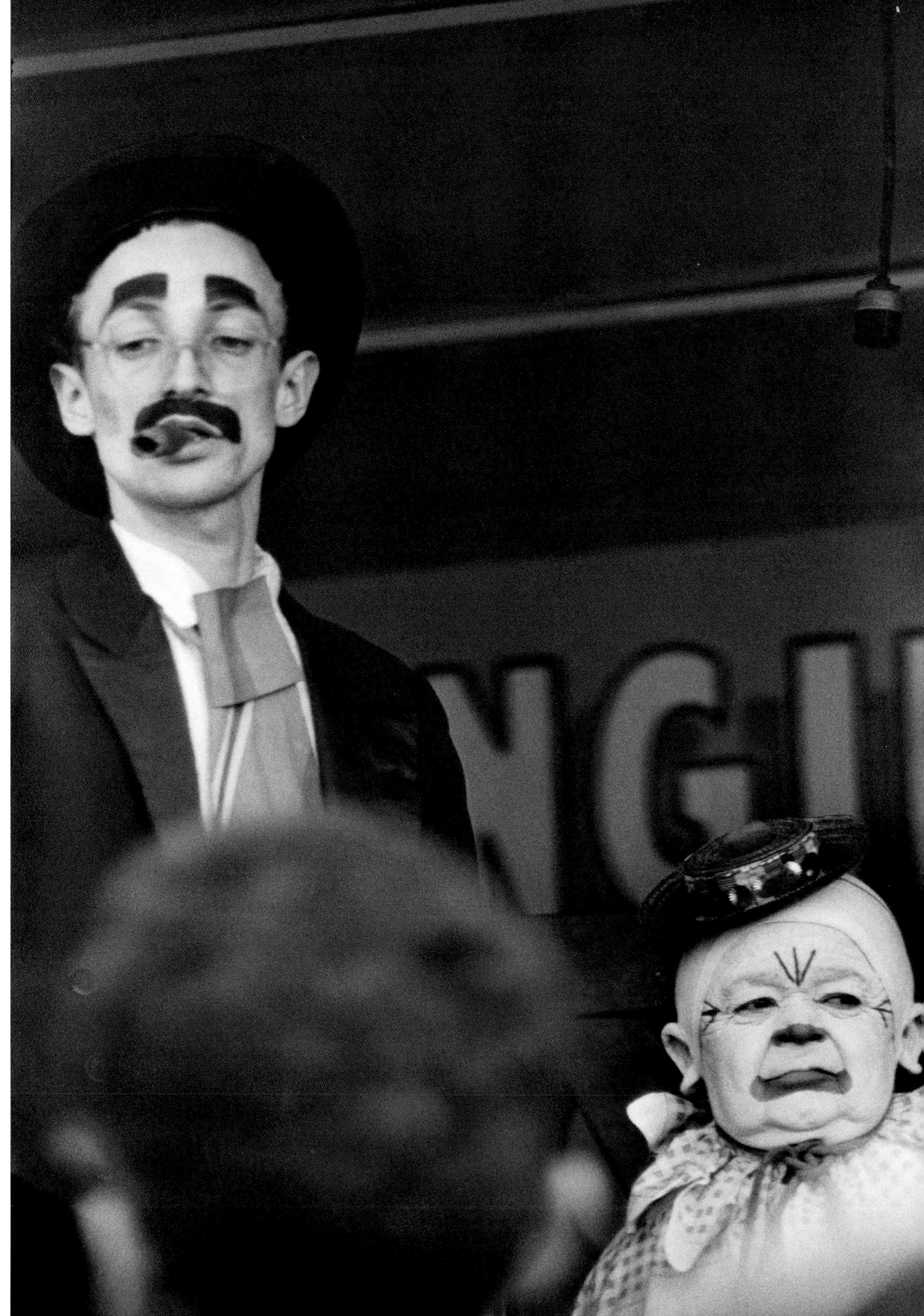

NGII

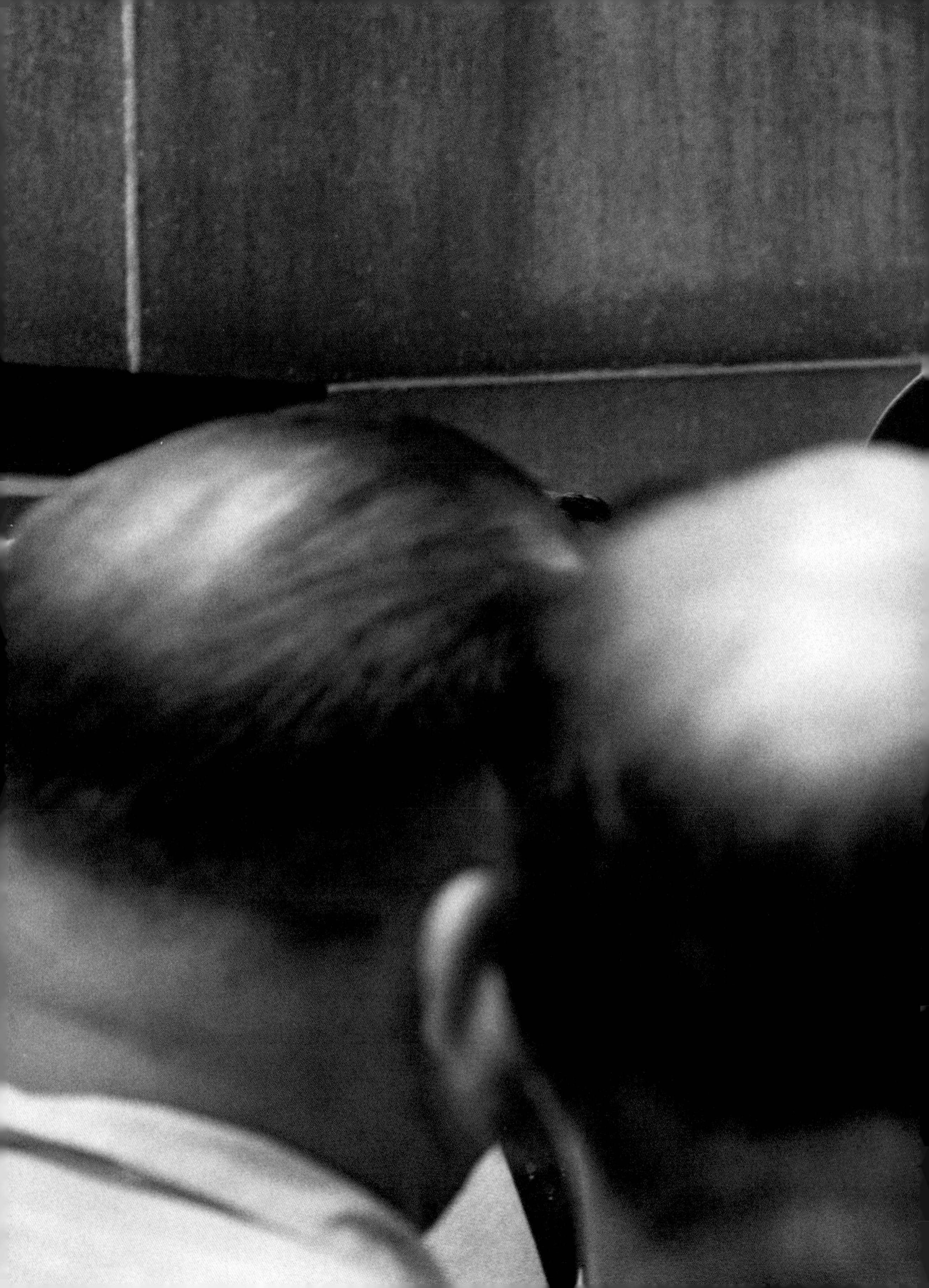

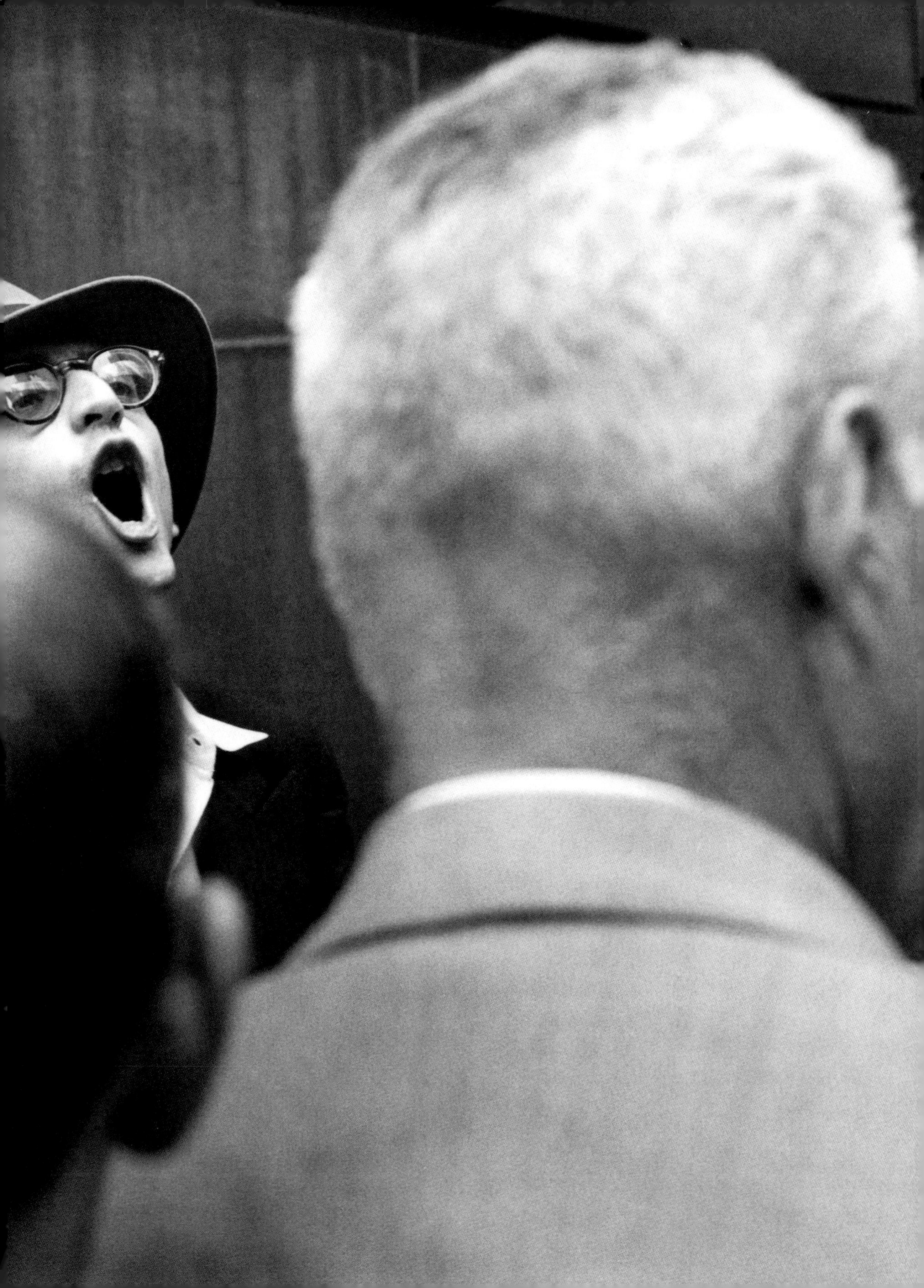

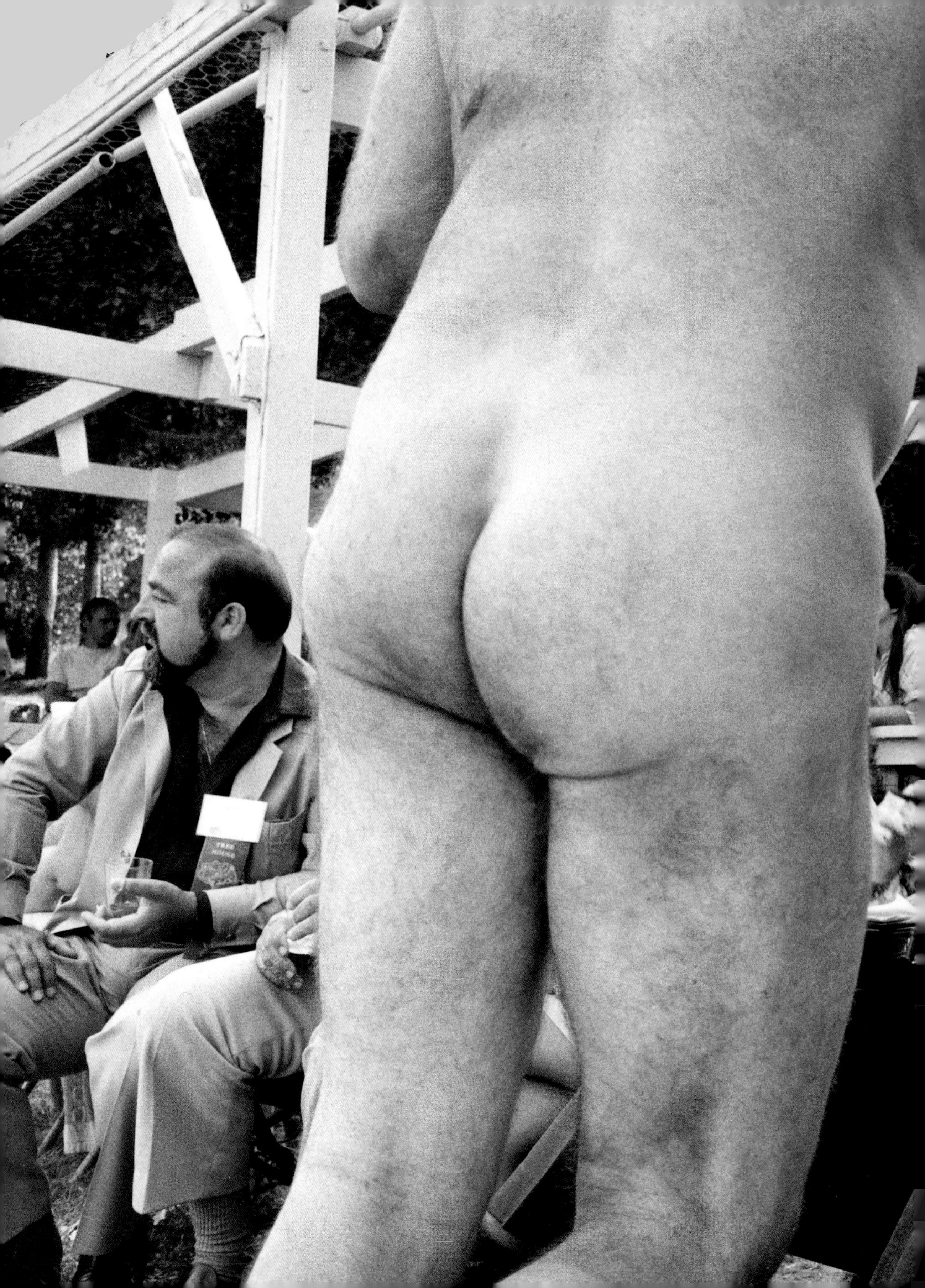

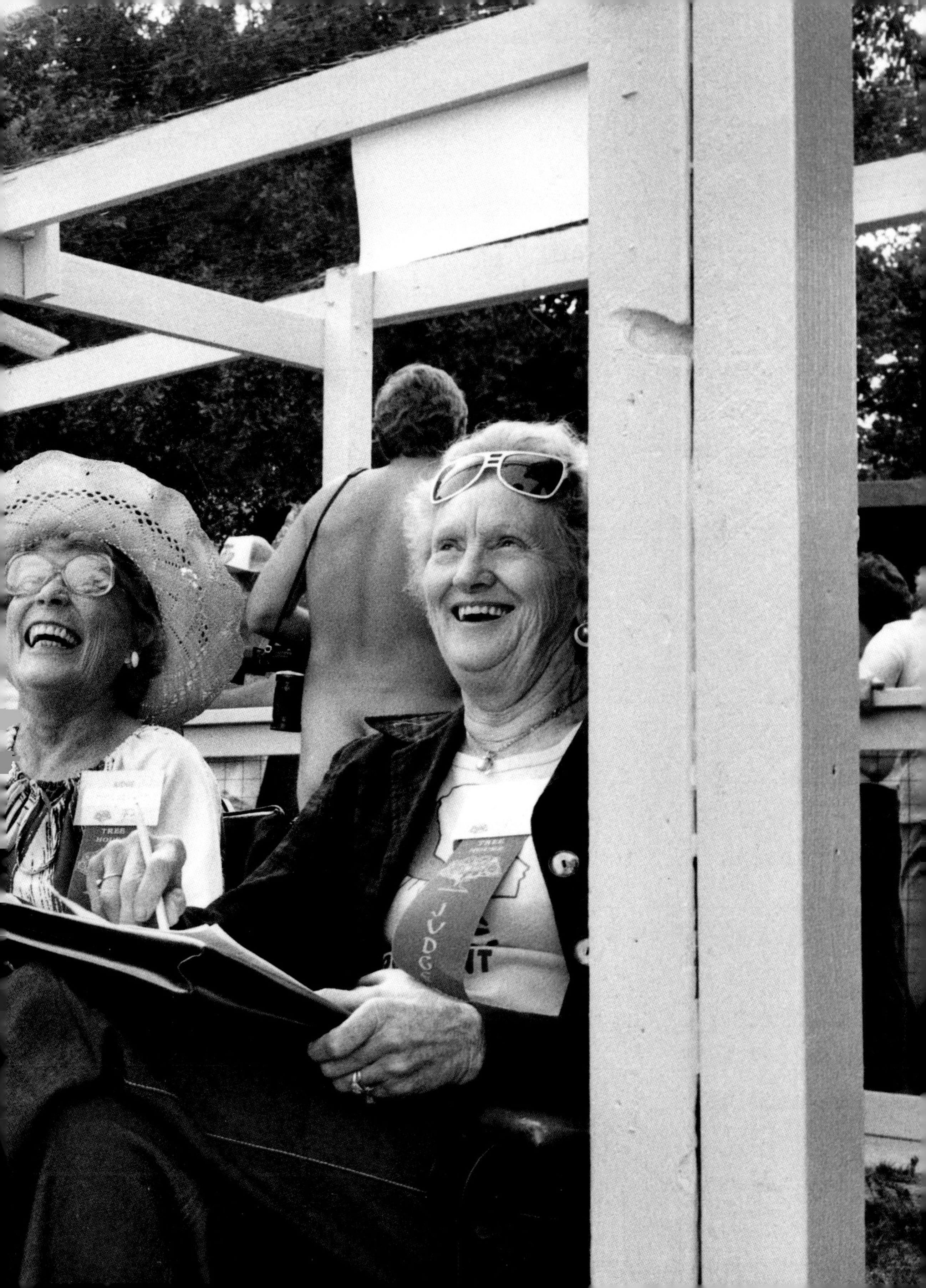

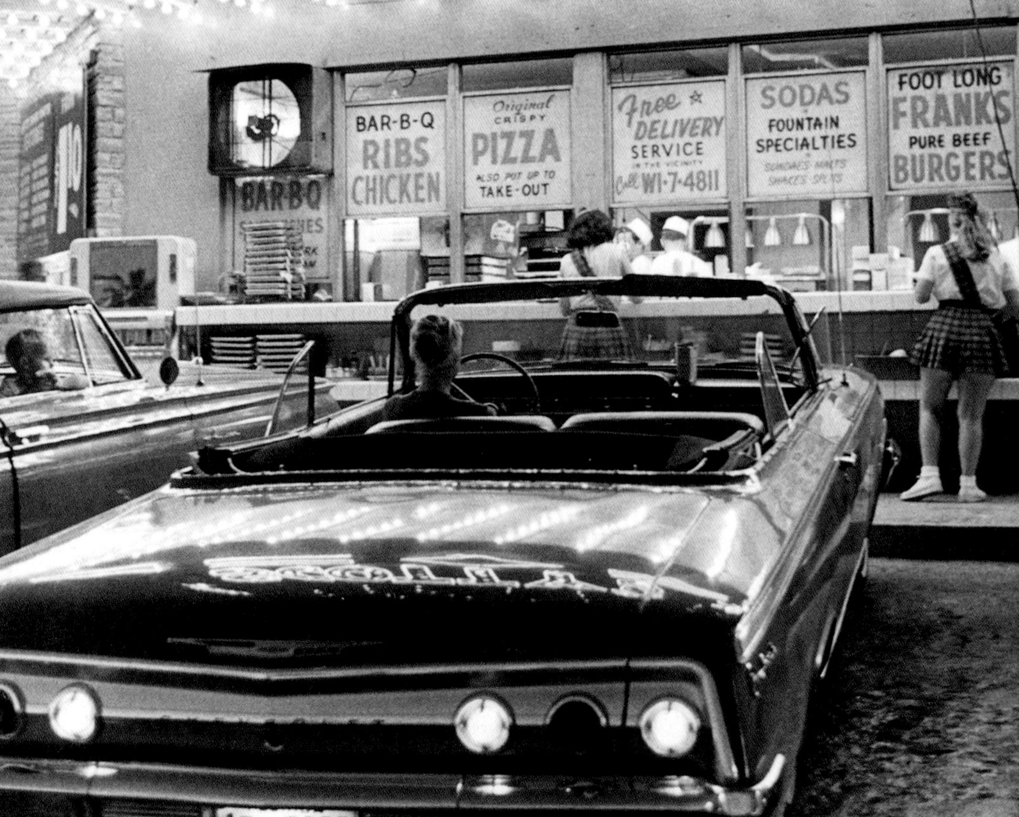

SCOTTY'S
-B-Q CHICKEN
B-Q RIBS
BAR-B-Q RIBS CHICKEN
Original Crispy PIZZA ALSO PUT UP TO TAKE-OUT
Free DELIVERY SERVICE IN THE VICINITY Call WI-7-4811
SODAS FOUNTAIN SPECIALTIES SUNDAES MALTS SHAKES SPLITS
FOOT LONG FRANKS PURE BEEF BURGERS
CURB AREA only
1E-8830

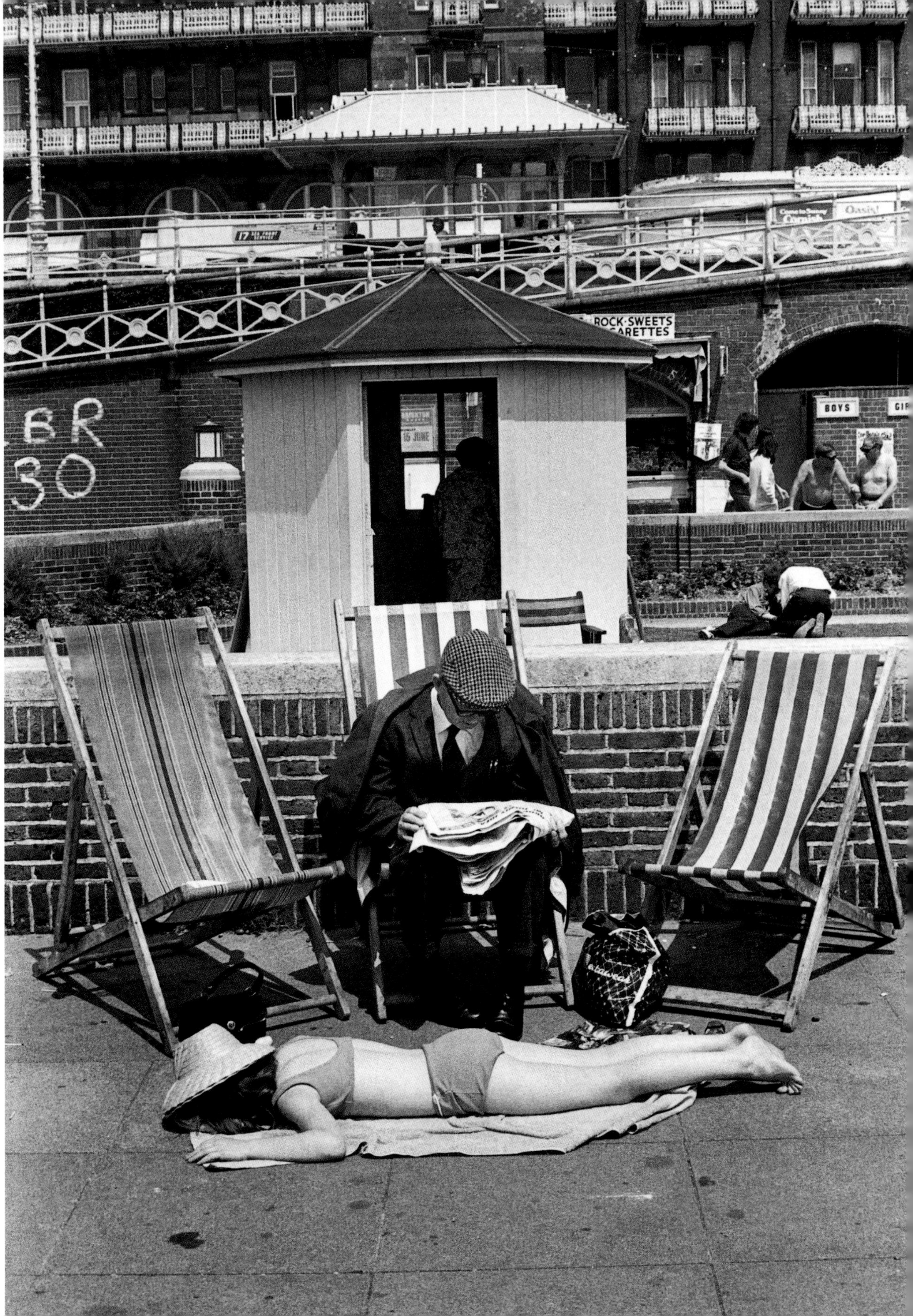

ROCK · SWEETS
CIGARETTES
BOYS
GIR
15 JUNE
BR
30

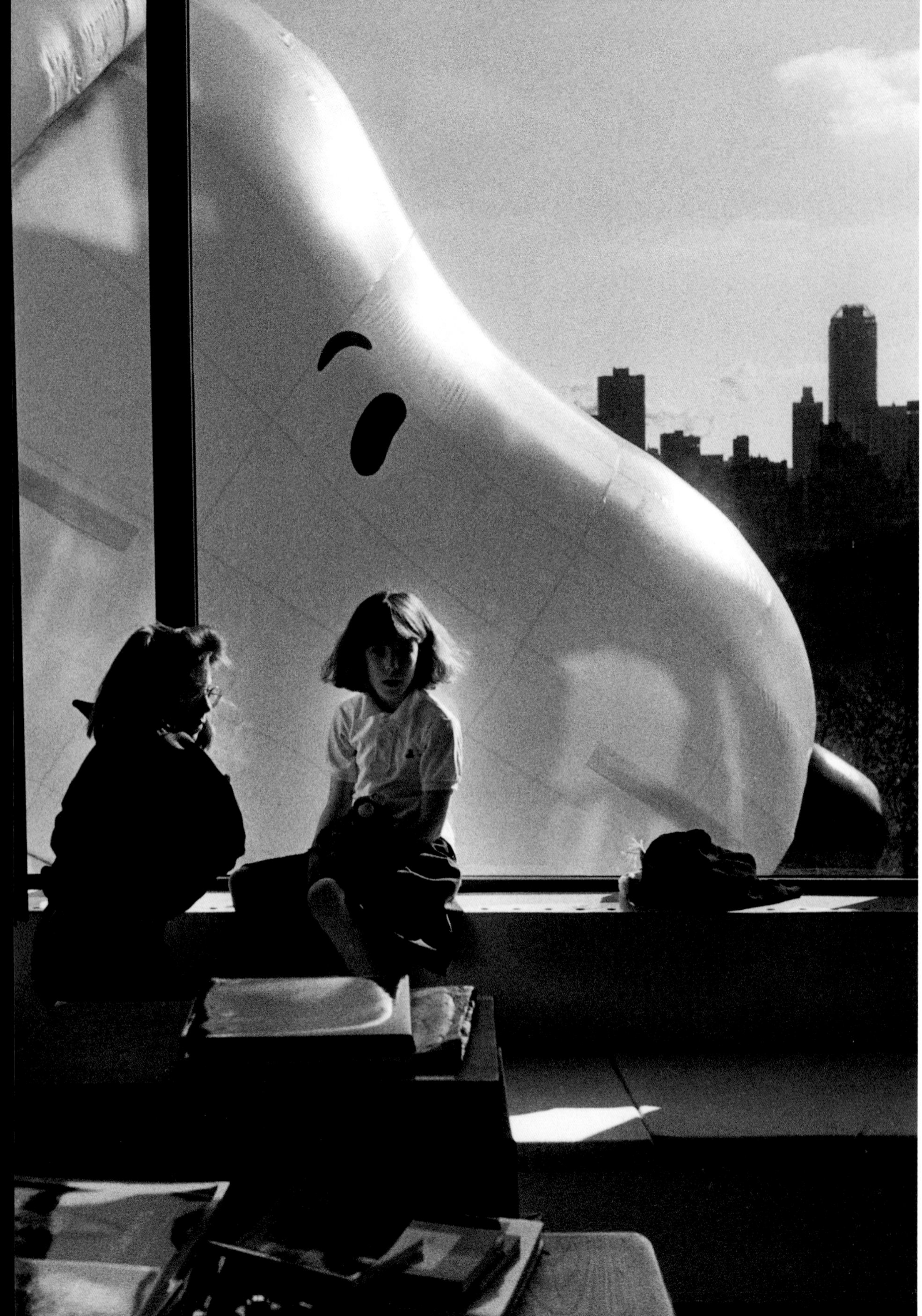

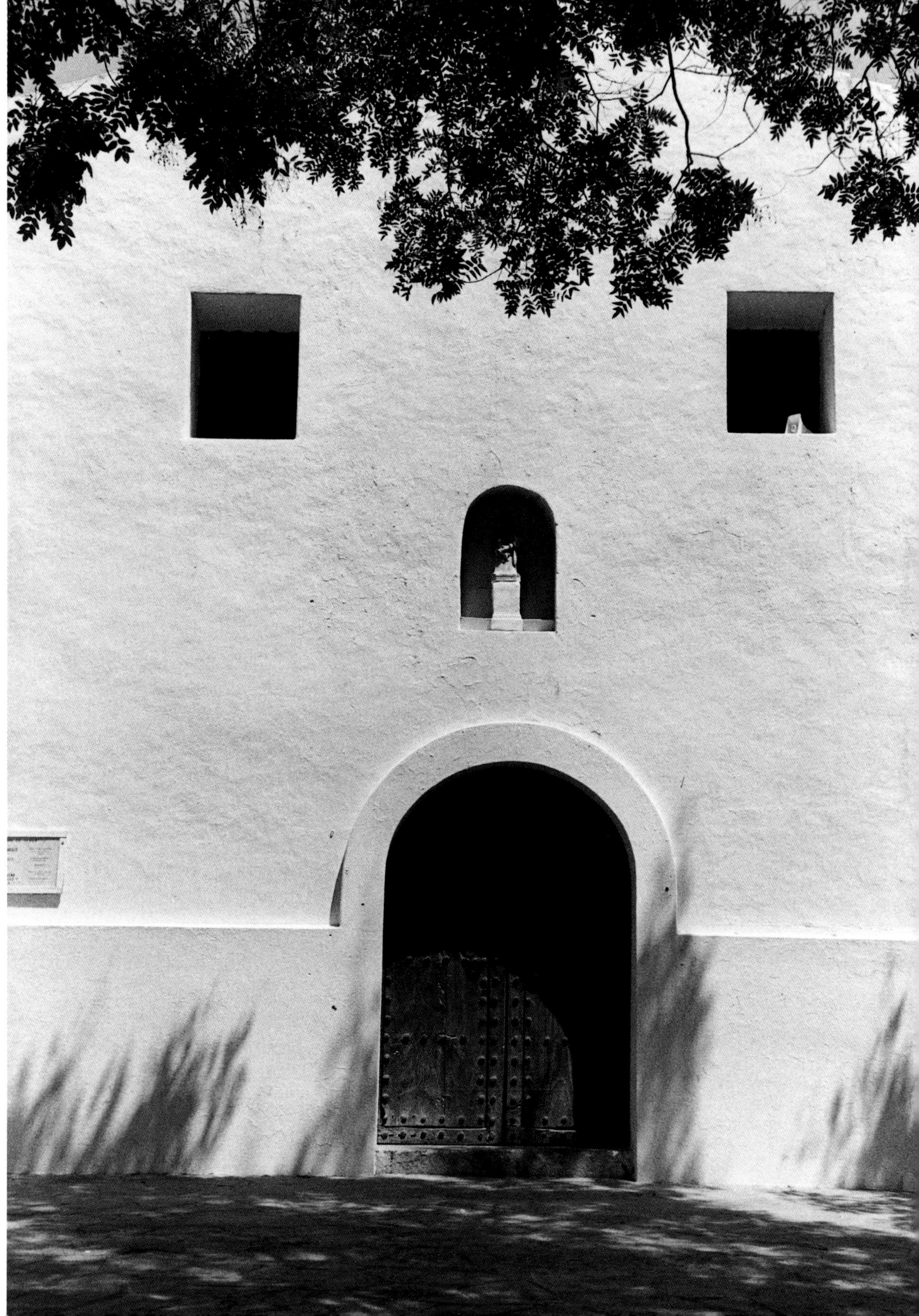

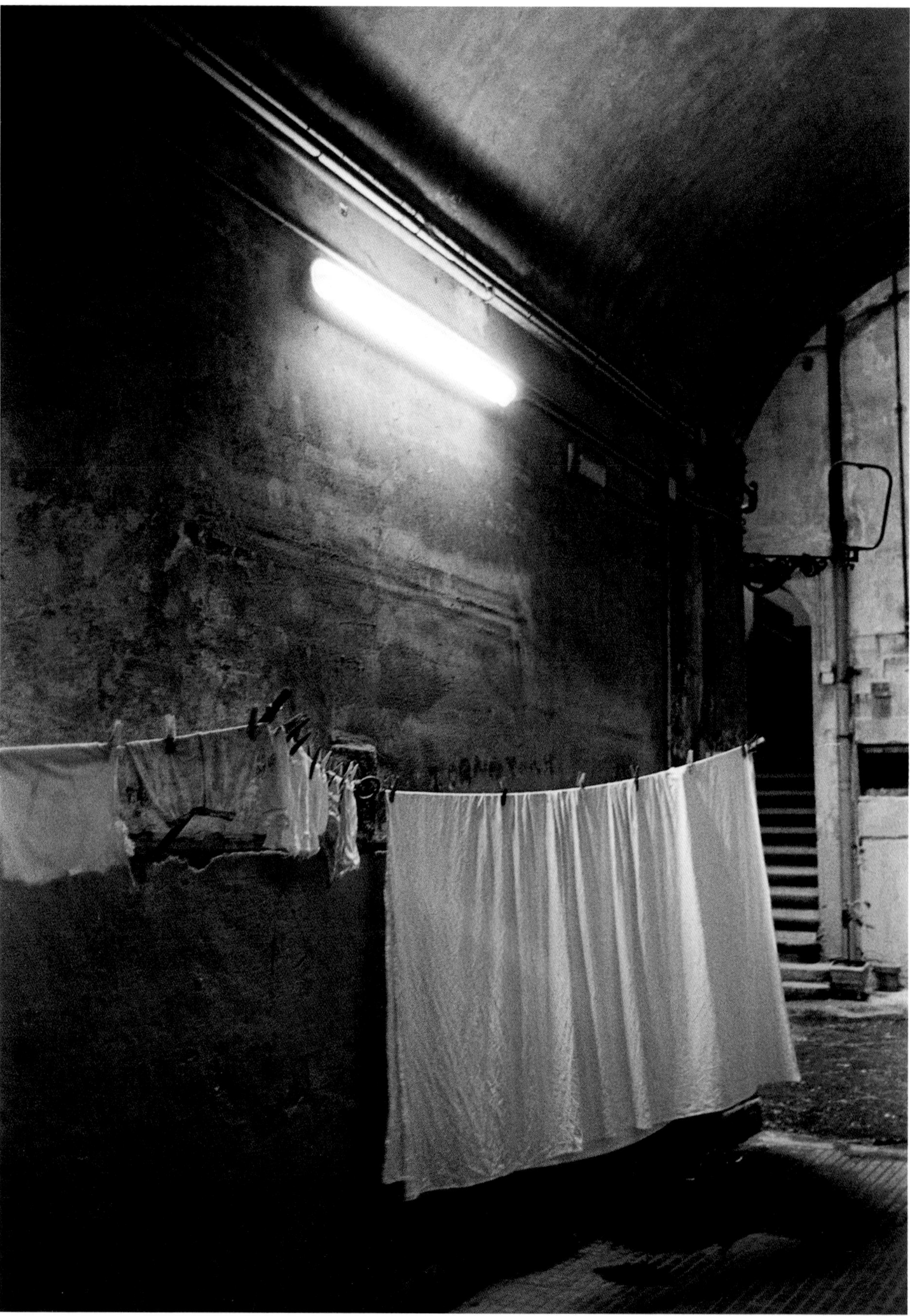

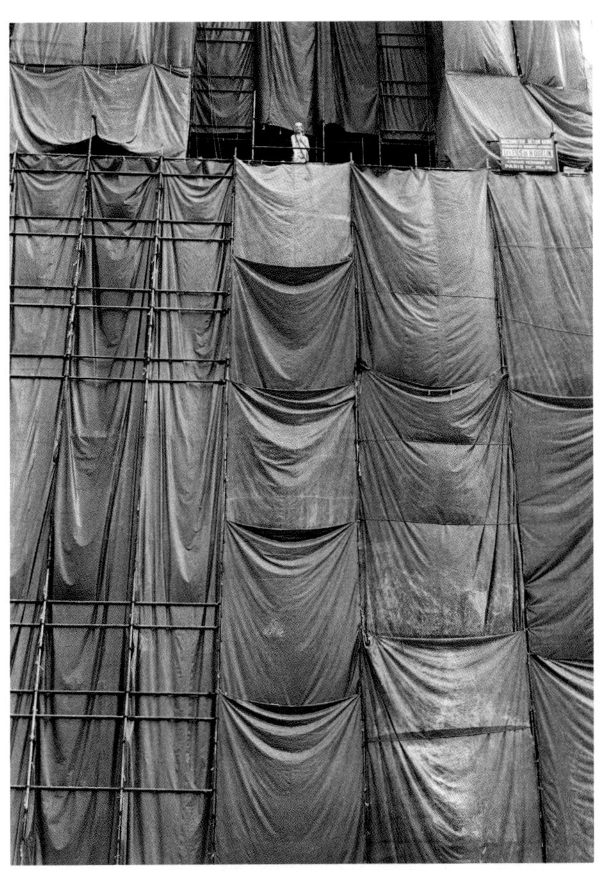
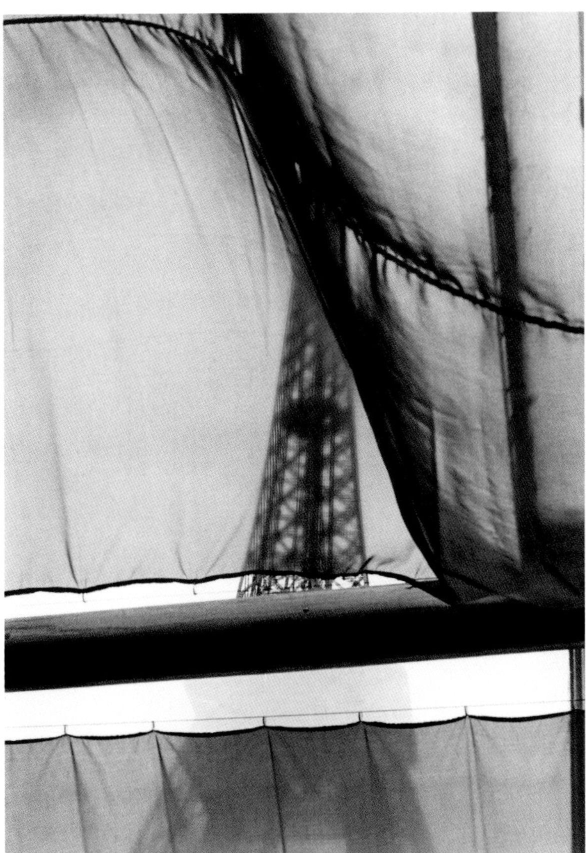
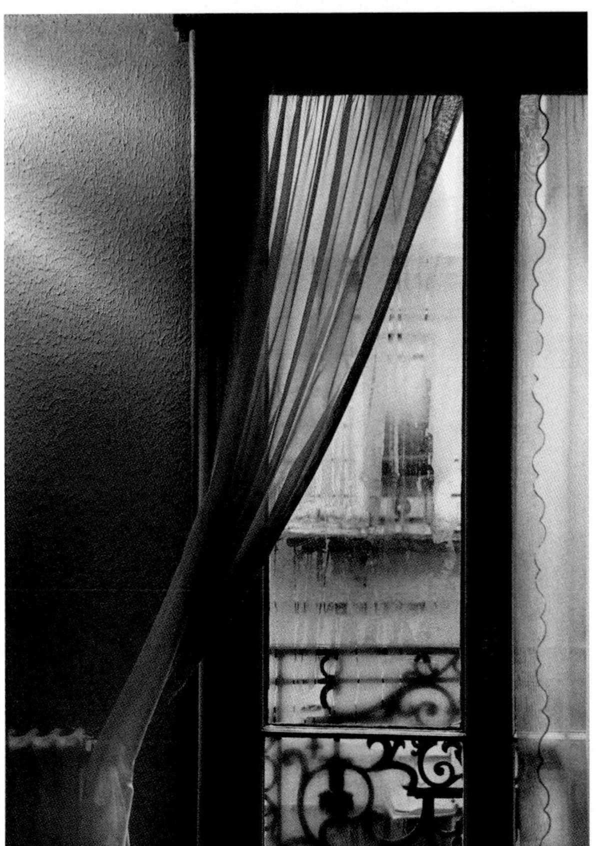
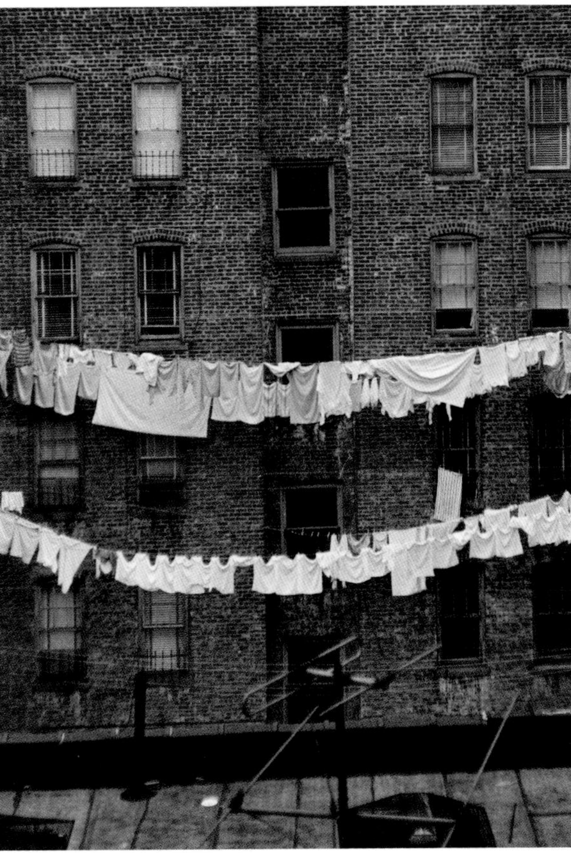

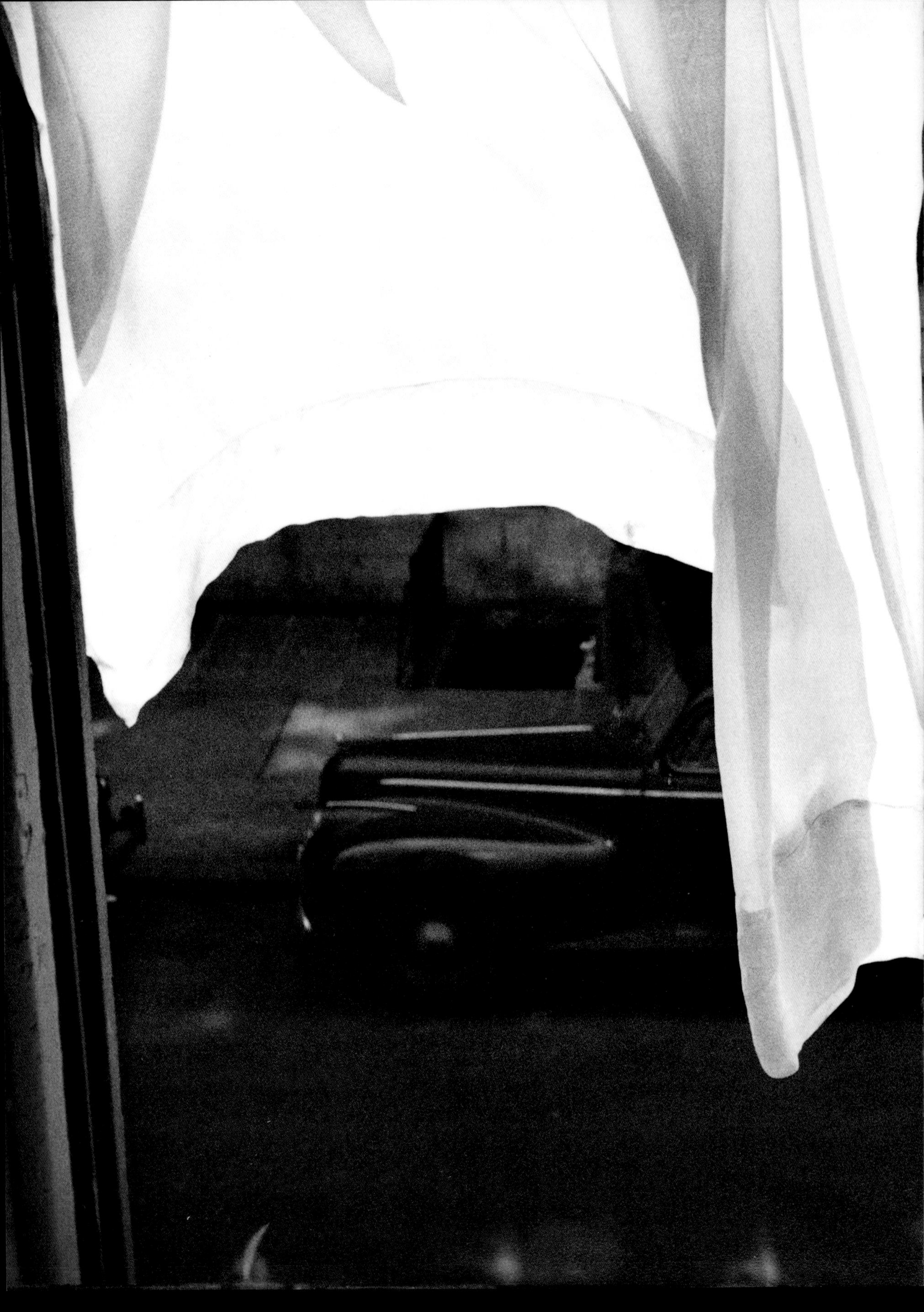

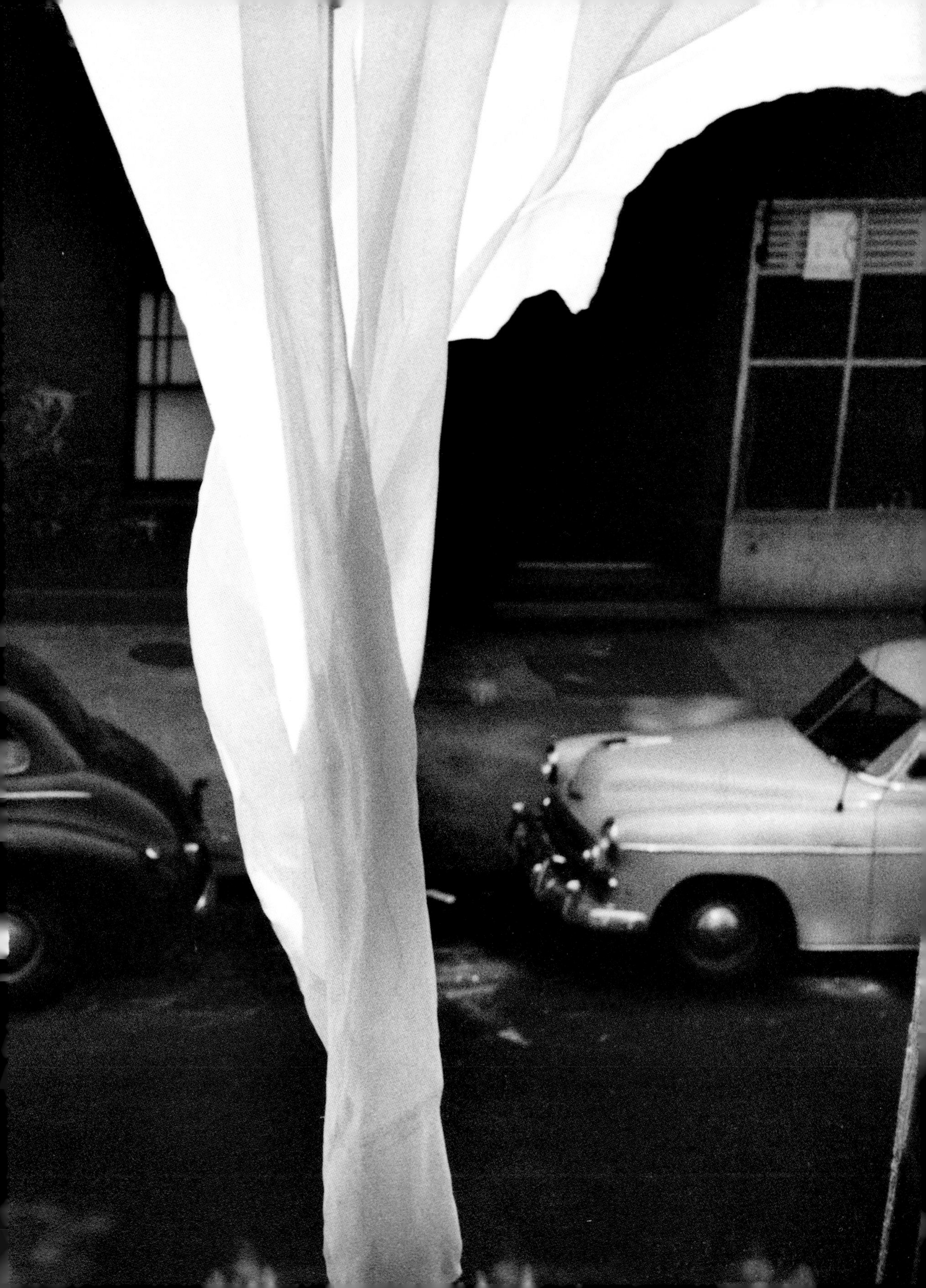

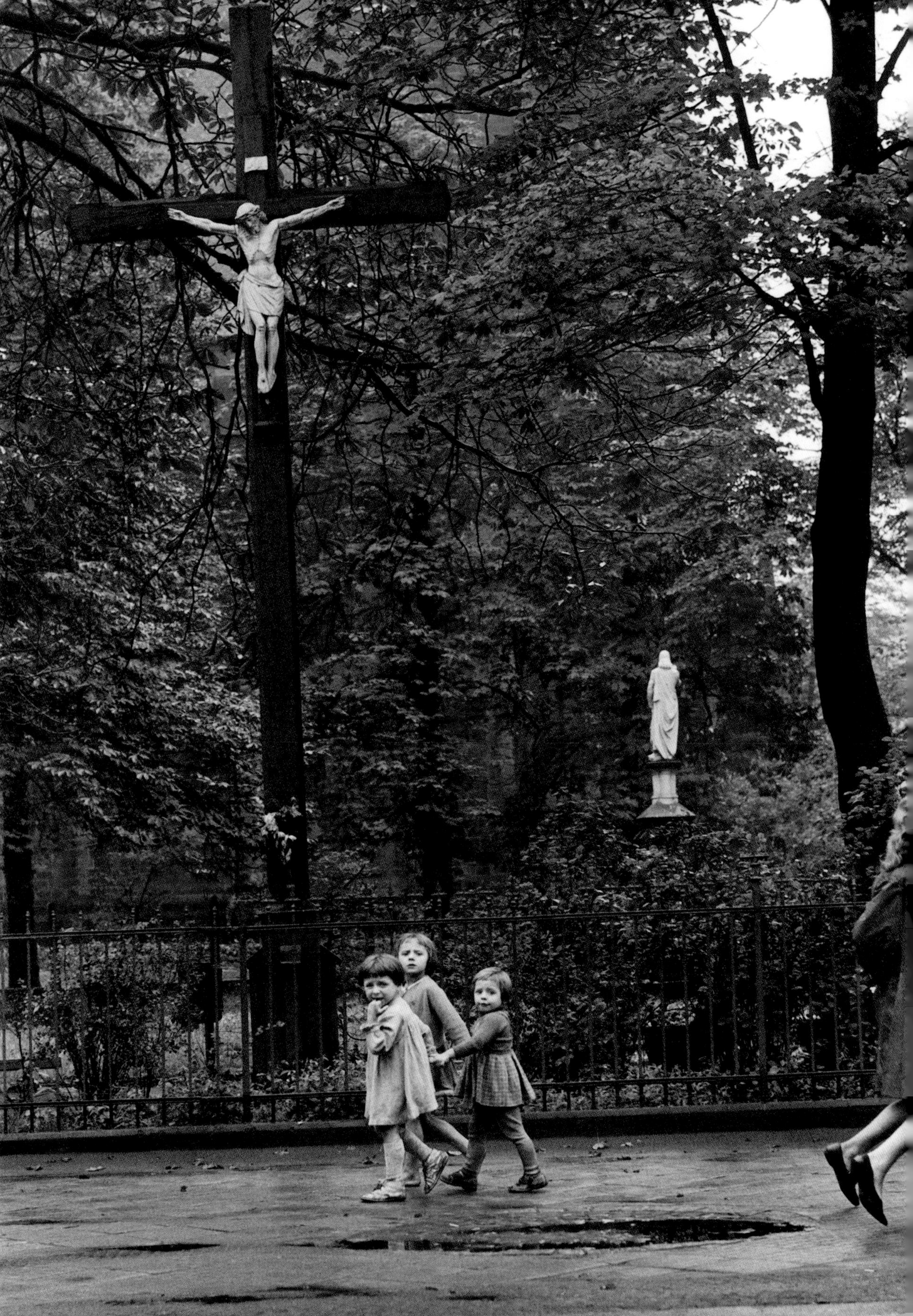

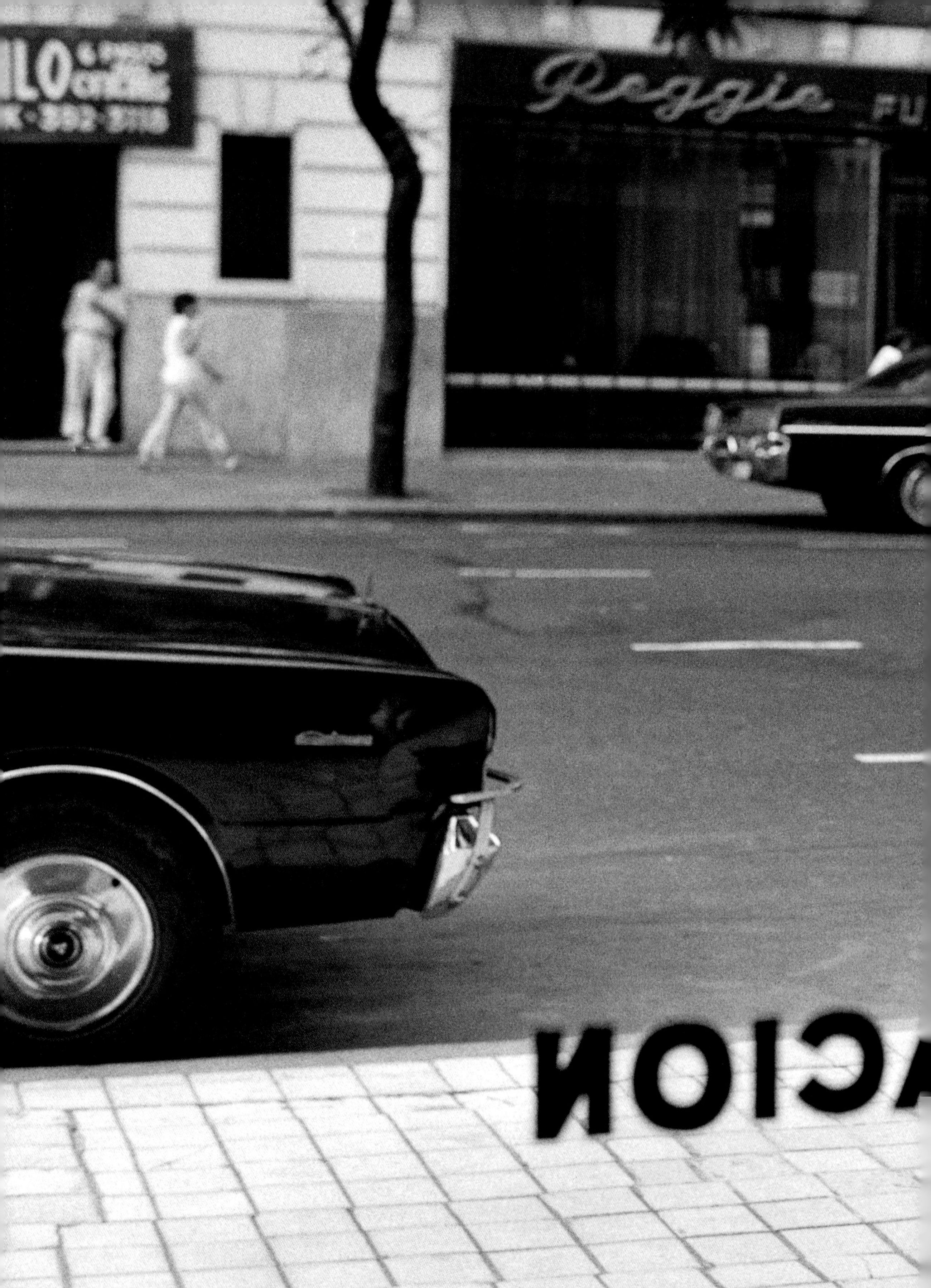

Reggia
ACION

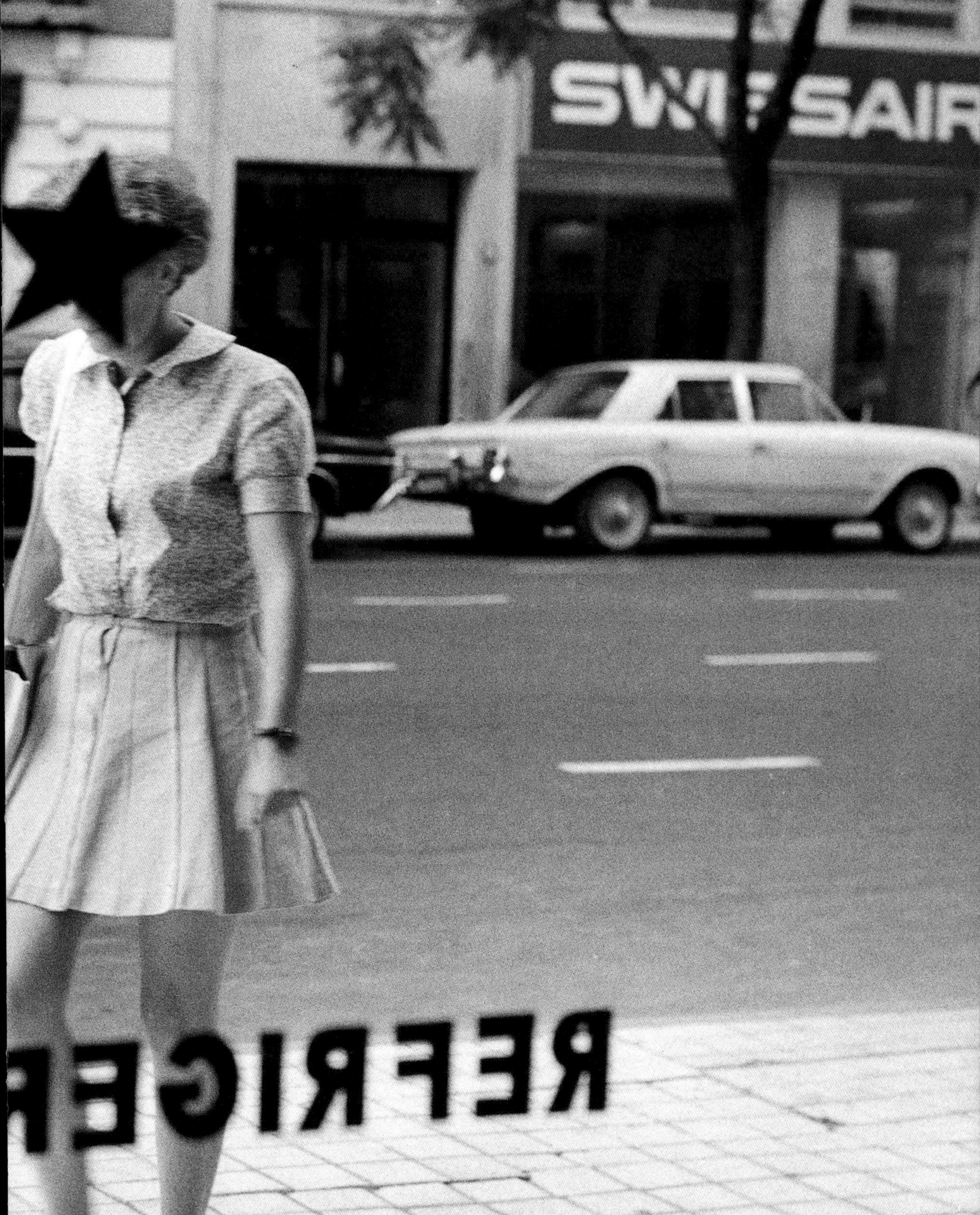

SWISSAIR
REFRIGER

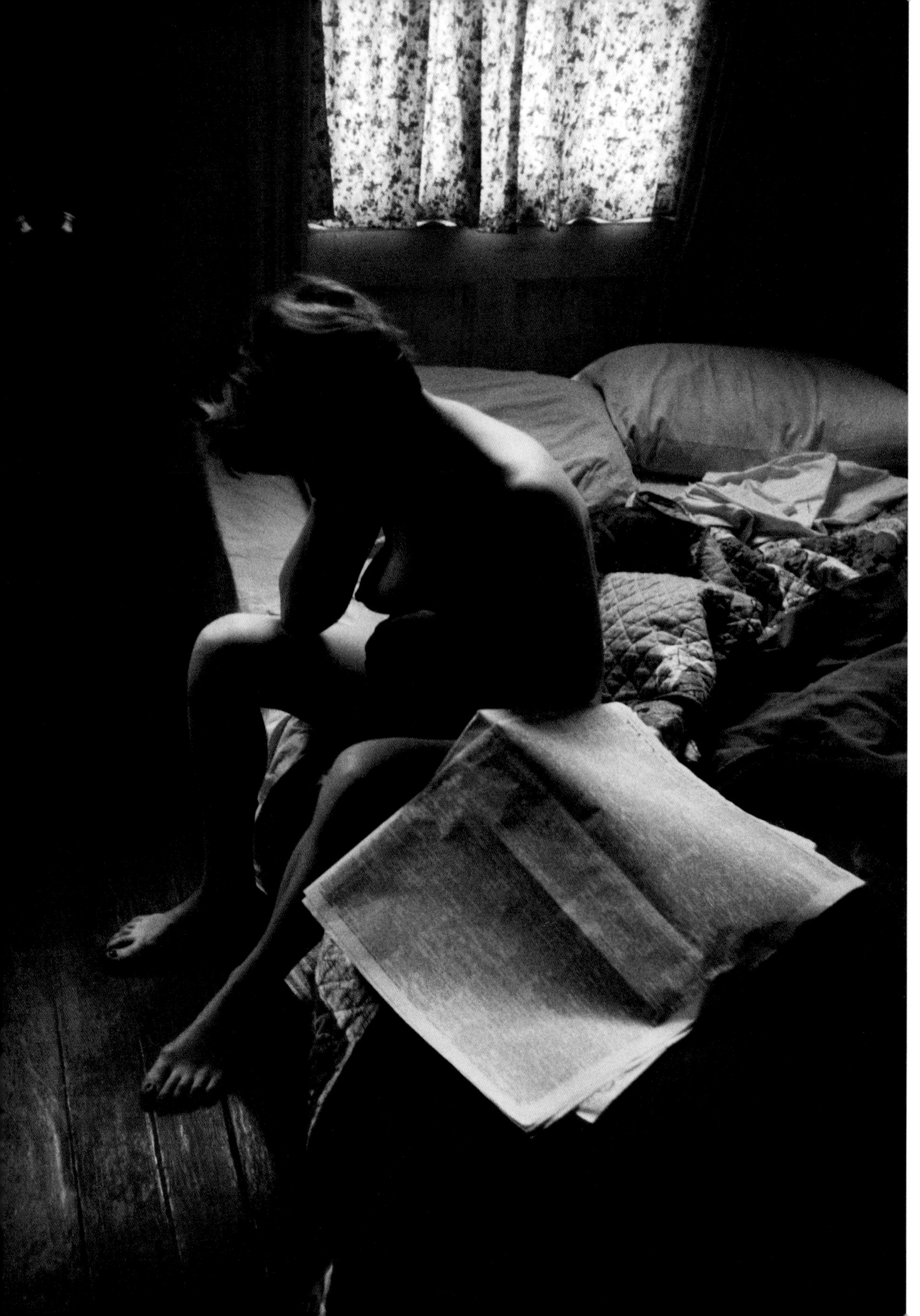

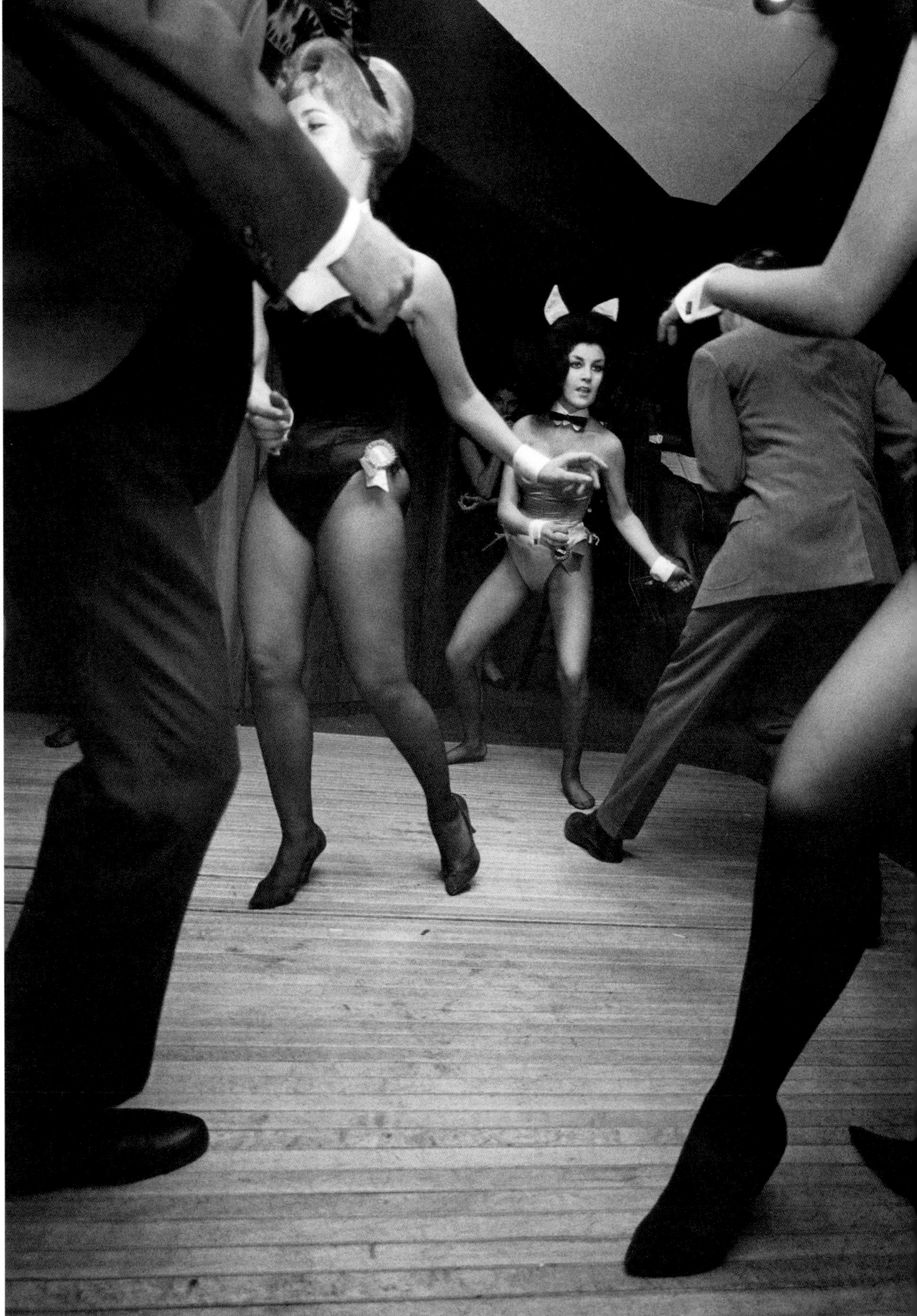

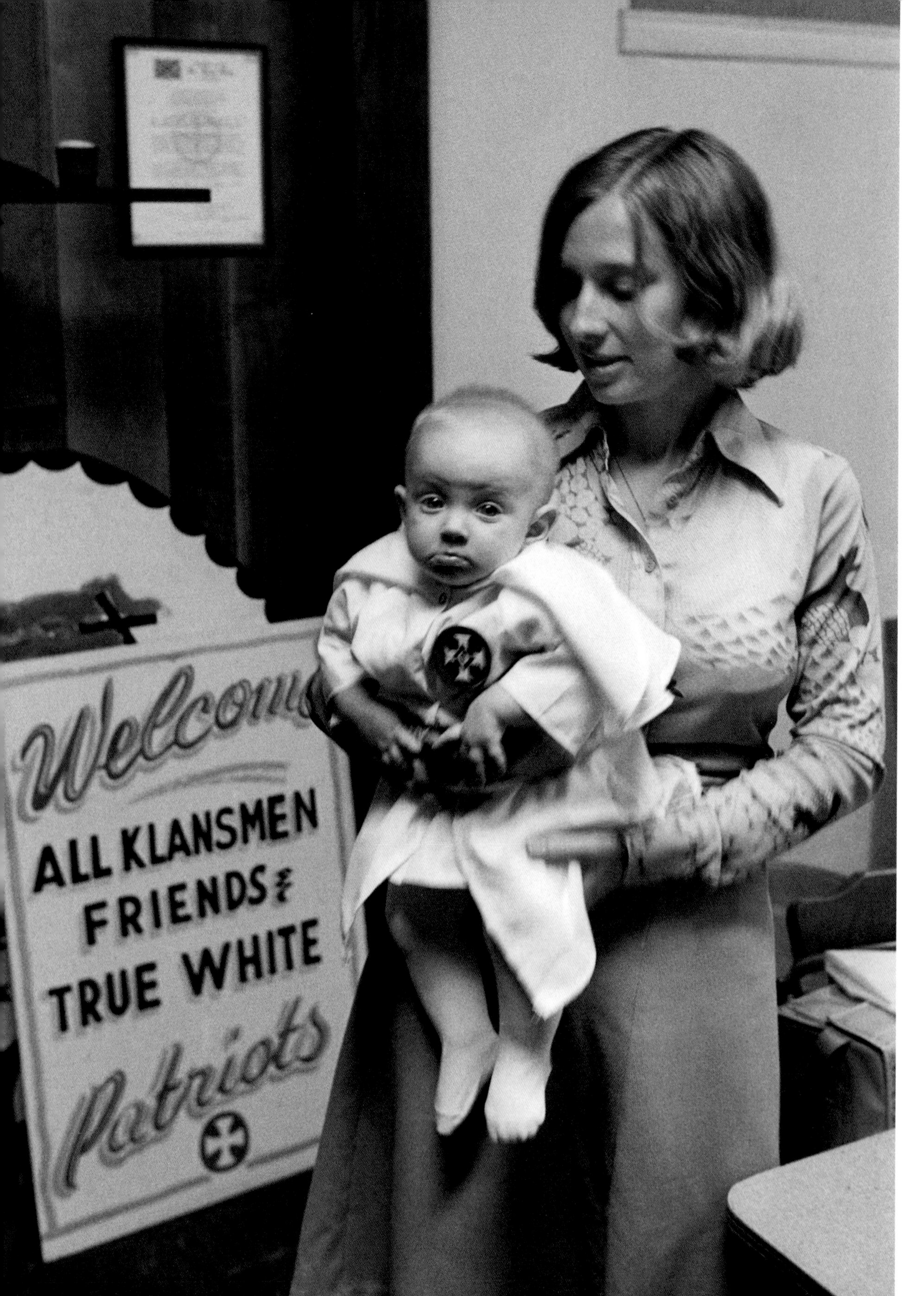

Welcome
ALL KLANSMEN
FRIENDS &
TRUE WHITE
Patriots

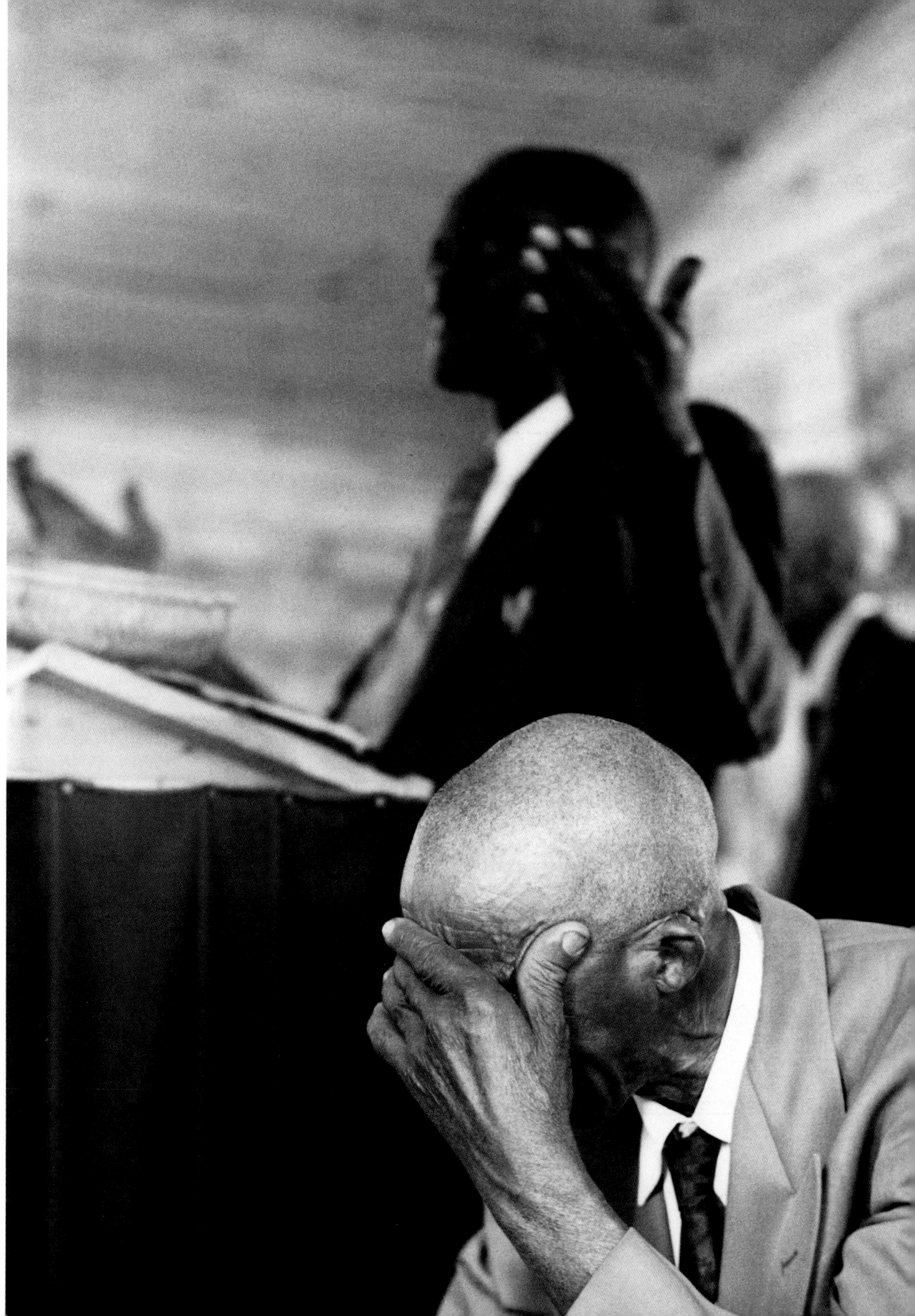

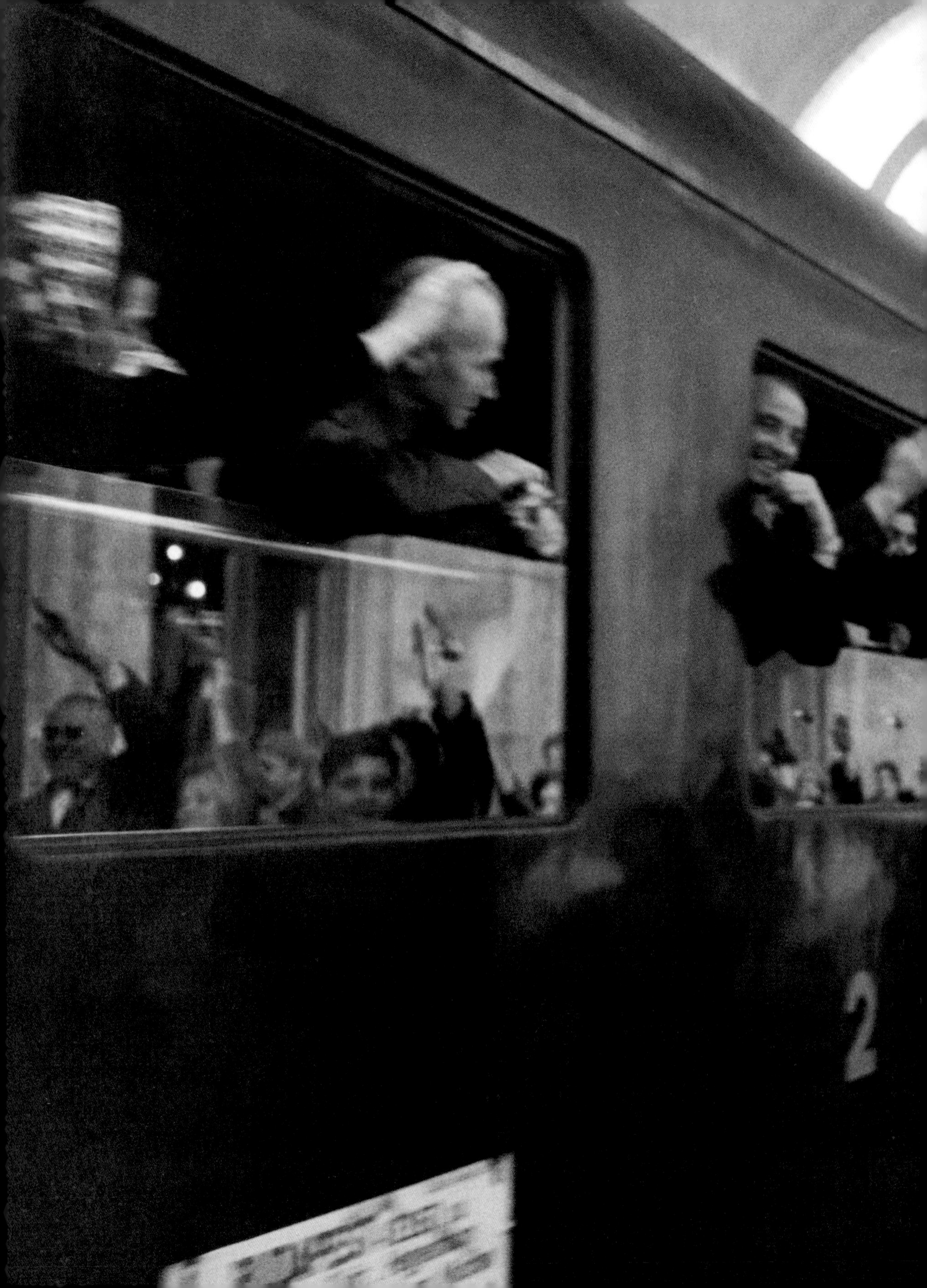

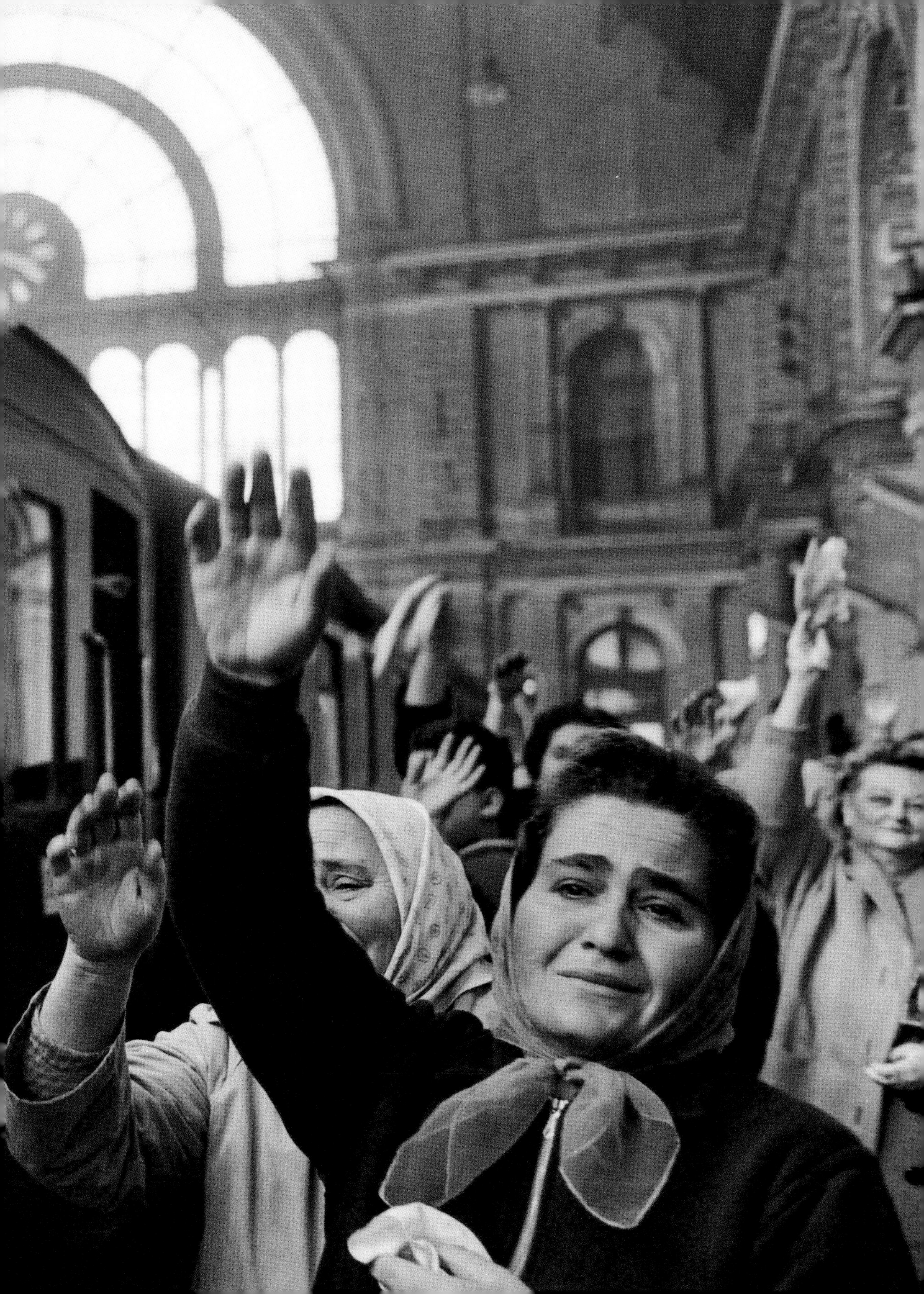

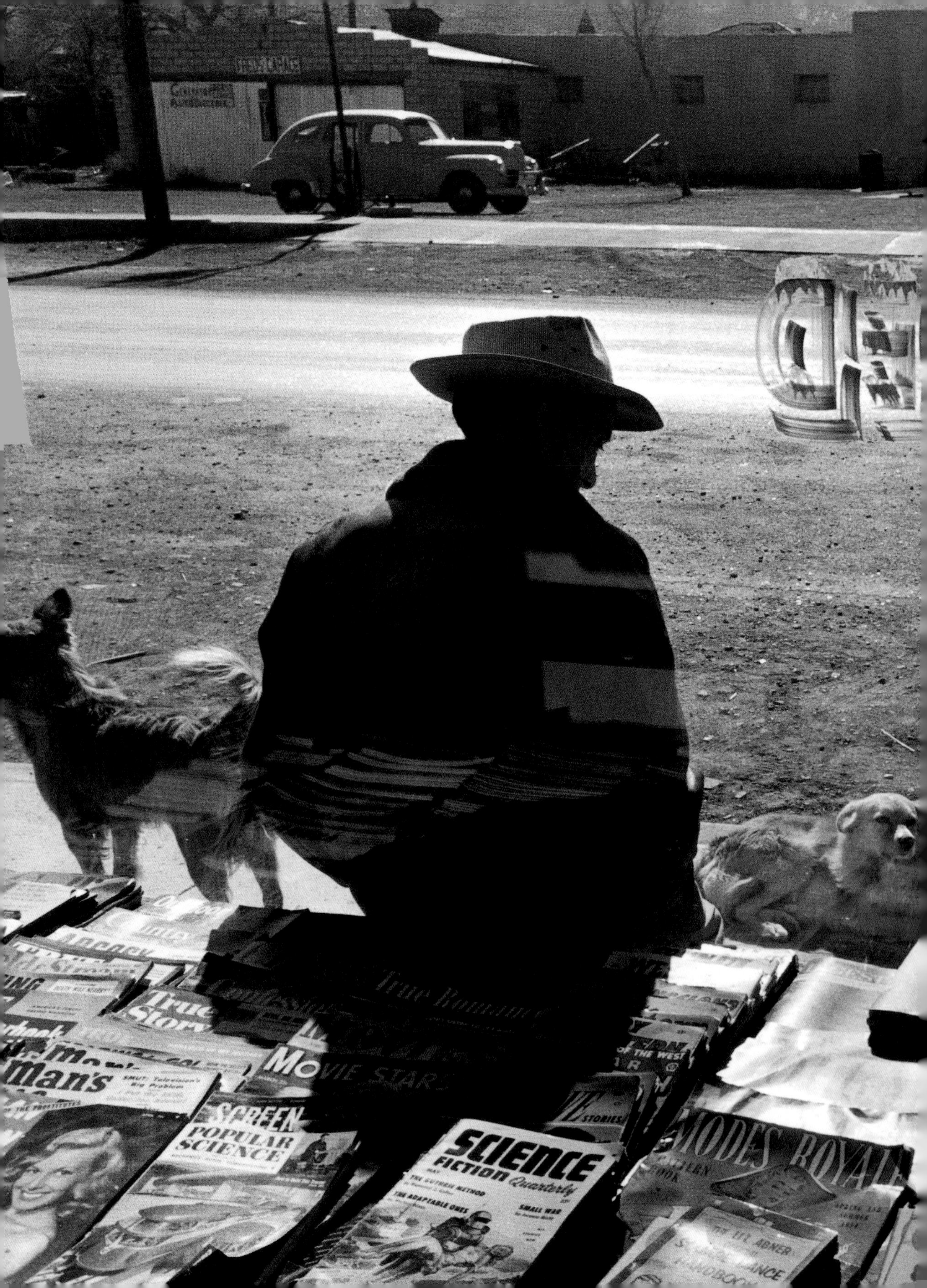
True
Story
Movie Stars
SCREEN
POPULAR
SCIENCE
SCIENCE
FICTION
Quarterly
THE ADAPTABLE ONES
SMALL WAR
MODES ROYAL

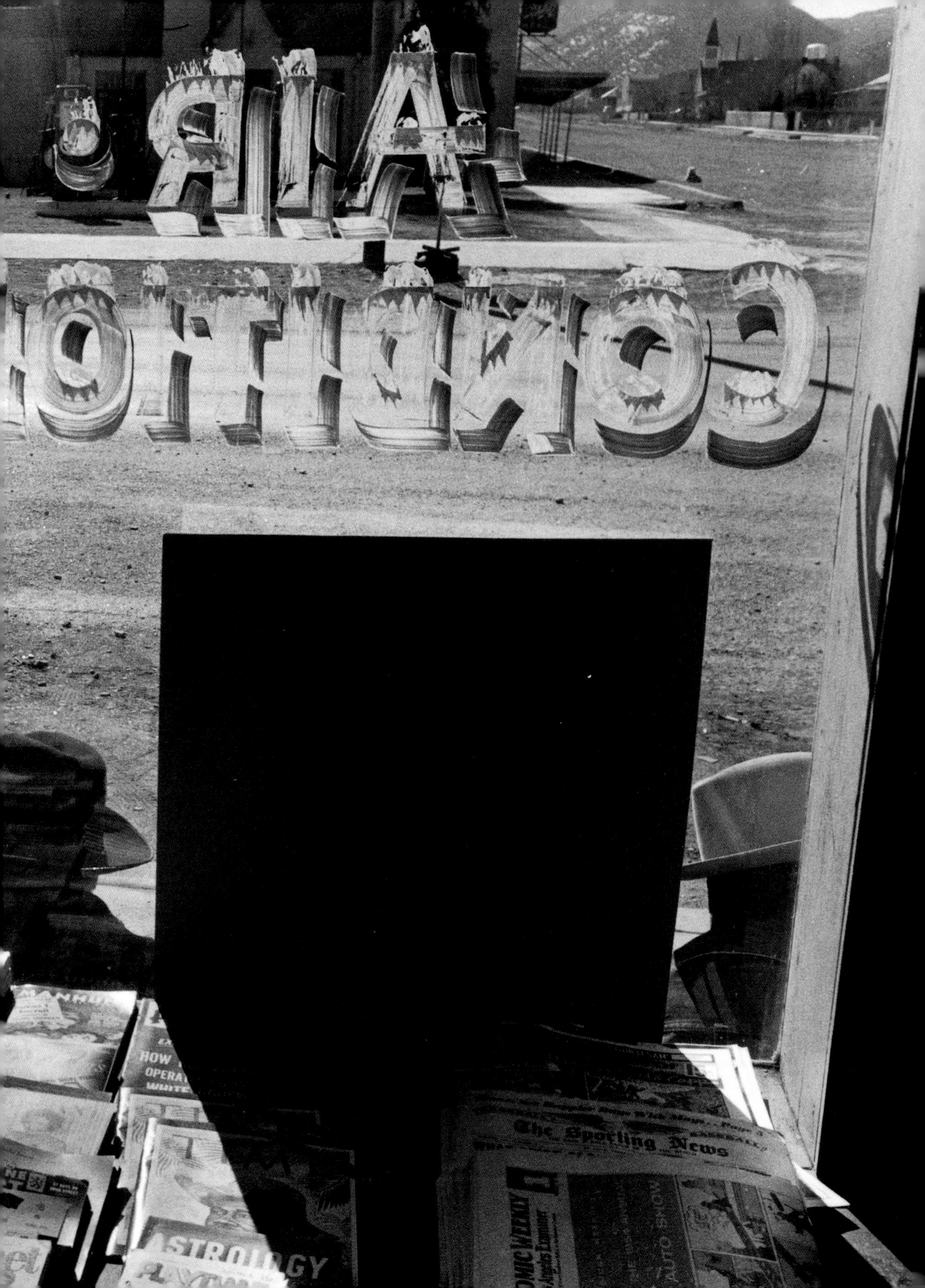
AIR
CONDITIO
The Sporting News
ASTROLOGY
COMIC WEEKLY
Los Angeles Examiner

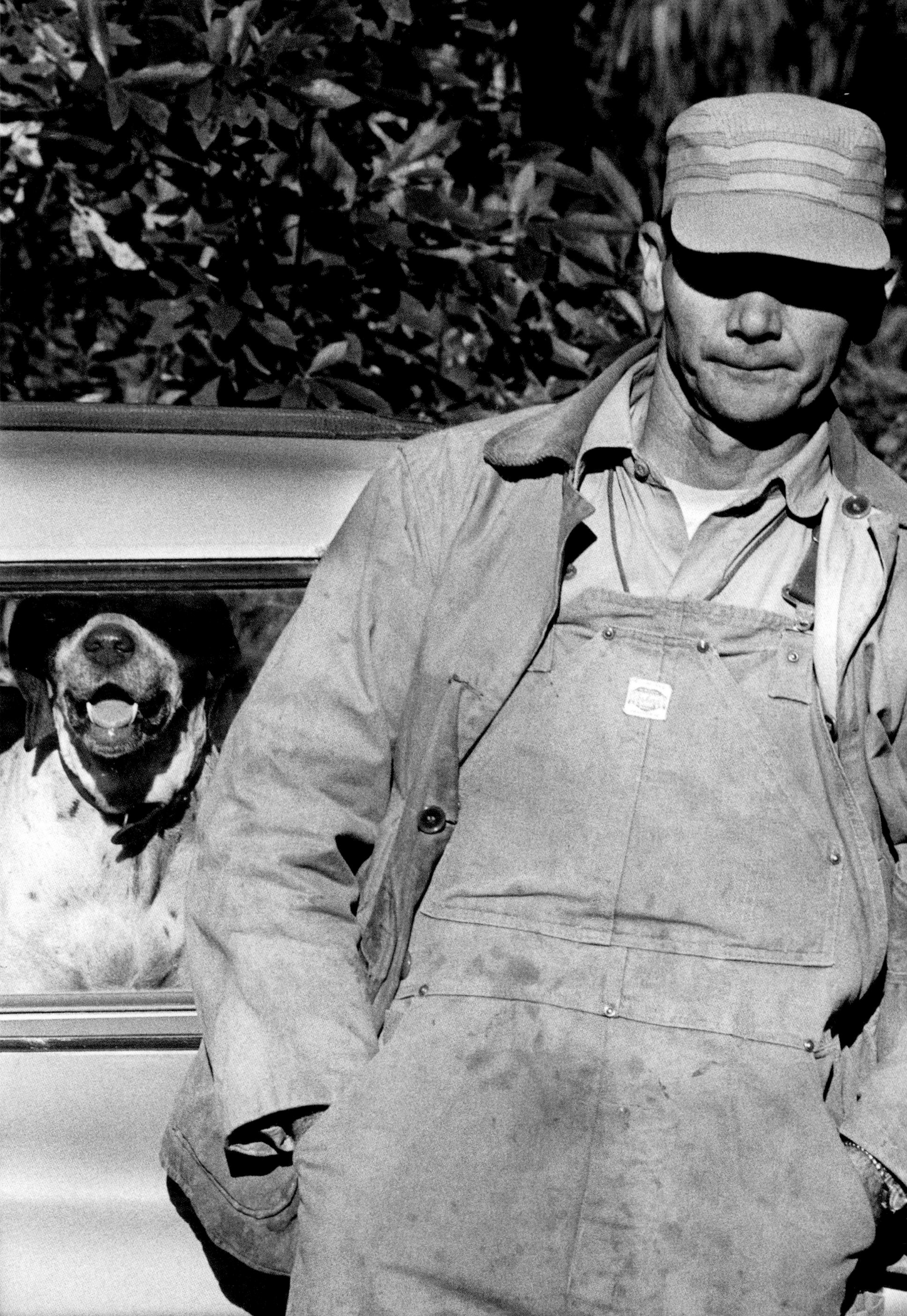

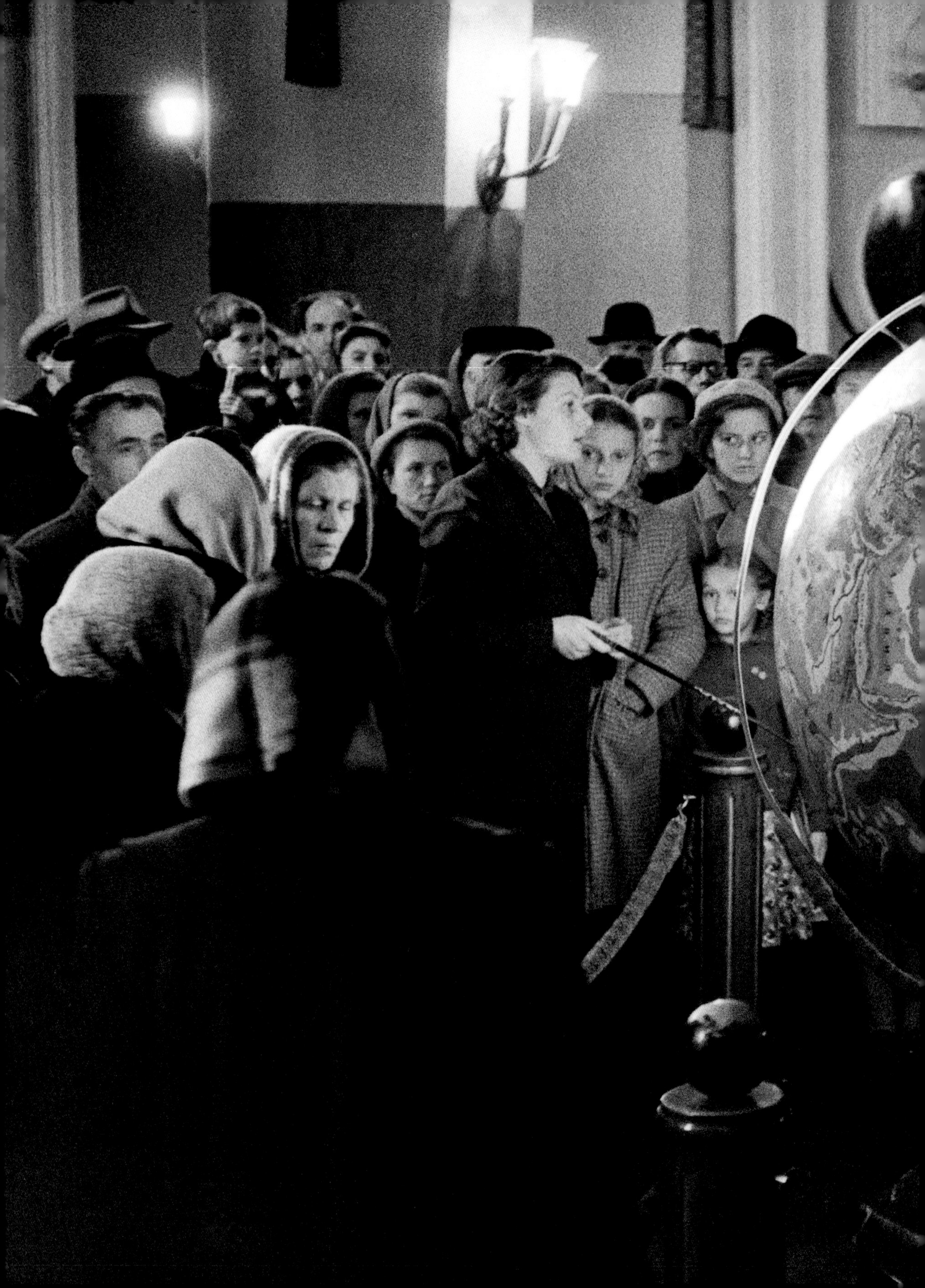

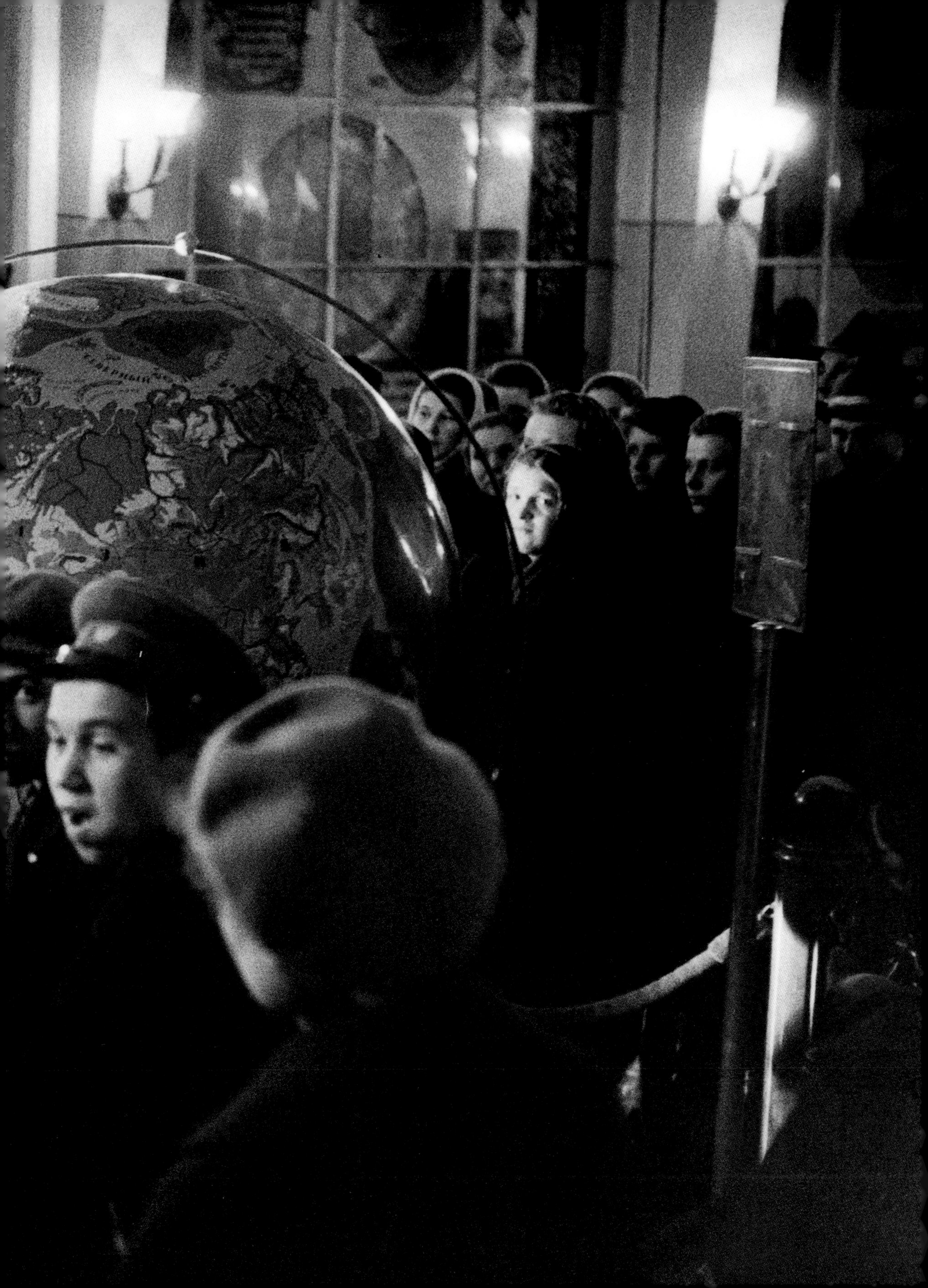

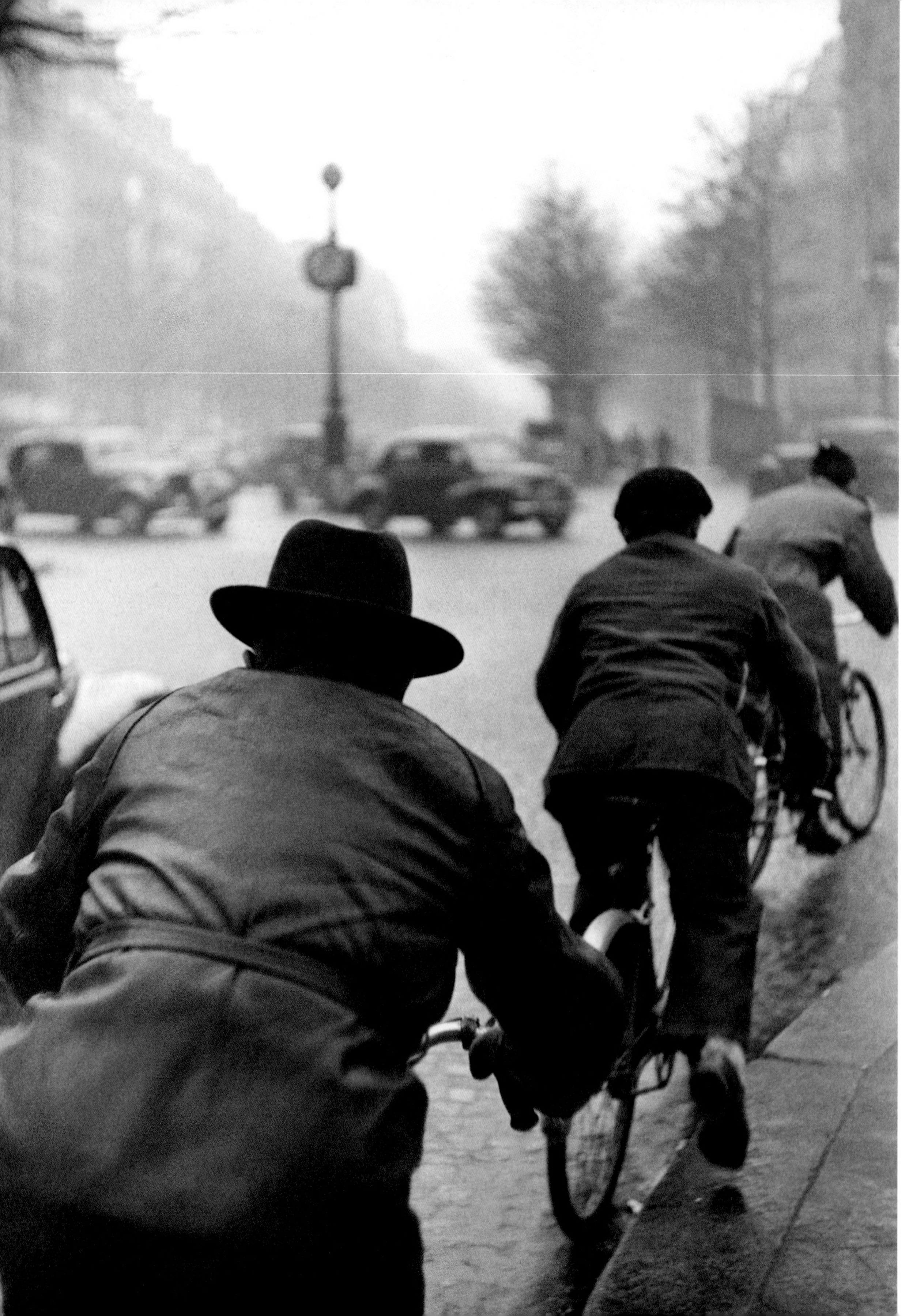

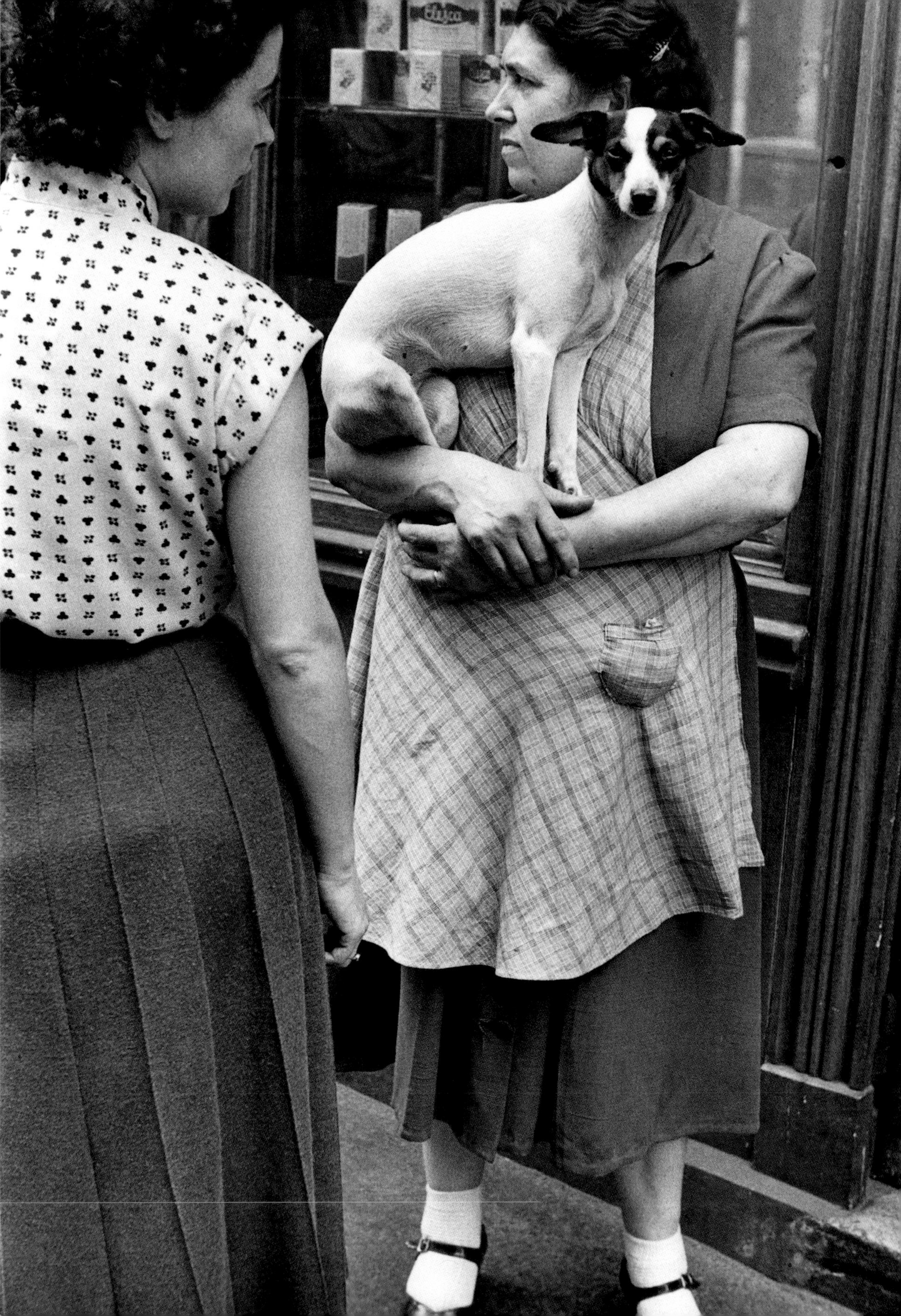

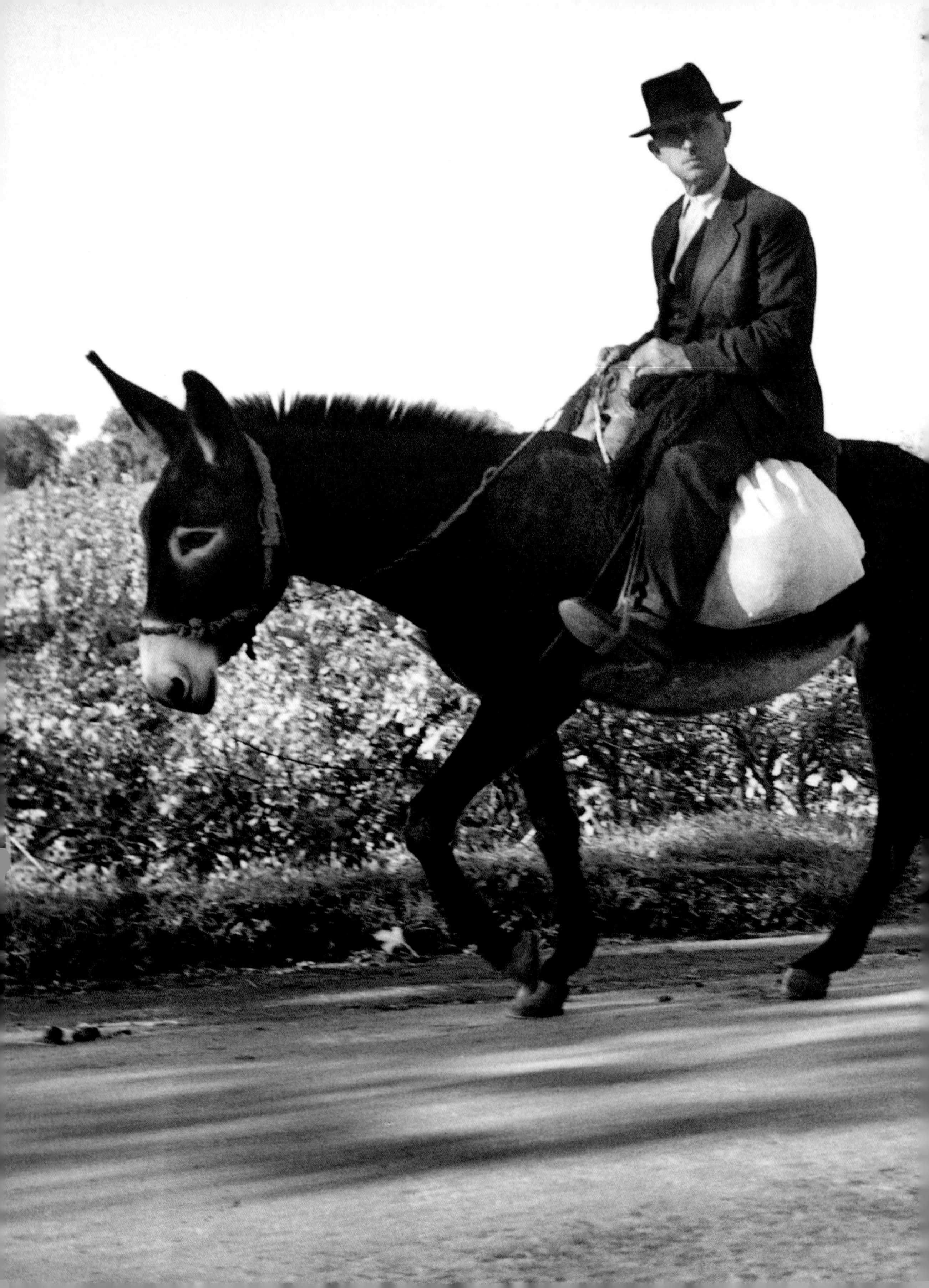

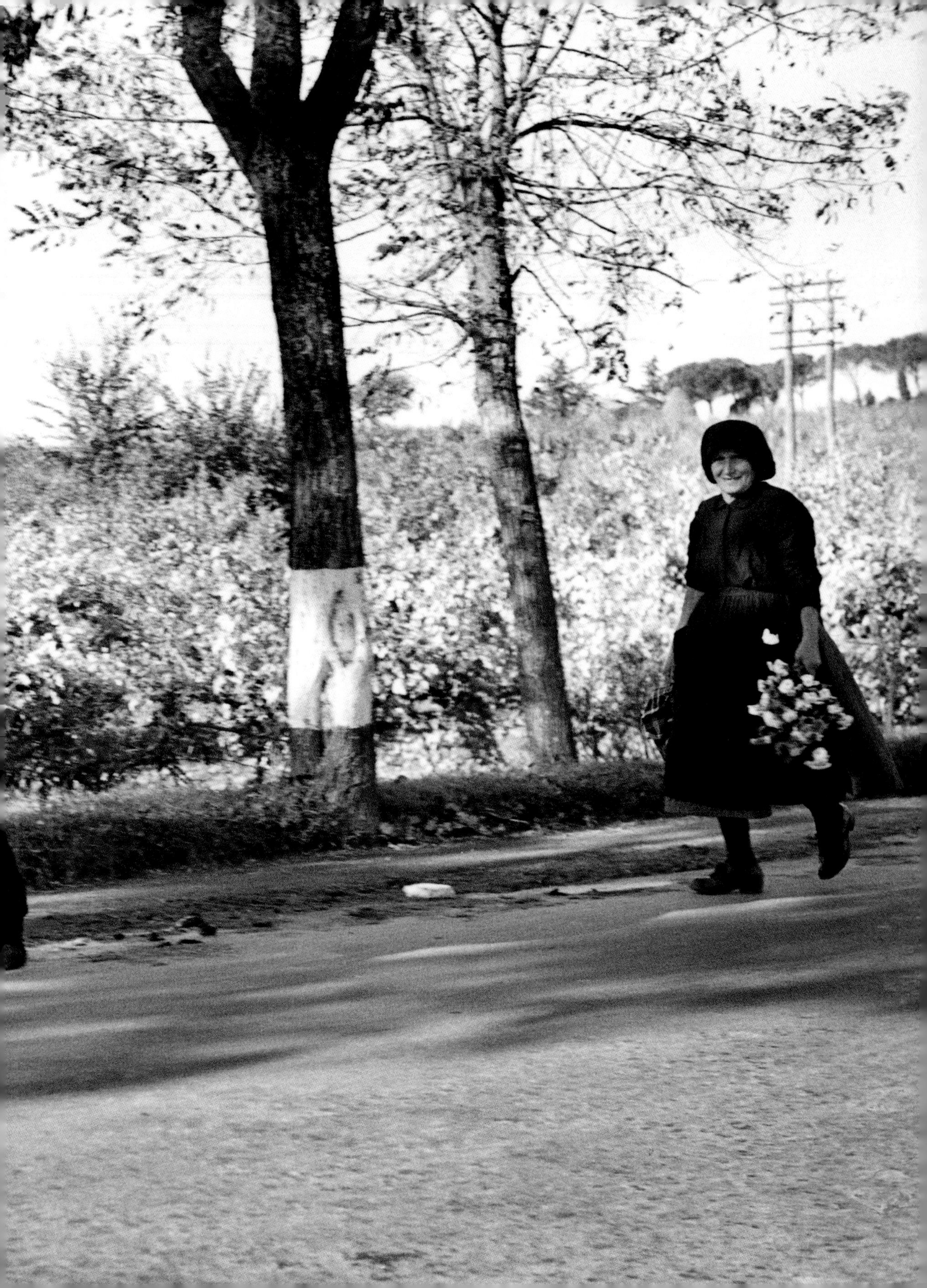

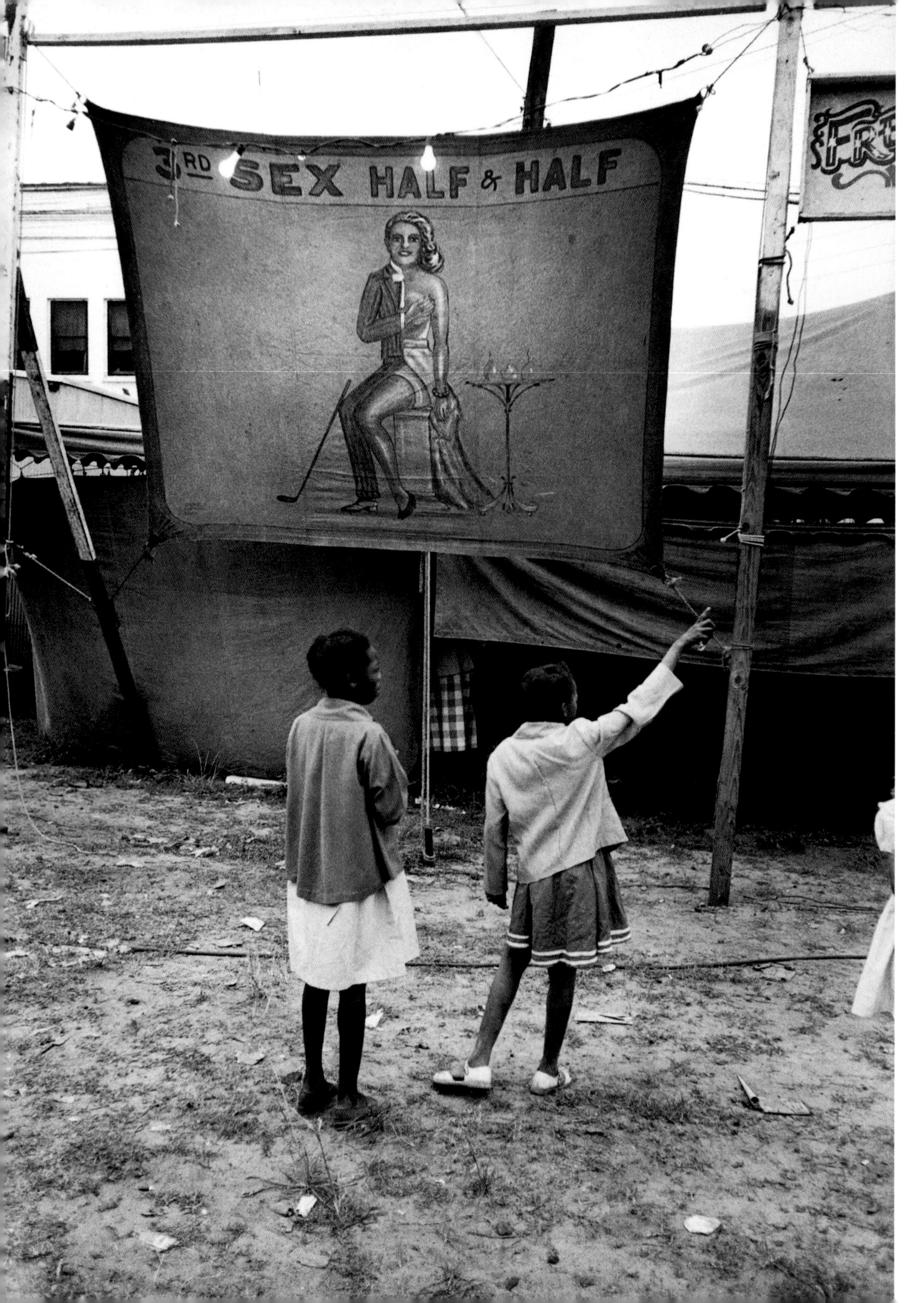
3RD SEX HALF & HALF

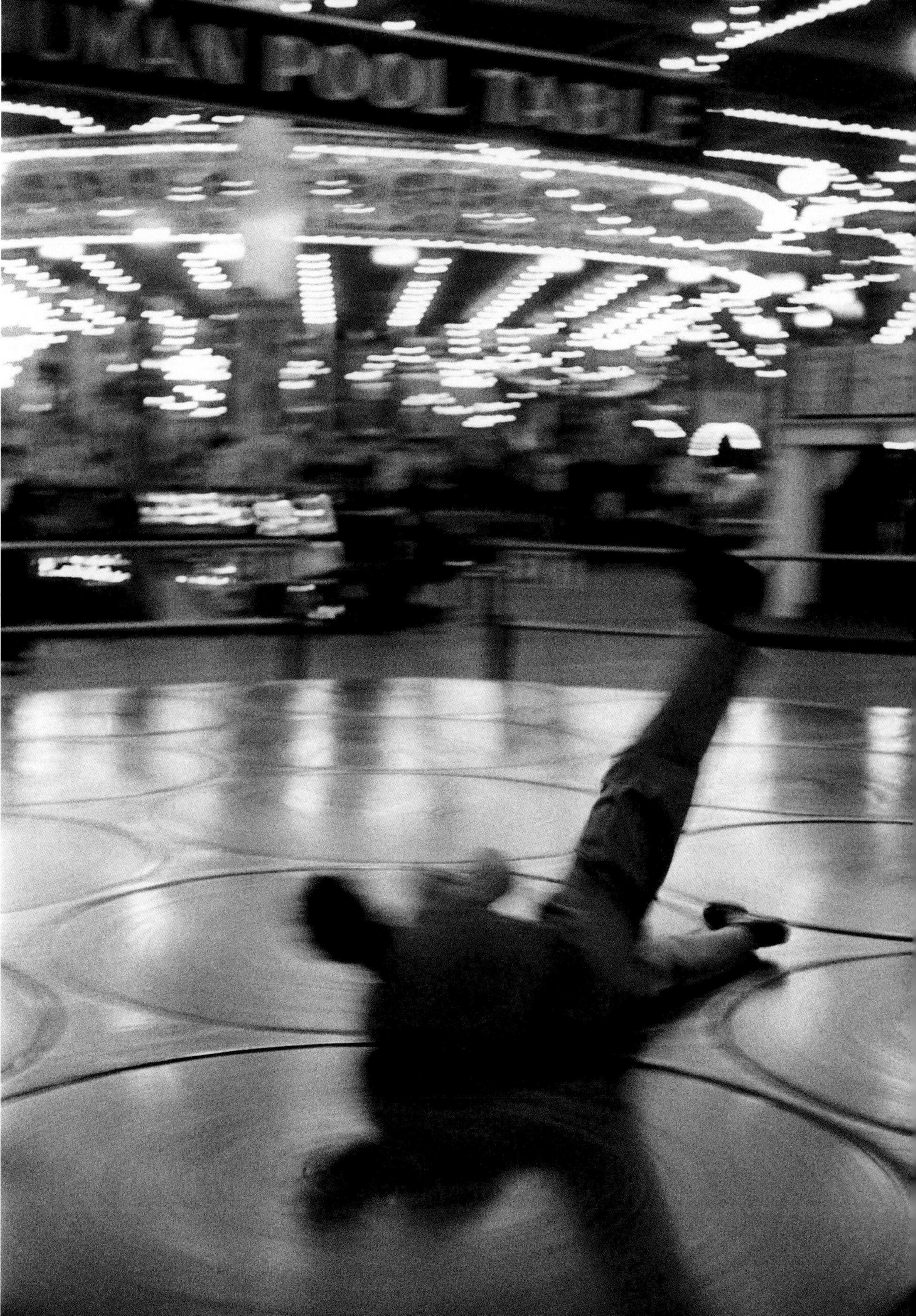

MAN POOL TABLE

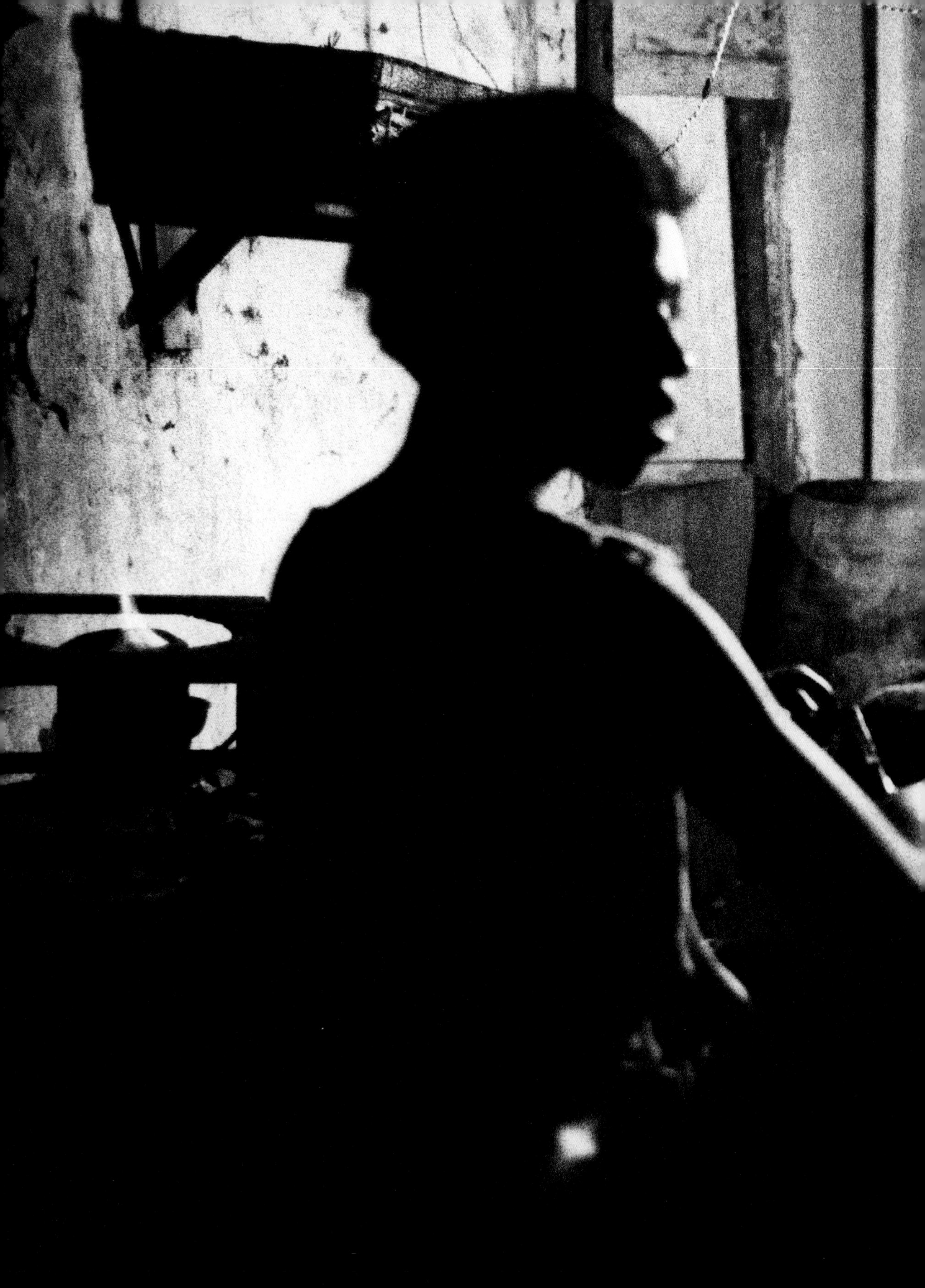

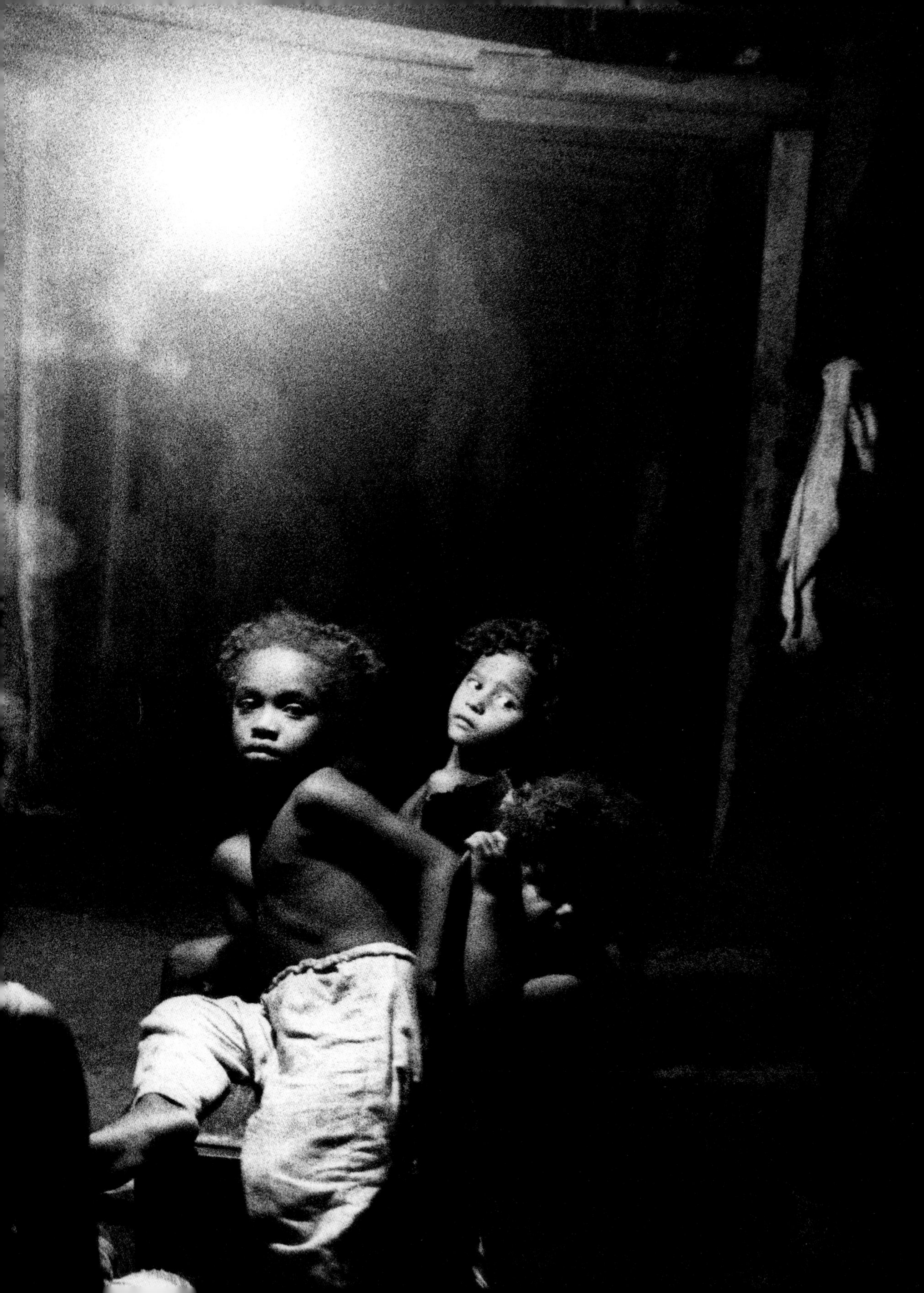

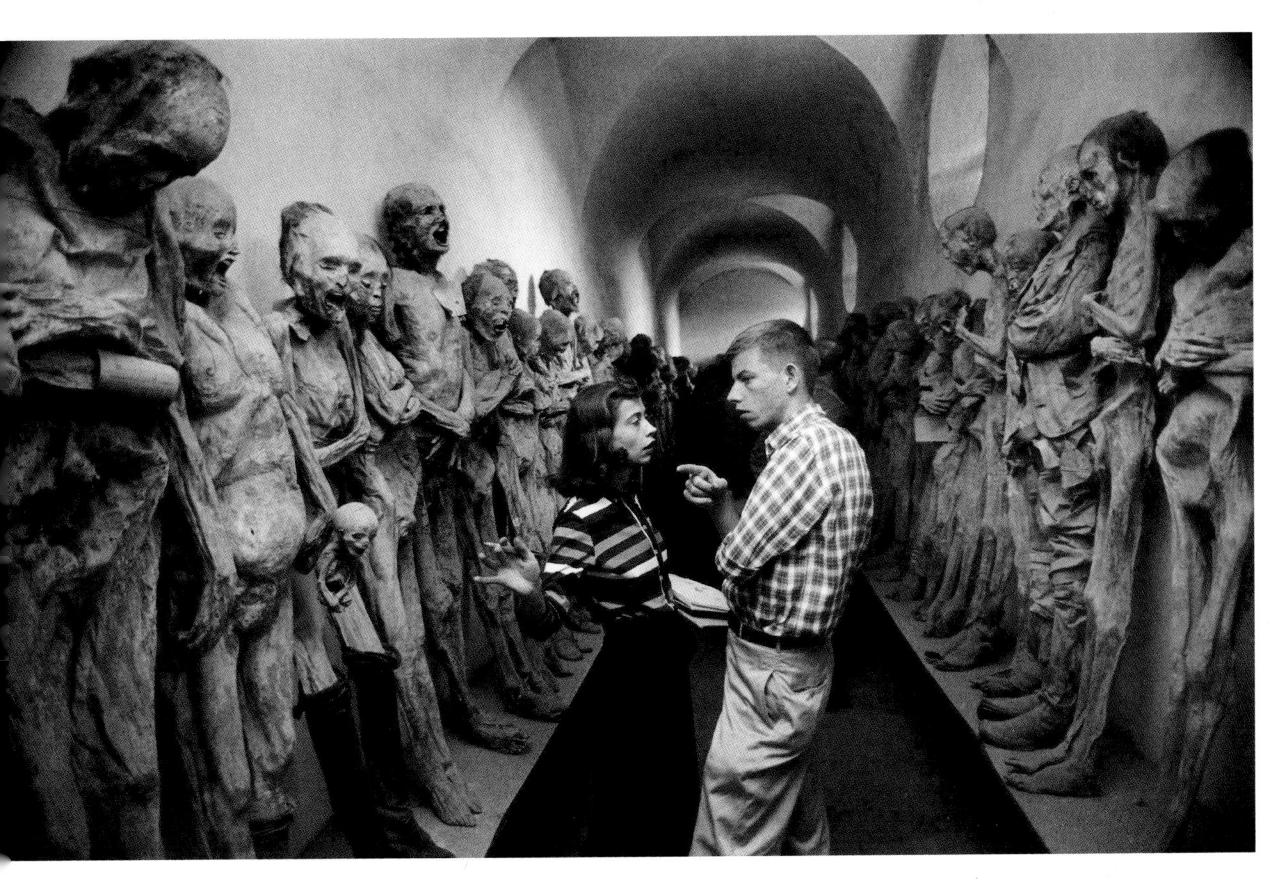

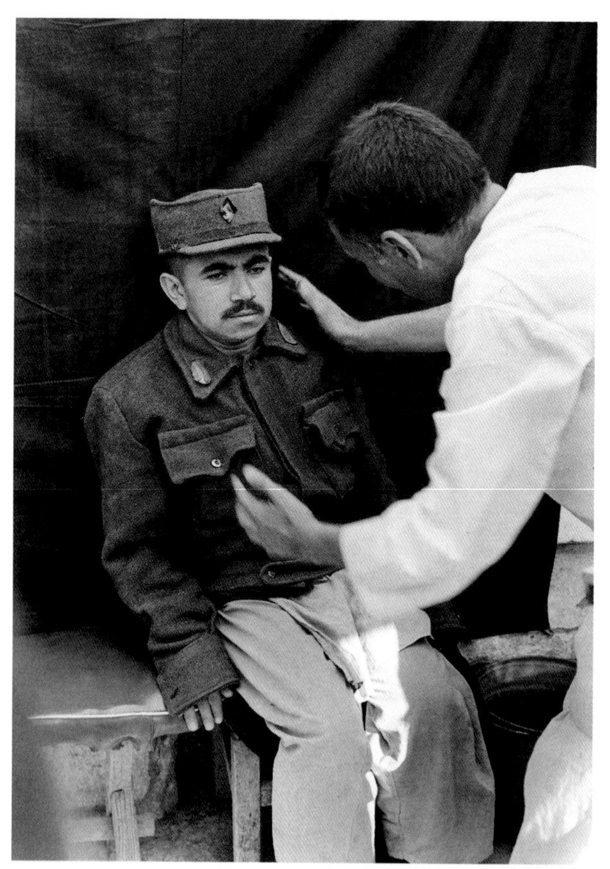
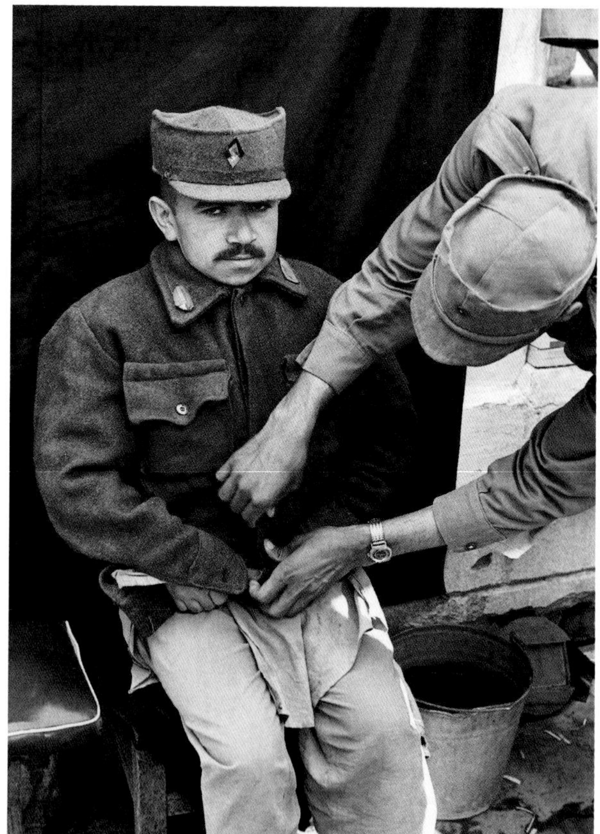
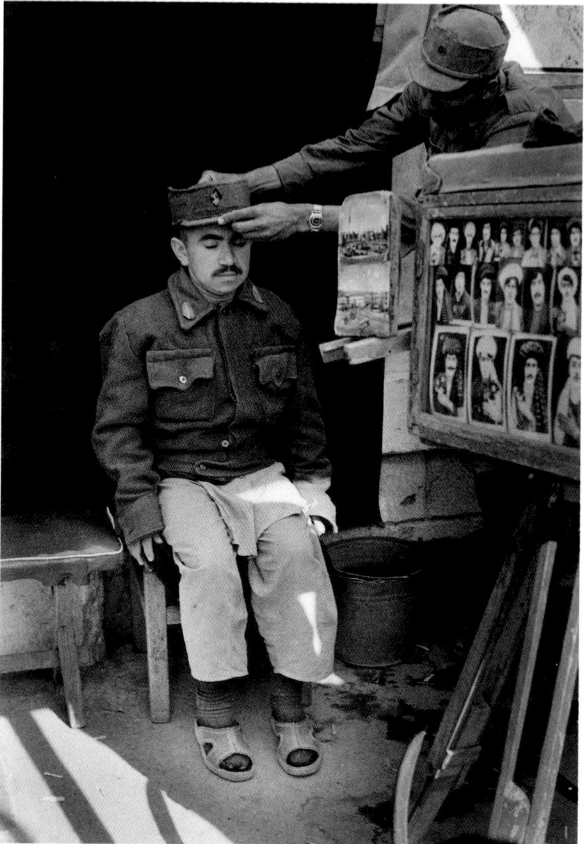
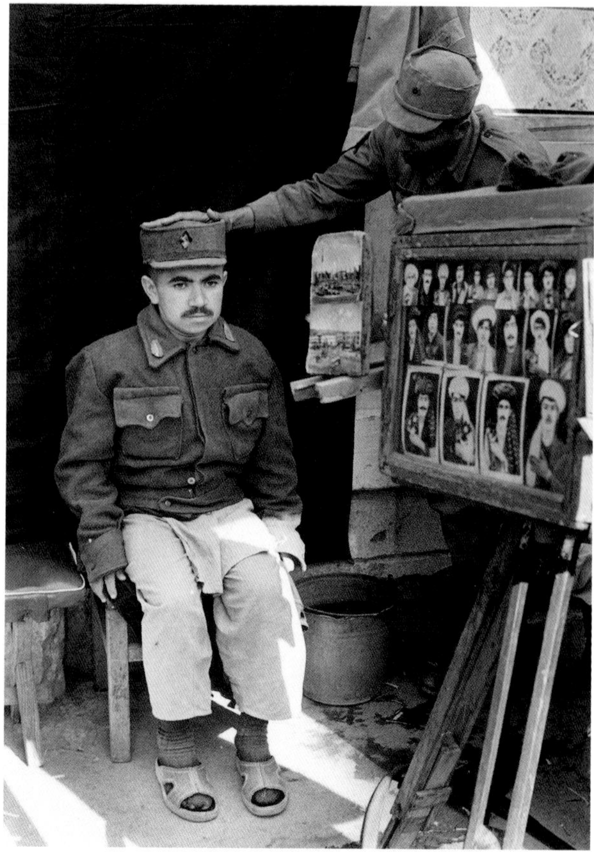

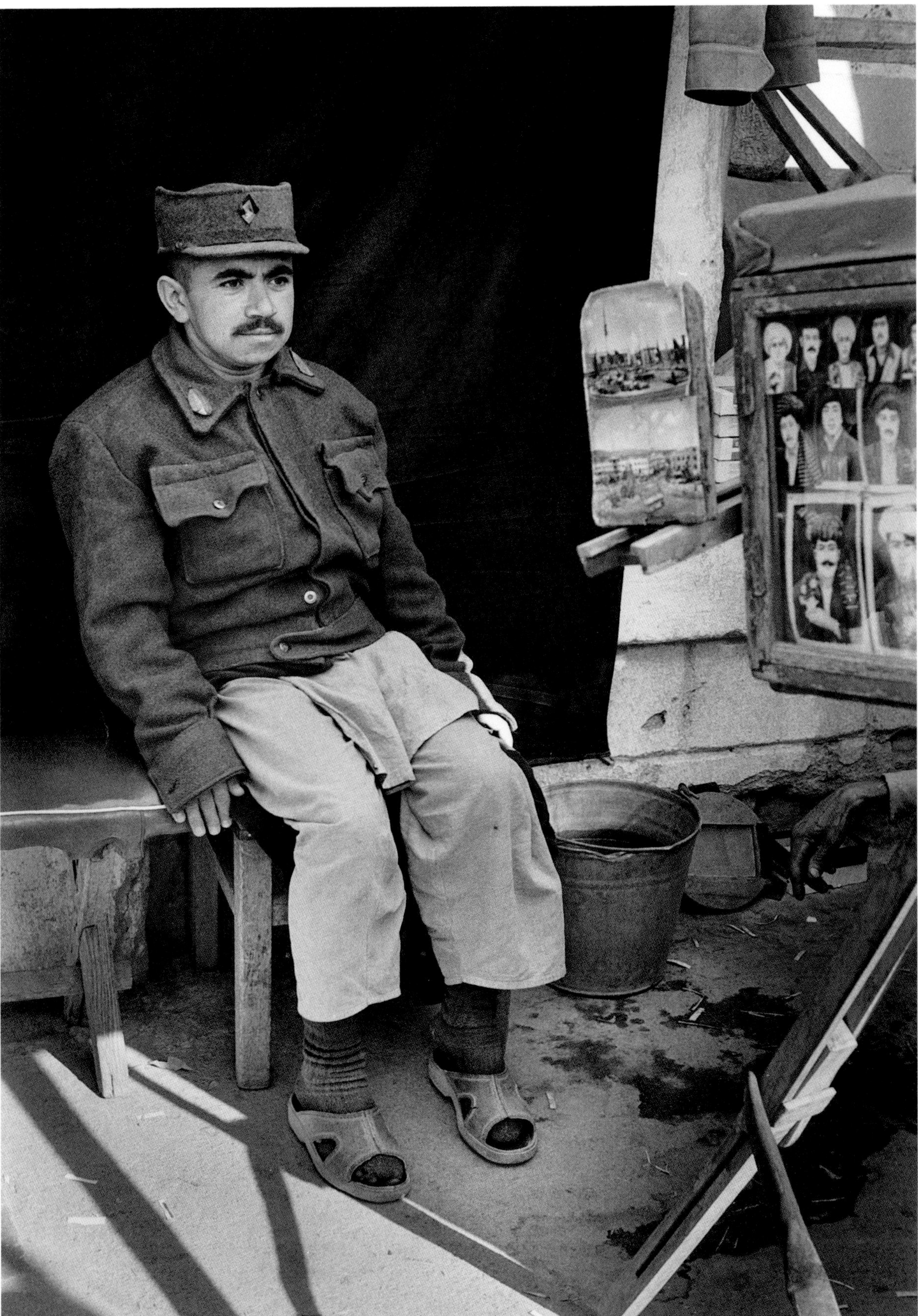

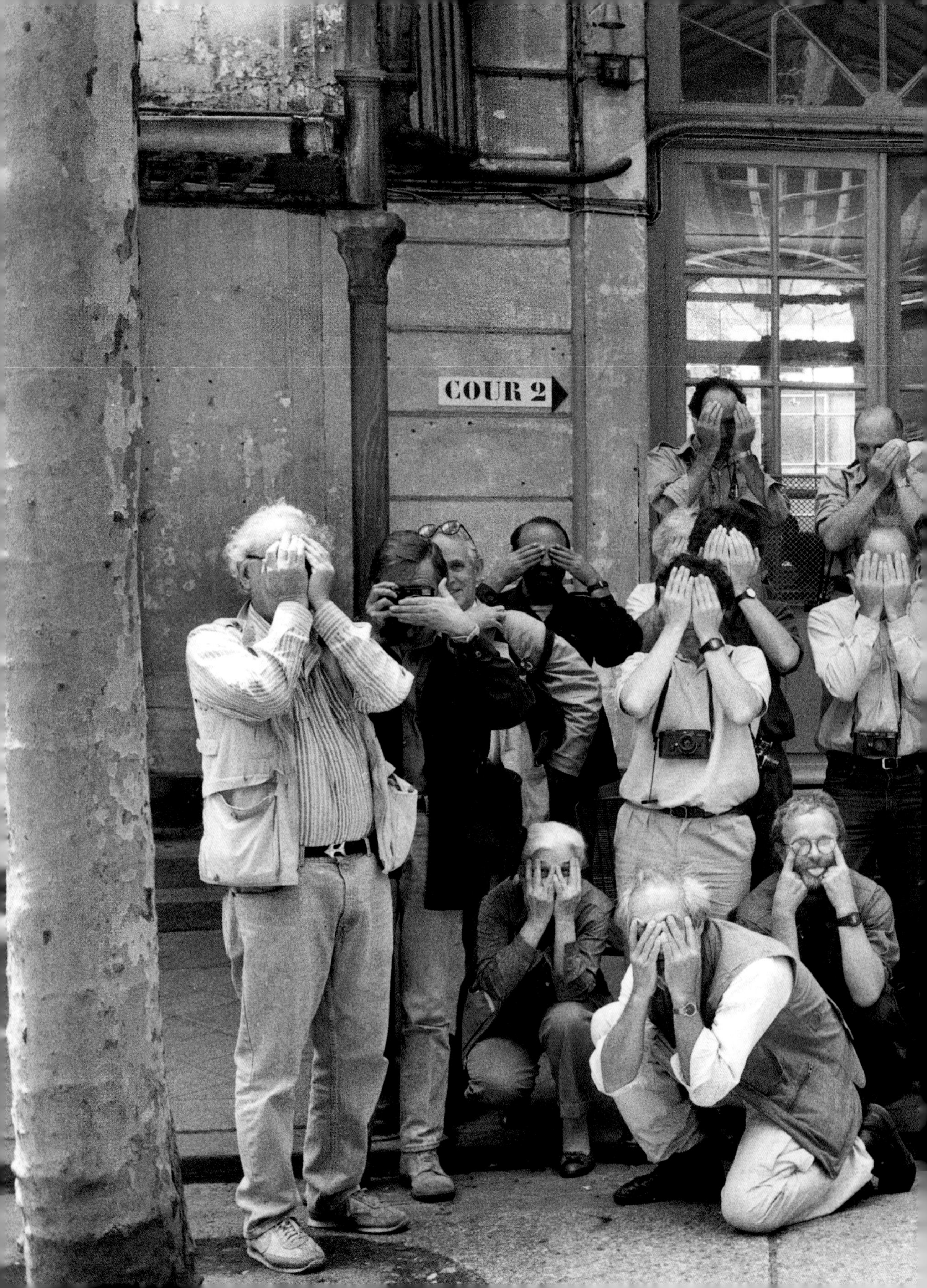
COUR 2

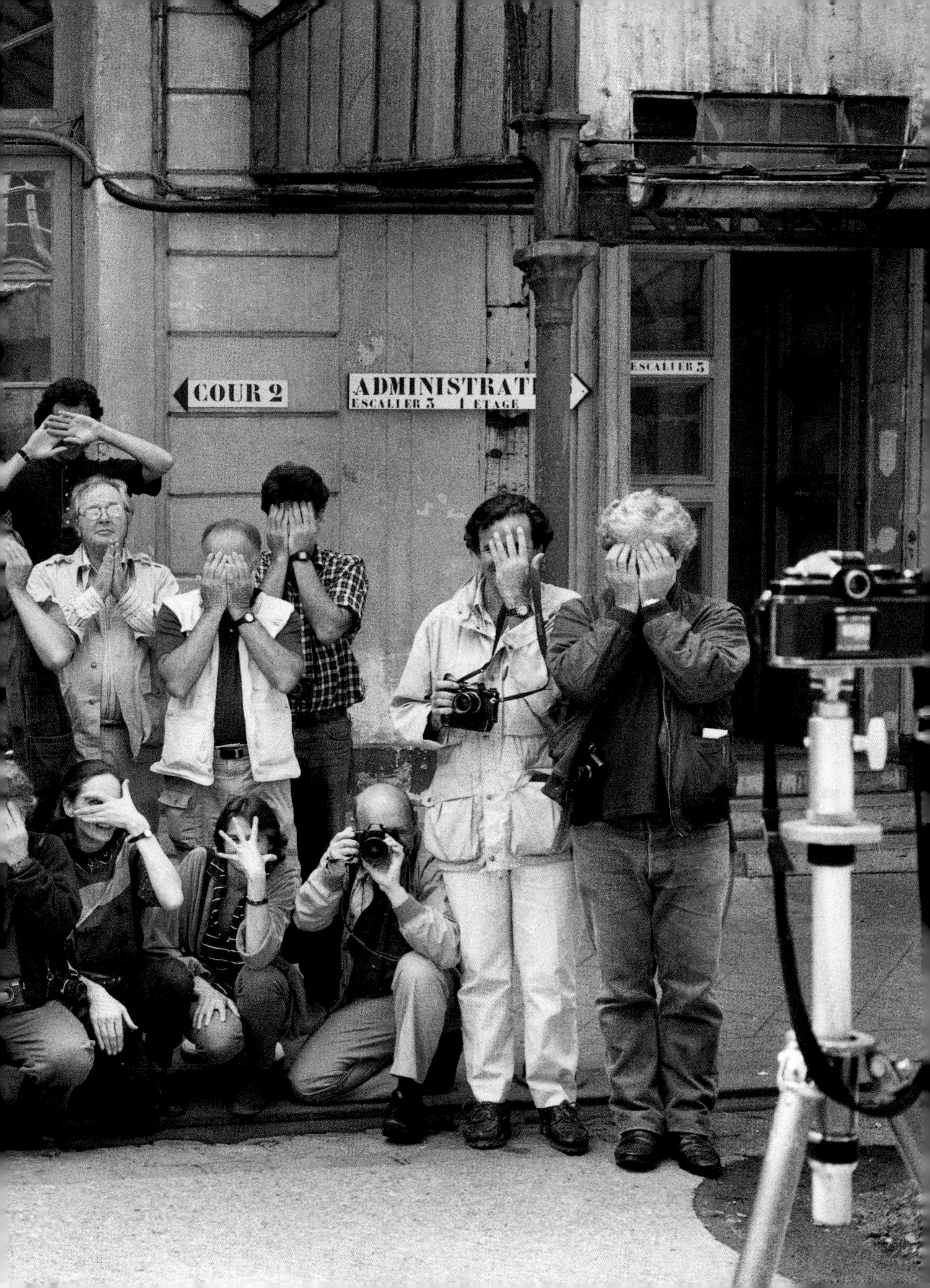

◄ COUR 2
ADMINISTRATION ►
ESCALIER 3   1 ETAGE
ESCALIER 5

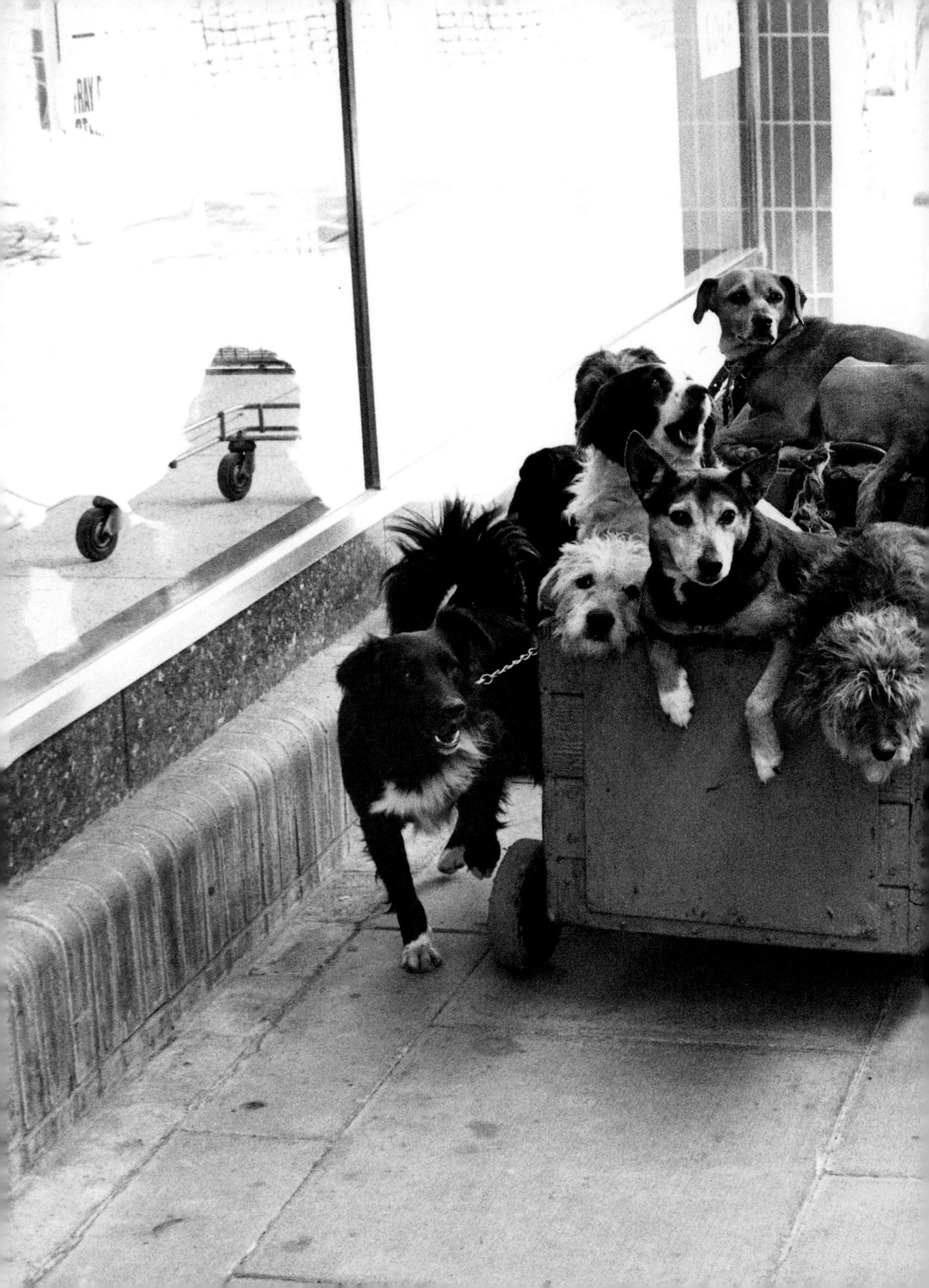

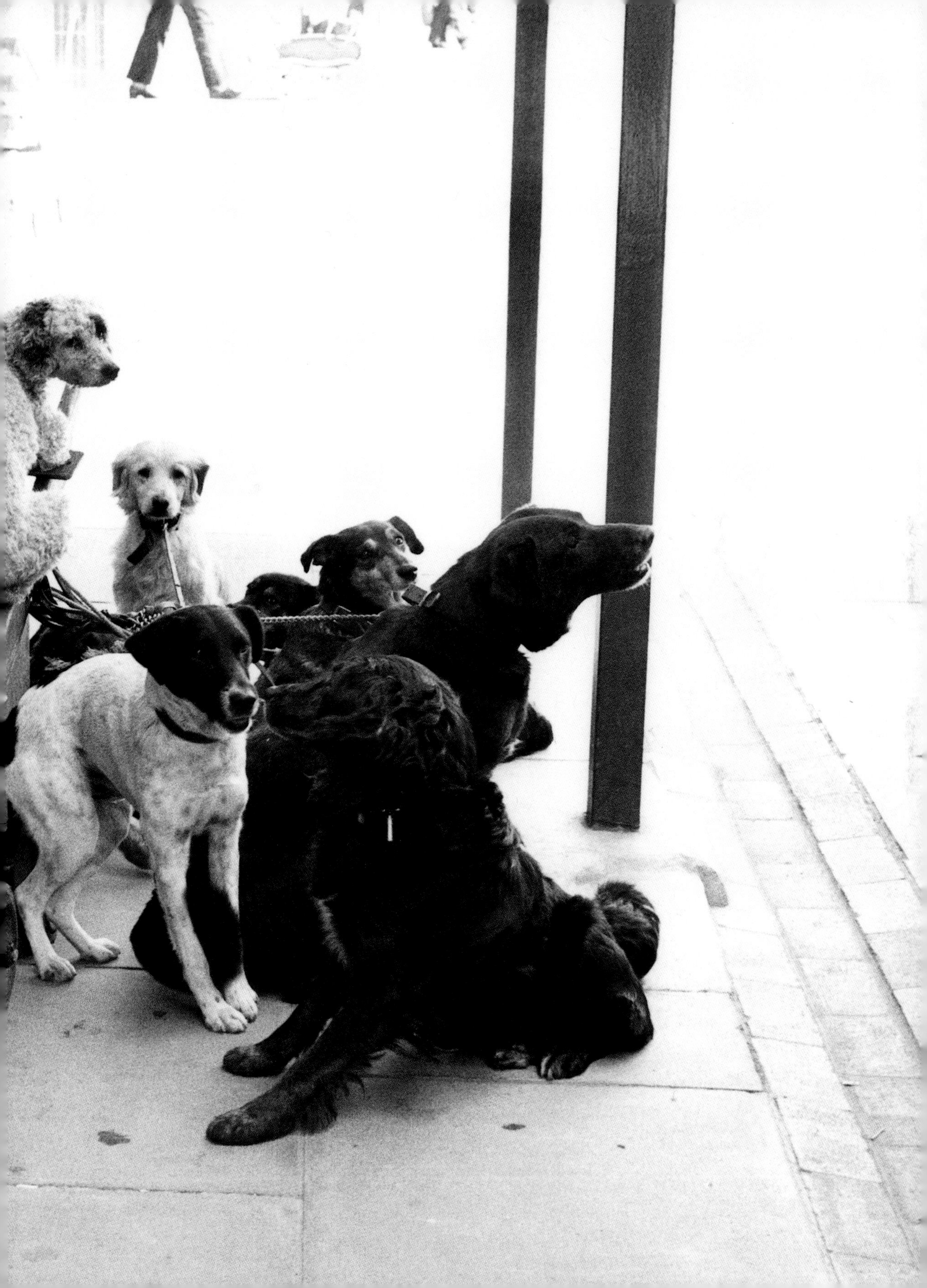

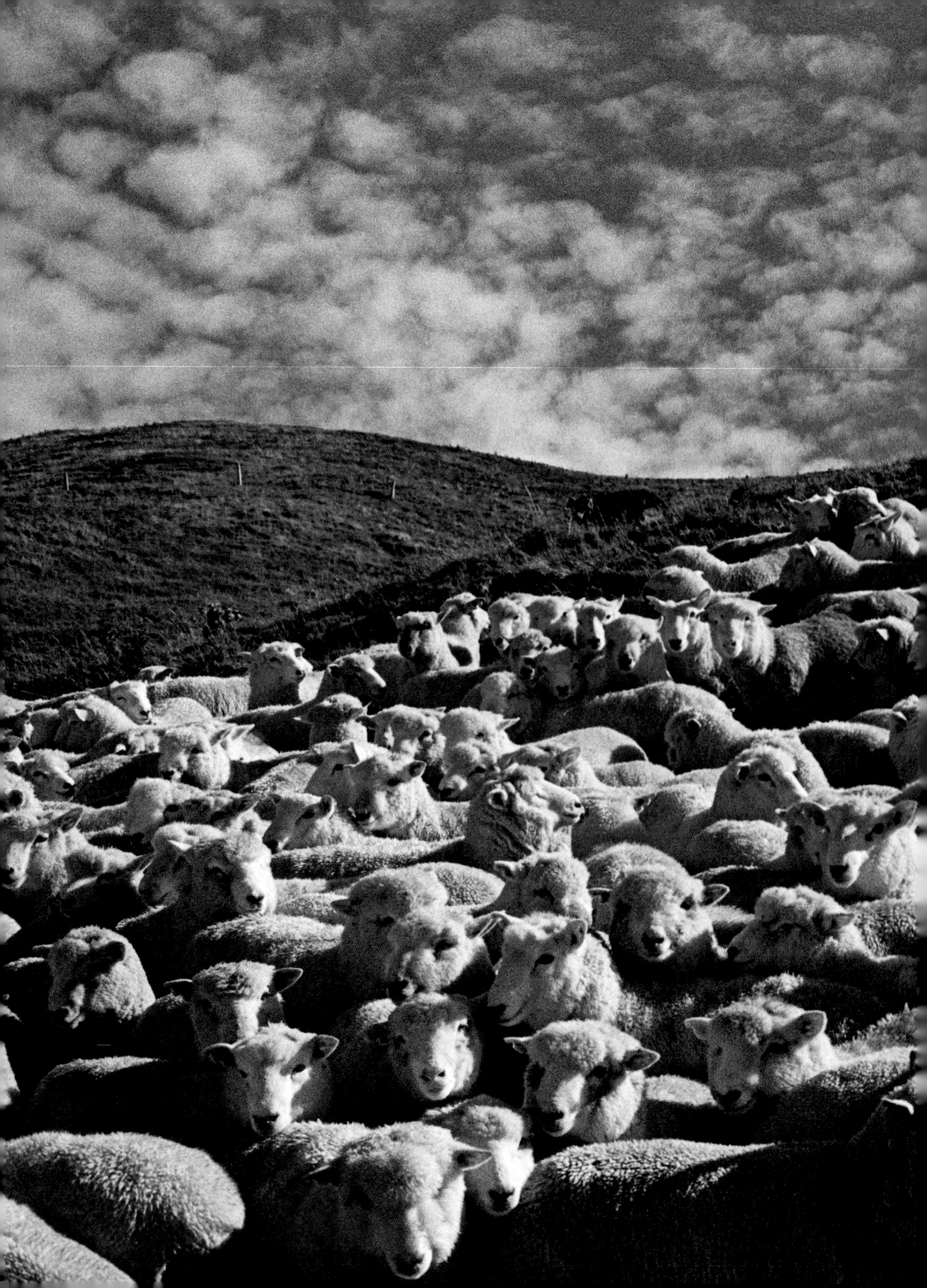

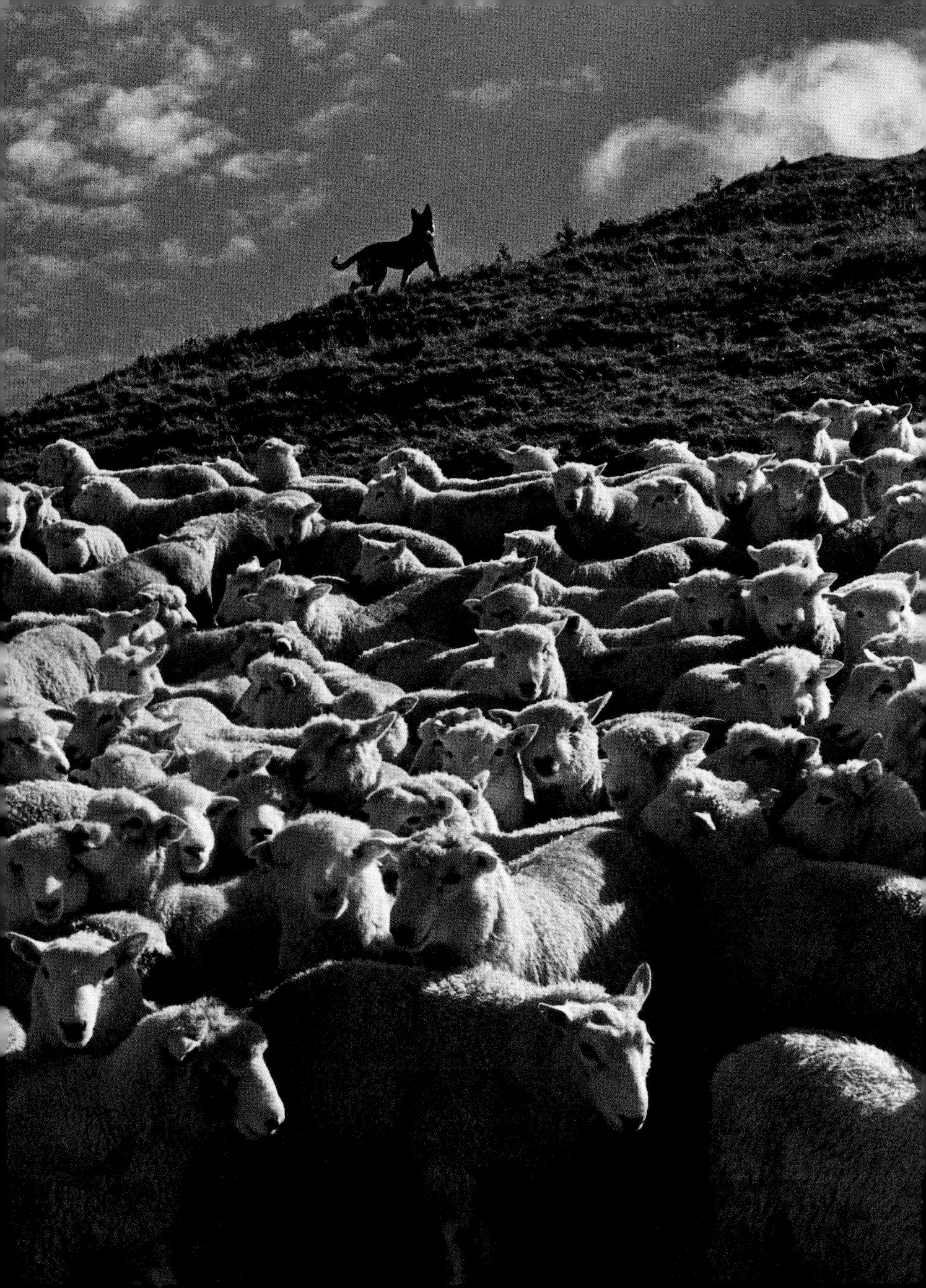

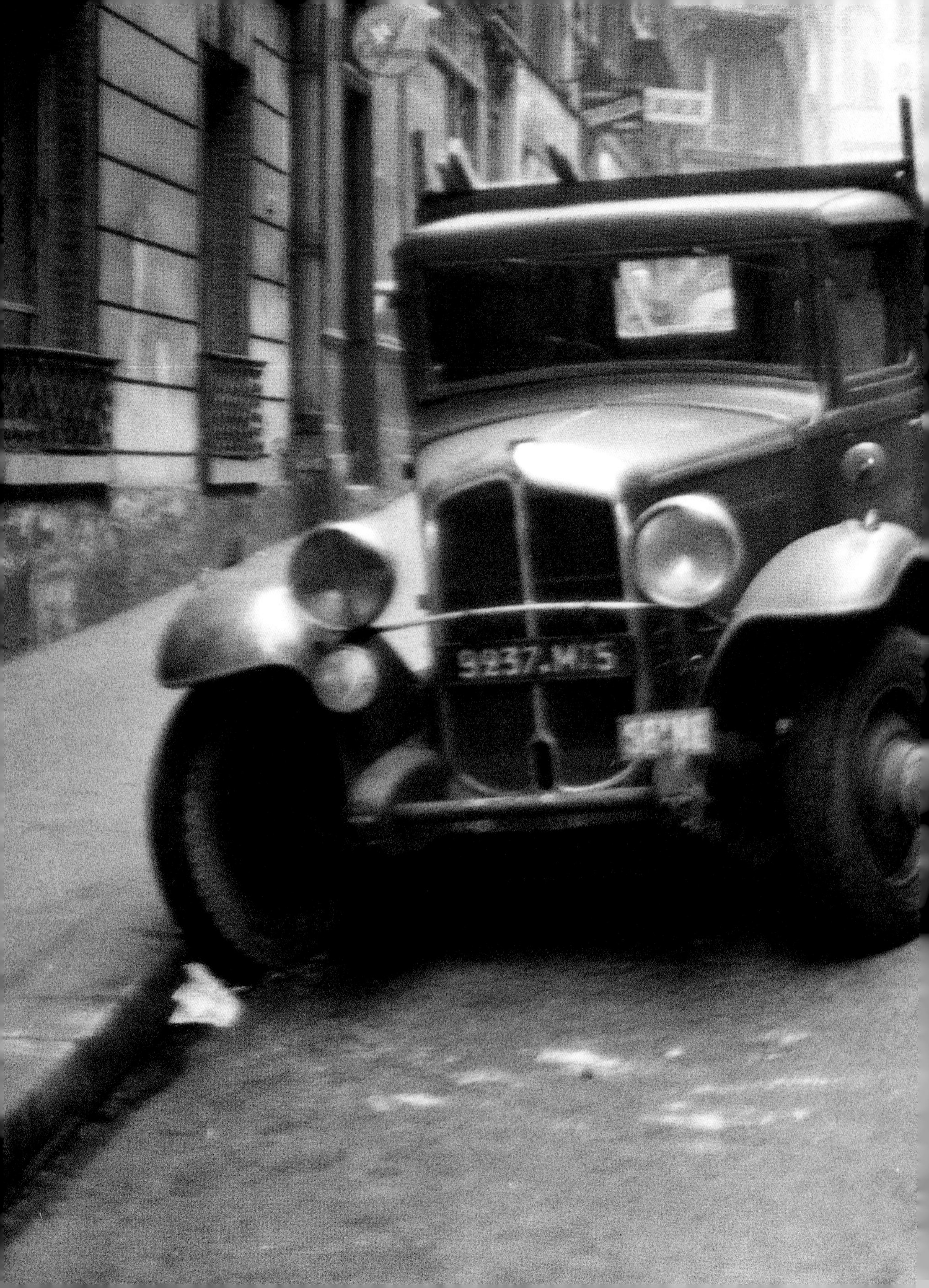
9937 M 5

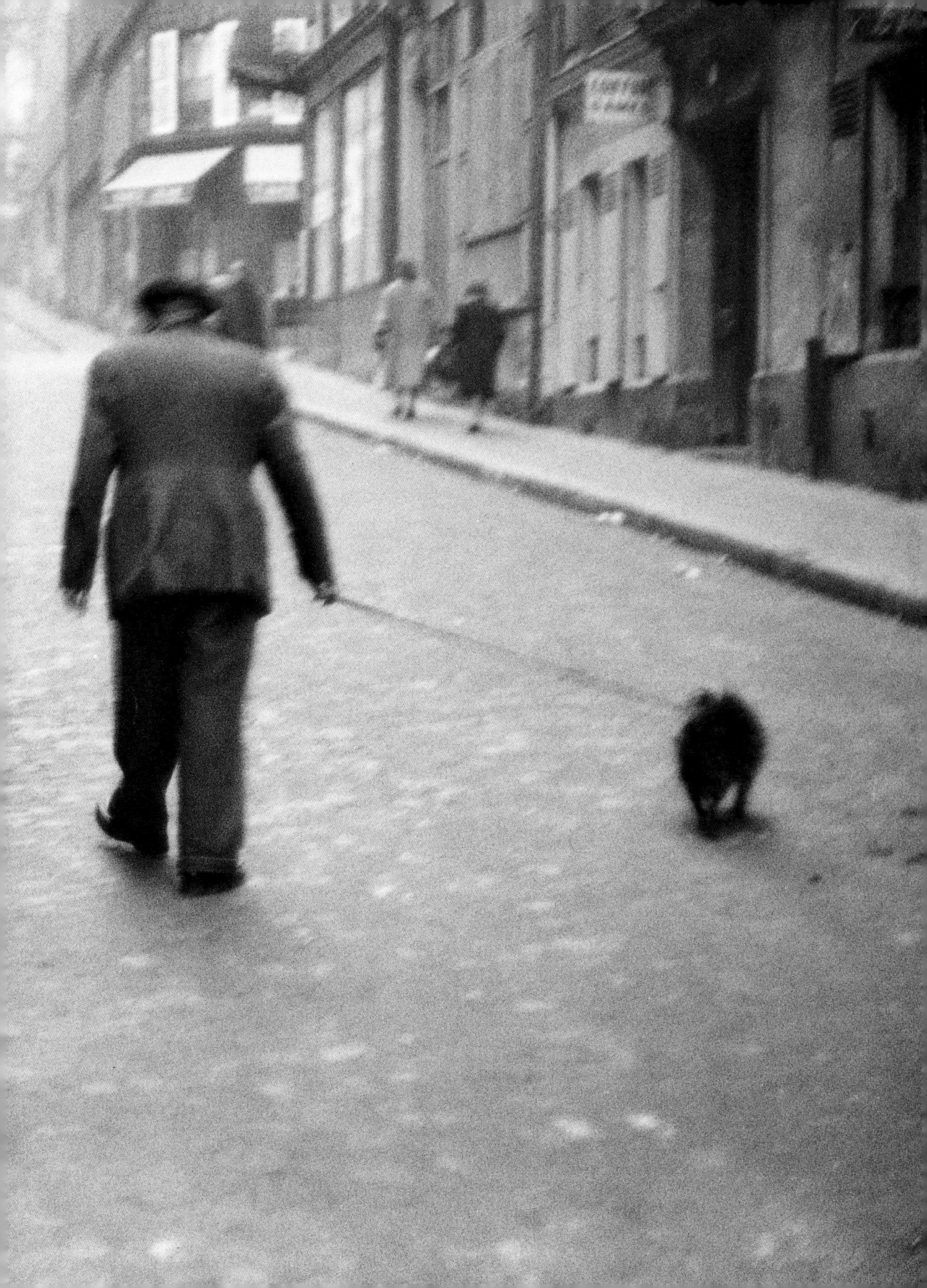

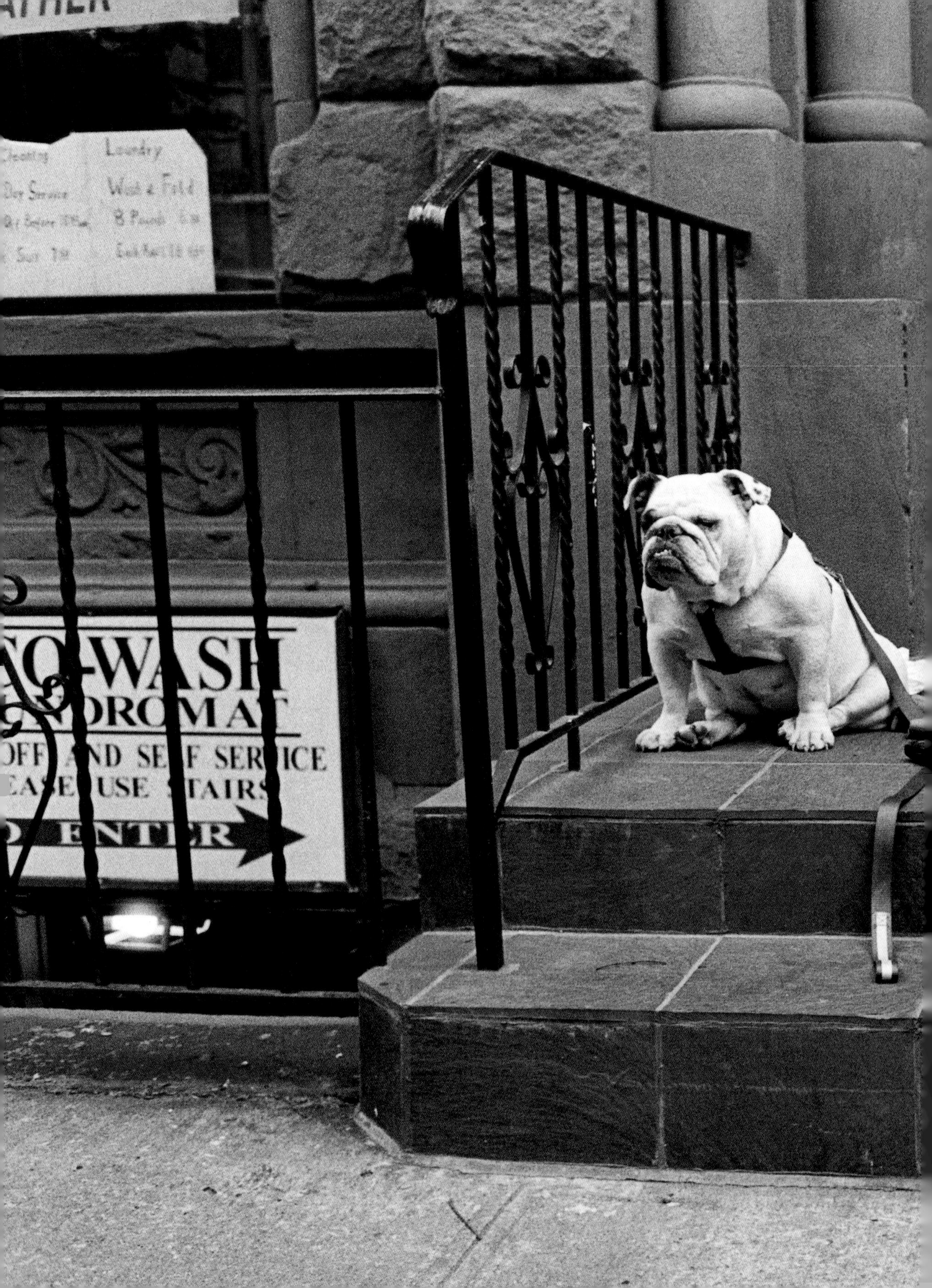
LAUNDROMAT
Cleaning   Laundry
Dry Service   Wash & Fold
O-WASH
DROMAT
OFF AND SELF SERVICE
EASE USE STAIRS
D ENTER

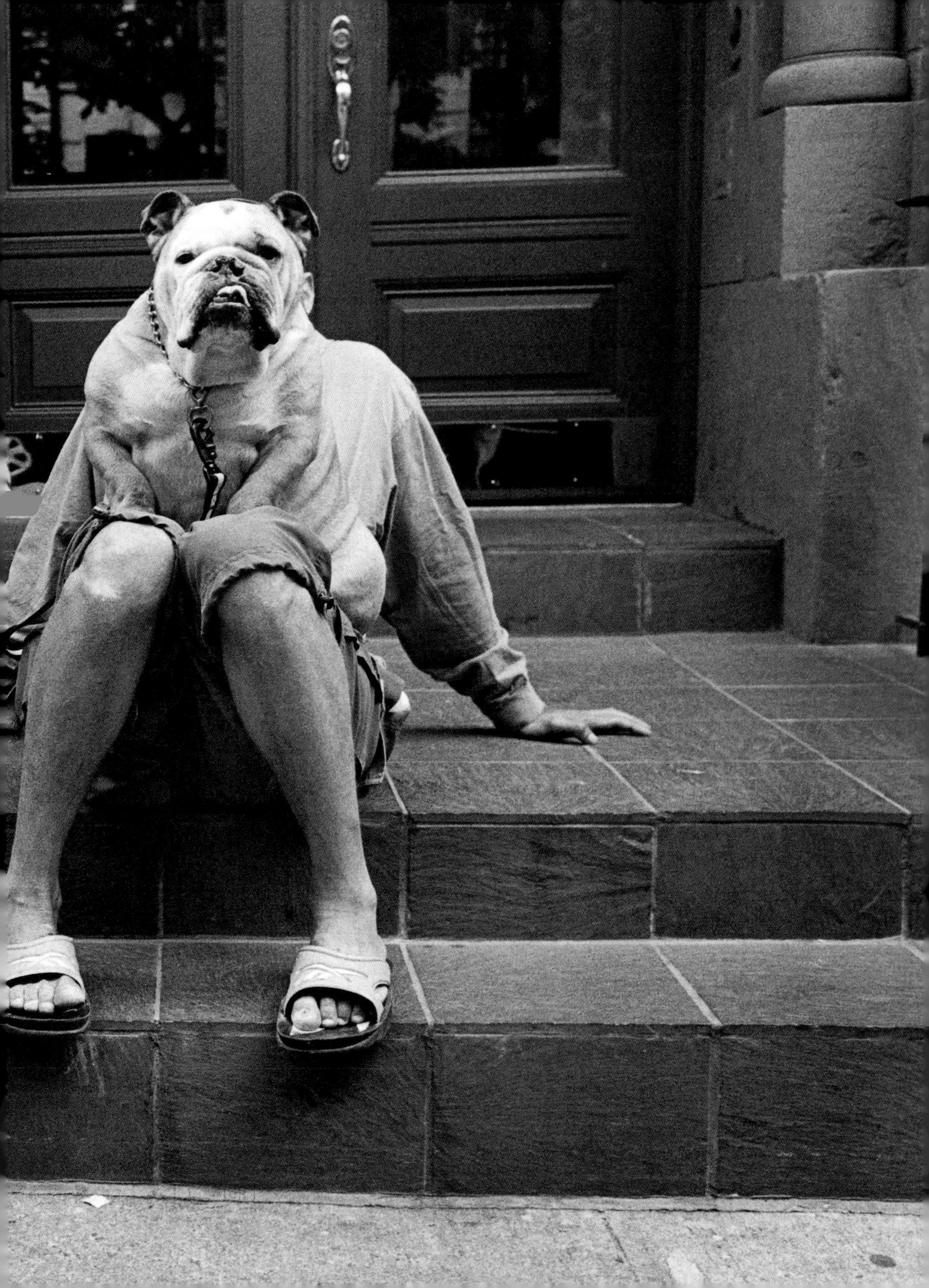

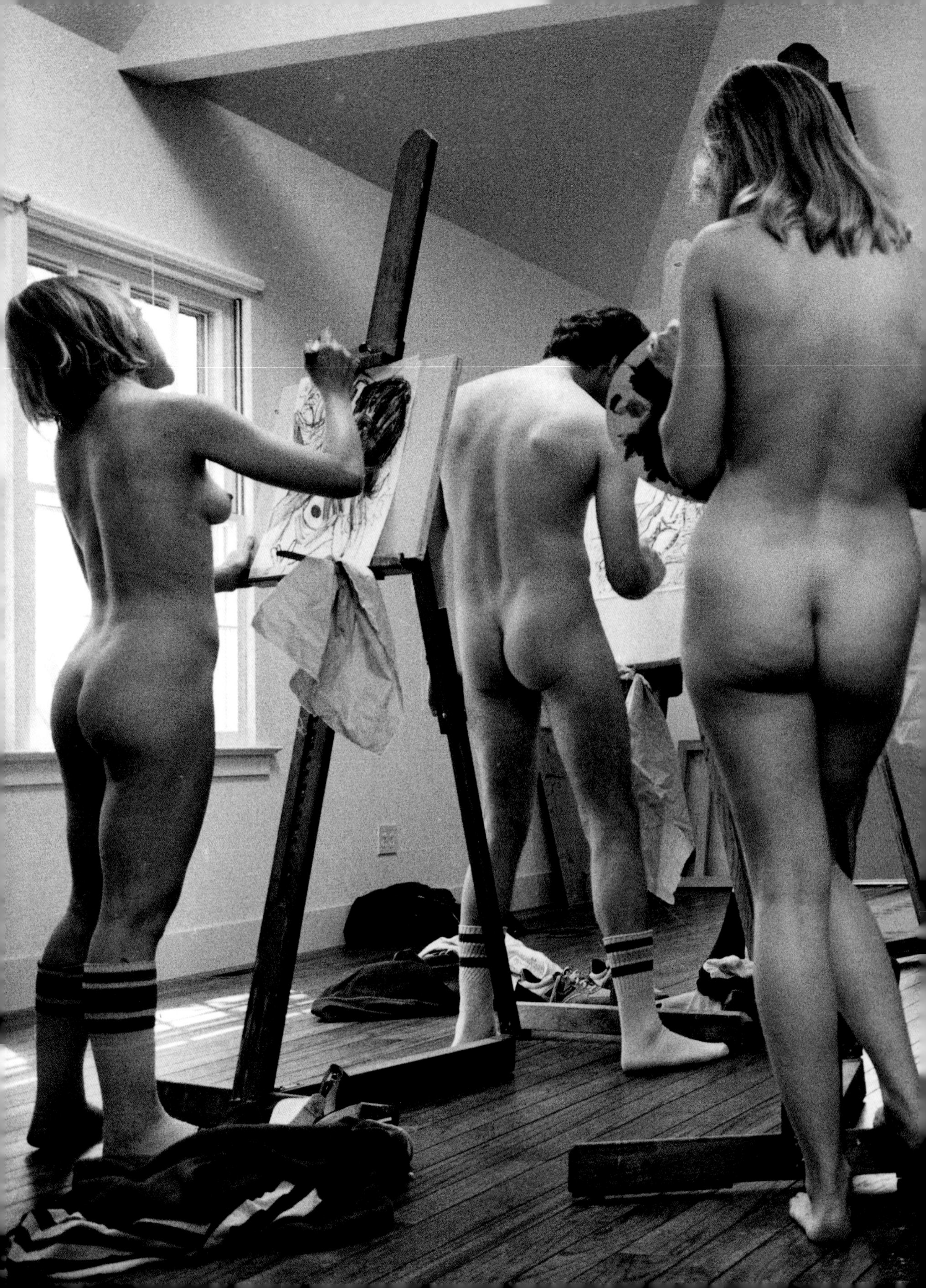

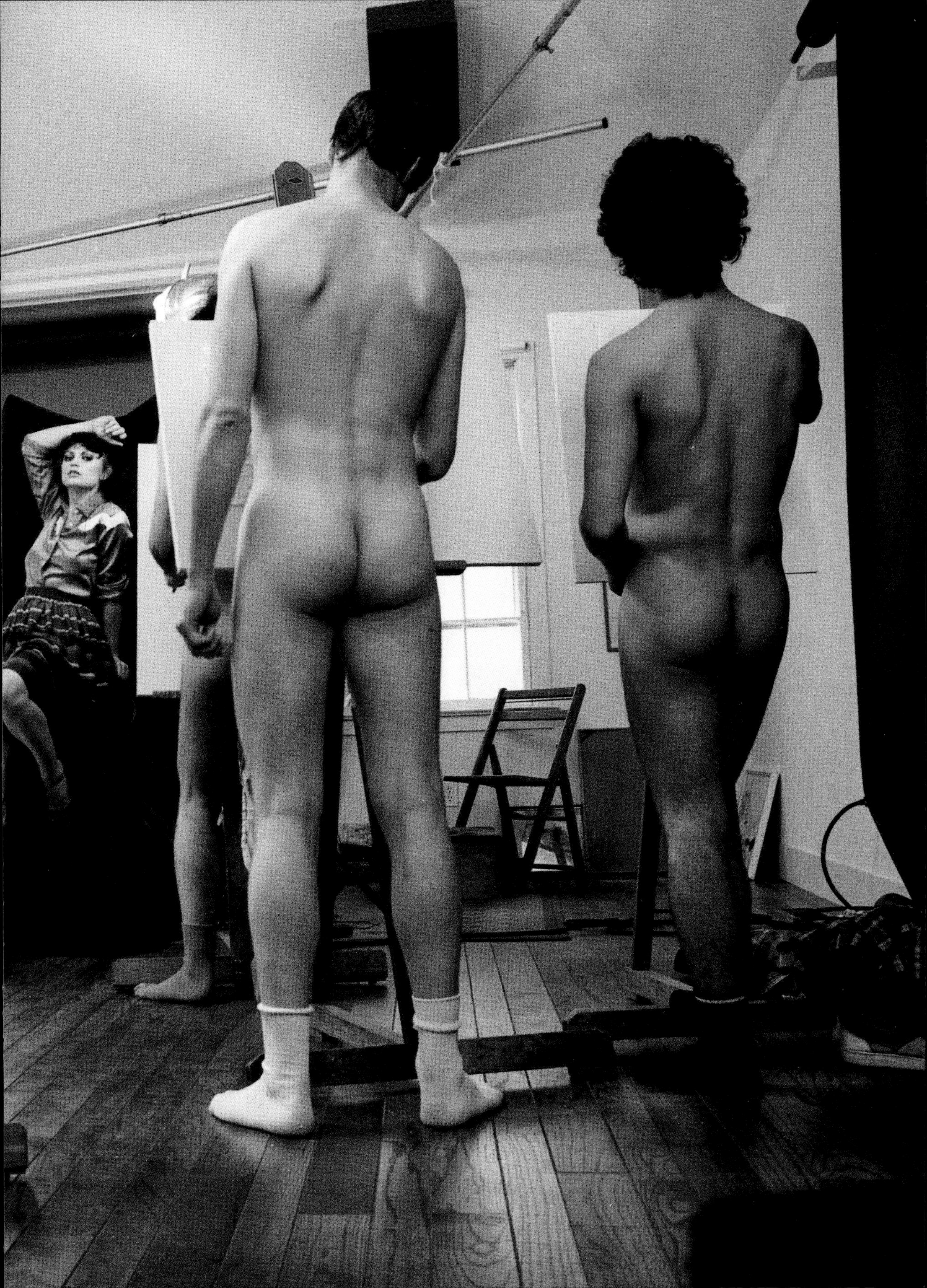

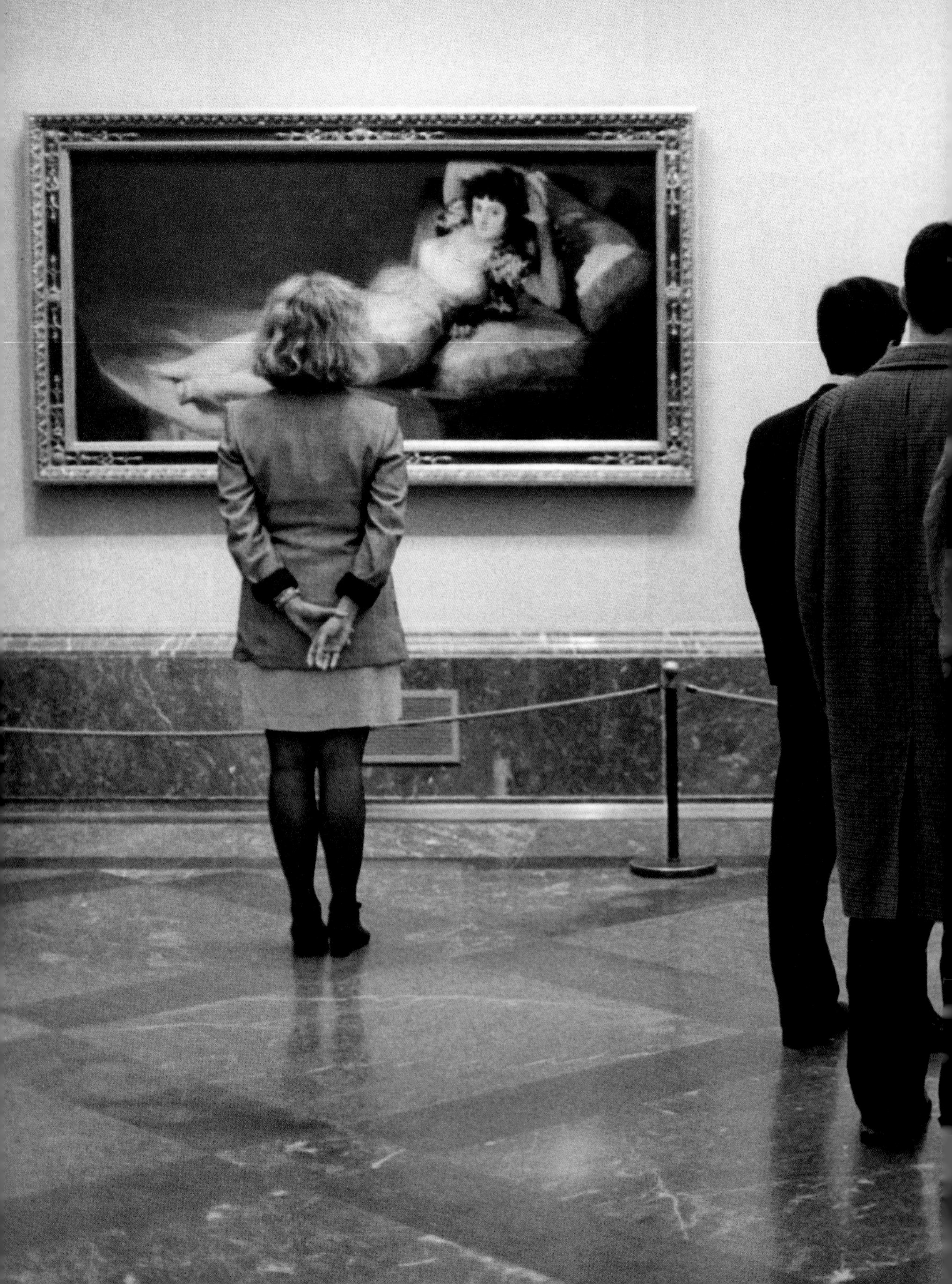

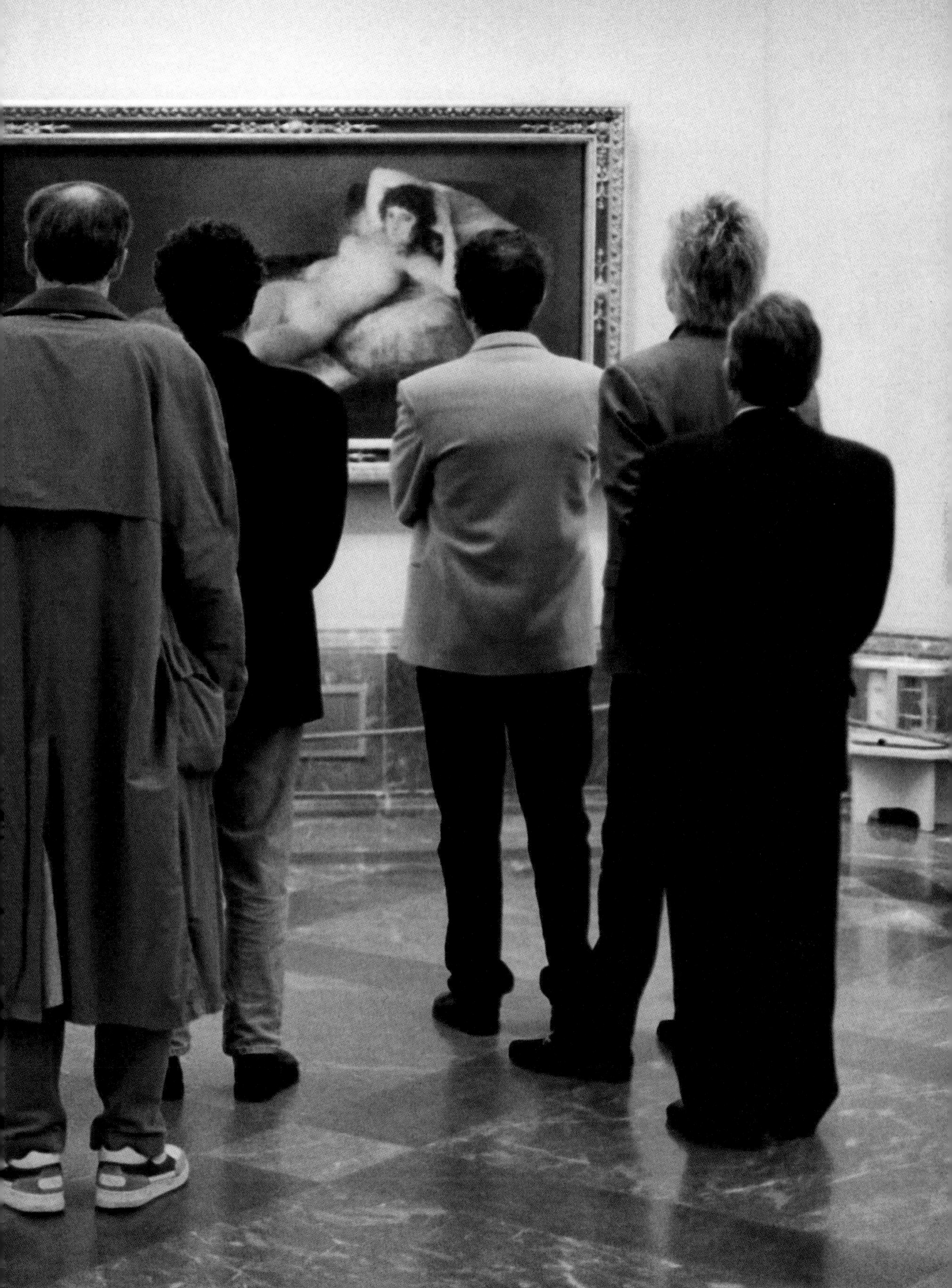

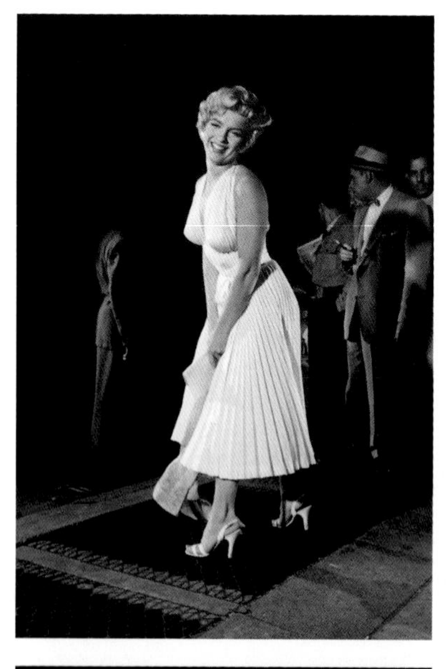
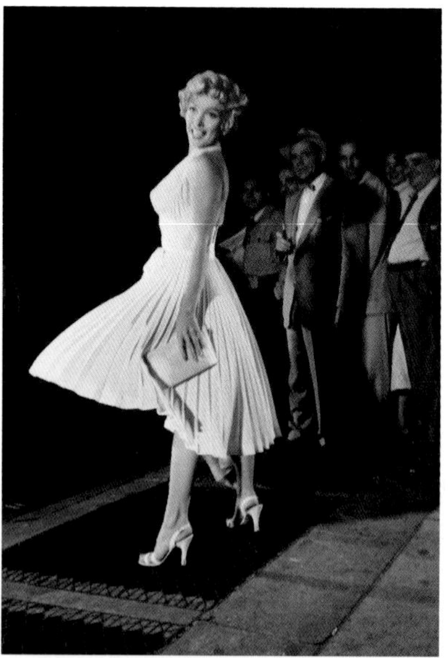
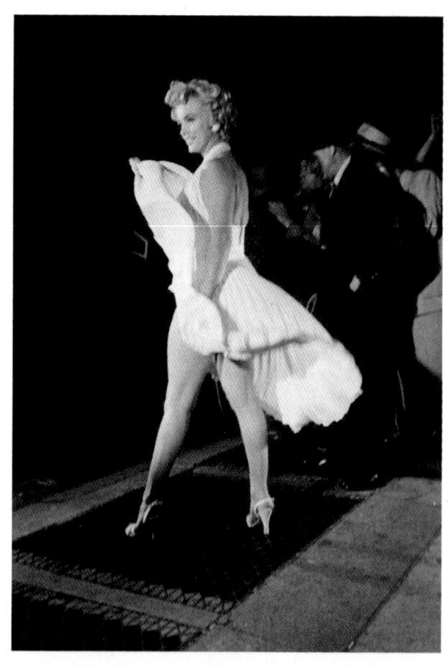
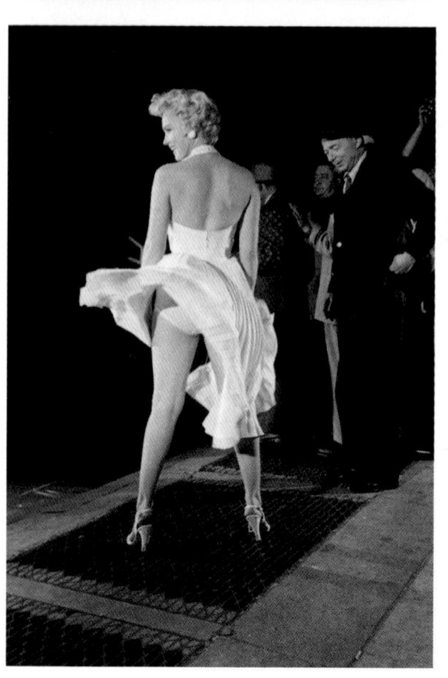
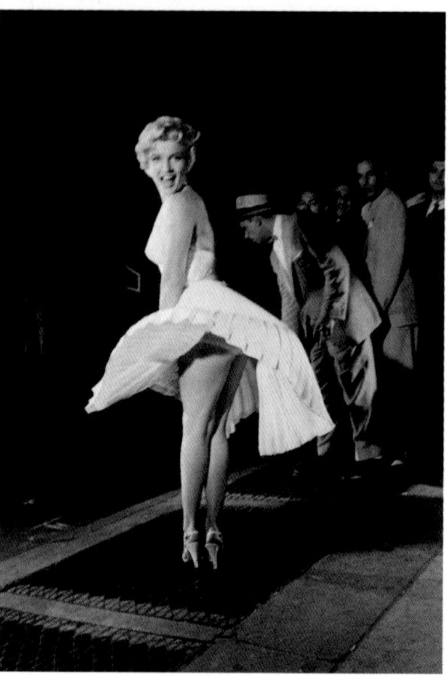
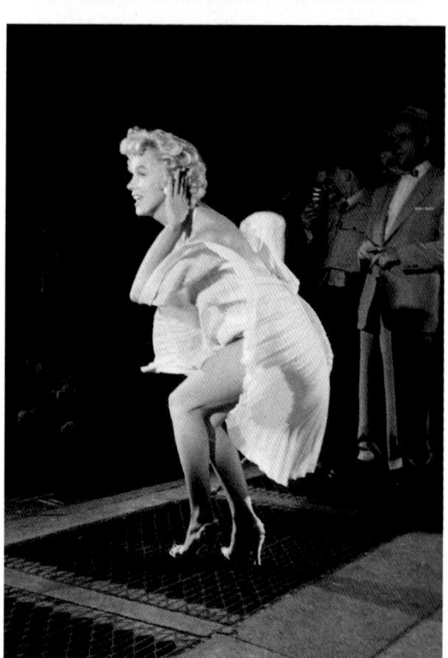

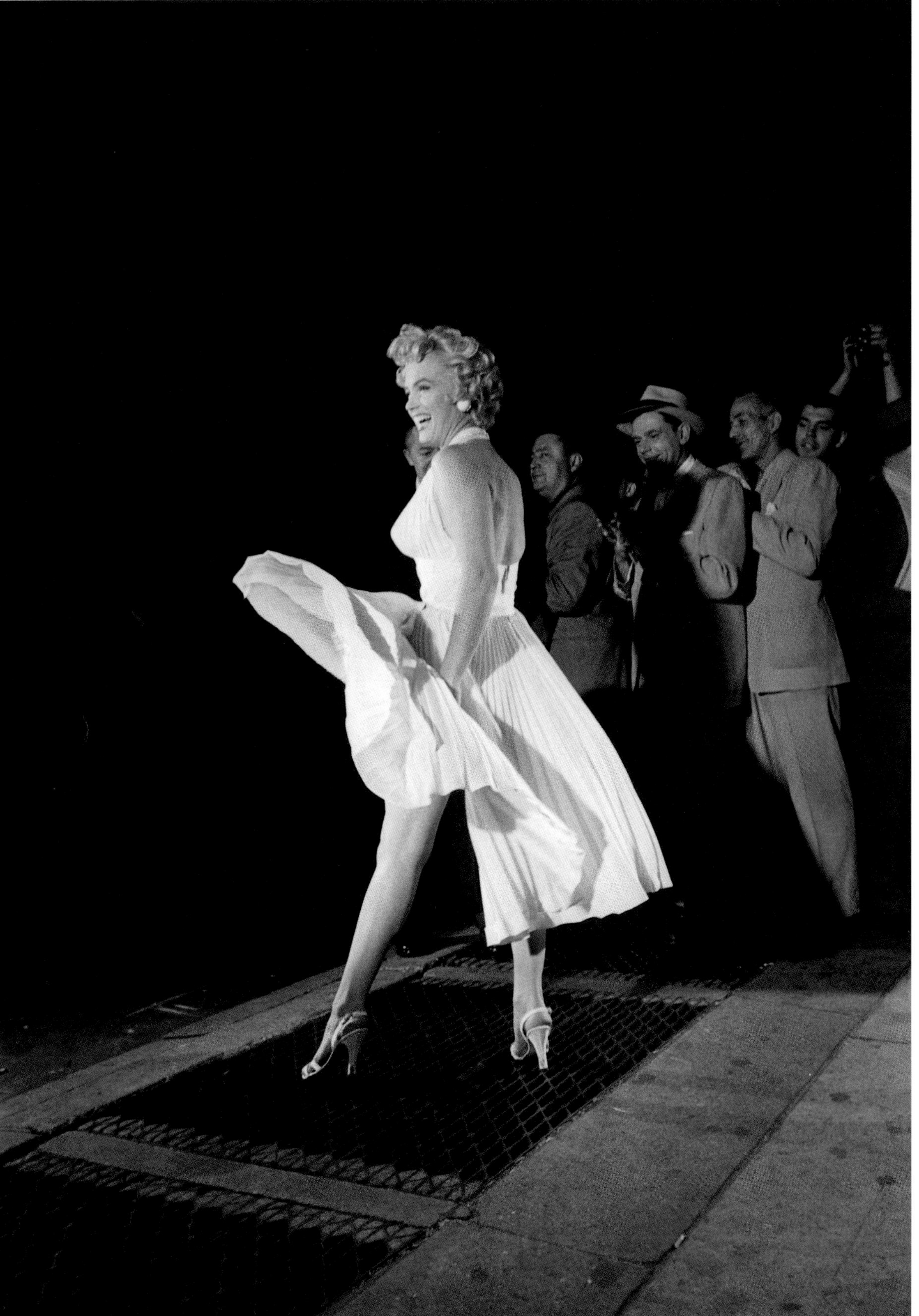

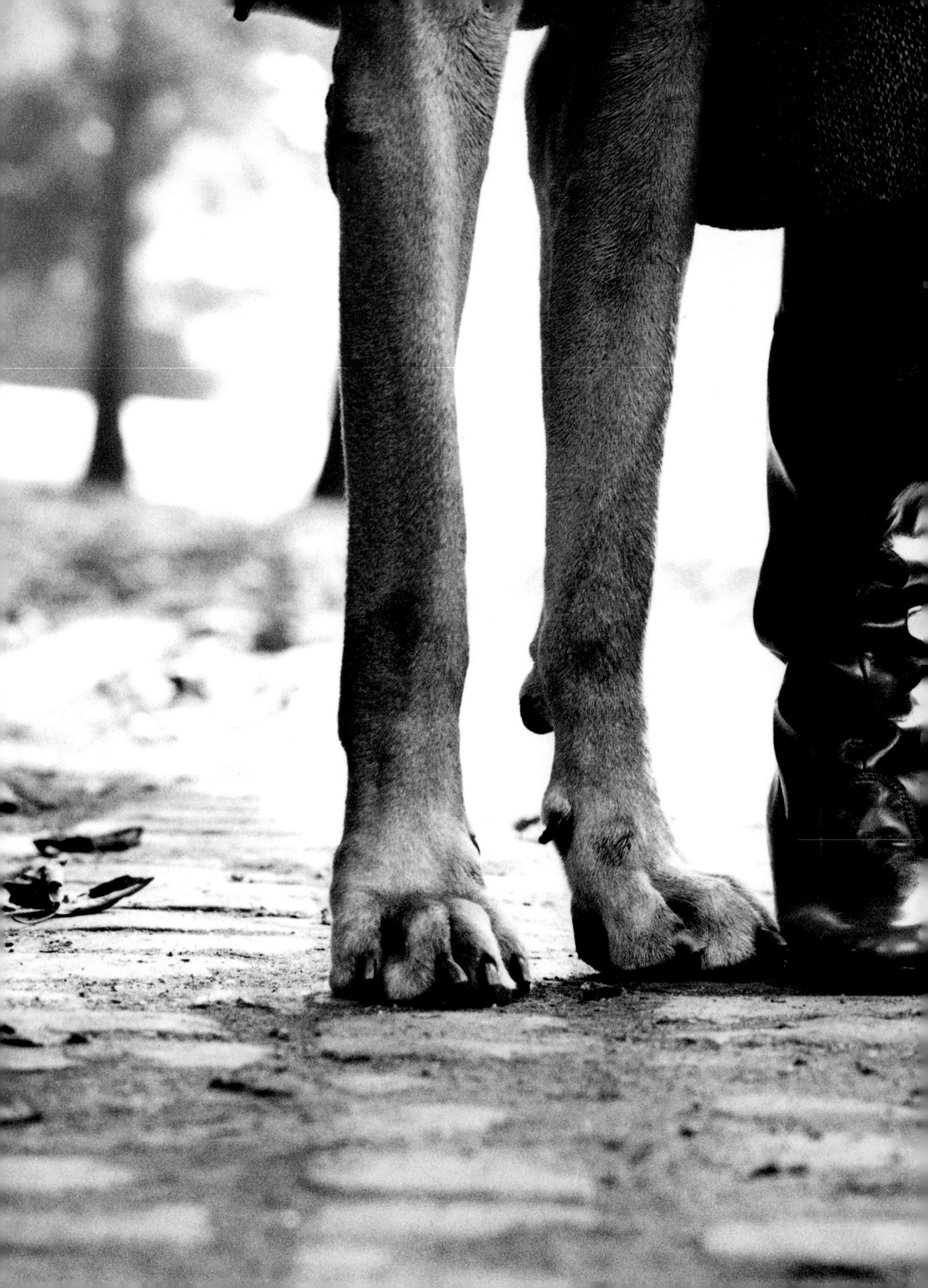

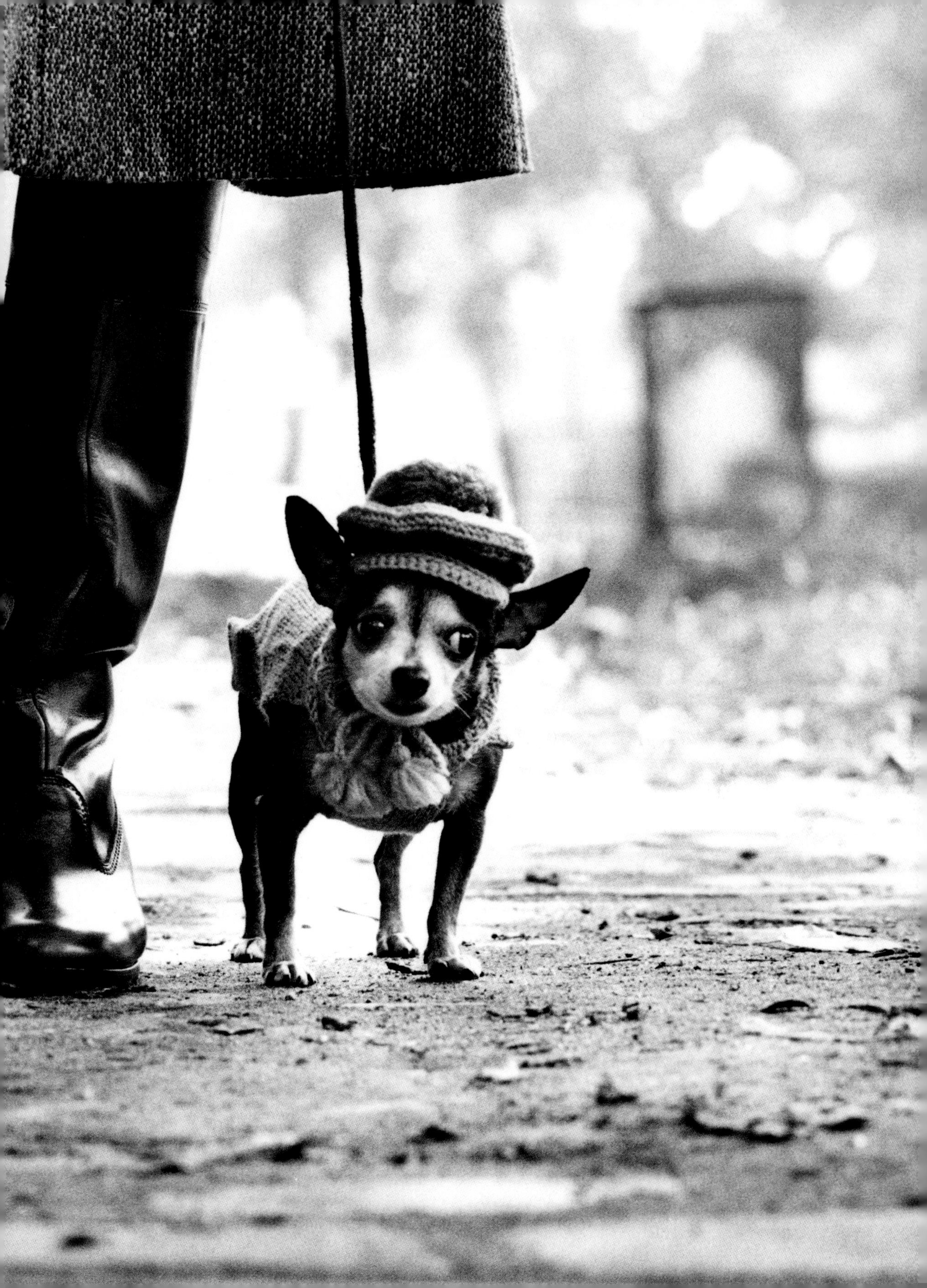

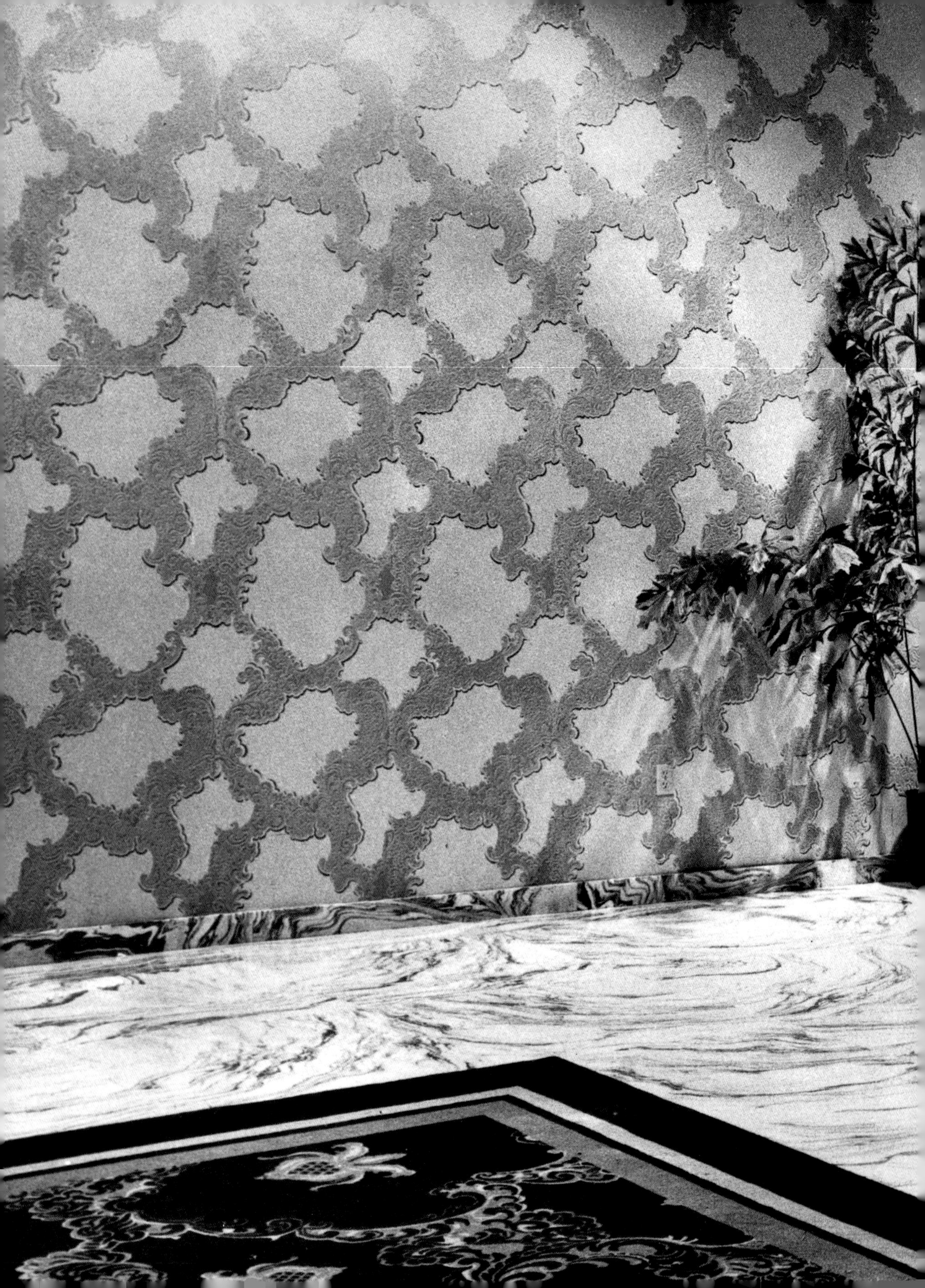

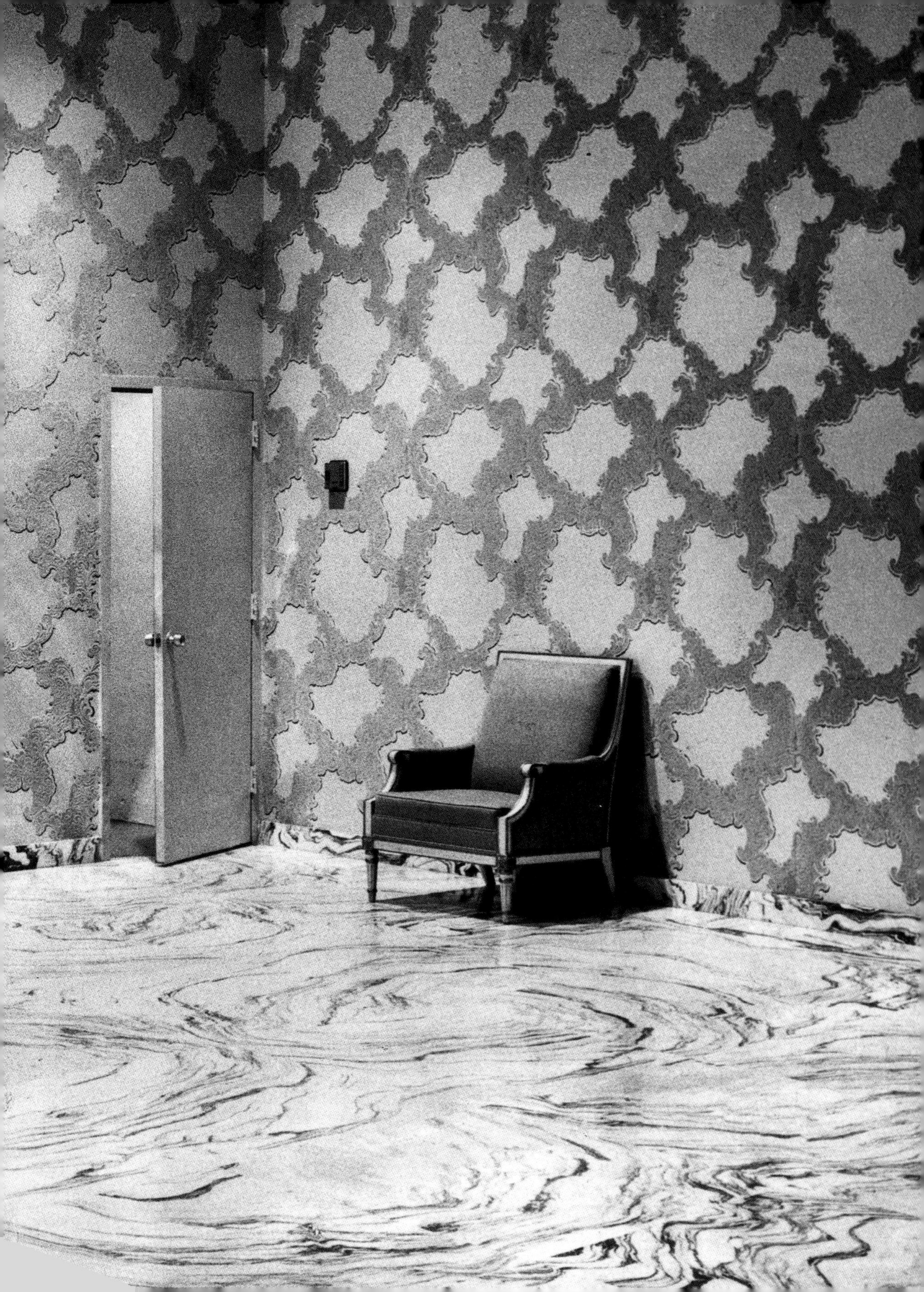

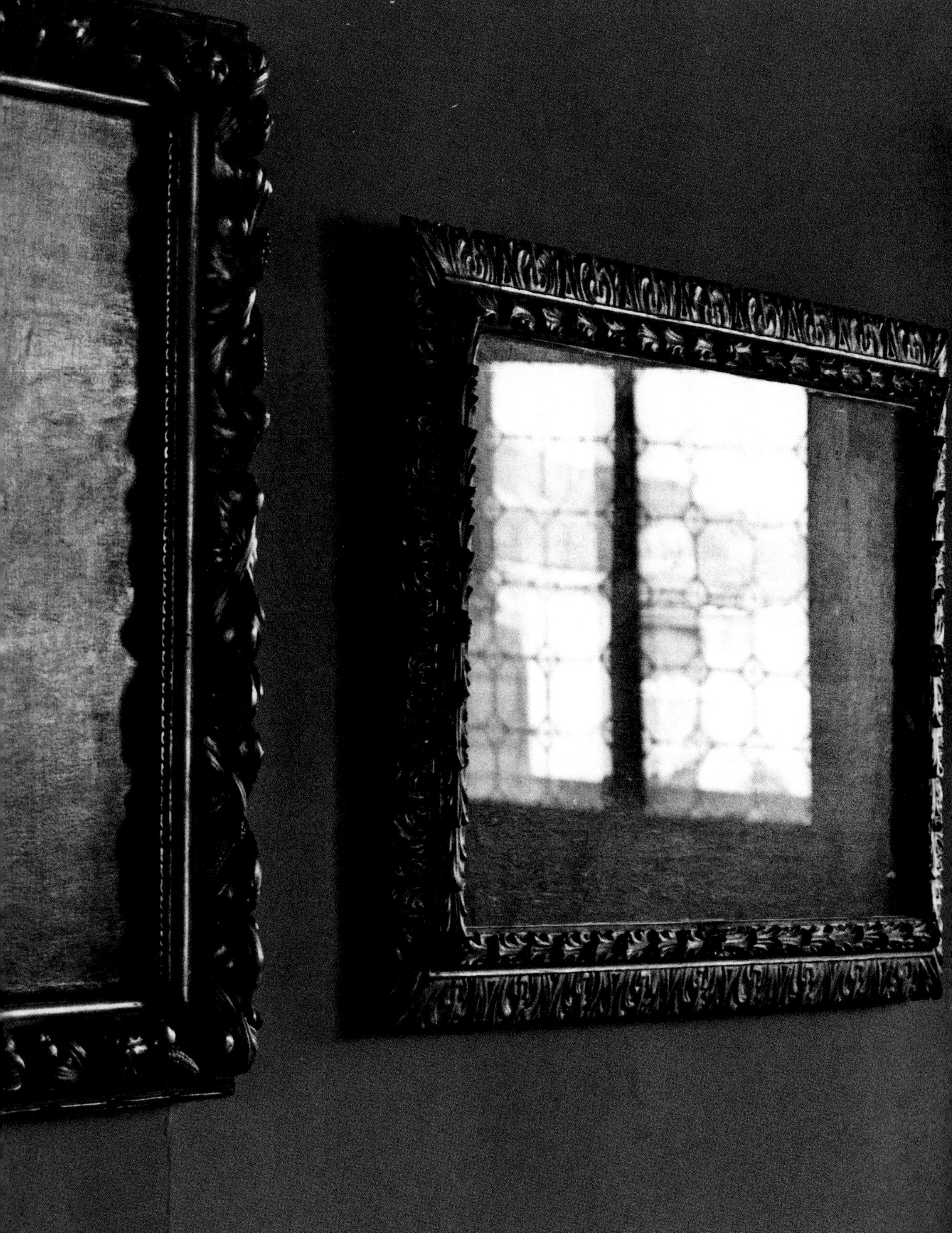

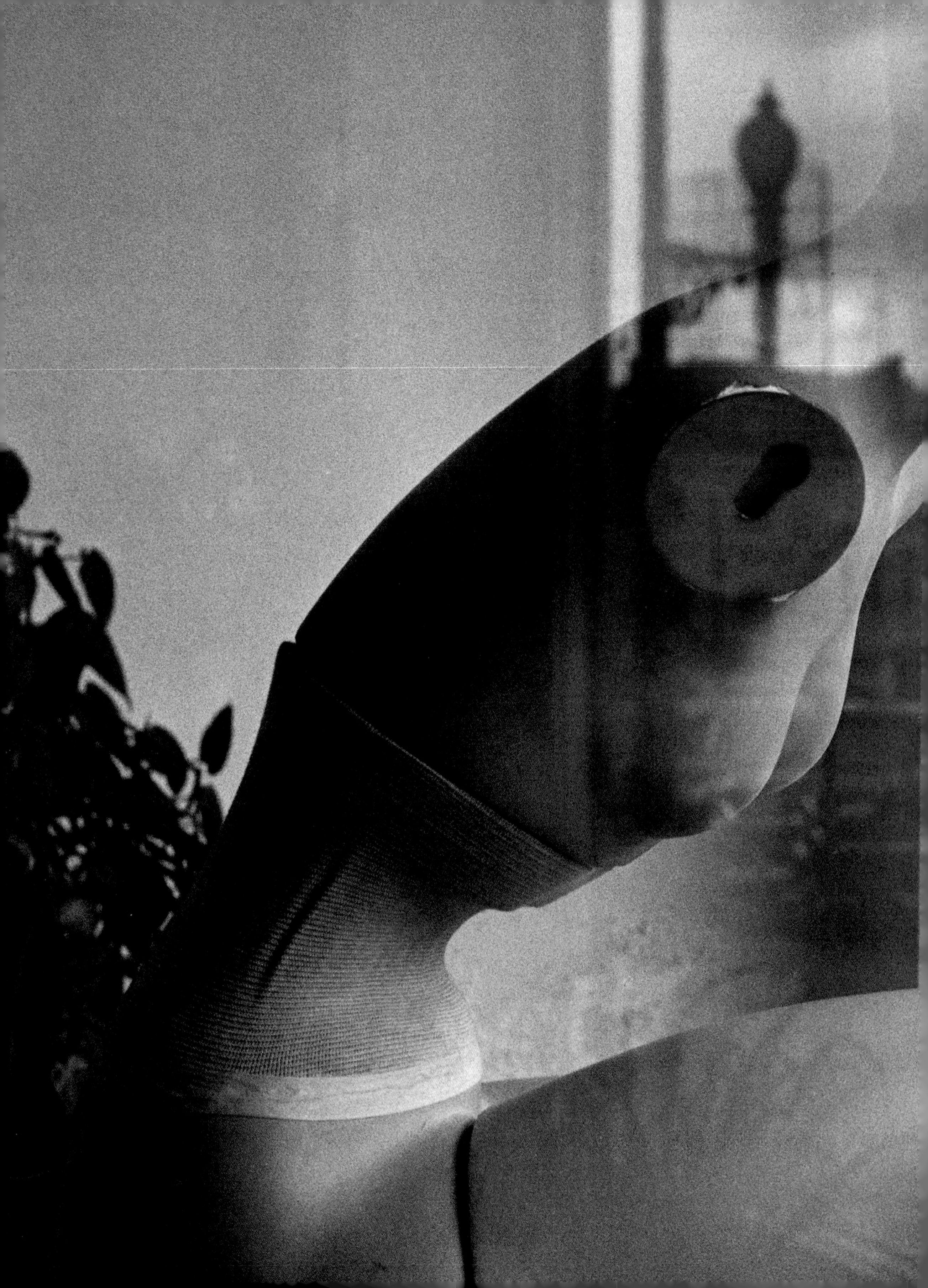

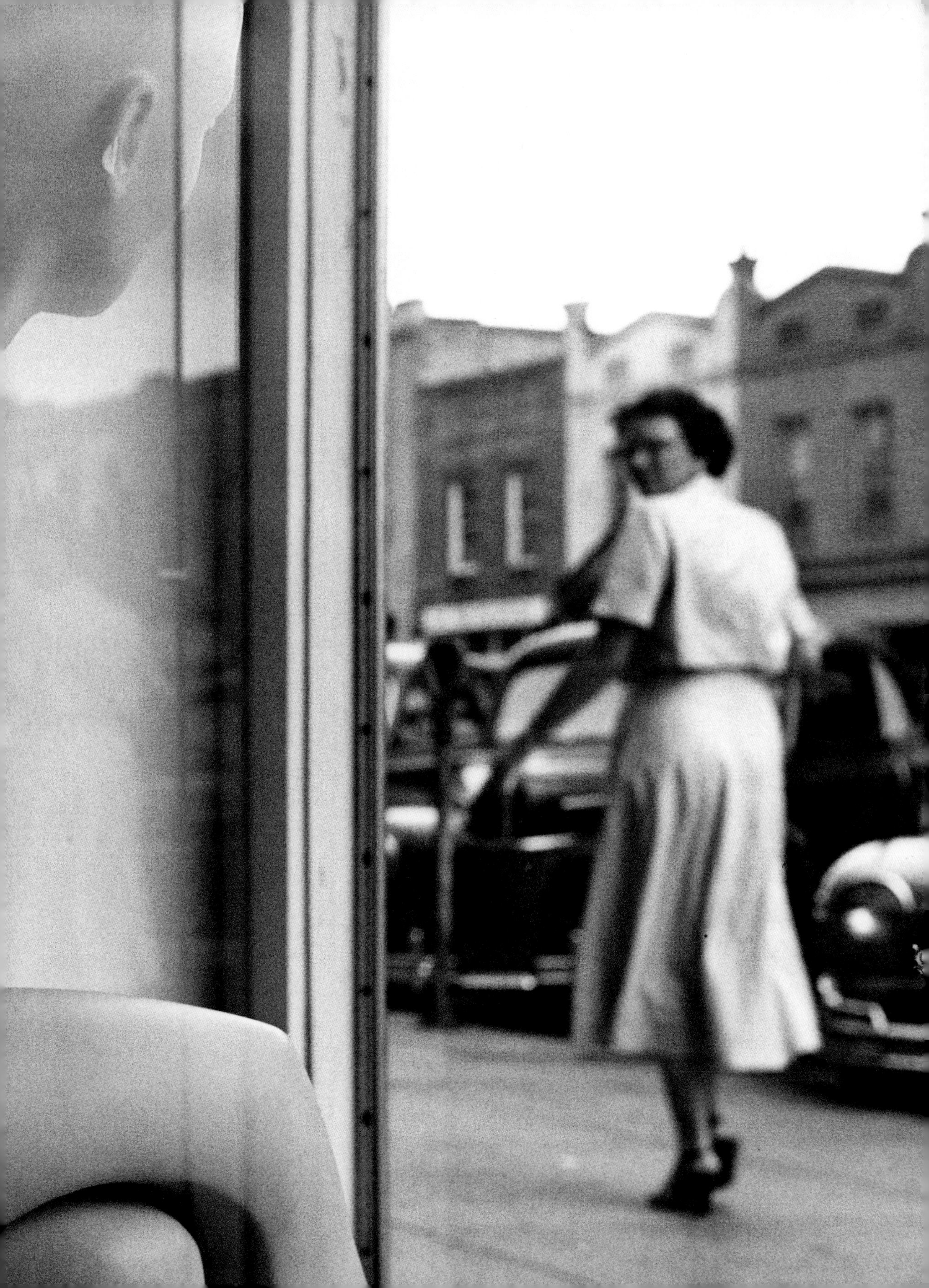

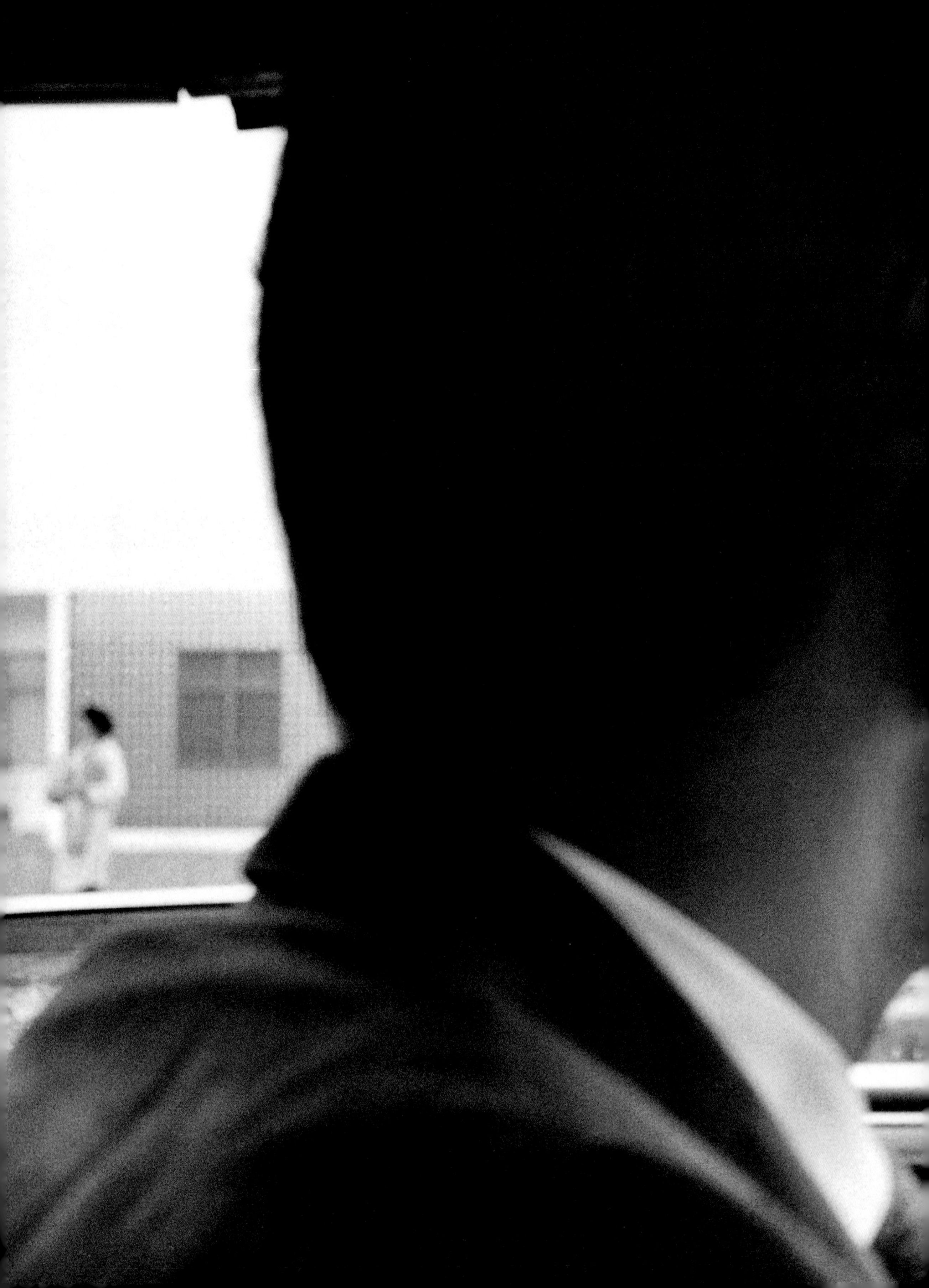

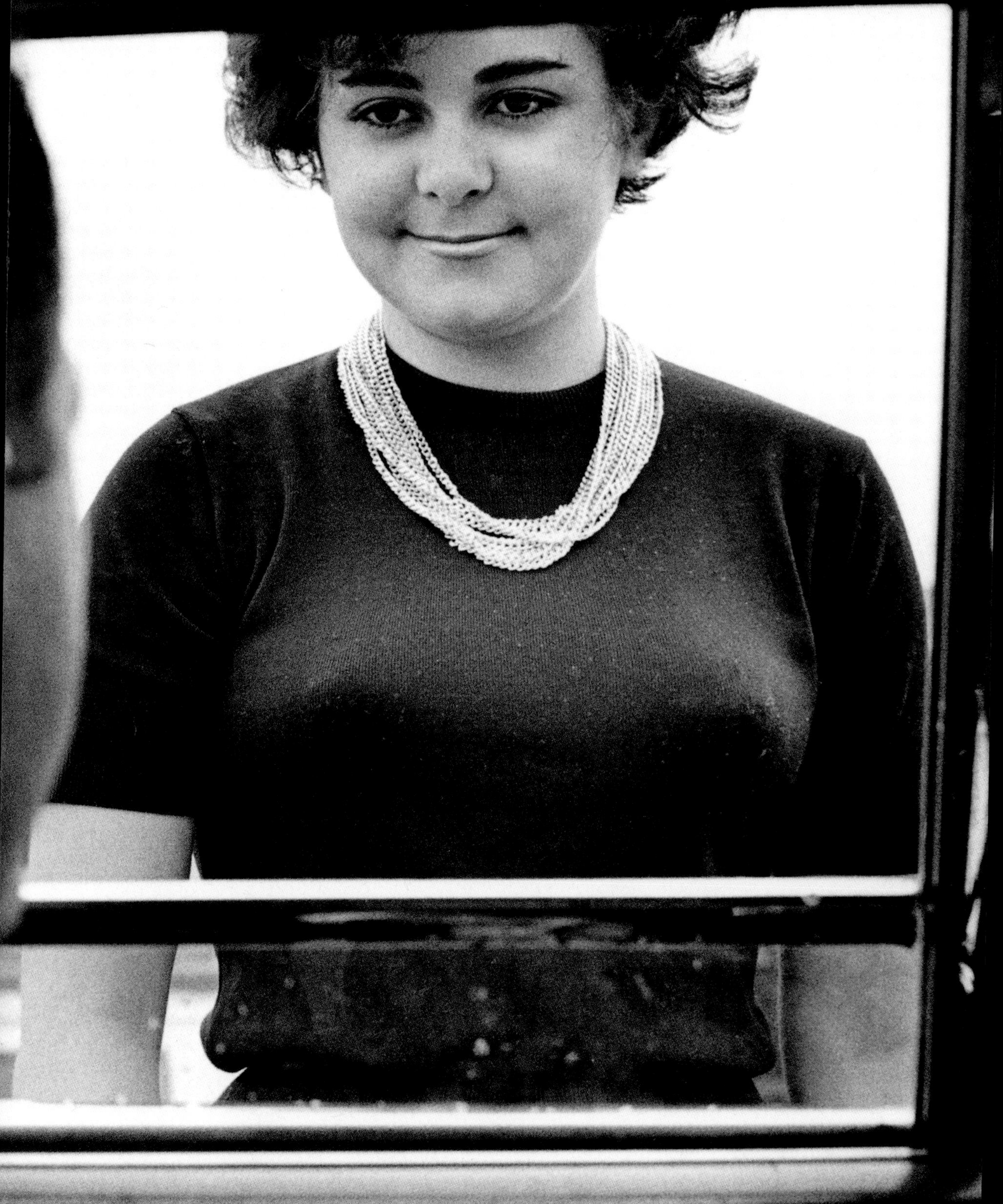

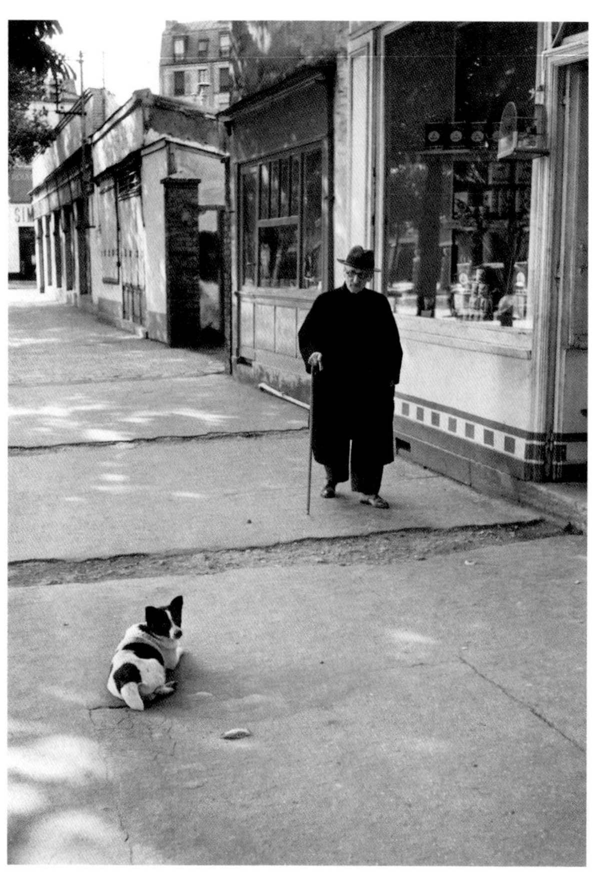
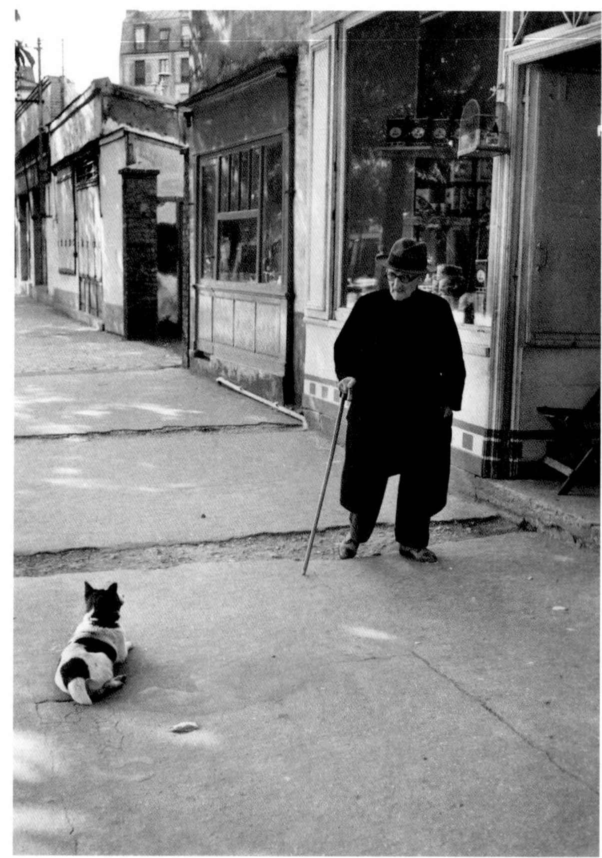

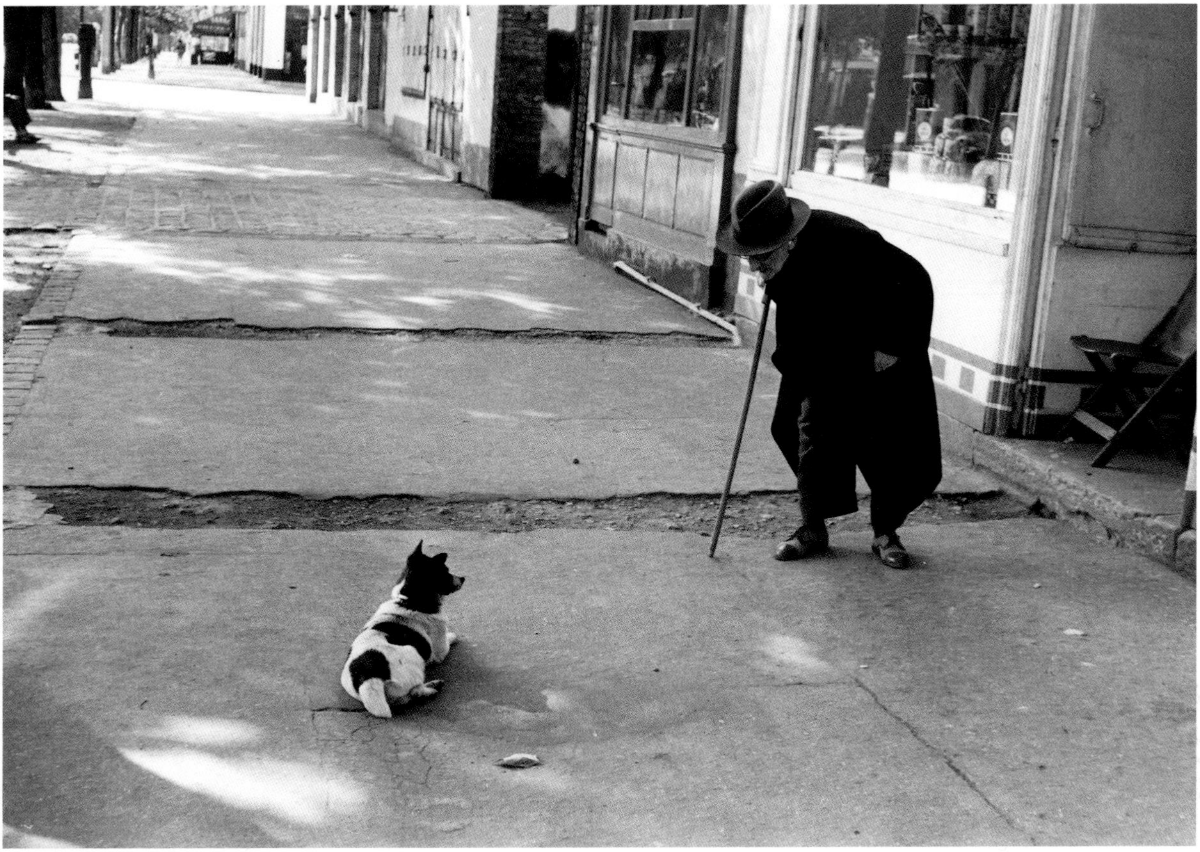

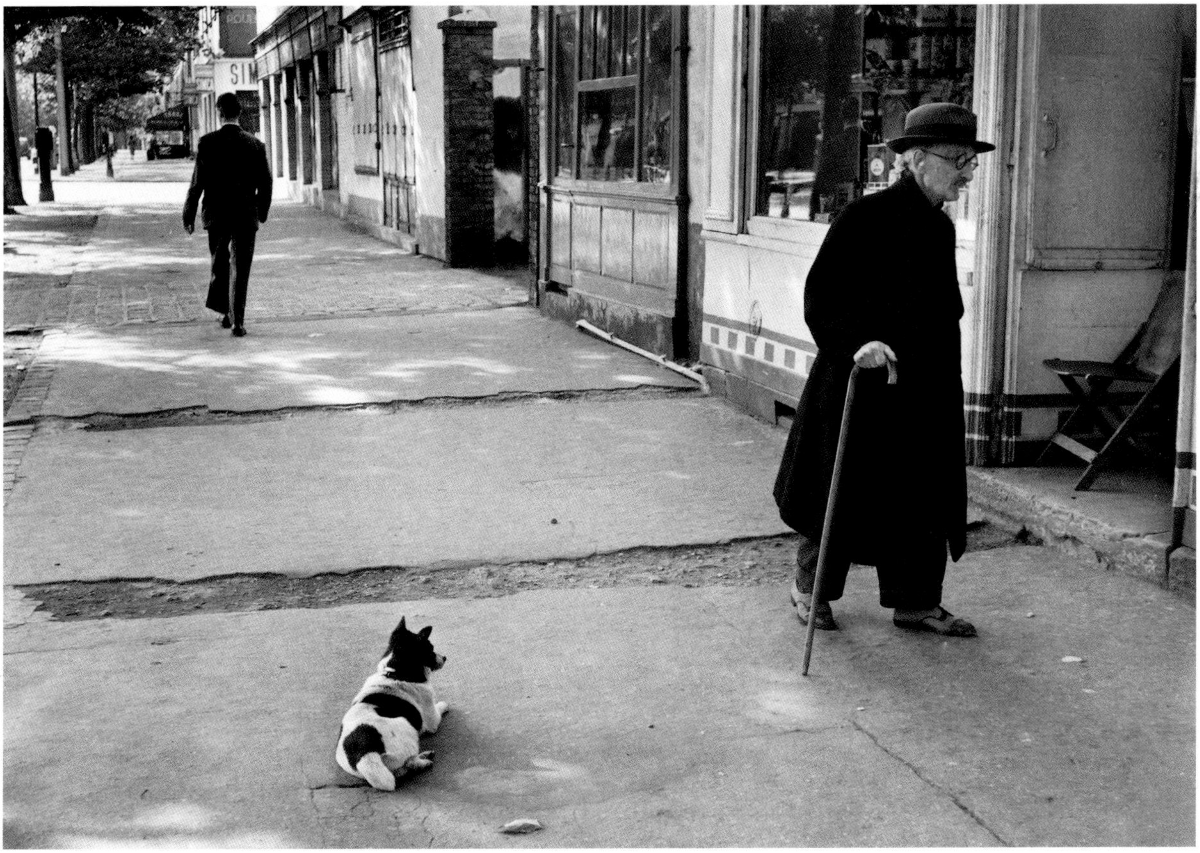

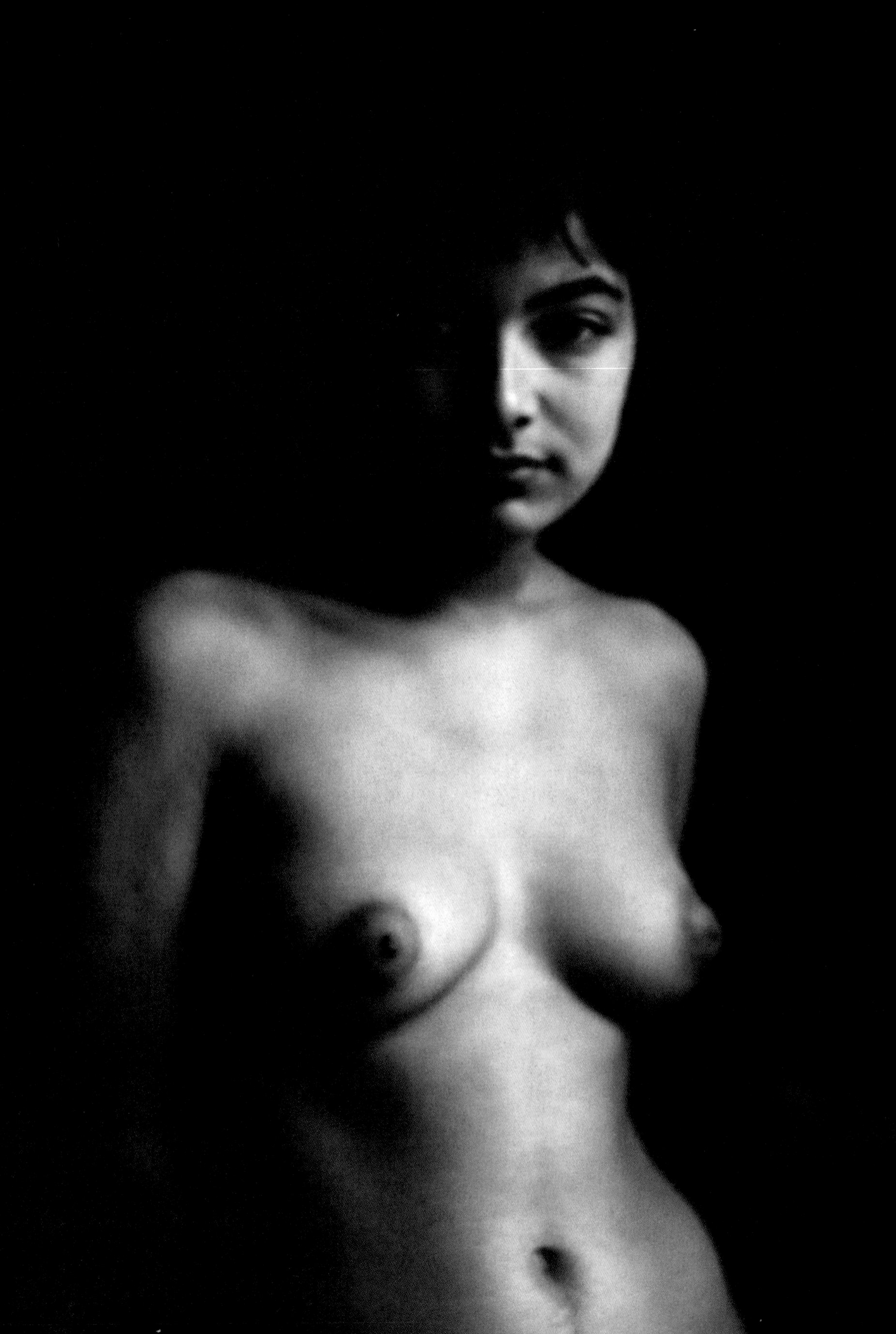

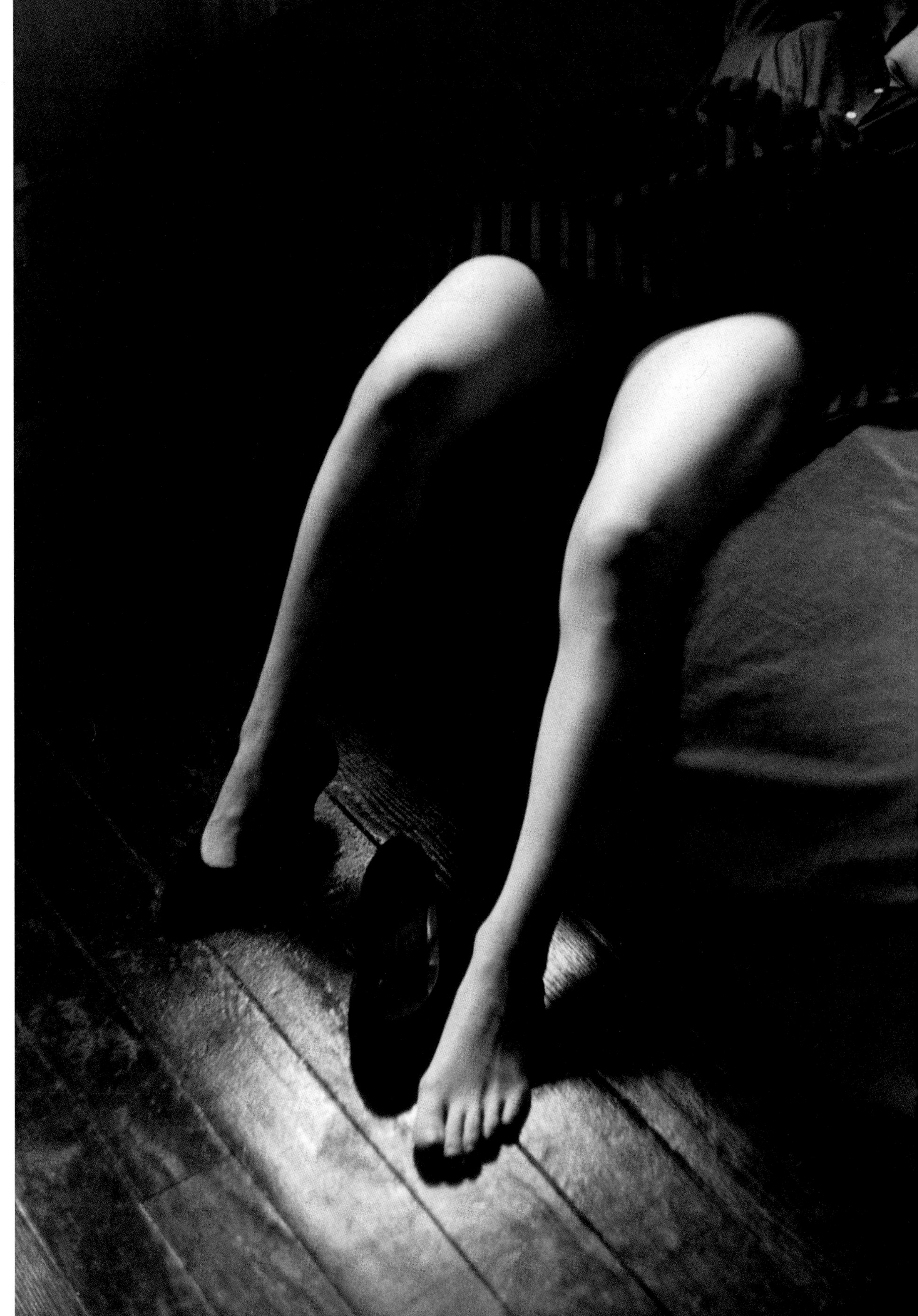

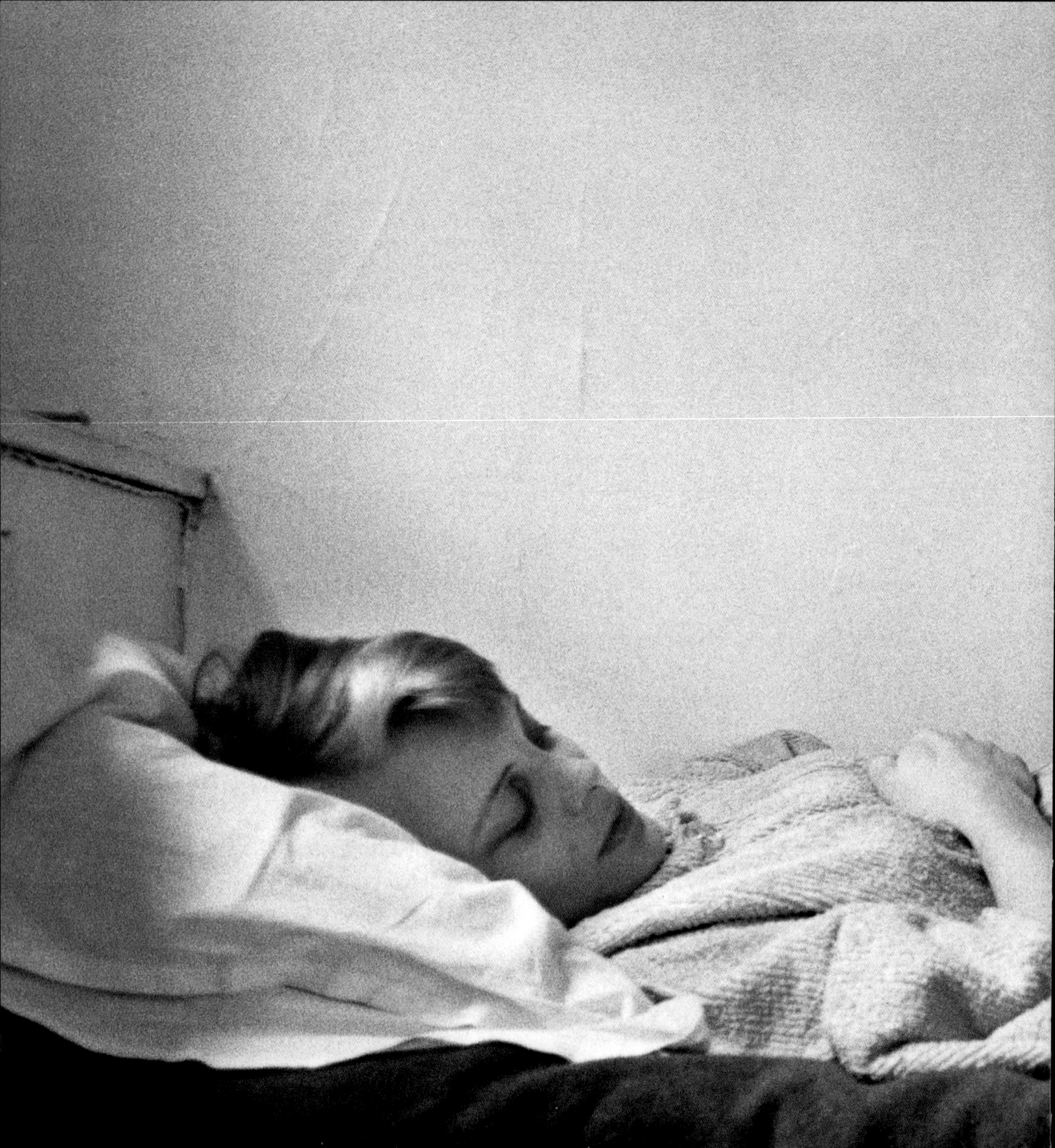

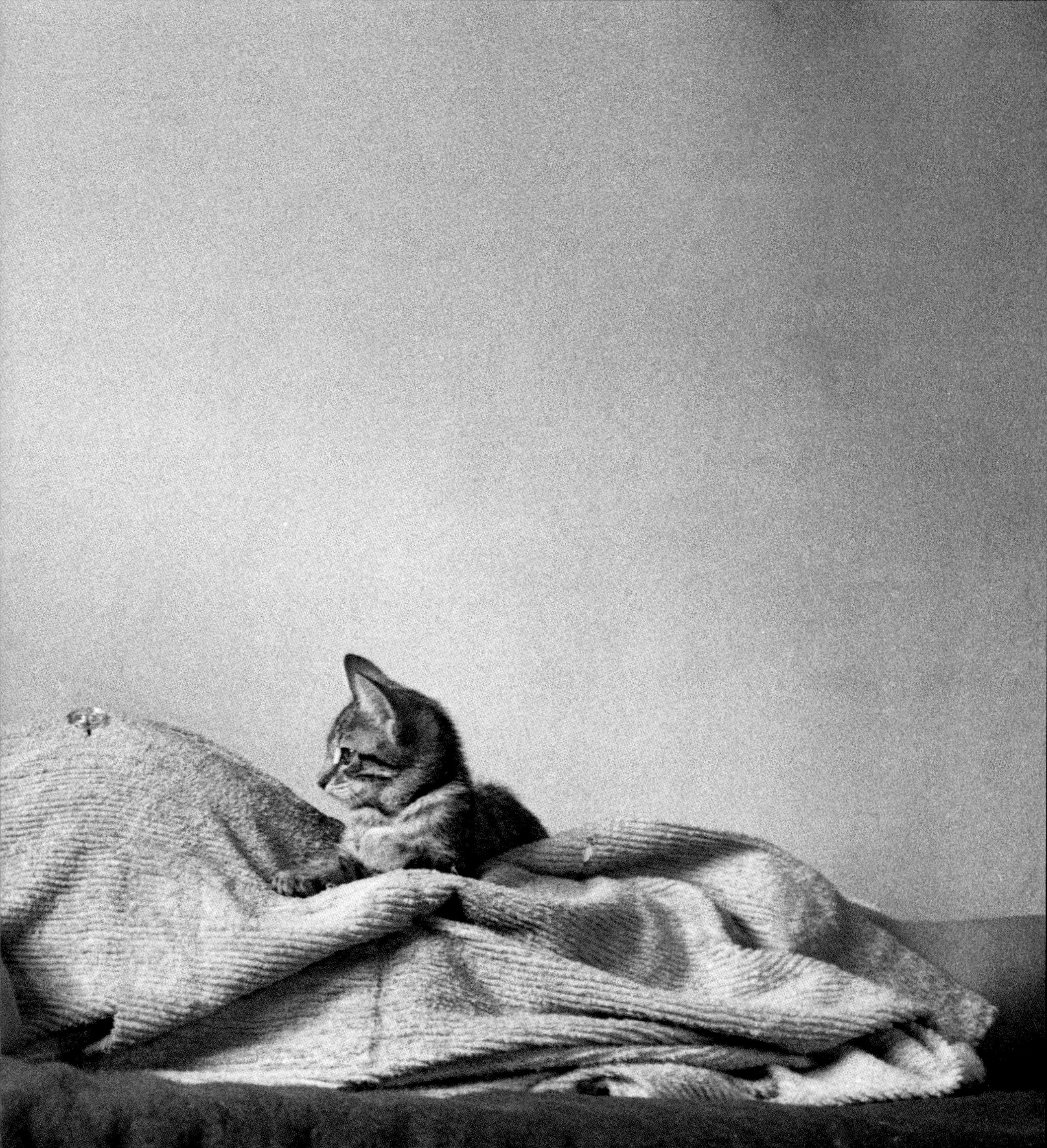

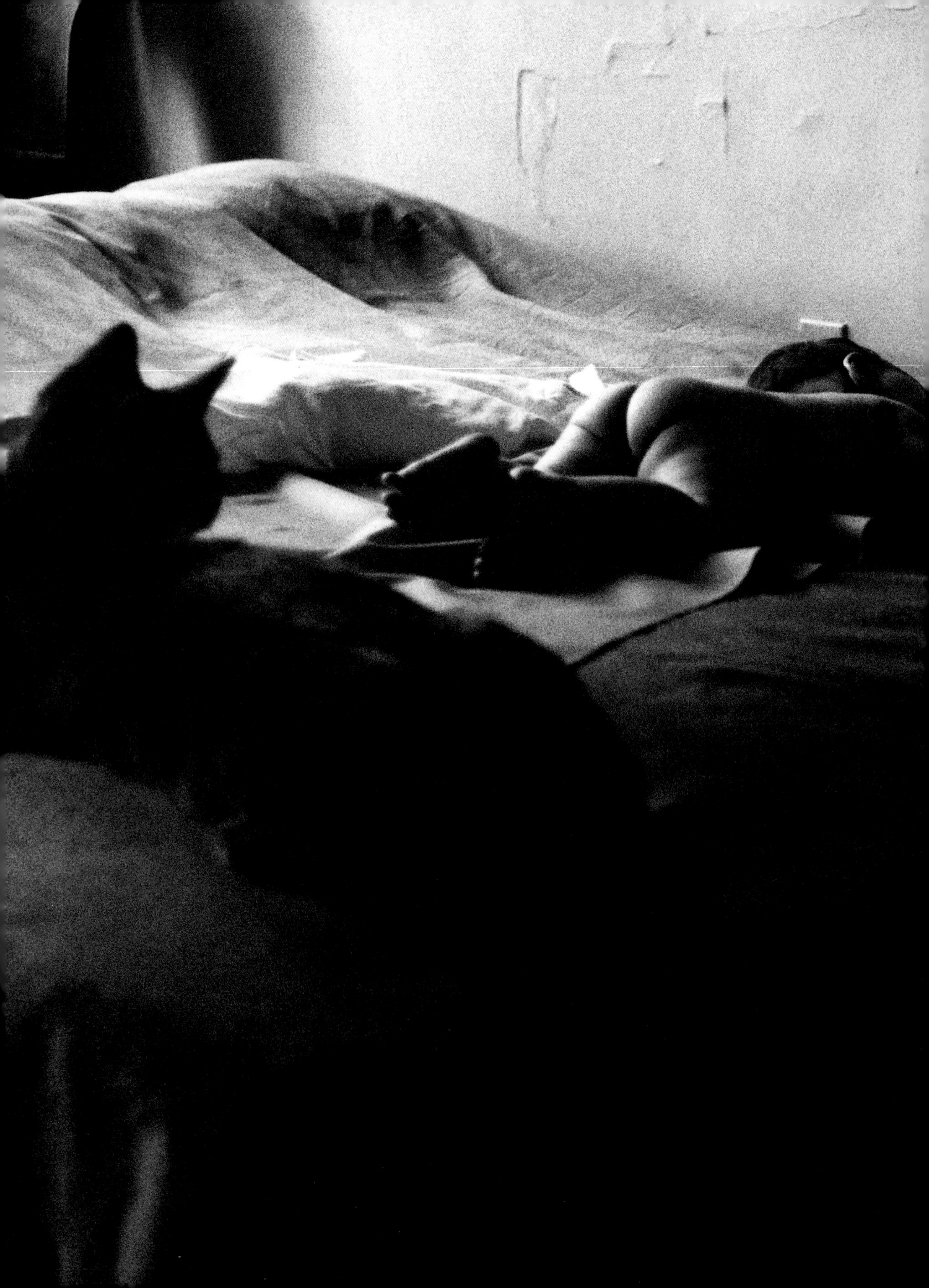

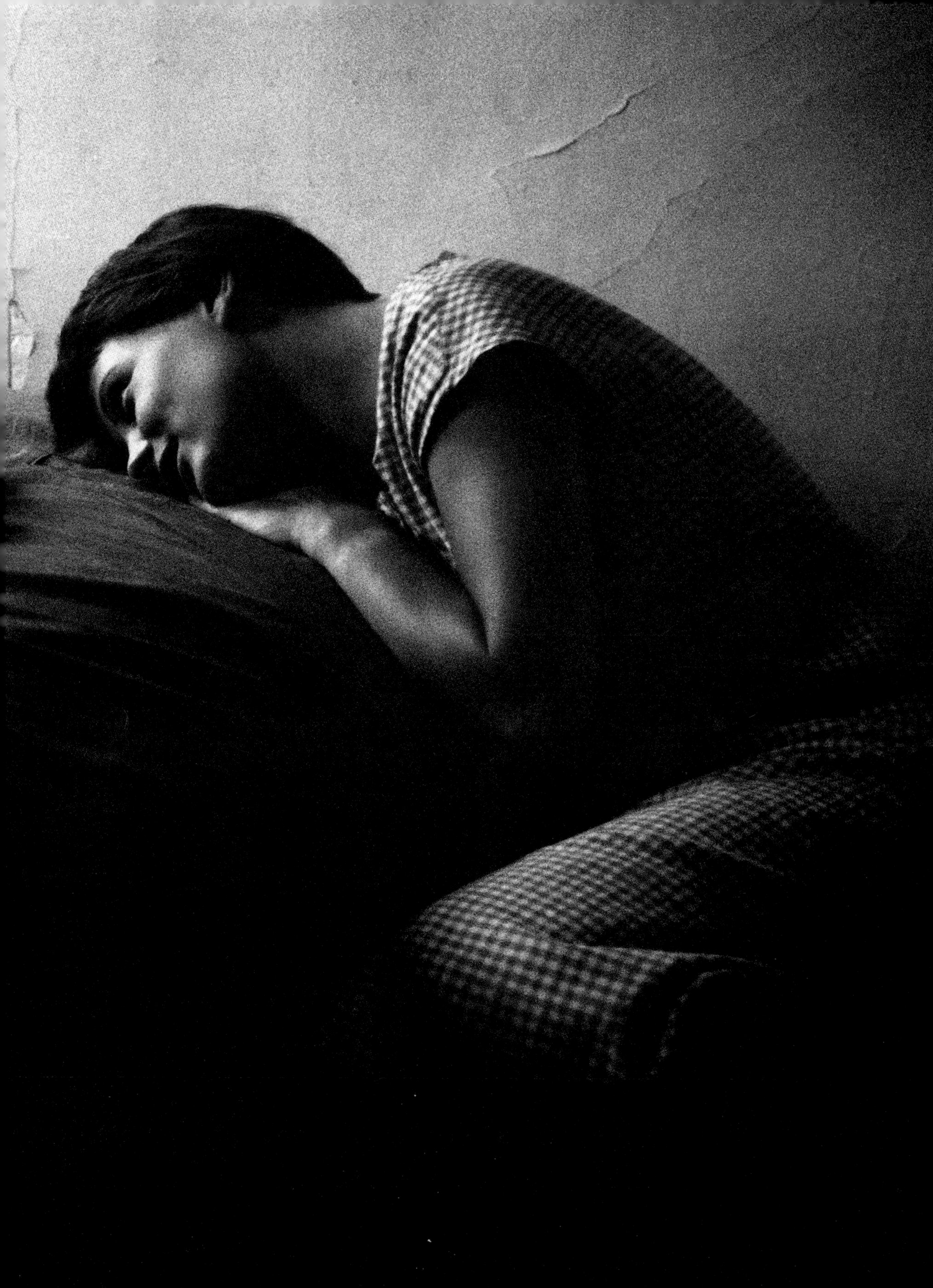

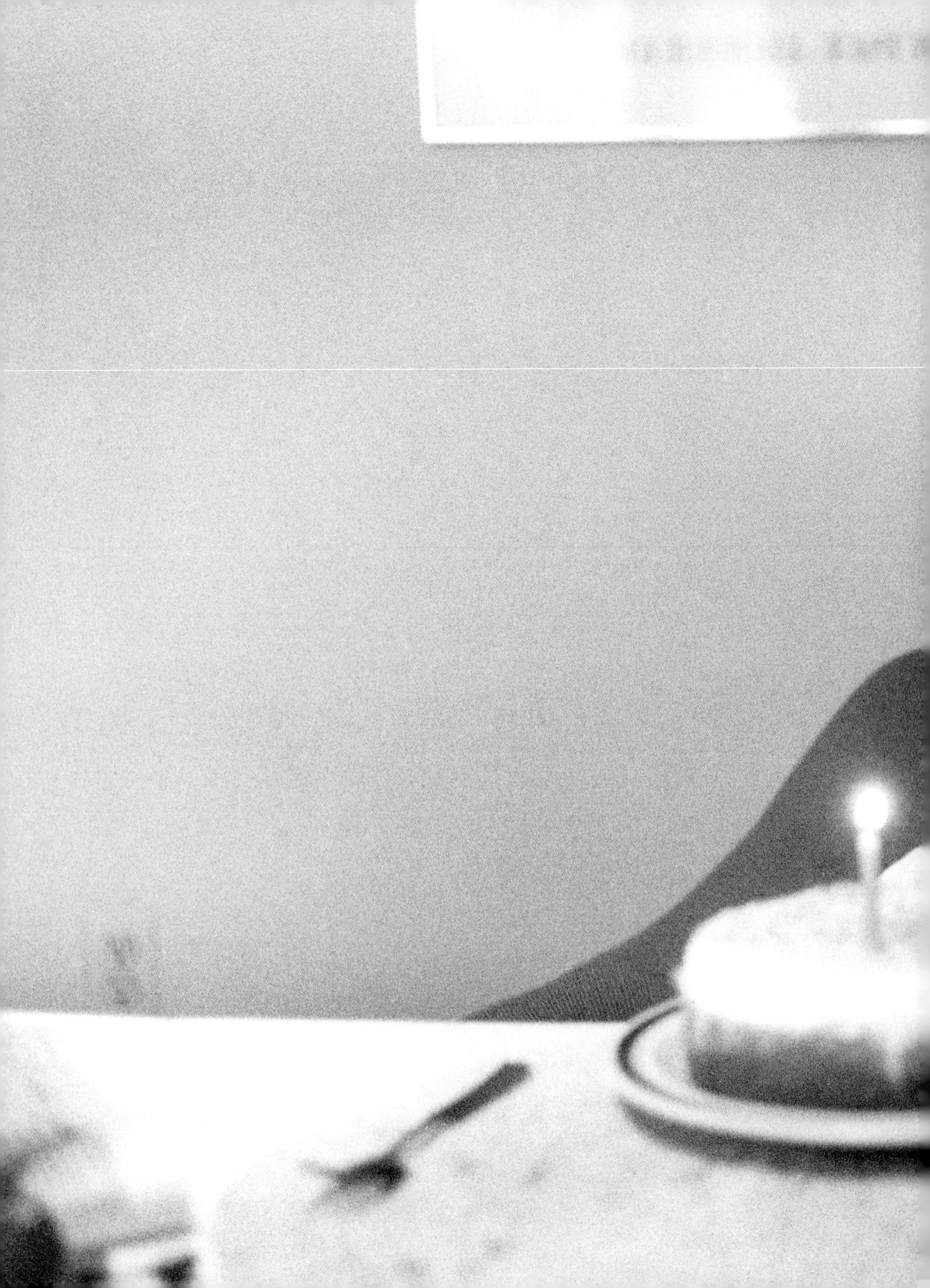

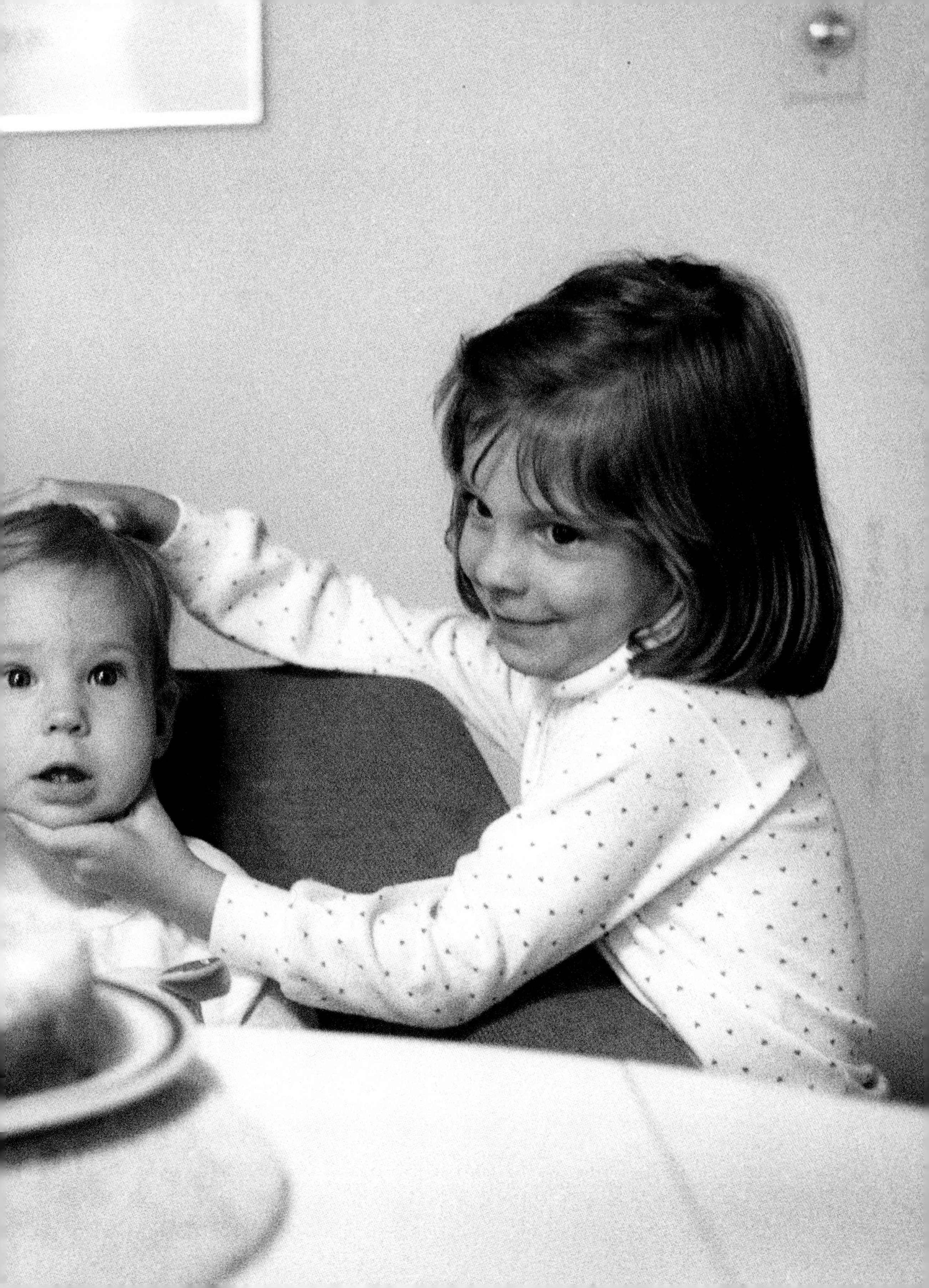

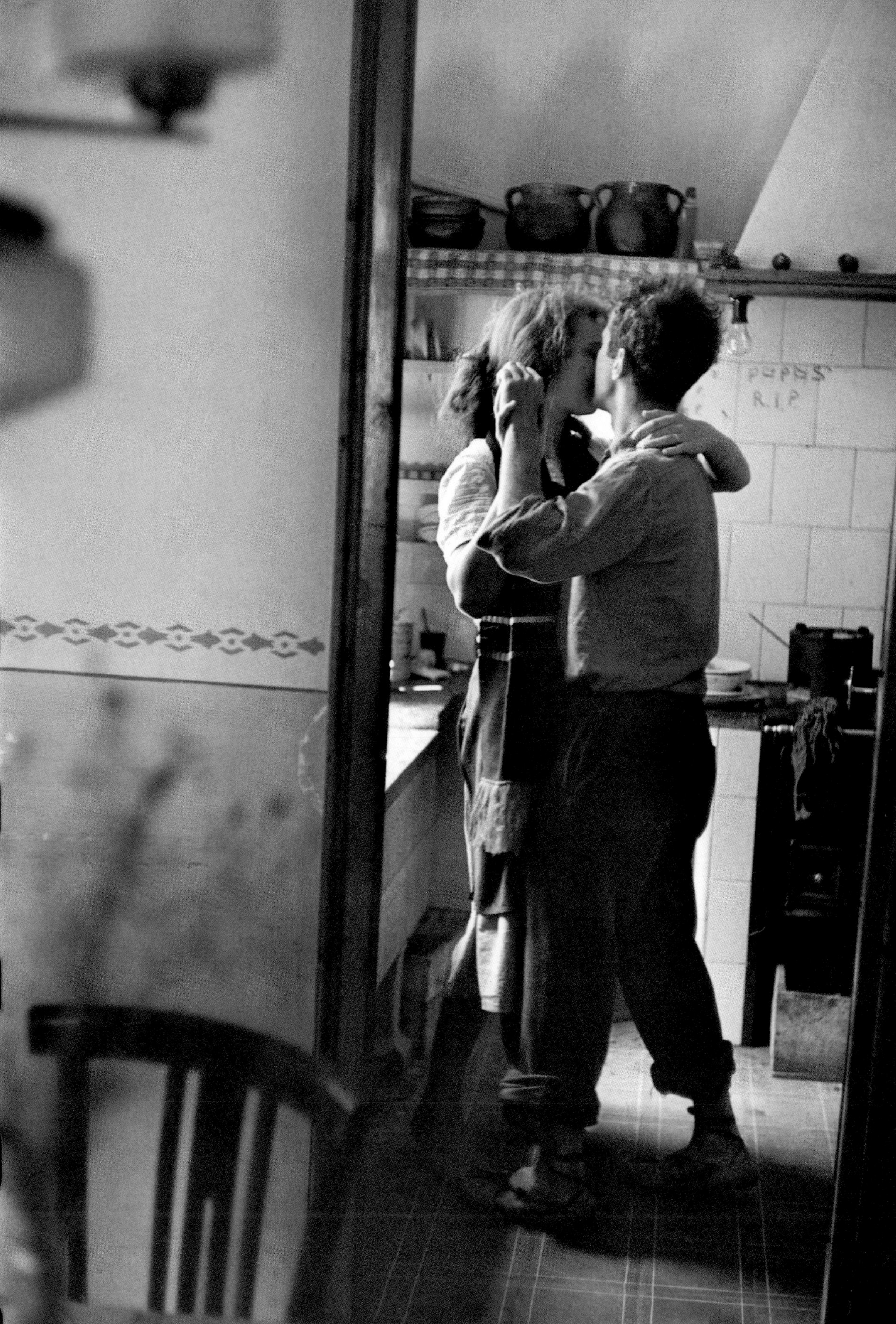

PEPAS
R.I.P

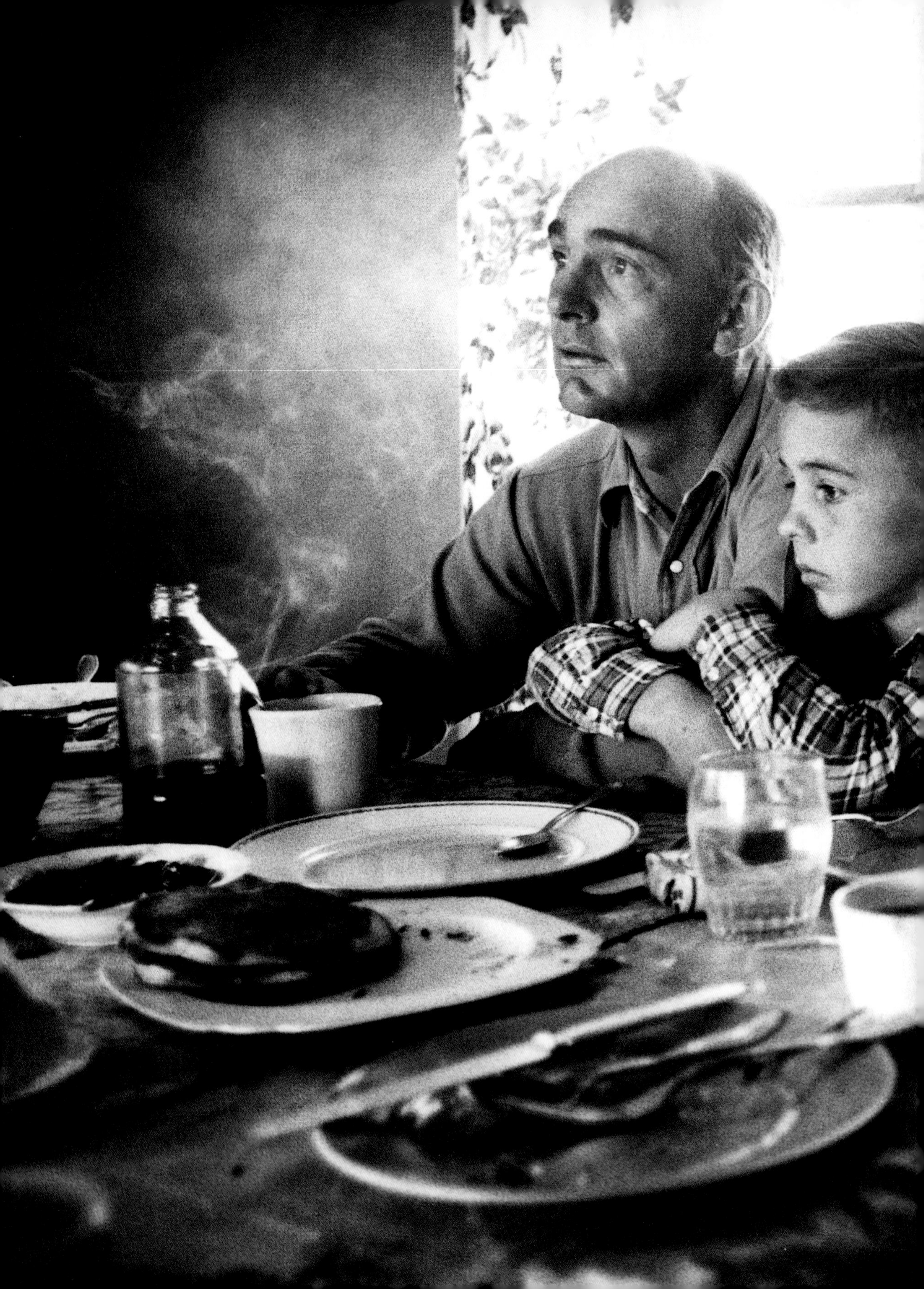

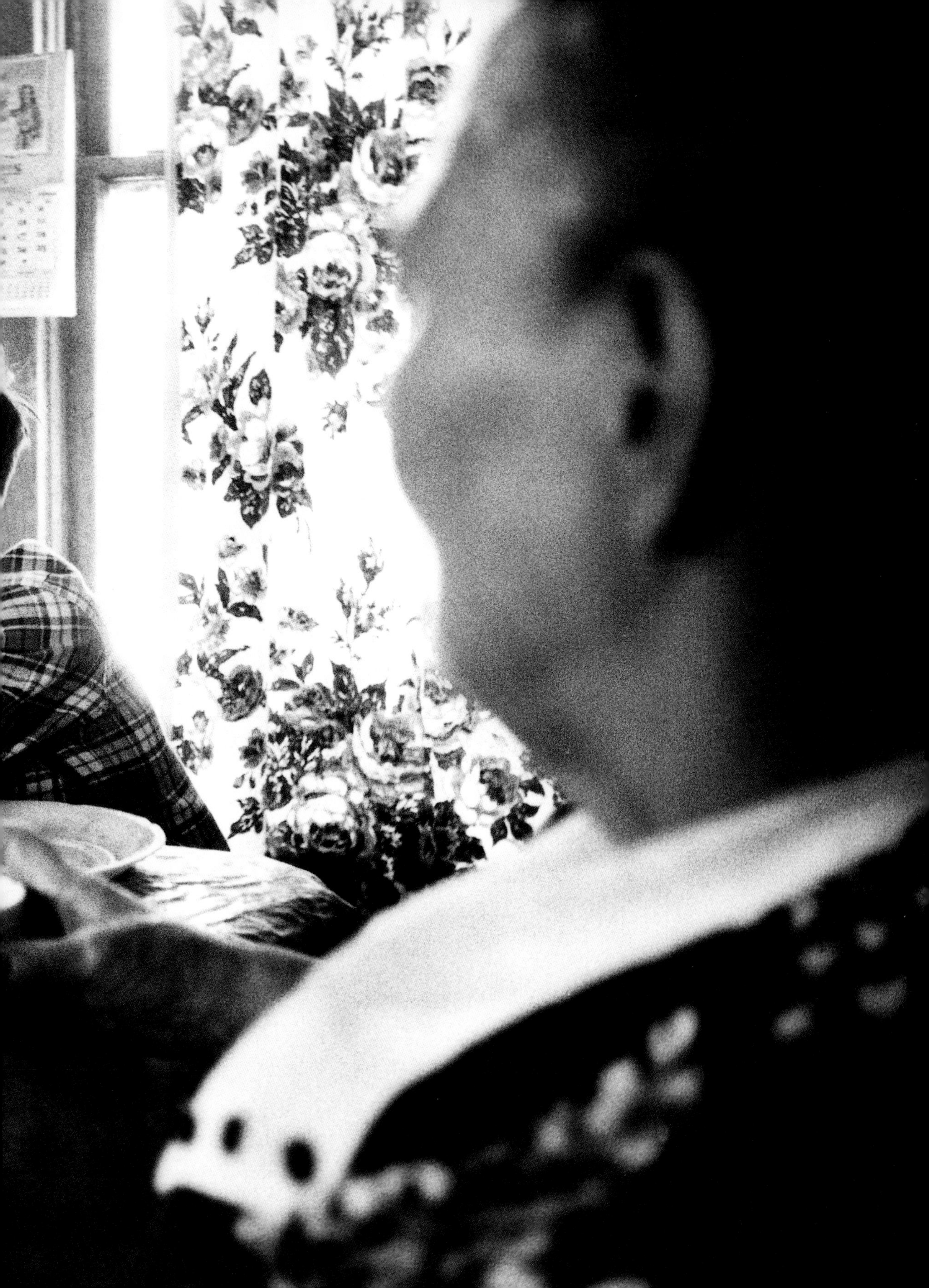

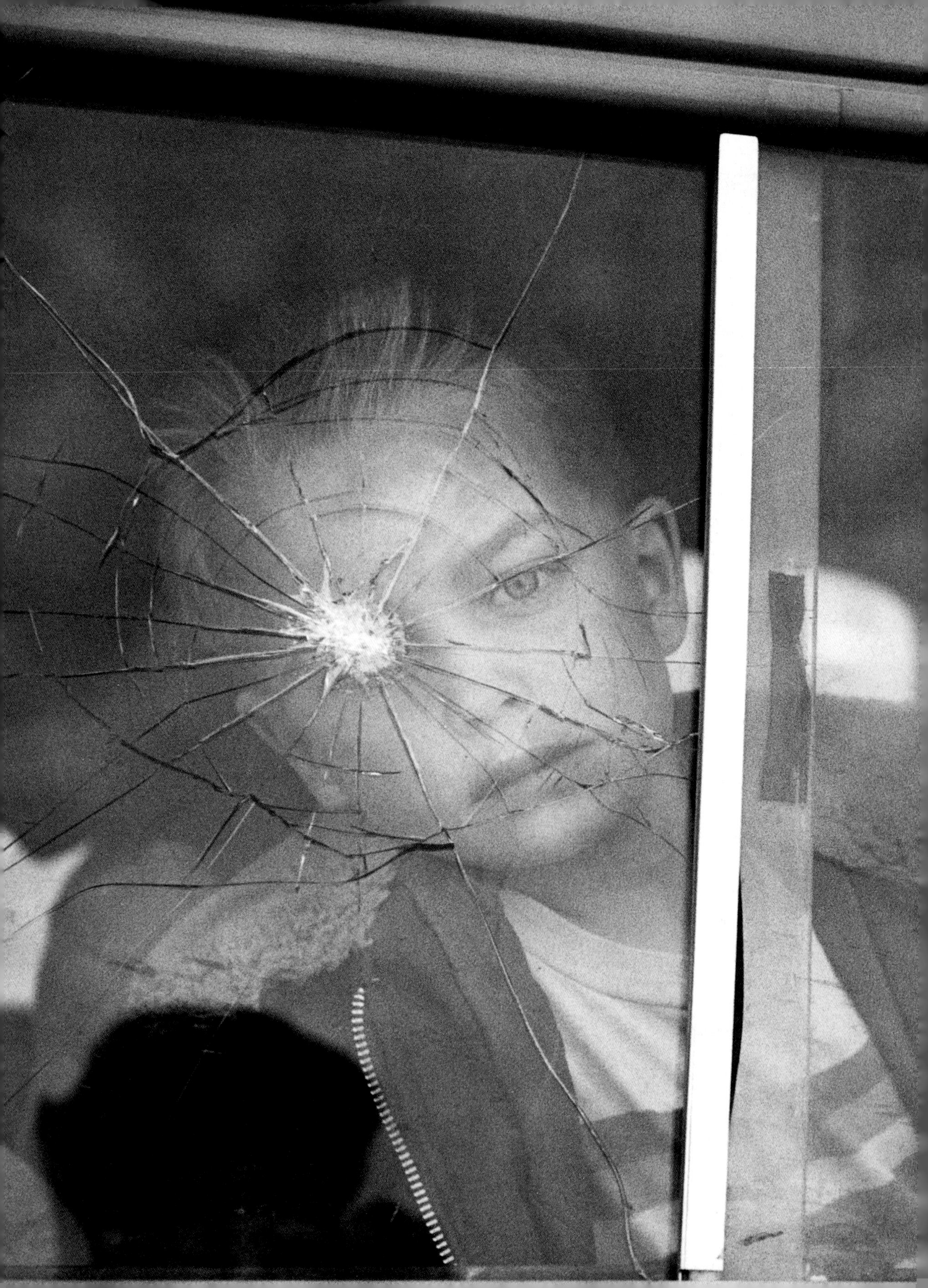

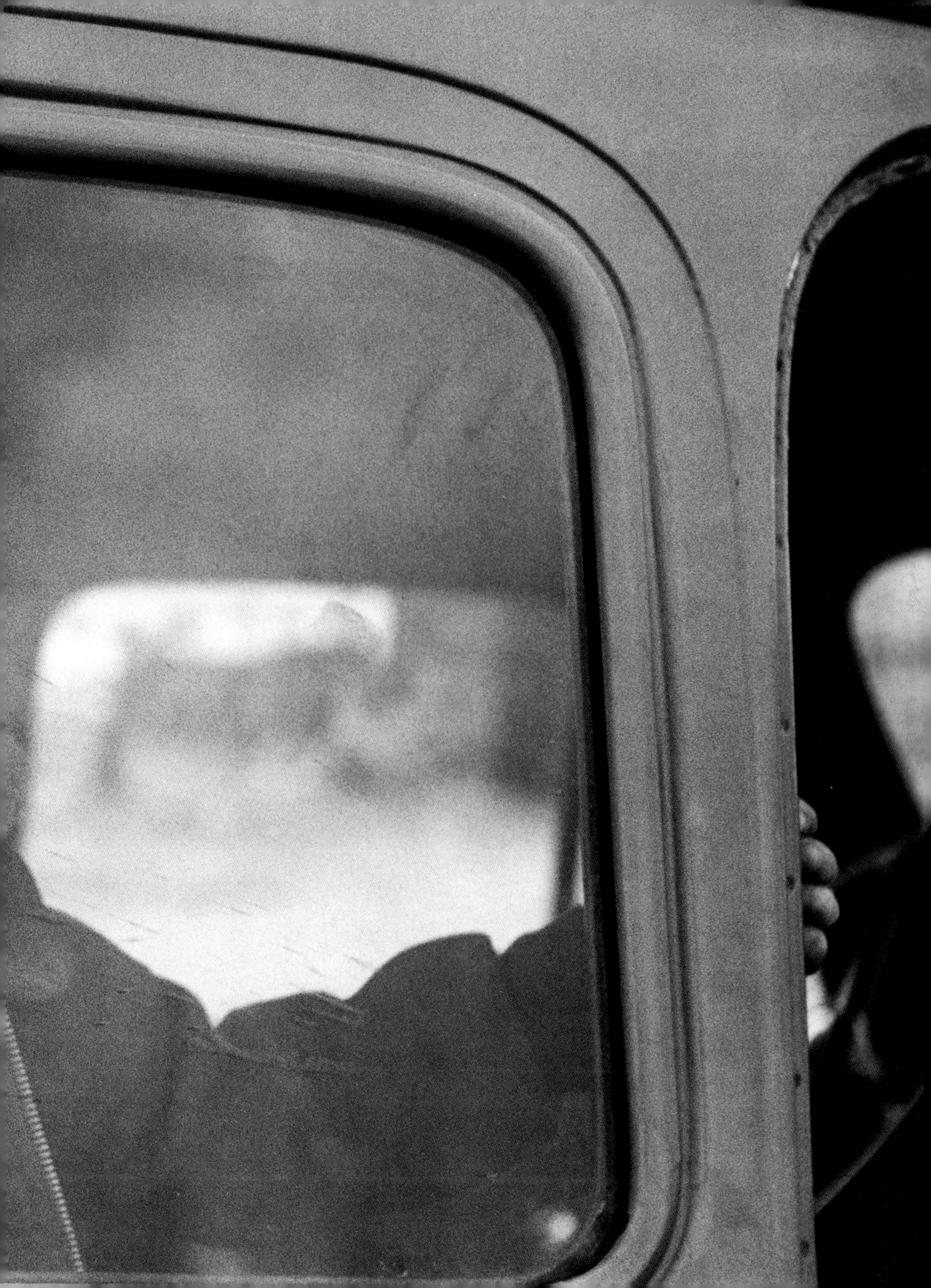

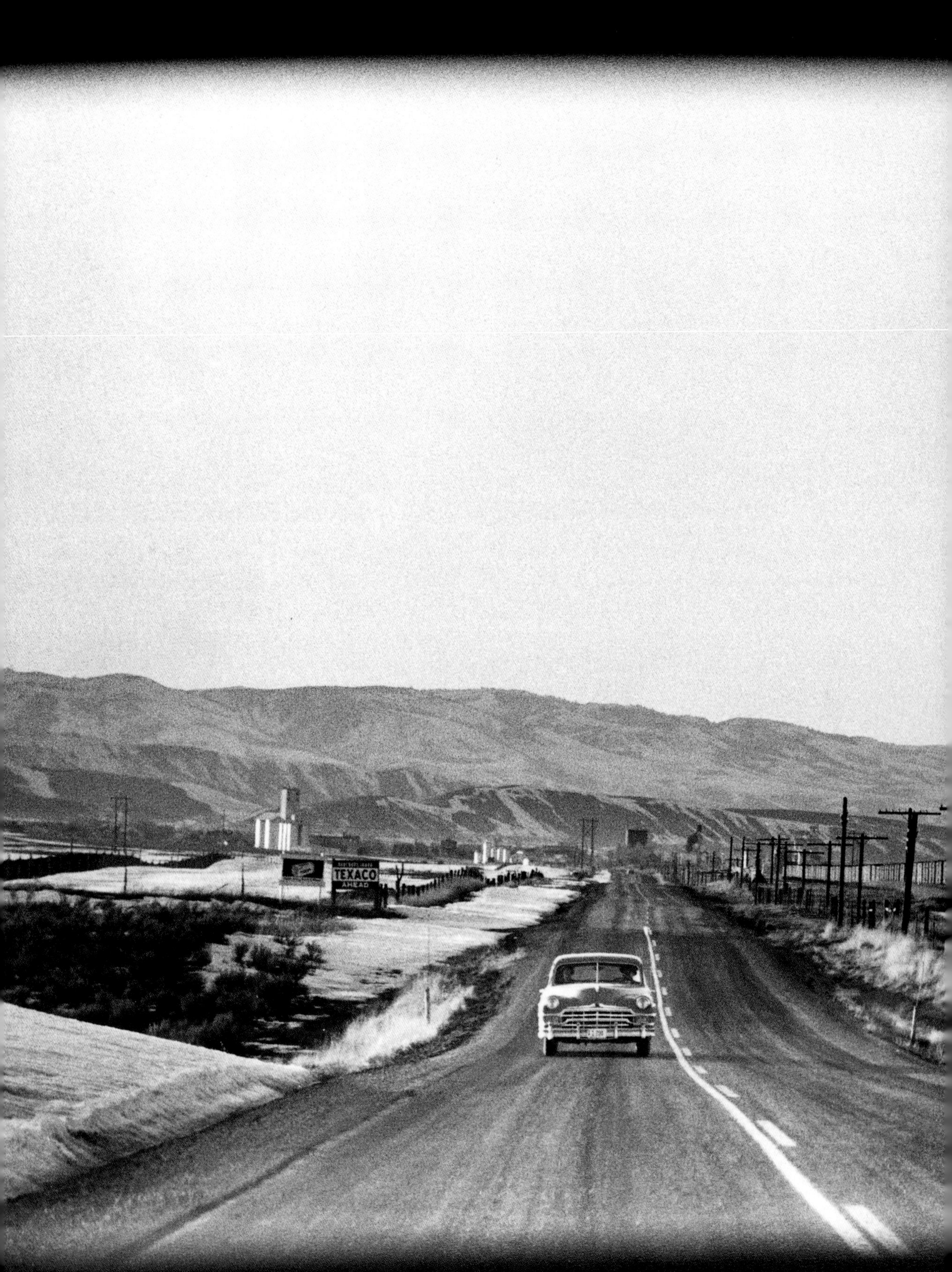

TEXACO
AHEAD

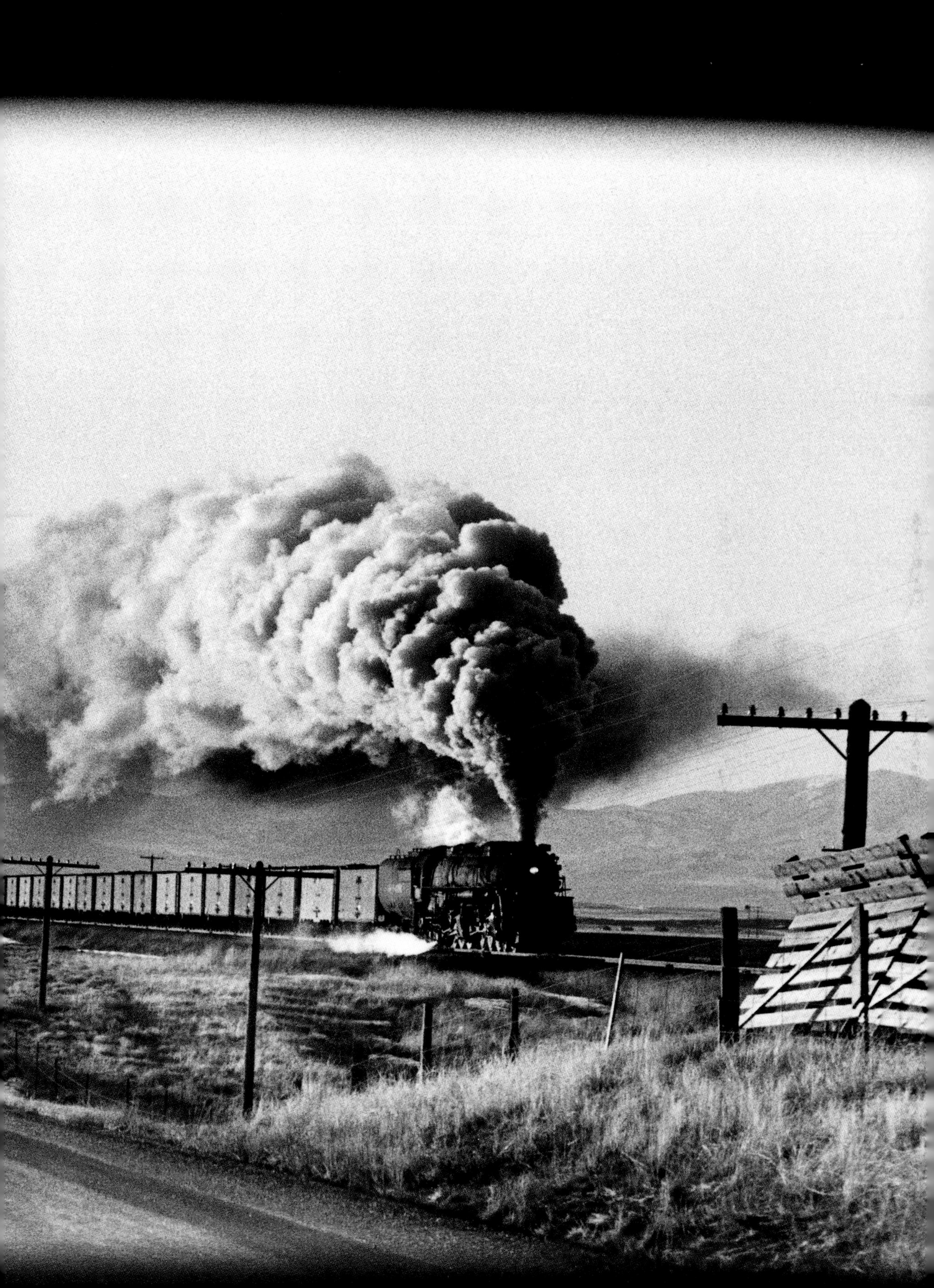

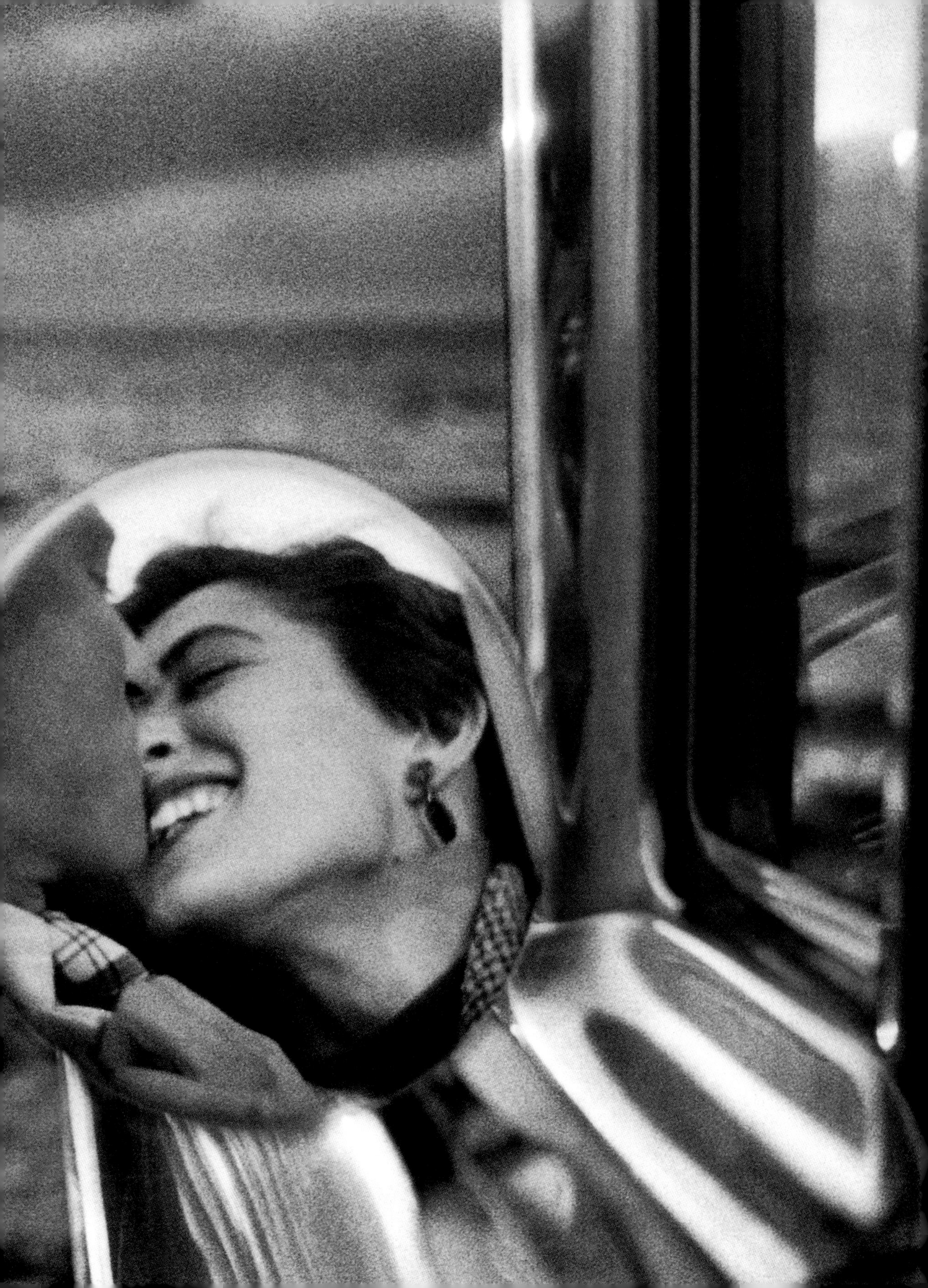

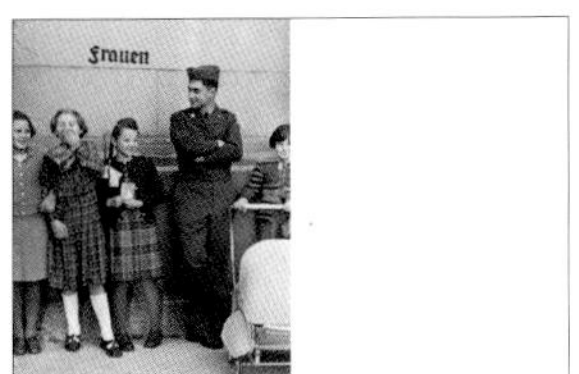

2. Karlsruhe, Germany, 1951

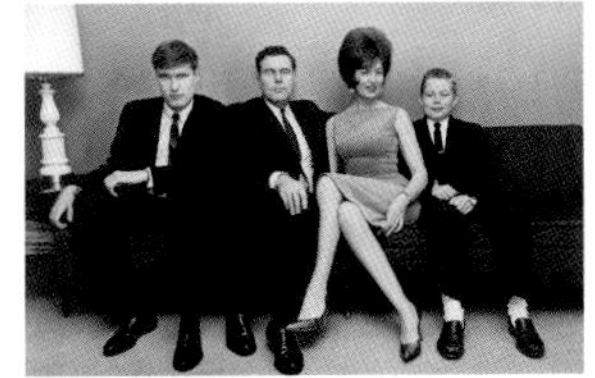

10. USA, 1962

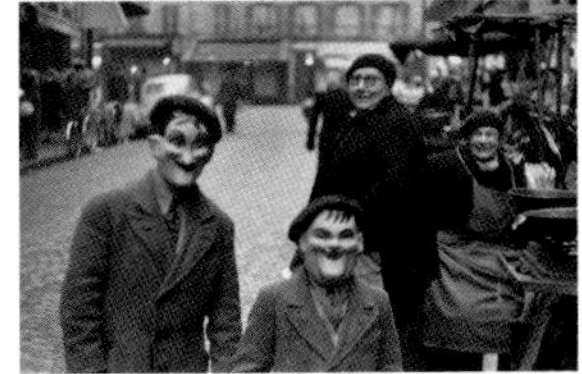

12. Paris, France, 1949

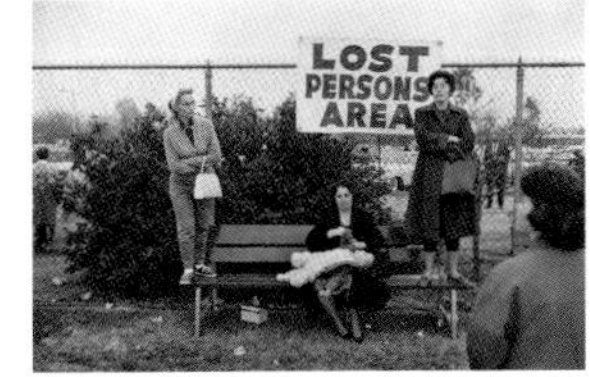

14. Pasadena, California, 1963

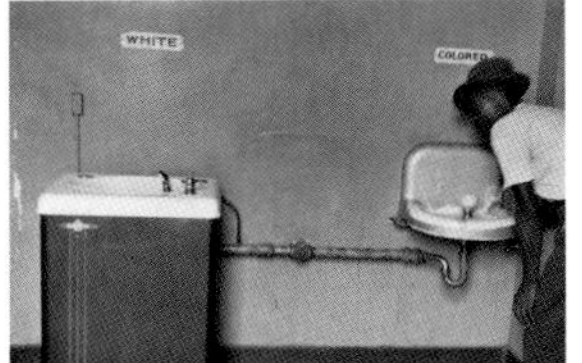

16. North Carolina, USA, 1950

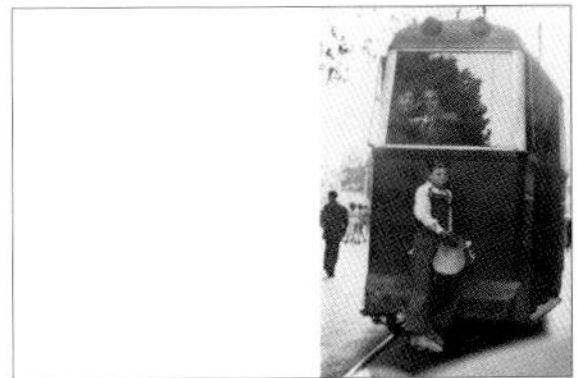

19. Barcelona, Spain, 1952

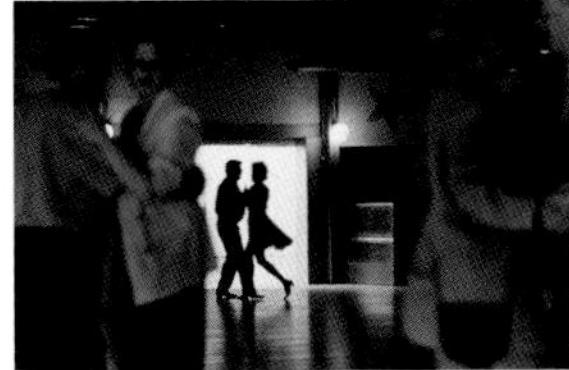

20. Finland, 2001

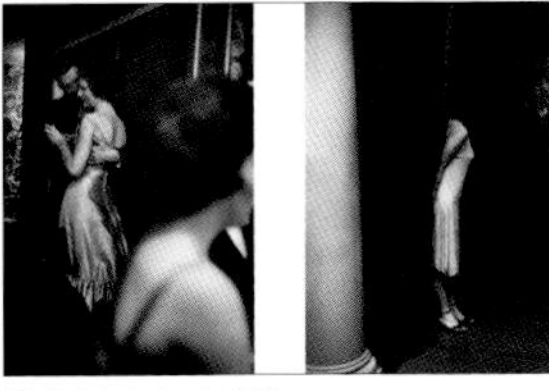

22. Dublin, Ireland, 1962
23. San Francisco, California, 1955

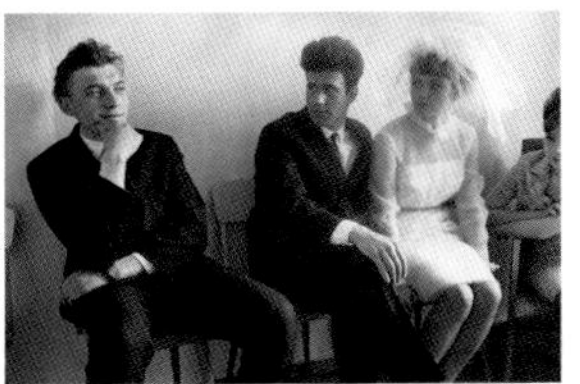

24. Bratsk, Siberia, USSR, 1967

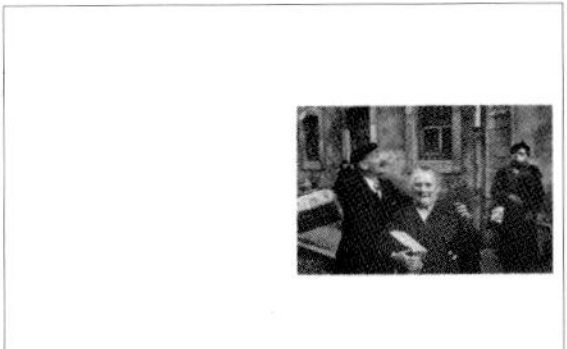

27. Verdun, France, 1951

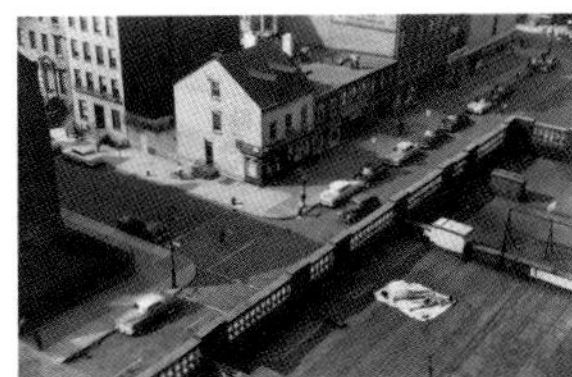

28. New York City, 1954

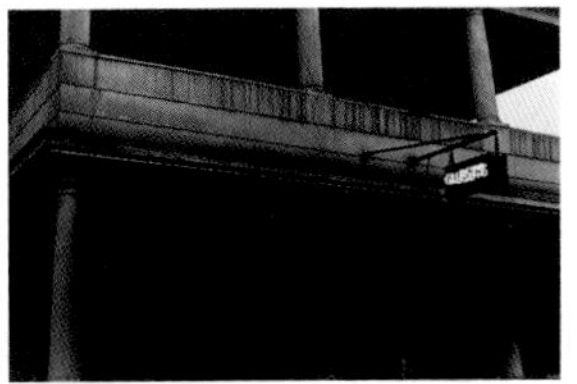

30. Cassadaga, Florida, 1956

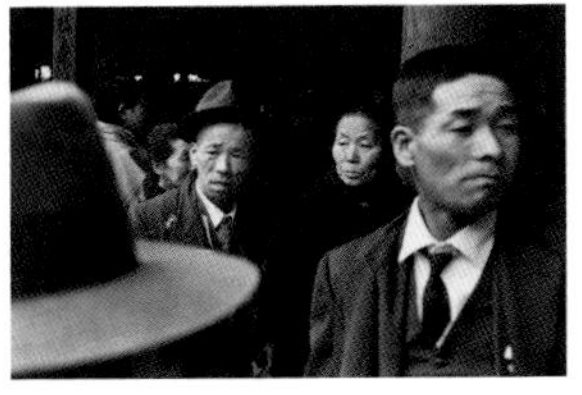

32. Tokyo, Japan, 1956

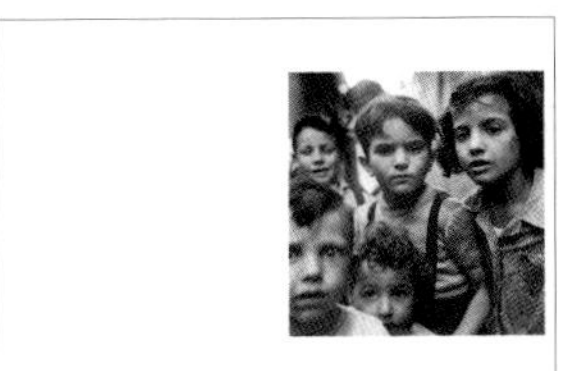

35. Venice, Italy, 1949

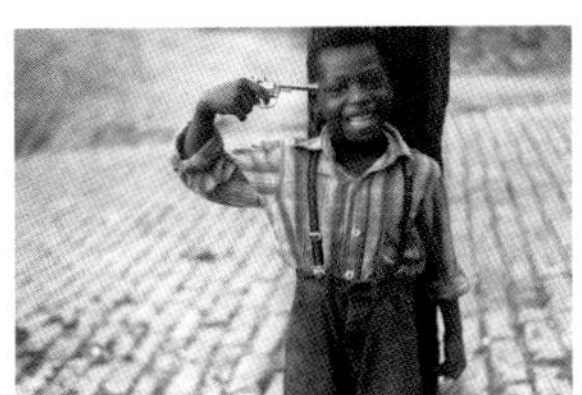

36. Pittsburgh, Pennsylvania, 1950

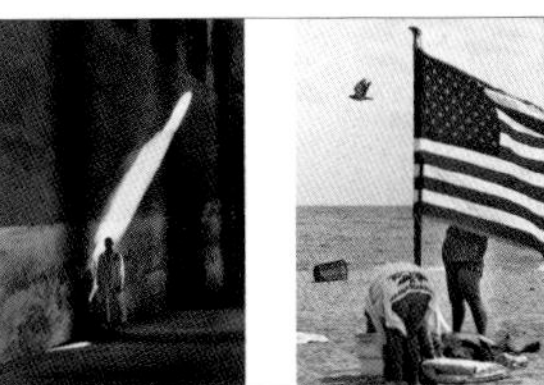

38. Cairo, Egypt, 1958
39. Coney Island, New York, 1975

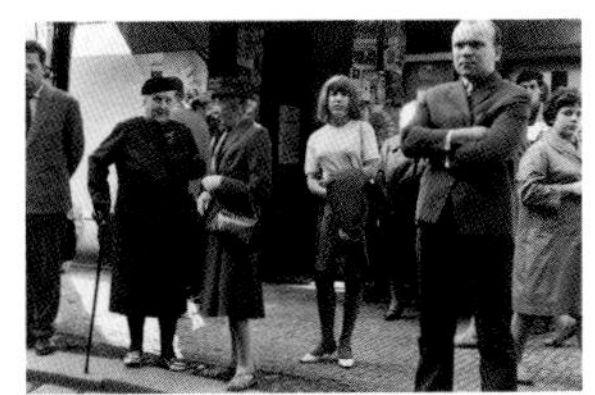

40. Prague, Czechoslovakia, 1964

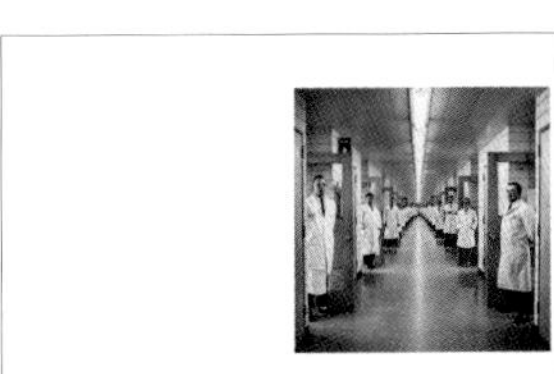

43. New Jersey, USA, 1966

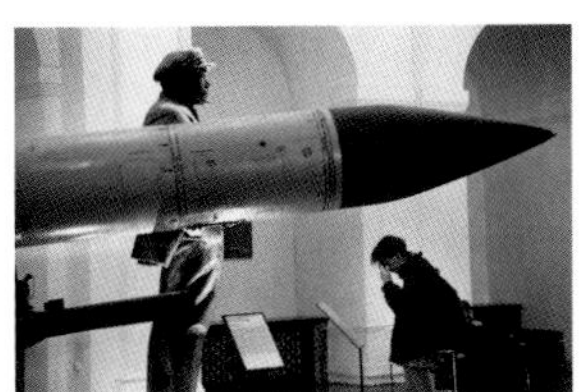

44. Berlin, Germany, 1995

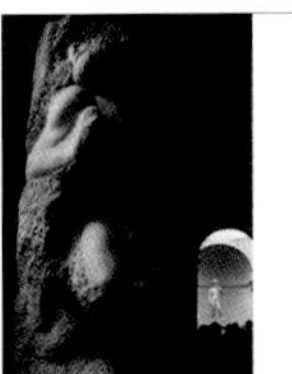

46. Florence, Italy, 1976
47. Cachoeira, Brazil, 2005

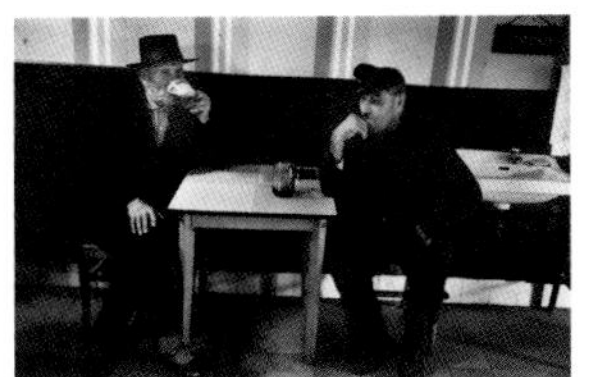

48. Hungary, 1964

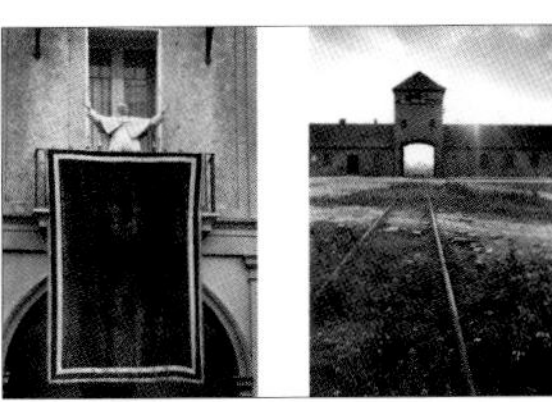

50. Pope Pius XII, Castel Gandolfo, Italy, 1956
51. Auschwitz, Poland, 1964

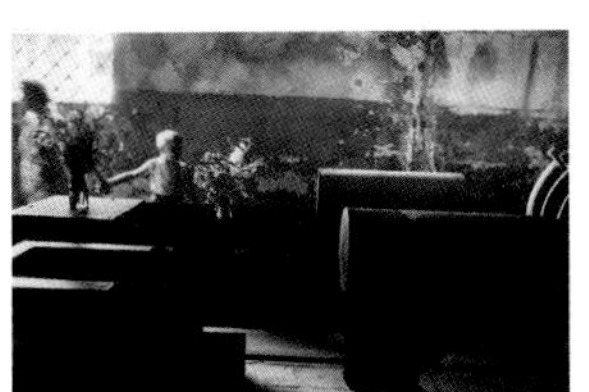

52. Auschwitz, Poland, 1964

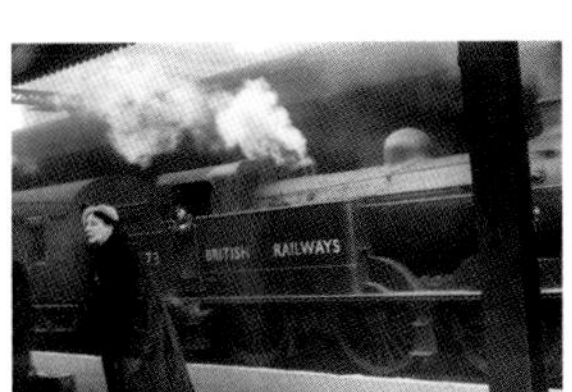

54. London, England, 1952

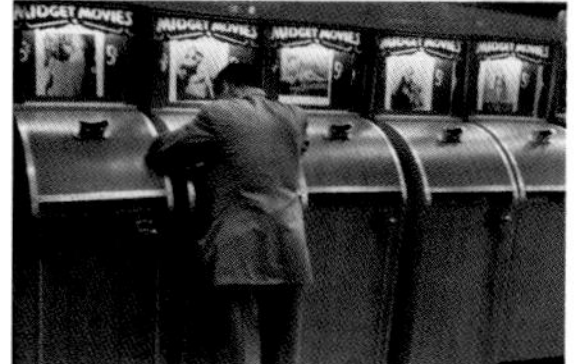
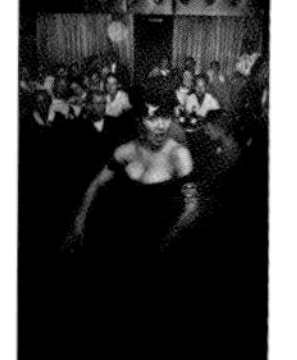
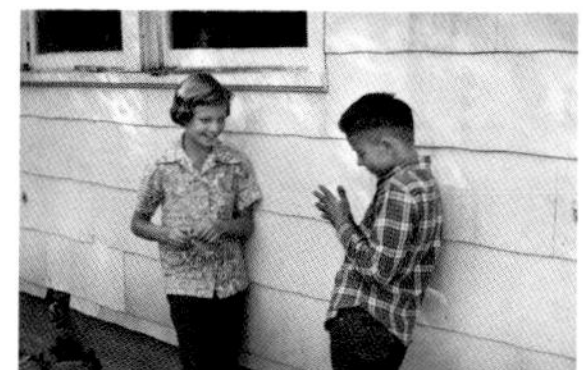
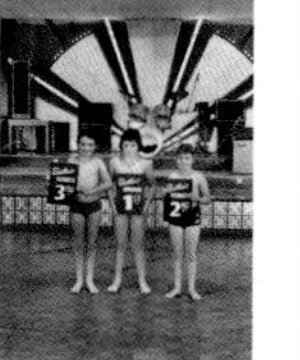

56. New York City, 1950

58. Des Moines, Iowa, 1955
59. Times Square, New York, 1950

60. Wyoming, USA, 1954

62. Barry Island, Wales, 1978
63. Honfleur, France, 1968

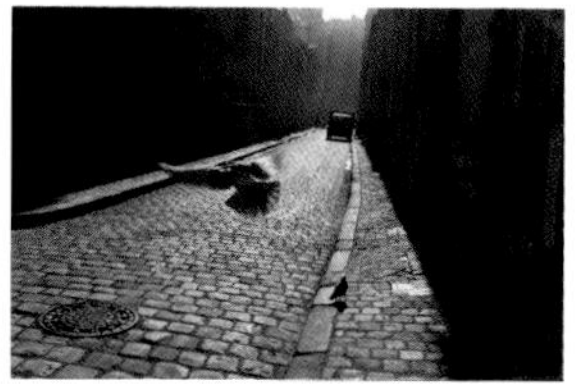
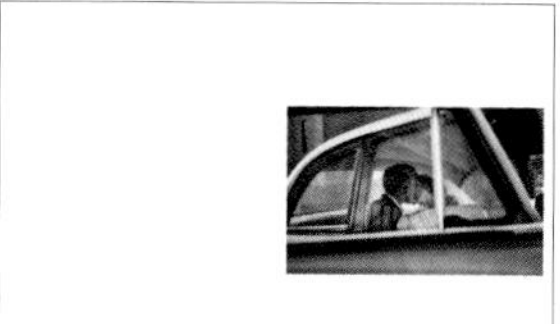
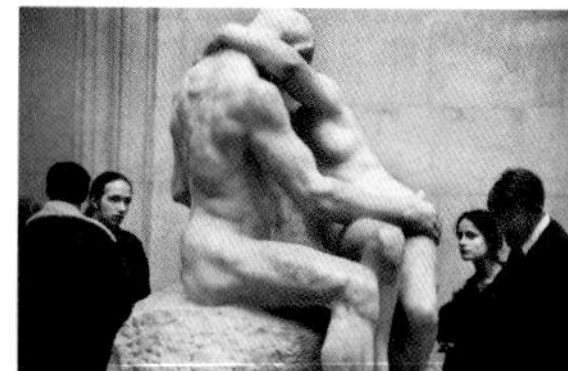
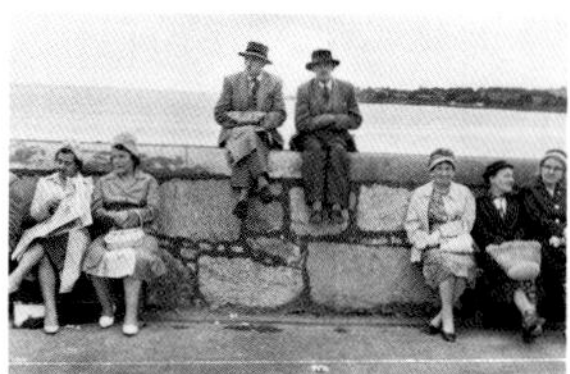

64. Orleans, France, 1952

67. New York City, 1955

68. Tate Gallery, London, England, 1993

70. Dún Laoghaire, Ireland, 1962

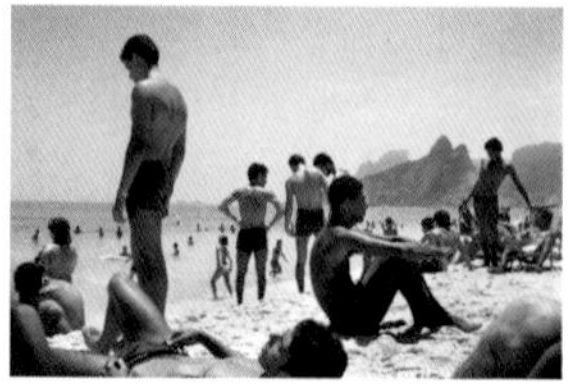
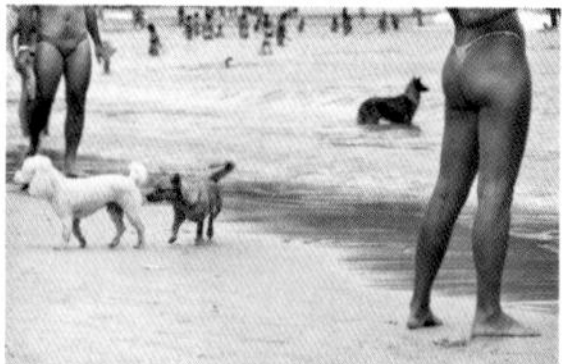
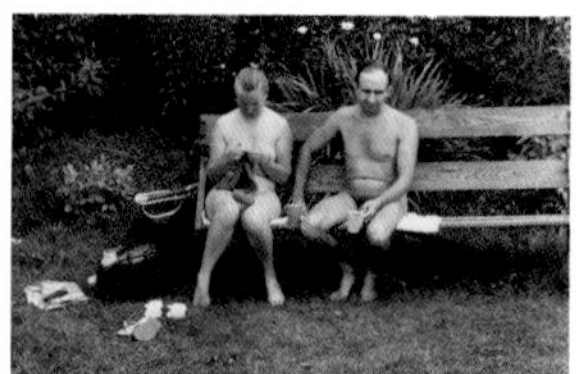
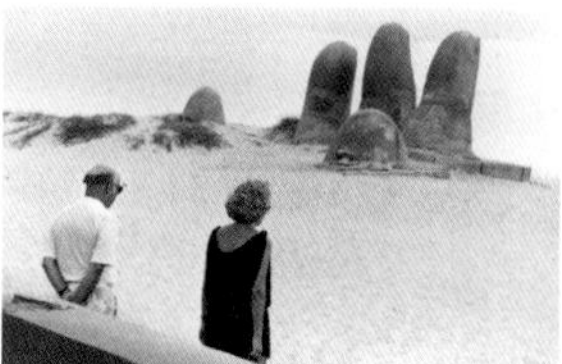

72. Rio de Janeiro, Brazil, 1984

74. Búzios, Brazil, 1990

76. Kent, England, 1968

78. Punta del Este, Uruguay, 1990

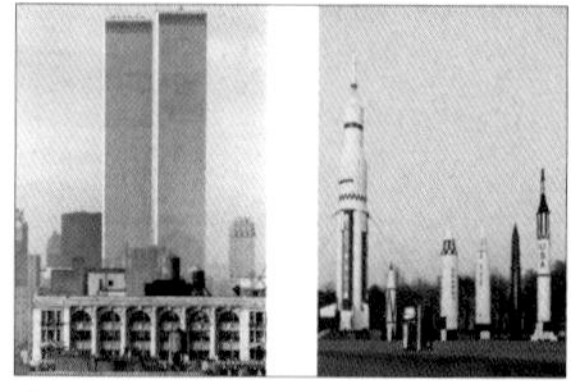
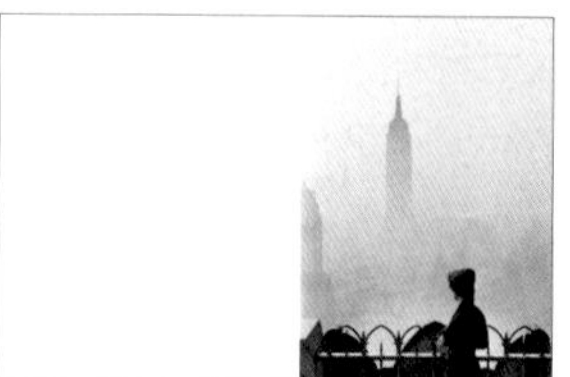
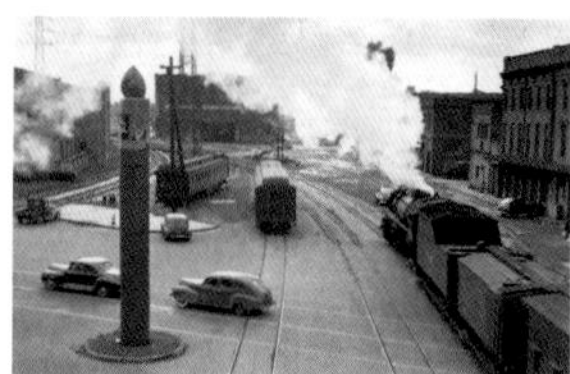
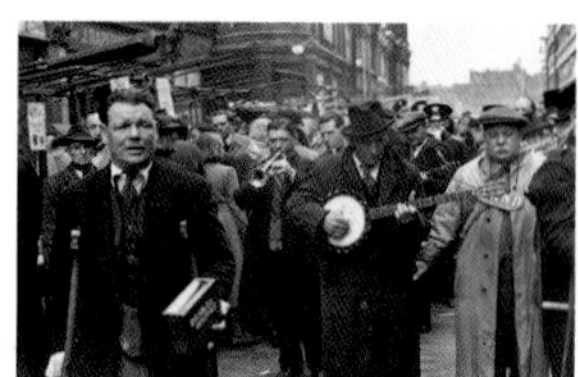

80. New York City, 1979
81. Huntsville, Alabama, 1974

83. New York City, 1955

84. New Orleans, Louisiana, 1950

86. London, England, 1952

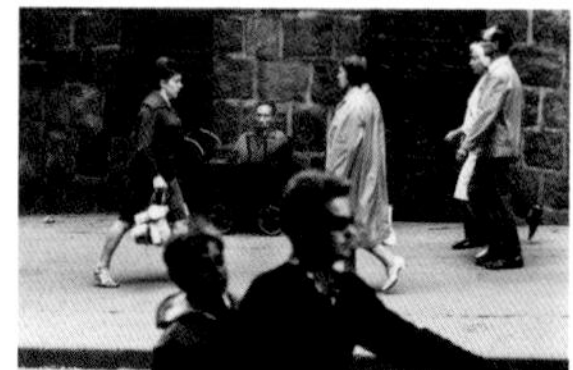
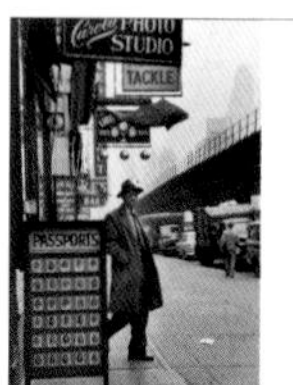
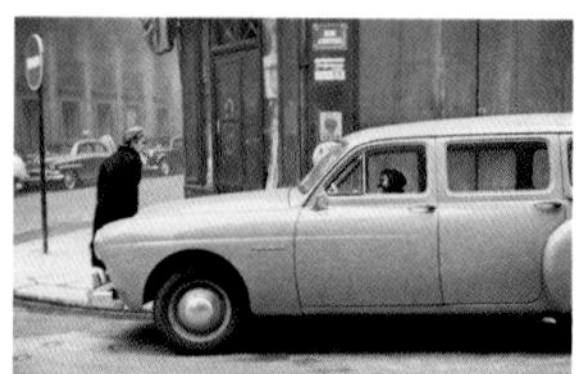
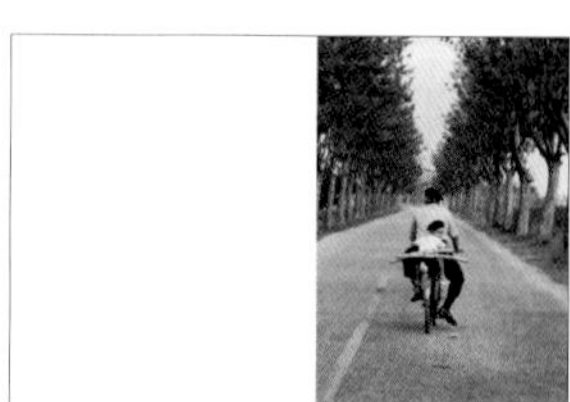

88. Gdansk, Poland, 1964

90. New York City, 1955
91. New Mexico, USA, 1962

92. Paris, France, 1957

95. Provence, France, 1955

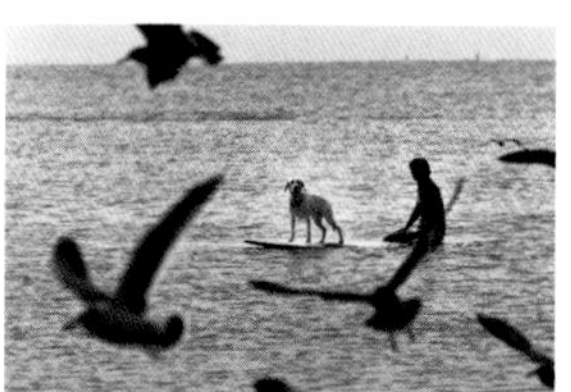
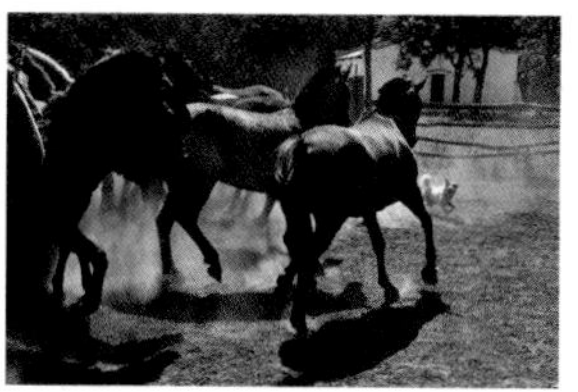
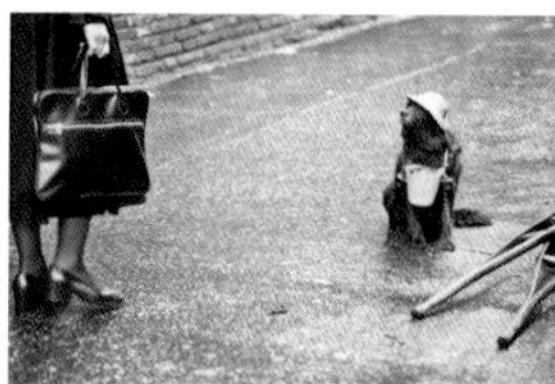
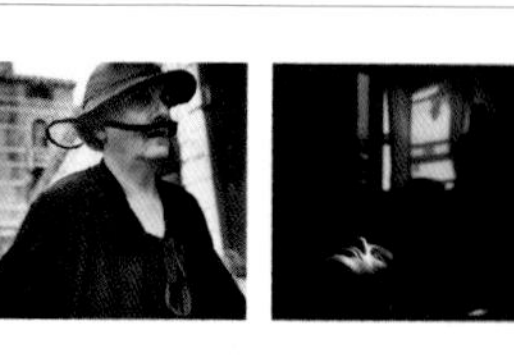

96. Enoshima, Japan, 2003

98. Argentina, 1972

100. Rome, Italy, 1978

102. Milan, Italy, 1949
103. Los Angeles, 1947

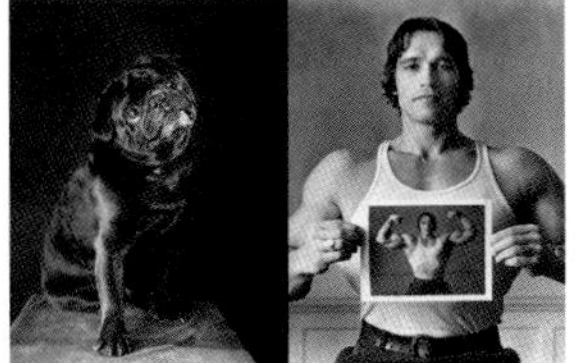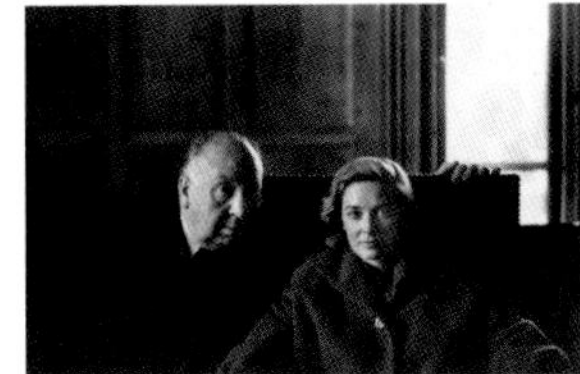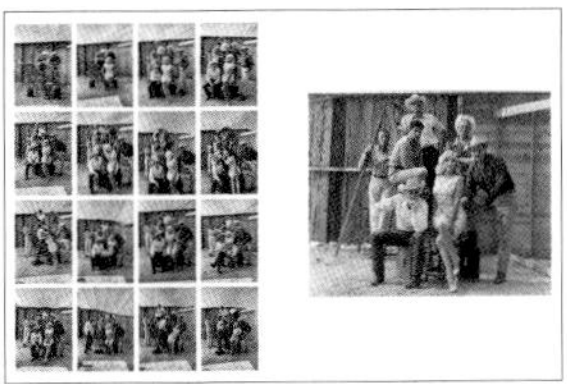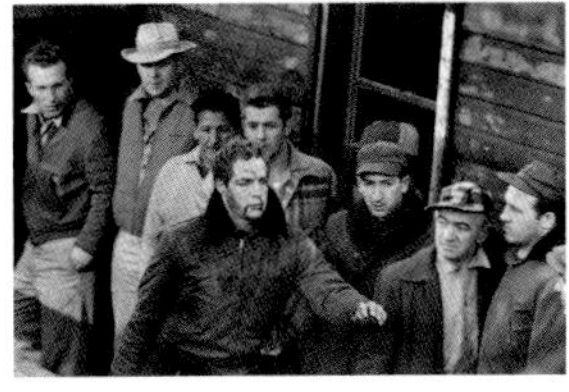

104. New York City, 1991
105. Arnold Schwarzenegger, New York City, 1977

106. Alfred Hitchcock and Vera Miles, New York City, 1950

108. Arthur Miller, Frank Taylor (producer), Ely Wallach, John Houston, Montgomery Clift, Marilyn Monroe and Clark Gable, "The Misfits" set, Reno, Nevada, 1961

110. Marlon Brando, "On the Waterfront" set, Hoboken, 1954

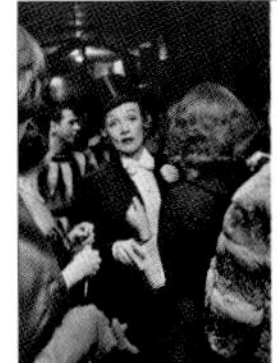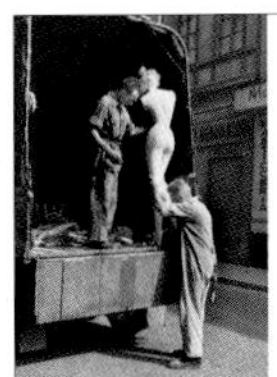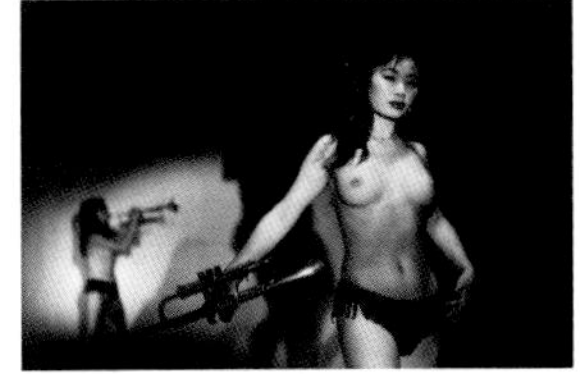

112. Marlene Dietrich, New York City, 1959
113. Marilyn Monroe, Reno, Nevada, 1960

114. Grace Kelly, New York City, 1955

116. Milan, Italy, 1949
117. New York City, 1955

118. Tokyo, Japan, 1960

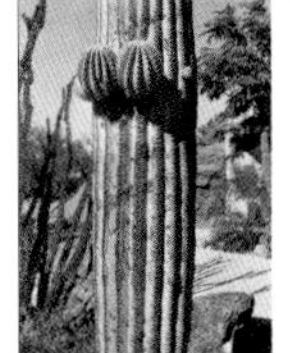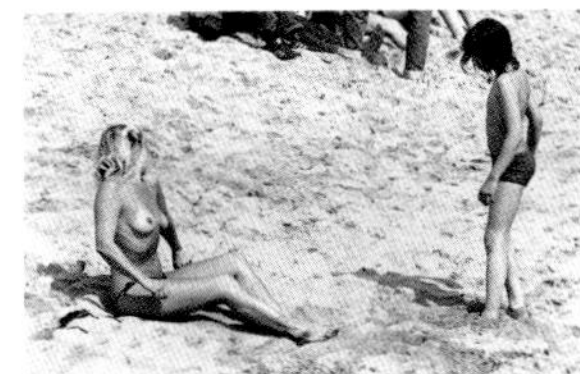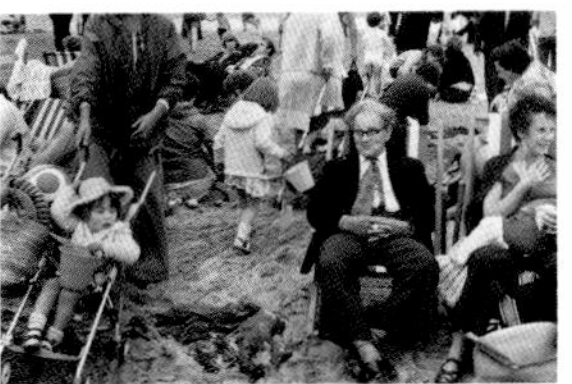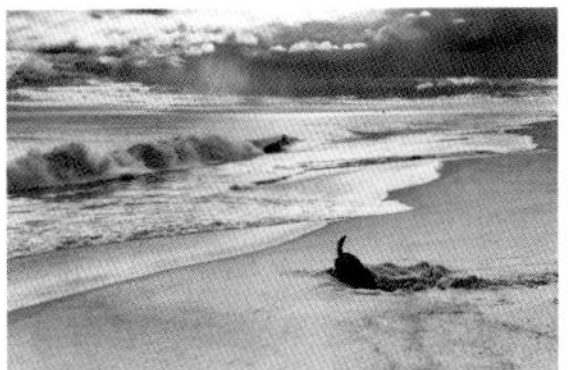

120. Arizona, USA, 1978
121. Chicago, Illinois, 1949

122. St. Tropez, France, 1980

124. Liverpool, England, 1978

126. East Hampton, New York, 1998

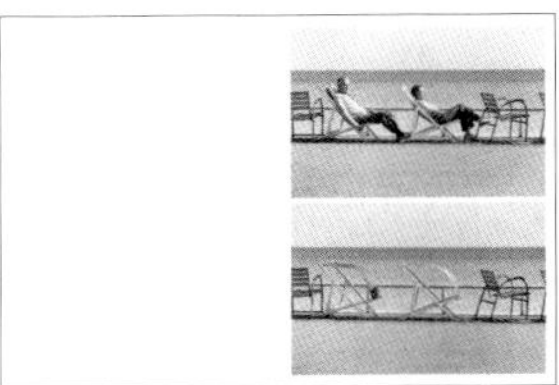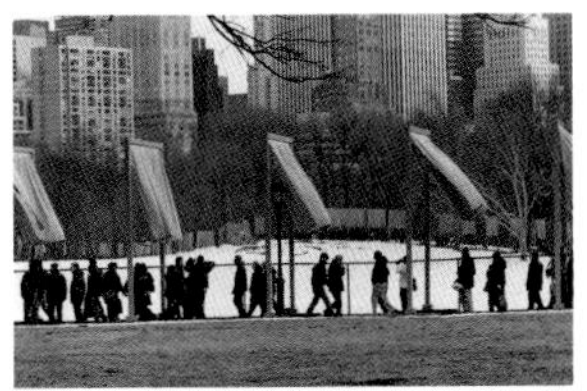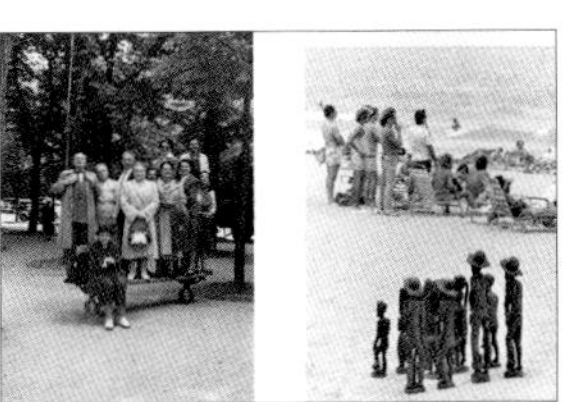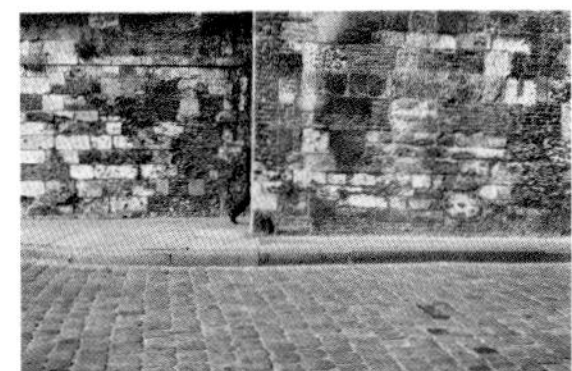

129. Cannes, France, 1975

130. Central Park, New York City, 2005

132. Paris, France, 1951
133. San Juan, Puerto Rico, 1978

134. Honfleur, France, 1968

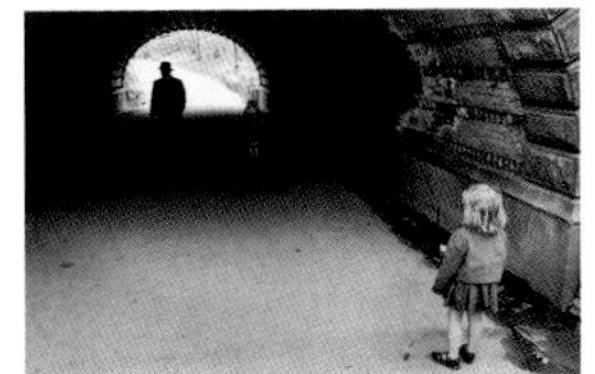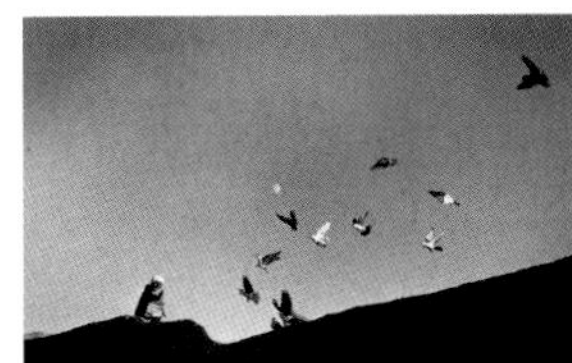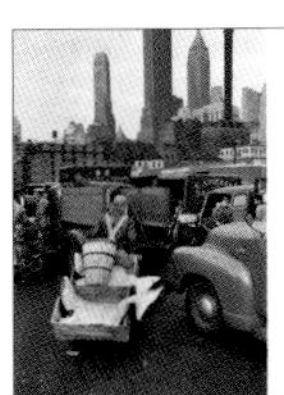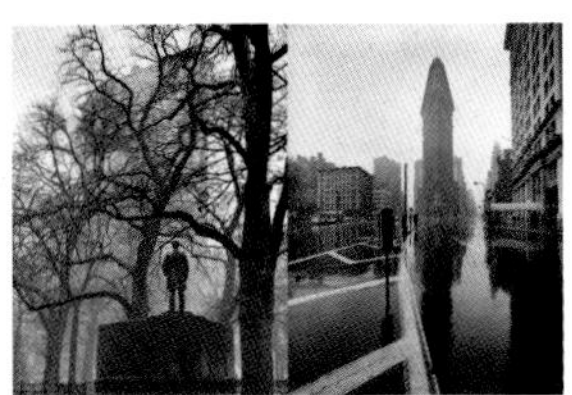

136. New York City, 1953

138. Herat, Afghanistan, 1977

140. New York City, 1953
141. New York City, 1978

142. New York City, 1969
143. New York City, 1969

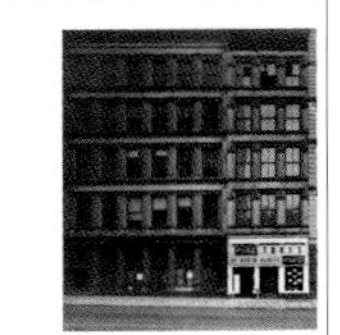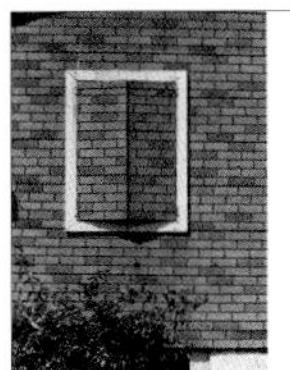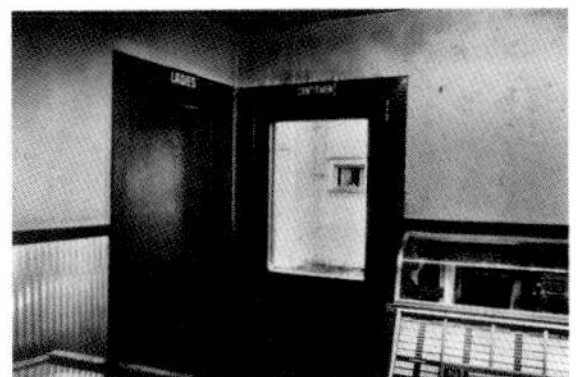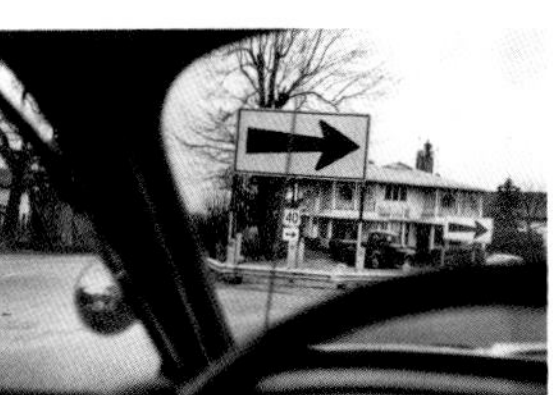

145. New York City, 1969

146. Puerto Rico, 1969
147. Motel room, Texas, USA, 1962

148. Western USA, 1954

150. Idaho, USA, 1954

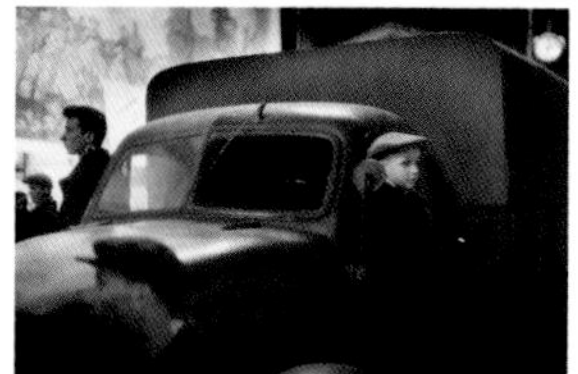

152. Moscow, USSR, 1957

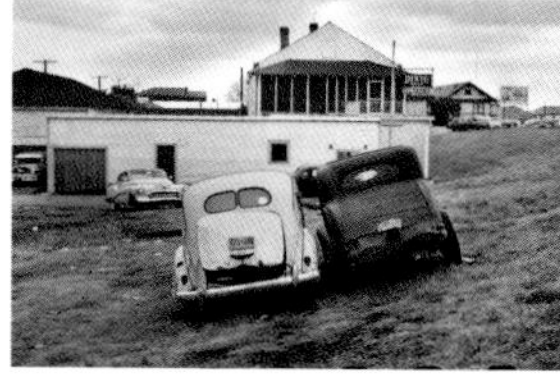

154. New Orleans, Louisiana, 1950

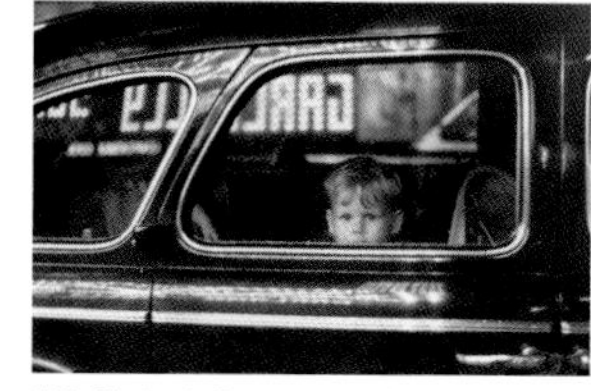

156. Pittsburgh, Pennsylvania, 1950

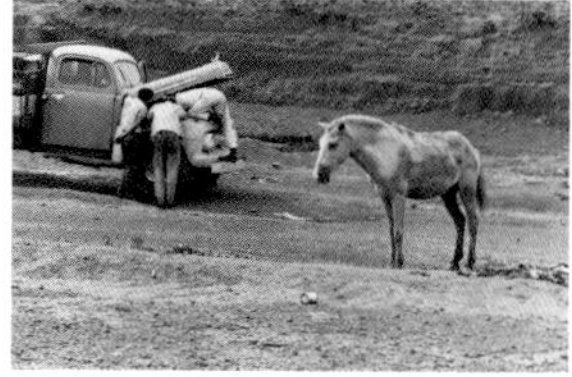

158. Brasilia, Brazil, 1961

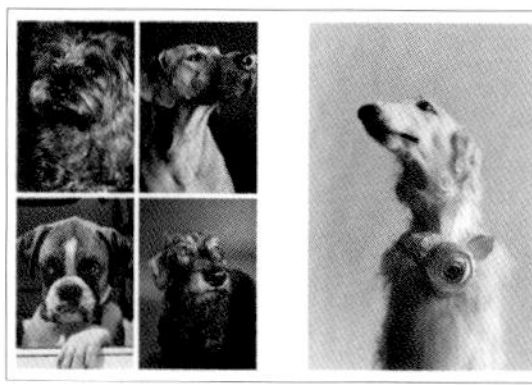

160. (from top left clockwise)
New York City, 1996. New York City, 2003.
New York City, 2002. Tokyo, Japan, 2003
161. New York City, 1999

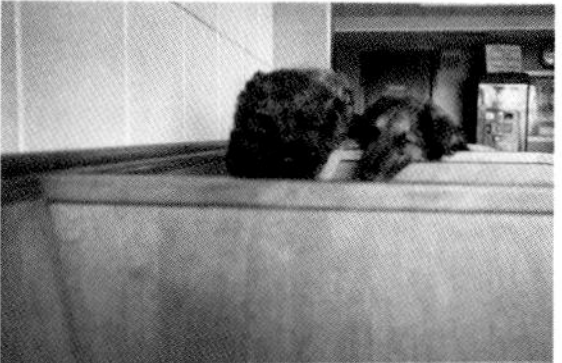

162. New York City, 1953

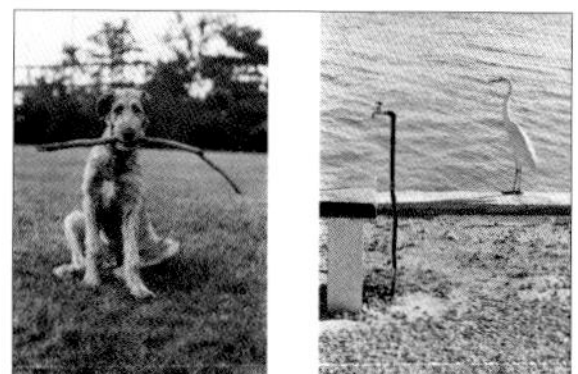

164. New Jersey, USA, 1971
165. Florida Keys, USA, 1968

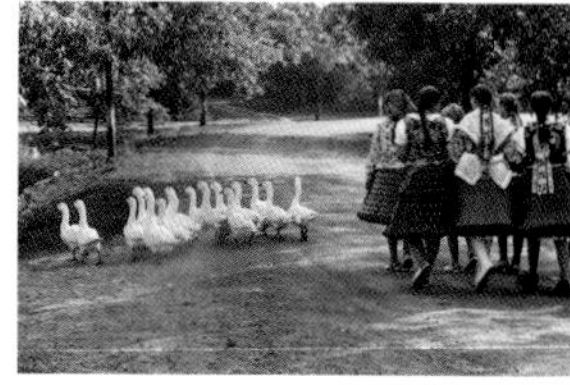

166. Hungary, 1964

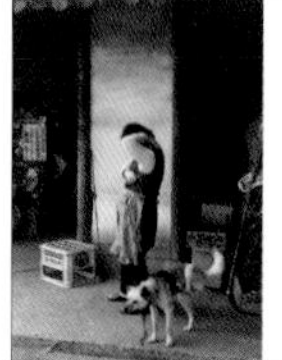

168. Kyoto, Japan, 1977
169. Krakow, Poland, 1964

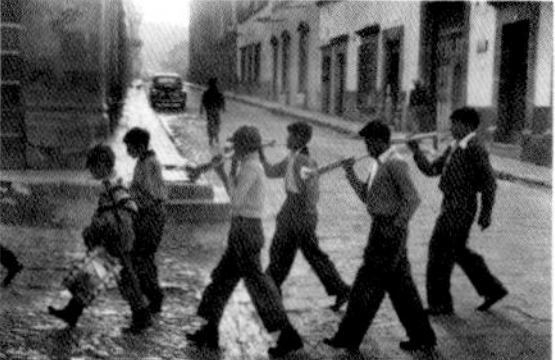

170. San Miguel de Allende, Mexico, 1957

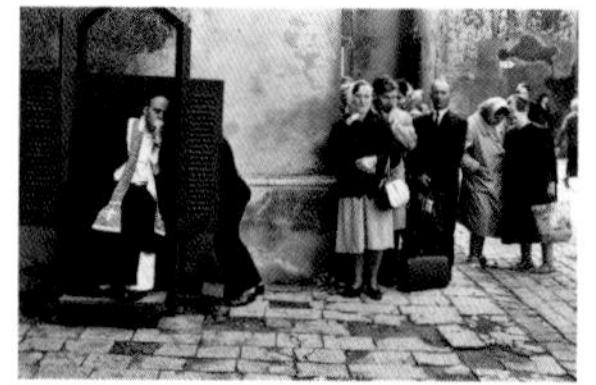

172. Czestochowa, Poland, 1964

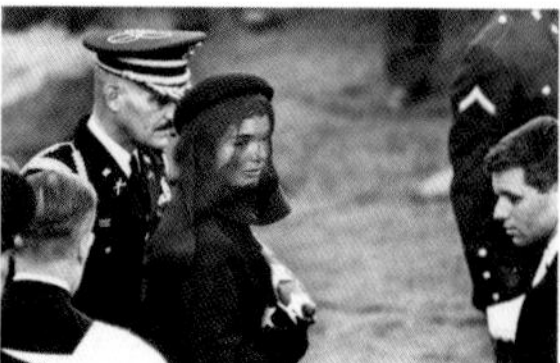

174. Jacqueline Kennedy, Arlington, Virginia, 1963

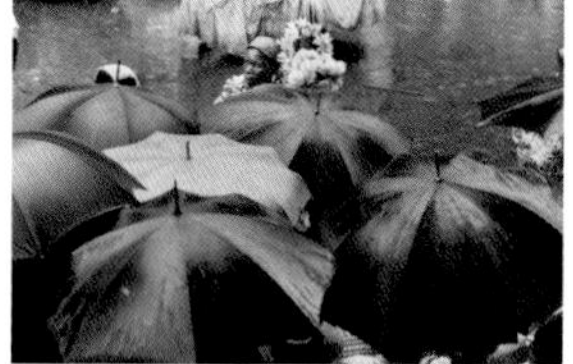

176. Brasilia, Brazil, 1961

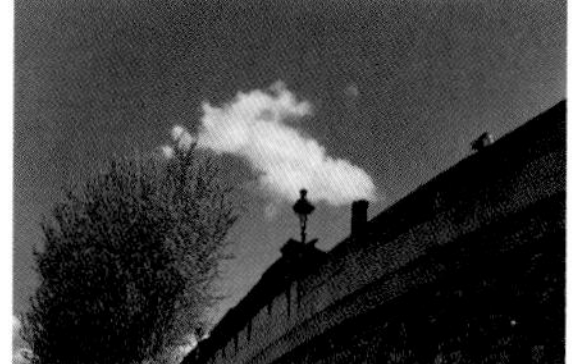

178. Paris, France, 2004

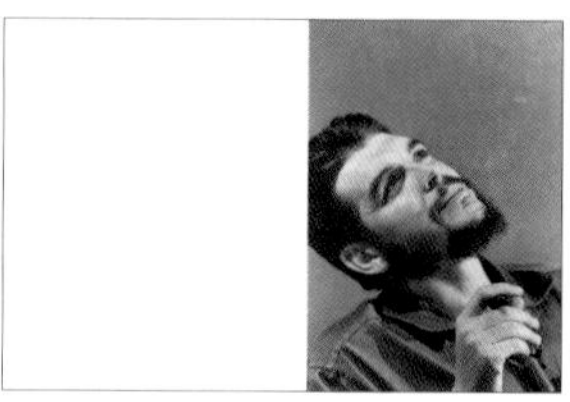

181. Che Guevara, Havana, Cuba, 1964

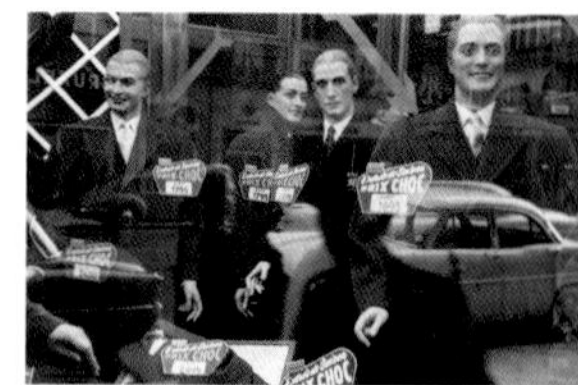

182. Brussels, Belgium, 1957

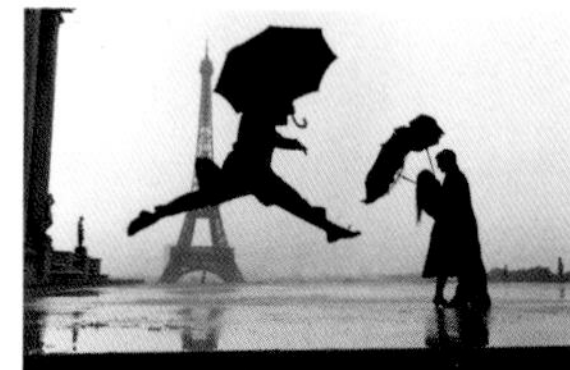

184. Paris, France, 1989

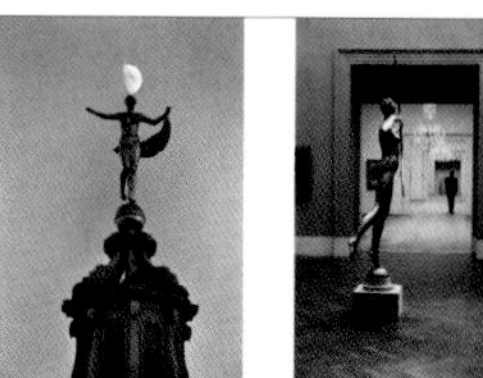

186. Berlin, Germany, 1995
187. Metropolitan Museum, New York City, 1949

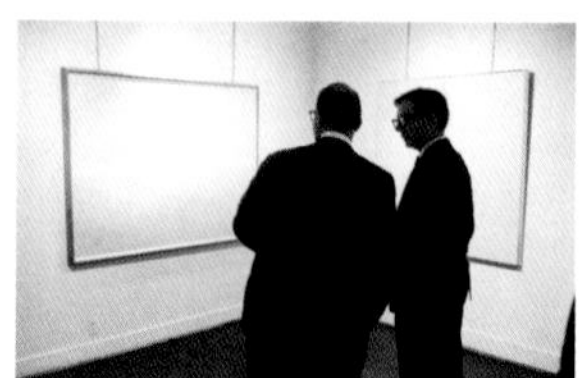

188. New York City, 1963

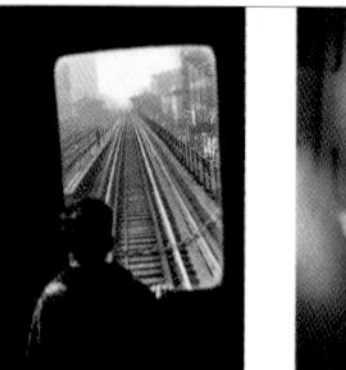

190. New York City, Third Avenue L, 1955
191. John F. Kennedy, Los Angeles, California, 1960

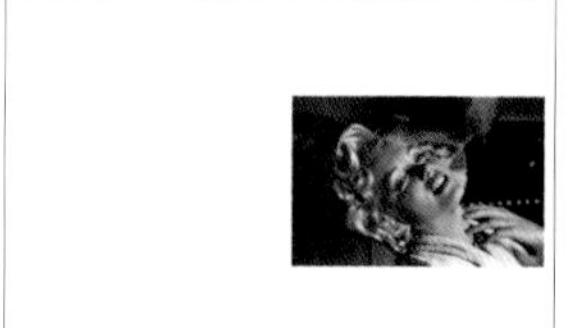

193. Marilyn Monroe, New York City, 1956

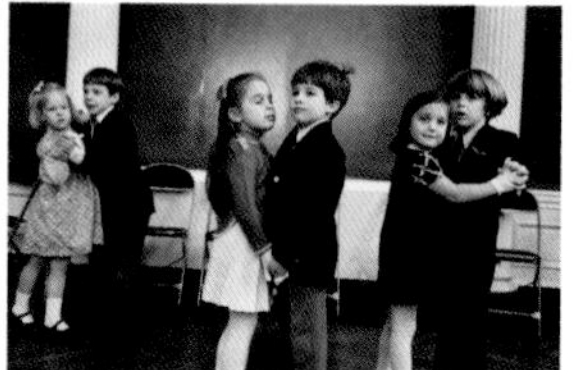

194. New York City, 1977

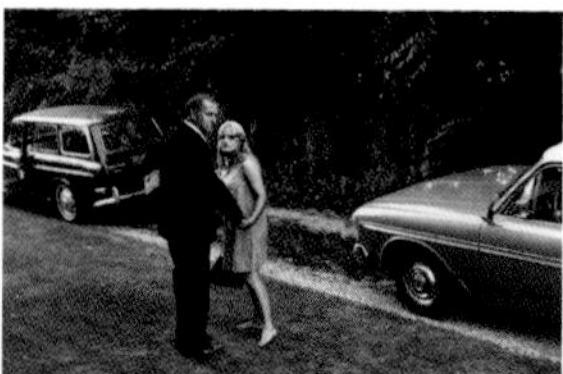

196. East Hampton, New York, 1966

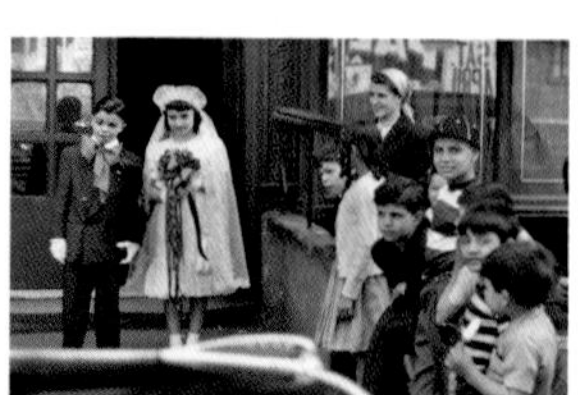

198. New York City, 1950

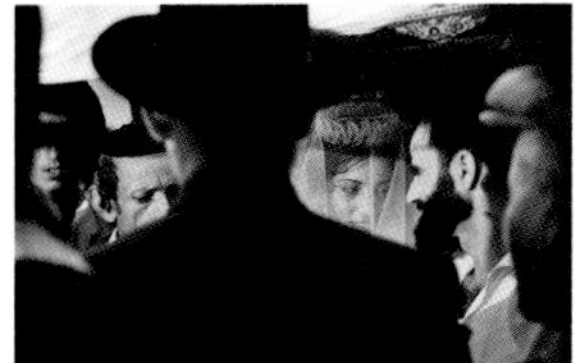

200. Israel, 1962

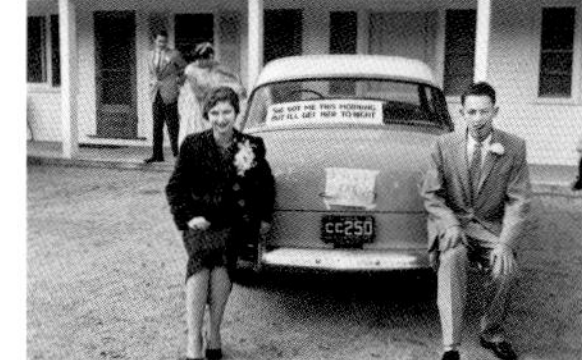

202. New Hampshire, USA, 1958

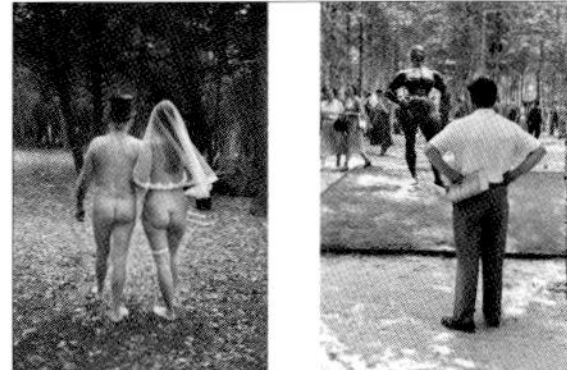

204. Kent, England, 1984
205. Moscow, USSR, 1959

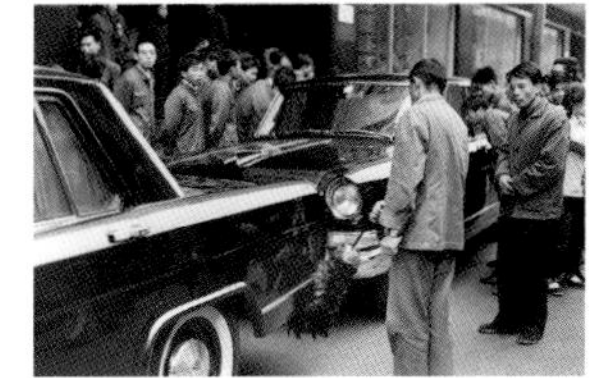

206. Beijing, China, 1978

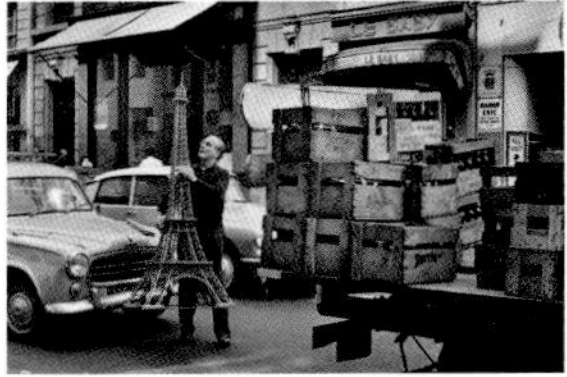

208. Paris, France, 1966

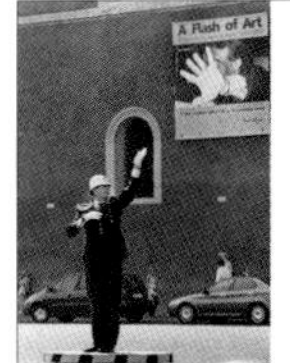

210. Rome, Italy, 2004
211. Florida, USA, 1968

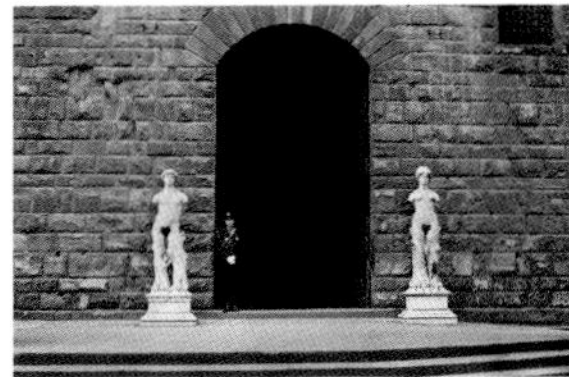

212. Florence, Italy, 1949

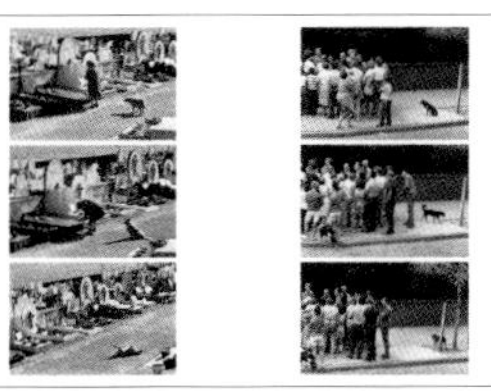

214. St. Tropez, France, 1979
215. Albany, New York, 1962

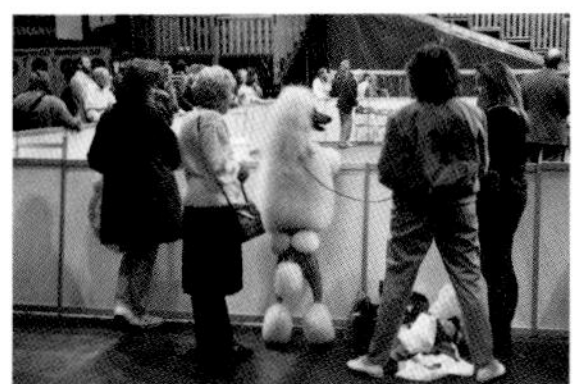

216. Birmingham, England, 1991

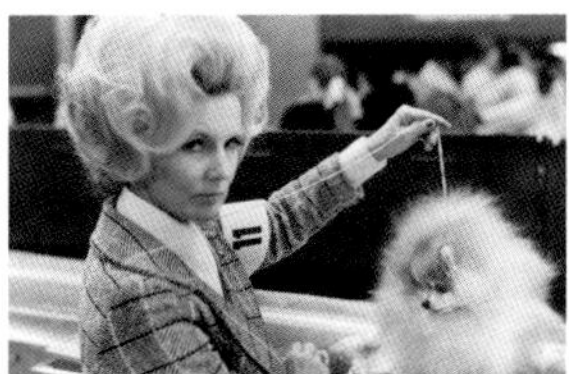

218. New York City, 1973

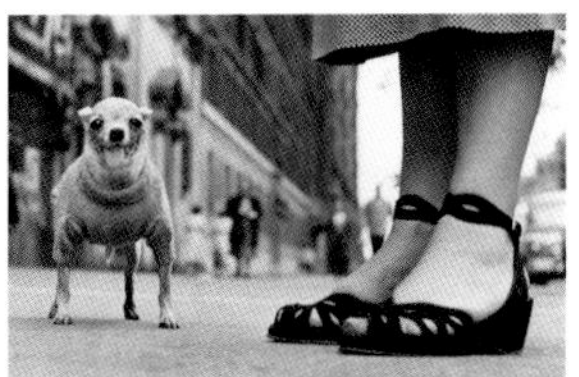

220. New York City, 1946

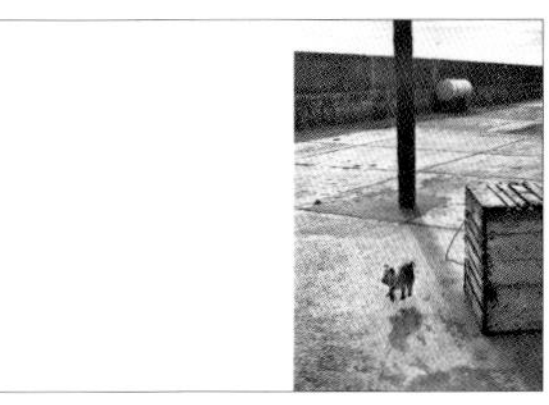

223. Ballycotton, Ireland, 1968

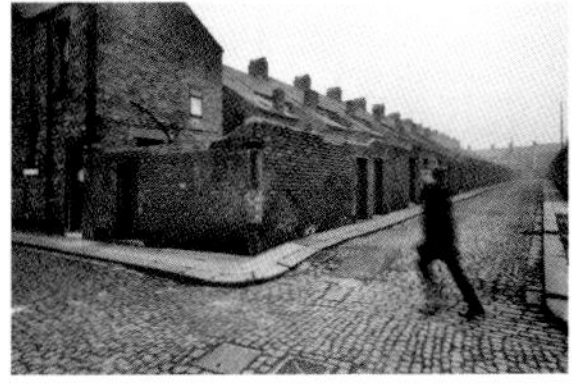

224. Newcastle, England, 1969

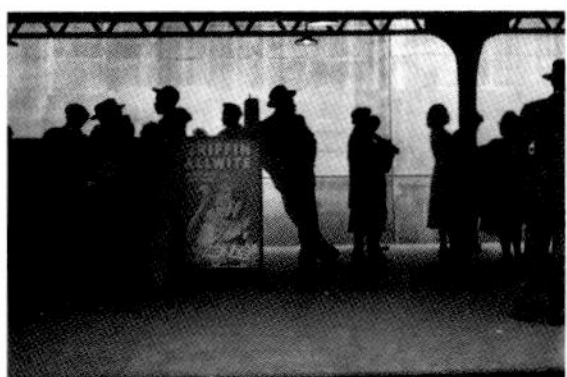

226. New York City, 1948

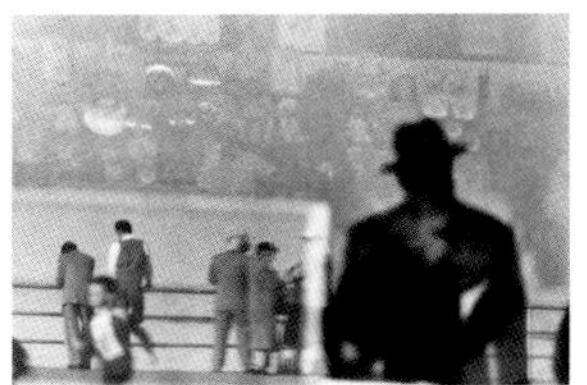

228. Coney Island, New York, 1956

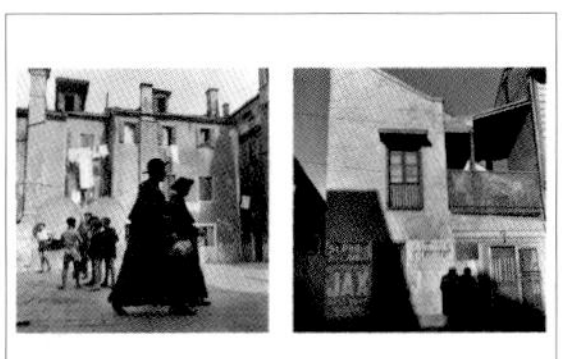

230. Venice, Italy, 1949
231. New Orleans, Louisiana, 1949

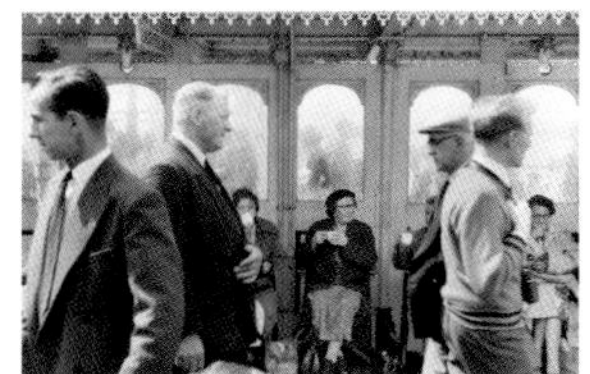

232. Brighton, England, 1958

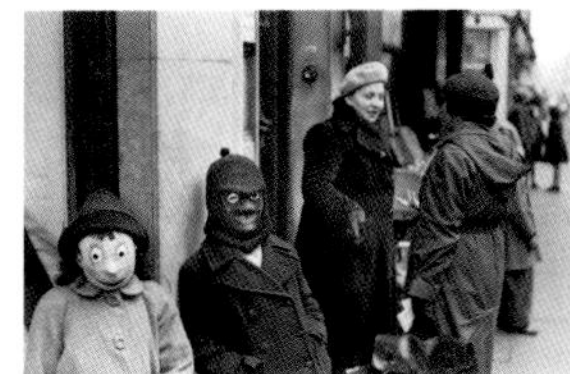

234. Paris, France, 1949

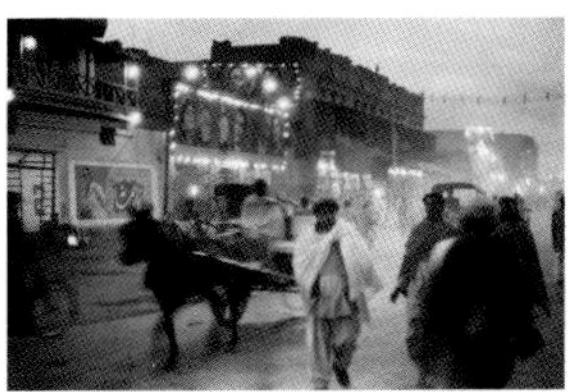

236. Lahore, Pakistan, 1954

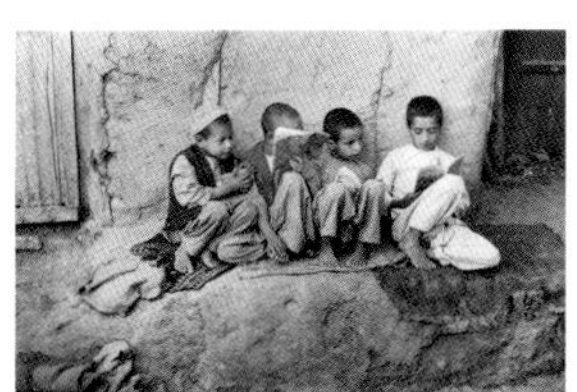

238. Herat, Afghanistan, 1977

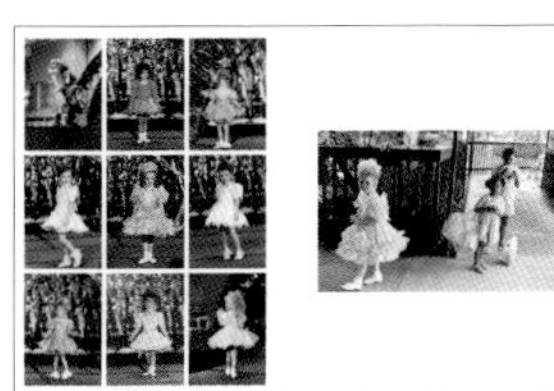

240. Kissimmee, Florida, 1997

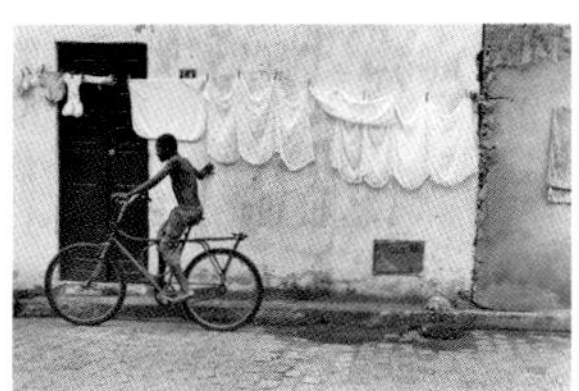

242. Cachoeira, Brazil, 2005

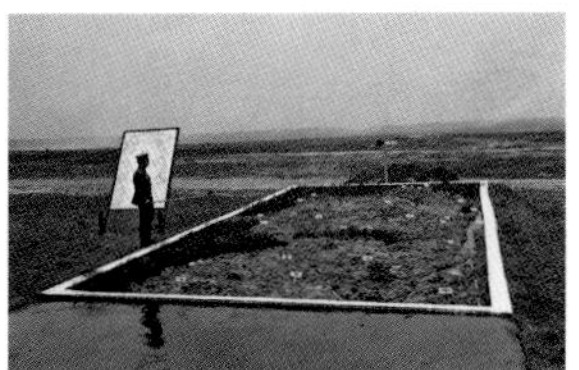

244. Near Moscow, USSR, 1966

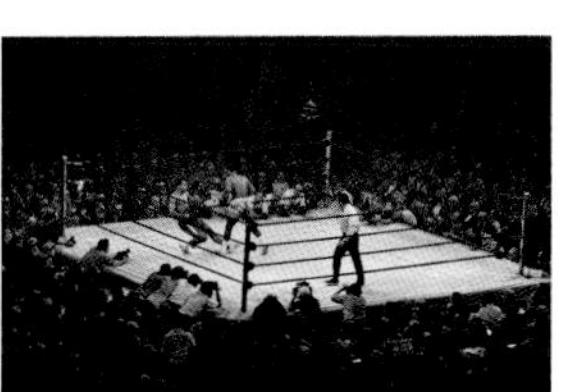

246. Mohammed Ali and Joe Frazer bout,
New York City, 1971

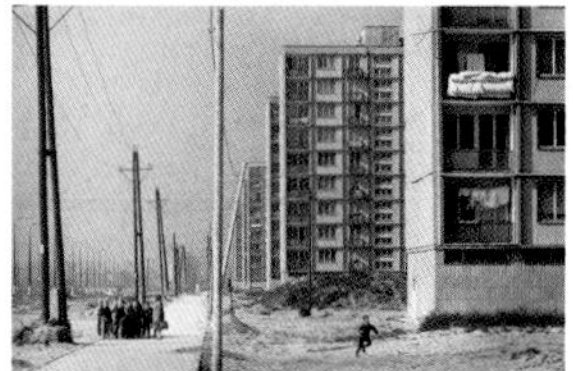

248. Prague, Czechoslovakia, 1964

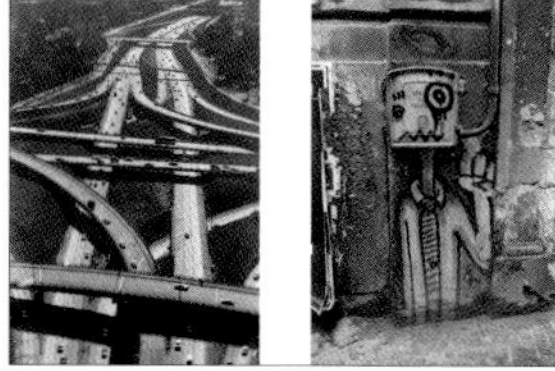

250. Detroit, Michigan, 1961
251. Naples, Italy, 2004

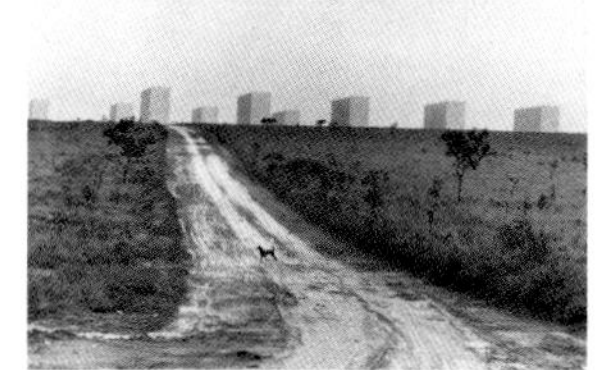

252. Brasilia, Brazil, 1961

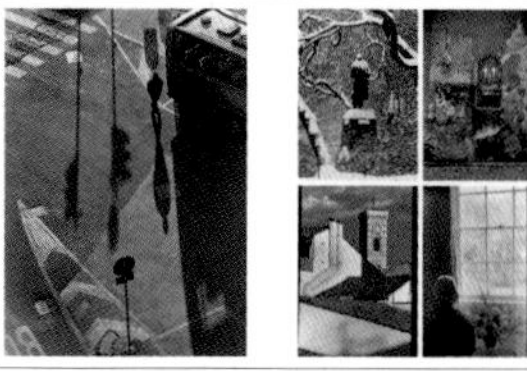

254. Milan, Italy, 2000
255. (from top left clockwise)
New York City, 2006. Naples, Italy, 2004.
Florence, Italy, 2004. Ireland, 1968

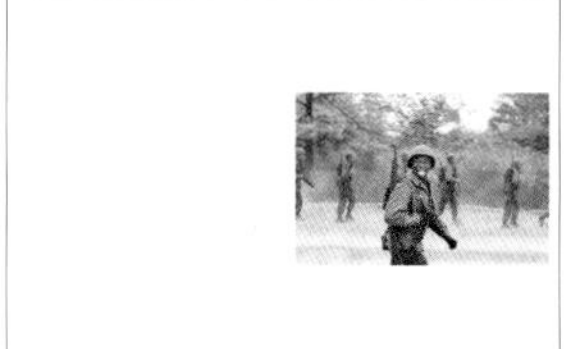

257. Fort Dix, New Jersey, 1951

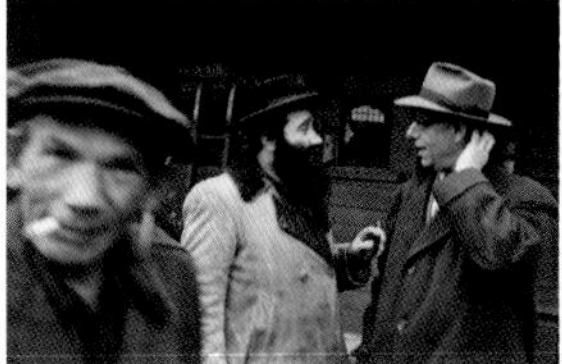

258. Fulton Fish Market, New York, 1953

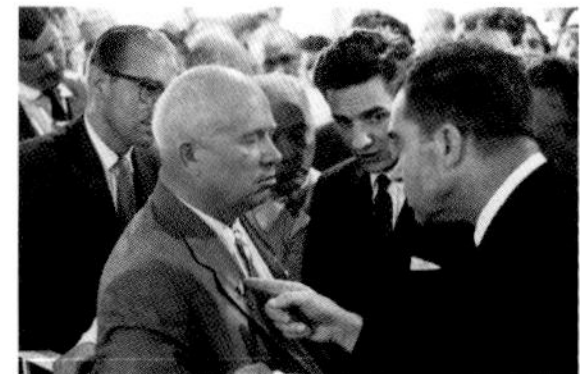

260. Nikita Khrushchev and Richard Nixon,
Moscow, USSR, 1959

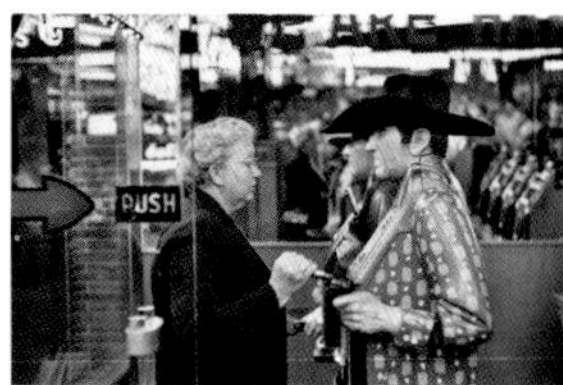

262. Las Vegas, Nevada, 1954

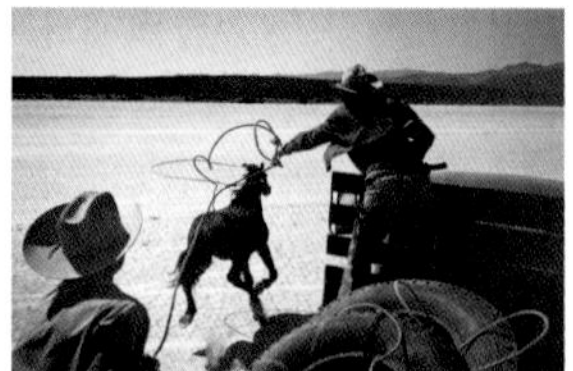

264. Reno, Nevada, 1960

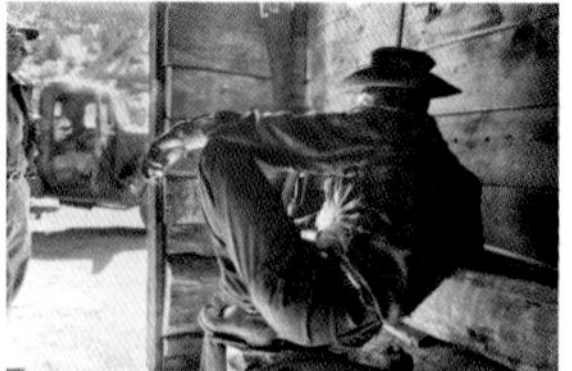

266. Montana, USA, 1954

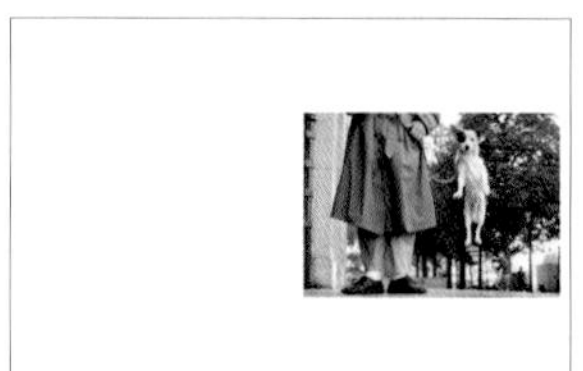

269. Paris, France, 1989

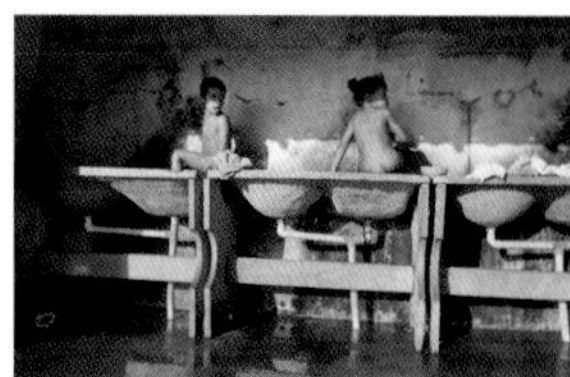

270. Cachoeira, Brazil, 2005

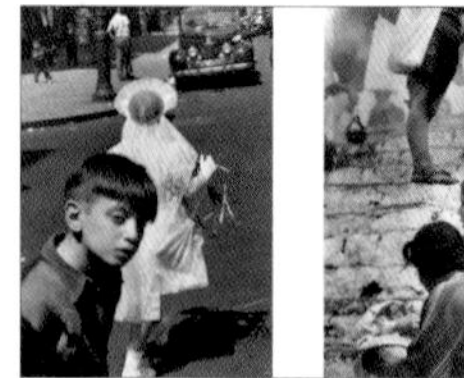

272. New York City, 1950
273. Cicicastenango, Guatemala, 1955

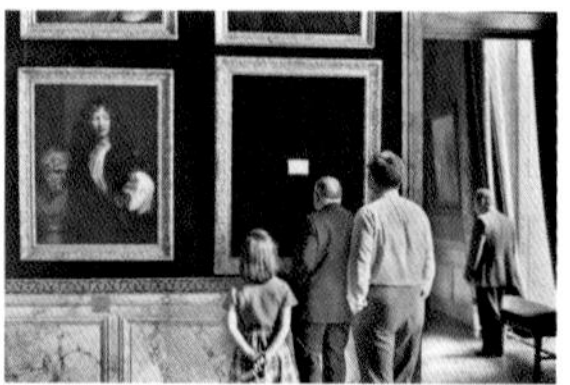

274. Versailles, France, 1975

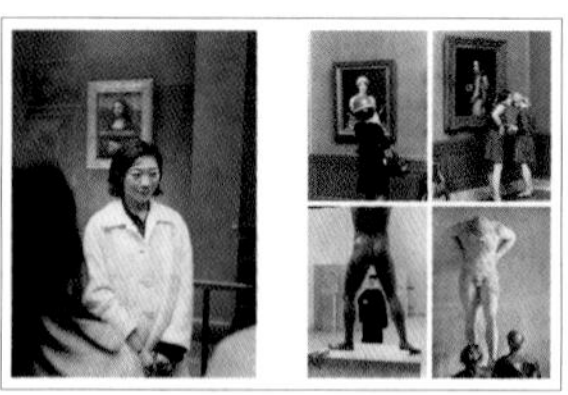

276. Paris, France, 1997
277. (from top left clockwise)
New York City, 1969. New York City, 1969.
Athens, Greece, 1963. Paris, France, 1993

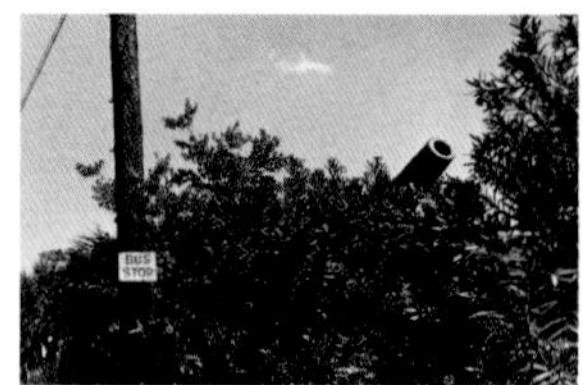

278. Fort Dix, New Jersey, 1951

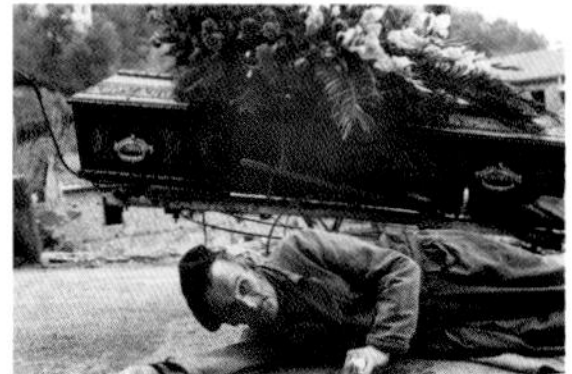

280. Tuscany, Italy, 1949

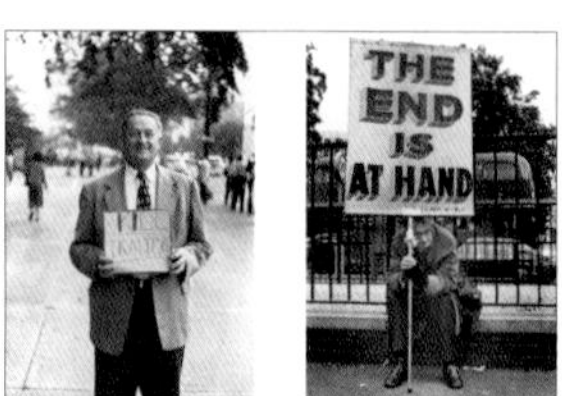

282. Washington DC, 1953
283. London, England, 1978

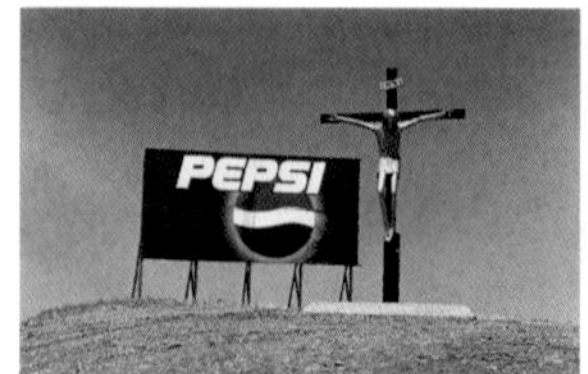

284. Valdez Peninsula, Argentina, 2001

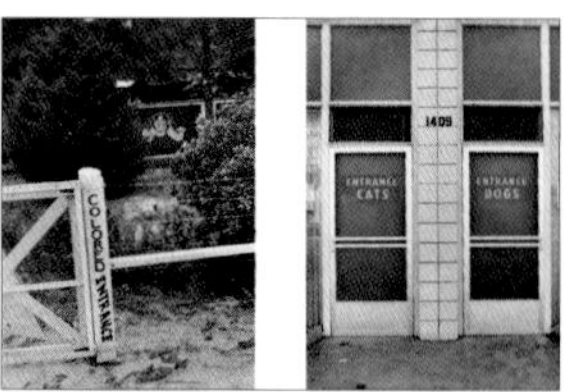

286. Mississippi, USA, 1954
287. Alameda, California, 1975

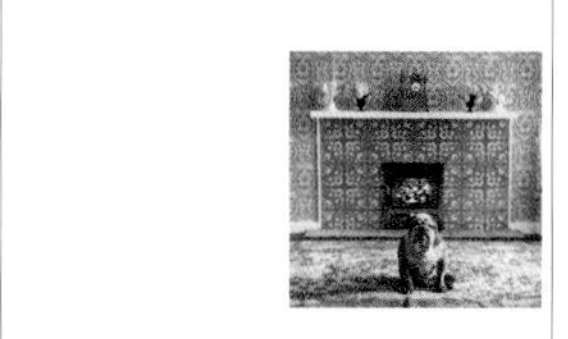

289. London, England, 1966

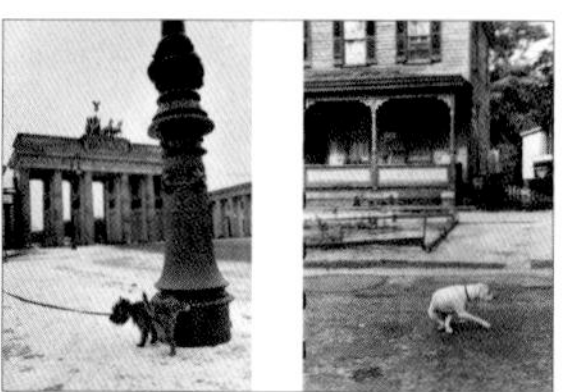

290. Berlin, Germany, 1995
291. Wilmington, North Carolina, 1950

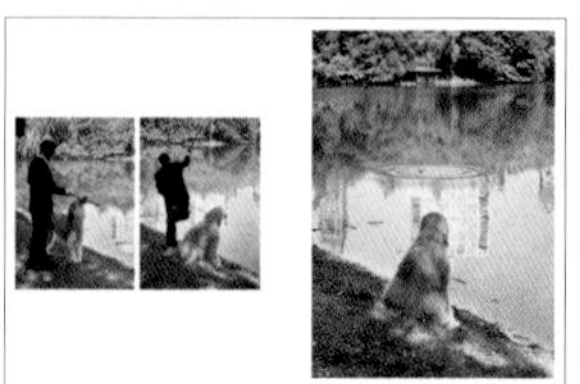

292. Central Park, New York City, 1990

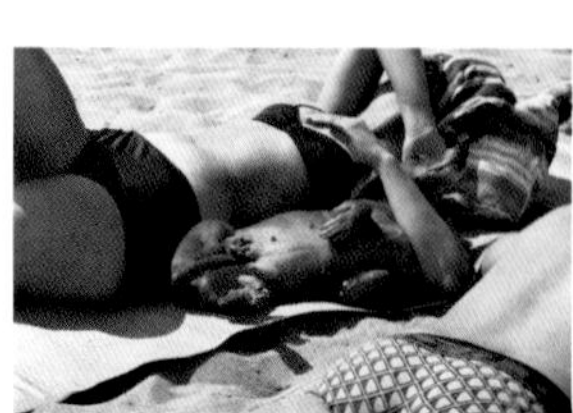

294. Saintes-Maries-de-la-Mer, France, 1977

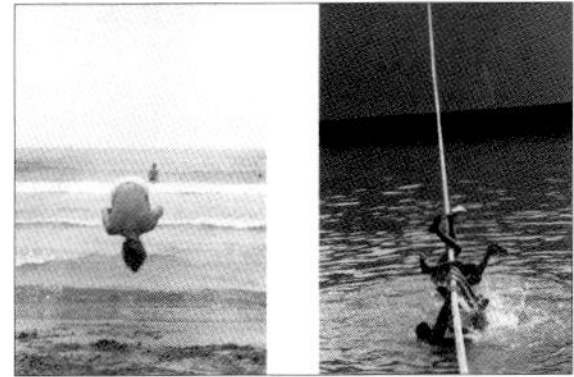

296. Saintes-Maries-de-la-Mer, France, 1977
297. Tahiti, 1980

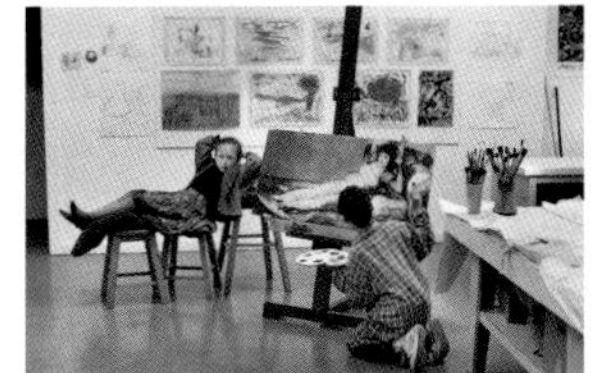

298. Bridgehampton, New York, 1990

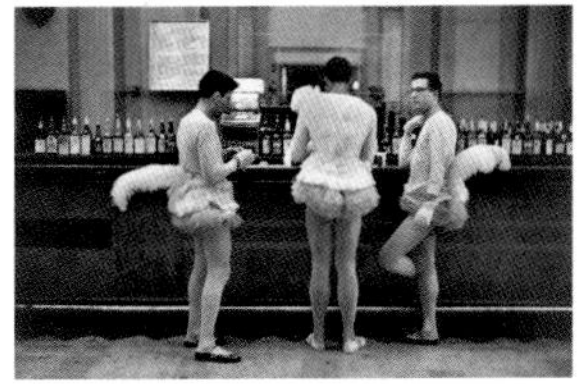

300. New York City, 1956

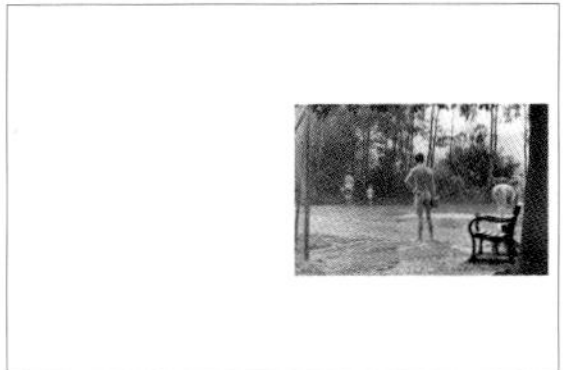

303. Kent, England, 1968

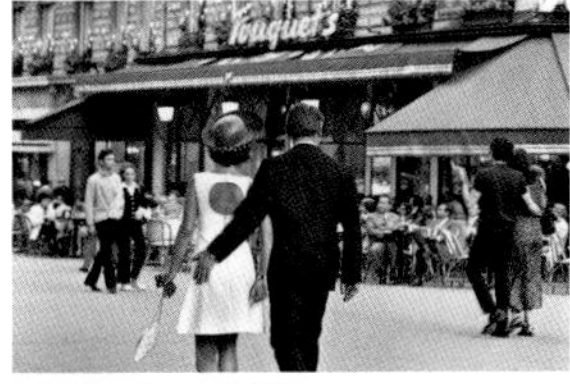

304. Paris, France, 1970

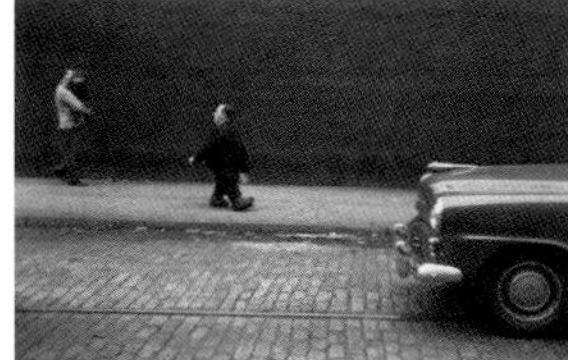

306. Pittsburgh, Pennsylvania, 1950

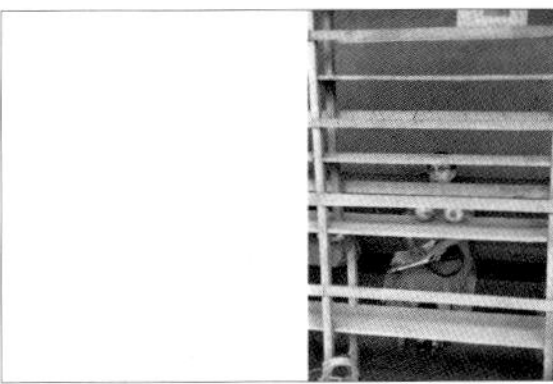

309. Managua, Nicaragua, 1957

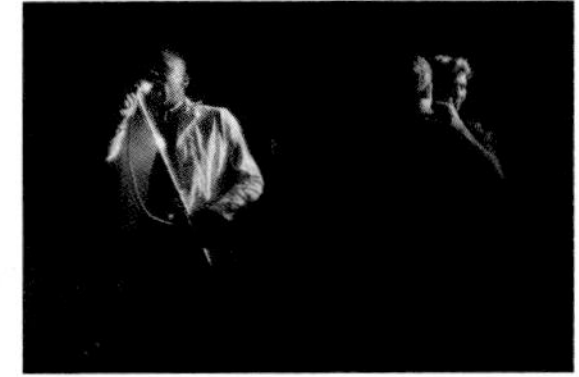

310. Karlsruhe, Germany, 1951

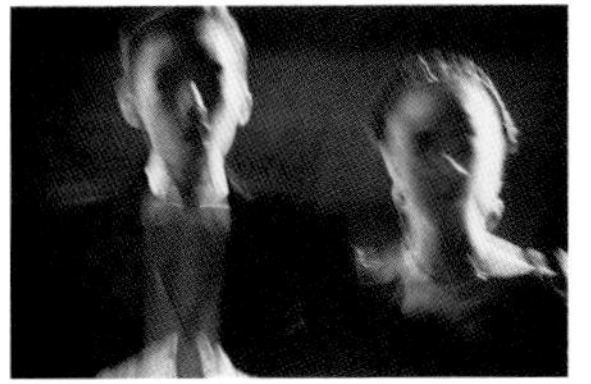

312. Tokyo, Japan, 1995

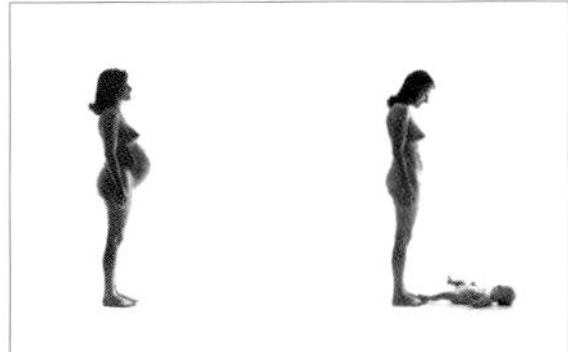

314. New York City, 1977

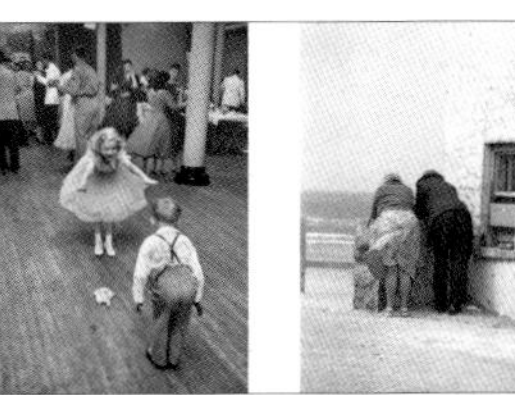

316. New York City, 1955
317. Ireland, 1964

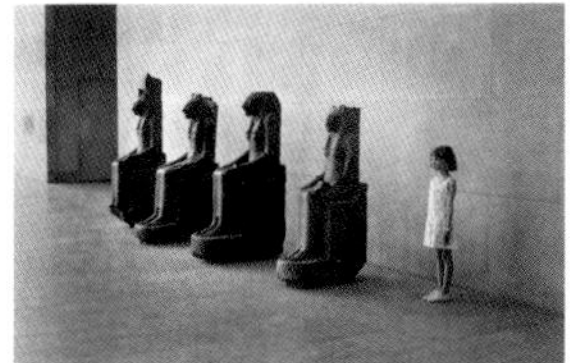

318. Metropolitan Museum, New York City, 1988

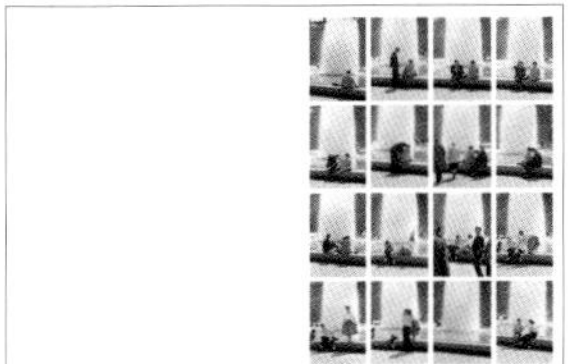

321. Paris, France, 1989

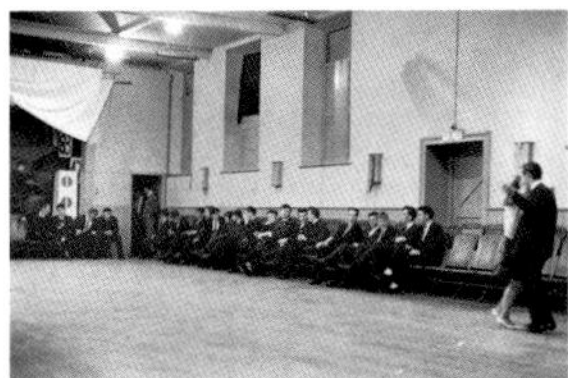

322. Ireland, 1965

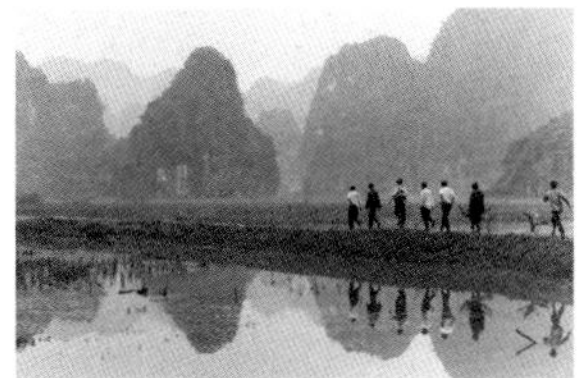

324. Northern Vietnam, 1994

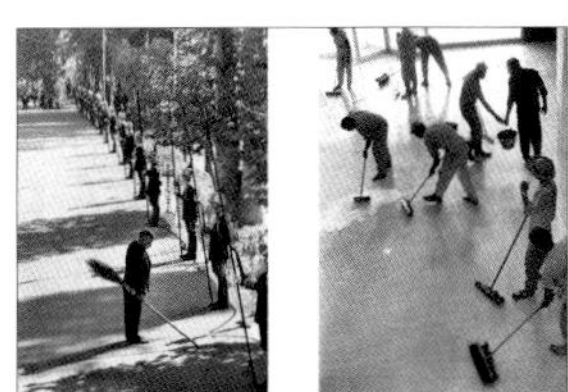

326. Tehran, Iran, 1967
327. Tehran, Iran, 1967

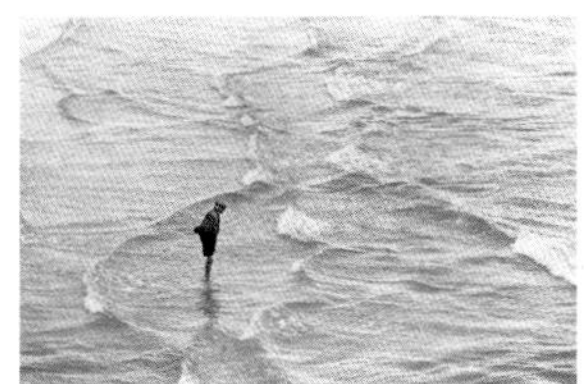

328. Brighton, England, 1966

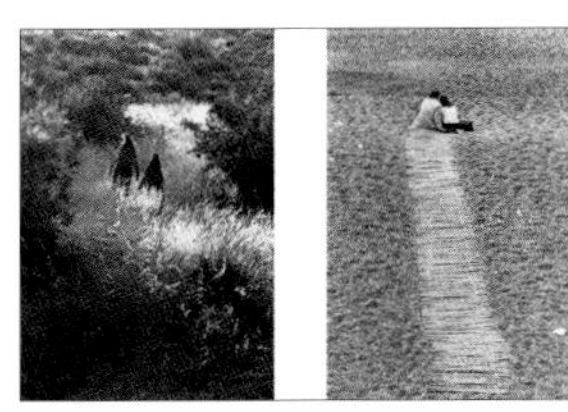

330. Punta Tombo, Argentina, 2001
331. Brighton, England, 1966

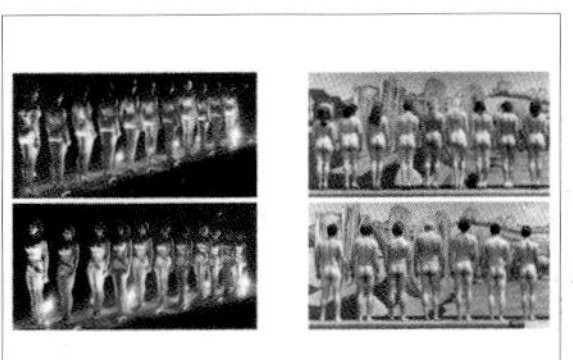

332. Arkansas, 1954
333. Bakersfield, California, 1983

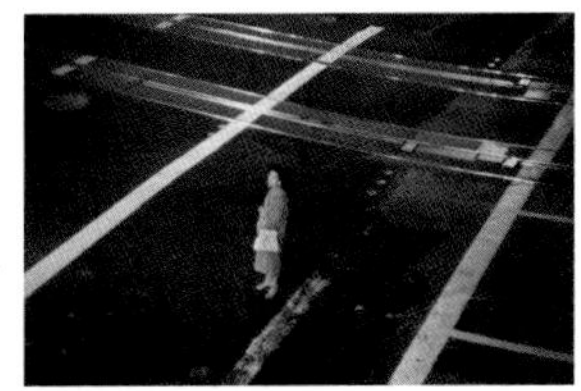

334. San Francisco, California, 1958

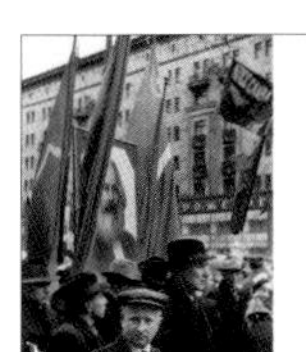

336. Moscow, USSR, 1957
337. Detroit, Michigan, 1961

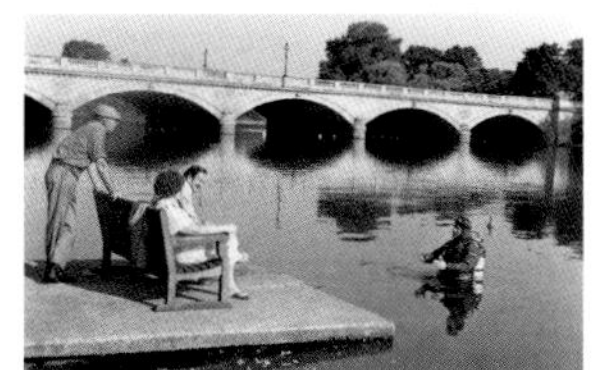

338. London, England, 1978

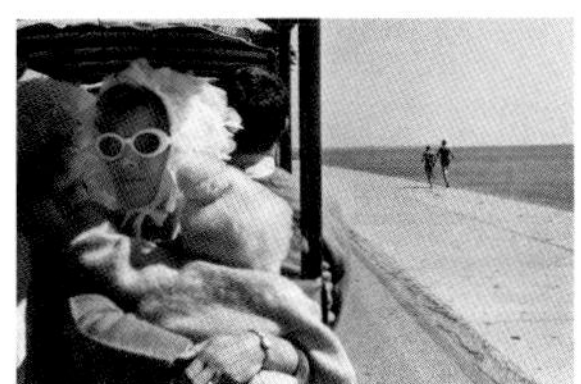

340. Key West, Florida, 1968

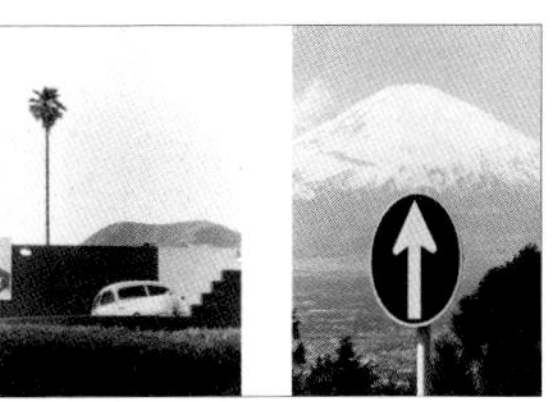

342. Hollywood, California, 1956
343. Mt. Fuji, Japan, 1977

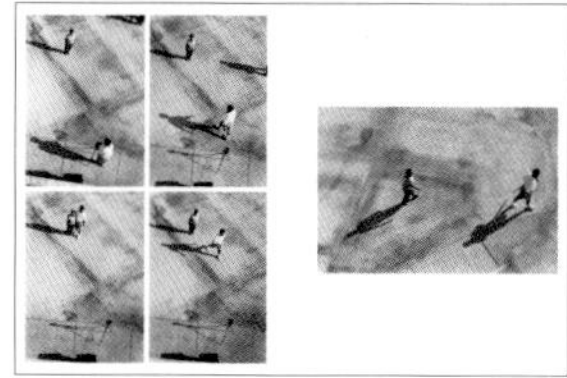

344. Los Angeles, California, 1997

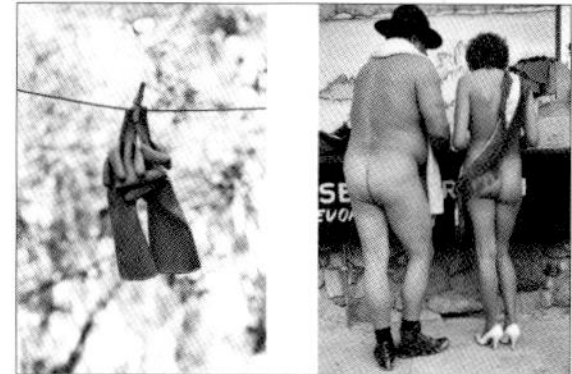

346. Sicily, Italy, 1965
347. Bakersfield, California, 1983

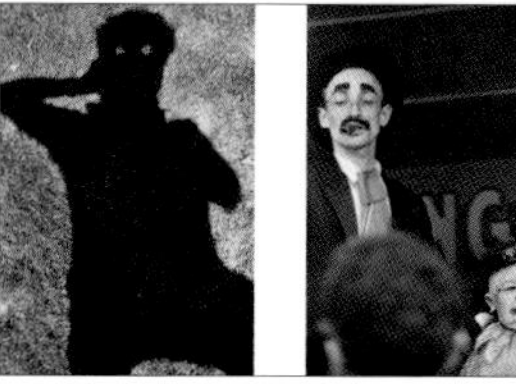

348. Ireland, 1961
349. Coney Island, New York, 1956

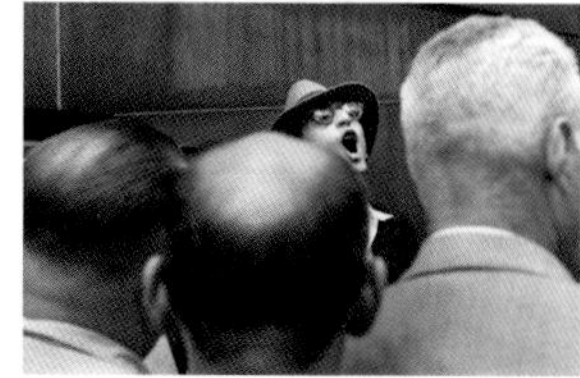

350. New York City, 1955

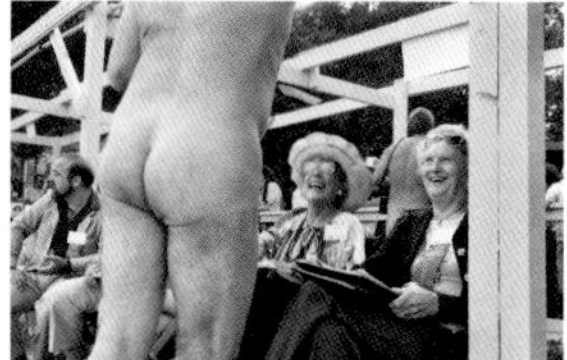

352. Bakersfield, California, 1983

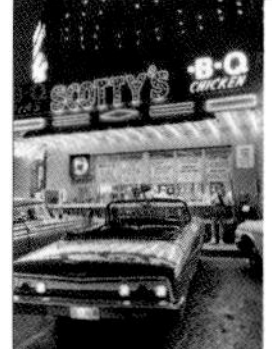

354. Miami Beach, Florida, 1962
355. Brighton, England, 1970

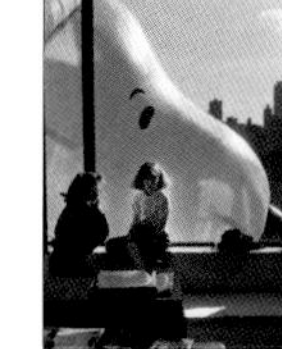

356. Macy's balloon, New York City, 1988
357. Ibiza, Spain, 2000

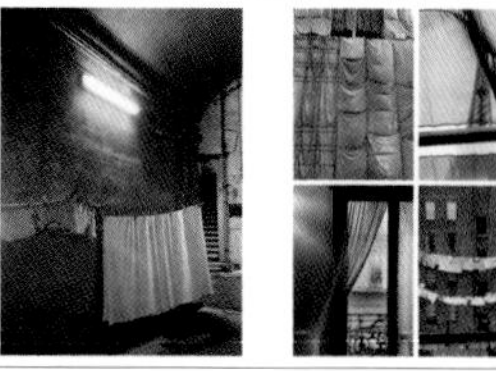

358. Naples, Italy, 2004
359. (from top left clockwise)
Paris, France, 1968. Paris, France, 1968.
Paris, France, 1992. New York City, 1955

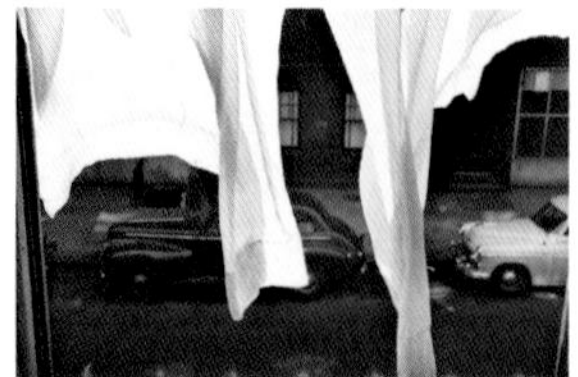

360. New York City, 1954

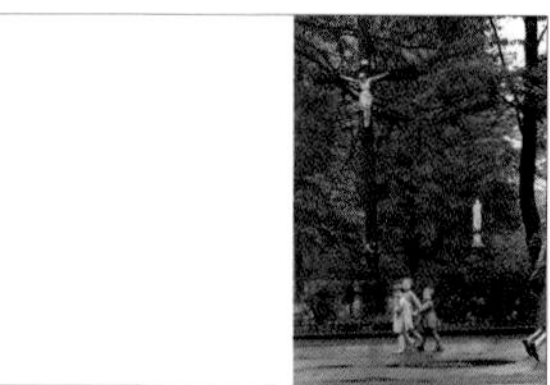

363. Poland, 1964

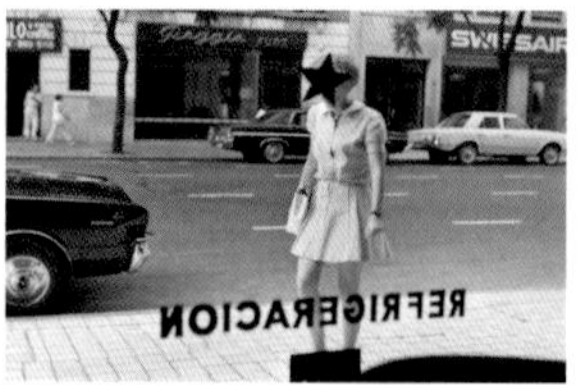

364. Buenos Aires, Argentina, 1972

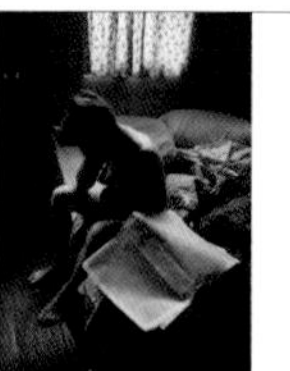

366. New York City, 1953
367. Chicago, Illinois, 1962

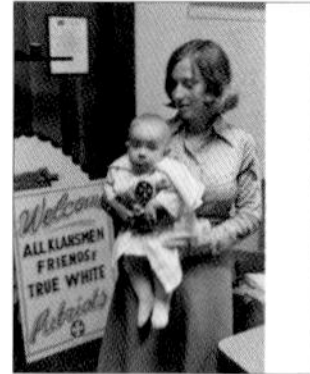

368. Baton Rouge, Louisiana, 1976
369. Arkadelphia, Alabama, 1954

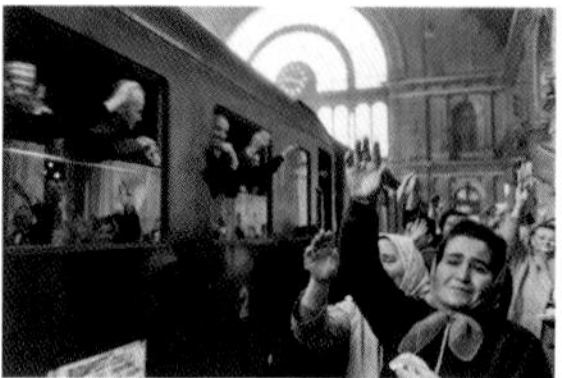

370. Budapest, Hungary, 1964

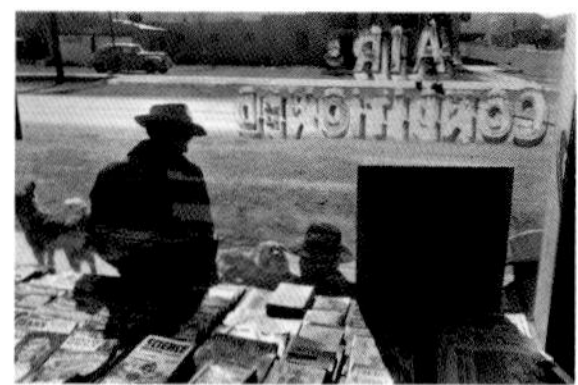

372. Idaho, USA, 1954

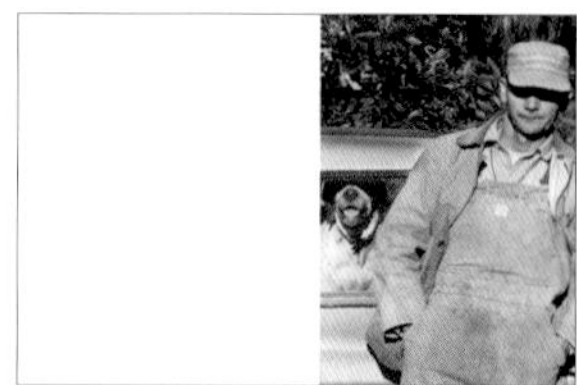

375. South Carolina, USA, 1962

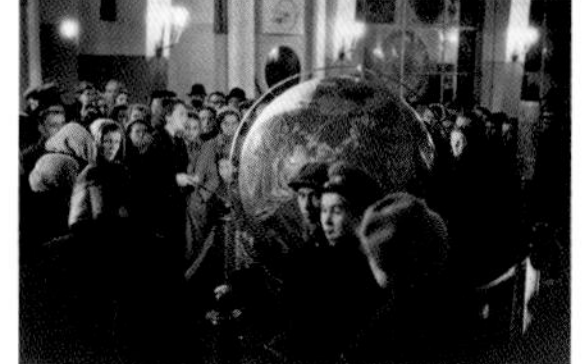

376. Moscow, USSR, 1957

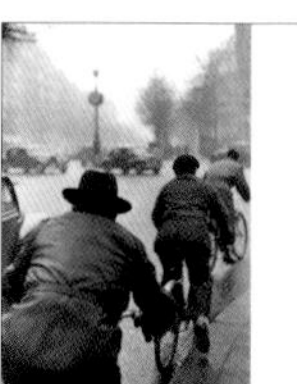

378. Paris, France, 1952
379. Paris, France, 1952

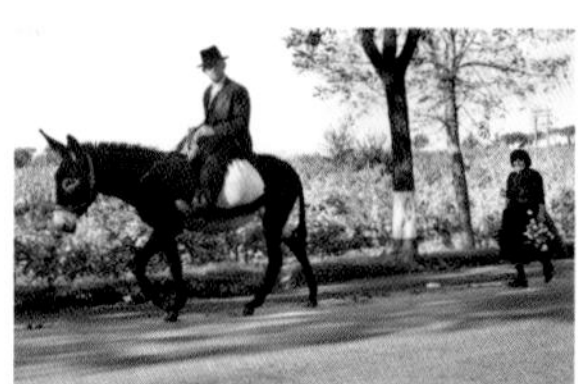

380. Tuscany, Italy, 1949

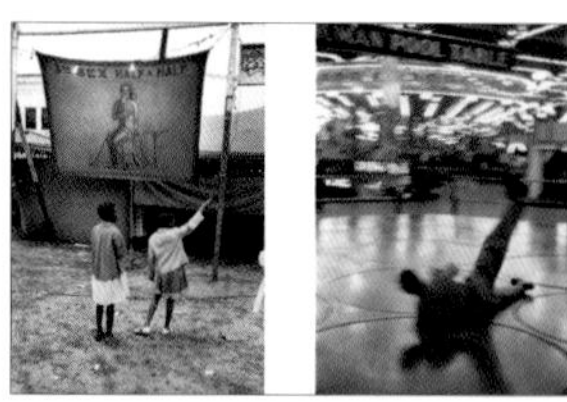

382. South Carolina, USA, 1954
383. Coney Island, New York, 1955

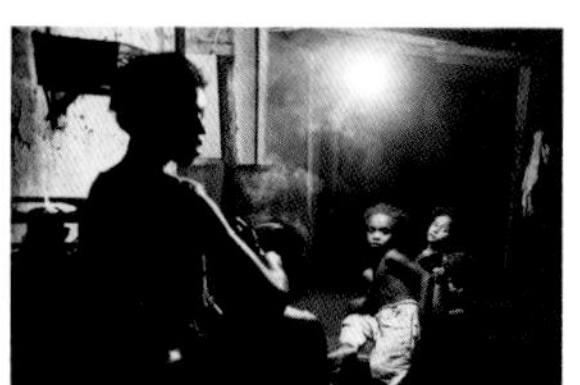

384. Brazil, 1961

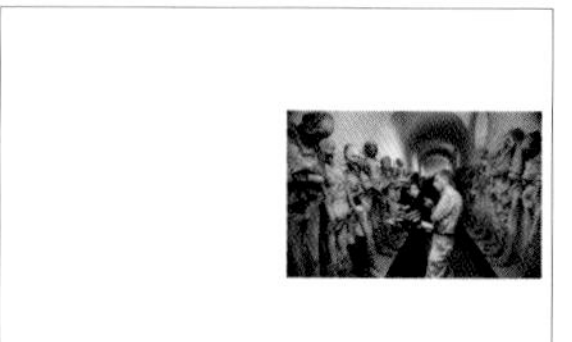

387. Guanajuato, Mexico, 1957

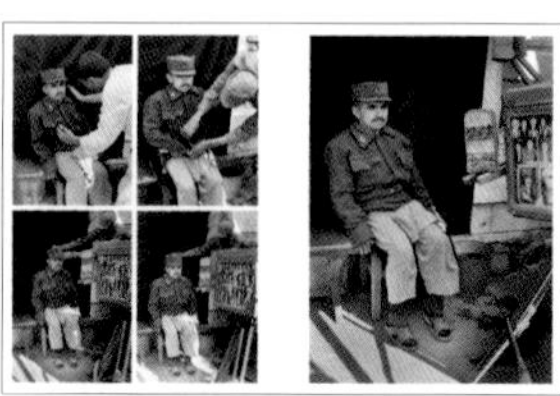

388. Herat, Afghanistan, 1977

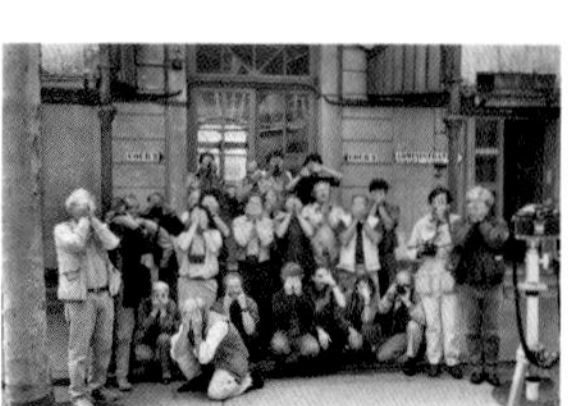

390. Magnum photographers, Paris, France, 1988

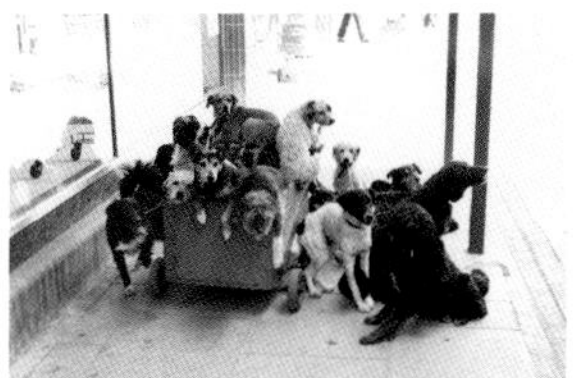

392. Near London, England, 1974

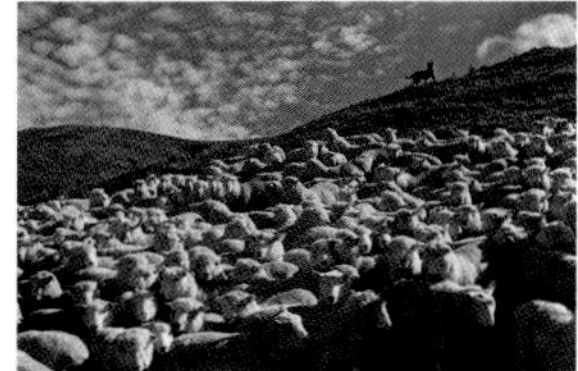

394. New Zealand, 2004

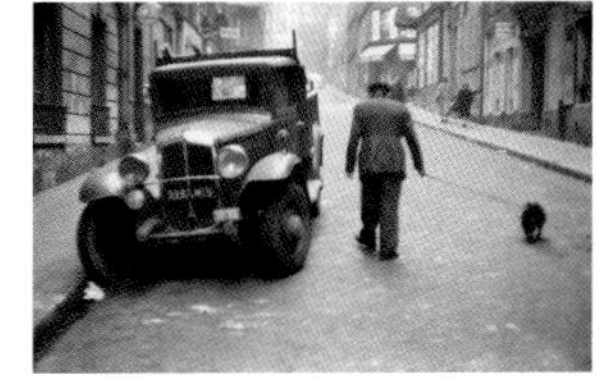

396. Paris, France, 1952

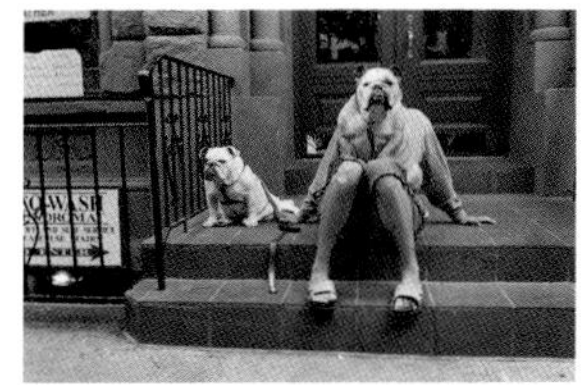

398. New York City, 2000

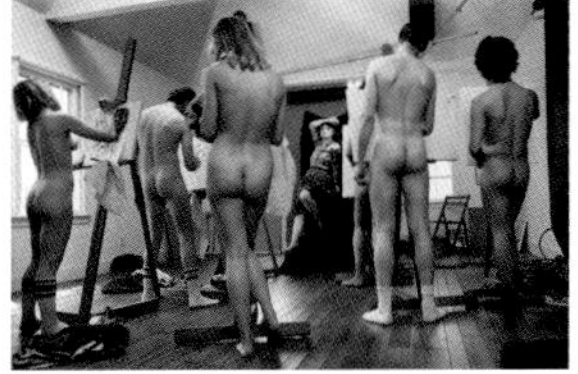

400. East Hampton, New York, 1983

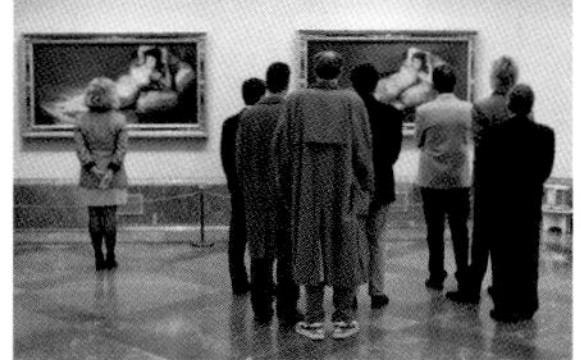

402. Prado Museum, Madrid, 1995

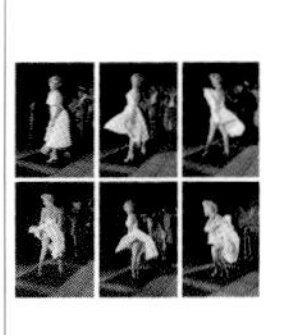

404. Marilyn Monroe on the "Some Like It Hot" set, New York, 1956

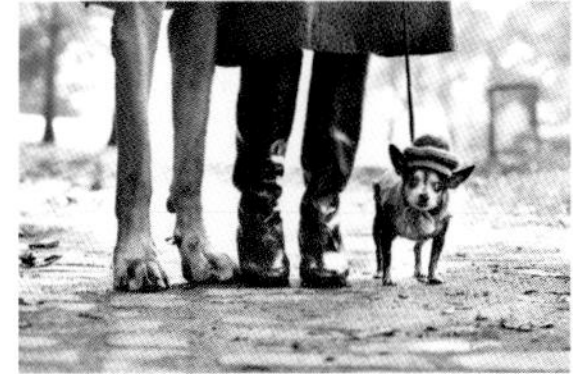

406. New York City, 1974

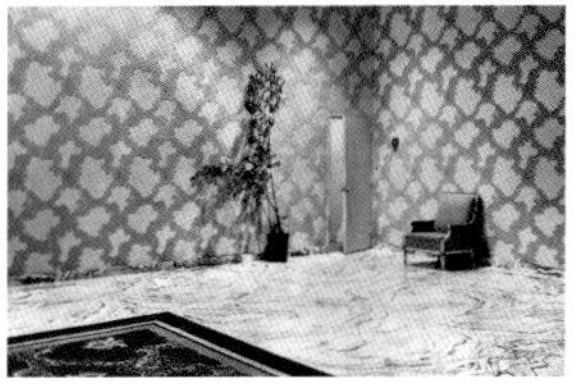

408. Miami Beach, Florida, 1962

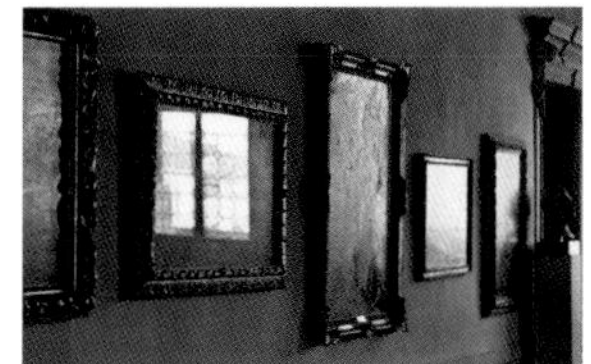

410. Venice, Italy, 1965

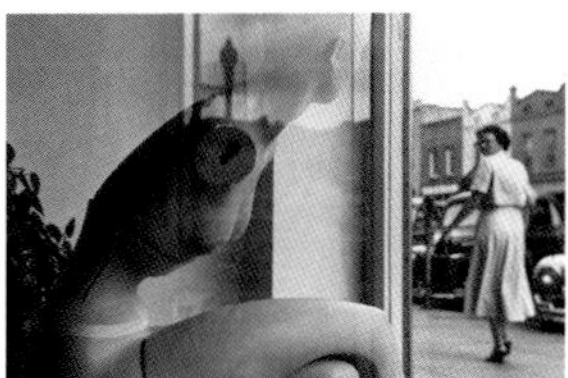

412. Wilmington, North Carolina, 1950

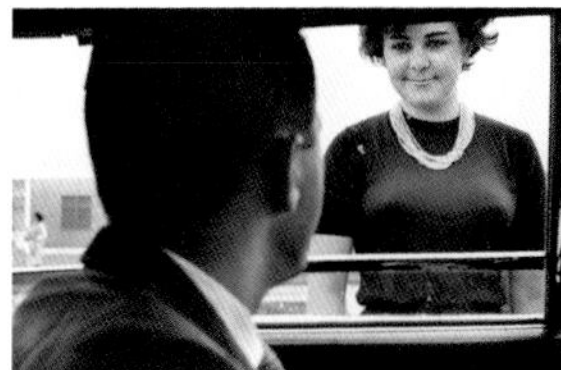

414. Brasilia, Brazil, 1961

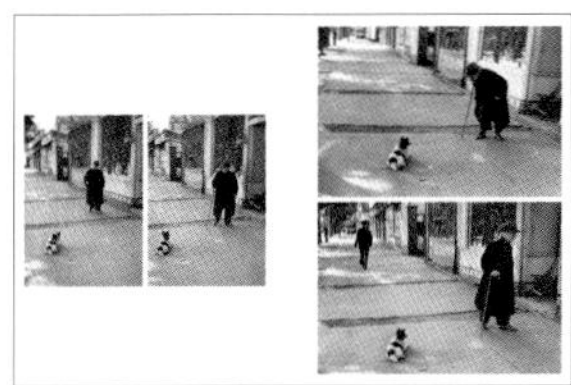

416. Paris, France, 1952

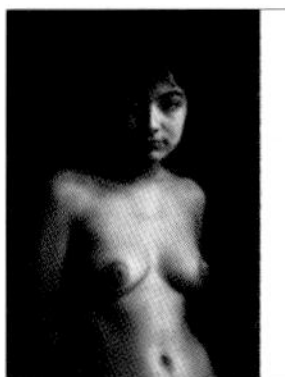
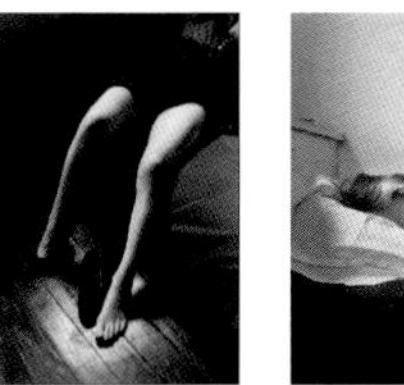

418. Milan, Italy, 1949
419. New York City, 1954

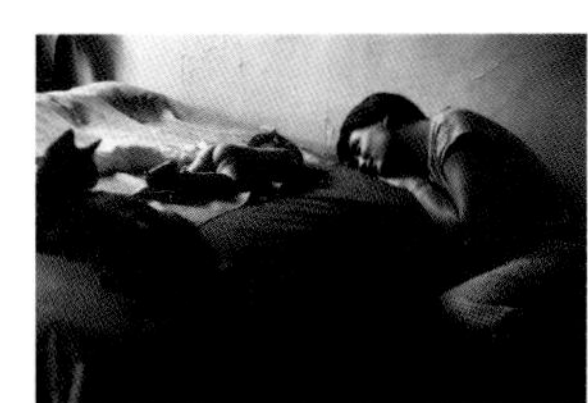

420. New York City, 1953

422. New York City, 1953

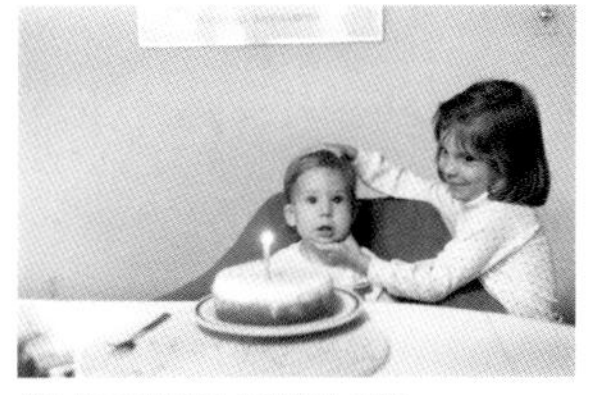

424. East Hampton, New York, 1981

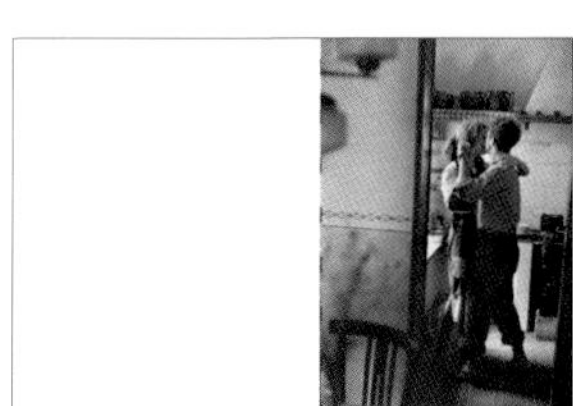

427. Valencia, Spain, 1952

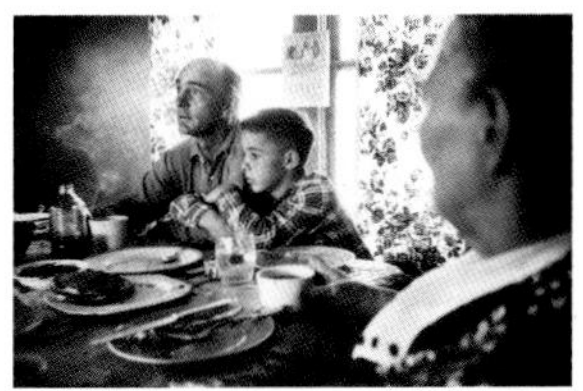

428. Wyoming, USA, 1954

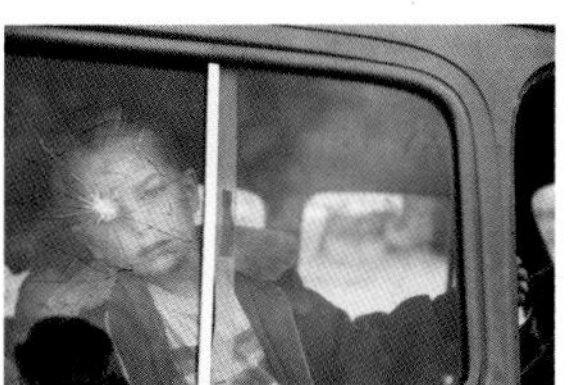

430. Colorado, USA, 1955

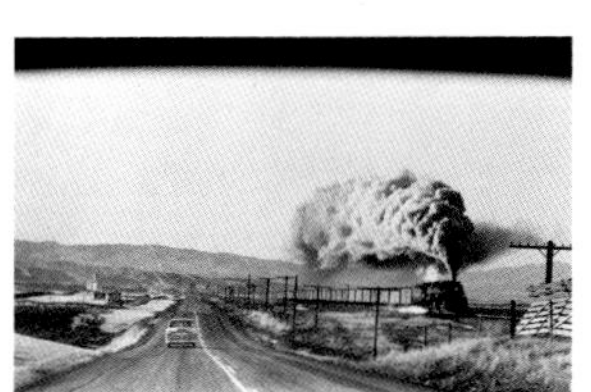

432. Wyoming, USA, 1954

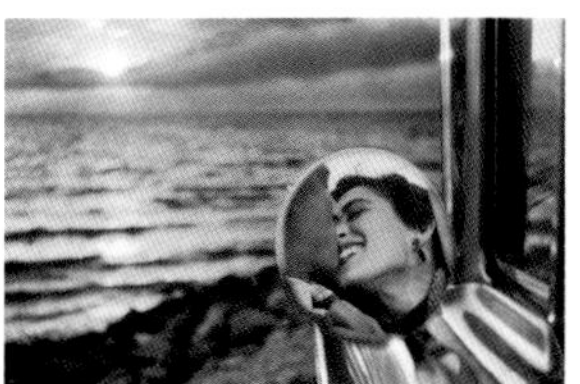

434. Santa Monica, California, 1955

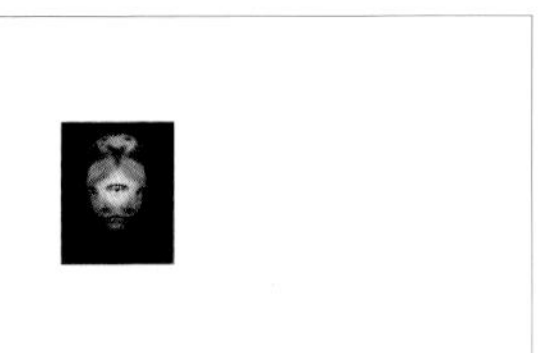

446. Hollywood, California, 1944

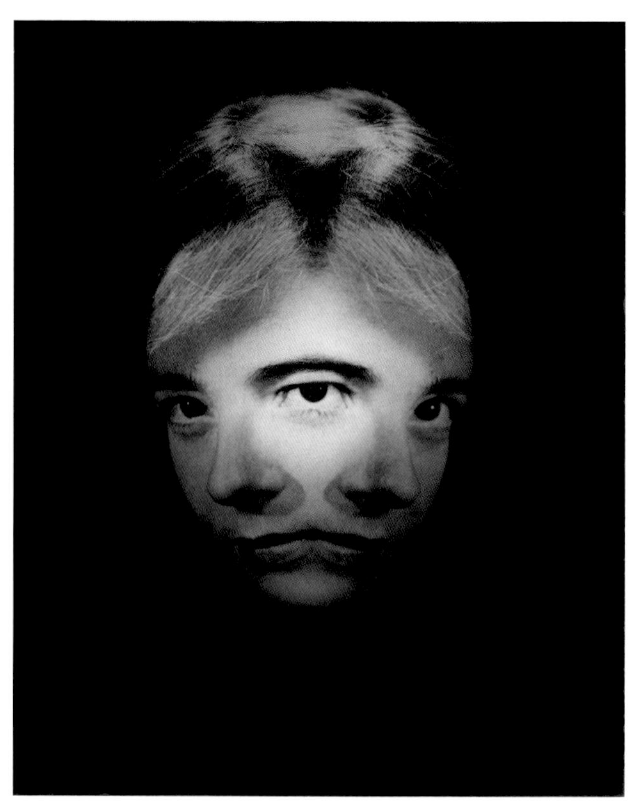

A Brief Biography

Born on July 26, 1928, in Paris, Elliott Erwitt spent his childhood in Milan. His family moved back to Paris in 1938, and immigrated to New York the following year, then moved to Los Angeles in 1941. His interest in photography began while he was a teenager living in Hollywood. In 1948 Erwitt moved to New York, there he met Edward Steichen, Robert Capa and Roy Stryker. After spending the year 1949 traveling in France and Italy, Erwitt returned to New York and began working as a professional photographer. Drafted into the army in 1951, he continued to take photographs while stationed in Germany and France.

Elliott Erwitt was invited to join Magnum Photos in 1953 by Robert Capa. A member of the prestigious agency ever since, Erwitt has served several terms as its president. One of the leading figures in the competitive field of magazine photography, Erwitt's journalistic essays, illustrations, and advertisements have been featured in publications around the world for more than forty years. In addition to his work as a still photographer, Erwitt began making films in 1970. He has published several books and has had one-man exhibitions in numerous museums and galleries around the world including New York's Museum of Modern Art, the Smithsonian Institution, the Art Institute of Chicago, Paris' Museum of Modern Art, and Zurich's Kunsthaus.

Based in New York City, Elliott Erwitt travels obsessively. He likes children and dogs.

Eine kurze Biografie

Elliott Erwitt wurde am 26. Juli 1928 in Paris geboren und verbrachte seine Kindheit in Mailand. Die Familie zog 1938 zurück nach Paris und emigrierte im darauf folgenden Jahr nach New York. Später, im Jahr 1941, zog sie nach Los Angeles. Sein Interesse an der Fotografie erwachte, als er als Teenager in Hollywood lebte. 1948 zog Erwitt nach New York, wo er Edward Steichen, Robert Capa und Roy Stryker kennen lernte. Nachdem er 1949 einige Zeit durch Frankreich und Italien gereist war, kehrte Erwitt nach New York zurück und begann seine Arbeit als professioneller Fotograf. Als er 1951 in die Armee eingezogen wurde, fotografierte er auch während seiner Stationierung in Deutschland und Frankreich.

Elliott Erwitt wurde 1953 von Robert Capa eingeladen, für Magnum Photos zu arbeiten. Seitdem ist Erwitt Mitglied dieser angesehenen Agentur und hat mehrmals als ihr Präsident fungiert. Er ist eine der führenden Figuren auf dem stark umkämpften Gebiet der Magazin-Fotografie. Erwitts journalistische Essays, Illustrationen und Werbeanzeigen werden seit mehr als vierzig Jahren weltweit veröffentlicht. Neben seiner Arbeit als Fotograf begann Erwitt 1970 auch Filme zu drehen. Er hat mehrere Bücher veröffentlicht und war mit Einzelausstellungen in zahlreichen Museen und Galerien auf der ganzen Welt vertreten, darunter das Museum of Modern Art in New York, das Smithsonian und das Art Institute of Chicago sowie das Museum für Moderne Kunst in Paris und das Kunsthaus Zürich.

Seinen Lebensmittelpunkt hat Elliott Erwitt in New York City, aber er ist nahezu ununterbrochen auf Reisen. Er mag Kinder und Hunde.

Brève Biographie

Né le 26 juillet 1928, à Paris, Elliott Erwitt a passé son enfance à Milan. Sa famille retourna à Paris en 1938 et émigra à New York l'année suivante. Elle s'établit ensuite à Los Angeles en 1941. Son intérêt pour la photo s'éveilla lors de son adolescence à Hollywood. En 1948, Erwitt s'installa à New York, où il fit connaissance d'Edward Steichen, Robert Capa et Roy Stryker. Après avoir voyagé en France et en Italie en 1949, Erwitt regagna New York et commença à travailler comme photographe professionnel. Militaire en 1951, il continua à prendre des photos en Allemagne et en France.

Elliott Erwitt fut invité à rejoindre Magnum Photos en 1953 par Robert Capa.

Erwitt a réalisé plusieurs contrats en tant que président de cette prestigieuse agence. Un des acteurs principaux dans le domaine compétitif du magazine photo, les essais journalistiques d'Erwitt, les illustrations et les publicités ont été publiées dans des revues du monde entier pendant plus de quarante ans. En marge de son travail de photographe, Erwitt commença à faire des films en 1970. Il publia plusieurs livres et exposa dans de nombreux musées et galeries mondiaux y compris le Musée d'Art Moderne de New York, la Smithsonian Institution, l'Art Institute of Chicago, le Musée d'Art Moderne de Paris, et le Kunsthaus de Zürich.

Vivant à New York, Elliott Erwitt est constamment en voyage. Il aime les enfants et les chiens.

Biografía Breve

Elliott Erwitt nació en París el 26 de julio de 1928 y pasó su infancia en Milán. Su familia regresó a París en 1938 y emigró a Nueva York al año siguiente. En 1941, la familia se trasladó a Los Ángeles, donde comenzó el interés de Erwitt por la fotografía mientras transcurría su adolescencia en Hollywood. En 1948 volvió a Nueva York, donde conoció a Edward Steichen, Robert Capa y Roy Stryker. Después de pasar 1949 de viaje por Francia e Italia, Erwitt volvió a Nueva York y comenzó su trabajo como fotógrafo profesional. En 1951 le llamaron a las filas y continuó tomando fotografías en sus destinos en Alemania y Francia.

En 1953, Robert Capa le invitó a formar parte de Magnum Photos, agencia de la cual ha sido miembro desde entonces y que ha presidido en varias ocasiones. La obra de Erwitt, una de las figuras líder en el duro campo de la fotografía para revistas, compuesta por ensayos periodísticos, ilustraciones y anuncios, ha venido apareciendo en publicaciones de todo el mundo durante más de cuarenta años. Además de su trabajo como fotógrafo, Erwitt comenzó a rodar películas en 1970. También ha publicado varios libros y ha expuesto muestras personales en numerosos museos y galerías de arte de todo el mundo, entre ellos el Museo de Arte Moderno de Nueva York, la Institución Smithsonian, el Instituto de Arte de Chicago, el Museo de Arte Moderno de París y en el Kunsthaus de Zúrich.

Elliott Erwitt viaja incansablemente desde su sede en la ciudad de Nueva York. Le gustan los niños y los perros.

Breve Biografia

Nato il 26 luglio 1928 a Parigi, Elliott Erwitt trascorre la sua infanzia a Milano. Nel 1938 insieme alla famiglia torna a Parigi ed emigra a New York l'anno seguente. Nel 1941 la famiglia si trasferisce a Los Angeles. A Hollywood, ancora adolescente, Erwitt inizia ad interessarsi alla fotografia. Nel 1948, Erwitt si trasferisce a New York, dove conosce Edward Steichen, Robert Capa e Roy Stryker. Dopo diversi periodi passati in Francia e in Italia, nel 1949 Erwitt torna a New York e dà inizio alla sua carriera di fotografo professionista. Nel 1951 si arruola nell'esercito e continua a scattare fotografie durante le sue guarnigioni in Germania e in Francia.

Nel 1953, Robert Capa lo invita ad associarsi all'agenzia Magnum Photos. Membro della prestigiosa agenzia da allora, Erwitt viene più volte designato presidente. Considerato una delle principali icone nel mondo concorrenziale della fotografia da rivista, Erwitt firma reportage, illustrazioni e fotografie pubblicitarie che compaiono su riviste di tutto il mondo da oltre quarant'anni. Oltre al suo lavoro di fotografo da posa, nel 1970 Erwitt inizia a produrre film. L'artista ha pubblicato diversi libri ed organizzato mostre personali in numerosi musei e gallerie internazionali tra cui il Museum of Modern Art di New York, lo Smithsonian Institution, l'Art Institute di Chicago, il Museo di Arte Moderna di Parigi e la Kunsthaus di Zurigo.

Attualmente residente a New York, Elliott Erwitt è appassionato di viaggi, ama i bambini e i cani.

My appreciation goes to friends and colleagues who helped me put this volume together and to my publisher who made the swift journey from concept to publication so easy, direct and efficient.

Specifically, my grateful thanks go to Yayoi Sawada, Jeff Ladd, Karl Shanahan, Christina Burns, Alwine Krebber, Sean Callahan, Stout Thomas & Johnson and especially the designer Stuart Smith, with whom I have been collaborating joined at the hip doing our "Personal Best".

None of the photographs in this book have been electronically manipulated. One pre-digital exception is the picture on page 446 which I made by printing two negatives sandwiched together in my enlarger. I was just 16-years-old, did not know any better and soon got over it.

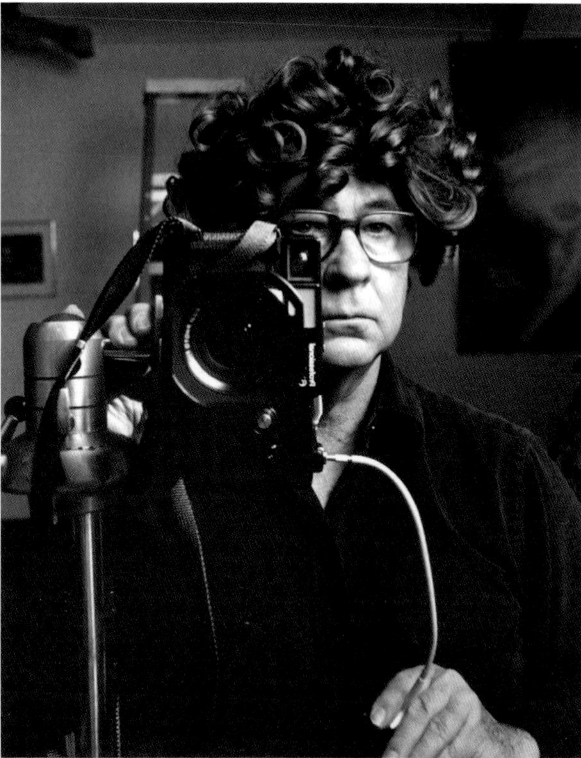

East Hampton, New York, 1998

© teNeues, an Imprint of
Die Gestalten Verlag GmbH & Co. KG, Berlin 2025
© 2024, Elliott Erwitt LLC. All rights reserved.

Second edition

Photographs by Elliott Erwitt
Design by SMITH, London
Victoria Forrest, Heather McDonough, Karl Shanahan

Introduction by Sean Callahan

Translations by The Translation Department ·
Andrea Wiethof (German translator),
Susanne Schnitzler (German editor),
Diana Donzelli-Gaudet (Italian translator),
Paola Bortolotti-van Loon (Italian editor),
Lidia Oliveira (French translator),
Jean-Marie Léger (French editor),
Mar Rodriguez (Spanish translator),
Nelson Luis Sanchez Oliva (Spanish editor)

Editorial Coordination by Christina Burns, teNeues
Production by Alwine Krebber, teNeues
Color separation by ORT Medienverbund, Krefeld, Germany

ISBN 978-3-96171-632-6

Printed in Bosnia and Herzegovina by GPS

For more information and to order books, please visit
www.teneues.com and www.gestalten.com

Die Gestalten Verlag GmbH & Co. KG
Mariannenstrasse 9–10
10999 Berlin, Germany
hello@gestalten.com

Düsseldorf Office
Waldenburger Straße 13
41564 Kaarst, Germany
verlag@teneues.com

teNeues Press Department
press@gestalten.com

Bibliographic information published by the Deutsche Nationalbibliothek. The Deutsche Nationalbibliothek lists this publication in the Deutsche Nationalbibliografie; detailed bibliographic data is available online at www.dnb.de

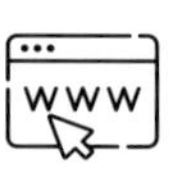

www.teneues.com

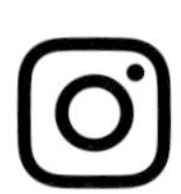

https://instagram.com/teneuespublishing